THE INSTITUTE FOR POLISH–JEWISH STUDIES

The Institute for Polish–Jewish Studies in Oxford and its sister organization, the American Association for Polish–Jewish Studies, which publish *Polin*, are learned societies that were established in 1984, following the International Conference on Polish–Jewish Studies, held in Oxford. The Institute is an associate institute of the Oxford Centre for Hebrew and Jewish Studies, and the American Association is linked with the Department of Near Eastern and Judaic Studies at Brandeis University.

Both the Institute and the American Association aim to promote understanding of the Polish Jewish past. They have no building or library of their own and no paid staff; they achieve their aims by encouraging scholarly research and facilitating its publication, and by creating forums for people with a scholarly interest in Polish Jewish topics, both past and present.

To this end the Institute and the American Association help organize lectures and international conferences. Venues for these activities have included Brandeis University in Waltham, Massachusetts, the Hebrew University in Jerusalem, the Institute for the Study of Human Sciences in Vienna, King's College in London, the Jagiellonian University in Kraków, the Oxford Centre for Hebrew and Jewish Studies, the University of Łódź, University College London, and the Polish Cultural Institute and the Polish embassy in London. They have encouraged academic exchanges between Israel, Poland, the United States, and western Europe. In particular they seek to help train a new generation of scholars, in Poland and elsewhere, to study the culture and history of the Jews in Poland.

Each year since 1987 the Institute has published a volume of scholarly papers in the series *Polin: Studies in Polish Jewry* under the general editorship of Professor Antony Polonsky of Brandeis University. Since 1994 the series has been published on its behalf by the Littman Library of Jewish Civilization, and since 1998 the publication has been linked with the American Association as well. In March 2000 the entire series was honoured with a National Jewish Book Award from the Jewish Book Council in the United States. More than twenty other works on Polish Jewish topics have also been published with the Institute's assistance.

Further information on the Institute for Polish–Jewish Studies can be found on their website, <www.polishjewishstudies.pl>. For the website of the American Association for Polish–Jewish Studies, see <www.aapjstudies.org>.

THE LITTMAN LIBRARY OF
JEWISH CIVILIZATION

The Littman Library of Jewish Civilization is a registered UK charity
Registered charity no. 1000784

POLIN

STUDIES IN POLISH JEWRY

VOLUME TWENTY-FOUR

Jews and their Neighbours in Eastern Europe since 1750

Edited by

ISRAEL BARTAL, ANTONY POLONSKY

and

SCOTT URY

Published for
The Institute for Polish–Jewish Studies
and
The American Association for Polish–Jewish Studies

Oxford · Portland, Oregon
The Littman Library of Jewish Civilization
2012

The Littman Library of Jewish Civilization

Chief Executive Officer: Ludo Craddock
Managing Editor: Connie Webber

PO Box 645, Oxford OX2 OUJ, UK
www.littman.co.uk

_____

Published in the United States and Canada by
The Littman Library of Jewish Civilization
c/o ISBS, 920 NE 58th Avenue, Suite 300
Portland, Oregon 97213-3786

A catalogue record for this book is available from the British Library

Library of Congress Cataloging-in-Publication data applied for
ISSN 0268 1056

ISBN 1-978-904113-91-1
ISBN 1-978-904113-92-8 (pbk)

Publishing co-ordinator: Janet Moth
Production: John Saunders
Copy-editing: George Tulloch
Proof-reading: Mark Newby and Joyce Rappaport
Index: Bonnie Blackburn
Design: Pete Russell, Faringdon, Oxon.
Typeset by: John Saunders Design & Production
Printed in Great Britain on acid-free paper by
the MPG Books Group, Bodmin and King's Lynn

Articles appearing in this publication are abstracted and indexed in
Historical Abstracts and America: History and Life

This volume is dedicated to

PROFESSOR JERZY TOMASZEWSKI

*eminent scholar of twentieth-century Polish history and of the
Jews and other minorities in Poland, a long-standing member of our
editorial collegium, on the occasion of his eightieth birthday*

———

This volume benefited from grants from

THE MIRISCH AND LEBENHEIM CHARITABLE FOUNDATION

THE LUCIUS N. LITTAUER FOUNDATION

CHARLES MERRILL AND JULIE BOUDREAUX

Editors and Advisers

Preface

THIS VOLUME OF *Polin* attempts to re-evaluate the relations between Jews and their neighbours in modern eastern Europe. Instead of viewing these as a series of ongoing religious and economic competitions that inevitably led to political and ideological conflict, contributors to this volume were asked to explore new or neglected aspects of inter-group interaction and exchange in the vast area between the Elbe and the Urals populated by Jews, Poles, Russians, Ukrainians, Germans, and other groups. The essays in the volume thus seek to establish new intellectual and methodological paradigms that can enable scholars of Jewish and east European histories and cultures to better understand and represent relations between Jews and their neighbours. In addition they aim to contribute to a deeper understanding of Jewish history and culture and to illuminate how relations between Jews and other groups reflect broader patterns of interaction, exchange, and division between members of different communities.

As in other volumes of *Polin*, the New Views section examines a number of important topics. These include the synagogue architecture of Volhynia and Podolia in the seventeenth and eighteenth centuries; the attitude of American Jews and American diplomacy towards the bill banning *sheḥitah* in Poland in the second half of the 1930s; British perspectives on the situation of Jews in Poland between 1944 and 1946; and the persistence of antisemitic stereotypes in the Polish countryside.

Polin is sponsored by the Institute of Polish–Jewish Studies, which is an associated institute of the Oxford Centre for Hebrew and Jewish Studies, and by the American Association for Polish–Jewish Studies, which is linked with the Department of Near Eastern and Judaic Studies, Brandeis University. As with earlier issues, this volume could not have appeared without the untiring assistance of many individuals. In particular, we should like to express our gratitude to Professor Jehuda Reinharz, president of Brandeis University, and to Professor Frederick Lawrence, who succeeded him as president in January 2011; to Mrs Irene Pipes, president of the American Association for Polish–Jewish Studies; and to Professor Jonathan Webber, treasurer of the Institute for Polish–Jewish Studies. These three institutions all made substantial contributions to the cost of producing the volume. A particularly important contribution was that made by the Mirisch and Lebenheim Foundation; the volume also benefited from a grant from the the Lucius N. Littauer Foundation. As is the case with earlier volumes, this one could not have been published without the constant assistance and supervision of Connie Webber, managing editor of the Littman Library, Ludo Craddock, chief executive officer, Janet Moth, publishing co-ordinator, Pete Russell, designer, and the tireless copy-editing of George Tulloch and Joyce Rappoport. Anat Vaturi of

Tel Aviv University was also kind enough to take time off from her doctorate on Jews and Protestants in early modern Kraków to proofread many of the contributions to this volume.

Plans for future volumes of *Polin* are well advanced. Volume 25 will analyse the history of Jews in Lithuania since 1772; volume 26 will be devoted to the history of Jews in Ukraine; and volume 27 will investigate the situation of the Jews in the Kingdom of Poland between 1815 and 1918. Future volumes are planned on Polish Jewish literature, on the historiography of Jews in the Polish lands, and on Jewish education in eastern Europe. We would welcome articles for these issues, as well as for our New Views section; in particular we are always grateful for assistance in extending the geographical range of our journal to Ukraine, Belarus, and Lithuania, both in the period in which these countries were part of the Polish–Lithuanian Commonwealth and subsequently.

We note with sadness the deaths of Józef Życiński, archbishop of Lublin, one of the main voices in the Polish Catholic hierarchy calling consistently and boldly for closer Christian–Jewish and Polish–Jewish relations; of Professor Ihor Shevchenko, a great Byzantist and active member of the American Association for Polish–Jewish Studies; of Jana Prot, a distinguished doctor and also an active member of the American Association for Polish–Jewish Studies; and of Professor Stanisław Litak, a longstanding member of our Advisory Board.

POLIN

We did not know, but our fathers told us how the exiles of Israel came to the land of Polin (Poland).

When Israel saw how its sufferings were constantly renewed, oppressions increased, persecutions multiplied, and how the evil authorities piled decree on decree and followed expulsion with expulsion, so that there was no way to escape the enemies of Israel, they went out on the road and sought an answer from the paths of the wide world: which is the correct road to traverse to find rest for their soul? Then a piece of paper fell from heaven, and on it the words:

Go to Polaniya (Poland)!

So they came to the land of Polin and they gave a mountain of gold to the king, and he received them with great honour. And God had mercy on them, so that they found favour from the king and the nobles. And the king gave them permission to reside in all the lands of his kingdom, to trade over its length and breadth, and to serve God according to the precepts of their religion. And the king protected them against every foe and enemy.

And Israel lived in Polin in tranquillity for a long time. They devoted themselves to trade and handicrafts. And God sent a blessing on them so that they were blessed in the land, and their name was exalted among the peoples. And they traded with the surrounding countries and they also struck coins with inscriptions in the holy language and the language of the country. These are the coins which have on them a lion rampant from the right facing left. And on the coins are the words 'Mieszko, King of Poland' or 'Mieszko, Król of Poland'. The Poles call their king 'Król'.

And those who delve into the Scriptures say: 'This is why it is called Polin. For thus spoke Israel when they came to the land, "Here rest for the night [*Po lin*]." And this means that we shall rest here until we are all gathered into the Land of Israel.'

Since this is the tradition, we accept it as such.

S. Y. AGNON, 1916

POLIN
Studies in Polish Jewry

Contents

PART II

NEW VIEWS

OBITUARIES

Note on Place Names

POLITICAL connotations accrue to words, names, and spellings with an alacrity unfortunate for those who would like to maintain neutrality. It seems reasonable to honour the choices of a population on the name of its city or town, but what is one to do when the people have no consensus on their name, or when the town changes its name, and the name its spelling, again and again over time? The politician may always opt for the latest version, but the hapless historian must reckon with them all. This note, then, will be our brief reckoning.

There is no problem with places that have accepted English names, such as Warsaw. But every other place name in east-central Europe raises serious problems. A good example is Wilno, Vilna, Vilnius. There are clear objections to all of these. Until 1944 the majority of the population was Polish. The city is today in Lithuania. 'Vilna', though raising the fewest problems, is an artificial construct. In this volume we have adopted the following guidelines, although we are aware that they are not wholly consistent.

1. Towns that have a form which is acceptable in English are given in that form. Some examples are Warsaw, Kiev, Moscow, St Petersburg, Munich.

2. Towns that until 1939 were clearly part of a particular state and shared the majority nationality of that state are given in a form which reflects that situation. Some examples are Breslau, Danzig, Rzeszów, Przemyśl. In Polish, Kraków has always been spelled as such. In English it has more often appeared as Cracow, but the current trend of English follows the local language as much as possible. In keeping with this trend to local determination, then, we shall maintain the Polish spelling.

3. Towns that are in mixed areas take the form in which they are known today and which reflects their present situation. Examples are Poznań, Toruń, and Kaunas. This applies also to bibliographical references. We have made one major exception to this rule, using the common English form for Vilna until its first incorporation into Lithuania in October 1939 and using Vilnius thereafter. Galicia's most diversely named city, and one of its most important, boasts four variants: the Polish Lwów, the German Lemberg, the Russian Lvov, and the Ukrainian Lviv. As this city currently lives under Ukrainian rule, and most of its current residents speak Ukrainian, we shall follow the Ukrainian spelling.

4. Some place names have different forms in Yiddish. Occasionally the subject matter dictates that the Yiddish place name should be the prime form, in which case the corresponding Polish (Ukrainian, Belarusian, Lithuanian) name is given in parentheses at first mention.

Note on Transliteration

HEBREW

An attempt has been made to achieve consistency in the transliteration of Hebrew words. The following are the key distinguishing features of the system that has been adopted:

1. No distinction is made between the *alef* and *ayin*; both are represented by an apostrophe, and only when they appear in an intervocalic position.

2. *Veit* is written *v*; *ḥet* is written *ḥ*; *yod* is written *y* when it functions as a consonant and *i* when it occurs as a vowel; *khaf* is written *kh*; *tsadi* is written *ts*; *kof* is written *k*.

3. The *dagesh ḥazak*, represented in some transliteration systems by doubling the letter, is not represented, except in words that have more or less acquired normative English spellings that include doublings, such as Hallel, kabbalah, Kaddish, rabbi, Sukkot, and Yom Kippur.

4. The *sheva na* is represented by an *e*.

5. Hebrew prefixes, prepositions, and conjunctions are not followed by a hyphen when they are transliterated; thus *betoledot ha'am hayehudi*.

6. Capital letters are not used in the transliteration of Hebrew except for the first word in the titles of books and the names of people, places, institutions, and generally as in the conventions of the English language.

7. The names of individuals are transliterated following the above rules unless the individual concerned followed a different usage.

YIDDISH

Transliteration follows the YIVO system except for the names of people, where the spellings they themselves used have been retained.

RUSSIAN AND UKRAINIAN

The system used is that of British Standard 2979:1958, without diacritics. Except in bibliographical and other strictly rendered matter, soft and hard signs are omitted and word-final -й, -ий, -ый, -ій in names are simplified to -*y*.

PART I

Jews and their Neighbours in Eastern Europe since 1750

Between Jews and their Neighbours

Isolation, Confrontation, and Influence in Eastern Europe

ISRAEL BARTAL and SCOTT URY

THE QUESTION OF INFLUENCE AND THE END OF JEWISH HISTORY

OVER SEVENTY-FIVE years ago, in a time and place that often seem to be far, far away, the young, engaged, and ever impassioned historian Emanuel Ringelblum observed that the nascent, already embattled field of Polish Jewish history stood at a methodological impasse. Ringelblum was particularly disturbed by the academic trend that seemed to dominate Polish Jewish history, or, as he put it, 'the legend of the Chinese Wall that separates Jewish society from Christian society'.[1] While a world war, the Nazis' attempts to exterminate the Jews of Europe, four and a half decades of communist rule, the isolation of the Cold War, and the integration of much of what was once referred to as 'Eastern Europe' into the European Union all separate Ringelblum's seemingly prophetic comments from the present collection, many observers will be struck by how little both popular perceptions and academic representations of relations between Jews and their neighbours in eastern Europe have changed. This volume is designed to help effect that long-awaited change: methodologically, intellectually, academically, culturally, and even politically and ideologically. The task, as we shall explain, is neither simple nor easy.

For far too long, the study of relations between Jews and members of other groups in eastern Europe has been told as the story of two (at times more) communities in a

We would like to thank those students and scholars whose participation in various methodological seminars at the Hebrew University helped us think through many of the questions raised in this essay as well as in other studies.

[1] See E. Ringelblum, *Żydzi w Warszawie: Od czasów najdawniejszych do ostatniego wygnania w r. 1527* (Warsaw, 1932), 129. On Ringelblum, see the recent biography by S. D. Kassow, *Who Will Write Our History? Emanuel Ringelblum, the Warsaw Ghetto, and the Oyneg Shabes Archive* (Bloomington, Ind., 2007). We are indebted to Natalia Aleksiun for her comments on this issue (London, 2008). For more on this generation of historians, see D. Engel, 'On Reconciling the Histories of Two Chosen Peoples', *American Historical Review*, 114 (2009), 915–22; M. Rosman, *How Jewish Is Jewish History?* (Oxford, 2007), 83.

permanent state of endless conflict, if not actual war. Indeed, study after study has asked questions and pursued research agendas that simultaneously assume and reinforce a binary, at times impenetrable, divide between Jews and Xs, representatives of some other ethnic group (Germans, Poles, Russians, Ukrainians, etc.). Either under the influence of Marxist concepts regarding the dialectical nature of society and the inevitable historical process, or because of the rise of national divisions in eastern Europe, the Middle East, and other centres of Jewish life, relations between Jews and members of other groups in eastern Europe are often represented as the history of competition, contestation, and ultimately conflict between two 'always-already' oppositional camps that share little save a mutual need for division. Another critical intellectual dilemma inherent in such conceptualizations is that these studies often revolve around questions of who did what to whom and why. The result is a series of studies that leave the impression of an endless game of intramural ping-pong. In fact, these representations of inter-group relations seem to be tailor-made to fit Homi Bhabha's comments regarding 'the binary logic through which identities of difference are often constructed'.[2] Over time, this fundamental, underlying assumption of a perennial, if not inevitable or inherent, divide and subsequent state of isolation and conflict between members of different groups has shaped not only popular and academic interpretations of relations between Jews and their neighbours but also the very definition and image of the entire region itself, 'Eastern Europe'.[3] As the editors of a collected volume on Yiddish culture in Montreal casually noted,

The Jewish immigrants of that era, who gave the Montreal Jewish community its special character, came predominantly from the countries of Eastern Europe and spoke a language called Yiddish . . . Jewish immigrants came to Canada bearing a heavy weight of cultural baggage, the residual legacy of their centuries-old civilization which, under the conditions prevailing in Europe, had resulted in a near-autonomous, self-enclosed cultural realm.[4]

Aware of and somewhat disturbed by the state of academic affairs and accompanying popular images, the contributors to this collection have taken it upon

---

[2] See H. K. Bhabha, 'Introduction: Locations of Culture', in id., *The Location of Culture* (London, 1994), 3. On history as a constant struggle between two opposing forces, see K. Marx and F. Engels, *Manifesto of the Communist Party*, in K. Marx, *Later Political Writings*, ed. and trans. T. Carver (Cambridge, 1996), 12, 29–30.

[3] See e.g. the recent essay by O. Bartov, 'Eastern Europe as the Site of Genocide', *Journal of Modern History*, 80 (2008), 557–93.

[4] I. Robinson, P. Anctil, and M. Butovsky, *An Everyday Miracle: Yiddish Culture in Montreal* (Downsview, Ont., 1990), 11. For additional examples, see A. Hertzberg, *The Jews in America: Four Centuries of an Uneasy Encounter* (New York, 1989), 168, 170, 175, 280; H. R. Diner, *The Jews of the United States, 1654–2000* (Berkeley, 2004); A. Shapira, *Brener: sipur ḥayim* (Tel Aviv, 2008), 45; R. R. Wisse, *The Modern Jewish Canon: A Journey through Language and Culture* (New York), 21–2; R. S. Wistrich, *Laboratory for World Destruction: Germans and Jews in Central Europe* (Lincoln, Nebr., 2007), 48–9. We are indebted to Kalman Weiser for his insightful comments on this and many other issues.

themselves to re-evaluate and reinvigorate the study of relations between Jews and their neighbours in eastern Europe. Instead of viewing and representing relations between Jews and members of other groups as a series of ongoing religious and economic competitions that inevitably led to political and ideological conflicts, contributors to this volume were asked to explore new or otherwise neglected aspects of inter-group interaction and exchange in that vast expanse between the Elbe and the Urals populated by Jews, Poles, Russians, Ukrainians, Germans, and members of other groups. In addition to looking at new aspects of social, cultural, and economic life in eastern Europe, authors were also encouraged to think about different ways to research, interpret, and represent interactions between members of different groups. Are there new intellectual and methodological paradigms that can enable scholars of Jewish and east European histories and cultures better to understand and represent relations between Jews and their neighbours? If so, what can these methodological and theoretical frameworks contribute to the study of Jewish society and culture, eastern Europe, and, ultimately, inter-group relations? Most importantly, how can this collective effort to re-evaluate the very nature of relations between Jews and their neighbours in eastern Europe contribute to our larger understanding of Jewish history and culture, as well as of the extent to which relations between Jews and representatives of other local groups reflect larger, more universal patterns of interaction, exchange, and division between members of different communities?

Among the different topics that authors were asked to examine while preparing their contributions were questions related to moments of inter-cultural exchange and patterns of reciprocal influence.[5] Instead of assuming that ideologies of isolation lead to hermetically sealed societies and that the politics of confrontation was an all-encompassing experience, contributors were asked to (re)consider the extent to which Jews and non-Jews regularly participated in common social, cultural, political, and economic spheres and how their involvement in these spheres depended upon and reinforced common activities, institutions, practices, mores, beliefs, and ultimately cultures. Another critical question was how these common structures, institutions, and practices helped create and institutionalize specific modes of inter-action and patterns of influence that very often circumvented whatever social isolation and ideological confrontation may have theoretically separated—and de facto defined—members of different groups. In this case, society and culture were assumed to be composed not solely of lofty ideas, critical actions, or dramatic developments that historical subjects consciously chose to embrace and undertake but, rather, of more fundamental, at times elusive, social, cultural, religious, political, and intellectual aspects of everyday life that historical subjects could not help but

---

[5] For a larger discussion of influence, see H. Bloom, *The Anxiety of Influence: A Theory of Poetry* (Oxford, 1973). See also S. Bassnett, 'Influence and Intertextuality: A Reappraisal', *Forum for Modern Language Studies*, 43 (2007), 134–46. On the use of influence within the framework of Jewish history, see Rosman, *How Jewish Is Jewish History?*, 140–3.

partake in and, therefore, be shaped by.[6] Our working assumption was that these moments of exchange and patterns of influence ran far deeper than those addressed by more traditional historiographical models of inter-group relations in eastern Europe, in particular those that revolve around questions regarding languages spoken, books read, parties voted for, neighbourhoods lived in, and the like.

Although some studies have criticized the concept and model of influence as a unidirectional process in which influence passes vertically from dominant cultures to more dependent (or colonized) ones, we maintain that influence is, in fact, a reciprocal if not multi-directional process, and, as such, has much to offer to the study of inter-group relations in eastern Europe.[7] Searching for and tracing patterns of influence also allows scholars to explore less obvious examples of interaction and exchange as well as the multifaceted web of daily life that so often characterized the many layers of interaction between Jews and their neighbours in eastern Europe. Indeed, much like the cases of African Americans or Israeli Arabs (Palestinian Israelis), not only were Jews in eastern Europe influenced by their neighbours' habits, the whims of ruling powers, and cultural developments in the region, but they too exerted a discernible influence on the surrounding cultural, political, and social milieu, one that they not only shared, but that they also helped to create. This model of reciprocal influence, one that allows for Jews (and others) to be simultaneously the agents and the receivers of influence, will help guide this essay and the volume that it introduces.

Like many other methodological paradigms, attempts to trace patterns of cultural exchange and influence present several problems to the scholar of Jewish history. Unfortunately, the very components of culture and society that often bind members of different, if not at times oppositional, groups in common frameworks are, by their very nature, the most elusive aspects of any culture, and, therefore, the most difficult to uncover, trace, pinpoint, and prove.[8] Thus, the first methodological problem inherent in this project is the editorial request that scholars shift their attention from traditional topics of historical analysis to more elusive historical processes and fleeting moments. In many cases, scholars have had a far easier time pointing to similar or parallel developments and phenomena than to actual

---

[6] See Bahktin's discussion of unconscious hybridity: M. M. Bakhtin, *The Dialogic Imagination: Four Essays*, trans. C. Emerson and M. Holquist (Austin, Tex., 1981), 358–61, cited in R. J. C. Young, *Colonial Desire: Hybridity in Theory, Culture, and Race* (London, 1995), 21.

[7] For critiques of 'influence' as a tool for academic research, see Graham Allen on Bloom in G. Allen, *Intertextuality* (New York, 2006), 133–44. See also D. N. Myers, *Resisting History: Historicism and its Discontents in German-Jewish Thought* (Princeton, 2003), 162–8; A. Rodrigue, 'The Ottoman Diaspora: The Rise and Fall of Ladino Literary Culture', in D. Biale (ed.), *Cultures of the Jews: A New History* (New York, 2002), 879; Rosman, *How Jewish Is Jewish History?*, 140–3; K. Ashley and V. Plesch, 'The Cultural Processes of "Appropriation"', *Journal of Medieval and Early Modern Studies*, 32 (2002), 2–4.

[8] Note Rosman's comment that 'Moreover, the usual impossibility of tracing modes of transmission renders the question of who influenced whom moot': Rosman, *How Jewish Is Jewish History?*, 142.

examples of cross-cultural adaptation, borrowing, or influence.[9] Cultural history, by its very nature, does not rely upon the search for a smoking gun; and yet that does not mean that where there is smoke there is no fire.[10] In an effort to resolve some of the methodological disagreements between the volume's three editors, we have agreed to grant contributors a reasonable degree of leeway—as opposed to the quasi-legal 'burden of historical proof'—in their search for such patterns of influence and moments of exchange. Designed to move the study of east European Jewry beyond the intellectual and academic impasse that has long troubled scholars, this volume is intended to create an academic space for new modes of inquiry that will contribute to our understanding of how members of different groups operate and interact on a myriad of different levels, some explicit, others implicit. While some critics may charge that our editorial policy is too liberal, we believe that this intellectual exercise is a necessary step in our efforts to expand the intellectual and academic discourse on these and related topics.

Beyond the methodological problems associated with 'proving' influence, the question of influence raises several additional questions regarding the very nature and borders of the field of 'Jewish history', matters that at least one scholar has referred to as *hashpa'itis*, or, in its rough English translation, the fear of influence.[11] Thus, another trap embedded deep within this intellectual exercise is the one that threatens to take the study of Jewish history to the very point at which Jewish history ceases to exist as an autonomous, independent field, and becomes part of a larger Polish, Russian, or East European history in which Jews in eastern Europe have more in common with Poles, Russians, Ukrainians, or members of other local groups than with Jews in other times and places.[12] Or, to put it somewhat less academically: how far can we stretch the limits—intellectual, methodological,

[9] See e.g. J. Sanders, *Adaptation and Appropriation* (London, 2006); Ashley and Plesch, 'Cultural Processes of "Appropriation"'; C. Sponsler, 'In Transit: Theorizing Cultural Appropriation in Medieval Europe', *Journal of Medieval and Early Modern Studies*, 32 (2002), 36: 'Difficult though it may be to scrutinize processes of appropriation—rather than fixed texts, objects, and events—let us glimpse that history being written.'

[10] See L. Hunt (ed.), *The New Cultural History* (Berkeley, 1989); V. E. Bonnell and L. Hunt (eds.), *Beyond the Cultural Turn: New Directions in the Study of Society and Culture* (Berkeley, 1999).

[11] On the anxiety of influence, see Bloom, *Anxiety of Influence*; Allen, *Intertextuality*, 133–44. On *hashpa'itis*, see Myers, *Resisting History*, 157–72, as well as D. N. Myers, 'Simon Rawidowicz, "Hashpaitis", and the Perils of Influence', *Transversal*, 7 (2006), 13–25.

[12] See Rosman's typically prescient comments in his *How Jewish Is Jewish History?*, 35–40, 82–104. For a discussion of similar phenomena in German, French, and American contexts, see N. Roemer, 'Outside and Inside the Nations: Changing Borders in the Study of the Jewish Past during the Nineteenth Century', in A. Gotzmann and C. Wiese (eds.), *Modern Judaism and Historical Consciousness: Identities, Encounters, Perspectives* (Leiden, 2007), 28–53. Thanks to Noah Gerber for bringing the latter source to our attention. See also E. Barkan, 'Historical Crimes and National Identity', in K. Almqvist and E. Wallrup (eds.), *Cosmopolitanism* (Stockholm, 2006), 195, 197; B. Lang, 'Hyphenated-Jews and the Anxiety of Identity', *Jewish Social Studies*, 12, no. 1 (2005), 4–5; I. Bartal, 'Bein historiyah imperialit lehistoriografiyah le'umit', in *Toldot yehudei rusiyah*, ed. A. Kulik (Jerusalem, 2010), 7–16.

cultural, ideological, and political—of the field of Jewish history and society as we wrestle with questions of influence, appropriation, and exchange?[13] Reflecting a very real case of *hashpa'itis* in the early twentieth century, the great master of modern Jewish literature, culture, and nationhood Yitzhak Leibush Peretz notes: 'Peoples whose blood is mixed, who are united neither in their land, their language, nor their economic institutions—are not possible. Different blood and different cultures, various world views—these can be maintained temporarily and kept together artificially only by external factors. Take them away, and the people will fall apart.'[14]

Despite our own individual cases of *hashpa'itis*, as well as the fervent arguments presented by some of the more outspoken opponents of this approach,[15] we fear that a conscious decision—or an even more problematic passive non-decision— not to pursue these questions would only further the intellectual, academic, and cultural stalemate exemplified by the binary 'Jews and Xs' school of research. Determined to move beyond this academic, cultural, and political gridlock and to explore these moments and patterns of inter-cultural exchange and mutual influence, we are confident that the field, its scholars, and its students can not only handle the question of influence, but that the turn to these questions will ultimately help us all overcome our individual and collective cases of *hashpa'itis* and, in the process, invigorate and advance the state of research on relations between Jews and members of different groups in lands east of Germany and west of the Urals.[16]

RELATIONS BETWEEN JEWS AND NON-JEWS IN JEWISH HISTORIOGRAPHY

In approaching the problem of the relations between Jews and their neighbours in eastern Europe, we come up against a long historiographic tradition from Heinrich Graetz to Simon Dubnow to Shmuel Ettinger which has seen this issue as central to any understanding of the Jewish past. Indeed, one is hard pressed to find any historian of 'the Jews' who did not view the issue as one that went to the very core of Jewish civilization. Although the place and role of non-Jewish society in the very construction of 'Jewish history' deserves a much longer, more systematic study, we shall attempt here to outline the various representations of relations between Jews

[13] For similar observations regarding the dilemmas inherent in writing Ukrainian history, see S. Plokhy, 'Beyond Nationality', *Ab Imperio*, 4 (2007), 29–30.

[14] Y. L. Peretz, 'Al sifrut yidish', in id., *Kol kitvei y. l. perets*, trans. S. Meltzer (Tel Aviv, 1962), 141–2 (Hebrew pagination).

[15] See D. G. Roskies, 'Border Crossings', *Commentary*, 115 (2003), 62–6; Rosman, *How Jewish Is Jewish History?*, 140–3.

[16] We would like to thank Gershon D. Hundert for supplying this definition of 'east European Jewry' within the context of the encyclopedia recently published under his editorship, *The YIVO Encyclopedia of Jews in Eastern Europe*, 2 vols. (New Haven, 2008).

and non-Jews as they appear in key works of Jewish history composed over the past one hundred and fifty years.[17]

The two major forces that shaped the interpretation of relations between Jews and their neighbours in eastern Europe were the ideas of the European Enlightenment and the struggle for civic and political equality for Jews within the framework of the modern state. These two processes, one intellectual, the other political, have left an indelible mark on the writing of Jewish history throughout the modern era. Ultimately, the acceptance of the central tenets of the Enlightenment and the fundamental goal of Jewish emancipation was based upon a total rejection of 'traditional Jewish' society. In order to achieve this transvaluation of Jewish values, a new historical narrative was created which portrayed traditional Jewish society as one stuck in a primitive cultural and intellectual state. A central part of this view of traditional Jewish society was the portrayal of relations between Jews and non-Jews as a never-ending saga of isolation that engendered a protracted social and moral crisis.

As elsewhere, this new Jewish narrative was the by-product of ideologies, politics, and societies that its authors were exposed to in London, Amsterdam, Berlin, and Vienna. In addition to thinking about the past, many figures of the Jewish Enlightenment also played active roles in various conceptualizations of the (Jewish) future. New cultural organizations and political movements offered them opportunities from the end of the eighteenth century up to today to work towards the reconstruction and rehabilitation of Jewish society. This deep connection between Enlightenment ideals and projects for equal citizenship influenced historiographical interpretations of both those Jews who continued to live according to traditional Jewish ways as well as non-Jews in the past, present, and future. As a result of this intellectual, ideological, and political position, historians' understanding of the Jewish past as well as their interpretation of the nature of relations between Jews and members of other ethnic and religious groups created the image of an enclosed and separate traditional Jewish society that should eventually be replaced by an open, liberal society in which Jews would integrate freely into their surroundings. Thus, the (Jewish) Enlightenment was responsible for the early interpretations of traditional Jewish society as an isolated body that had limited contact with the surrounding society.

The early generations of Jewish historians created a style of writing which was not only new to Jewish society but was also identified with and loyal to imperial rule and culture (Graetz was deeply committed to the supremacy of German culture while Dubnow believed in the need to maintain the territorial integrity of the tsarist empire). As such, the historiographical models that they used in order to frame and write about the Jewish past were simultaneously modern and colonial ones. In fact, they themselves served as agents of Westernization and modernization of those

---

[17] For more on this, see N. H. Roemer, *Jewish Scholarship and Culture in Nineteenth-Century Germany: Between History and Faith* (Madison, 2005).

Jews who continued to dwell on the margins of European society in areas that were often viewed as 'non-European' regions. The motif of a traditional Jewish society that kept its members bound in a state of non-European darkness and impatiently awaited the agents of modern, Western enlightenment, albeit in a Jewish key, to deliver them from their abysmal, primitive state would characterize and define the writing of Jewish history for generations. If the Enlightenment was the cure and the Jews were the patient, then traditional Jewish society was the disease.

Thus, the Jewish search for a new, non-traditional Jewish identity depended upon the internalization of key European ideas, whether they be those of the German philosophical tradition or those of new national movements. Another key idea that Jewish society inherited and internalized from the Enlightenment was the separation of the religious aspects of Jewish history and society from the political ones. This divide was evident in different writings about the Jews' status in the post-corporative era, whether the focus was on religious life and reform, which dominated research in western Europe, or on the ethnic aspects of Jewish life, which remained the preferred topic of research for Jews in the multinational empires of eastern Europe.

Heinrich Graetz (1817–91), one of the most prominent historians who contributed to the development of a modern Jewish historical consciousness, embodies this synthesis of imperial and modern ideologies and functions. Graetz, who was born in the Polish territories that were annexed by Prussia in the late eighteenth century, fully identified in mind and in spirit with German culture. As such, his relationship to 'Eastern Europe' in general, and to the Jews of eastern Europe, the *Ostjuden*, in particular, is a clear marker of Graetz's own role as an agent of German imperial culture who was committed to disseminating Western culture among the ostensibly backward Jewish residents of 'the East'. In his eyes, the 'Polish' essence of east European Jewish society was the main reason for its essential separation from the surrounding German environment and long-term Jewish residents.[18]

Moreover, the behaviour of east European Jews in accordance with traditional Jewish culture and folk ways engendered the hatred of other groups in central and eastern Europe. Although he was not the only one who voiced this opinion in the second half of the nineteenth century, Graetz went so far as to declare that the immigration of Jews from eastern Europe to German lands prevented the integration of other Jews into the non-Jewish surroundings and kept European Jewry trapped in 'a new middle ages': 'In the century of Descartes and Spinoza, when the three Christian nations, the French, English and Dutch, gave the death-blow to the middle ages, Jewish-Polish emigrants, baited by Khmelnytsky's bands, brought a new middle ages over European Judaism, which maintained itself in full vigor for more than a century, to some extent lasting to our time.'[19]

[18] See e.g. H. Graetz, *History of the Jews*, 6 vols. (Philadelphia, 1967), v. 16: 'The Cossack persecution of the Jews, in a sense, remodeled Judaism. It became polonized, so to speak.'   [19] Ibid. 17.

At the same time, many Jewish intellectuals, including those who helped create the new Jewish history and historiography, were well aware of the growing gap between the Enlightenment ideal of amicable relations between Jews and non-Jews and the increasingly bitter confrontations with and expressions of prejudice on the part of many of their non-Jewish neighbours. In response to these developments as well as to the rise of different movements for national liberation, several of the more prominent historians of east European Jewry advocated the adoption of a Jewish ethnic identity (and later the development of this identity into a national one) as a replacement for the earlier religious-corporate identity. Part of this transformation included a conscious effort to integrate a new memory of the pre-modern past into the socio-political framework of multinational empires in which many Jews lived. That said, the rise of a Jewish national historiography did not lead to the disappearance of universal, Enlightenment trends and their emphasis on tolerance and integration. If anything, these two trends continued side by side and together highlight the deep, inherent contradiction that haunts the field of Jewish history to this day.

These larger processes often led to new readings of historical sources and a fervent search for the roots of an ethnic (or national) identity in pre-modern Jewish society. One of the more prominent representatives of this new school of east European Jewish history was the Russian Jewish historian Simon Dubnow (1860–1941). After the First World War, when nation states were created in eastern Europe in which there was a direct correlation between 'the nation' and 'the state', this spirit of national historiography became even more prominent. Among Dubnow and his peers in the inter-war era there was now a connection between an emphasis on Jewish ethnic and cultural characteristics and the search for various political solutions to the problems that arose, including Europe's 'Jewish question'.

Often viewed as an intellectual disciple of Dubnow, the Kiev-born Israeli historian Shmuel Ettinger (1919–88) combined social radicalism with his fervent commitment to Jewish nationalism to construct narratives that represented a dichotomous, binary interpretation of relations between Jews and their neighbours. The synthesis of his radical political views with a deep consciousness of a unique Jewish ethnic identity continued, in many senses, the tensions that characterized the historical writings of earlier generations that combined the Enlightenment tradition of universalism with a Romantic, atavistic nationalism. At one extreme of his historical approach were those forces that opposed the integration of the Jews with Christian Slavs in their Russian imperial and Soviet permutations. At the other extreme, Ettinger regularly found expressions of tolerance and openness as well as the influence of rationalism and the Enlightenment. He looked towards the historical roots of eastern Europe and suggested a model of reciprocal, ongoing connections and relations between Jews and members of other ethnic groups. According to Ettinger, the starting point for the long story of tense relations between Jews and their neighbours in the territory of Rus was the adoption of the Christian Byzantine tradition by the Slav principalities beginning in the late tenth century.

Caesaro-papism and the hostility of the Byzantine Church to Judaism laid the foundations for negative attitudes towards the Jews in the Russian empire up until the early twentieth century. In a short article published in 1973, Ettinger brought together several pieces of extant information regarding the presence of Jews in Kievan Rus that highlighted the atmosphere at the time. What is most interesting is that, even though he repeatedly emphasized the fact that the sources were limited, Ettinger himself adopted the position of the historian Georgy Petrovich Fedotov regarding the centrality of anti-Jewish attitudes in ancient Russia. Ettinger wrote:

The increasing centrality of the argument against the Jews can be explained via the Jewish–Christian disputations that took place in Kievan Rus at the time the work was written. This disputation between the young Russian church (according to the Byzantine rite) and the Jews also aimed at other religions, and, in particular, against the Roman Catholic faith . . . From everything mentioned above, we can assume that the Jews were a significant factor in the cultural and religious life of Kievan Rus; they were a key factor in the religious disputations and it stands to reason that there were attempted conversions.[20]

Ettinger viewed the Jewish influence on Muscovite Russian culture in the following centuries as one that was associated with the West and described it as a clear expression of the influence of 'the rational Jewish thought of the Middle Ages . . . similar to that of Jewish centres in western Europe in the thirteenth and fourteenth centuries'.[21] Thus, Russian opposition to Jewish influences as well as to the physical presence of members of the Jewish faith in the empire between the sixteenth century and the twentieth century was anti-Western in its character and also opposed to the concept of progress. This Byzantine spirit, according to Ettinger, shaped the anti-Jewish policies of Muscovite Russia as well as those in imperial Russia from the days of Ivan the Terrible in the middle of the sixteenth century till the collapse of the Russian empire in 1917. The struggle of the Russian state against the 'Judaizing heretics' and the repression of this heretical movement, wrote Ettinger, brought to an end the

relative religious tolerance [that] characterized the reign of Ivan the Third and provoked a reaction which led to a break in cultural relations with the West and a repression of the intellectual activity that was brought to Russia by Jews and Hebrew translations. A number of researchers saw this heresy as a Renaissance and Reformation in Russia; however, even if this opinion is accepted with reservations, one cannot deny that its failure actually pushed back the wheels of progress even further in the country.[22]

---

[20] S. Ettinger, 'Rusiyah haki'evit', in B. Roth (ed.), *Tekufat ha'ofel: hayehudim be'eiropah hanotserit 711–1096* (Tel Aviv, 1973), 189.

[21] S. Ettinger, 'Hahashpa'ah hayehudit al hatesisah hadatit bemizraḥ eiropah besof hame'ah ha-15', in id., *Bein polin lerusiyah* (Jerusalem, 1994), 55 (this article first appeared in 1961).

[22] S. Ettinger, 'Hahashpa'ah hayehudit al kefirat hamityahadim berusiyah hamoskva'it', in id., *Bein polin lerusiyah*, 69–70 (this article only appeared after the death of the author); see also 'Medinat moskvah beyaḥasah el hayehudim', ibid. 72–104 (this article first appeared in 1953).

This hostility which came to the eastern half of Europe from the western half was one of the central themes around which Ettinger reconstructed relations between Jews and their neighbours. Jewish communities, which represented a distinct urban stratum in the socio-economic system of the Polish–Lithuanian Commonwealth, were, in his eyes, European islands surrounded by neighbours who were inferior to them in their communal organization, economic activities, and cultural affairs. In the face of all this stood the centralized Russian state—either the Russian imperial one or the Soviet one—determined to integrate its Jewish subjects. Ettinger described relations between Jews and Russians in the following terms:

It seems as though the readiness to accept the Jews and to grant them a place in Russian society was more likely when Russia's residents were interested in accepting Western ideas and living according to their model; and that a rejection of the Jews and the adoption of actions harmful to them occurred when Russia was pulling away from the West and returning to more traditional values and ways. However, the liberal periods of looking westward have been relatively infrequent over the past two hundred years.[23]

Ettinger's summary was consistent with the classic Zionist model which viewed the rise of Jewish nationalism as a result of Jewish realizations regarding the illusory nature of the Enlightenment's claims that surrounding societies were ready to accept the Jews into their fold.[24]

Israel Bartal's doctoral dissertation, which was written under the supervision of Ettinger and Chone Shmeruk at the Hebrew University, addressed the various permutations of the non-Jewish east European in the Jewish imagination in a period of rapid modernization. Based on a large pool of literary sources in Hebrew and Yiddish, the thesis traced these transformations from pre-modern models of inter-group relations in a corporate setting of the Polish–Lithuanian Commonwealth to a new type of relations in an urban environment that were rooted in the capitalist system as well as modern means of communication. This analysis revealed that the processes of modernization in eastern Europe had far-reaching implications for the interactions between Jews and representatives of other groups:

During this period there was an intensification of contact between the Jews of Eastern Europe and the non-Jewish population. Social and cultural processes which had already begun in the first half of the nineteenth century were accelerated, and literature evolved in Hebrew, Yiddish, Russian, German and Polish, in which expression was given to the image of the non-Jewish environment in relationship to these changes. This was a transitional period at the start of which a system of contacts and relationships of a medieval character was dominant between Jews and Gentiles. By its end, a number of different views of the relations between Jews and Gentiles competed for dominance in the Jewish environment.

[23] S. Ettinger, 'Rusiyah vehayehudim: nisayon shel sikum histori', in id., *Bein polin lerusiyah*, 439 (this article first appeared in 1971).

[24] A similar view is expressed by Ruth Wisse in her *If I am not for Myself . . .: The Liberal Betrayal of the Jews* (New York, 1992).

These ranged from the acceptance of the conceptual and literary influences of the outside world while rejecting assimilation, to the negation of a specific Jewish identity.[25]

Like Ettinger, Bartal drew a connection between changes in the images of the non-Jew that appeared in Jewish modernist writings and the transition from a world of traditional concepts to one of modern concepts such as hope and disappointment. These changes are most apparent when looking at the gap between the hopes that grew out of the Enlightenment and the disappointments that arose out of repeated political and social crises. One key aspect of these Enlightenment visions was the hope for a new solidarity between Jews and non-Jews. Moreover, in each and every case, disappointment among Jewish writers and Jewish historians was viewed as the result of the actions of the ruling powers, who failed to behave according to the proper European model. By placing the onus for these political failures on ruling parties, Jewish historians and ideologues were able to continue believing in both the state of conflict between Jews and non-Jews, and the possibility of openness, integration, and co-operation. This concept of good people who are misled by bad leaders is exemplified in the following quotation from an article entitled 'I Give Up', in which Yitzhak Leibush Peretz condemns the Polish nobility and praises the Polish peasants (and people):

It was not I who allowed Poland to be partitioned, because of family intrigue and hope for material gain. It was not I who put foreign rulers on the Polish throne . . . It was not I who brought modern civil law from Paris. It was not I who brought religion and the Jesuits from Rome. It was not I who delayed the emancipation of the peasants, so that it had to come from Petersburg. Dear nobleman, this culture, with all its virtues, is *yours* . . . my only sorrow is that in this Poland which is *yours*, besides me, who works and trades in the town, so, also, the peasant, who ploughs and sows had no share![26]

The identification of a particular historian with the position expressed by a specific source regarding the degree of proximity or distance between Jews and Poles originates, no doubt, in the political disposition of the historian in question. Peretz's comments regarding those Poles that he does not want to be close to (the nobles), and those that he does want to join (the peasants), are not that different in principle, structure, and attitude from Graetz's comments regarding the impact that Jews from Polish lands had on German–Jewish interaction. Generations of historians who wrote about the history of the Jews in eastern and central Europe repeatedly searched for an openness and toleration among Russians, Poles, Ukrainians, or Germans that would have made possible Jewish integration in accordance with the principles of the Enlightenment project and emancipation contract. Indeed, without that openness there could be no integration, let alone the

[25] I. Bartal, 'Non-Jews and Gentile Society in East European Hebrew and Yiddish Literature, 1856–1914', *Polin*, 4 (1989), 53–4.

[26] Cited ibid. 68–9. For Bartal's model of the three phases in the relations between the Jews and their surroundings in eastern Europe, see I. Bartal, *The Jews of Eastern Europe, 1772–1881*, trans. C. Naor (Philadelphia, 2005), 157–68.

dream of integration and acceptance. According to each particular historian's understanding of Jewish history, it was either Russian liberals, Polish intellectuals, or Ukrainian workers who determined the degree of openness or isolation that would ultimately be granted to Jews in eastern Europe. Moreover, in almost every case, this was a binary, either/or equation, a social contract par excellence that knew no shades of grey. One was either accepted into the surrounding society or, conversely, one's attempts to integrate were ultimately rejected. For generations, the search for and historiographical construction of a middle ground eluded historians of the Jews, in particular those who researched and wrote about Jews in the Russian empire and its successor states.

Nor was this larger historiographical approach limited to turn-of-the-century ideologues like Dubnow or early Israeli historians like Ettinger.[27] In a recent Hebrew book, the Israeli scholar Havi Dreifuss (Ben Sasson) examines the Jewish view of relations between Poles and Jews during the Holocaust. Her survey of an impressive array of archival and published sources in a variety of languages leads her to conclude:

It seems that in the later years of the war there appeared a contradiction between the image of the 'good Pole' that many Jews had created in the early days of the war and the reality that they experienced later on. The disappointment felt by many Jews in light of the behaviour of Poles did not fit their earlier visions and led to a dramatic shift in their interpretation of their surroundings. The positive image disappeared and was replaced by an extremely hostile one. From this point on, many Jews saw Poles as partners in their persecution. There were even those [Jews] who attributed to them [Poles] the German designs for extermination.[28]

According to Dreifuss's interpretation, the experience of Polish Jews during the Second World War was another chapter in a long chain of great expectations and bitter disappointments. The vision of toleration was there, as was the expectation that this openness would be adopted by those on the other side of the religious-national divide. However, once again, true to the classic model of Zionist historiography—only this time in ways that were unprecedented in their catastrophic dimensions and horrific in their results—the other partner in the 'Enlightenment contract' did not respond as so many Jews had hoped and, perhaps, even prayed.

For almost two hundred years, modern Jewish historiography, whether integrationist or national, has seen such disappointments as the very litmus test of the Jewish historical experience and of European liberalism. Some have seen these repeated cases of disappointment as a reflection of a depressing reality, and others will claim that it is a narrative construct that obscures more complex social and

---

[27] See e.g. works by the authors of this essay: M. Opalski and I. Bartal, *Poles and Jews: A Failed Brotherhood* (Hanover, NH, 1992), and S. Ury, *Red Banner, Blue Star: The Revolution of 1905 and the Transformation of Warsaw Jewry*, forthcoming, esp. ch. 6.

[28] H. Dreifuss, *Anu yehudei polin? Hayeḥasim bein yehudim lepolanim bitkufat hasho'ah min hahebet hayehudi* (Jerusalem, 2009), 192.

historical processes. Either way, 'the greater the expectations, the greater the disappointment', and within this historiography the theme of bitter disappointment in the wake of the unfulfilled promises of the Enlightenment plays a central role in the construction of relations between Jews and 'Others'.

HISTORIOGRAPHICAL CHALLENGES FROM WITHIN AND FROM BEYOND

While the historiography of Jews in eastern Europe very often stresses their separation from the societies in which they lived, the study of inter-group relations and interactions has gone through a series of theoretical and intellectual transformations over the past two decades. As a result, many works in fields as varied as literary, cultural, and post-colonial studies no longer speak of how ethnic identities were inherited and then maintained, but rather of the ways in which different political settings and cultural developments contributed to the construction of hybrid identities in which no specific political or cultural unit or individual is completely isolated and separate from surrounding cultures or societies. Thus, while questions of influence provide one of the main themes for this volume, discussions of hybridity are also relevant for any study of inter-group relations, including those between Jews and their neighbours in eastern Europe.

Among prominent thinkers, Mikhail Bakhtin, Homi Bhabha, and Edward Said have all advocated various interpretations of a hybrid self that arises out of colonial or other settings. For these and other scholars, modern selves are shaped by constant exposure to and negotiations between different cultures, which inevitably lead to repeated moments of exchange, cases of borrowing, and unconscious patterns of adaptation and acts of resistance. Originally borrowed from the nineteenth-century sciences of biology and botany and then translated into an assault on early twentieth-century theories of master races as well as somewhat newer ones regarding the essential nature of ostensibly holistic identities and communities, hybridity, like so many concepts, can mean, has meant, and will continue to mean many things to many people, from linguistic fusion to rebellions against colonial authority.[29]

That said, Robert Young is fair in summarizing hybridity in the following manner:

[29] For an overview of the history of the term and its different uses, see Young, *Colonial Desire*, 6–28. On linguistic, colonial, and post-colonial discussions of hybridity, see, respectively, Bakhtin, *Dialogic Imagination*, 358–61; E. W. Said, *Out of Place: A Memoir* (New York, 2000); H. K. Bhabha, 'Signs Taken for Wonders: Questions of Ambivalence and Authority under a Tree outside Delhi, May 1817', in id., *Location of Culture*, 102–22, esp. 111–15. See also Rosman's discussion of this issue, as well as his critique of Bhabha: Rosman, *How Jewish Is Jewish History?*, 94–104, 183. For a thought-provoking critique of Bhabha and other advocates of post-colonial hybridity, see P. Cheah, 'Given Culture: Rethinking Cosmopolitical Freedom in Transnationalism', in P. Cheah and B. Robbins (eds.), *Cosmopolitics: Thinking and Feeling beyond the Nation* (Minneapolis, 1998), 290–328.

At its simplest, hybridity, however, implies a disruption and forcing together of any unlike living things, grafting a vine or a rose on to a different root stock, making difference into sameness. Hybridity is a making one of two distinct things, so that it becomes impossible for the eye to detect the hybridity of a geranium or a rose . . . Hybridity thus makes difference into sameness, and sameness into difference, but in a way that makes the same no longer the same, the different no longer simply different.[30]

Or, as Said put it in regard to the legacy of his parents' lives in colonial Egypt, Lebanon, and Palestine:

His parents were themselves self-creations: two Palestinians with dramatically different backgrounds and temperaments living in colonial Cairo as members of a Christian minority within a large pond of minorities, with only each other for support, without any precedent for what they were doing except an odd combination of prewar Palestinian habit; American lore picked up at random in books and magazines from my father's decade in the United States . . . the missionaries' influence; incompleted and hence eccentric schooling; British colonial attitudes that represented both the lords and the general run of 'humankind' they ruled; and, finally, the style of life my parents perceived around them in Egypt and which they tried to adapt to their special circumstances. Could 'Edward's' position ever be any thing but out of place?[31]

Under the influence of these and other thinkers, scholars of Jewish history and culture have similarly begun to re-evaluate the fundamental historical maxim regarding the 'great Chinese Wall' that has long separated Jews and non-Jews in the annals of Jewish history.[32] Scholars of medieval Jewish history, in particular, have produced a series of works that are clearly influenced by larger discussions of hybridity and exchange. While scholars such as Mark Cohen and Mark Meyerson are out to correct what they believe are historiographical misconceptions regarding

[30] Young, *Colonial Desire*, 26.

[31] Said, *Out of Place*, 19. See also ibid. 92, 95, 179, 184, 190, 236. Or, as Bernhard Felsenthal, the legendary rabbi of Chicago's Congregation Sinai, once described himself: 'Racially I am a Jew, for I have been born among the Jewish nation. Politically I am an American as patriotic, as enthusiastic, as devoted an American citizen as it is possible to be. But spiritually I am a German, for my inner life has been profoundly influenced by Schiller, Goethe, Kant, and other intellectual giants of Germany': cited in A. A. Goren, *The American Jews* (Cambridge, Mass., 1982), 34. See also C. Lévi-Strauss, 'Cosmopolitanism and Schizophrenia', in id., *The View from Afar*, trans. J. Neugroschel and P. Hoss (New York, 1985), 184–5.

[32] Note Rosman's comment that 'Once upon a time Jewish scholars posited that traditional Jews of the past lived in cultural and—to a great degree—social isolation from the Gentile world. Jewish life was seen as autonomous in the broadest sense, based on the classic Jewish past and driven by an independent, internal Jewish dynamic . . . In practice, the hundreds of studies documenting social and cultural ties between Jews and Christians cast doubt that there was real isolation': M. Rosman, 'A Jewish Guide to Medieval Domestic Europe', review of E. Baumgarten, *Mothers and Children: Jewish Family Life in Medieval Europe*, in *Jewish Quarterly Review*, 98 (2008), 419. See also Y. Zerubavel, 'Memory, the Rebirth of the Native and the "Hebrew Bedouin" Identity', *Social Research*, 75 (2008), 315–52.

the study of pre-modern Jewish history,[33] Gil Anidjar, Elisheva Baumgarten, David Nirenberg, and Israel J. Yuval have all gone at least one step further by putting forward provocative—and, in the eyes of some, controversial—theses regarding the very nature of relations between Jews and their neighbours.[34] Yuval's discussion of Jewish–Christian relations in medieval Ashkenaz seems to go the furthest by suggesting that the mutual (mis)interpretations of images and motifs surrounding the First Crusade led to repeated, unconscious acts and patterns of cultural borrowing and reciprocal influence between Jews and Christians.[35] Nirenberg is similarly provocative in his contention that religious confrontations and inter-group violence were not barriers to the creation of a common cultural sphere, but, in fact, were integral and accepted aspects of one larger society.[36] Not to be outdone, Baumgarten's analysis of Jewish–Gentile relations through the lens of gender opens an entirely new set of questions and topics for historians. Lastly, despite the many methodological, ideological, and intellectual differences among these and other works, together they represent a discernible shift in the way that Jewish and non-Jewish histories and societies in the medieval era are viewed and represented. No longer marginal or angrily rejected, moments of cultural exchange and the accompanying questioning of historical and disciplinary borders are central to the study of medieval Jewish society.[37]

Nor are such efforts to re-evaluate relations between Jews and non-Jews and, in the process, the very nature, structure, and limits of Jewish history restricted to one particular sub-field. The recent collection *Cultures of the Jews* is designed, as the volume's editor David Biale writes in his programmatic introduction, to demonstrate how 'For every period of history, interaction with the non-Jewish majority has been critical in the formation of Jewish culture. Even those Jewish cultures thought to be the most insular adapted ideas and practices from their surroundings.'[38]

---

[33] M. R. Cohen, *Under Crescent and Cross: The Jews in the Middle Ages* (Princeton, 1994), and M. D. Meyerson, *A Jewish Renaissance in Fifteenth-Century Spain* (Princeton, 2004). See also J. Elukin, *Living Together, Living Apart: Rethinking Jewish–Christian Relations in the Middle Ages* (Princeton, 2007).

[34] See G. Anidjar, '*Our Place in al-Andalus': Kabbalah, Philosophy, Literature in Arab Jewish Letters* (Stanford, Calif., 2002); Baumgarten, *Mothers and Children*; D. Nirenberg, *Communities of Violence: Persecution of Minorities in the Middle Ages* (Princeton, 1996); I. J. Yuval, *Two Nations in Your Womb: Perceptions of Jews and Christians in Late Antiquity* (Berkeley, 2006).

[35] Yuval, *Two Nations in Your Womb*.

[36] See Nirenberg, *Communities of Violence*, 9–10, 13, 201–2, 227–8, 245.

[37] I. G. Marcus, 'Israeli Medieval Jewish Historiography: From Nationalist Positivism to New Cultural and Social Histories', *Jewish Studies Quarterly*, 17 (2010), 244–85.

[38] D. Biale, 'Preface: Towards a Cultural History of the Jews', in id. (ed.), *Cultures of the Jews*, p. xx. Note Rosman's comment that 'Many chapters in the recent *Cultures of the Jews*, for example, imply the claim that there were many Jewish cultures and each one was more closely tied to its geographic and chronological cultural context than to Jewish culture in the past or the present': Rosman, 'Jewish Guide to Medieval Domestic Europe', 419. As an example, see Rodrigue, 'Ottoman Diaspora'.

These new voices from fields as diverse as medieval Jewish history and cultural studies are not the only ones that challenge the traditional conceptualization and representation of Jewish history and culture. Thus, the fall of the Berlin Wall and the subsequent restructuring of Polish society has led to a new generation of studies in Poland dedicated to re-evaluating the nature of Polish–Jewish relations and the place of 'the Jews' in Polish history and culture. Critical studies by scholars such as Agnieszka Jagodzińska, Adam Kaźmierczyk, Annamaria Orla-Bukowska, Eugenia Prokop-Janiec, and Marcin Wodziński have all begun to question many of the long-standing assumptions regarding Jews and their neighbours.[39]

Over time, exchanges, conferences, and central journals like *Polin* and *Gal-ed* have brought these and other studies to the attention of scholars in the United States and Israel. The influence of these academic and intellectual exchanges can be seen in several recent works on Jewish history and society in the early modern era. Indeed, studies by scholars such as Paweł Maciejko and Adam Teller have contributed immeasurably to earlier works by Jacob Goldberg, Gershon Hundert, and Moshe Rosman on the very nature and margins of Jewish society in the early modern Polish lands.[40] The publication of volume 22 of *Polin* under the editorial stewardship of Teller and Magda Teter has helped solidify this challenge to early modern Jewish history and society in eastern Europe and also lay the intellectual foundations for this present volume.[41]

Yet despite the influence of these and other works addressing the early modern period, the study of Jewish history and culture in modern eastern Europe has seen far fewer challenges similar to those of Nirenberg and Yuval, and even that of Biale.[42] Indeed, none of these studies has yet led to a fundamental reassessment of the field similar to the one produced by the combined impact of the recent wave of

---

[39] See e.g. the following works in English by key Polish scholars: A. Jagodzińska, 'The Importance of Being Beautiful: The Jews of Warsaw and their Aesthetic Declarations in the Second Half of the 19th Century', *Pinkas*, 1 (2006), 76–96; A. Kaźmierczyk, 'Converted Jews in Kraków, 1650 1763', *Gal-ed*, 21 (2007), 17–52; A. Orla-Bukowska, 'Maintaining Borders, Crossing Borders: Social Relationships in the *Shtetl*', *Polin*, 17 (2004), 171–95; E. Prokop-Janiec, *Polish-Jewish Literature in the Interwar Years*, trans. A. Shenitzer (Syracuse, NY, 2003); M. Wodziński, 'Good Maskilim and Bad Assimilationists; or, Toward a New Historiography of the Haskalah in Poland', *Jewish Social Studies*, 10, no. 3 (2004), 87–122. See also A. Landau-Czajka, *Syn będzie Lech...: Asymilacja Żydów w Polsce międzywojennej* (Warsaw, 2006), as well as A. Cała, *Asymilacja Żydów w Królestwie Polskim (1864–1897): Postawy, konflikty, stereotypy* (Warsaw, 1989).

[40] P. Maciejko, *The Mixed Multitude: Jacob Frank and the Frankist Movement, 1755–1816* (Philadelphia, 2011); A. Teller, '"In the Land of their Enemies"? The Duality of Jewish Life in Eighteenth-Century Poland', *Polin*, 19 (2007), 433–4, 446; J. Goldberg, *Hamumarim bemamlekhet polin-lita* (Jerusalem, 1985); M. J. Rosman, *The Lords' Jews: Magnate–Jewish Relations in the Polish–Lithuanian Commonwealth during the Eighteenth Century* (Cambridge, Mass., 1990); G. D. Hundert, *The Jews in a Polish Private Town: The Case of Opatów in the Eighteenth Century* (Baltimore, 1992). See also Rosman, *How Jewish Is Jewish History?*, 182–6.

[41] See *Polin*, 22 (2010), devoted to 'Social and Cultural Boundaries in Pre-Modern Poland'.

[42] For an overview of parallel changes in the study of German Jewry, see Myers, *Resisting History*, 168–72.

studies on medieval Jewish culture and society. And the pivotal question remains: why not?

Although the study of east European Jewish history has long outgrown Dubnow's stress on the separateness of the autonomous Jewish society, the following considerations may help explain the present state of academic affairs. First, Jewish historiography and the contemporary Jewish discourse on community have a long and deeply embedded fear of 'assimilation' as one of the more menacing threats to the theoretical sanctity of the Jewish community.[43] Ever since Arthur Ruppin canonized the scientific study of 'the Jews', assimilation has stood as one of the most pressing threats that modern society poses to 'the Jews'.[44] The long-standing association of any and all signs of 'assimilation' with the beginning of a slippery slope that inevitably leads to the end of all things Jewish has led many to label any sighting of interaction and influence as the early stages in assimilationist fantasies of Jewish self-hatred and accompanying drives for collective self-destruction.[45] Speaking about the connection between the fear of assimilation and the commitment of many Jewish scholars of Jewish studies to the very concept of 'a Jewish community', Andreas Gotzmann points to the tendency of many academics to downplay or even ignore moments of influence and exchange between Jews and non-Jews. 'Jewish history,' he notes, 'while continuing to be an enterprise aimed primarily at a Jewish and only later a non-Jewish readership, increasingly accentuated the "Jewish" features of its object.'[46] Thus, while many scholars of 'the Jews' in America, Europe, and Israel have long distanced themselves from Ruppin's doomsday predictions, Peretz's angry admonishments, and Dubnow's calls for national revival, the vestiges of these early foundations of modern Jewish studies and culture often remain.[47] Indeed, while the field of Jewish studies is far more diverse and varied than it was a generation or two ago, there are still several fundamental tenets that unite the vast

[43] In the contemporary North American Jewish discourse this is also referred to as the matter of 'Jewish continuity', and now with the similarly vague term 'Jewish peoplehood'.

[44] See A. Ruppin, *Hasotsiologiyah shel hayehudim: hamivneh hasotsiali shel hayehudim* (Berlin, 1931–3), ii. 83–92, 247–54. For an opposing viewpoint, see H. Arendt, *The Origins of Totalitarianism* (New York, 1973), 84: 'Assimilation, whether carried to the extreme of conversion or not, never was a real menace to the survival of the Jews.' For discussions of these issues, see A. Morris-Reich, *The Quest for Jewish Assimilation in Modern Social Science* (London, 2007); S. DellaPergola, 'Arthur Ruppin Revisited: The Jews of Today, 1904–1994', in S. M. Cohen and G. Horenczyk (eds.), *National Variations in Jewish Identity: Implications for Jewish Education* (Albany, NY, 1999), 53–84. Also note that Bar Ilan University in Israel has an academic centre dedicated to the study of 'assimilation as the primary danger to the future of the Jewish people'. See <http://www.biu.ac.il/JS/rappaport/English/aboutE.htm>, accessed 25 Oct. 2010.

[45] See e.g. Y. L. Peretz's vituperative assault on the assimilationist camp in turn-of-the-century Warsaw and, in particular, on Warsaw's pro-assimilation Polish weekly, *Izraelita*: Dr Shtitzer [Y. L. Peretz], *Der veg*, 18 (31) Aug. 1905, p. 1; Dr Shtitzer [Y. L. Peretz], *Der veg*, 30 Aug. (12 Sept.) 1905, p. 2; Dr Shtitzer [Y. L. Peretz], *Der veg*, 3 (16) Sept. 1905, p. 1.

[46] A. Gotzmann, 'Historiography as Cultural Identity: Toward a Jewish History beyond National History', in Gotzmann and Wiese (eds.), *Modern Judaism and Historical Consciousness*, 512.

[47] See e.g. the sources cited in n. 4 above.

majority of its practitioners within the framework of an academic community, and one of these underlying assumptions is a commitment to 'the Jews' as a cohesive social, political, and cultural entity.

In the case of east European Jewry, this faith in and commitment to the very concept of community has consistently found its way back into the scholarship. Indeed, from Dubnow to Ettinger to the present, the study of east European Jewry has often been the study of 'the Jews' as a community, a people, a nation (in waiting).[48] Grounded in Dubnow's search for a communal past and strengthened by early Zionist thinkers like Leon Pinsker, Theodor Herzl, and Ruppin, who looked to east European Jewry as the heart, soul, and future of the Jewish people, scholars have more often than not imagined, researched, and portrayed the Jews of eastern Europe as a community. Unlike quintessential figures of Jewish modernity in western Europe and North America such as Georg Simmel's stranger, Walter Benjamin's *flâneur*, and Woody Allen's Zelig, who slip into hyper-individuality if not beyond, modern Jewish society and history in eastern Europe is very often seen as one of community, belonging, and nation; and community, belonging, and nation are fundamentally opposed to if not inherently threatened by influence and hybridity.

The overriding faith in and loyalty to an organic, if at times even essentialist, conception of Jewishness grounded in and bound by an all-encompassing concept of community has been further fortified over the past six decades by the creation of the State of Israel and the construction and solidification of the new Israeli self in the Old New Land.[49] Unlike many of their immediate ancestors or colleagues outside Israel, most contemporary Israeli scholars have spent the majority of their lives in one particular nation state where one Jewish language reigns and a state-sponsored, Jewish-oriented culture maintains a dominant, hegemonic presence.[50] Hence, while the Zionist project to create a brave new Jewish (or Israeli) world may not have succeeded on all fronts, it has succeeded in creating a new Jewish society in which millions of Israeli Jews have state-supported, and in many situations state-mandated, ethnic, linguistic, religious, cultural, and civic identities as 'free people in our land'. Ironically, one of the central tensions and sites of hybridity that exists in this framework is a strange, yet to be fully deciphered intersection between an imagined Jewish past and an omnipresent Israeli present.[51] For better

[48] One notable exception is B. Nathans, *Beyond the Pale: The Jewish Encounter with Late Imperial Russia* (Berkeley, 2002). However, here too the author cannot escape what one of his Berkeley teachers, Amos Funkenstein, masterfully termed 'the dialectics of assimilation'. See A. Funkenstein, 'The Dialectics of Assimilation', *Jewish Social Studies*, 1, no. 2 (1995), 1–14.

[49] On Zionist attempts to engineer the creation of a New Jew, see A. Shapira, *Yehudim ḥadashim, yehudim yeshanim* (Tel Aviv, 1997), 155–74; O. Almog, *Hatsabar: deyokan* (Tel Aviv, 1997). See also Yuri Slezkine's comments on this issue in his polemical work *The Jewish Century* (Princeton, 2004), 204 ff.

[50] See D. N. Myers, 'Is There Still a "Jerusalem School"? Reflections on the State of Jewish Historical Scholarship in Israel', *Jewish History*, 23 (2009), 389–406.

[51] We would be grateful to anyone who would take the study of this new Israeli–Jewish hybridity on

or for worse, the Zionist revolution has succeeded in creating a New Israeli Jew, one that knows neither the blessings nor the challenges of Galut—or, in the language of this essay, hybridity. Furthermore, many Israeli academics are—whether they like it or not—by-products of this national project and the new post-Galut cultural environment and parallel conceptions of community and self that it has so desperately (and at times successfully) tried to create.[52] Indeed, while no one culture is the by-product of one particular overriding force, neither is any one individual immune from the influence of the dominant culture which he or she dwells, works, and participates in, contributes to, and produces. In the light of this situation, many of the all-too-human by-products of the ethno-national Jewish state of Israel seem averse—on both the conscious and the subconscious levels—to the use of theories of hybridity and influence as methodological prisms for understanding what are often seen and presented as organic, holistic conceptions and practices of Jewish culture, history, and self.

None of these factors, however, explains sufficiently a perceived lack of interest in, if not at times a palpable hostility towards, models of influence, hybridity, and exchange and their potential use for furthering our understanding of east European Jewry, its history, and its culture.[53] Indeed, many of the same factors also weigh heavily upon those who research medieval Jewish history and culture, a field that has passed through an intellectual and theoretical renaissance in the past generation. Thus, the key to understanding the state of the field rests in the very image of east European Jewry in contemporary Jewish society. For many observers, the Jews of eastern Europe have become the representation of an authentic, unadulterated pre-modern Jewish past that often stands for all that was beautiful and pure about Jewish society, from Yiddish lullabies to plates of gefilte fish.[54] Discussed at length and with much clarity elsewhere, this romanticization and essentialization of east European Jewry is further exacerbated by the seemingly sacred role that it plays as the consummate victim of the ultimate horror of the

themselves as their next academic project. In the meantime, see A. Morris-Reich, '"End on Surface": Teleology and Ground in Israeli Culture', *Representations*, 97 (2007), 123–50; G. Zukermann, *Yisre'elit safah yafah: az eizo safah hayisre'elim medaberim?* (Tel Aviv, 2008).

[52] Note that one of the central historical museums in Israel today, Beit Hatefutsot, the Museum of the Jewish People, is housed on Tel Aviv University's campus adjacent to the Department of Jewish History. Architecturally and ideologically, the original designers of the university–museum complex some forty years ago believed that the Jewish Diaspora belonged in the past, either as a dead culture on display in a museum case or as a topic researched and taught within the protected realm of an academic institution on the outskirts of the new Hebrew city of Tel Aviv.

[53] Engel claims that this resistance lies in a 'narrative of unique righteousness' common to both Poles and Jews: Engel, 'On Reconciling the Histories of Two Chosen Peoples', 925.

[54] On earlier images of east European Jews in German lands, see S. Aschheim, *Brothers and Strangers: The East European Jew in German and German-Jewish Consciousness, 1800–1923* (Madison, 1982). On the different roles played by Yiddish culture and the legacy of east European Jewry in contemporary American Jewish society, see J. Shandler, *Adventures in Yiddishland: Postvernacular Language and Culture* (Berkeley, 2006).

modern world, the Holocaust.[55] Nor are such romantic myths limited to the collective and individual imaginations of Jews in America, Israel, or Europe.[56] Indeed, the continued popularity of Jewish festivals in Poland, the array of Jewish-theme cafés in central and eastern Europe, and the wooden figurines that dot the urban landscape of cities like Kraków testify to the globalization of the now iconic myth of east European Jewry as the ultimate victim of the Holocaust, if not of modernity itself.[57]

As a result of this iconic role, the passive historical actor of 'east European Jewry' remains trapped in a historical *telos*, one that passes directly from the Khmelnytsky pogroms of 1648–9, to the massacre in Jedwabne in 1941, to the gates of Auschwitz in 1942–4, only to reach its final, post-Shoah postscript in the bloody pogrom in the Polish city of Kielce on 4 July 1946.[58] Once cast in this role in Jewish history, there appear to be few parts available to the Jews of eastern Europe beyond the lachrymose narrative of hatred, violence, genocide, and victimhood. And so, east European Jewry remains frozen and sacralized in a myth as the ultimate victim of Nazi policies. As such, it is particularly resistant to any attempts to problematize, theorize, or even humanize this past. Often it seems as if one slight adjustment to this paradigm of victimhood would lead to another catastrophe, the destruction of east European Jewry as the symbol of Jewish suffering and the subsequent collapse of the Jewish master narrative of the Holocaust, the twentieth century, and modern Jewish history and society. While these myths draw their strength from the realm of popular culture and the politics of community, where they are particularly well entrenched, they also maintain their influence in the hallowed corridors of academia. As a result, except for several recent studies of early modern Jewry, there are few attempts to create an alternative story of east European Jewry that do not revolve around powerlessness and victimhood and an accompanying Zionist postscript of rebirth and redemption.[59]

These, in short, are the myths that we wish to challenge, the problem that we want to resolve, the discussion that we would like to begin. The question that we

[55] For more on this topic, see S. J. Zipperstein, *Imagining Russian Jewry: Memory, History, Identity* (Seattle, 1999), 87–105; P. Wróbel, 'Double Memory: Poles and Jews after the Holocaust', *East European Politics and Societies*, 11 (1997), 560–74; Bartov, 'Eastern Europe as the Site of Genocide'. We would like to thank François Guesnet for his prescient comments regarding the 'essentialization of east European Jewry' in conversations in Budapest in 2007 and London in 2008.

[56] See e.g. the ground-breaking work by Jackie Feldman, including 'Marking the Boundaries of the Enclave: Defining the Israeli Collective through the Poland "Experience"', *Israel Studies*, 7, no. 2 (2004), 84–114.

[57] On the various representations of Jews and Judaism in contemporary eastern Europe, see E. Lehrer, 'Repopulating Jewish Poland—in Wood', *Polin*, 16 (2003), 335–55; R. E. Gruber, *Virtually Jewish: Reinventing Jewish Culture in Europe* (Berkeley, 2002).

[58] On the events in Kielce, see J. T. Gross, *Fear: Anti-Semitism in Poland after Auschwitz* (New York, 2006), 81–166.

[59] On this, see D. Biale, *Power and Powerlessness in Jewish History: The Jewish Tradition and the Myth of Passivity* (New York, 1986).

want to ask is: 'Must east European Jewish history revolve around a master narrative of victimhood and redemption?'

JEWS AND THEIR NEIGHBOURS IN EASTERN EUROPE

The chapters making up the section 'Jews and their Neighbours in Eastern Europe since 1750' attempt to challenge these myths and to move the study of east European Jewry out of the realm of the mythical and into a more real, human mode of cultural imagination. Based on a series of panels at the Fourteenth World Congress of Jewish Studies in Jerusalem that were sponsored, in part, by the Hebrew University's Leonid Nevzlin Research Center for Russian and East European Jewry as well as by the Israeli, Polish, and Russian foreign ministries, the essays collected in this volume are part of an ongoing discussion between students, researchers, and scholars in America, Europe, and the Middle East on the very nature and limits of national histories and societies.[60] While they are in no way exhaustive, these chapters represent a wide cross-section of opinions and approaches to many of the questions raised above. In addition to historical works addressing the eighteenth, nineteenth, and twentieth centuries, we have also included contributions from such other disciplines as literature and politics, as well as studies that address questions of culture and memory. Moreover, while any attempt at balance and parity would ultimately prove counter-productive, contributions were originally written in English, German, Hebrew, and Polish by authors working in Canada, England, Germany, Israel, Poland, and the United States. In this and other ways, this collection reflects the very processes of cultural exchange that it attempts to uncover.

In addition to essays considering interactions between Jews and Poles, there are also contributions examining relations between Jews and representatives of other ethnic groups (Lithuanians, Russians), discussions of negotiations with various governments (Habsburg, Lithuanian, Polish, Russian, and Soviet), analyses of exchanges between Jews and different cultural realms (German, Polish, and Russian), and an examination of how the politics of memory affects contemporary interpretations of these and related phenomena. Moreover, by amassing an array of authors and approaches, this volume not only reconsiders the construction of borders and the creation of divisions in eastern Europe, but also contributes to larger discussions regarding the nature and study of inter-group relations in a myriad of related but distinct academic fields, from history to memory and from literature to political science.

The dismemberment of the Polish–Lithuanian Commonwealth and the imposition on its Jewish subjects of Austrian, Prussian, and Russian rule mark the beginning of a new era of ongoing negotiations between Jews and government authorities in all three regions. Government attempts to reform 'the Jews' and to

---

[60] Our thanks to Jonathan Dekel-Chen and Haim Weiss for helping organize these panels.

codify their place and function in the late eighteenth and early nineteenth centuries are the topic of the first essay in this volume, by Marcin Wodziński. By analysing reform plans drawn up by members of the Polish intelligentsia and officials in the period, Wodziński brings forward a fascinating set of documents that tell us much about early attempts at rehabilitating 'the Jews' and the ways in which these projects reflect changes in the Polish Enlightenment. Starting with the programme of the priest Franciszek Ksawery Szaniawski, continuing with the key government figure Stanisław Staszic, and concluding with the work of the middle-level bureaucrat Gerard Witowski, Wodziński traces the crystallization of Polish designs for 'the Jews' from productivization to ghettoization and eventually to expulsion. Like many other scholars of the Enlightenment, Wodziński also touches upon questions regarding the possible connection between the disastrous developments of the twentieth century and early reform experiments in the Enlightenment era.

In 'Praying at Home' Rachel Manekin continues the theme of relations between Jews and government officials by looking at the daily, seemingly prosaic intersection of Jewish society and modern governance in the Habsburg city of Lemberg (Lwów, Lviv). Focusing on the enigmatic figure of Sara Ornstein, the widow of the Rabbi Jacob Meshulam Ornstein, Manekin argues that government efforts to stem movements of religious enthusiasm among various Christian groups such as Pietists, Quakers, Rosicrucians, and Martinists affected Jewish attempts to operate private prayer groups, *minyanim*. Unlike earlier scholars of Jewish history in Galician lands, such as Raphael Mahler, Manekin argues that the so-called *minyan* law was not aimed at restricting the burgeoning Jewish movement of hasidism, but, in fact, was an outgrowth of government fear of the 'disturbance of peace, order, and public safety that "irrational" and fringe religious groups might cause'. Regardless of the direct impetus for this legislation, Manekin shows how Jews had to modify their daily affairs in accordance with the wishes and machinations of the modern state.

Government attempts to reform and modernize 'the Jews' figure prominently in the next chapter, by Agnieszka Jagodzińska, on the cultural aspects of Jewish acculturation in nineteenth-century Warsaw. Unlike many other students of that mixed blessing of integration, Jagodzińska focuses on aspects of relations between Jews and Poles that are often overlooked, the realm of the aesthetic. Starting with government decrees aimed at restricting and standardizing dress codes and facial hair in the 1840s and continuing with the responses made by different Jewish communities and leaders, Jagodzińska carries forward many of the themes addressed by Wodziński and Manekin regarding government interference in Jewish lives (and bodies) and lays the groundwork for many of the questions addressed by other contributors, such as Bauer, Guesnet, Horowitz, and Neuburger, regarding the individual motivations for cultural adaptation and integration.

In her analysis of 'The Ideological Roots of the Polish Jewish Intelligentsia' Ela Bauer examines the various permutations and uses of the concept of 'the intelligentsia' as it passed back and forth between different European cultures and societies. Starting with a discussion of the image of the intelligentsia in western Europe, Bauer moves on to discuss how the same concept, 'the intelligentsia', was imported into Polish society and reinterpreted, and then again retranslated as it found its way into Jewish society in the Polish lands. While the general trend described is one in which ideas, concepts, and perhaps influence move from West to East and from European realms to European Jewish ones, Bauer shows the many different layers of negotiation and directions of exchange at play as representatives of the Polish and Jewish intelligentsia consciously and subconsciously responded to and mimicked one another. The final product is a hybrid concept that developed in European, Polish, and Jewish cultural spheres. François Guesnet continues this look at the role played by the Jewish intelligentsia by turning to the historical works of the long-overlooked figure Ezriel Natan Frenk. Frenk was an indefatigable and prodigious author whose works spanned several different genres, including journalism, drama, folklore, and popular histories. Writing in Yiddish and in Hebrew, Frenk not only introduced a geographically centred concept of the history of the Jews in Poland to his readers, but by writing about relations between Jews and non-Jews in the urban environment as well as about the history of converts from Judaism, he also reminded his readers that their society was intimately related to another, larger one and, thus, was shared by others. This sense of a shared historical and cultural space was reinforced by Frenk's translations of different works—including Polish classics by Prus, Orzeszkowa, and Sienkiewicz—into both Yiddish and Hebrew. In this and in other ways Frenk both advocated and thrived in what Guesnet terms as the '"semi-permeable" or "selectively permeable" boundary between the Jewish and Polish worlds'.

While Frenk stood between Jewish and Polish societies, few figures embody the connection between Jewish and Russian societies better than An-sky (Shmuel Zanvil Rappoport), who lived 'between two worlds'. In his chapter on this celebrated figure, Brian Horowitz shows how An-sky's literary œuvre exposes the intricate layers of relations between Jewish neighbours. His discussion of An-sky's fictional renditions of Jewish society further complicates, and at times even threatens to subvert, this volume's goal of discussing Jews and their implicitly non-Jewish neighbours. Moreover, An-sky's portrayal of 'revolutionaries and nationalists, young and old, rich and poor, women, men, children, and even their animals' highlights another way of understanding the mixture of cultures and sub-groups that defined eastern Europe for centuries. According to Horowitz, An-sky is able to achieve this level of narrative sophistication through the use of the 'dialogic method', which allows him to present a wide variety of perspectives. This literary analysis of An-sky's fictional renditions of worlds lost also raises a litany of questions regarding the methodological differences and the different narrative possibilities embedded within various disciplines.

An-sky, of course, was not the only Jewish intellectual whose works expressed the divisions within Jewish society across Europe. Karin Neuburger's analysis of Uri Zvi Greenberg (1897–1981) sheds much light on another aspect of this multi-directional maze of exchange by focusing on the influence of German culture on this Jewish writer. Born in Galicia and raised in Lviv, Greenberg was, like many other members of the Jewish intelligentsia, drawn to and enamoured with German high culture. Throughout her analysis of Greenberg's story 'Memoirs (from the Book of Wanderings)' Neuburger argues that the author repeatedly struggled with his own conception of self, one which juxtaposed his Jewish origins with his European yearnings. Like Horowitz's, Neuburger's literary analysis takes the reader out of the realm of high politics and into the inner struggles of a central literary figure in Jewish society and culture. Focusing on personal dilemmas, Greenberg's story exposes the 'tension between the young author and his family and community', which repeatedly deny the individual the right to self-actualization on his path to becoming a 'free Jew'. Another tension that shapes this story is that between the Jewish East and the European West. For Neuburger, the story reveals the extent to which European Romantic visions of 'the self', 'who is independent of any external factor, who exists in and of himself alone, and who operates autonomously', influenced Greenberg's writings and thoughts. Here as well, the turn to literature offers the reader a different perspective on the many ways in which Jewish and non-Jewish societies, cultures, and individuals were inextricably intertwined across the European continent.

Jeffrey S. Kopstein and Jason Wittenberg take this collection and its readers away from individual case studies and into the scientific study of society. In their thought-provoking contribution 'Did Ethnic Balance Matter?' the authors examine the relationship between ethnic demographics and electoral behaviour in inter-war Poland in order to ask: 'did the encounter between Poles, Ukrainians, Jews, Germans, and Belarusians induce political moderation, or lead to political polarization?' While national politics in inter-war Poland has been discussed at length elsewhere, this quantitative analysis of demographic records and their potential influence on voting patterns in the elections to the Polish Sejm in 1922 and 1928 highlights the debates that preoccupied different political groups as well as the delicate balancing act that many societies attempt to strike between democracy and nationalism. Here too the disciplinary turn—from history and literature to the social sciences—demonstrates the various ways in which scholars from different fields understand, construct, and address the same topic of 'Jews and their neighbours'.

Piotr Wróbel continues this discussion of Poles and Jews in the political realm with an analysis of the attempted integration of Jews into revolutionary groups between the wars. By carefully examining relations between Jews and the Polish Communist Party up to the outbreak of the Second World War, Wróbel takes on one of the trickier and more delicate aspects of Polish–Jewish relations, the image and charge of the *żydokomuna* ('Judaeo-communism'). Undaunted by the particularly problematic politics of Polish memory, Wróbel shows that, despite the vision of unity between Polish and Jewish workers, 'this unity was never achieved' and that most Jews 'had serious difficulties with integration into socialist and communist parties'. Referring to the oft-repeated charge that the Jews invented, developed, and administered communism, the author concludes that 'Jews could not dominate the Polish communist movement because most of them were not able to integrate into it and remained strangers even among the internationalists.'

Few figures embody the trials and tribulations of inter-war Polish Jewry more than the political leader, cultural activist, and diehard believer in the inherent beauty of 'the folk', Noah Prylucki. Kalman Weiser's analysis of Prylucki's attempts to secure a position as the Chair in Yiddish Language and Literature in Vilna highlights additional aspects of this ongoing mixture of co-operation, isolation, and influence in eastern Europe. Weiser's analysis of the intense negotiations between representatives of the Lithuanian government and leaders of the Jewish Scientific Institute (YIVO), including Prylucki, Zelig Kalmanowicz, and others, reveals the many different levels of intrigue and conflict that often plagued efforts at inter-ethnic co-operation. Moreover, like Horowitz's discussion of An-sky, Weiser shows how relations between Jews and other Jews were often just as intricate, complicated, and difficult as those between Jews and their neighbours.

Inter-group relations from 1939 to 1941 have attracted a great deal of interest in the wake of Jan T. Gross's explosive book *Neighbors*. By examining the violence that followed the Soviet withdrawal from Poland's eastern borderlands and the subsequent Nazi invasion, Kai Struve's chapter 'Rites of Violence? The Pogroms of Summer 1941' should be seen, in part, as a response to Gross's study. Concentrating on three separate concentric circles, Struve argues that the Nazis' association of Jews with Soviets, the radicalization of national resistance among Lithuanian and Ukrainian nationalist groups, and the legacy of popular antisemitism among local populations proved to be a volatile combination that both legitimized and encouraged anti-Jewish excesses and pogroms. Once synthesized, these different forces led to a certain layering of the violence against Jews in the region, one that proved to be particularly deadly.

In her chapter '*Nusekh poyln*? Communism, Publishing, and Paths to Polishness among the Jewish Parents of 16 Ujazdowskie Avenue', Karen Auerbach examines how, in the period after 1944, publishing offered a way into Polishness for a number of Jews who sought to find a place for themselves in the new political system. Many of them were also supporters, even if with reservations, of the new communist orthodoxy. Their careers offer a picture of the reasons why some Jews were attracted to Marxism-Leninism that is very different from the antisemitic trope of the vengeful Jew in the security apparatus.

The fall of communism and the reconfiguration of the European continent have led to a series of questions in Poland and neighbouring states regarding social cohesion. In her essay on 'Changing Images of "the Jews" in Polish Literature and

Culture, 1980–2000' Dorota Glowacka argues that literary representations of Jews in recent years reflect 'important political and cultural changes' while also serving as influential factors 'shaping attitudes towards Jews'. By examining a wide range of Polish works penned by Polish and Polish Jewish writers, Glowacka lends a certain degree of continuity and also closure to this admittedly open-ended volume. Moreover, her conclusion that literary representations of Jews have recently taken on 'positive connotations and have begun to function as a symbol of democratic hope in the country and of Polish society's opening up to pluralistic, more welcoming forms of being with others in the world' provides the reader with several rays of hope. Lastly, Glowacka's contribution highlights the extent to which relations between Jews and their neighbours remain a critical and definitive topic for a variety of thinkers in contemporary eastern Europe.

As diverse and varied as they may be, these chapters raise far more questions than answers regarding relations between Jews and their neighbours in eastern Europe. In view of this, we ask that each contribution be seen as an initial foray into a particular topic. Moreover, a number of key aspects of inter-group relations are not addressed in this collection. We invite other scholars to begin looking into questions related to gender, the role of the economy, and the place of the arts in the matrix of relations that shaped and defined society and culture in modern eastern Europe. Other, theoretical, angles are similarly missing, including a discussion of the very concept of 'the neighbour', as well as comparisons with inter-group relations in other regions and other cases of interaction between dominant and subaltern societies and cultures. In sum, this collection should not be seen as a definitive statement on any particular historical period, cultural phenomenon, or social development, but, rather, as part of an ongoing discussion.

A CONFESSIONAL POSTSCRIPT

It should perhaps come as no surprise that three scholars with such radically different life stories should combine their efforts to discuss the relevance of theories of hybridity and influence to the study of society and culture in eastern Europe. In many ways, our own lives can be seen as stories of repeated layers of intersecting languages, cultural adaptations, and conflicting questions of society and self that cross a variety of periods and settings. One could even argue that these individual negotiations are reflected through our own stories and then reinterpreted back onto the canvas of history, or in this case, the history of the writing of history. As he grew up outside Tel Aviv in the early years of Israeli statehood, Israel Bartal's childhood was divided between the celebration of Yiddish language and culture in the home and an adamantly Hebrew Israeli culture and society. For Antony Polonsky, life and work have been divided between the fields of Jewish and Polish histories in three different countries: South Africa, England, and the United States. And Scott Ury's life path has been divided between two radically different settings—America's pastoral Midwest and the Middle East's Jewish state. Hence, our co-operative search for new tools, methods, and means for uncovering the multiple layers of intersection, influence, and exchange between Jews and their neighbours in eastern Europe is far more than a work of history; and it is also very much a work in progress. Moreover, despite our diverging paths and opinions, our point of intersection—a desire to move the study of relations between Jews and their neighbours beyond binary, dichotomous models of good and bad, friend and foe, redeemed and damned—has served as a point of convergence and discussion for the three editors of this volume. In this way, the innumerable exchanges, disputations, and compromises between the editors over the course of this project should be seen as an example of the very same processes of isolation, exchange, and influence that characterized relations between Jews and their neighbours in eastern Europe for centuries.

Reform and Exclusion

Conceptions of the Reform of the Jewish Community during the Declining Years of the Polish Enlightenment

MARCIN WODZIŃSKI

IN THE LAST DECADES of the eighteenth century the reform of the Jewish community, along with reform of the peasantry and the urban question, was considered one of the most important and urgent tasks facing the Polish–Lithuanian Commonwealth. This task was taken over by those states which saw themselves as its heirs, the Duchy of Warsaw and the Kingdom of Poland. Beginning in the 1780s, the issue of the position of Jews in Polish society was discussed repeatedly during all major public debates. Although Jewish reform was addressed during the last great attempt to put the Polish–Lithuanian Commonwealth in order at the Four Year Sejm (1788–92), such efforts did not come to fruition because of the partitions. The subject was raised again during the formation of the Duchy of Warsaw (1807) and subsequently in the first years of the Kingdom of Poland (1815–30), each time resulting in a lively discussion about the place and organization of the Jewish community in the new state. The last of the major debates on the reform of Polish Jewry in the first half of the nineteenth century took place between 1815 and 1822. The surviving brochures, treatises, press articles, and even works of fiction comprise one of the richest collections of documents on the debate on the 'Jewish question' in nineteenth-century Europe. Importantly, the arguments and positions formulated during those debates largely determined the subsequent course of thinking on the place of the Jewish community in Poland, on the direction of reforms, and on Polish–Jewish relations for many decades to come.

All these debates and the policy recommendations which resulted from them have aroused considerable interest among historians. The pronouncements of the period of the Four Year Sejm have been particularly closely examined, but later debates somewhat less so, including that which took place between 1815 and 1822.[1]

---

[1] The essential works on the Jewish question and the reforms of the period of the Four Year Sejm are N. M. Gelber, 'Żydzi a zagadnienie reformy Żydów na Sejmie Czteroletnim', *Miesięcznik Żydowski*, 1/2 (1931), 326–44, 429–40; E. Ringelblum, 'Projekty i próby przewarstwienia Żydów w

And in spite of the generally good state of our knowledge, the topic as a whole still lacks a definitive treatment. The dominant characteristic of almost all historical publications on this subject is the tendency to focus on public pronouncements and policy initiatives. However, these programmatic declarations and opinions are only one aspect of the attitudes of the Polish political elites towards the Jewish community and are thus insufficient for a comprehensive analysis and understanding both of the issues involved and of the beliefs which guided the men of the Enlightenment who determined policy. What we intuitively understand today, listening with scepticism to present-day politicians, is still not fully appreciated by the historians who study political pronouncements made two centuries ago. These debates deserve a new critical analysis that will give more attention to issues that may not have been explicitly articulated, but which shaped the opinions of the politicians and the actions taken by successive state authorities in respect of the Jews. The most characteristic feature of these debates was the ambivalence reflected, on the one hand, in the declared goal of full social integration of the Jewish population, and, on the other, in the expression of implicitly anti-Jewish prejudices and phobias and consequent xenophobic attitudes which led to the complete opposite of the declared aspiration towards integration, namely to a call for the isolation of the Jewish community. These tendencies became especially intense during the decline of the Polish Enlightenment in the first decades of the Congress Kingdom (1815–30), and found their expression in many aspects of that state's Jewish policy. Perhaps the most striking examples are the projects for Jewish agricultural settlement and the formation of Jewish districts in several

epoce stanisławowskiej', *Sprawy Narodowościowe* (1934), 1–30, 181–224, also published separately as *Projekty i próby przewarstwienia Żydów w epoce stanisławowskiej* (Warsaw, 1934); A. Eisenbach, *Emancypacja Żydów na ziemiach polskich, 1785–1870, na tle europejskim* (Warsaw, 1988), English version *The Emancipation of the Jews in Poland, 1780–1870*, ed. A. Polonsky, trans. J. Dorosz (Oxford, 1991); A. Eisenbach, 'The Four Years' Sejm and the Jews', in A. Polonsky, J. Basista, and A. Link-Lenczowski (eds.), *The Jews in Old Poland, 1000–1795* (Oxford, 1993), 73–89; J. Michalski, 'Sejmowe projekty reformy położenia ludności żydowskiej w Polsce w latach 1789–1792', in id. (ed.), *Lud żydowski w narodzie polskim: Materiały sesji naukowej w Warszawie 15–16 września 1992* (Warsaw, 1994), 20–44; K. Zienkowska, 'Citizens or Inhabitants? The Attempt to Reform the Status of the Polish Jews during the Four Years' Sejm', *Acta Poloniae Historica*, 76 (1977), 31–52; G. D. Hundert, *Jews in Poland–Lithuania in the Eighteenth Century: A Genealogy of Modernity* (Berkeley and Los Angeles, 2004), 211–31. The most important studies of the debates and reforms of the constitutional period of the Kingdom of Poland (1815–30) are M. L. Wishnitzer, 'Proekty reformy evreiskogo byta v Gertsogstve Varshavskom i Tsarstve Pol'skom', *Perezhitoe*, 1 (1909), 164–221; N. M. Gelber, 'She'elat hayehudim bepolin beshenot 1815–1830', *Tsiyon*, 13–14 (1948–9), 106–43; id. 'Di yidn-frage in kongres-poyln in di yorn 1815–1830', *Bleter far geshikhte*, 1/3–4 (1948), 41–105; R. Mahler, *Divrei yeme yisra'el: dorot aharonim*, v (Merhavia, 1970), 153–72. See also R. Mahler, *A History of Modern Jewry, 1780–1815* (New York, 1971), 303–13. Two studies that paint a broad picture of the two phases of the 'Jewish debate'—Eisenbach's *Emancypacja Żydów na ziemiach polskich* and Mahler's *Divrei yeme yisra'el*—ignore the continuity of these debates, and the ideological bent of these works diminishes their value. Furthermore, Eisenbach concentrates one-sidedly on the legal aspects of emancipation, while Mahler only briefly touches on the reforms of the Four Year Sejm.

dozens of cities of the kingdom, which have attracted the attention of historians in recent years,[2] and the fascinating but less well-known plans for establishing an autonomous region or even a 'Jewish state'.

We still know very little about the most glaring examples of the oxymoronic policy of integration by exclusion—the plans for the establishment of a Jewish autonomous region and the expulsion of the Jews from Poland. This subject is worthy of interest not only because it is the least known, but also because, in my view, it is the best example of the general ideological tendencies of the Polish political elite and their attitudes towards the Jewish population and the reform of their community in the late Enlightenment period.[3] The evolution of this theme also reflects the general direction of the development of the Jewish question among the opinion-forming elites of the Kingdom of Poland in the last years of the Polish Enlightenment. Finally, the debate is the best illustration of the theme of the Enlightenment and its dissonances: the ambiguities and conflicts between the declared and the hidden ideas, objectives, and motives of the men of the Enlightenment. The so-called Jewish question appears, thus, to be a test case for the culture of the European Enlightenment torn between the enlightened ideas of liberty, equality, and fraternity, on the one hand, and suppressed phobias, thoughtless stereotypes, intellectual dishonesties, and simple irresponsibilities on the other. The contradictions of the Enlightenment will be a theme running through this essay.

SZANIAWSKI: TO HAVE THEIR OWN COUNTRY, THEIR OWN GOVERNMENT—THESE ARE THE WISHES OF THE JEWS

As with many other things, the men of the Enlightenment did not come up with entirely novel ideas on the state of Jewish society and the means of improving it. In fact, projects for the resettlement of the Jewish population to the south-eastern border area of the Polish–Lithuanian Commonwealth had been developed in Polish culture from at least the sixteenth century, appearing in the works of such well-known anti-Jewish writers as Jan Achacy Kmita, Sebastian Miczyński, and

---

[2] On Jewish districts, see E. Bergman, 'The *Rewir* or Jewish District and the *Eyruv*', *Studia Judaica*, 5 (2002), 85–97. On the proposed agricultural colonization, see M. Wodziński, 'Clerks, Jews, and Farmers: Projects of Jewish Agricultural Settlement in Poland', *Jewish History*, 21 (2007), 279–303, or the abridged Polish version '"Wilkiem orać": Polskie projekty kolonizacji rolnej Żydów, 1775–1823', in M. Wodziński and A. Michałowska-Mycielska (eds.), *Małżeństwo z rozsądku? Żydzi w społeczeństwie dawnej Rzeczypospolitej* (Wrocław, 2007), 105–29.

[3] The only text devoted to this subject is the article by N. M. Gelber, 'Ein "Krim-Projekt" aus dem Jahre 1818', *Die Stimme*, 1/24 (1928), 2–4. It also receives a mention in M. Janion, 'Mit założycielski polskiego antysemityzmu', in J. Hensel (ed.), *Społeczeństwa europejskie i Holocaust: Poszerzona dokumentacja konferencji w Żydowskim Instytucie Historycznym w Warszawie 30 września 2004 r. z okazji 75. urodzin Feliksa Tycha* (Warsaw, 2004), 19–21, German version M. Janion, 'Der Gründungsmythos des polnischen Antisemitismus', in J. Hensel (ed.), *Europäische Gesellschaften und der Holocaust* (Warsaw, 2004).

Sebastian Śleszkowski.[4] Basically, however, these were marginal antisemitic pronouncements that had no real consequences and provoked no wide response, and
were connected with more general projects for agricultural colonization. These
writers most often called for the compulsory concentration of the Jewish population in agricultural communities in the south-eastern borderlands of Poland–
Lithuania, where they would have the social status of serfs.[5] Similar projects were
repeatedly proposed during the many debates on the status of the Jewish population and on the attempts to resettle Jews on agricultural land. These projects were
not necessarily of an antisemitic nature, though it should be noted that they quite
regularly resorted to the stock motifs of antisemitic literature.[6]

   A turning point came during the debates in the reign of King Stanisław August
Poniatowski, especially during the Four Year Sejm, when projects for Jewish settlement on the land were proposed both by Polish reformers, some of them very well
disposed towards the Jewish community, and by the Jews themselves. The idea of
the settlement of Jews on agricultural land in clusters of homogeneously Jewish
communities, with a high level of autonomy, had already been expressed in the
projects of Chancellor Andrzej Zamojski (1717–92), the author of a monumental
scheme for the legal reform of the Polish–Lithuanian Commonwealth, and of
another leading court official, August Moszyński (1731–86).[7] In May 1785 the well-
known journalist Piotr Świtkowski (1744–93), editor of *Pamiętnik Historyczny i
Polityczny*, put forward a project for an all-Jewish agricultural settlement.[8] A similar plan was proposed by a royal factor, the Jew Abraham Hirszowicz. In his *Projekt
do reformy i poprawy obyczajów starozakonnych mieszkańców Królestwa Polskiego*
('Project for the Reform and Improvement of the Customs of the Jewish Inhabitants
of the Kingdom of Poland') he suggested Jewish colonization of the steppes in
Ukraine and Podolia, because 'there are a lot of empty steppes in Ukraine, as well as
large parcels of fallow land . . . which, if given to Jews for cultivation, will bring

---

   [4] On this, see K. Bartoszewicz, *Antysemityzm w literaturze polskiej XV–XVII w.* (Warsaw, 1914),
23; R. Kaśków, 'Zainteresowanie Żydami i kulturą żydowską w XVI i na początku XVII w. w Polsce',
Ph.D. thesis (Wrocław University, 1996), ch. 2; see also Ringelblum, *Projekty i próby przewarstwienia
Żydów*, 62.

   [5] See e.g. Dawid Origaniusz, *Prognosticon; albo, Zalecenie cieliencia smrodliwego narodu żydowskiego
na ten nowy rok 1629* (Prague, 1629), p. 7; J. Jurkowski, *Dzieła wszystkie*, ii: *Utwory panegiryczne i
satyryczne*, ed. C. Hernas and M. Karplukówna (Wrocław, 1968), 264–93; Kaśków, 'Zainteresowanie
Żydami i kulturą żydowską'.

   [6] It should be remembered that, although they were of rather marginal importance before the nine-
teenth century, projects for the creation of Jewish districts—whether in Europe or, more often, in
Palestine—appeared in the sociopolitical journalism of many European countries. See N. M. Gelber,
Zur Vorgeschichte des Zionismus: Judenstaatsprojekte in den Jahren 1695–1845 (Vienna, 1927).

   [7] Ringelblum, *Projekty i próby przewarstwienia Żydów*, 64–5, 68; J. Michalski, 'The Jewish Question
in Polish Public Opinion during the First Two Decades of Stanisław August Poniatowski's Reign',
Scripta Hierosolymitana, 38 (1998), 123–46.

   [8] E. Ringelblum, 'Żydzi w świetle prasy warszawskiej wieku XVIII-go', *Miesięcznik Żydowski*, 2/1
(1932), 502.

prosperity to the country and populate empty land'.[9] At the same time, Tadeusz Czacki (1765–1813), the renowned Polish reformer and author of a leading mono- graph on the Jews in Poland, also proposed the formation in the southern provinces of the state of rural settlements made up exclusively of Jews.[10]

Two elements differentiate the projects initiated during the reign of Stanisław August from earlier antisemitic writings. First, by contrast with the proposals of Kmita or other early anti-Jewish writers, all these projects for the settlement of Jews in Jewish-only agricultural colonies in a region set aside for them were the result neither of repressive intentions nor of a desire to exclude the Jews from other territories. Second, their fundamental goal was not to create autonomous Jewish regions but to achieve a change in the occupational structure of the Jewish popula- tion and to establish, at least for some Jews, ties to the land. Discussions of the pos- sibility of self-government for the areas settled by Jews were rather a by-product of these plans and not their main purpose. Thus, up to the end of the eighteenth cen- tury, schemes for the creation of a Jewish state did not arouse much interest in Poland, and their discussion occurs only on the periphery of other visions of reform.

The first project which proposed an autonomous Jewish state unconnected to plans for agricultural settlement and which gave it a central place in ideas for the reform of the Jewish community is found in an anonymous article in the journal *Pamiętnik Warszawski* in 1815. Its author was most probably the priest Franciszek Ksawery Szaniawski (1768–1830), a lawyer and professor at Warsaw University and a well-known Enlightenment publicist.[11] Szaniawski correctly observed that all previous attempts to deal with the 'Jewish question' had been very limited in scope and had not achieved—indeed, could not achieve—the desired results. Each new government proposed partial legal solutions that had no chance of success, because the future benefits were not obvious to Jews affected by the proposed reforms, and as a consequence they had no faith in them and did not support them. He argued that what was needed was a simple but potent incentive which would induce the Jews to make efforts to reform themselves. Such an incentive could be the creation of something resembling a Jewish state, or rather an autonomous Jewish district. He argued that 'To have their own country, their own government—these are the wishes of Jews attached to their religion.'[12] He believed also that circumstances had developed which made possible the realization of this unusual plan. Szaniawski, like many Europeans of the time, was impressed by Russia's victory over Napoleon,

[9] See A. Hirszowicz, *Projekt do reformy i poprawy obyczajów starozakonnych mieszkańców Królestwa Polskiego*, in *Materiały do dziejów Sejmu Czteroletniego*, vi, ed. A. Eisenbach et al. (Wrocław, 1969), 521.

[10] 'In the southern provinces, special settlements consisting only of Jews will be established': T. Czacki, *Rozprawa o Żydach i Karaitach* (Warsaw, 1807), 227–9. See also Ringelblum, *Projekty i próby przewarstwienia Żydów*, 67.

[11] X.S. [Franciszek Ksawery Szaniawski], 'Rzeczy rozmaite o żydach', *Pamiętnik Warszawski*, i/1 (1815), 438–41. For more about Szaniawski, see H. E. Wyczawski (ed.), *Słownik polskich teologów katolickich*, iv (Warsaw, 1982), 248–50.   [12] [Szaniawski], 'Rzeczy rozmaite o żydach', 440.

and saw in Russia the basis for a new European order. It should be remembered that this was at a time when the 1815 Congress of Vienna was deciding the new borders of Europe, including those of Poland. Tsar Alexander I, who took the title of King of Poland, formally returned the name of Kingdom of Poland to the political map of Europe, where it had been absent for twenty years. Despite the fact that the territory of the new state was substantially reduced in comparison with the Duchy of Warsaw, the tsar led Poles to hope that this restricted Kingdom of Poland could in the future be enlarged by the addition of lands annexed by imperial Russia during the partitions. Because of his charismatic personality, Tsar Alexander was able to persuade even those sceptical of, or indeed hostile to, the Russian state and its policies towards Poland, to accept his political vision. Hopes for new political solutions seemed well grounded and were quite widespread, though of course were not necessarily uncritical or naive. Even the most far-reaching changes appeared possible. Szaniawski considered (or at least wrote to this effect) that Alexander I, and other rulers influenced by him, were in a position to take unprecedented steps to resolve the 'Jewish question' in a way not possible before then. 'The magnanimity of monarchs that strive for a general peace—could it not also be applied to designate some provinces as a Jewish state?'[13]

The establishment of a Jewish state was intended to have two consequences. In the first place, the generous fulfilment of the Jews' most cherished dream would persuade them to make all possible efforts to attain this goal, and in this way it would be a positive incentive which would convince the Jews of the advantages of reform. This could be considered a positive element, reflecting the Enlightenment principles of equality and the rational nature of all human beings. Szaniawski made an appeal for rational choices to be made: 'Jews are human beings . . . We should treat them as human beings and try, as far as possible, to use their blind attachment to old customs for the real advantage of the entire population.'[14] His pronouncement was in keeping with the main current of Enlightenment rhetoric on the Jews, which saw as its goal the productivization of the Jewish community, a current which had dominated Polish public discussions from the period of the Four Year Sejm.[15]

The second consequence of the creation of a Jewish state was that it would be a kind of blackmail, because

it may be assumed that Jews now living in various lands, who would like to continue living there and to enjoy the full freedom of their own religion, could be required to comply fully with the outward customs of other inhabitants in matters such as attire and other superficial characteristics; or, on the other hand, if they want to remain slaves and adhere to all, even the least important, contemporary customs of their people, they could be required to remove themselves to the Jewish state.[16]

---

[13] [Szaniawski], 'Rzeczy rozmaite o żydach' 440.   [14] Ibid.

[15] See the analysis of Enlightenment discussion of the Jewish question in my '*Cywilni chrześcijanie*: Spory o reformę Żydów w Polsce, 1789–1830', in G. Borkowska and M. Rudkowska (eds.), *Kwestia żydowska w XIX w.: Spory o tożsamość Polaków* (Warsaw, 2004), 9–42.

[16] [Szaniawski], 'Rzeczy rozmaite o żydach', 440.

The Jewish state would thus constitute an asylum for those who did not want to abandon their fanatical customs; and it would serve as a means of coercion of those who remained in the Kingdom of Poland, obliging them to abandon any signs of differentiation and to integrate fully. Despite the amicability shown to the Jews by this project, which established that their settlement in the new state would be voluntary and that the goal would be full integration combined with full emancipation, a certain ambivalence can be observed here. It is expressed in the suspicion that such a created state could be used as a pretext for the forced unification or deportation of the Jewish population, and that this population, or at least a significant proportion of it, might not be willing to choose any of the offered options. This reflected a broader ambiguity of both the Polish and the European Enlightenments, unable to resolve the dilemma between a liberal, optimistic view of human nature in general, and suspicions and fears of anti-Jewish stereotypes in particular.

However, it needs to be repeated that, despite this ambivalence, Szaniawski's proposals sought a solution beneficial not only to the Christian majority, but also to the resettled Jews. In addition, these proposals would be realized through the free consent and agreement of those Jews. 'To have their own country and their own government' was, according to the author, a dream expressed by the Jews themselves.

STASZIC: REMOVE THEM FROM THE COUNTRY, AS OTHER NATIONS HAVE DONE

In the next few years, during the lively debates about the reform of the Jewish population in the Kingdom of Poland, several projects were initiated which were similar to the ideas articulated by Szaniawski. One of them was advanced by Stanisław Staszic (1755–1826), the most important ideologue writing on the Jewish question in the Kingdom of Poland.[17] In 1816 Staszic published in *Pamiętnik Warszawski*— the same journal that had published Szaniawski's proposal—an important programmatic article on the Jewish issue.[18] He provided a detailed (although far from accurate) analysis of the position of Jews in the society of the Kingdom of Poland and proposed a multifaceted project for reform. After asserting that the Jews were the biggest threat to the development of Polish 'civilization' and then analysing the

[17] The views of Staszic on the Jewish issue have not been comprehensively described. The most recent studies on this subject include S. Czarniecki, 'Staszic myśliciel i Staszic działacz — o stosunku Stanisława Staszica do Żydów w Polsce', *Zeszyty Staszicowskie*, 3 (2002), 137–45; A. Kuczyński, 'Stanisław Staszic i Abraham Stern: Spojrzenie na wzajemne kontakty', in J. Olejniczak (ed.), *Stanisław Staszic: Materiały sesji staszicowskiej* (Piła, 1995), 125–36. See also Eisenbach, *Emancypacja Żydów na ziemiach polskich*, index; B. Szacka, *Stanisław Staszic: Portret mieszczanina* (Warsaw, 1962), 147–9.

[18] S. Staszic, 'O przyczynach szkodliwości Żydów i o środkach usposobienia ich, aby się społeczeństwu użytecznemi stali', *Pamiętnik Warszawski* (1816). Subsequent references to this work are to the critical edition of Staszic's writings: S. Staszic, *Dzieła*, iv (Warsaw, 1816), 217–48.

nature of this threat, Staszic claimed that there were only two ways to solve the problem, both based on the establishment of 'mutual physical exclusivity'.[19] One was 'to remove [the Jews] from the country, as other nations have done'; the second, a consistent policy of their isolation and ghettoization (a term consistently avoided in the debate) within the borders of the Kingdom of Poland. Staszic developed in detail the second option. This was not because he considered the first to be inhumane or less efficacious. Quite the contrary—he believed that 'it is too late for us to expel the Jews',[20] probably alluding to the loss of both independence and the ability to move all Polish Jews to the sparsely populated regions of eastern Poland such as the Ukrainian steppes. (Staszic was probably familiar with earlier ideas of this sort, which had appeared in Polish publications beginning in the sixteenth century.) Moreover, Staszic was convinced that the rapid growth of the Jewish population in the territories of central Poland (the area of the Kingdom of Poland) was the result of a conscious policy of the partitioning states, which planned to use Jews as a means to undermine the Polish character of the kingdom—'to change the Polish land into a Judaean land' (*ziemia judzka*)[21]—and, at the same time, to rid themselves of Jews in the lands they had acquired in the partitions. Staszic was therefore very sceptical about the possibility of obtaining the support and goodwill of the leaders of the partitioning states, including Tsar Alexander, in this matter. Nevertheless, he emphasized that

the most effective means of liberating Europe from the Jews and eliminating those obstacles and corruptions by which the Jews contaminate or hinder the progress of civilization in Christian societies rest solely in the authority and power of the Russian tsars. They can allocate them space and settle them in Bessarabia and Crimea, regions uninhabited until now, whose location is best suited to the character and industry of the Jewish nation.[22]

In other words, Staszic fully agreed with Szaniawski's suggestion, yet—owing to lack of support from the tsar—he believed that the plan of creating Jewish settlements in southern Russia was unrealistic and as such not worthy of serious consideration. As an active politician, he instead set out in detail a programme which could be carried out by the government of the Kingdom of Poland, on whose 'Jewish policy' he had a direct and often decisive influence.

It is interesting that, despite the obvious agreement between Szaniawski and Staszic that the best solution to the Jewish question would be the resettlement of the Jews in the sparsely populated territories of the Russian empire, the views of these two authors were different in all other aspects. While Szaniawski postulated the resettlement of only those Jews who refused to conform to the laws of the land, Staszic proposed the application of this 'civilizing' policy to all Jews in the Polish Kingdom, changing the nature of the project from liberal to repressive. He did not believe that Jews could make a choice that would be advantageous to society at large, or if they did so, the choice would not be sincere. In his view, the civilizing of

---

[19] Staszic, *Dzieła*, iv. 237.   [20] Ibid.   [21] Ibid. 247.   [22] Ibid. 248.

the Jews would be a lengthy process and would proceed against their will. The main concern of the reformers should not be how to persuade the Jews to accept the civilizing process, but rather how to forestall those abuses which would result from the Jews having ostensibly accepted these changes. In his judgement, the Jews 'fail to advance themselves even in the midst of a people that is becoming more civilized, they do not accept any aspects of its civilization, they do not change for the better, and they only become more ingenious in their harmful ways'.[23]

Along with resettlement, Staszic also proposed the creation of Jewish ghettos on the territory of the Kingdom of Poland. His two plans were alternative versions of the same repressive and isolating concept. His remarks about resettlement are too brief to allow far-reaching conclusions to be drawn, and they did not affect further debate on this project. However, they are interesting and important in that they signal an evolution of Staszic's views, and a change in the political climate and general mood that was to find expression two years later in the most radical project of the entire debate, that published by Gerard Witowski.

For Staszic, however, the two most characteristic features of the change were the move of the 'Jewish threat' to centre stage and its demonization. Staszic had already been expressing hostile views about the Jews in his earliest writings on current affairs, including the well-known political treatise *Przestrogi dla Polski* published during the deliberations of the Four Year Sejm in 1790.[24] However, of the thirty-nine chapters devoted to almost all the major social and political issues in the Polish–Lithuanian Commonwealth, only one short chapter discusses the Jewish question (chapter 35, a little over five pages out of 170 pages in total). A considerable part of this chapter is devoted to the Polish gentry rather than the Jews. Listing 'the classes less useful to society', Staszic put the Jews in last place after 'clergy, gentry, patrons, doctors, actors, street vendors, pedlars'.[25] Although the Jews were judged negatively, in the greater scheme of socio-political processes as understood by Staszic, they played a marginal role. Around 1815, however, Staszic's views on the negative influence of the 'Jewish question' on the fate of Poland and Poles underwent a dramatic shift. He wrote in 1816 that of the three major misfortunes of the old Polish–Lithuanian Commonwealth—the absence of a hereditary monarchy, the absence of a permanent army, and the influx of Jews—it was precisely the Jews who were the largest and most permanent misfortune, because 'even if the body [the Polish–Lithuanian Commonwealth] had not been partitioned, or after partitioning were to be united again, with this inner flaw it would never be able to regain its strength and vigour'.[26] Staszic believed that in the twenty years since the final partition and extinction of the Polish–Lithuanian

---

[23] Ibid. 234.

[24] The most recent critical edition is S. Staszic, *Przestrogi dla Polski* (Wrocław, 2003). On the opinions that it expresses about the Jews, see C. Leśniewski, *Stanisław Staszic: Jego życie i ideologia w dobie Polski niepodległej, 1755–1795* (Warsaw, 1925), 325–8.

[25] Staszic, *Przestrogi dla Polski*, 113. [26] Staszic, 'O przyczynach szkodliwości Żydów', 218.

Commonwealth, the Poles had been compelled to wage a battle against the Jews and the partitioning states over whether 'the Jews will end up becoming Poles, or the Poles become Jews'.[27] Jews, in his view, had now become the principal and most dangerous threat to Polish independence and to the preservation of identity and national culture. The resolution of so central a problem had to become a key goal and had to be approached in a comprehensive manner.

The evolution of Staszic's views reflected changes which took place in public discourse as a whole after 1815 in Poland, and which could in general be characterized as the conservative crisis of Enlightenment ideology.[28] As always in such cases, the crisis exposed weaknesses, paradoxes, and unresolved ambivalences between the ideas and the practices of the men of the Enlightenment. The fall of the Commonwealth and the series of violent political changes in the following years led to a general reformulation of conceptual categories, in which the state and the 'political nation' were replaced as principal category by the nation as defined by its spirit and culture. At the same time, 'society' became a rather unclear concept, based more in the cultural life of the nation than in state structures.[29] Of course, the new guiding categories did not fit well into the general conceptual apparatus of the Enlightenment, which by its very nature was interested more in state and society than in culture and nation. Moreover, these changes coincided with both a growing retreat from the optimistic and universalistic ideas of the Four Year Sejm and an intensification of xenophobic, or at least mistrustful, attitudes towards all categories of 'alien', which of course included the Jewish population. This was tied to disillusionment with the results of the planned reforms of the Jewish population—a disillusionment which was evident almost from the beginning of the debate on the Jewish question in the Kingdom of Poland, although at the outset somewhat marginally. Politicians who were negatively disposed towards the Jews correctly pointed out that the reforms which had been planned several decades earlier had transformed neither the occupational structure nor the inner group dynamics of the Jewish community, nor had they brought about any change in Polish–Jewish and Christian–Jewish relations. The blame for this state of affairs was laid on the Jewish community and its 'stubborn obstinacy', rather than on the simple fact that none of the projected reforms had been implemented. Significantly, Stanisław Staszic was the most vocal among the disillusioned, proving once again that he was a particularly astute observer of new tendencies in society and a pioneer in articulating nascent views.

[27] S. Staszic, 'Uwagi nad Projektem organizacji Żydów', Archiwum Główne Akt Dawnych, Warsaw (hereafter AGAD), Centralne Władze Wyznaniowe Królestwa Polskiego, 1418, p. 15.

[28] See T. Kizwalter, *Kryzys Oświecenia a początki konserwatyzmu polskiego* (Warsaw, 1987).

[29] For the evolution of the definition of 'nation' and 'society' in political discourse in Poland during this period, see A. Walicki, *Philosophy and Romantic Nationalism: The Case of Poland* (Notre Dame, 1994), 64–85; J. Jedlicki, *Jakiej cywilizacji Polacy potrzebują: Studia z dziejów idei i wyobraźni XIX wieku* (Warsaw, 1988), 26–7, 37. On the consequences of this evolution for the debate on the Jewish question, see my *'Cywilni chrześcijanie'*.

* WITOWSKI: MARCH THEM . . . TO THE BORDERS OF GREAT TARTARY

Before it found its most extreme expression in the pronouncements of Gerard Witowski, to whom I shall turn presently, the question of the establishment of a Jewish state, or its equivalent, was discussed in the following years by a number of authors. Opinions similar to those of Szaniawski and Staszic were expressed a number of times, especially during the revived debate on Jewish reform held in the Sejm of the Kingdom of Poland in 1818 and 1820. However, this issue remained peripheral to the main plans for social change and the reform of the Jewish population. Among the authors of such observations were the liberal members of the Sejm Ludwik Łętowski (1786–1868) and Adam Feliks Bronikowski (1758–1829). Łętowski proposed designating 'certain towns for Jewish settlement only, facilitating the removal of the small number of Catholics'.[30] At the same time, he believed that the Jews should be guaranteed legal rights and autonomy in governing their own affairs. He even suggested the creation of such Jewish districts on the outskirts of Warsaw and Lublin, places that would make it possible for the Jews to continue their business activities. This project combined elements of the proposals of both Szaniawski and Staszic, accepting Szaniawski's call for the creation of autonomous Jewish regions, but agreeing with Staszic that these regions should be located in the territory of the Kingdom of Poland.

This project was opposed by Adam Feliks Bronikowski, who believed that it was not viable because it undermined Poland's economic well-being, since in the regions of Poland from which Jewish entrepreneurs were excluded the entire Polish economy would collapse.[31] The author of the most scholarly contribution to this debate, Jan Alojzy Radomiński (1789–1864), a mid-level official, argued that the establishment of a Jewish state would be detrimental to the Jews themselves because, as a result of centuries of demoralization, they would be unable to sustain their own state. 'The character, way of thinking, and spirit of contemporary Jewry are antisocial, which allows me to assert that, even if they were assigned a separate country, unless they organized their affairs differently from how they conduct them here today, they would be extremely unhappy.'[32]

Despite the scepticism of Staszic, Bronikowski, and Radomiński, a project did, however, surface at this time on the periphery of international diplomacy. Lewis Way (1772–1840), a British religious activist and sponsor of Protestant missions to eastern European Jews, brought to the attention of Tsar Alexander in 1817 a project for the establishment of a zone of Jewish settlements in the south of Russia or in Palestine. In accordance with Alexander's wishes, Way presented this project the

---

[30] L. Łętowski, *O Żydach w Polsce* (Warsaw, 1816), 24.

[31] A. F. Bronikowski, *Myśli względem reformy Żydów w Królestwie Polskim* (Warsaw, 1819), 7–9.

[32] [J. A. Radomiński], *Co wstrymuje reformę Żydów w kraju naszym i co ją przyspieszyć powinno?* (Warsaw, 1820), 66.

next year at the Congress of Aix-la-Chapelle. In the end, the plan was abandoned and did not influence other schemes aimed at regulating the status of the Jewish population in Europe.[33]

It is possible that it was precisely this international interest in projects for the creation of a 'Jewish national home', as well as the lively debate on the Jewish issue in the Sejm of the Kingdom of Poland in 1818, that led Gerard Witowski, a medium-rank government official responsible for Jewish issues (and in later years also government secretary to the Jewish Committee—Komitet Starozakonnych), to publish an anonymous pamphlet in which he took up Father Szaniawski's proposals.[34] This was the most radical project of the debate so far.

Witowski began with a review of a brochure written by General Wincenty Krasiński (1782–1858), father of the famous Romantic poet Zygmunt and—according to the expert on nineteenth-century Polish culture Maria Janion—a founding father of 'antisemitic fantasy' in nineteenth-century Poland.[35] This brochure, he claimed, had inspired him to take up the topic. Continuing Krasiński's arguments, Witowski came to the conclusion that attempts hitherto to reform the Jews had not brought about the expected results, but rather the very opposite. Despite all efforts to reform them, the Jews would always remain harmful to Polish society. Moreover, 'civilized' and baptized Jews would become even more harmful, because 'he who has shaved off his beard is no less a Jew than he who still has a beard; the latter has a better character because he does not hide it; while the other hides his treason under the mask of civilization and regards his new position only as a new means to acquire wealth'.[36] According to Witowski this was proof that the transformation of Jewish society was impossible. As a result, one ought to use a 'surgical' method, a complete separation of the two societies. This aspect of his argument was directly connected to Staszic's proposal. Witowski also mentioned, rather sarcastically, that although it might make no difference to cosmopolitans 'who should be sacrificed, the Jews for the Christians, or the Christians for the Jews', from a technical standpoint it would be easier to resettle 300,000 Jews than three million Poles.

Concretely, Witowski suggested an appeal to the new king of Poland, Tsar Alexander I, requesting that he designate some uninhabited territory for the Jews: '. . . to allot to the Jews in the borderlands of Great Tartary, or somewhere else in the southern parts of his spacious realm, a piece of land which will allow them to

---

[33] See N. M. Gelber, *Zur Vorgeschichte des Zionismus: Judenstaatsprojekte in den Jahren 1695–1845* (Vienna, 1927), 49–55; N. Feinberg, 'The Jewish Question at the Congress of Aix-la-Chapelle, 1818', *Israel Yearbook on Human Rights*, 2 (1973), 179, 185. For more about the activities of Lewis Way, see J. Parkes, 'Lewis Way and his Times', *The Jewish Historical Society of England: Transactions*, 20 (1959–61), 189–201.

[34] [G. Witowski], *Sposób na Żydów; czyli, Środki niezawodne zrobienia z nich ludzi uczciwych i dobrych obywateli: Dziełko dedykowane posłom i deputowanym na Sejm Warszawski 1818 roku* (Warsaw, 1818).

[35] Janion, 'Mit założycielski polskiego antisemityzmu'. See [W. Krasiński], *Aperçu sur les Juifs de Pologne par un officier général polonais* (Warsaw, 1818).   [36] [Witowski], *Sposób na Żydów*, 10.

live comfortably, and comfortably increase their tribe'.[37] Once such a province on the southern borders of the Russian empire had been chosen, all the Jews of the Kingdom of Poland should be transported there as soon as possible. The transport would proceed in 300 columns of 1,000 people each, which would move on foot from central Poland to the steppes of southern Russia. In developing his project, the author attended to minute details, such as the organization of living quarters and the provision of food during the stages of the march, 'of course paid for by the Israelites themselves' from the money and land confiscated from them earlier, as well as the length of the daily march (14 kilometres) and that it should commence 'immediately after the Jewish Passover'.

Praising the virtues of his plan, Witowski enumerated the advantages that its realization would bring for Poland, Russia, and the Jewish population itself. The new situation would awaken in Jews a feeling of citizenship and would prevent further exploitation of the Polish peasantry, the main offence of the Jews, and so 'as a result of separation, whether willingly or unwillingly, the Jews must needs become honest people'.[38] The Russian government would gain new land, populated and bringing profit, as well as new taxpayers and, first and foremost, new army recruits, because a people with its own autonomous province would have to provide its own military contingent. Poles would also gain from the exile of the Jews, because after the initial period of economic downturn, peasants and small business owners would occupy the places vacated by the Jews, leading to an economic upturn and demographic growth. The nation would regain its health as if after the removal of a 'tumour constantly consuming its breast'.[39]

Witowski's opinions carried great weight and stimulated a lively discussion, being both typical of their time and yet unique. Witowski gave expression to shared frustrations that were appearing ever more frequently in the writings of other journalists and political figures of the day. These included Staszic, as noted above; Stanisław Kostka Potocki, the minister for religious affairs, including Jewish issues; Adam Jerzy Czartoryski, one of the most influential politicians and a close collaborator with the tsar; the viceroy (*namiestnik*) Józef Zajączek; the distinguished politician and Enlightenment writer Julian Ursyn Niemcewicz; Tadeusz Mostowski, minister for internal affairs; and a great many others.[40] Witowski was particularly indebted to the work of Wincenty Krasiński, who was exceptionally ill disposed towards the Jewish population. However, Witowski was even more radical then Krasiński, as he believed that 'love of humankind, this true hallmark of chivalry, prevented him [Krasiński] from seeking the medicine which would effectively cure the disease'.[41] Witowski intentionally presents in radical form ideas which, up to that time, even those journalists most resentful towards the Jews had

---

[37] Ibid. 13.   [38] Ibid. 17.   [39] Ibid. 20.

[40] For a discussion of these and other examples, and more about the phenomenon of disillusionment and its consequences for the public debate on the status of the Jews, see my '*Cywilni chrześcijanie*'.

[41] [Witowski], *Sposób na Żydów*, 3.

hidden under the rhetoric of the humanism of the Enlightenment and the love of humanity.

As I have noted, these frustrations can be summed up as an outspoken expression of impatience with the decades-long process of attempting to reform the Jewish population and its failure to produce any concrete results. However, their roots lay deeper, in fundamental structural changes in the societies of contemporary Europe—changes which many in the political elite in Poland (and elsewhere) were not fully aware of, far less in accord with. At this time, social and political changes were undermining the old class order and making possible the extension of freedoms to wider sections of the population, including the Jews.[42] The glittering financial careers of some Jewish families, the growing, if always marginal, participation of Jews in the public life of the country, and even the political involvement of some Jews—all this caused a growing fear that the reforms begun during the period of the Four Year Sejm were bringing results opposite to those intended (or rather imagined). There was a widespread view that, instead of destroying the Jewish 'state within the state' (or, as it was sometimes described, the 'Jewish corporation'), they had actually strengthened the Jews in their harmful, antisocial attitudes and activities. In 1818 members of the State Council of the Kingdom of Poland, during a discussion on the establishment of a Rabbinical School in Warsaw, agreed that Jewish reform needed to proceed very cautiously, 'so that education might not strengthen the "harmful corporation"' of the Jews, and so that civilization, instead of transforming them, might not offer the Jews an additional instrument for the sly swindling of Christians.[43] In a similar way, an influential politician from the liberal camp, Marcin Badeni (1751–1824), wrote in 1819: 'we should slow down the process of the civilization of the Jews, because it might open up more ways for them to oppress the masses, which are already oppressed by them today as it is. In introducing or broadening the scope of civilization we should follow the rule that the civilization of Christians should be speeded up, and that of Jews slowed down.'[44] Witowski's declarations were entirely in line with a whole series of Polish publications and policies reflecting this anxiety. In his words: 'Until we adopted this disastrous idea of "civilizing" the Jews, contempt was to some extent an obstacle to their advance: an unshaven Jew was harmful, but only to simple folk, for he could not even enter the hallway; but as soon as we admitted the "baptized" to the sanctuary of citizenship, there was no dam which could contain their depravity.'[45]

Witowski expressed his frustration in an unusually sharp tone, which clearly departed from the existing rules of Enlightenment discourse, which demanded

[42] For more on societal integration at this period, see Eisenbach, *Emancypacja Żydów na ziemiach polskich*, 251–93.

[43] AGAD, I Rada Stanu Królestwa Polskiego, 436, p. 857. Compare with this a very similar statement made by the minister of internal affairs Tadeusz Mostowski in 1816, cited in Eisenbach, *Emancypacja Żydów na ziemiach polskich*, 199.

[44] As cited by M. Mycielski, *Marcin Badeni (1751–1824): Kariera kontuszowego ministra* (Warsaw, 1994), 86.   [45] [Witowski], *Sposób na Żydów*, 22–3.

political correctness, even in the otherwise openly anti-Jewish writings of Wincenty Krasiński. Still, despite its most radical nature, Witowski's voice is very instructive, as it can be understood as expressing the inherent ambiguities of the ideology and practice of the Polish Enlightenment, the dissonances common to both its more radical and its many other, more conciliatory, proponents.

Two elements in Witowski's pamphlet must have been especially shocking to the Enlightenment public. First, he rejected the basic tenet of Enlightenment philosophy that all human beings shared a common nature which made possible, through the educational process, the elimination of all existing defects both of individuals and of entire social groups. Witowski stated openly that the Jewish nature could not be reformed and that 'reform of the Jews does not lead anywhere, which we have learned after eight hundred years of experience'.[46] Although he referred to Krasiński, his opinion was much more radical, since he attributed the 'corruption' of Jewish society not to the demoralizing influence of a hostile environment, but rather to the inherent character of the Jews. The only solution was banishment. The only way that the Jews could become 'useful citizens of the country' would be through their disappearance. Witowski thus rejected the beliefs common to all reform-seeking Poles ever since the projects of the author who signed himself 'Anonymous' and of Mateusz Butrymowicz in the final decades of the eighteenth century, and at the same time questioned one of the principal dogmas of Enlightenment discourse.

Equally shocking to those who participated in this debate was the fact that Witowski discarded the traditional separation between the good religion established by Moses and the mistakes of the Talmud. This age-old distinction was important to the ideologists of the Enlightenment, because it allowed them to criticize Judaism and the social order based upon its norms, while at the same time keeping at least an appearance of neutrality in matters of personal faith, as well as a pose of enlightened tolerance—important elements in the self-image of the men of the Enlightenment. For Witowski, however, the entire Jewish religion without exception was a source of evil that contributed to the perpetuation of the depraved Jewish nature, rendering futile any attempts at reform. He felt that Jews would stop cheating only when forced to do so—in this particular case, after resettlement in a Jewish province on the borders of the civilized world where they would have nobody to deceive, because there would be no non-Jews in the neighbourhood.

Aspects of Witowski's ideas were undoubtedly inspired by Szaniawski. Witowski, like his predecessor, did not envisage the new Jewish province as solely based on agriculture; he planned that the Jews, as its exclusive population, would have to engage in all occupations, including trading, military, and even, it may be surmised, administrative. The core of the project was not settlement on the land and productivization, but rather the creation of a territorially compact Jewish com-

---

[46] Ibid. 6, 11.

munity: one could say (using terminology from another discourse) the creation of a
'Jewish national homeland'. At the same time, Witowski adapted Szaniawski's
ideas to a purpose that was actually the very opposite of the original, shifting the
emphasis from granting autonomy and educating the Jews into responsibility for
their future, to group imprisonment—the sequestering of a whole people in a new
province. Unlike Szaniawski, Witowski sought the forced resettlement of all Polish
Jews and the obligatory deportation of any other Jews that happened to find themselves on Polish soil; implicitly, Jews would not be permitted to leave the new
Jewish province. Such a project was clearly repressive and its main assumption was
a complete, radical, and obligatory separation.

Witowski was criticized from all possible quarters of the contemporary political
scene. The very liberal Walerian Łukasiński (1786–1868) pointed out, for example,
that it was nonsensical to declare that the reforms of the Jewish community had not
brought about the expected results, since no such reforms had yet been implemented in Poland. The few attempts to introduce reforms of Jewish life had been
incomplete and lacking in logic.[47] Minister of state Stanisław Kostka Potocki
(1755–1821), who was considerably more critical of the Jews, rejected Witowski's
project on technical grounds, as he believed that it would be easier to reform
300,000 Jews than to resettle them.[48] Most interesting was the reaction of Jakub
Tugendhold (1794–1871), in later years a well-known representative of the Polish
Haskalah and a very productive author, who at the time was a 24-year-old novice in
the public forum. In a brochure *Jerobaał; czyli, Mowa o Żydach* ('Jerubbaal; or, A
Discourse on the Jews'), he rejected Witowski's arguments, not only because of
their clearly antisemitic character, but primarily because—despite Jewish aspirations for a messianic return to Zion—Poland was the fatherland of Polish Jews.
Any plans for a Jewish province were nothing more than a return to the Middle
Ages and an attempt to revert to the shameful practice of expelling Jews from their
place of residence.[49] Tugendhold thus struck a well-aimed blow at the most
sensitive spot for Polish Enlightenment reformers, exposing clearly the anti-
Enlightenment character of their phobias and the projects motivated by them.

CONCLUSION

Calls for the establishment of an autonomous Jewish province continued to appear
during subsequent years and decades. However, beginning with Witowski's pamphlet, their character was almost always anti-Jewish and they neither attempted
to fulfil the assumed desire of the Jews to have their own country, nor sought to

[47] W. Łukasiński, *Uwagi pewnego oficera nad uznaną potrzebą urządzenia Żydów w naszym kraju i
nad niektórymi pisemkami w tym przedmiocie teraz z druku wyszłemi* (Warsaw, 1917), 8–9.

[48] S. K. Potocki, *Żyd nie żyd? Odpowiedź na głos ludu izraelickiego* (Warsaw, 1818), 16.

[49] J. Tugendhold, *Jerobaał; czyli, Mowa o Żydach, napisana z powodu wyszłego bezimiennie pisemka
pt. 'Sposób na Żydów'* (Warsaw, 1818).

promote educational and productivizing goals in relation to Jews.[50] They essentially promoted separation, or in other words, 'there will be no Jews here'. In this sense they vividly reflected the path travelled by Enlightenment philosophy, from the idea of integration to the idea of separation. A near-exact replica of Witowski's project is contained in a sizeable booklet written in 1841 (but not published until 1854) by the Romantic philosopher and messianic writer Józef Wojciech Gołuchowski (1797–1858).[51] Gołuchowski proposed the establishment, under the protection of the Russian tsar, of a Jewish province near either the Black Sea or the Caspian Sea, or in the Caucasus (in more or less the same regions as proposed by Witowski), the compulsory organization of the Jews in military fashion, and their gradual resettlement—at their own expense, naturally.

The subject continued to be raised in later years by antisemites of all shades; it lay, for example, at the roots of both the plan for the Jewish colonization of Madagascar and the support given by Polish right-wing nationalists to the emigration of Jews to Palestine between the world wars. The fascist journal *Polska Błyskawica* called for the immediate forced evacuation of the entire Jewish population to Palestine, because 'the continuation of the present state of affairs, especially in Poland, will have a negative effect particularly on the Jews themselves, forcing the [Polish] population to defend themselves energetically, using any available means'.[52] In the influential paper of the Silesian conservatives, *Kuźnica*, Edward Handke repeated the projects of Witowski and Gołuchowski almost word for word.[53] He remarked that the immediate expulsion of the entire Jewish population from Poland was impossible owing to the sheer number of them as well as their economic importance. The emigration would have to continue, Handke wrote, for twenty to thirty years, assuming optimistically that more than 100,000 individuals would be moved each year. Physical force (by pogroms) was not a good way to compel emigration because it would cause the depravation of the Polish community, negatively influencing the international position of the Polish Republic and, in the event of military conflicts, would make the Jewish population dangerous. It would also be difficult to sustain economic pressure by boycott for such an extended period of time. According to Handke, forced emigration should be

---

[50] Very unusual was a pronouncement of the Polish National Committee in 1832, which upon the initiative of Joachim Lelewel contained a note concerning the help that Jews would receive from the Polish nation towards the formation of a national state in Palestine. See A. Eisenbach, *Wielka Emigracja wobec kwestii żydowskiej, 1832–1849* (Warsaw, 1976), 110–24; Gelber, *Zur Vorgeschichte des Zionismus*, 90–1.

[51] K. Przezor [Józef Gołuchowski], *Kwestia reformy Żydów przez Klemensa Przezora* (Lipsk, 1854). For more on this project, see Gelber, *Zur Vorgeschichte des Zionismus*, 213–20; A. Eisenbach, *Kwestia równouprawnienia Żydów w Królestwie Polskim* (Warsaw, 1972), 305–6. See also Janion, 'Mit założycielski polskiego antysemityzmu', 30.

[52] 'Rezolucja Partii Narodowych Socjalistów uchwalona w dniu 17.XI.33. na posiedzeniu Obwodowego Zarządu PNS na Śląsk i Zagłębie Dąbrowskie w Katowicach', *Polska Błyskawica*, 1/2 (1933), 3.

[53] E. Handke, 'Jaki charakter nadać emigracji żydowskiej?', *Kuźnica*, 3/1 (1937), 4.

applied to only one age cohort, for example 18-year-olds, since young people of that age are energetic and would eagerly wander the world without taking too much capital with them: 'In order to ensure the emigration of 18-year-olds, they should be interned in cultural concentration camps paid for by their families until such time as they cross the border.'[54] By Handke's calculation, in that way about 60,000 people would leave each year; after twenty years the birth rate would have dropped to zero; and after thirty years the emigration law could be taken off the books, as the elderly would have died off. In his view his project had the virtue that Jews would disappear from schools within five years and from the learned professions in twenty years.

These are just a few examples. The darkest day came in October 1943, when an anonymous antisemitic journalist expressed anxiety in an underground nationalist publication that too many Polish Jews were surviving the Holocaust. Therefore, after victory, it would be necessary to find a 'civilized' solution to this issue, the best being the evacuation of the Jews from Poland to 'as yet uninhabited territories of southern Russia'.[55] To be sure, this is not to be understood as proof of a link between the dissonances of the Enlightenment and the Holocaust. The antisemitic journalist did not express the desire to murder Jews, 'merely' to expel them from Poland. Still, it demonstrates that the ambiguities of the Enlightenment did not recede despite even the most appalling expressions of anti-Jewish xenophobia. The resemblance to Witowski's project reminds us that these ideas had their roots in some not very enlightened ideals of the Polish Enlightenment, and that the suppressed phobias, stereotypes, and obsessions which the men of the Enlightenment did not possess the strength to confront remained, paradoxically, the most persistent elements of their sorry legacy, even in face of the horrors of the Holocaust. From the projects for social integration and emancipation, motivated by the highest Enlightenment ideals of human equality, later generations chiefly inherited ideas of Jewish separation and enclosure in larger or smaller ghettos or concentration camps, sometimes as large as an entire province in the 'as yet uninhabited territories of southern Russia'.

Translated from the Polish by Alexandra Hawiger

---

[54] E. Handke, 'Jaki charakter nadać emigracji żydowskiej?'
[55] As cited by J. T. Gross, *Upiorna dekada: Trzy eseje o stereotypach na temat Żydów, Polaków, Niemców i komunistów, 1939–1948* (Kraków, 1998), 43.

Praying at Home in Lemberg
The Minyan *Laws of the Habsburg Empire 1776–1848*

RACHEL MANEKIN

ONE OF THE MOST important legacies of the Josephinian regime in the Habsburg empire was its policy of religious toleration, generally understood as freedom of worship.[1] Since Austria was a confessional state, and membership in a particular religion determined the legal status of the individual, the policy of religious toleration had implications also for the civil sphere.[2] Starting with the first Edict of Toleration towards Lutherans, Calvinists, and Greek Orthodox in 1781, freedom of worship was generally limited to the private sphere. Non-Catholic houses of worship were not allowed to display external signs such as bells and towers or have public street entrances. A Christian non-Catholic community of a hundred families or more was allowed to build a meeting place for prayers and employ a religious leader, but smaller communities could meet only at private homes. Still, the measure of religious freedom granted to non-Catholics was sometimes greater than that granted to Catholics, since the government did not interfere in the internal religious matters of non-Catholics.[3]

In the following years, edicts of toleration were issued for Jews in the different Habsburg crown lands, the last and most progressive one being to the Jews of Galicia in 1789. The first paragraph of the Galician edict declared that Jews were free to practise their religion without any interference, as long as this did not violate the laws of the land.[4] As a result of their status as members of a tolerated religion,

The research for this essay was completed when I was a fellow at the Katz Center for Advanced Judaic Studies at the University of Pennsylvania in spring 2010. I would like to express my gratitude to its director, David Ruderman, and to its staff.

[1] C. H. O'Brien, 'Ideas of Religious Toleration at the Time of Joseph II: A Study of the Enlightenment among Catholics in Austria', *Transactions of the American Philosophical Society*, 59, pt. 7 (1969), 1–80; R. J. W. Evans, *Austria, Hungary, and the Habsburgs: Central Europe, c.1683–1867* (Oxford, 2006), 44–9; P. Zagorin, *How the Idea of Religious Toleration Came to the West* (Princeton, 2003), 291.

[2] I. Gampl, *Staat — Kirche — Individuum in der Rechtsgeschichte Österreichs zwischen Reformation und Revolution* (Vienna, 1984), 65–6.   [3] O'Brien, 'Ideas of Religious Toleration', 23–5.

[4] 'Die gesamte Judenschaft soll in Ausübung ihrer väterlichen Religion und angeerbten Gebräuche,

Jews were exempted from giving testimonies in court on the sabbath and from fees on contracts documenting the sale of chametz (leavened bread) to Christians, and they could provide kosher meals for Jewish prisoners (Jewish prisoners were also exempted from forced public labour on the sabbath).

Some of the restrictions on Jews were intended to maintain the superiority of the Christian religion. For example, open public trade was prohibited on Catholic holidays, and Jews were forbidden to employ Christian maids except on the sabbath and Jewish holidays; such help had to be limited to the most necessary. Jews had to stay inside their homes during Christian public processions; they could not have balls on Christian fast days; and they were not allowed to participate in the interior renovation of churches. In addition, they were not allowed to fire guns during Jewish celebrations or march in public with torches or candles during weddings and other celebrations, or to use too much candlelight in their synagogues.

Jews were required to help extinguish fires even on the sabbath, and, like Christians, they had to say the special prayers for the welfare of the emperor as well as special prayers during times of war. They could erect an *eruv* (an enclosure around a neighbourhood to enable the carrying of objects on the sabbath in accordance with Jewish law), but had to finish it in a short time and without ceremony, and only provided it did not hinder other people from walking or driving. They could not collect money for the poor in Palestine, but collections for local Jews were permitted. The government authorities declared that they would not involve themselves with the question of sects within Judaism, that hasidim were tolerated, and that it was forbidden to persecute them. There were four specific areas of Jewish religious life in which the government reserved its right to intervene: the appointment of district rabbis, the building of synagogues, the building of cemeteries, and the conducting of prayers in private homes, referred to in the government documents as 'Miniamim' (*sic*).[5] In those areas there were special regulations that stipulated the conditions for official approval, which was generally granted by the district authorities.[6]

Of all the restrictions listed above, it seems that the intervention in the area of private *minyanim* had the most far-reaching consequences for Jewish society, since

soweit solche mit dem gegenwärtigen Gesetze und den allgemeinen Landesgesetzen nicht im Widerspruche stehen, durchaus frei und ungehindert sein': J. Karniel, 'Das Toleranzpatent Kaiser Josephs II. für die Juden Galiziens und Lodomeriens', *Jahrbuch des Instituts für Deutsche Geschichte*, 11 (1982), esp. 75.

[5] 'Miniam' or 'Minjam' are the only terms used in government documents to denote prayer gatherings in private homes. Only in 1852 did a Jew writing to the district authorities use the term 'Klausen (Winkelbethstuben)' to describe hasidic *minyanim*: see the letter by Michael Goldberg from Żółkiew, 15 Mar. 1852: Tsentral'nyi derzhavnyi istorychnyi arkhiv Ukrayiny, Lviv (hereafter TsDIAL), 146-14-298, pp. 69–79, esp. p. 77, in microfilm copy in Central Archives for the History of the Jewish People, Jerusalem (hereafter CAHJP), HM2/8613.2.

[6] M. Stöger, *Darstellung der gesetzlichen Verfassung der galizischen Judenschaft*, 2 vols. (Lemberg, 1833), i. 91–103.

it provided a legitimate exit path for those Jews who wished to abandon the communal synagogues in favour of a more intimate prayer service. Jews who embraced this option did so in accordance with their social status or religious sensibilities and thus created new social and religious networks, something that had been much more restricted before the partition of Poland. The private *minyanim* created a sphere where religion could be experienced in a free and individual manner, in contrast to the established synagogues, where the time and format of prayers, seating arrangement, and expected behaviour were determined by the community. It was the legal system of the state that enabled this individual experience and not the communal leadership, which, after all, had to preserve the received customs and traditions. Religious life, it seems, was shaped and reshaped, or at least enabled, not only by religious leaders and communal authorities, but also by the state. Statistically, on average about sixty-three permits for *minyanim* were granted annually. From many archival documents it is clear that many more operated without any permit. The official calculation was to allow one *minyan* per fifty families in the countryside, and two *minyanim* for that number in the cities.[7]

Why would the government be concerned with that aspect of religious life and not leave it to the responsibility of the Jewish community councils? In general, during the reign of Joseph II, the Austrian government consolidated the process that Maria Theresa had started, of exercising power and control over all areas of life, including religion. In most cases it was not religion per se that interested the government,[8] but mainly the management and administration of the religious communities and their institutions, allowing no independent bodies to function outside the jurisdiction of the centralized state.[9] Since private *minyanim*, by definition, constituted an independent and unregulated sphere, the government regulations functioned as a form of control mechanism. In the official documents there is no answer to the question why the Jewish community councils, which supervised the synagogues, were kept out of any decisions concerning private *minyanim*. One possibility is that the mere decision to allow private *minyanim* to function, even under certain restrictions, was against the interests of the community councils because of the loss of control they suffered, whether monetary or religious. Another possible reason is the lack of space in the main synagogues, to which private *minyanim* provided a solution without increasing the visibility of the Jewish presence in the urban landscape, as well as in the eyes of their Christian neighbours. This seemed to serve well the interests of the Catholic state.[10]

---

[7] Ibid. 110.

[8] Joseph II did, however, interfere in the practice of the Catholic religion by closing monasteries, restricting pilgimages and the number of religious holidays, controlling the Catholic seminaries, etc.: see E. Winter, *Der Josephinismus und seine Geschichte: Beiträge zur Geistesgeschichte Österreichs, 1740–1848* (Brünn, 1943), 127–270.

[9] See H. E. Strakosch, *State Absolutism and the Rule of Law: The Struggle for the Codification of Civil Law in Austria, 1753–1811* (Sydney, 1967).

[10] A community that wanted to build a synagogue had to pay for the required permission of the

Another explanation may be deduced from a reference to this subject in a report of 1842 summarizing the legal status of the Jews. In it the writer concludes from several sources that the practice of Jewish religion requires prayer, but not necessarily prayer services in a synagogue. That was why it was thought that prayers at home or in private *minyanim* needed to be taken into consideration.[11] It seems that the authorities' sensibilities as *Catholics*, for whom the church is an indispensable space for the practice of religion, led them to make this particular observation regarding Jews. Regulating *minyanim* ensured that individual Jews could fulfil the religious requirement to pray under various circumstances, which would be duly registered.

What motivated Jews to pray in such *minyanim*? In the historiography of Galician Jews, the topic of private *minyanim*, especially the government policy towards them, is usually discussed within the context of hasidism,[12] but as we shall see below, the context was much wider than hasidism, even if we assume that private *minyanim* became the most important tool in its spread. From the different cases that I have examined, all based on newly discovered archival documents, it is clear that many Jews looked for an intimate place where they could pray with like-minded Jews of the same class, age, or religious sensibilities. I shall use some of them for my analysis, especially those which contain appeals against rejections of petitions to establish *minyanim*. I shall concentrate here on cases from the city of Lemberg in the 1840s, because of the richness of the documents from this time and place.

Interestingly, after 1848 the Austrian authorities transferred decisions regarding *minyanim* to the Jewish community councils.[13] In one of the paragraphs of a draft document regulating the activities of the Jewish communities in the 1850s, it

district authorities a cameral tax of 2,000 gulden, a huge amount, in addition to an annual tax of 100 gulden. This annual tax applied only to synagogues built after the promulgation of the Edict of Toleration of 1789: see Stöger, *Darstellung der gesetzlichen Verfassung*, 67.

[11] 'Ausser dem öffentlichen Gottesdienste der Juden in der Synagoge kömmt auch noch die häusliche Religions-Übung oder der Privat-Gottesdienst Miniam genannt um so nothwendiger in Betracht zu ziehen, als wie an mehreren Orten berührt wird, ersterer keinswegs eine unerlässliche Bedingung der israelitischen Religion ist': see Haus-, Hof- und Staatsarchiv, Vienna, Alter Kultus/Israelitischer Kultus, Ktn. 1, 5981 1842, p. 17.

[12] See e.g. R. Mahler, *Hasidism and the Jewish Enlightenment: Their Confrontation in Galicia and Poland in the First Half of the Nineteenth Century*, trans. E. Orenstein, A. Klein, and J. Machlowitz Klein (Philadelphia, 1985), 69–103.

[13] The title page of one of the 1848 Yiddish pamphlets explains to the Jewish masses the meaning of the Pillersdorf constitution: 'Constitution: The Imperial Decree with All [its] Fifty-Nine Paragraphs: According to this Constitution there will be an End to the Two Shameful Taxes, Candle and Meat, and the 1,000 Gulden Tax that Had to be Paid When a New Synagogue was Built, and it will be Possible to Make Public the *Minyanim*, and there will be Other Freedoms': see *Konstitutsyon: dos keyzerlikhe patent mit alle nayn und finftsig pinkte fun der konstitutsyon* (Lemberg, 1848). Apparently the author speaks about the illegal *minyanim* that will be able to function in the open. Listing this alongside such issues as heavy taxes is a proof of how central *minyanim* had become to Jewish life in Galicia.

was stipulated that 'Die sogenannten Miniamins (Winkelstuben)' should be reported to the government authorities only if there were complaints regarding sanitation and the like. Otherwise, it would be the community council that would grant the permits for private *minyanim* in exchange for an annual tax of 25 florins paid to the community. The participants in a *minyan* without such a permit, as well as the householder in whose premises the *minyan* took place, would be fined by the local authorities.[14] By contrast, the draft of the regulations for the Bohemian Jewish communities that served as a model for the Galician one stipulated that private *minyanim* were prohibited, with the exception of those that had been allowed by the rabbi in agreement with the community council.[15]

ORIGINS

The first legal reference to places of Jewish worship in eastern Galicia, following its annexation to Austria in 1772, is in Maria Theresa's Galician *Judenordnung* (1776).[16] Jews, according to this new law, could continue to conduct public prayers, marriages, circumcision, and other ceremonies, in the synagogues or in the *kahals* (the term used in the pre-partition period that was later replaced with the term *Kultusgemeinde*, or religious community), but conducting those ceremonies in private homes was forbidden. Building new synagogues or renovating the old ones required the permission of the highest Austrian authorities in Galicia. In villages where the Jewish population was too small to establish its own synagogue, Jews were permitted to pray in private homes, but without reading from the Torah or carrying out religious ceremonies. It seems that Maria Theresa was interested in a tight control over the newly annexed Jewish population, and a stricter hierarchical order of the Jewish institutions provided just that. Otherwise, she left the legal status as it had been in the pre-partition period.

A reversal of the policy towards private *minyanim* occurred in 1788, during the reign of Joseph II, when maintaining private *minyanim*, including those in which the Torah was read, was allowed to all. But this permission was not granted for nothing, as it required the payment of an annual imperial tax (*Cameral-Taxe*) of 50 gulden.[17] The tax was levied only on *minyanim* in which the Torah was read. In

[14] 'Entwurf eines die Reglung der jüdischen Kultusanstalten bezweckenden Gesetzes', §61, Miniamins: TsDIAL, 146-14-298, pp. 88–103, esp. p. 99, in microfilm copy in CAHJP, HM2/8613.2.

[15] 'Der von der k. k. Statthalterey richtig gestellte Entwurf einer Cultusgemeindeordnung für die Israeliten im Kronlande Böhmen', §82, Winkelbethsstuben: ibid., pp. 11–19, esp. p. 16.

[16] 'Allgemeine Ordnung für gesammte Judenschaft der Königreiche Galizien und Lodomerien', Zweiter Abschnitt, Vierter Artikel, 1, 16 July 1776, in *Continuatio Edictorum et Mandatorum Universalium in Regnis Galiciae et Lodomeriae* (Lviv, 1776), 76–121, esp. 91.

[17] Stöger, *Darstellung der gesetzlichen Verfassung*, 67. The laws were summarized in a law of 1836: see 'Privatgebeth der Juden (Miniam) ohne Ausstellung der Thorah bedarf keine kreisämtlichen Bewilligung', 21 Apr. 1836, Z. 14338, in *Provinzial-Gesetzsammlung des Königreichs Galizien und Lodomerien für das Jahr 1836* (Lemberg, 1838), 366–9.

effect, this ruling kept the Jewish community council out of the whole procedure and made the establishment of a private *minyan* a matter between the individual Jew and the government. A year later, it was included in the Edict of Toleration (1789): 'When a Jew, *for his very own convenience*, wishes to obtain a permit to conduct prayers in his home with reading from the Torah, he has to pay an annual tax of 50 florins, to be used for the Jewish *Normalschulen*' (emphasis mine).[18] 'Convenience' was not what determined in the pre-partition period the rights of the individual Jew in the religious sphere, at least not in the legal sense, and it was introduced here for the first time. Still, the change was not that great, because the community was not in a position to decide if such a *minyan* could be established or how to use the tax receipts. In 1792 the government accepted the suggestion of the school inspector Herz Homberg to cut the tax by half, since it was too high for most Jews, but to levy it on all private *minyanim*, regardless of whether they included reading from the Torah or not.[19] With the closure of the German Jewish schools in Galicia in 1806, the school tax was annulled,[20] and the authorization for *minyanim* was carried out by the leaseholders of the candle tax payments. The procedure included also a tax payment of 3 ducats to be transferred to the police, in addition to a stamp fee payable to the district authorities.[21]

In the legislation of 1798 for western Galician Jews (part of the Austrian empire between 1795 and 1809), there is a definition of three types of places of Jewish worship: *Synagogen*, *Schulen*, and *Privathäuser*. The synagogue was defined as a place where, in the centre, there was a raised covered table, and which contained an ark with at least three scrolls of Torah, but no cooking oven. A *Schule* (*beit midrash*) was defined as a larger place furnished with an oven, and which like the synagogue was designated for worship and was the property of the Jewish community. The *Privathaus*, or 'Minjam', was a private home where the owner conducted prayers on the sabbath and weekdays, with or without reading from the Torah.[22] It seems that this description was taken from the pre-partition period, since it was formulated just three years after western Galicia was annexed to Austria. It should be emphasized that the term *shtibl*, common in Jewish historiography to designate a private *minyan*, does not appear in any of the official documents examined in this essay.[23]

---

[18] 'Wenn aber ein Jud die Erlaubniss zu erhalten wünschet, für sich allein zur eigenen Bequemlichkeit das Gebet in seinem Hause mit Aufstellung der Thoras zu verrichten, so hat er dafür eine Taxe von 50 fl. rhn. jährlich zu entrichten, die für die jüdischen Normalschulen zu verwenden ist': Karniel, 'Das Toleranzpatent Kaiser Josephs II.', §9, pp. 76–7.

[19] See 'Privatgebeth der Juden', esp. 368; Stöger, *Darstellung der gesetzlichen Verfassung*, 67.

[20] Also because it constituted a restriction contrary to what was required of Jews in the other 'Slavonic provinces': Stöger, *Darstellung der gesetzlichen Verfassung*, 67. 'Slavonic provinces' is probably a reference to Bohemia.

[21] 'Privatgebeth der Juden', 368; Stöger, *Darstellung der gesetzlichen Verfassung*, 68.

[22] Stöger, *Darstellung der gesetzlichen Verfassung*, 64–5 n. 1.

[23] In a letter of 1838 written by Sacher, the chief of the Lemberg police, there is a reference to 'Chassidenstube, Clasel genannt', so it seems that at that time a hasidic *minyan* was called a *klayzl*: see R. Mahler, *Ḥaḥasidut vehahaskalah* (Merhavia, 1961), 438–49, esp. 445.

MINYANIM AND SECRET SOCIETIES

New legislation published in 1810 altered significantly the status of the private *minyanim*. The *minyan* tax was abolished, and anyone wishing to establish a private *minyan* in his house was able to do so, provided he obtained an annual permit from the district authorities. Authorizations were issued at no cost other than the 20 gulden stamp fee required for official documents. The novelty of the new law was its definition of an unauthorized private *minyam* as a 'secret society' (*geheime Gesellschaft*), and those attending the *minyan* as members of such a society, who were thus liable to the appropriate punishment specified in the penal code.[24] Although maintaining *minyanim* was legal, there remained the suspicion that they might become a cover for illegal activities against the security and peace of the country. It is possible that what sparked off suspicion was the atmosphere created by the Napoleonic wars. In any event, the law was noticed by a London magazine, which reported: 'The tax on Jews who maintained in their own houses private acts of their religion, known by the name of *miniam*, should be abolished. Permission will be freely granted to all who desire it *gratis* only on *stamped* paper. All Jews performing *Miniam* without this, will be considered as forming a new sect, and punished accordingly.'[25] The interpretation of *geheime Gesellschaft* as 'sect' here is incorrect, since the Polish version of the law published alongside the German uses the term *tajne towarzystwo*, which means 'secret society' and not 'sect'.[26]

MINYANIM AND CHRISTIAN CHAPELS

On 22 August 1823 an amendment to the 1810 *minyan* law was published, representing yet another shift in the government attitude towards *minyanim*. This time the legislature brought the application procedure for establishing Jewish private *minyanim* into line with that of private Christian chapels (*Privat-Kapellen*).[27] Because of the importance of this law, I shall present here its full translation:

[24] See 'Kreisschreiben: Wegen der Bedingungen unter welchen die Abhaltung der Miniam für die Zukunft gestattet wird', 1 Oct. 1810, in *Continuatio Edictorum et Mandatorum Universalium in Regnis Galiciae et Lodomeriae* (Lviv, 1810), 164–5. The law was supposed to be binding from 1 November 1811. The treatment of secret societies is included in the chapter dealing with serious crimes against national security and public peace: see *Gesetzbuch über Verbrechen und schwere Polizey-Uebertretungen*, 2. Aufl. (Vienna, 1816), pt. ii, §§37–50, pp. 20–5. Austrian policy towards secret societies was established in parallel with its attitude towards the freemasons, whose activities were not forbidden at first. This began to change in 1785, when they were allowed only one meeting place in each of the provincial capitals. From 1794 onwards, secret societies were banned completely, mainly out of fear that they would serve as a cover for subversive political activities. See P. P. Bernard, *Jesuits and Jacobins: Enlightenment and Enlightened Despotism in Austria* (Urbana, Ill., 1971), 121; J. Van Horn Melton, *The Rise of the Public in Enlightenment Europe* (Cambridge, 2001), 269–70.

[25] *The Universal Magazine*, NS, 15 (1811), 152.   [26] 'Kreisschreiben', 165.

[27] 'Abänderung des Kreisschreibens vom Jahre 1810 hinsichtlich der unbefugten jüdischen Privatandacht (Miniams-)Hälter, dann diesfällige Strafen', 22 Aug. 1823, Z. 44076, in *Provinzial-Gesetzsammlung des Königreichs Galizien und Lodomerien für das Jahr 1823* (Lemberg, n.d.), 156–7.

Amendment to the provincial decree [Kreisschreiben] of 1810 regarding those who conduct unauthorized Jewish private prayer services (Miniam), and the due penalties thereof

The decree of the Court Chancellery of 17 July of this year, Z. 22353, revokes the provincial decree of 1 October 1810, Z. 33776, the main substance of which is the announcement that conducting a Jewish private prayer service (Miniam) is considered [to be the activity of] a secret society and its founder and participants will be punished under clauses 41 and 42 of the second section of the penal code,[28] and [this new amendment lays down] the following:

1. Gathering for the sole purpose of conducting a private Jewish prayer service (Miniam) with reading from the Torah,[29] without obtaining a provisional authorization from the district authorities, is a punishable offence.
2. A Jewish householder who conducts a private prayer service of this kind will be punished in accordance with the circumstances, with a fine or imprisonment.
3. The circumstances according to which the punishment will be fixed will depend on the following factors:
    (*a*) The number of years that the Miniam has been operating.
    (*b*) The amount of tax that the Miniam operator and participants were attempting to evade through lack of registration with the district authorities.
    (*c*) The position the operator and participants of the Miniam would have been in, had it been impossible to reject their application [i.e. if it is clear that the application would have been successful].
4. In general, an authorization for maintaining a Miniam will only be granted under those conditions that would allow a Christian householder to operate a private chapel [*Privat-Kapelle*]. This authorization will therefore only be issued where:
    (*a*) The householder making the application and the other named participants are known as law-abiding people, and are not suspected of religious enthusiasm [*Religionsschwärmerei*].
    (*b*) Age, illness, or distance of residence make visits to the synagogue impossible.

Clause 4 is in fact the most important part of the new law, and it asserts that Jewish prayer services and worship in Christian chapels in private homes should from now on be subject to the same legal requirements. Legal uniformity became an important principle in the legal thinking during the reign of Joseph II and was ultimately expressed in the *Allgemeines bürgerliches Gesetzbuch für die gesammten Deutschen Erbländer*, which was issued on 1 June 1811. This general civil code

---

[28] According to these clauses, the founder of a secret society and its leaders will be liable to strict imprisonment (meaning that the regime includes irons on the hands, legs, and body, receiving a hot meal only every other day, sleeping on bare planks, and not being able to receive visitors) of three to six months, and other participants face imprisonment of between a week and a month for the first offence, with sentences of one to three months for subsequent offences. See *Gesetzbuch über Verbrechen*, pt. ii, §§41–2, p. 22.

[29] In effect, the 1823 law exempted *minyanim* with no Torah reading from the need for a permit. This was later repeated and re-emphasized in a specific law: 'Privatgebeth der Juden', esp. 368.

included also special considerations for Jews, for example in the marriage laws.[30] In addition to the general civil law code there were also provincial decrees (*Kreisschreiben*) issued in the various provinces of the empire, called political laws, which were intended to correct or to amend specific laws. As far as the Jews were concerned, a number of decrees reflected a departure from the uniformity represented in the general law code, by imposing restrictions or special demands aimed exclusively at Jews. Examples of this are the special 'Jewish taxes' (the meat tax and the candle tax) and the demand that Jewish couples receive approval from the district authorities prior to their marriage in order for it to be considered legal.[31]

In this case, though, it seems that what stood behind the 1823 law was indeed considerations of legal uniformity. In the Catholic case private chapels were associated with the rich or with religious confraternities (*Bruderschaften*). The legislature, which feared that the law on private chapels would benefit mainly the rich, ruled that the permits should not be granted lightly ('nicht so leicht ertheilen'), especially since such chapels might cause division and other abuses. Granting permits was, in the Catholic case too, in the hands of the political authorities and not the religious ones, and it was they who were supposed to enquire whether the conditions of sickness or age were fulfilled. Still, the law enabled bishops to allow the functioning of private chapels without the need for preliminary enquiries.[32] Religious confraternities had been forbidden since 1783, except for one state-supported confraternity,[33] so it is clear why they would not be allowed to conduct private prayers.

The term *Religionsschwärmerei*, 'religious enthusiasm', was frequently used in the context of the German Enlightenment in reference to sectarians and religious groups with a mystical tinge, such as the Pietists, the Quakers, the Rosicrucians, the Martinists, and others, who were considered to be irrational, responsible for the spread of superstition and fanaticism, and a threat to Enlightenment ideals.[34] In the Austrian context, this attitude was also reflected in the law, specifically in a

---

[30] Only Jews were required to obtain an authorization for marriage from the district authorities, and this constituted one of the most discriminatory clauses of the law. See *Allgemeines bürgerliches Gesetzbuch für die gesammten Deutschen Erbländer der Oesterreichischen Monarchie* (Vienna, 1811), §124.

[31] In Galicia there were additional requirements for Jewish marriages, such as presentation of various documents in order to receive the district administration's approval.

[32] 'Die Gestattung von Hauscapellen auf eine kürzere, durch persönliche Verhältnisse, als: Krankheit, Alterschwäche, beschränkte Zeit, steht der politischen Landesstelle zu': see J. T. F., von Barth-Barthenheim, *Oesterreich's geistliche Angelegenheiten in ihren politisch-administrativen Beziehungen* (Vienna, 1841), §§1033–40, pp. 554–6 ('Von den Andachten in Nebenkirchen, Hauscapellen in Privatvereinen, Brüderschaften und Leichenvereinen'), esp. §1035, p. 555. See also Gampl, *Staat — Kirche — Individuum*, 113.

[33] Barth-Barthenheim, *Oesterreich's geistliche Angelegenheiten*, §§1041–7, pp. 557–62; Gampl, *Staat — Kirche — Individuum*, 67.

[34] On the discourse regarding *Schwärmerei* in the European Enlightenment, see L. E. Klein and A. L. La Vopa (eds.), *Enthusiasm and Enlightenment in Europe, 1650–1850* (San Marino, Calif., 1998).

clause defining the establishment of sects as a crime.[35] The Austrian legislature was not only wary of attacks against the Catholic religion but also fearful of the disturbance of peace, order, and public safety that 'irrational' and fringe religious groups might cause.[36] It is understandable why a Christian wishing to conduct private prayer services at home would have to prove that he was not suspected of sectarian activity or *Religionsschwärmerei*.

In the Jewish context there was no definition of the term *Religionsschwärmerei*. An attempt by several maskilim to have hasidism considered as a form of *Religionsschwärmerei* failed. The Lemberg police chief, Sacher, also wished to treat the hasidim as *Religionsschwärmer* and argued that the state should treat them no differently from their Catholic counterparts.[37] But the Austrian authorities rejected the argument and continually stressed that hasidim were *not* included in this category.[38] Moreover, they emphasized that the government had no interest in the question of sects within Judaism, and regarding *minyanim* it was solely concerned whether the petitioner was a law-abiding person.[39] Hasidim could enjoy the policy of religious toleration just like other Jews; they had the right to practise their religion unhindered, including the establishing of *minyanim*, provided this did not contravene the civil laws. The parity of *minyanim* with Christian chapels under the law introduced a new restriction: from now on only a limited group of people could apply to maintain a *minyan* in their homes. But the old liberal policy still applied to those attending the private *minyan*, a group with no restriction whatsoever.

[35] 'wer Unglauben zu verbreiten, oder eine der christlichen Religion widerstrebende Irrlehre auszustreuen, wer Sectirung zu stiften, sich bestrebt . . .': *Gesetzbuch über Verbrechen*, pt. ii, §107*d*, p. 51. It seems that sectarianism was forbidden as early as 1803: see Gampl, *Staat — Kirche — Individuum*, 127 n. 74.

[36] As a historian of the period writes: 'From the time of the ecclesiastico-political measures taken by Joseph II, the Austrian Josephine policies had adopted a strong stand against any religious "*Schwärmerei*", meaning any non-rationalistic form of religiosity. Aversion to religious *Schwärmerei* among Catholics, in different locations and different periods, speaks for itself': F. Valjavec, *Der Josephinismus: Zur geistigen Entwicklung Österreichs im 18. und 19. Jahrhundert* (Brünn, 1944), 73 (translation mine).

[37] See *Haḥasidut vehahaskalah*, 438–49, esp. 447. This paragraph from Sacher has been mistranslated in several recent scholarly works, and its correct translation should be: 'Indeed, it could be argued that the laws forbid hasidic gatherings from the standpoint of their being considered *Bruderschaften*, and that all Jews seeking to conduct a *minyan*, in exchange for the prescribed fee, would need to produce in advance a certificate that they were not hasidim or *Schwärmer*. But what value would such certifications have, since they are issued by the district rabbis, who are themselves mostly inclined towards the sect of the hasidim?'

[38] R. Manekin, 'Hasidism and the Habsburg Empire', forthcoming in *Jewish History*.

[39] See TsDIAL, 146-85-2310, no. 17158 1823 72617, pp. 46–52, in microfilm copy in CAHJP, HM2/8343.5. See also 'Behandlung der jüdischen Frömmlersekte Chasiden genannt', 26 Apr. 1824, Z. 23819, in *Provinzial-Gesetzsammlung des Königreichs Galizien und Lodomerien für das Jahr 1824* (Lemberg, n.d.), 67–9, esp. 68: 'dass sich die Regierung in die ohnehin erfolglosen Nachforschung, ob ein Jude zu dieser oder jener Sekte gehöre, nicht einzulassen, sondern bei Behandlung der einzelnen Individuen nur ihre persönlichen Eigenschften im Auge zu behalten'.

WHO CAN ATTEND A PRIVATE *MINYAN*?

An examination of the many government records dealing with petitions and appeals about *minyanim* reveals that Jews who were interested in having their own *minyanim* included hasidim, rabbinical figures, members of the upper and professional classes, and even women. Some of them were indeed too old or infirm to walk to the synagogue, but others clearly used age and health only as an excuse. The number of such records is particularly large in the early 1840s and this allows us to discover other considerations of the government policy towards *minyanim*.

This period saw a rise in rejections of petitions for *minyanim*, apparently because of a new interpretation of clause 4 of the 1823 law. The phrase in question was at the beginning of paragraph 4*a*: 'The householder making the application and the other named participants'. Until that time, this was understood as applying only to paragraph 4*a*, meaning that the householder and all the participants had to be law-abiding people and not suspected of *Religionsschwärmerei*. According to the new interpretation this opening phrase should apply also to paragraph 4*b*, meaning that it was not only the householder that had to be old, sick, or living far from the synagogue, but also all the participants in the *minyan*. This condition was almost impossible to fulfil and hence petitions for *minyanim* were rejected in large numbers.

The central authorities in Galicia discussed this issue in a report of a meeting of the Gubernium (the central Austrian authority in Galicia) that dealt with the appeal of Nochim Taubes, which I shall describe below. One of the participants in the proceedings explained that the logic and the wording of the text of the 1823 law was unclear and that as a result there was a misunderstanding of the law. He stressed in particular three points:

1. The permission to conduct prayers in private homes should be granted to Jews under the same conditions granted to Christians, which is not the case if one accepts the new interpretation. The law regarding private Christian chapels does not indicate that the participants too should be people who cannot attend services in the church because of age, illness, or distance. It concerns only the householder.

2. If one were to accept the new interpretation, then neither the family members who live in the same household nor other people who live in the house would be able to participate in the prayers unless they were old or sick, which is contrary to the spirit of the law.

3. According to the Jewish religion one needs at least ten men in order to conduct prayers. Under the new interpretation there would be no way to maintain a private *minyan* in Lemberg; the young and healthy would have no reason not to

attend the synagogue, and the sick and the old who were not able to walk to the synagogue would not be able to walk to the *minyan* either.[40]

He proposed that the opening phrase apply only to paragraph 4*a* and not 4*b*, that is, only to the householder and not to the participants. But, in the end, only three of those present at the meeting supported him, while the majority voted for accepting the new interpretation of the 1823 law.

From the report we also see that the strict application of the 1823 law was a reaction to what the members of the Gubernium perceived as preferential treatment of Jews. Christians, they claimed, sometimes needed to walk for a whole hour to get to church,[41] while Jews had to walk for no more than ten minutes in order to get to one of the many synagogues or *batei midrash* in Lemberg.[42] Moreover, Christian requests for private chapels were in general treated in a very strict manner.[43] Another hint of the new severity in the application of the 1823 law is found in the deliberations of the case of Jacob Glanzer, who petitioned for a permit to turn a wing of his house into a synagogue.[44] In the report written by the Lemberg district authorities to the Gubernium in 1843 the writer stated clearly that the number of permits for *minyanim*, which in the past were granted very frequently, had recently been reduced, something that 'should be welcomed'. Those permits are 'now' granted rarely by comparison with the situation before.[45]

The worsening of the *minyanim* situation is reflected also in a provincial decree of 1840, according to which the punishment for operating a *minyan* without a permit applies also to the participants and not only to the householder, as stated in clause 2 of the 1823 law.[46] Jews reacted to the new policy by appealing to the higher authorities, that is the Gubernium and even the Court Chancellery. In what follows I shall present a few such examples, all drawn from archival documents. They will include the cases of Fischel Mieses, one of the richest Jews in Lemberg; Leib

[40] TsDIAL, 146-85-2370, no. 1844 39009 11/h/1, pp. 21–2, in microfilm copy in CAHJP, HM2/9574.3.

[41] In general, the rule was that 'no parishioner would have more than an hour's walk to his or her parish church': see W. D. Bowman, *Priest and Parish in Vienna, 1780 to 1880* (Boston, 1999), 39.

[42] The large number of *minyanim* in Lemberg was noted by a missionary visiting the city: 'There are [in Lemberg] two large synagogues, four smaller ones, and a great many in private houses': see A. A. Bonar and R. M. M'Cheyne, *Narrative of a Mission of Inquiry to the Jews from the Church of Scotland in 1839* (Philadelphia, 1845), 465.

[43] 'weil ebenfals bei Bewilligung von christlichen Hauskapellen mit der grössten Strenge vorgegangen wird — diese jüdischen Privat-Andachten in keinem Falle eine Begünstigung verdienen': TsDIAL, 146-85-2370, no. 1844 39009 11/h/1, p. 30, in microfilm copy in CAHJP, HM2/9574.3. The strictness in granting permits for Christian chapels was required by law, as mentioned above. [44] Manekin, 'Hasidism and the Habsburg Empire'.

[45] TsDIAL, 146-85-2369, no. 25621 4 1843 72872 11/h, pp. 68–71, esp. p. 70, in microfilm copy in CAHJP, HM2/9774.2.

[46] 'Straffälligkeit der Theilnehmere an unbefugten jüdischen Privatandachten (Miniam)', Gubernial-Kundmachung vom 11. September 1840 Gubernial-Zahl 53081, in *Zweite Abtheilung der Provinzial-Gesetzsammlung des Königreichs Galizien und Lodomerien für das Jahr 1840* (n.p., n.d.), 572.

Bochmes, the controller of the Jewish hospital in Lemberg; two known rabbinical figures, Nochim Taubes and Markus Wolf (Mordecai Zev) Ettinger (Itinga); and Sara Ornstein, the widow of the late district rabbi of Lemberg.

Fischel Mieses, whose daughter Lena was married to the son of Rabbi Jacob Meshulam Ornstein (1775–1839), the rabbi of Lemberg and district,[47] lived in the inner city (most Jews lived in Jewish neighbourhoods in the suburbs), in house no. 332. Mieses was informed in 1842 that his petition for a *minyan* in his home had been denied because he had not proved that the participants in his *minyan* could likewise not attend the synagogue. Mieses, age 75, appealed against this decision, and claimed that he had operated a *minyan* in his home for many years, always receiving the required annual permit after attesting that he and the other participants were law-abiding people who were not suspected of *Religionsschwärmerei*. He said that the participants included his children as well as Jews who lived close by, such as the lawyer (Leo?) Kolischer and the doctor (Izak) Epstein. Both, it should be noted, were active members of the Jewish community and were among the members of the group that initiated the plan to establish a Temple in the city.[48] It is obvious that his circle included progressive and professional Jews. Mieses argued against the new interpretation of the 1823 law that required in effect that a private *minyan* should include ten sick or old men. His appeal proved successful, and the Gubernium ordered the district authorities in September 1842 to grant Mieses the annual permit, since he had proved that he fulfilled the necessary conditions for maintaining a *minyan*.[49] Mieses, it seems, was treated favourably by the Gubernium because of his status.

But status alone was not always a guarantee of preferential treatment. In 1842 the petition of Leib Bochmes, the controller of the Jewish hospital in Lemberg, was rejected. Bochmes claimed that he lived very far from the synagogue, and that not just his advanced age, but also his duties in the hospital prevented him from walking to the synagogue. The district authorities claimed that he lived close to the synagogue, and, they added drily, his duty as controller required even more strength than walking to the synagogue. It is interesting to note that the Jewish community council and the magistrate spoke strongly on his behalf, describing him as an active member of the community who had helped those in need in the hospital for many years without any pay. They too claimed that he could not attend the synagogue because someone might be seeking his help at the same time. Despite his status and connections, the Gubernium rejected his appeal in September 1842, claiming simply that the necessary conditions outlined in the

[47] On the description of Mieses as one of the richest men in town, see TsDIAL, 146-85-2348 ad 50757 11/B 31170/1668 1819, pp. 30–3, esp. p. 30, in microfilm copy in CAHJP, HM2/8344.5. See also M. Bałaban, 'Shalshelet hayaḥas shel mishpaḥat orenshtain-broda', *Sefer hayovel likhvod doktor mordekhai ze'ev broda* (Warsaw, 1931), 38.

[48] See M. Bałaban *Historia lwowskiej Synagogi Postępowej* (Lwów, 1937), 18.

[49] Archiwum Państwowe, Kraków (hereafter APKr), Teki Schneidera, 1001, no. 9471 1842 50536 11/h/1, pp. 73–6, in microfilm copy in CAHJP, HM2/5784.

1823 law had not been fulfilled.[50] It seems that, in this case, the explanations presented were simply not believed. The fact that an individual was a professional of a higher status was not enough to guarantee a permit.

Also denied a permit in the same year was a well-known rabbinical figure in Lemberg, Rabbi Markus Wolf Ettinger (1804–53)—after maintaining a *minyan* at his home for six years. Although Ettinger provided a certificate from Dr Gerbel, one of the city's physicians, attesting to his physical weakness, the district doctor, Dr Machold, claimed that Ettinger, though elderly, was perfectly healthy, and walking to the synagogue would not harm him. According to the authorities, Ettinger lived in the city, house no. 265, which was only a few steps from the synagogue.[51] Ettinger appealed this decision to the Gubernium. He claimed that, since he could not walk to the synagogue, the rejection of his petition would hinder his ability to practise his religion, a right that is granted in the first paragraph of the Edict of Toleration. Ettinger was not as fortunate as Mieses, and in April 1843 the Gubernium confirmed the rejection by the district authorities.[52] As a last resort, Ettinger petitioned the Court Chancellery the following year. But in March 1844 Vienna decided to reject his petition and to uphold the previous decisions in his case.[53] It seems that it is the proximity of his house to the synagogue that was the reason why his permit was denied. The various authorities were not swayed by the considerations he presented, and decided on the basis of a strict interpretation of the 1823 law.

Since I discuss the issue of hasidic *minyanim* elsewhere,[54] I shall mention here only the case of Jakob Huss, whose petition was denied in 1842. The district authorities asserted that, although he was indeed old, he was still strong and healthy and could walk to the synagogue, which was close to his home. Huss's appeal to the Gubernium was unsuccessful, and the Gubernium even criticized the previous decisions of the district authorities (in 1839 and 1840) to grant Huss such a permit. According to the Gubernium this was an administrative offence (*Ordnungswidrigkeit*).[55] What is interesting in Huss's case is his description as someone who belongs to the sect of the 'half hasidim' (*Halb-Chasiden*),[56] probably a reference to Jews who are not followers of a particular hasidic leader but adopt some hasidic customs.[57] Apparently, the authorities were well aware of this group.

[50] APKr, Teki Schneidera, 1001, no. 10265 1842 54555 11/h/1, pp. 90–3, in microfilm copy in CAHJP, HM2/5784.

[51] I wish to thank Sergey Kravtsov, who checked and confirmed that this claim is indeed correct.

[52] APKr, Teki Schneidera, 1001, no. 12945 11/h/1, pp. 72, 78–9, in microfilm copy in CAHJP, HM2/5784.

[53] TsDIAL, 146-85-2370, no. 8903/517 20522 11/h/1, pp. 10–16, in microfilm copy in CAHJP, HM2/9574.3.   [54] Manekin, 'Hasidism and the Habsburg Empire'.

[55] APKr, Teki Schneidera, 1001, no. 12945 11/h/1, pp. 111–12, in microfilm copy in CAHJP, HM2/5784.

[56] 'Nach der vorliegenden Äusserung der Polizei-Direktion zur K.Z.2918/842 gehört Jakob Huss zur Sekte der Halb-Chasiden, ist zwar alt, aber noch kräftig und gesund, und kann das seiner Wohnung nahe liegende Bethhaus in der Lietubker Gasse besuchen': ibid. 111.

[57] This group is described in the scholarly literature as a 'hasidic periphery': see U. Gelman, *Sefer ḥasidim: ḥibur ganuz bigenutah shel haḥasidut* (Jerusalem, 2007), 38.

As previously noted, there were women who maintained private *minyanim* in their homes. One such woman was Feige Fried, who appealed in 1842 to the Gubernium against a fine of 40 florins that was imposed on her for maintaining a *minyan* at her home without a permit. Fried used for that purpose part of the bequest that her husband had left her, and continued to maintain the *minyan* even after her permit was not renewed. The Gubernium instructed the district authorities to reconsider the treatment of her case, since it was not clear why a fine had been imposed only on her, and not on the other participants, as required by the 1840 decree.[58]

As mentioned above, Rabbi Nochim Taubes appealed to the Gubernium in 1844 to reverse the rejection of his petition. Taubes (1820–70) was among the close friends of Rabbi Jacob Ornstein and served later as rabbi of Kolomea.[59] The reason for the rejection was that Taubes did not prove that the participants in his *minyan* could not attend the synagogue because of age, poor health, or distance. Taubes argued in his appeal against the new interpretation of the 1823 law, claiming that for the purpose of conducting a *minyan*, a minimum of ten adult males must be present. If all ten of them are unable to walk to the synagogue owing to their age or health, it is surely likely that they will also be unable to walk to a private *minyan*. Taubes presented certificates issued by two doctors as well as by the district doctor confirming that he had been suffering from bad headaches and chronic inflammation in his right eye, and recommending that he should avoid crowded places. He also presented a confirmation from a rabbi that neither he nor other participants in his *minyan* were suspected of *Religionsschwärmerei*.

In the discussion of his case in July 1844, a majority supported the new interpretation of the law, pointing out that other appeals had already been rejected for the same reason in 1842 and 1843, such as that of Sara Ornstein, and saw no reason to accept his appeal.[60] Although a few participants were convinced by Taubes's arguments, the main reason for the rejection was the desire to limit the number of permits for private *minyanim*, so that it would not look as if the law accorded Jews preferential treatment by comparison with Christians.

SARA ORNSTEIN

Sara Ornstein was the widow of Rabbi Jacob Meshulam Ornstein, the late rabbi of Lemberg and district. Mrs Ornstein continued to maintain the private *minyan* at

[58] APKr, Teki Schneidera, 1001, no. 63344 Curr. 11/h/1, pp. 88–9, in microfilm copy in CAHJP, HM2/5784.

[59] M. Vunder, *Me'orei galitsiyah: entsiklopediyah leḥakhmei galitsiyah*, 6 vols. (Jerusalem, 1978–2005), iii. 55. Taubes was considered a zealot operating close to Rabbi Ornstein. He was referred to in a Viennese Jewish newspaper as 'ein zweiter Domingo beim Grossinquisitor Ornstein': see *Wiener Blätter*, 27 Feb. 1851, p. 113.

[60] TsDIAL, 146-85-2370, no. 1844 39009 11/h/1, pp. 19–31, in microfilm copy in CAHJP, HM2/9574.3.

her home, house no. 425 in Kraków suburb 2/4, after her husband died, apparently with the authorization of the district authorities. In 1841 her petition for renewal was rejected. The reason given for the rejection was that she had not proved that the other participants fulfilled condition 4*b*. Ornstein appealed this decision to the Gubernium, claiming that:

1. Her petition for a permit was not to establish a new *minyan* but to continue an existing one. Her husband had maintained the *minyan* with the required annual permission for thirty years without any interruption. She herself had received permission for the year 1841 (her husband probably managed to get the permission for 1840 just before his death).

2. The participants were the same ones for whom the permission had been granted before. They included relatives as well as great money-lenders ('grosse Capitalisten'). For the latter, walking to the faraway main synagogue presented a real danger, since money might be stolen from them (the *minyan* operated daily).

3. She herself was unable to walk to the synagogue because of her age and ill health. She presented affidavits from the Jewish community council and the police that she and the participants were respectable people of good standing and were not suspected of *Religionsschwärmerei*.

The Gubernium accepted her appeal and instructed the district authorities to grant Sara Ornstein a permit to operate her *minyan* for the year 1842.[61]

But this was not the end of her fight.[62] Ornstein continued to receive annual permits until February 1845, but her petition for the following year was rejected. This time, the reason given was a decree of the Court Chancellery of 31 December 1844, no. 38566/2392, ordering that the number of permits granted for private *minyanim* in Lemberg should be limited, since the existing synagogues and prayer houses in the city were not far from the areas where Jews resided. Ornstein appealed again to the Gubernium, stressing the fact that the *minyan* had started in her house thirty years previously; that there were sixteen participants; and that she was 70 years old and suffered from weak eyesight, which made it impossible for her to walk to the synagogue. In addition, the participants were not suspected of *Religionsschwärmerei*, and in any event, this was not a petition for a new *minyan*, but for the renewal of an existing one. The court decree, she claimed, called for the permits to be limited and not for eliminating *minyanim* altogether. On 31 March 1845 the Gubernium rejected Ornstein's appeal, upholding the reasons given by the district authorities.

Ornstein's last recourse was to appeal to the Court Chancellery in Vienna, using the same arguments as she had used before. The Gubernium submitted to Vienna

---

[61] APKr, Teki Schneidera, 1001, no. 15438 1842 82834 11/h/1, pp. 108–10, in microfilm copy in CAHJP, HM2/5784.

[62] Haus-, Hof- und Staatsarchiv, Alter Kultus/Israelitischer Kultus, Ktn. 4, ad 36590-845.

on 18 February 1846 its reasons for rejecting Ornstein's appeal. It mentioned the court decree of December 1844, which called for the number of permits for *minyanim* to be limited as much as possible, both in general and in Lemberg in particular. It emphasized that the number of prayer houses in Lemberg—one of them close to Ornstein's house—was large enough, and even older Jews were able to get there. There was no reason to make an exception for this particular petitioner, especially since she had not proved that the other participants were not able to attend the synagogue because of age, health, or distance, as the 1823 law required.[63]

The Court Chancellery discussed Ornstein's case on 1 May 1846, in a committee composed of such members as Franz Freiherr von Pillersdorf, the famous Austrian statesman. In its reply to the Gubernium, the committee clarified the two decrees quoted by the Gubernium: the court decree of 1844, and paragraph 4*b* of the 1823 *minyanim* law. As to the 1844 decree, the Court Chancellery declared that it did not by any means call for a prohibition on the authorizing of *minyanim*, it merely required that the conditions and demands of clause 4 of the 1823 law be met strictly. In the case of Sara Ornstein, these conditions had been fulfilled, as it had been confirmed that she and the other participants were known as honest people and that they were not suspected of *Religionsschwärmerei*. Additionally, her age and the distance from her house to the synagogue, as proved, did not allow her to attend the synagogue. The committee added that, as the widow of the late district rabbi who had served his community for many years, she deserved reasonable consideration of her case, particularly as it was not an application for a new private *minyan*.

As to the claim that the applicant had not proved that all participants in her *minyan* were unable to attend the synagogue for reasons of age, ill health, etc., the Court Chancellery replied that this claim was based on a wrong interpretation of the law. The suggestion that paragraph 4*b* of the law referred not only to the master of the house or mistress of the house who applied for the permit, but also to the participants in the *minyan*, was simply incorrect. The committee suggested that the Galician authorities should grant Sara Ornstein the required permit and correct its misinterpretation of the law, also with regard to future applications for the authorization of *minyanim*, that is to require the conditions of paragraph 4*b* only with regard to the masters or mistresses of houses ('Hausväter oder Hausmütter') who applied for a permit.[64] It is important to note that paragraph 4*a* of the 1823 law used only the term *Hausvater*, and the *Hausmütter* added now was in consideration of such future cases as Sara Ornstein's.

As a result of the Court Chancellery's decision on Ornstein's case the interpretation of the law was indeed amended and the Court Chancellery issued a special order to clarify the 1823 law.[65] Mahler, who mentioned this clarification, was not

---

[63] The report to the governor is signed by Referent Gubernial-Sekretär Hofmann, 18 Feb. 1846.

[64] The reply from the Court Chancellery was signed by Hofrath Ritter von Zaleski.

[65] 'This situation [requiring that the participants too need to fulfil condition 4*b* of the 1823 law]

aware that it was the result of Sara Ornstein's appeal to Vienna. In his effort to interpret the issue of private *minyanim* exclusively within the context of the struggle against hasidim, Mahler missed the more common aspect of the issue of *minyanim*, which was not dictated solely by the hasidic or maskilic angle. The issue of private *minyanim* did not relate only to hasidim, and in our case, not even only to men. The importance of this example lies also in the fact that even the rabbi of the city maintained his own private *minyan*. Large as his house must have been, it is hard to believe that there were more than a few dozen participants there. The public synagogue seems almost to be a place serving the less fortunate Jews, those with a lower socio-economic or intellectual status.

WOMEN AND SYNAGOGUES

In the documents relating to Ornstein, or the cases of other women, there is no specific reference to the fact that the applicant is a woman, and no particular questions or surprises arise in consequence. As the law applied equally to Christians and Jews, one can guess that instances where women applied for permission to hold prayers in their homes were more frequent among Christians. I have been unsuccessful in locating any study of this issue within an Austrian Christian context, but within a German Pietist context we know of prayer meetings and Bible studies being held in women's homes.[66] It may be that meetings of this kind also took place among the German Evangelical colonists in Galicia who had been brought there by the Austrian emperors,[67] but this requires further research. Also, in the Christian case the authorities were more sensitive to the question of sectarianism,[68] and this may be the reason for the extra strictness in the authorization of private Christian prayer, as pointed out in the documents cited above. The efforts of the authorities in Galicia to apply more strictness towards Jewish *minyanim* did not prove successful in the end, thanks to the persistence of one woman, Sara Ornstein.

The information we have on the connections between women and synagogues is not plentiful, but certain facts can be gleaned from the documents on applications for the establishment of private *minyanim* and from contemporary press reports.

---

continued until 1846, when an imperial decree made it clear that not all members of the *minyan* must prove that they were ill, infirm, or lived too far from the synagogue, and that an official permit to conduct a *minyan* should also be issued in cases where the householder alone was forced to worship at home because of one of these difficulties': Mahler, *Hasidism and the Jewish Enlightenment*, 82.

[66] J. Van Horn Melton, 'Pietism, Politics, and the Public Sphere in Germany', in J. E. Bradley and D. K. Van Kley (eds.), *Religion and Politics in Enlightenment Europe* (Notre Dame, Ind., 2001), esp. 322–4.

[67] On these colonies, see I. Röskau-Rydel, *Deutsche Geschichte im Osten Europas: Galizien* (Berlin, 1999), 57–66.

[68] G. Wanner, 'Aufklärung, Religionsschwärmerei und Aberglaube in Vorarlberg: Eine Studie über religiöse Verhältnisse in der ersten Hälfte des 19. Jahrhunderts aus Akten des Generalvikariats-archives in Feldkirch', *Montfort*, 20 (1968), 444–63.

For example, Jacob Glanzer of Lemberg, a rich hasidic Jew who was granted permission to establish a synagogue in a wing of his house in 1843, reported that it contained 262 seats, 198 for men and 64 for women.[69] An 1844 report tells us that in the Great Synagogue of Lemberg, in the corners and at the pillars, 'those who sit far away, i.e. the women', cannot hear (the prayers) properly.[70] Two years later, in a report on the Temple established in Lemberg, the same newspaper reports that Jews 'dressed like Polish Jews (in traditional rather than modern style)' also attend, together with their wives, on Friday evenings and on the sabbath, as they have realized that 'here too, one can pray with concentration'.[71] There was a great cultural distance between Glanzer's synagogue and the Temple, but we see that facilities for women were not left out of either place of worship.

The *minyan* for which Sara Ornstein sought a permit was, as mentioned above, one that was maintained in her house for some thirty years. The existence of a *minyan* of this kind required suitable physical conditions, financial means, and the intellectual ability to satisfy all the formalities and bureaucracy required to obtain the necessary permit. Anyone fulfilling these conditions could by law run a *minyan*, with no discrimination based on gender. If there were other women who operated private *minyanim*, they were surely widows of means and standing like Sara Ornstein, who did so in memory of their husbands or as an expression of piety.

Sara Ornstein's case accords well with the literary description of her as penned by Joseph Perl, who, when writing of her husband, Rabbi Jacob, added:

I have heard that he [Rabbi Ornstein] has kept apart from his wife for some years, since she does not want to [ritually] purify herself because of her physical health. She is also quite righteous, and is very strict with herself, since she wears a four-cornered garment with *tsitsit*, and on Hoshana Rabba, while saying the Hoshanot, she holds a *lulav* and *etrog* in her hand, which she bought especially for herself. I have also heard that in the house where she lives there is a regular *minyan*, and there was one man there who had directed the *ba'al toke'a* in blowing the *shofar* since this *minyan* was established, but once, when she had to pray at the *minyan* in her home on Rosh Hashanah, she did not allow that man to direct the *shofar*-blowing as he was not God-fearing enough in her eyes; from this incident, I saw how fervent she was. She curries favour with no one, either Jew or non-Jew, for I have heard that she lends her money to the [Polish] nobility and does not curry favour with them, charging them unbelievable amounts of interest, and even though she also collects large sums from Jews on the basis of a *heter iska*; still, in order to distance herself from the prohibition on charging [Jews] interest altogether, she only lends money to Jews when there are no members of the nobility to lend to.[72]

---

[69] TsDIAL, 146-85-2370, no. 1844 5885 11/h, pp. 6–7, esp. p. 7, in microfilm copy in CAHJP, HM2/9774.3.

[70] *Allgemeine Zeitung des Judentums*, 25 Nov. 1844. The report relates to a sermon delivered there by Rabbi Abraham Kohn, and points out that the women could not hear significant parts of the sermon.

[71] *Allgemeine Zeitung des Judentums*, 30 Nov. 1846, pp. 718–21, esp. p. 719.

[72] J. Perl, *Boḥen tsadik* (Prague, 1838), 50. On this book, see J. Meir, 'Midrash shemot besefer boḥen tsadik', *Tarbiz*, 76 (2007), esp. 570.

From this description we gain an impression of a strong and independent woman, who conducted a money-lending business, dealt with non-Jews, and was knowledgeable and pious in her religion. Her piety, as described by Perl, is not the stereotypical 'female' piety, generally represented by acts of kindness or the reading of popular religious texts, but a piety based on her confidence in her knowledge of Jewish law. Perl's description, whether realistic or literary and imaginary, is based on the reputation Ornstein had earned for herself, which accords with her conduct in the case discussed here, both in her desire to maintain the *minyan* in her home and in her dogged attempts to preserve its existence.

CONCLUSION

The Jewish communal leadership was never favourably disposed towards private *minyanim*. They brought about a reduction in revenue from contributions made when members were called to the Torah, as well as a certain loss of communal control over religious life, not to mention halakhic considerations. Rabbi Ezekiel Landau, the rabbi of Prague, lamented this in strong words:

Because of our many sins, an evil custom has spread whereby individuals, great and small, conduct *minyanim* in their houses. No one protests or prevents it. Who knows how many husks [*kelipot*] and harmful things are spawned there . . . Worse, 'the secondary has become primary' and 'the servant girl has supplanted her mistress', for these *minyanim* are full while the synagogogues are empty. These *minyanim* are full of adolescent boys and girls conversing during the prayer service, and Scripture cries out, 'Why have I come to a *minyan* with no men, just empty youths?' I read that the sexton calls the worshippers to the synagogue, but no one answers. Because of our many sins, the disease has spread, first breaking out among the great, and now everyone builds an altar for himself. Were I to have the power, I would protest against all of them, no matter who they are. Those [conducting *minyanim*] who don't have permits, as well as anyone who has the ability to protest but doesn't do so out of favouritism, will be held to account in the future.[73]

Although the rhetoric might be somewhat exaggerated, Landau demonstrates here the weak control he had over the situation. Clearly, as someone who occupied an official position, he could not prohibit something that the government had allowed. At the time he wrote this, the law enabled every individual to receive a permit for his own *minyan* in exchange for an annual tax.

The intervention of the enlightened-absolutist monarchy in these matters stemmed from its belief in the sovereignty of the state in all areas of life, including religious life.[74] Because of its tolerance towards the Jewish religion, the state did not interfere in Jewish religious customs, but did lay down the 'administrative' rules for religious institutions or so-called 'external' religious affairs, as opposed to

---

[73] Y. Landau, *Derushei hatsalah* (Jerusalem, 1966), *derush* 3, para. 14, pp. 12–14, esp. p. 13*b*. I am grateful to Shnayer Leiman for directing me to this source.

[74] See Strakosch, *State Absolutism and the Rule of Law*, 137–42.

'internal' affairs, which were left to the religious clergy.[75] The Jewish religious communities viewed this as unwarranted interference and an affront to the religious autonomy that they had enjoyed for a long time. However, from the point of view of the individual member of the Jewish community, male or female, the law constituted a guarantee of the protection of individual rights, even in the religious sphere. This applied to those individuals who understood the meaning of the law, even if they belonged to minority groups such as Jews or women. In pre-partition Poland the sphere of religion was perceived as a corporate privilege, applying to the community as a whole. Under the Habsburg regime another dimension was added to the communal sphere, and that is the right of the individual to practise his religion without the mediating role of the community. The result was the freedom to experience religious life in different individual settings other than those that could be offered by the traditional community, thus creating new norms and expectations for worship.

[75] Government interference was greater in Catholic religious institutions since Catholicism was considered the national religion On the Josephine policy regarding relations between religion and state, see O'Brien, 'Ideas of Religious Toleration', 25.

Overcoming the Signs of the 'Other'

Visual Aspects of the Acculturation of Jews in the Kingdom of Poland in the Nineteenth Century

AGNIESZKA JAGODZIŃSKA

THE ACCULTURATION of a minority group, defined as the acceptance of the cultural patterns of the dominant majority, in practice usually translates itself into the adoption of the majority's names, language, dress code, and other customary behaviour.[1] The acculturation of Jews in the nineteenth-century Kingdom of Poland followed this general pattern. Cultural changes which had been initiated by both the Polish Enlightenment and the Jewish Haskalah accelerated in the second half of the nineteenth century. Modernization challenged the traditional Jewish way of life, and the different responses to it divided Polish Jewry ideologically. Cultural transformation along with social and political changes led to the ideological fragmentation of Jewish society at the turn of the nineteenth and the twentieth centuries.

There were many sides to nineteenth-century Jewish acculturation in the Kingdom of Poland. In this essay I wish to focus on various aspects of visual change. The transformation of the iconosphere, by which I understand the entire visual universe of the past, is a broad subject. I shall limit myself to the discussion of changes in Jewish dress and in Jewish appearance (including hair, beards, side-locks, and wigs). Photographs, drawings, paintings—and descriptions, in cases in which images have not been preserved—enable us to reconstruct the appearance of Jews in the changing iconosphere of the nineteenth century and to document how this appearance was modified over time.

The visual acculturation of the Jews living in the Kingdom of Poland in the nineteenth century occurred in two ways, 'compulsory' and 'voluntary'. These different types of acculturation affected different groups. The first, aimed primarily

[1] An explanation of 'acculturation' as a term and concept, and a definition of its relation to other terms and concepts used in the literature (such as assimilation, integration, emancipation), can be found in T. Endelman, 'Assimilation', in G. D. Hundert (ed.), *The YIVO Encyclopedia of Jews in Eastern Europe*, 2 vols. (New Haven, 2008), i. 81–7. In this essay I follow Endelman's terminology.

at traditional Jews, was imposed by laws promulgated by the government of the Kingdom of Poland, which, particularly after 1830, was closely linked with the Russian authorities.[2] In theory, at least, it had broader consequences than the second type. The laws which attempted to 'normalize' or to 'correct' the situation of Jews living in the Kingdom of Poland focused on 'distinctive' Jewish clothing, amongst other things. They affected, above all, the traditional sectors of the Jewish community, the majority of Polish Jewry at this time. These were the Jews who up until the state reforms in the 1840s and 1850s had not changed their dress and appearance and were reluctant to do so when these reforms were implemented, in contrast to some of their modernization-oriented brethren.

Voluntary acculturation, by contrast, did not depend on government legislation, but was the result of the personal choice of individual Jews of the 'progressive' (*postępowy*) camp. They were supporters of Jewish acculturation and integration into Polish society and identified themselves as 'Poles of Mosaic faith'.[3] Progressive Jews were most numerous in large cities (especially Warsaw) and less well represented in small towns. They constituted a not very large, but culturally and politically significant, part of Jewish society in the Kingdom of Poland and expressed their views in the weeklies *Jutrzenka* (1861–3), edited by Daniel Neufeld, and *Izraelita* (1866–1915), edited by Samuel Peltyn. They emerged from the Jewish intellectual circles and the new growing bourgeoisie and ideologically were the heirs of the Haskalah (Jewish Enlightenment).[4] Their goals included the dissemination of education and progressive ideas, the legal emancipation of Jews, the modernization of many aspects of Jewish life (including religion), acculturation (defined as the abandonment of distinctive attire, language, and custom), and integration with Polish society. As far as religion was concerned, they did not wish to abandon Judaism, yet at the same time they developed many projects of religious reform.

In this essay I shall discuss the specifics of both types of visual acculturation and investigate the relationship between the progressive and conservative Jews of the Kingdom of Poland, especially in Warsaw, the capital of Jewish acculturation and integration. Dress was at this time a way of expressing one's cultural, religious, and even political identity. In the case of progressive Jews, visual acculturation was not only a matter of social fashion but a manifestation of changes in their self-perception. The new identity of 'Poles of Mosaic faith' involved both a commitment to identify oneself as a Jew and the adoption of a 'modern' lifestyle. Conversely, the

[2] For detailed information on the Kingdom of Poland and its dependence on Russia, see M. Wodziński, *Haskalah and Hasidism in the Kingdom of Poland: A History of Conflict*, trans. S. Cozens (Oxford, 2005), 34–9.

[3] In the historiography the members of this sector of Jewish society are defined as 'integrationists', 'acculturated Jews', 'Poles of Mosaic faith', or 'progressive Jews' (the latter is an element of their self-description and has nothing in common with Progressive Judaism), and in the older literature as 'assimilators' or 'assimilated Jews'.

[4] On the formation of the Warsaw bourgeoisie, see M. Siennicka, *Rodzina burżuazji warszawskiej i jej obyczaj* (Warsaw, 1998), 25–9.

pre-modern construct of Jewish identity, in which a special dress and appearance were believed to be the outer indication of Jewishness, resulted in the retention of the traditional style of dress by more conservative Jews. Their fear of losing this identity was translated into their refusal to become visually modernized. Traditional Jews believed that they could not be Jewish and look 'modern'.

CIVILIZING THE 'OTHER': LAW AND JEWISH DRESS

The beginnings of the modernization of social life coupled with post-Enlightenment ideological changes exerted a major influence on the Jewish iconosphere, especially on the dress traditionally worn by Polish Jews.[5] The problem of the visual distinctiveness of the Jews had already been discussed by the reformers of the Four Year Sejm (1788–92), summoned to improve the situation of the country and expected to 'solve', among other problems, the 'Jewish question'.[6] At the end of the Polish–Lithuanian Commonwealth, Christian as well as Jewish reformers proposed various plans for the improvement of the situation of the Jews, and the problem of dress was a constant subject of political debate; it continued to be so in the period of the Grand Duchy of Warsaw and the Kingdom of Poland.[7] In reality, large-scale changes in the appearance of Polish Jews took place only in the nineteenth century. These were connected to other changes in Jewish life which were stimulated by both internal and external pressures. While the voluntary transformation took place throughout the nineteenth century, the compulsory modernization of Jewish dress, imposed from above, coincided mainly with the 1840s and the attempt by the tsar to intervene in this matter in the Kingdom of Poland.

The efforts to civilize and modernize the tsarist empire and the lands it conquered, begun by Peter the Great, influenced the political behaviour of his successors. After the partitions of Poland between 1772 and 1795 a large number of Jews became subjects of the tsar, and the 'Jewish question' had to be taken into consideration in the planned reforms. One of these measures included the elimination of distinctive Jewish clothing and other visual elements of Jewish 'otherness'. Such reforms were intended, on the one hand, to ensure better control over this population and, on the other, to bring about 'normalization'—to lead to the 'fusion' of the

---

[5] On the traditional dress of Polish Jews, see I. Turnau, 'Jewish Costume in Sixteenth–Eighteenth Century Poland', in J. Kruppé and A. Pośpiech (eds.), *Omnia res mobilia: Polish Studies in Posthumous Inventories of Movable Property in the 16th–19th Century*, trans. A. Kinecka (Warsaw, 1999), 281–9. A. Rubens also wrote about this in his *A History of Jewish Costume* (London, 1973), 103–13, but one should treat his statements with care, because they are often imprecise or even erroneous.

[6] For the Sejm's debates on the subject of Jewish dress, see R. Żebrowski, 'Zagadnienie stroju żydowskiego w dobie Sejmu Czteroletniego: Projekt reformy', *Biuletyn Żydowskiego Instytutu Historycznego*, 131–2 (1984), 31–47.

[7] See A. Eisenbach, *Emancypacja Żydów na ziemiach polskich, 1785–1870, na tle europejskim* (Warsaw, 1988), 90, 105–6, 189, 345, 404, 434; Żebrowski, 'Zagadnienie stroju żydowskiego'.

Jews with the Christians among whom they lived. Tsarist policy, based on the larger concept of 'civilization', put pressure upon the Jews to meet the cultural standards of 'modernity'.

On 18 November 1845 a tsarist decree concerning the obligatory change of the dress code of Jews in the empire was extended to the territories of the Kingdom of Poland.[8] In accordance with the decree, from 1 July 1846 Jewish dress could be worn only after payment of a fee; after 1 January 1850 a general prohibition of Jewish dress would take place.[9]

The fees (*konsensowe*) for wearing Jewish dress during the planned interim period were not uniform. They varied according to which of six classes a Jew was assigned. The accompanying table shows the criteria used in the creation of the class structure and the corresponding fees.

Fees payable for the right to wear Jewish dress in the Kingdom of Poland, 1846–1849
(*silver roubles*)

Fee class	Class membership by occupation	Annual fee
I	Wholesale merchants, landowners, holders of the right to distil and sell alcohol in the city or countryside, collectors of state or municipal taxes, government suppliers	50
II	Retail merchants, butchers, tavern-keepers	30
III	Stall-keepers, pedlars, factors	20
IV	Small-scale urban manufacturers	10
V	Craftsmen, rural labourers engaged in farming, clerks, servants, workmen	5
VI	All other Jews not included in classes I–V	3

Source: Based on AGAD, KRSW, 6643, fo. 10, item 6.

Permits had to be purchased by each family member, while the cost of the permit was established according to the profession of the father of the family. The only exemptions were the elderly (aged over 60) and children below 10.[10] Older children, whether attending Christian schools or Jewish schools, were expected to change their appearance because 'the schools cannot accept children in Jewish dress'.[11] The fee was intended to encourage the abandonment of traditional dress: 'all those who switch from Jewish dress to dress similar to that of their neighbours or to the Russian style will be exempt from the fee from the moment of the said change'.[12] Those who returned to traditional Jewish dress would again be liable to pay the fee.

[8] See Archiwum Główne Akt Dawnych, Warsaw (hereafter AGAD), Komisja Rządowa Spraw Wewnętrznych (KRSW), 6643, fo. 3.   [9] AGAD, KRSW, 6643, fo. 10, item 1.

[10] Contrary to the popular interpretation of this law, only elderly people who had reached the age of 60 before 1 July 1846 were exempt from paying fees. The legal documents state that 'people who reach the age of 60 after the appointed date cannot avail themselves of exemption from payment': ibid., fo. 12, item 4.   [11] Ibid., fos. 35–6, item 2.   [12] Ibid., fo. 10, item 7.

A person who wished to dress in the traditional Jewish manner—or even just retain an element of the dress—had to carry a receipt for the fee and an identity card which could be shown on demand to the police or military.[13] Anyone wearing traditional attire who did not purchase a permit would be fined. Exemption was granted to 'rabbis and clergy of the Mosaic faith' but only during the time they were performing certain religious functions.[14] After they ceased to perform the function, they would either have to purchase the permit (in the interim period when Jewish traditional dress was still acceptable) or dress as non-Jews.

A description of prohibited Jewish dress can be found in the instruction sent to each province (*gubernia*) and to the magistrate of Warsaw:

Prohibited Orthodox dress comprises:

For males: silk or satin long caftans (coats); sashes (garter belts); fur headdresses called kalpaks and yarmulkes and other distinctive Jewish hats; knee-breeches; slippers; beards and twisted sidelocks (peyes).

For females: turbans; headbands; Jewish-style dresses; colourful shoes; and other distinctive dress and adornments.[15]

The types of dress permitted were also specified by law. Jews could choose one of two options: accept the dress code of other inhabitants of the Kingdom of Poland, or accept Russian dress (sometimes called Russian merchant dress). The law regulated precisely what was acceptable:

For males: hats with a brim proportional in width to those worn by other inhabitants; normal caps without yarmulke and sidelocks; short coats of linen, wool, tweed, or thick cotton, without belts but with buttons, or simple Russian-style coats, with which the hair may be cut in the Russian style [*v skobku*].

For females: head covered with a simple cap or woman's hat; dresses of usual German cut or attire as worn by Russian women.[16]

Instructions concerned not only the type and size of dress but also the material from which it was made. For example, those who accepted the Russian style of dress could not wear clothes made out of silk.[17]

Jewish appearance and attire in the Pale of Settlement (that part of the Russian empire where the Jews were permitted to settle) were regulated in the same way. In

---

[13] Ibid., fo. 13, item 14.

[14] 'Jewish clergy' comprised first and foremost dayans (assistants to the rabbi). It is significant that, when the dress law was first introduced, a large number of Jews began to petition the government to obtain 'clergy' status for themselves (which petitions were usually denied) and thereby receive permission to wear traditional attire. See M. Wodziński, *Władze Królestwa Polskiego wobec chasydyzmu: Z dziejów stosunków politycznych* (Wrocław, 2008), ch. 4. The problem of deciding who should be styled as 'Jewish clergy' is noted in the KRSW records: see, for example, AGAD, KRSW, 6646, fo. 337, or 6650, fo. 35.

[15] AGAD, KRSW, 6643, fo. 17, item 2. [16] Ibid., item 6.

[17] Ibid., fo. 10, item 5. Silk was an emblematic material for various groups of hasidim: see G. Dynner, *Men of Silk: The Hasidic Conquest of Polish Jewish Society* (Oxford, 2006).

Figure 1. 'Russian' attire for a Jewish man, 1847
AGAD, KRSW, 6644

Figure 2. 'Russian' attire for a Jewish woman, 1847
AGAD, KRSW, 6644

this respect the situation of Jews in Warsaw did not differ significantly from, say, that of Jews in Vilna. In the Vilna province Jews who accepted 'German' or 'Russian' dress style were exempt from the requirement to purchase a permit. The allowed dress styles were similar to those in the Kingdom:

For males: French hats or ordinary military hats without yarmulke and sidelocks; cloth, wool, or linen coats with no velvet borders and no belts with buttons; or simple caftans of Russian style, with which the hair may be cut in the Russian style; simple pants, knee-length or inserted into the boots.

For females: the head is covered with a simple cap or German-style hat or Russian head-dress. For single women: a Russian-style *sarafan* [a type of Russian long dress], the head without cover or headband; or German attire, with a braid fastened with a comb.[18]

The two styles were required by law to retain their specific characteristics, and elements of one were not to be combined with elements of the other. This meant that, for instance, in Vilna a Jewish woman could not wear a Russian headband with German-style attire, or have a braid with a comb along with Russian attire.[19]

What were the specifics of 'local', 'German', and 'Russian' dress styles? How did they differ? First of all, the local and German styles had many similarities, rendering them nearly identical. Compared with the Russian style, the German/local style was more modern and closer to the standards of Western fashion. Because the coats worn in this style were shorter than the Russian coats, it was regarded as a more radical version of non-Jewish attire. This is especially true given that Jews dressed in the German style, wearing dress coats or *surduty* or *paletoty* (types of overcoats), could not wear beards.[20] The German style took its name from German Jews in general, and in particular from the Prussian Jewish families who moved to Warsaw in the first half of the nineteenth century.

Those Jews who dressed in German style did not actually differ from other inhabitants of the Kingdom of Poland of the same social class who wore the local style. The modernization and urbanization taking place in the nineteenth century brought democratic changes to fashion and made it more international than it had been in the past. This local/European dress style was often accepted by progressive Jews, who attempted to achieve integration and cultural adaptation to Polish society.

Traditional Jews much preferred variants of the Russian style (see Figures 1 and 2). This style may be described as follows: 'a longer dress coat or *kapota* with buttons, pants worn over the shoes or inserted in the boots, scarf at the neck, and ordinary hat or military-style cap'.[21] All Russian clothing had to be made from approved fabrics. In the summer months the same dress could be made from

---

[18] AGAD, KRSW, 6643, fos. 37–8.

[19] For more on the modernization of Jewish dress in Vilna, see I. Klauzner, 'Hagezirah al tilboshet hayehudim, 1844–1850', *Gal-ed*, 6 (1982), 11–26. On the interesting ups and downs of the Russian textile industry and on the meeting of East and West in fashion, and also on the connections between industrial change and fashion in Russia, see C. Ruane, 'Clothes Make the Comrade: A History of the Russian Fashion Industry', *Russian History/Histoire Russe*, 23 (1996), 311–43.

[20] AGAD, KRSW, 6649, fo. 365, item 5.

[21] *Dziennik Urzędowy Guberni Augustowskiej Suwałki*, 31 Dec. 1849/12 Jan. 1850: AGAD, KRSW, 6646, fo. 213.

Figure 3. 'German' attire of Nuchem Salomon Brünner, a Prussian Jew living in Warsaw in the early nineteenth century

From I. Schiper, A. Tartakower, and A. Hafftka (eds.), *Żydzi w Polsce Odrodzonej* (Warsaw, 1932–3), i. 440

Figure 4. 'German' attire of Amalia Brünner, a Prussian Jew living in Warsaw in the early nineteenth century

From I. Schiper, A. Tartakower, and A. Hafftka (eds.), *Żydzi w Polsce Odrodzonej* (Warsaw, 1932–3), i. 441

lighter fabrics.[22] This attire could be worn with a short beard, but without sidelocks, and the hair had to be cut evenly on both sides, no longer than 1½ *vershki* (barely 7 cm). Yarmulkes were prohibited.[23] Jews trying to circumvent the law began wearing small knitted skullcaps under a normal cap. The government decided that these skullcaps were practically a substitute for yarmulkes and made them illegal.[24]

The problems involved in implementing this legislation led to some modifications in its character, above all in 1848 and 1853. Jews were allowed to wear some special elements of Jewish dress on the sabbath and other holidays, and during reli-

[22] The Jews tried to have themselves exempted from this, asking for permission to wear Russian dress made either of cloth or of lighter fabrics independently of the season: see AGAD, KRSW, 6647, fo. 87, item 4. This appeal was granted by the Government Commission on Internal and Religious Affairs in 1853 in a routine resolution pertaining to Jewish dress and appearance: see AGAD, KRSW, 6649, fo. 365, item 6.

[23] Dziennik Urzędowy Guberni Augustowskiej Suwałki, 31 Dec. 1849/12 Jan. 1850: AGAD, KRSW, 6646, fo. 213.

[24] Archiwum Państwowe, Lublin, Rząd Gubernialny Lubelski, Adm. 1808, p. 133. I am indebted to Marcin Wodziński for this reference.

gious ceremonies.[25] In accordance with the decree of 1853, the police were not to interfere with Jews wearing religious dress on their way to prayer houses or returning home, and they could not intrude upon places of religious assembly on festivals or during religious rituals. They were not supposed to 'search for those items of dress, which are not externally visible', for example the *talit*.[26] The police did, however, have permission to check whether, under the pretext of wearing 'religious attire', Jews were actually wearing other elements of prohibited traditional dress, such as a yarmulke.[27]

How successful were these reforms? In February 1850 an official reported: 'As a result of all these regulations, only a small number of religiously Orthodox Jews have continued to follow the old customs and attire regardless of the approach of the 1850 deadline [when the old dress would become illegal]; by far the greater part of the Jews, namely the wealthiest classes, have adopted the dress worn by the native inhabitants or by the Russian merchants.'[28] This claim proved too optimistic. A decade later, the civilian governor of Augustów province in Suwałki stated in his report:

Many inhabitants of the Mosaic faith try to escape the eyes of the police. It might have been expected that, having been forced to change their dress, they would keep to the new one, but instead they return to the old dress as soon as they can escape the supervision of the authorities. This stubbornness is rooted in the superstition and false belief that the maintenance of the old manner of dress is required by religion. These false convictions could be most effectively countered by the Israelite clergy, and I believe that this clergy will not refuse to help, especially now that followers of the Mosaic faith [*ludność starozakonna*] have received equal rights with the other inhabitants of the country.[29]

The claim that the reform had proved successful was valid for the middle-class and wealthy Jews who lived in the large cities such as Warsaw. However, the situation was different in rural areas and small towns. Active opposition to the reforms and their total rejection was especially strong in hasidic circles. Some officials even feared that the reform would be undermined by their influence: 'those who have changed their dress may be forced gradually to return to the old manner of dress as a result of hatred and attacks from those who stubbornly follow old religious rules—namely the sect of hasidim or *hussyty*—and in this way they could bring to naught several years' work undertaken by the government to such favourable effect'.[30] However, it appears that the negative influence of the hasidim on the

---

[25] AGAD, KRSW, 6649, fo. 356, item 10.

[26] Ibid., item 11.   [27] Ibid., item 10; see also AGAD, KRSW, 6649, fos. 246–7.

[28] Letter from the Office of General Administration (section 1) to the Secretary of State, Board of Administration, 11/23 Feb. 1850: AGAD, KRSW, 6646, fo. 205.

[29] Report of the civilian governor of Augustów province in Suwałki to the Government Commission on Religion and Public Education, 26 Dec. 1862/7 Jan. 1863: AGAD, KRSW, 6650, fos. 266–7.

[30] Letter from the Office of General Administration (section 1) to the Secretary of State, Board of Administration, 11/23 Feb. 1850: AGAD, KRSW, 6646, fo. 206.

reforms was exaggerated and reflected a generally hostile view of this group among officials.[31]

Hasidism was not the only factor thwarting the dress reform. The authorities soon came to understand that enforcement of the law was encountering great difficulties not only because of opposition motivated by religion or ideology but also because of the economic situation of a large part of Polish Jewry. This meant that the Jewish 'poor classes' were unable to afford new clothing. All that such Jews could do in the face of the new law was simply shorten their long *kapoty*. Thus in the interim period Jewish dress remained significantly unchanged and only minor adjustments were made.[32] In Warsaw the wealthy and 'enlightened' members of the Jewish community tried partially to resolve this problem by establishing a special fund for the purchase of new clothing for the poorest members of the community. The Warsaw banker Mathias Rosen first initiated such a programme and others soon followed in his steps.[33]

SIDELOCKS, BEARDS, AND WIGS

The tsarist reforms aimed not only to modernize Jewish dress but also to remove other distinctive traits. Besides dress, male Jews differed from Christians by virtue of their sidelocks and long, sometimes split, beards; married women shaved their heads and wore wigs made of hair or ribbons, or special head coverings. By the legislation, the beard—cut substantially shorter—could be worn only with Russian dress; it was forbidden with local or German attire. Jews who wished to retain facial hair had few options. In the interim period, they had to pay fees as if they had not modernized their dress and appearance, and later were forced to choose one of the options permitted by the law: 'Russian' with the short beard or 'local'/'German' without it.

The law concerning the dress and appearance of religious Jews also interfered with the traditional appearance of women. Married Jewish women were now forbidden to shave their heads after marriage. The law also prohibited the wearing of wigs or fabric coverings, which were often made of illegal silk, in place of hair. Jewish women, like Christians, were required to keep their own hair and were allowed to cover it only with a hat or cap. In this matter attempts were made to determine that the law was not contrary to Jewish religious law. Jakub Tugendhold, a member of the Jewish Community Board and censor in Warsaw, who was called to testify before the Government Commission on Internal and Religious Affairs (Komisja Rządowa Spraw Wewnętrznych i Duchownych), confirmed that head-shaving was not obligatory under Jewish law. He did, however, point out that 'for a Jewish woman, exposing her hair in public is against tradition and against moral and religious precepts'.[34]

[31] On the stereotypical, strongly ideologized portrayal of hasidim in the nineteenth century and its evolution, see Wodziński, *Haskalah and Hasidism in the Kingdom of Poland*.

[32] AGAD, KRSW, 6643, fo. 10, item 4.

[33] AGAD, KRSW, 6646, fos. 147–9.

[34] AGAD, KRSW, 6649, fo. 9.

Figure 5. Type of haircut and beard prescribed to accompany 'Russian' attire, 1847
AGAD, KRSW, 6644

As regards beards and sidelocks, as well as shaven heads and wigs, traditional Jews tried not to violate tradition. Some decided to pay the fee and some simply ignored the law, while others wrote petitions for exemption from fee payments on the grounds of difficult circumstances and poverty, as well as health problems, which the government sometimes accepted.[35]

In the 1850s the implementation of the reform of dress and appearance became stricter. The police now made use of personal searches, searches of localities, reprimands, fines, and arrests. If these were ineffective, 'personal constraint' (*przymus osobisty*) was employed, in which the police cut off the sidelocks and long beards of Jews who failed to observe the reform. It should be noted here that in theory, by contrast with actual practice, this law should not necessarily be seen as motivated by hostility to Jews. Such 'personal constraint' was standard practice in tsarist Russia, a manifestation of the government's goal of 'civilizing' its subjects. Jews were only one of the target groups of such repression. Polish and Russian nobles wearing long beards shared the same fate.[36] But of course theory must be distinguished from practice, which could take violent forms with judaeophobic overtones. Violent scenes often occurred in the transitional period when the police discovered that an individual did not have a permit to wear Jewish dress, or later, when the law was in full operation, that someone was illegally wearing Jewish dress or its elements.

[35] AGAD, KRSW, 6644, fos. 185–6; 6647, fo. 104; 6648, fo. 45; 6649, fo. 356, item 20.

[36] Compare, for example, the 'cultural reforms' of Peter the Great, who ordered boyars to shave off their beards, imposed taxes on those who wished to retain the old style of dress, and in an equally drastic way controlled the introduction of the new attire. See L. Bazylow and P. Wieczorkiewicz, *Historia Rosji*, 4th, rev., edn. (Wrocław, 2005), 151; M. Heller, *Historia Imperium Rosyjskiego*, trans. E. Melech and T. Kaczmarek (Warsaw, 2000), 349–50.

The problem of how to deal with such situations created the need for legislation on enforcement of the law. In 1853 a decree of the Government Commission on Internal and Religious Affairs updated the dress reform and gave more explicit guidelines both for control of the Jewish population and for the enforcement of the dress laws. Personal constraint was now to be the final step in enforcing the government's will. This included the forcible shaving of beards, cropping of sidelocks, and shortening of overcoats, and in the case of women, removing their wigs. However, in order to avoid public disturbance these actions were to take place under strictly defined conditions. According to the decree:

If a Jew stubbornly continues to refuse to abandon old Jewish dress, or wears a beard with dress other than in the Russian style . . . or in other ways disobeys the regulations concerning changes in Jewish dress, then by the decision of the Administrative Board issued on 14 February 1851, no. 20,209, he is to be forced to obey such regulations even by means of personal constraint, which must be carried out by the police, exclusively at the local police station, and only after drafting a detailed protocol documenting how the guilt of the accused was confirmed and what methods of constraint were applied on him.[37]

It is clear that the goal of this decision was to limit the arbitrary behaviour of the police. It was feared that they might use violent means in public places, causing disturbances of public order and initiating highly undesirable social unrest. Evidence for such incidents can be found in the archival records. There are known reports of cases of personal constraint carried out by police in public places and also against Jews who were not subjects of the tsar.[38] Personal constraint and searches were used not only against individuals: there were occasions when such methods were used during public gatherings (for example fairs), where a significant number of traditionally dressed Jews were present.[39] The new legal regulations were intended to prevent similar occurrences.

The 1853 decree also regulated in a wide-ranging fashion the upholding of the law concerning the dress and appearance of Jewish women. The main problem in this case turned out to be not so much dress itself as the custom that married Jewish women had of shaving their heads and wearing wigs. The law permitted these women who were ashamed to show their own hair to wear a cap covering the forehead, 'as some Christian women do, and even some Jewish women, especially those of advanced years'.[40] Jewish women who did not follow the regulations had to pay a five-rouble fine each time they were found to be violating the law. Before

[37] AGAD, KRSW, 6649, fo. 356, item 12.

[38] See, for example, the testimony of Markus Rosenstrauch from Kraków against police inspector Jaśkiewicz from Piotrków, who had committed an act of personal constraint on him: AGAD, KRSW, 6647, fos. 271–2, item 18.

[39] Letter of Majer Izyk Grynberg of Maków to Governor General, Prince Mikhail Gorchakov, in which Grynberg files a complaint about a personal constraint, consisting of the trimming of beards and sidelocks, imposed by the mayor of Pułtusk on about a hundred Jews who had come to a fair in that town in 1847: AGAD, KRSW, 6645, fos. 32–3.   [40] AGAD, KRSW, 6649, fo. 356, item 18.

the fine was paid, the offence had to be documented in a detailed record which clearly explained the nature of the violation and the guilt of the accused. However, a personal search of an accused woman could take place only at the local police station, to which the woman was to be accompanied by her husband or close relative, and only after receipt of a written denunciation. It was not unusual for such denunciations to be made by fellow Jews against their co-religionists who were violating the dress laws or were trying to find various ways to circumvent them.[41]

Severe punishments were imposed on rabbis and 'Jewish clerics' who advocated the shaving of women's heads after marriage. According to the decree of 1853 those who did so could be punished by confinement in a 'correction house' (i.e. prison) for two to three years, along with the loss of certain rights and privileges. If they committed the same offence a second time, they could be drafted into the army or, if they were unfit for military service, they could be detained in corrective squads for ten to twelve years.[42]

The resistance of a majority of traditional Polish Jews to the dress reform should be interpreted as their refusal to abandon the outer, visual signs of their Jewishness, which they considered to be a crucial component of their identity. However, this form of acculturation, which was forced on the Jewish community from the middle of the nineteenth century, failed to eliminate the 'otherness' of Jewish dress and appearance. This occurred not so much because of Jews' resistance but because of the fact that, when the Russian law was applied in the Kingdom of Poland, two types of dress ('Russian' and 'local') were prescribed for Jews. Traditional Jews overwhelmingly chose the 'Russian' option, which was already distinct from the dress worn by Poles, as it allowed them to keep their beards.[43] Thus the law did not overcome the 'otherness' of Jewish dress and appearance but merely exchanged one version of foreign dress for another. Compared with Poles, traditional Jews were visually different before the reform and continued to be so after it. Compulsory acculturation failed to modernize Jewish appearance. The true transformation came through voluntary acculturation.

'OTHER' BECOMING 'OUR': FASHION AND POLITICS IN 1861–1866

Voluntary visual acculturation initially encompassed only the relatively small, 'enlightened' part of the Jewish community. While traditional Jews, when forced by law, preferred Russian dress, progressive Jews usually chose German dress,

---

[41] See the convoluted denunciation by Herszlik Nejmark: AGAD, KRSW, 6646, fos. 14, 16, 17, 18–20, 27–8, 37, 38, 45, 226, 231–2, 255, 256–7.   [42] AGAD, KRSW, 6649, fo. 356.
[43] On the importance of the beard in Jewish culture, see E. Horowitz, 'The Early Eighteenth Century Confronts the Beard: Kabbalah and Jewish Self Fashioning', *Jewish History*, 8 (1994), 95–115; id., 'Visages du judaïsme: De la barbe en monde juif et de l'élaboration de ses significations', *Annales: histoire, sciences sociales*, 49 (1994), 1065–90.

which resembled local styles of clothing. The result of this situation was that progressive Jews—unlike the Jewish traditionalists whose Russian dress did not evolve much after the reform—were in practice open not to one but to many changes. The constant transformation of their dress and appearance was dictated by current trends in fashion which also affected Polish society. In this context the dress chosen by progressive Jews should be viewed as the fulfilment of their aesthetic, cultural, and sometimes national preferences. Integrationists, especially at the beginning of modernization, were conscious of the fact that their appearance was a manifestation of their choice of lifestyle. The statement they made in this way was addressed not only to Polish society, but also to the rest of the Jewish community. Appearance thus functioned as a message that signalled one's ideological choice.

The message conveyed by the dress worn by progressive Jews became particularly critical in the early 1860s, the period of Polish–Jewish brotherhood (1861) and of the January Uprising (1863–4).[44] The events of the early 1860s brought fundamental changes in the social function of dress and altered the approach to the actual implementation of the reform. After the experience of legally imposed change, whose impact had been a dispiriting experience for both the Jews and the authorities, attempts were now made to influence Jewish society from within and to modify traditional dress and appearance using more diplomatic means. In this period the semiotics of dress came to be very rich and value-laden, as the iconosphere became the space in which not only aesthetic but also political choices were manifested. Jews who first took part in the demonstrations of Polish–Jewish solidarity and then supported the Polish struggle for independence showed their allegiance to the Polish cause not only by verbal declarations but also by their appearance. The events of the 1860s produced a unique situation which was not to recur in the subsequent history of the nineteenth century; its specific nature requires special treatment.

From the beginning of the Polish–Jewish brotherhood in 1861 until the tsar's amnesty in 1866, the style of dress in the Kingdom of Poland was constantly influenced by the political situation and became itself a reaction to these political changes. One sign of the intensification of revolutionary sentiment in the fashion of this period was the collective wearing of black. This represented national mourning for the current situation of the Polish lands divided by the partitions.[45] Mourning garb was a popular form of social response to daily events and a way of expressing patriotic sentiments. Warsaw was at the centre of these manifestations.

---

[44] The Polish–Jewish brotherhood of 1861 was a specific instance of the widely manifested solidarity of Christians and Jews against the common enemy (tsarist Russia). The pact found its fullest expression in Warsaw, where its course was also the most dramatic. For more on the character, development, and further fate of the pact, see M. Opalski and I. Bartal, *Poles and Jews: A Failed Brotherhood* (Hanover, NH, 1992).

[45] M. Możdżyńska-Nawotka, *O modach i strojach* (Wrocław, 2004), 229–35.

It was at this time that the legend of 'the people of Warsaw' was born—the belief in the unity of members of different social classes, political opinions, and religious beliefs all supporting 'the cause' against the common enemy. The common wearing of black was one manifestation of the solidarity that for some time united people of all classes and religions.

What was specific about dress and fashion in the early 1860s? The research of Małgorzata Możdżyńska-Nawotka has demonstrated that the fashion of this period had its own peculiar rules. The attire worn during the period of national mourning was in shades of black or other dark colours. Houses, shops, churches, and public buildings were also decorated in black. Mourning fashion included also children's clothes, and even the dress of dolls. Participation in mourning was further expressed by black bands or tape worn on clothing. When the tsarist government prohibited black, the colour purple—a colour of semi-mourning—was used as a substitute. Important dress accessories included specific items of jewellery: the motif of chains, for example, symbolized the situation of the politically oppressed Polish lands, or a crown of thorns or palm branch alluded to martyrdom. In addition, white was used to invoke associations with ideas of freedom. During national holidays, such as the anniversary of the Constitution of 3 May, white or coloured clothes were worn.

Tsarist repressions in regard to dress increased significantly in the autumn of 1863. Now mourning dress could be worn only by women who had lost a husband, mother, or father and who could prove such loss with a special document. All others were subject to severe punishment for wearing black attire. The prohibition of dress accessories in black and white encompassed gloves, veils, hat feathers, and all kinds of kerchiefs and shawls. Overcoats could be black, but without white accessories. Men were totally prohibited from wearing mourning attire.[46]

Jews who decided to manifest their solidarity with the Poles and participate in patriotic demonstrations and public gatherings dressed according to this particular dress code. From photographs of this period, we can learn not only how they looked but also the social roles they wished to assume: those of freedom fighter, insurgent, soldier, martyr.[47] Political fashion influenced not only Jewish men's attire but also women's. One example can be seen in a photograph from 1862 of Karolina Orgelbrand, daughter of a well-known Warsaw Jewish bookseller and publisher, in which she wears a modest dark dress decorated solely with a heavy chain with martyrological associations.[48] In addition, Jewish women manifested their engagement in current events by manufacturing special patriotic mementoes,

---

[46] Ibid.

[47] For more on the photographs of Jews from this period and on the roles assumed by Jews, see A. Jagodzińska, *Pomiędzy: Akulturacja Żydów Warszawy w drugiej połowie XIX wieku* (Wrocław, 2008), 112–16.

[48] Her picture can be found in A. Grupińska and B. Burska (eds.), *Żydzi Warszawy, 1861–1943* (Warsaw, 2003), 37.

such as a banner made in Kalisz in 1863 by 'Polish Israelite women', who dedicated it in the accompanying inscription to their 'Valiant Brothers'.[49]

The increase in patriotic feeling was accompanied by a renewed interest in national historical dress, a special, emotionally charged, concept of 'our dress'.[50] Its main element was the *czamara*, a covering worn over a coat, similar to the *kontusz* worn by nobility, but without an opening and with a flat-lying collar with trimmed fastening.[51] Another element of male patriotic clothing was the *konfederatka*, whose tradition began in the times of the Bar Confederation. It was a four-pointed cap with a square base and no peak, made of red cloth and trimmed with black sheepskin.[52] The tsarist authorities strongly prohibited this type of dress. Incidents occurred in which policemen flung down *konfederatki* from their wearers' heads or cut up with scissors the *czamary* of those who had manifested their patriotism using such elements of dress.[53]

Some progressive Jews also accepted these symbols, since *konfederatki* and *czamary* were so dramatic in their expression. A *konfederatka* was worn, for example, by Izydor Brünner, the son of Nuchem and Amalia Brünner (see Figures 3 and 4), wealthy, 'progressive' Jews who came to Warsaw from Prussia in the early nineteenth century. The Brünner family was quickly Polonized and Izydor became a soldier in the Mickiewicz Legion of 1848 and took part in the January Uprising.[54] Another example is provided by Izydor Kamioner, the 19-year-old son of a Warsaw merchant and a graduate of the Rabbinical School, who wore such clothing during the funeral of Archbishop Antoni Melchior Fijałkowski, which turned into a popular demonstration.

During the funeral, Izydor marched in the cortège, dressed in an old Polish *czamara* and carrying the 'revolutionary flag' with Polish and Lithuanian arms. With government repression becoming more severe, he was forced to flee to France—which his father, during the subsequent inquiry, tried to explain as a 'business trip'.[55] As the example of Kamioner illustrates, demonstrations organized on occasions of historical national anniversaries, as well as at funerals of important personalities, became forums where Jews could manifest their solidarity with Polish society.

During patriotic demonstrations the national function of dress became dominant, while other functions (such as aesthetic or practical) became secondary.[56]

---

[49] A photograph of the banner is reproduced in I. Schiper, A. Tartakower, and A. Hafftka (eds.), *Żydzi w Polsce Odrodzonej: Działalność społeczna, gospodarcza, oświatowa i kulturalna*, 2 vols. (Warsaw, 1932–3), i. 466.

[50] On the character and importance of 'our dress', see P. Bogatyriew, 'Funkcje stroju ludowego na obszarze morawsko-słowackim', in id., *Semiotyka kultury ludowej* (Warsaw, 1975), 86–90.

[51] Możdżyńska-Nawotka, *O modach i strojach*, 268.   [52] Ibid. 272.   [53] Ibid. 199, 202.

[54] A portrait of Izydor Brünner wearing patriotic dress can be found in Schiper, Tartakower, and Hafftka (eds.), *Żydzi w Polsce Odrodzonej*, i. 451.

[55] *Żydzi a powstanie styczniowe: Materiały i dokumenty*, ed. A. Eisenbach, D. Fajnhauz, and A. Wein (Warsaw, 1963), 70, 199, 208–9.

[56] See Bogatyriew, 'Funkcje stroju ludowego na obszarze morawsko-słowackim'.

Figure 6. Two groups of Jews at the funeral of Archbishop Melchior Fijałkowski, 1861.
On the left, young Jews in Polish national dress, and on the right, Jews dressed traditionally
Fragment of a lithograph by Maksymilian Fajans, *Exportacya Zwłok Nieodżałowanej Pamięci
Najdostojniejszego Arcybiskupa Metropolity Ks. Antoniego Melchiora Fijałkowskiego*, Fine Prints and
Drawings Collection of the National Library, Warsaw, Sz. 3 G. 23.213

According to Piotr Bogatyriew, a researcher into the semiotics of dress, 'In regions
where the difference between the oppressed class and its oppressor is very large,
the oppressed people carefully cultivates the tradition of its dress as a manifestation of national identity', and such was the case of the Poles rebelling against the
Russian authorities.[57] In the 1860s specific dress and its elements became a way of
informing others of one's stance towards the political situation. Those Jews who
decided to enter the formerly alien circle of Polish values and attitudes expressed
their cultural and political preferences in the visual sphere. For Poles of Mosaic
faith, dress and appearance became means of articulating their own complicated
identity.

The Polish–Jewish brotherhood of 1861 actively involved Jews in the existing
conventions of Polish fashion and behaviour. This was a time when the attitudes,
expectations, and hopes of a part of Warsaw's Jews corresponded to those of the
rest of the city's inhabitants. The phenomenon of brotherhood in these years was
grounded in joint endeavours and a common set of values accepted by both
Christian Poles and Poles of Mosaic faith. The widely understood visual sphere

[57] Ibid. 47.

became one of the foundations for the construction of this unity. In the early 1860s the ideas of Polish–Jewish union found their expression in the dress worn by Jews. In the visual sphere, brotherhood was expressed not only through the wearing of dark clothing or black mourning bands, or the use of black decoration on houses.[58] Complying with current fashion in those times not only had aesthetic meaning, but was also a political testimony. The visual sphere became an important space for the formation of modern Polish Jewish identity. The acceptance of specific forms of 'our dress', with strong semiotic and emotional undertones, was regarded as an acceptance of the meanings which these symbols represented. It was perceived as such by those who made these choices, as well as by those who took note of them. In this respect, the 'other' was becoming the 'our'.

PROGRESSIVE JEWS FIGHTING THE OTHERNESS OF POLISH JEWRY

Progressive Jews, or Poles of Mosaic faith, who advocated the cultural adaptation of Jews to Polish society (which included change of language, names, and dress) had to be prepared to meet the opposing views of the traditionalists (*shamranim*). The greatest worry of the conservative members of the Jewish community was that the transformation of Jewish society, taking place under the catchword of 'progress', would result in the undermining of Judaism. Therefore, progressive Jews, fighting their *Kulturkampf* for the modernization of Jewish life and for integration into Polish society, were forced to use religious arguments in order to prove that the changes proposed by them or by the government were not only not antireligious, but were in fact prescribed by religion.[59]

In such polemics they most often used citations from the Talmud or references to the authority of a rabbi or other religious authority. For example, rabbinical proclamations on government restrictions on Jewish dress and appearance were used in polemics by progressive Jews directed against Jewish traditionalists. Three such statements may be noted: Chief Rabbi Chaim Dawidsohn's of 1849, Chief Rabbi Ber Meisels's of 1851, and Chief Rabbi Jakub Gesundheit's of 1871. All of them advised obedient acceptance of the law regarding appearance. Rabbi Dawidsohn warned that 'every member of our faith, with care and eagerness, should try to carry out the government's instructions. Any person who does not comply immediately will not only sin against God, by being the cause of much evil, but will also be punished by the government and will become one of those who, crying out too late, are unworthy to be heard.' Ber Meisels pointed out that one should

---

[58] The use of black by Jews as a sign of mourning is recalled by M. Jastrow, 'Bär Meisels, Oberrabiner zu Warschau: Ein Lebensbild auf historischem Hintergrunde, nach eigener Anschauung entworfen', *The Hebrew Leader*, 15/25 (1870), p. [2].

[59] This concerned, of course, only those changes introduced from above which were in accord with the direction of modernization mapped out by the progressives.

Figure 7. Jews in various attires, 1853: modern dress (foreground)
and traditional Jewish dress (background)
Lithograph by Jan Feliks Piwarski, in J. F. Piwarski,
Kram malowniczy warszawski; czyli, Obrazy miejscowe z ubiegłych czasów
(Warsaw, 1855–9), pl. 3

not disregard the rules, because that would cause a 'much greater affront to the entire community'. Jakub Gesundheit urged his followers to comply with the government rules promptly and unconditionally in order to prevent the use of personal constraint, emphasizing that these rules did not contradict religious principles. All three statements were cited by *Izraelita* on the occasion of the promulgation in 1871 of government decrees confirming the previous rules and making known that they would be unconditionally enforced.[60] These statements, so the integrationists thought, would provide an excellent incentive to traditionalists and Orthodox to comply with the rules on dress.

We should, however, be conscious of the conditions in which these rabbinical

[60] *Izraelita*, 1871, no. 13, pp. 103–4.

appeals were issued. The rabbis were obliged to publish such proclamations by the government, which sought to achieve the most efficient enforcement of the law by ensuring the support of the religious leaders of the Jewish community. But although they were forced to encourage their brethren to accept the changes required by the law, their real position on this matter was very different. The law was regarded by the traditional members of the Jewish community as an assault against religious principles and tradition, and the methods by which it was implemented, including the personal constraint that violated personal dignity, met with particular disapproval. As writings from the period of Polish–Jewish brotherhood show, the reform was regarded as a form of religious persecution. A document written by (or accepted by) Meisels in about 1861 posed the question:

Who among us does not remember the atrocities of those who violated our dignity when the instruction concerning the change of dress was issued?—how they dishonoured the old and did not spare the young; how the grey-haired were dragged through the streets to have their beards cut; how they wanted to destroy our holy Torah and force us to violate the laws of our religious teachings.[61]

When discussing the methods used by the government and the Jewish proponents of integration in their fight against the signs of Jewish 'otherness', it is essential to bear in mind how the methods used by the reformers were perceived by those whom they tried to reform.

In order to persuade the Orthodox members of the Jewish community to modernize their appearance, the progressive Jews attempted to use halakhah (prescriptive Jewish law) to prove that such a transformation was not prohibited by religious law. This applied particularly to the law prohibiting Jewish women from shaving their heads and wearing wigs. In 1871 *Izraelita* published an article full of citations from legal and religious works, which concluded that 'the Talmud and all compendiums of Mosaic religious law agree that it is only walking in the street with an uncovered head that is forbidden to a married Jewish woman'.[62] The solution proposed in the article consisted simply of wearing a cap or other head covering similar to those used by Christian women.

Progressive Jews also had another strategy for persuading Jewish traditionalists. They published 'morally uplifting' stories about and by 'enlightened' Orthodox Jews.[63] In most cases, such examples of 'good traditionalists' invoked on the pages of the integrationist press as examples to follow were fictitious. Progressive Jews merely put their own arguments into these Orthodox mouths, presenting their own critique of traditional society as Orthodox self-criticism. Some of these

[61] *Żydzi a powstanie styczniowe*, ed. Eisenbach, Fajnhauz, and Wein, 15.

[62] [J. G…n], 'Zwyczaj golenia głów przez mężatki żydowskie uważany ze stanowiska halachicznego (z hebrajskiego)', *Izraelita*, 1871, no. 11, pp. 82–3.

[63] See I. L. Grosglik, 'List do Redakcji "Izraelity"', *Izraelita*, 1870, no. 6, pp. 44–5, and correspondence in 'Pogadanki', *Izraelita*, 1872, no. 33, p. 266.

manipulations are surprising even today in their lack of realism. It is hard to believe, for example, the story of a 'progressive' hasidic Jew from the provinces who remarked on the use of force in implementing the dress reform: 'The repressive measures that were embarked upon last year were met with no small pleasure, because we expected that they would bring us full redemption for ever from our exclusiveness; but unfortunately those measures soon weakened and our hopes came to nothing.'[64]

In order to win over traditionalists, Poles of Mosaic faith used yet another strategy. They often accused the traditionalists of committing the sin of *ḥilul hashem* ('profanation of the name', an insult to God), criticizing them for offending, through their behaviour or dress, against the good name of Israel and bringing disgrace on Judaism: 'A separateness of dress causes disrespect, insults our religion, and leads to *ḥilul hashem.*' Christians, observing in traditional Jews an 'unyielding stubbornness in their attachment to unimportant forms of dress' and an 'empty conservatism', were said to form 'very negative views' about these Jews and their religion.[65] The progressive Jews also argued that a specific form of dress had little to do with the fundamentals of the Mosaic faith and that abandoning it did not cause any religious harm, whereas maintaining it ran the risk of making Jews a laughing stock while also insulting the honour of Israel:

Can anyone, even the most devoted adherents of tradition, prove that the cut or the form of our dress has anything in common with our religion? Do we not, on the contrary, find in our own history irrefutable evidence that our forebears always dressed in the same way as the natives of the land where they dwelt . . . ? Why should we now—with such obstinate resistance, looking for any way to circumvent the law—try to keep those distinctive features which, without having any religious merit, bring disgrace on the name of Israel and impose constraints on the stubborn that are an affront to human dignity?![66]

The proponents of integration warned traditional Jews of the fatal consequences of their 'sinful stubbornness'. They tried to prove that the path to progress, which does not preclude being a Jew, brings more advantages to Judaism than stubborn behaviour that is mistakenly attributed to tradition. In their view, unnecessary conservatism in dress and appearance induced in Christians a dislike for Jews or even a hatred of them, as it offended and repelled. The traditionalists were reproached most of all for an attachment to unimportant relics of the past and not to the everlasting values of Judaism, which did not depend on any particular form of attire. The proponents of integration accused the traditional Jews of 'not paying attention to the persistent calls of the present, instead devoting their present and future to nursing dead forms of the past', asking rhetorically, 'is not the stubborn maintenance of superficial distinctive features, unconnected to religion or custom

---

[64] Correspondence in 'Pogadanki', *Izraelita*, 1872, no. 33, p. 266.
[65] [S. H. Peltyn], 'Grzeszny upór: Ku rozwadze współwierców zachowawców', *Izraelita*, 1882, no. 7, p. 50.   [66] *Izraelita*, 1871, no. 17, p. 129.

and intended only to demonstrate separateness from the rest of the people, the cultivation of something long dead?'[67]

Very few traditional Jews could read Polish and so could not have been exposed to the opinions expressed in *Izraelita*. Rather, the writing was motivated by the progressives' fear that traditional Jews, by maintaining their style of dress, were exposing them—the integrationists—to the contempt and mockery of non-Jews. Their appeals to traditional Jews were intended to show Polish society at large that they too believed that all Jews should adopt the dress of the country. Those who wanted social integration with the Poles were afraid that they might suffer rejection and contempt because of the strange, outlandish, even comical—as it was perceived—appearance of some members of the Jewish community. They feared contempt more than hatred, as Samuel Peltyn admitted: 'Hatred and envy may turn into goodwill and friendship; the ditch that separates them may be filled with a better understanding, with a more just judgement of each other's merits. However, between esteem and contempt lies an abyss which nothing can ever fill.'[68]

The conflict with the traditional part of the community over dress was not only verbal. Jews in modern dress, with an appearance similar to Poles, won entrance to the public spaces of Christian society (such as parks, gardens, pubs), from which the *kapota* Jews were barred. At the same time, acceptance from the Polish side was met with ostracism from the Jewish side, especially in the first half of the nineteenth century, when the changes in dress were only beginning. According to Hilary Nussbaum, the chronicler of the Jewish community in Warsaw,

It was not easy at the beginning for those European-dressed ladies to go out and make their way unscathed through Jewish districts. They were met each time with hissing, pointing fingers, laughter, jibes, name-calling, threats, and curses, such that many of them would leave the house only in the evening, or they would send the maid out in advance with a hat wrapped up and with other articles of toilet, and would meet her at a pre-arranged entrance to a street forbidden to Jews [*egzymowana ulica*], where the lady would change her clothes.[69]

The situation described by Nussbaum shows that the progressive Jews lived at the boundary between two worlds: both metaphorically, in the cultural sphere, and physically, in the urban space between Poles and Jews (or between other Poles and other Jews, as they would have put it). The change to new visual standards and aesthetic norms took place in both of these spheres. In the perception of Poles of Mosaic faith, acculturation was the way to overcome the sign of the 'other' in themselves and in the rest of the Jewish community.

---

[67] [Peltyn], 'Grzeszny upór', 49–50.   [68] Ibid. 50.
[69] H. Nussbaum, *Szkice historyczne z życia Żydów w Warszawie od pierwszych śladów pobytu ich w tem mieście do chwili obecnej* (Warsaw, 1881), 61.

CONCLUSION

The alteration of dress and appearance became one of the most important determinants of the dynamics of Jewish acculturation in the Kingdom of Poland. Of all the key elements of cultural change (language, dress, names, customs), visual transformation was considered to be the first phase of a more profound metamorphosis. That is precisely why traditional Jews refused to accept the dress reform, fearing that soon other changes would follow that would lead them away from the tradition of Judaism. Progressive Jews, on the other hand, promoted the visual adaptation of the Jews as much as they could, believing that it would be the first, necessary, step to integration with the Poles. In that sense, the dress question proved to be more closely connected to the question of identity and self-perception than it might at first glance seem to be.

The visual separateness of Jews was to be eliminated through either 'compulsory' or 'voluntary' acculturation. Neither of them, however, became quite what it was expected to be. Compulsory acculturation, demanded by the state legislation, instead of eliminating the 'otherness' of Jewish dress and appearance, in practice led only to exchanging one type of visual distinctiveness for another. Even when the traditional Jews were forced to accept the reform, they continued to be 'different' within Polish society. Their Russian attire became distinguishing and stigmatic as much as their previous Jewish dress had been. In this respect the reform missed its goal completely.

The second, 'voluntary', form of acceptance of non-Jewish dress was expected to become, along with other cultural changes, a tool for the successful social integration of Jews into Polish society. However, this form also proved problematic. The very term 'voluntary acculturation' needs to be reinterpreted against the historical evidence and understood more as an acculturation that was not enforced by state legislation than as one that was completely voluntary in its character. Many of the actions and choices of Poles of Mosaic faith (as is true of any social interaction) were not entirely free but were shaped by the expectations of Polish society. Poles were expected to verify and approve the acculturation when it was completed. In addition, the integrationists were clearly a minority within the Jewish community. Their will to conform to the Polish expectations was not shared by the traditional majority, which led to tension with the traditional sector of the Jewish community. It was also a problem that Polish expectations were ambiguous and inconsistent. Progressive Jews were supposed to adopt Polish cultural standards, but even when they did so they were still not fully accepted, or were even rejected in spite of their efforts. Sander L. Gilman wrote about a similar paradox:

The more one attempts to identify with those who have labeled one as different, the more one accepts the values, social structures, and attitudes of this determining group, the further away from true acceptability one seems to be. For as one approaches the norms set by the reference group, the approbation of the group recedes. In one's eyes, one becomes identical with the definition of acceptability and yet one is still not accepted. For the ideal state is never to have been the Other, a state that cannot be achieved.[70]

Acculturation, which offered to bring progressive Jews to the Polish 'promised land', in fact left them somewhere between Polish and Jewish culture. It caused the erosion of the traditional ethno-religious Jewish identity, which was replaced by an identity with multiple components. Jews started to believe that their identity could encompass many factors, even some that were once considered contradictory. The fragmentation of an individual identity went along with the ideological fragmentation and division of the Jewish community. Progressive Jews seeking an understanding with Polish society distanced themselves from traditional Jews. In fact, as Anna Landau-Czajka has suggested, writing on Jewish assimilation in the inter-war period, they formed a 'third nation', considered neither as Poles by Poles nor as Jews by Jews.[71] Poles of Mosaic faith spoke Polish, used Polish names, and dressed similarly to other Poles, but were still perceived as 'other'—or, perhaps, a new 'other'.

Translated from the Polish by Alexandra Hawiger

---

[70] S. L. Gilman, *Jewish Self-Hatred: Anti-Semitism and the Hidden Language of the Jews* (Baltimore, 1986), 2–3.

[71] A. Landau-Czajka, *Syn będzie Lech...: Asymilacja Żydów w Polsce międzywojennej* (Warsaw, 2006).

The Ideological Roots of the Polish Jewish Intelligentsia

ELA BAUER

AT THE BEGINNING of the twentieth century, two articles appeared in Hebrew periodicals in Warsaw and in Kraków.[1] Jewish society was portrayed in them as suffering from a serious leadership crisis. Moshe Kleinman wrote in *Luaḥ aḥiasaf* that the intelligentsia, the maskilim, who should serve as a 'fruit of life' of the nation and were expected to be the class representing their ideals and hopes, were in fact unsuited to assuming leadership roles.[2] The author of an article published in *Eshkol*, probably E. Gintzig, wrote that the Hebrew intelligentsia was dying off and not fulfilling its purpose in leading the people, because it did not have the knowledge or the ability to lead the masses in the right way. What the articles share is dissatisfaction with the activities of the Jewish intelligentsia. This disappointment was also expressed in other articles published in Polish Jewish newspapers in various languages. They present the Polish Jewish intelligentsia as a ruling class that has reached the end of its useful life, having to make place for a new leadership. Earlier, during the latter part of the nineteenth century, the Polish Jewish intelligentsia had been considered to be the class suited to the leadership of Polish Jewish society. The object of this essay is to explain how the Jewish intelligentsia in the Polish lands was first seen as the obvious leader of Jewish society and how, by the beginning of the twentieth century, this stratum was no longer considered worthy of such a role and was subjected to sharp criticism.

THE MEANING OF 'INTELLIGENTSIA'

The concept of 'intelligentsia'[3] has long been discussed by many researchers, yet

---

[1] M. Kleinman, 'Mi yelekh lefaneinu', *Luaḥ aḥiasaf* (Warsaw), 10 (1902), 398–403, and an article written anonymously, 'Penei hador', *Eshkol* (Kraków), 5 (1902), 5–6.

[2] Kleinman, 'Mi yelekh lefaneinu', 403.

[3] There is a rich literature on the term 'intelligentsia' and its origin, including the following: A. Gella, *Development of Class Structure in Eastern Europe: Poland and her Southern Neighbors* (Albany, NY, 1989); id., 'An Introduction to the Sociology of the Intelligentsia', in id. (ed.), *The Intelligentsia and the Intellectuals: Theory, Method and Case Study* (London, 1976); id., 'The Life and Death of the Old Polish Intelligentsia', *Slavic Review*, 30 (1971), 1–27; J. Jedlicki, 'Inteligencja', in J. Bachórz and

the discussion has not produced an agreed definition.[4] Many of the scholars that study this sociological and intellectual phenomenon refrain from defining the term and prefer to leave it as a broad and even vague concept.[5] During the course of the nineteenth century, the word 'intelligentsia' became used in many European languages not just to describe brain-power, inborn talents, and the ability to learn, but also to describe a social phenomenon.[6] The term was defined in many different ways, above all because of a variety of geographical and cultural factors.

German scholars were the first to consider the intelligentsia as constituting a new social class. According to Richard Pipes, they were also the first to give the term a broader meaning.[7] The varied explanations that developed in relation to the term 'intelligentsia' during the first half of the nineteenth century are connected to the philosophical ideas of Hegel and to German Romantic idealism. They are also the product of the development of the modern state and government bureaucracy in this period and the new opportunities for the middle classes to attain a higher education through studies at university and other institutions of higher education. These possibilities created new financial opportunities and increased social mobility. A new reservoir of people who had acquired academic education was created within European society, representing a new human resource, which in fact resulted in the problem of overproduction of the intelligentsia (a surplus of academically trained people).[8]

Karl Mannheim saw in the intelligentsia a modern bourgeois class whose only wealth was the academic knowledge it had acquired. He stressed the contribution of the intelligentsia to the rise of the modern German state, particularly in the creation of a government bureaucracy.[9] He describes the rise of this new social stratum, whose members stemmed from diverse backgrounds, but who shared a common interest and ideology, forming part of the new forces creating the modern state. Ralf Dahrendorf, following Mannheim, has emphasized not only the

---

A. Kowalczykowa (eds.), *Słownik literatury polskiej XIX wieku* (Wrocław, 1991); J. Jedlicki, *Jakiej cywilizacji Polacy potrzebują: Studia z dziejów idei i wyobraźni XIX wieku* (Warsaw, 2002); R. Pipes, *Russia under the Old Regime* (London, 1974); id. (ed.), *The Russian Intelligentsia* (New York, 1961); F. Björling and A. Pereswetoff-Morath (eds.), *Words, Deeds and Values: The Intelligentsias in Russia and Poland during the Nineteenth and Twentieth Centuries* (Lund, 2005); J. Mikułowski-Pomorski (ed.), *Inteligencja między tradycją a wyzwaniami współczesności* (Kraków, 2005). In 2008 a series of three books about the Polish intelligentsia was published under the general editorship of Jerzy Jedlicki: *Dzieje inteligencji polskiej do roku 1918* (Warsaw, 2008), i: M. Janowski, *Narodziny inteligencji, 1750–1831*; ii: J. Jedlicki, *Błędne koło, 1832–1864*; iii: M. Micińska, *Inteligencja na rozdrożach, 1864–1918*.

[4] A. Walicki, 'Polish Conceptions of the Intelligentsia', in Björling and Pereswetoff-Morath (eds.), *Words, Deeds and Values*, 3.

[5] Björling and Pereswetoff-Morath (eds.), *Words, Deeds and Values*, introduction, p. xvii.

[6] See Jedlicki, *Jakiej cywilizacji Polacy potrzebują*, 261–74; id., 'Inteligencja'.

[7] R. Pipes, '"Intelligentsia" from the German "Intelligenz"? A Note', *Slavic Review*, 30 (1971), 615–18.   [8] In Germany the term used was *geistige Überproduktion*.

[9] K. Mannheim, 'The Problem of the Intelligentsia: An Enquiry into its Past and Present Role', in id., *Essays on the Sociology of Culture* (New York and Oxford, 1956), 96–156.

creation of this bureaucracy, but the loyalty of this new class to the government and to authority.[10]

Mannheim's analysis has been accepted by many scholars who consider the development of the German intelligentsia to be connected to the Industrial Revolution and the German nationalist awakening. Other scholars emphasize the formation of the intelligentsia as a social class, an elite associated with scientific activity as a result of the advanced education acquired by its members, and with social and political activity revolving around identification with the state and the government. However, the attempt to use this same approach in relation to the situation outside Germany in order to understand the situation of the east European intelligentsia presents many difficulties.[11]

From the second half of the nineteenth century, the term 'intelligentsia' began to be used in the Russian and Polish lands to describe a social class whose members sought to guide and lead the rest of the society to which they belonged.[12] In some areas, the intelligentsia was identified with a revolutionary struggle, whereas in others it was identified with the avant-garde. According to Andrzej Walicki, 'In both countries [Poland and Russia] membership in the intelligentsia had an ethical component, requiring conscious commitment to the public welfare. In Poland however, this commitment was identified, as a rule, with national patriotism, whereas in Russia it necessarily involved social radicalism and political opposition.'[13]

Indeed, the term 'intelligentsia' can be defined from political and sociological angles as well as from cultural and literary. I follow Richard Pipes's definition, according to which the intelligentsia should be seen as a group or a class separated from the society in which it lives by its education and by its modern attitude. Pipes characterizes an individual belonging to the intelligentsia as one with a deep sense of duty who is prepared to devote himself to the betterment of the society in which he lives.[14] This definition emphasizes the societal framework in which the intelligentsia operates as a group whose members are working for a joint aim, out of a strong collective sense of duty towards society.[15]

[10] R. Dahrendorf, *Society and Democracy in Germany* (London, 1968).

[11] When investigating the intelligentsia, beyond the distinction that is required between western and eastern Europe, it must be emphasized (as has been done by various distinguished researchers) that the words 'intelligentsia' and 'intellectuals' are not synonymous. They refer to two distinct groups within both eastern and western Europe. As Isaiah Berlin writes, 'the concept of intelligentsia must not be confused with the notion of intellectuals. Its members thought of themselves as united by something more than mere interest in ideas: they conceived themselves as being a dedicated order, almost a secular priesthood, devoted to the spreading of a specific attitude to life, something like a gospel': I. Berlin, 'A Remarkable Decade: The Birth of the Russian Intelligentsia', in id., *Russian Thinkers*, ed. H. Hardy and A. Kelly (Harmondsworth, 1984), 117.

[12] Jedlicki, 'Inteligencja'; id., *Jakiej cywilizacji Polacy potrzebują*.

[13] Walicki, 'Polish Conceptions of the Intelligentsia', 3.

[14] Pipes, *Russia under the Old Regime*, 253.

[15] In an interview given by the Israeli historian Michael Confino, who studied the nineteenth-century Russian intelligentsia, he argues among other things that it does not matter whether we

The different ways in which the term 'intelligentsia' is understood can cause confusion. In the nineteenth century, German, French, and Russian society each produced a different understanding of the term that mirrored the differences in culture and social structure.[16] As a consequence, perhaps the best way to understand how the intelligentsia developed in different societies would be to ask, not when this group first emerged, but rather when it began to be aware of its social and national responsibilities.

THE POLISH INTELLIGENTSIA

Following Richard Pipes's definition, other scholars have stressed the distinctive development of the intelligentsia in different east European societies, as well as the fact that the position of the intelligentsia in Russian and Polish society had no equivalent in central and western Europe.[17] In Poland in the first half of the nineteenth century there was no term to describe the limited group of educated people who had a strong sense of national commitment. Hence, in the Polish lands the term 'intelligentsia' in its sociological sense was adopted from Germany. Around 1848 the 'intelligentsia' was identified with the class of journalists, writers, politicians, educators, and the like, and it soon became an accepted term.[18]

In the years following the 1863 uprising the number of young Poles who had obtained a higher education at universities in Poland and elsewhere was rising. However, employment opportunities for them were very limited. Positions were available mainly in the civil service, but following the crushing of the uprising these opportunities diminished because of the policy of Russification.[19]

It was between the uprisings of 1830 and 1863 that the Polish intelligentsia developed its self-understanding. Whereas in Germany the 'third class' (members of the professional intelligentsia) produced government officials, the Polish intelligentsia established itself as a unique, elite social group, with a belief that it should devote itself to society and to the state and should take up national tasks and goals.

After 1863 the acquisition of knowledge was considered a method of self-improvement, a means to achieve social mobility. At the same time, the belief that

understand the intelligentsia as a social entity or as an intellectual entity: the intelligentsia in eastern Europe is a significant phenomenon. See M. Confino, 'Diyakono shel historiyon', *Zemanim*, 105 (2009), 30.

[16] J. Jedlicki, 'Przedmowa', in Janowski, *Narodziny inteligencji*, 19.

[17] A debate has been going on for years between scholars studying the Russian intelligentsia and those studying the Polish intelligentsia as to which of them first used the term in intellectual and public discourse. Aleksander Gella in his various studies favours the Poles, but it appears that in fact the Russian intellectuals were the first to do so. For further information on this, see Pipes, '"Intelligentsia" from the German "Intelligenz"?'; N. Knight, 'Was the Intelligentsia Part of the Nation? Visions of Society in Post-Emancipation Russia', *Kritika: Explorations in Russian and Eurasian History*, 7 (2006), 733–58.

[18] Jedlicki, 'Przedmowa', 10.   [19] Jedlicki, *Jakiej cywilizacji Polacy potrzebują*, 264–5.

the acquisition of knowledge should be undertaken not solely for personal advancement but also for the benefit of society persisted. In the second half of the nineteenth century a new expression appeared in Polish intellectual discourse: *pomoc własna*, 'self-help'. The term was given various interpretations, and among them was the view that higher education should benefit society as a whole.[20]

These ideas can be identified in various articles that appeared in the late 1860s and early 1870s. In 1867 an article in *Przegląd Tygodniowy* referred to the intelligentsia as a group which contributes to human society and to science by means of its knowledge, but is not restricted to that function alone. The intelligentsia was a ground-breaking force, promoting far-reaching ideas which would modify the views of society as a whole in areas such as religion and attitudes to modernity. The author cautioned that not everyone possessing a higher education (or intelligence) should be considered part of the intelligentsia. Membership of this group required the possessor of 'intelligence' to use his knowledge for the improvement of the society and country in which he lived.[21] The distinction was made still more explicit a few years later in an article in *Niwa*. This claimed that the acquisition of knowledge merely to improve the status of a particular individual, as sometimes occurred, should be considered self-interest. The goal should be for the knowledge gained by individuals to be utilized for the benefit of society.[22]

There were, the article claimed, some features specific to the Polish situation. Here it was not only a question of organizing educated people for the benefit of society, for the relief of the poor, and for the advancement of talented members of the lower classes. Even more important in the Kingdom of Poland was the organization of the intelligentsia, given the absence of a legitimate Polish governmental authority. Political organization was being repressed and this limited the possibility of political activity: 'Wherever government bodies have neglected their duties, civilian groups must act in their place.'[23] This was not a merely theoretical question: the intelligentsia should undertake initiatives that would lead to the establishment of alternative social institutions, such as scientific societies, museums, libraries, reading rooms for the masses, and newspapers.[24]

An article written at the beginning of the 1880s already gives a clear insight into the changes which had taken place in the understanding of the tasks and goals of the intelligentsia within Polish society.[25] To Polish intellectuals, the concept of an intelligentsia was not only sociological but political. Subsequent articles further developed the distinction between enlightened individuals and the concept of an intelligentsia.

---

[20] For more on this concept in Polish society and discourse, see B. Porter, *When Nationalism began to Hate: Imagining Modern Politics in Nineteenth-Century Poland* (Oxford, 2000), 44–8.

[21] 'Systemat historyczny H. T. Buckle rozwinięty w dziele jego p.t. Historya cywilisacyi w Anglii', *Przegląd Tygodniowy*, 19 Nov. (1 Dec.) 1867.

[22] 'Niemoc inteligiencyi', *Niwa*, 19 June (1 July), 3 (15) July 1873.

[23] 'Niemoc inteligiencyi', 19 June (1 July) 1873.　　　[24] 'Niemoc inteligiencyi', 3 (15) July 1873.

[25] 'Zadania inteligencyi naszej', *Przegląd Tygodniowy*, 7 (19) Dec. 1880.

The article in *Niwa* made it clear that enlightened people would only become members of the intelligentsia when they used their acquired knowledge to advance in various ways the society to which they belonged.[26] In order to define the intelligentsia and to stress its importance, the writer refers to relations between the intelligentsia—the new order—and the old historical order of the Polish nobility, the *szlachta*. In this way the intelligentsia attempted to present itself as the heir of the *szlachta* and its culture and standards, despite the fact that the intelligentsia in fact rejected much of that heritage or adapted it to the requirements of the social conditions in which it lived and operated.[27]

In the second half of the nineteenth century, and in particular in the decades following the 1863 uprising, the Polish intelligentsia was identified with a new school of thought, that of the Warsaw positivists. This was a philosophical movement based on a more modest understanding of national goals, which it limited essentially to the struggle for economic and cultural survival. The Warsaw positivists proposed a new programme to the Polish intelligentsia which envisaged the reorganization of Polish life through a network of non-governmental institutions—educational, social, and economic—that would aim, above all, to integrate into the nation the newly enfranchised peasantry. The leaders of this programme should be the intelligentsia.[28]

Hence, under the influence of the Warsaw positivists, during the 1880s the position of the intelligentsia as a group with national and social obligations had already become crystallized. The goals of the Polish intelligentsia had become concrete and were based on the principles of working from the foundations (*praca u podstaw*). In order to be successful, the intelligentsia needed to mobilize all sectors of society. This would lead to the democratization of Polish society and to its transformation into new forms.[29] The intelligentsia was no longer considered a sociological category, a class of intellectuals, but rather as a stratum with the responsibility of leading Polish society. Among the goals of the intelligentsia, particular stress was laid on the advance of the Polish nation. Cosmopolitanism was explicitly rejected.[30]

In the last twenty years of the nineteenth century, after the period in which the unique character of the Polish intelligentsia was defined, it began to be tested on the basis of its achievements. Various writers sought to investigate to what extent this class had fulfilled its national and social goals, a process which led to criticism and even doubt. When *Ateneum* asked the question 'Do we have an intelligentsia at all?', it was clear that it was referring to a group of men of substantial intellect that placed itself above personal interest, representing society as a whole and even standing at the head of society, undertaking tasks and fulfilling responsibilities in

---

[26] 'Niemoc inteligiencyi', 19 June (1 July) 1873.

[27] J. Żurawicka, *Inteligencja warszawska w końcu XIX wieku* (Warsaw, 1978), 207.

[28] Walicki, 'Polish Conceptions of the Intelligentsia', 9–10.

[29] Żurawicka, *Inteligencja warszawska*, 207.

[30] Ibid.

the interests of its country and of the age.[31] Whereas in the earlier period the surplus of educated people had been a topic of discussion, given the limited opportunities available to them, this was no longer raised as a problem in the last decade of the century.[32] What was discussed was the way in which the intelligentsia was fulfilling its public duties. Members of the intelligentsia were no longer called upon to take particular goals and roles upon themselves, but were judged on the basis of their success in fulfilling their duties.

Writings about the intelligentsia changed and became more critical, and those responsible for these comments were members of the intelligentsia themselves.[33] During the 1890s, the critics claimed that the intelligentsia was incapable of coping with the task it had set itself. The critics by and large ignored the political conditions in which the intelligentsia had to operate.[34] Towards the end of the nineteenth century, changes occurred within the internal structure of the intelligentsia. Various writers on the intelligentsia began to differentiate between the sector of the intelligentsia that had begun to support socialism, and the nationalist intelligentsia. Some attribute this internal split to the development of capitalism that began during the last twenty years of the nineteenth century and to the political situation of Congress Poland.[35]

Beyond the internal division, it is indeed difficult to ignore the fact that at the end of the nineteenth century the intelligentsia was considered unsuited and even anachronistic to political and public life in the Polish lands. Political and social dynamics and the emergence of a mass society had the effect of creating a new political and social reality, in which the intelligentsia found it difficult to integrate. Its members therefore had to find themselves new political and social frameworks. However, this development did not diminish their role and their contribution to Polish political and public life. The intelligentsia remained the only force able to organize national, cultural, and social life at a time when there was no legitimate government in Russian Poland.[36]

THE POLISH JEWISH INTELLIGENTSIA

In many parts of eastern Europe there were also groups of Jewish intelligentsia. These various groups that were formed during the second half of the nineteenth century were influenced by the political and cultural atmosphere that characterized their places of activity. In the Polish lands the local Jewish intelligentsia groups were presented with an interesting and difficult challenge. In cities such as Warsaw there were a number of different patterns that they could draw on as sources of inspiration. The Polish intelligentsia was the dominant force, but one cannot disregard the

---

[31] W. M. Kozłowski, 'Czy mamy inteligencyą?', *Ateneum*, 1893, no. 1, pp. 242–3.
[32] Ibid. 245.   [33] Ibid. 251.   [34] Jedlicki, 'Inteligencja', 736.
[35] Żurawicka, *Inteligencja warszawska*, 141.   [36] Ibid. 270.

influence of other models, such as the Russian and the German.[37] The Jewish intelligentsia in Warsaw, like its Polish counterpart, did not provide an exact definition of the term 'intelligentsia'. Both groups preferred to leave the term vague and to develop around it a wide spectrum of explanations and options.[38] Both the Jewish and the Polish intelligentsias struggled to define their roles and tasks. Both groups were forced to deal with the same environment and political situation, which above all restricted them to very narrow spheres of activity.[39] As early as the 1840s and 1850s there were young educated Jews in Warsaw who were well established economically, had attained personal achievements worthy of distinction, and had even made attempts to penetrate the local community leadership. These included doctors, teachers, lawyers, journalists, writers, and publishers. During the second half of the nineteenth century, they were transformed into a concerned and informed group that wished to lead the rest of Jewish society, to be active within it, and to change its status. Their activity was mainly devoted to the social and cultural spheres, partly because of the recognition of the importance of these areas, but also because they gradually realized how limited were the opportunities for activity and how small the chances of effecting change in anything related to political matters, whether within the Jewish community or outside it.

The growth of this new class within the Jewish communities of eastern Europe was not easy or obvious. Jews wishing to study at universities across the Russian empire were forced to cope with a policy of hidden obstacles to their acceptance into institutions of advanced academic study, and sometimes they were even excluded owing to the discriminatory policies operating there. Some of these Jews also had to cope with a suspicious attitude from within the Jewish community itself towards everything related to their acquisition of academic knowledge, and many were at an additional disadvantage because there were gaps in their knowledge, as they were self-taught and lacked a systematic grounding in the subjects needed for success at university.

It appears from several sources that at the end of the nineteenth century there

[37] See, for example, the memoirs of Abraham Kottik, *Dos lebn fun yidishn inteligent* (New York, 1925), 26–66. Abraham Kottik and his family arrived in Warsaw from Kiev at the beginning of 1881. The young Kottik began to study at the local gymnasium. Owing to the policy of Russification, the studies were conducted in Russian in a rigid and sombre atmosphere. Pupils were forbidden to converse in Polish. Whereas the teachers are described by Kottik as being Polish patriots, the Lithuanian Jewish students were far removed from Polish culture. Despite everything, Kottik writes that the gymnasium environment turned him into a Russian intellectual: 'Reading had an influence not only on me, but on my entire generation. We were all influenced by Russian literature and culture; we became Jewish intellectuals who were influenced by Russification' (ibid. 65). Kottik goes on to describe how he began his revolutionary activities among the working classes (ibid.).

[38] L. Sadowski, *Polska inteligencja prowincjonalna i jej dylematy ideowe na przełomie XIX i XX wieku* (Warsaw, 1988), 10.

[39] For articles written by representatives of the Polish intelligentsia on the roles of this class, see nn. 22 and 25 above. For works on the roles of the Jewish intelligentsia, see E. Bauer, *Between Poles and Jews: The Development of Nahum Sokolow's Political Thought* (Jerusalem, 2005).

were about 1,200 Jews in Warsaw whom one could describe as belonging to the Jewish professional intelligentsia.[40] A section of the Jewish intelligentsia began its activities particularly within Polish liberal circles, in the belief that the Jewish intelligentsia should be active primarily within Polish society, thus furthering the improvement of relations between Poles and Jews. Jewish bourgeois families contributed significantly to the cultural and scientific spheres in Warsaw through their financial support for the activities of the Polish intelligentsia. These people funded the publication of newspapers and books and sponsored the Polish societies that wished to support research and the spread of scientific information.[41] Among these Jews were people like the Natanson brothers, Ludwik, Henryk, and Jacob. Henryk was a bookseller with a strong affinity for Polish culture. He was a graduate of the Rabbinical School of Warsaw and a leading activist in Jewish public life. In his business, he sold books in Polish, some of which were European classics. He was also a member of the Warsaw Stock Exchange. In the 1880s he and Jan Gottlieb Bloch, along with other progressive Jewish members of the Stock Exchange, prepared a memorandum to the Russian authorities in St Petersburg that eventually led the tsar to cancel plans to restore discriminatory legislation. Ludwik, who was the head of the Warsaw community, studied medicine, and was the publisher of the first Polish medical periodical, *Tygodnik Lekarski*. He was active in public health and other social projects on behalf of both Jewish and Polish organizations.[42] In addition to the Natanson brothers, there were other Jews who engaged with the Polish public and cultural spheres, such as Samuel Orgelbrand, who published a Polish encyclopedia, and Mathias Rosen and Leopold Kronenberg, who financed the publication of the important Polish periodical *Biblioteka Warszawska*. Jewish doctors were also influential in founding the Polish Medical Society (Polskie Towarzystwo Lekarskie). In addition, Orgelbrand and Jacob Natanson sponsored several public libraries in Warsaw.[43] Many, if not all, of these Jews who were engaged in different Polish cultural activities believed that this kind of involvement would help to improve the relationship between Jews and Poles.

Some scholars have argued that the varied support provided by Jews in Polish literary and cultural activities did not achieve this goal,[44] though it was considered that events such as the Polish revolts did bring Jews and Poles closer to each

[40] The following numbers of Jews in Warsaw that might count as belonging to the professional intelligentsia are derived from the census of 1897, as quoted in I. Gutman, S. Netzer, and A. Wein, *Toldot yehudei varsha* (Jerusalem, 1991), 69, and are all approximate. Teachers and educators, 750; medical personnel (doctors, medical assistants, paramedics, nurses), 230; scientists, literary people, journalists, 115; bureaucrats and administrators, 95; lawyers, 17.

[41] J. Shatzky, *Geshikhte fun yidn in varshe*, 3 vols. (New York, 1947–53), ii. 161–9.

[42] On the Natanson family, see e.g. I. Schiper, 'Di familie natanson', *Haynt*, 1935, nos. 142–56.

[43] More information on the Jewish involvement in Polish cultural and scientific life can be found in A. Hertz, *Żydzi w kulturze polskiej* (Paris, 1961).

[44] B. Garncarska-Kadary, *Ḥelkam shel hayehudim behitpathut hata'asiyah shel varsha bashanim 1816/20–1914* (Tel Aviv, 1985), 270.

other.[45] Nevertheless, as early as the late 1850s several intellectual and public debates indicated that there were those among the Polish intellectuals who did not approve of the rapprochement of certain Jewish circles with Polish society and the involvement of Jews in Polish culture. These Polish intellectuals thus attacked in 1857 the initiative of the Jewish publisher and bookseller Shmuel Merzbach to publish the writings of the famous Polish poet Adam Mickiewicz. Some Polish intellectuals argued, in various Polish periodicals, that Mickiewicz should not be published by a Jew.[46] Later, in 1859, the conservative newspaper *Gazeta Warszawska* attacked the attitude of Jews to Slav culture. As a result of this attack, an extensive public polemic about the involvement of the Jews in Polish society ensued.[47] These public debates, and later the events of the 1863 uprising and its aftermath, changed the course of the Warsaw Jewish intelligentsia. Various of its members began to seek ways in which they might act within their own Jewish society. In the 1860s and 1870s, a significant group of Jews in Warsaw who considered themselves as progressive Jews, some of them graduates of the Rabbinical School in Warsaw or of non-Jewish academic institutions, came to see themselves as representatives of and spokesmen for Jewish society in its dealings with Polish society and the Russian authorities.[48] Several of them wished to occupy central positions in the Jewish public sphere, and some of them saw themselves as guardians of the Jewish masses.[49]

It is also not impossible that this change was due to the Russian government's response to the 1863 uprising and the sanctions it imposed, and the fact that some of the sanctions were also directed towards Jewish groups. Further, the attitude taken to the Jewish question by the supporters of Polish positivism in Warsaw was that Jews, especially middle-class Jews, should be integrated into society for the common good. All these factors brought the Jewish intelligentsia back into Jewish society. But this did not change the central position of the Jewish intelligentsia, shared by its Polish counterpart, according to which belonging to the intelligentsia is not merely an improvement of one's personal situation: its essential principle is one of showing responsibility for the rest of society. Therefore, the direction of activity chosen by the Jewish intelligentsia was that of the modernization of Jewish society, which it believed would result in the public good. The same processes that took place within the Polish intelligentsia and moulded it as a class devoted to the

[45] See the Polish manuscript of Florian Sokolow, published in Hebrew as 'Tahalikhei hatemiah vehahitbolelut', in *Entsiklopediyah shel galuyot*, i: *varsha* (Jerusalem, 1953). The manuscript is in the archive of Nahum Sokolow, Central Zionist Archives, Jerusalem, A18 / box 227 (uncatalogued).

[46] Jedlicki, *Błędne koło*, 192.

[47] More information on this whole polemic can be found ibid. 194–200, and in A. Eisenbach, *Kwestia równouprawnienia Żydów w Królestwie Polskim* (Warsaw, 1972), 260–5.

[48] For additional information on this school, see Shatzky, *Geshikhte fun yidn in varshe*, ii. 19–111; A. Polonsky, 'Warszawska Szkoła Rabinów: Orędowniczka narodowej integracji w Królestwie Polskim', in M. Gałas (ed.), *Duchowość żydowska w Polsce* (Kraków, 2000), 287–307.

[49] Nahum Sokolow manuscript, Central Zionist Archives, A18 / box 227 (uncatalogued).

society in which it lived, can be identified within the Jewish intelligentsia during the last forty years of the nineteenth century. Just as the Polish intelligentsia presented itself as being the heir to the historical leadership of the Polish *szlachta*, so too did the Jewish intelligentsia see itself as a new leadership replacing the old Jewish leadership. Here too a process of differentiation took place. In their appeals to young people who stood at an important crossroads in their life, Jewish public figures and writers sought to make clear that not every intelligent and highly educated person automatically becomes a member of the intelligentsia. Not every doctor is an intellectual, and advanced academic study must be devoted to areas in which one can contribute to improving the welfare of society and to serving society; this should be done not merely for the love of science or for the sake of intellectual activity.[50] To be considered a member of the intelligentsia, one must be a person who sees himself as a prominent and leading member of society. The opportunities for leadership presented by the Jewish intelligentsia were broadened and within Jewish society were developed to include areas outside the scope of traditional Jewish leadership roles.

Like the members of the Polish intelligentsia, the Jewish intelligentsia sought to establish social organizations. Various writers encouraged the creation of new associations within Jewish society.[51] In 1866 Hilary Nussbaum pointed out that there was a need for change, which would entail the Jewish leadership taking on new roles. It should no longer be involved only in supervising and running institutions such as synagogues, but should lead Jewish society towards European culture and establish new Jewish institutions and public organizations that would benefit both Jewish society and society at large.[52]

In Polish society, as explained above, the purpose of these new organizations was to fill the gap in services caused by the fact that the government was not fulfilling its role in these areas, whereas among the Jews, the purpose of these societies was to make traditional Jews more progressive and transform them into useful members of society.[53] Many articles appeared in Warsaw's Jewish press seeking to encourage the establishment of new Jewish organizations that were to be different from the traditional Jewish associations, and they stressed the contribution to be made by these new groups towards both Jewish and the wider society. Special coverage was devoted to the Society for Hygiene and to the Jewish Teachers' Association. These organizations served as examples of the way in which advanced education could be channelled for the benefit of society as a whole, and of the way in which professional organizations too could work not only for the benefit of their

---

[50] M.S.T., 'Do naszej młodzieży', *Izraelita*, 27 June (9 July) 1870.

[51] For more on the new Jewish social and professional organizations and associations, see F. Guesnet, *Polnische Juden im 19. Jahrhundert: Lebensbedingungen, Rechtsnormen und Organisation im Wandel* (Cologne and Vienna, 1998), 161–78.

[52] H. Nussbaum, 'O instytucjach gminy staroz. w Warszawie', *Izraelita*, 15 (27) Apr. 1866.

[53] 'Pogadanki', *Izraelita*, 13 (25) July 1873.

members but for the good of society.[54] It was clear to the various writers that the establishment of these organizations was a part of the task of the Jewish intelligentsia, which was also involved in efforts to establish a variety of modern Jewish educational institutions.[55] These various efforts continued until the end of the nineteenth century.

CHALLENGING THE ROLE OF THE JEWISH INTELLIGENTSIA

The roles within society of both the Jewish and the Polish intelligentsia groups in Warsaw were formed without the creation of any binding definition of their responsibilities. The differences in their roles were accepted and understood by both the Jews and the Poles, and for this reason criticism of the role of the intelligentsia developed along distinctive lines within each group. But whereas the criticism of the Polish intelligentsia was focused on the extent to which it was taking its proper place within society, within Jewish society the intelligentsia faced an additional element of criticism related to the connections between the intelligentsia and Jewish society and its heritage.

The Jewish intelligentsia was being asked to raise the honour of Israel, to care for all levels of the social mosaic of Polish Jewry.[56] The intelligentsia was asked not to get involved in philosophical issues, but to meet the immediate requirements of Jewish society, without forsaking Jewry. As one of the most notable and distinguished publicists of *Hatsefirah*, Naftali Herz Neumanowitz, wrote under his pen-name 'Netz':[57]

Do not surround us with questions as [in the detailed talmudic discussion of the ritual status of] the oven of Akhnai. God forbid that we should expect all this of you. All the Jewish people ask of you is that you should justify your worthiness to the name you have chosen for your banner. We ask of you to be genuine intellectuals and not to bear the name of 'intelligentsia' in vain . . . My teachers! You should know that you have no right to call yourselves 'intelligentsia'. If you love the intelligentsia, study the Torah of Moses. What are the signs of life in the nineteenth century? Why should you be given the right to call yourselves 'the intelligentsia'? What is free Judaism? Not to renounce, for example, the lighting of Hanukah lights and the singing of 'Maoz tsur yeshuati'?[58]

A contributor to the Jewish Polish-language newspaper *Izraelita*, writing at the beginning of the twentieth century, not only claimed that the Jewish intelligentsia had cut itself off from the Jewish masses, but accused it of being in fact nothing

---

[54] See *Hatsefirah*, 9 (21), 13 (25) Jan. 1891; 15 (27), 14 (26) Apr., 12 (24) May 1899.
[55] B. Lauer, 'Samopomoc i straż pożarna', *Izraelita*, 16 (29) Nov. 1901.
[56] Netz, 'Berosh homiyot', *Hatsefirah*, 20 Apr. (2 May) 1890.
[57] For further details on this writer, see *Sefer zikaron lesofrei yisra'el haḥayim itanu hayom* (Warsaw, 1889), 75, and N. Sokolow, *Ishim* (Jerusalem, 1958), 214–23.
[58] Netz, 'Berosh homiyot', *Hatsefirah*, 27 Nov. (9 Dec.), 28 Nov. (10 Dec.) 1896.

more than a pseudo-intelligentsia—a criticism also raised against the Polish intelligentsia.[59]

It seems that in the new political and social reality that had developed at the end of the nineteenth century—the rise of new political players, together with the establishment of large numbers of new Jewish and Polish political parties—the aspirations of the intelligentsia to serve as the ruling class became irrelevant. Both Jewish and Polish intelligentsias became regarded as targets for attack. Indeed, in all aspects of the criticism levelled at the role of the intelligentsia, we find similarities between Polish society and Jewish society. Despite the almost complete identification of the Jewish intelligentsia circles with the assimilationists, it would be incorrect to attribute to them a total estrangement from Jewish society: some members of the Jewish intelligentsia did join the Jewish groups and parties formed at the end of the nineteenth century and beginning of the twentieth, and were in fact identified with Jewish nationalist and cultural initiatives. Around the turn of the century, the Polish Jewish intelligentsia split into different groups—a Jewish literary intelligentsia, a Jewish nationalist intelligentsia, and even a Jewish socialist intelligentsia. This divergence of various sub-groupings within the intelligentsia paralleled the divisions taking place within Polish society at large.

Furthermore, at the end of the nineteenth century and beginning of the twentieth, the Jewish intelligentsia was being assessed on the basis of its attitude to the Jewish masses, as was the Polish intelligentsia in its relations with the Polish masses. This was the viewpoint of Moshe Kleinman in an article 'Shenei ha'olamim' ('The Two Worlds') written in 1908. This was not the first time that Kleinman had criticized the Jewish intelligentsia. However, it was not only Kleinman that chose to present the Jewish intelligentsia in a most negative and unflattering light, as he claims that

The Jewish intelligentsia in each country is first and foremost part of the culture of that country and is nurtured from those roots. Is it not public knowledge that even the bearers of Hebrew and Jewish culture in Russia, for example, are deeply absorbed in Russian culture and that that is the source from which they feed? . . . Russian literature and society embody broad and glowing humanitarian ideals . . . whereas in Polish literature and society the bear shrinks into its own lair, continually sucking its paw—but only its own paw . . . There [we find] a broad discussion of matters of the highest importance—a battle between the powerful ones and the idealists regarding world happiness; [whereas] here there is a choking atmosphere of nationalist teeth-grinding chauvinism and the instigation of the lowest instincts of the masses . . . These are the two great seas whose spray rises and moistens the vineyard of the House of Israel; it will therefore be no surprise if one of them brings us good, healthy waters whereas the other brings foul waters.[60]

This is obviously exaggerated. On the other hand, one can see that Kleinman was aware of the fact that different Jewish intelligentsia groups drew inspiration from

[59] Lauer, 'Samopomoc i straż pożarna'.
[60] M. Kleinman, 'Shenei ha'olamim', *Revivim* (Lviv), 1 (1908), 13.

and were influenced by local intellectual circles. He also recognized the new social and political reality of the beginning of the twentieth century, which meant that the activity required of the Jewish intelligentsia in Polish areas could not be provided by its existing leaders, and a different type of leadership would have to emerge. When the Jewish intelligentsia began to be active during the 1860s, it had been seen as such a new leadership, and even as an alternative to the old traditional Jewish leadership, whereas by the beginning of the twentieth century it had become the 'old' leadership, which was considered unsuited to the Jewish political, social, and cultural reality.

CONCLUSION

For more than a century historians, sociologists, and other scholars have attempted to understand the nature of the intelligentsia. Although the term first developed in western Europe, the intelligentsia as a social group is a unique outcome of east European social, cultural, and political experience. In the Russian empire and the Polish lands the intelligentsia was recognized as an elite social group, a cultural and national leadership, and in some cases as an avant-garde.

Among the different intelligentsia groups that were active in eastern Europe there were various groups of Jewish intelligentsia. In the activities and the programmes of these groups one can recognize the influences of their surrounding environment. In the case of the Polish Jewish intelligentsia, one can recognize the influence exerted on their activities and dogmas by the Polish intelligentsia. Nevertheless, the relationships of the Polish Jewish intelligentsia with its parallel groups have scarcely drawn the attention of scholars. In the important set of books on the Polish intelligentsia that has been published recently, the Polish Jewish intelligentsia is mentioned only as part of the Polish intelligentsia (in a discussion of several members of the Polish intelligentsia who were of Jewish origin), and the books do not treat the Polish Jewish intelligentsia to a separate section.[61] This intelligentsia was nevertheless a significant social and intellectual phenomenon, which can incidentally serve as a mirror on Polish Jewish society and on the relations between Poles and Jews. In the second half of the nineteenth century, the Polish Jewish intelligentsia that was active in cities such as Warsaw wanted, among other things, to face the challenges that were the consequence of the complicated fabric of the Polish Jewish identity. The attempt to find the right balance between the Polish and the Jewish components of their identity, and the challenges posed by the circumstances of life in the Polish lands under the extended occupation, distinguished the Polish Jewish intelligentsia from other Jewish intelligentsia groups of nineteenth-century eastern Europe. Furthermore, the Polish intelligentsia's interpretation of the concept of leadership helped the Polish Jewish intelligentsia to define, up until the end of the nineteenth century, its tasks and aims. Under the

---

[61] Micińska, *Inteligencja na rozdrożach*, 32–8.

influence of Polish positivism some members of the Polish Jewish intelligentsia developed a moderate programme very different from those propounded by members of the Russian Jewish intelligentsia, and from the later programme developed by the socialist Jewish intelligentsia in Polish and other east European areas. On the basis of the assumption that the intelligentsia should be the leadership of Polish Jewish society, and in response to the variety of changes that had taken place in both Polish and Jewish societies in the second half of the nineteenth century, the tasks and duties of the Jewish Polish intelligentsia had been redefined. By the last years of the nineteenth century the Jewish intelligentsia could no longer manage to fulfil the missions and meet the challenges that were incumbent on it. This failure mirrored developments in Polish society at large. By the end of the century, new political frameworks had been established in Polish and Jewish society. Some of these new frameworks—such as those that were associated with the terms 'organic work' (*praca organiczna*) and 'working from the foundations' (*praca u podstaw*)—stood in opposition to previous methods and practices. The rise of new political forces, the era of the masses in the Polish lands and also in other parts of Europe, and the development of new political, social, and cultural frameworks—all this no longer matched the leadership models that the Polish and Jewish intelligentsias had created in previous years. Nevertheless, these new political, social, and cultural frameworks could not have formed without the preparatory activity and thought of both the Polish and the Jewish intelligentsias. In the transition from traditional and religious leaderships to the new political frameworks, the leadership models that both Polish and Polish Jewish intelligentsias created played a significant part.

Between Permeability and Isolation

Ezriel Natan Frenk as Historian of the Jews in Poland

FRANÇOIS GUESNET

UNJUSTIFIABLY, IN MY VIEW, Ezriel Natan Frenk (1863–1924) is a virtually forgotten author from the period of great flowering in Polish Jewish literary and intellectual creativity in Warsaw. At the end of the nineteenth and beginning of the twentieth centuries, the Polish metropolis grew into one of the world's most pulsating, vibrant centres of Jewish culture. Part of this ferment was the development of new forms of a culture of history, which in its complexity and constituent components characterized east European Jewish communities. Essential strands of this culture included a powerfully local—even parochial—orientation; a stress on the importance of prominent religious, especially hasidic, leaders; a generous way of handling anecdotal materials; and a combination of scholarly approaches with strong political committments.[1]

In these pages, I present Ezriel Natan Frenk as a compiler of these differing strands in the east European historical narrative. His driving ambition as a writer was marked by his desire to offer a comprehensive historical orientation to a readership limited to east European Jewry, as he wrote exclusively in Yiddish and Hebrew. Frenk integrated a broad spectrum of source material to this end: the archival tradition of individual Jewish *kehilot*, oral anecdotal traditions, legends of hasidic communities, and the scholarly research of his day. Part of Frenk's manner of shaping the past was based on his political independence. To preserve that demanded considerable personal sacrifice: although he had turned away from his hasidic education, in numerous publications he showed respect for hasidism as a religious and spiritual movement. Although he was active in Warsaw's enlightened Jewish circles and was proficient in Polish, he well understood the self-deceptions of that milieu, which strove for acculturation according to central and west

---

[1] The following comments cannot attempt to cover systematically the field of 'popular' historical writing in Yiddish and Hebrew in eastern Europe. A useful introduction, though it does not describe the phenomenon comprehensively as it is restricted to Yiddish texts, is I. N. Gottesman, *Defining the Yiddish Nation: The Jewish Folklorists of Poland* (Detroit, 2003), 3–74.

European paradigms. And although he was engaged in the Social Democratic movement, he did not reduce the history of Polish Jewry to a grand narrative of Jewish workers and peasants. Frenk also harboured some sympathy for Zionism, often writing for Zionist papers and periodicals, but it is clear that the east European Jewish world was his natural and declared homeland.

Frenk's work distinctly reflects the intellectual environment of his Warsaw, the first truly modern Jewish metropolis. Here, in the Polish capital, different religious and political ways of life coexisted and were able to unfold within a substantial array of important substructures which achieved a quasi-autonomous status. These encompassed the milieu of traditional Orthodoxy, competing hasidic communities, Russian Jewish migrants, 'assimilationists' keen to acculturate to Polish society, and followers of the Social Democratic movement. These groups were semi-permeable and sought supporters in the city's Jewish sub-metropolis; for example, the 'Litvaks', defined by their migration to the city and regarded among observant Jews as 'godless', combined a considerable level of socio-political dynamism with good organizational skills, and also sought and found diverse possibilities for connectivity in the religious and political environments in the capital. Ezriel Natan Frenk wrote for this highly dynamic and many-sided public as a whole.

A SURVEY OF FRENK'S LIFE AND WORK

Frenk's greatest achievement was as a writer of historical texts for both academic audiences and a broad reading public. He collected, edited, and published hasidic tales; translated excerpts from the Zohar, a central work in Jewish mysticism, into Hebrew; and translated leading Polish authors into his native Yiddish. In addition, he served for years as editor of the influential Hebrew-language weekly *Hatsefirah*. The broad spread of his creativity makes it impossible even in retrospect to categorize clearly his literary works. His popular historical writing would appear to undermine his classification as a serious scholar, as in these writings events of past or contemporary history are woven together and presented in melodramatic form. Thus, in 1908 he published a novella dealing with current events, the now nearly forgotten Alfonsn pogrom of May 1905. In that incident, enraged Jewish artisans and workers had demolished brothels run by Jews in Warsaw (the name 'Alfonsn' pogrom derives from the Yiddish slang word common in Jewish Warsaw for a procurer or flesh-pedlar). This small book, which by present-day criteria goes well over the line into kitsch, nonetheless depicts a singular eruption of violence within Jewish society that greatly disturbed Frenk's contemporaries.[2] Frenk devoted one monograph to the relations between Christian and Jewish townspeople,[3] and

[2] E. N. Frenk, *Der alfonsn-pogrom in varshe* (Warsaw, 1908). The novella will be discussed in detail below.

[3] E. N. Frenk, *Ha'ironim vehayehudim bepolin: masa histori* (Warsaw, 1921). The work was republished with the same title in Israel in 1969.

another one to Jewish–Christian conversions.[4] He also wrote a popular survey of Jewish history in Poland, which despite its appeal to a general audience is distinguished by numerous fresh perspectives on the topic, as well as original assessments.[5] In addition, Frenk published in the Jewish press a number of long articles or series of articles dealing with history; some of these were later released as monographs.[6] It is not yet possible to determine the total extent of Frenk's journalistic writings: in addition to the considerable number of historical monographs, we are still awaiting even an approximate listing of his full output of popular-historical publications as a journalist. These pieces were published in the major contemporary Yiddish and Hebrew periodicals from the 1880s until his death in 1924, and must amount to hundreds of articles. While their thematic focus was on the history and culture of east European Jews, and in particular Jews in the area of historical Poland, Frenk also familiarized his readership with key aspects of Jewish history in other parts of Europe. A further facet of his writing described hasidic Polish traditions and legends in detail.

Frenk himself stemmed from a wealthy hasidic merchant family in Wodzisław, near Kielce. This background evidently led to his conception of his role as an intermediary between hasidic traditions and the urban life of large Jewish cities. Among his works are biographies of leading hasidic figures; he also recorded hasidic legends, in both Hebrew and Yiddish.[7] Although Frenk grew up in an observant hasidic Jewish family, we do not know whether in his Warsaw years he was an active member of a hasidic community. However, that appears unlikely, since at an early age he turned away from religion and towards the beacon of the Jewish Enlightenment,[8] taking on the qualities of a modern intellectual.[9] Yet in his work as a historian and a writer, hasidism nevertheless played a substantial role. He wrote a large number of articles and monographs on legends about great hasidic leaders. With his popular and his scholarly writings, and his collections of folk stories, Frenk strove to open a window onto the Jewish past in Poland, from its beginnings down to his immediate present. His writings are noteworthy not least for their eschewal of interpretations based on ideology, religion, or the philosophy

[4] E. N. Frenk, *Meshumodim in poyln in 19tn yorhundert* (Warsaw, 1923).

[5] E. N. Frenk, *Di geshikhte fun yidn in poyln biz tsum yor 1907* (Warsaw, [1910]). See also F. Guesnet, *Polnische Juden im 19. Jahrhundert: Lebensbedingungen, Rechtsnormen und Organisation im Wandel* (Cologne and Vienna, 1998), 95–7, 183–4.

[6] E. N. Frenk, *Yehudei polin beyemei milḥamot napolion* (Warsaw, 1913); id., 'Letoldot haḥazakah', *Hashiloʻaḥ*, 1 (1896/7); id., *Di familie davidson* (Warsaw, 1924).

[7] E. N. Frenk, *Miḥayei haḥasidim bepolin* (Warsaw, 1895); id., *Yitsḥak meʻir beyaldutav* (Warsaw, 1904); id., *Agadot ḥasidim: levenei haneʻurim veleʻam* (Warsaw, 1923); and, published posthumously, id. *Mivḥar agadot haḥasidim* (Warsaw, 1924), reprinted several times in Israel, *inter alia* in 1954 in Tel Aviv.

[8] M. Bałaban, 'Ezriel-natan frenk', in *Yidn in poyln: studies un shilderungen fun fargangene tkufes* (Vilna, 1930), 314.

[9] As a rule, the extant photos and drawings show Frenk dressed in suit and tie, as in the photograph accompanying his obituary in *Nayer haynt*, 3 Feb. 1924.

of history. However, by focusing on the history of the Jews in Poland, he did present a picture of a specific encounter, characterized by autonomy, continuity, and integration into the political fabric of the Polish–Lithuanian Commonwealth.[10]

JOURNALISTIC ACTIVITIES

As a young man, Frenk was attracted to the Social Democratic movement, and soon after he settled in Warsaw, he became active in the social revolutionary organization Proletariat.[11] Its Jewish members established a cover organization, which functioned within the framework of the Association of Trade Clerks of Mosaic Faith (Stowarzyszenie Subjektów Handlowych Wyznania Mojżeszowego), a society of Jewish sales personnel that had been founded in 1856 with a strong orientation towards acculturation.[12] Frenk assisted them by translating Polish revolutionary writings into Yiddish. As a writer of original works, he initially established himself as a journalist, writing in Hebrew and Yiddish for the first important Jewish literary magazine published in Warsaw, the *Varshoyer yidishn kalendar*, issued by the hasidic publisher Heshel Epelberg. A number of important authors wrote for the *Kalendar*, such as the pioneer of Yiddish literary modernism, Yitzhak Leibush Peretz (1851–1915). Frenk also wrote for *He'asif*, the literary periodical published with some success by Nahum Sokolow (1859–1936), a well-known Warsaw journalist and later Zionist leader. The print runs of *He'asif* at times reached 3,000 copies.[13]

In Warsaw, Frenk also published his earliest historical works, which were articles for *Ha'eshkol*, the first Jewish encyclopedia project of that era, undertaken by Yitzhak Goldman (1812–88).[14] For all six instalments of this reference work, which ceased publication after the death of its editor, Frenk wrote about Polish and Polish Jewish history. Goldman and Frenk supported efforts to achieve Polish

---

[10] Frenk is listed in most relevant reference works, for example in *Pinkas varsha* (Buenos Aires, 1955), cols. 812–13; G. Kresel (ed.), *Leksikon hasifrut ha'ivrit bedorot ha'aḥaronim*, 2 vols. (Rehavia, 1965–7), cols. 682–3. For short biographical descriptions, see Bałaban, 'Ezriel-natan frenk', 314–19, and F. Guesnet, 'Frenk, Azriel Natan', in G. D. Hundert (ed.), *The YIVO Encyclopedia of Jews in Eastern Europe*, 2 vols. (New Haven, 2008), i. 548. S. D. Kassow, *Who Will Write Our History? Emanuel Ringelblum, the Warsaw Ghetto, and the Oyneg Shebes Archive* (Bloomington, Ind., 2007), 65, mentions Frenk briefly in the context of the formation of modern Polish Jewish historiography.

[11] J. Szacki, *Geshikhte fun yidn in varshe*, iii (New York, 1953), 273, 287, 397–8. Szacki gives 1883, and once also 1886, as the year Frenk arrived in Warsaw. On Proletariat, see N. M. Naimark, *The History of the 'Proletariat': The Emergence of Marxism in the Kingdom of Poland, 1870–1887* (New York, 1979), *passim*. [12] On this society, see Guesnet, *Polnische Juden im 19. Jahrhundert*, 162.

[13] Szacki, *Geshikhte*, 273, 287.

[14] Ibid. 255–9. Goldman stemmed from the region of Białystok and moved in 1837 to Warsaw. During the January uprising in 1863, he wrote appeals in Hebrew calling for the support of the Polish independence movement. Goldman was among the early arrivals of Lithuanian Jews in Warsaw, who were decried by local Warsaw Jews as 'Litvaks'. On this, see Guesnet, *Polnische Juden im 19. Jahrhundert*, 61–77, and id., 'Migration et stéréotype: Le Cas des Juifs russes au Royaume de Pologne à la fin du XIX siècle', *Cahiers du monde russe*, 41 (2000), 505–18.

independence, a not uncommon attitude at the time, especially in Polish Jewish circles close to Reform Judaism.

Frenk also showed his creativity as an freelance author for the Hebrew and Yiddish press in Congress Poland and Russia. Although he regularly wrote columns for the Warsaw periodical *Hatsefirah*, edited by Haim Zelig Slonimski (1810–1904), Frenk found its basic editorial policy 'too conservative' for his taste. More in keeping with his 'militant nature' was the daily *Hamelits* published in Russia under the editorship of Aleksander Cederbaum (1816–93), for which, under a pseudonym, he wrote a column of 'caustic correspondence' from Warsaw up to three times a week.[15] When *Hatsefirah* renewed publication in 1911 under changed conditions after a long period of official censorship, Frenk joined its editorial team as a regular staff member, becoming one of its main writers, along with Nahum Sokolow and Dovid Frishman (1859–1922). At this juncture, *Hatsefirah* was the most influential and largest Hebrew daily in Warsaw, with some 15,000 subscribers. During the First World War, Frenk and his colleague Efraim Singer effectively functioned as the sole editors, writing major sections of the paper, since the other staff members had left the capital. The paper's finances suffered under German occupation, and its modest survival was due in large part to Frenk's great personal sacrifice to keep it afloat. After the war, the paper was taken over by the Zionist movement and revamped.[16] In the framework of this reform, Frenk was not even retained as an editor, though he had been expecting to become the paper's director.[17] From that point on, Frenk signed his articles with the pseudonyms 'Cast-Off' and 'Outcast', until he was forbidden to do so.[18] Frenk voiced his bitterness over these developments in a long article in the Yiddish Warsaw daily *Moment*,[19] warning future editors of any Hebrew daily not to commit again those errors which were inevitably going to lead, in his eyes, to the downfall of *Hatsefirah*. Among the reasons for the newspaper's lack of success after the war, he names the partisanship of the new editors, their lack of devotion, their poor Hebrew, and their attempt to focus on local issues only, rather than to publish a newspaper that would bring news of the Jewish world to readers in Warsaw. Frenk's account of his personal fate of being abandoned by the new editors, and especially Shmuel Rosenberg, is a heart-rending testimony of utter despair. The article appeared on 2 February 1924, the day of Frenk's death. This coincidence suggests the possibility that he may have committed suicide, but this is not established fact.

Although he preferred to write his articles in Hebrew, Frenk also published

[15] Cederbaum (Tsederboym), born in Zamość in Lublin province, was among the leading east European Jewish publicists of his time, and had transferred his base of activity from the Polish Kingdom to St Petersburg.

[16] J. Pograbinski, 'Ha'itonut ha'ivrit', in *Entsiklopediyah shel galuyot*, i: *varsha* (Jerusalem and Tel Aviv, 1953), col. 483.   [17] Bałaban, 'Ezriel-natan frenk', 315.

[18] S. Niger and J. Shatzky (eds.), *Leksikon fun der nayer yidisher literatur*, 8 vols. (New York, 1956–81), viii. 516–20, s.v. 'Frenk, ezriel-natan'.

[19] 'Vegn dem kiyem fun a hebreisher tsaytung in varshe', *Moment*, 2 Feb. 1924.

regularly in the Yiddish papers and magazines, especially literary periodicals. He collaborated over many years in this type of writing with Peretz. Frenk wrote articles for Peretz's *Yidishe biblyotek*, *Literatur un lebn*, and *Yom-tov bleter*. In the pages of the *Hoyz-fraynd*, edited by Mordechai Spektor (1858–1925), Frenk published numerous articles, including a historical study of the legendary figure of Joseph Nasi.[20] Hence, Majer Bałaban's contention that Frenk published 'in all daily, weekly, and monthly papers in Hebrew and Yiddish appearing in Poland, Russia, and abroad' is probably a fairly accurate assessment.[21] Characteristic of Frenk's work was a fluid transition from genre to genre: he reworked some of his series of articles in daily newspapers into longer essays or books; turned some of his collections of historical material into literary works; and added anecdotal embellishments to his historical writing from the material he had collected on legends.

QUESTIONS OF LANGUAGE

Frenk published his articles, historiographical works, and collections of hasidic tales in just two languages: Hebrew and Yiddish. The sole exception was an essay, especially valued by Bałaban, on the structure of Jewish communities in Russia and Poland in the eighteenth century, which appeared in 1914 in a Russian-language work. This was a joint venture by the leading Polish Jewish and Russian Jewish historians of the time, and has, in my view, been unjustifiably overlooked within the historiography. The aim of the publishers was to compile an extensive compendium on the history of the Jewish people.[22] It is improbable that Frenk wrote this essay by himself in Russian; most likely it was translated. His motivation, despite his excellent knowledge of Polish, to write only in Yiddish and Hebrew cannot be explained by ideological motives alone. His early sympathies with the Social Democratic movement did not result in any attempt by him to write on Jewish history for the Polish reading public; he simply used the languages he deemed appropriate for his targeted audience. He viewed that history less as one of

[20] E. N. Frenk, 'Der yidisher firsht in zekhtsetn yor-hundert', *Hoyz-fraynd: a historish-literarishes bukh*, 3 (1908), 46–52. This is a brief factual biography of Joseph Nasi (1524–79) and his aunt Gracia Mendes (1510–69). According to Frenk, there is a connection here with Polish Jewry in that the Polish king Sigismund August made efforts to secure Nasi's diplomatic intervention with Sultan Suleiman I (1520–66), for which the king was supposedly prepared to grant extensive privileges to the Polish Jews in return (ibid. 52).

[21] Bałaban, 'Ezriel-natan frenk', 315. The list of Yiddish periodicals in which Frenk published, according to the *Leksikon fun der nayer yidisher literatur*, includes more than a dozen titles in addition to those already mentioned.

[22] Twelve volumes were planned, and the last two would deal with the history of the Jews in Russia. Owing to the outbreak of the First World War, however, only one volume was ever produced. Along with Simon Dubnow and Majer Bałaban, Isaac (Ignacy) Schiper, Ezriel Natan Frenk, and Israel Zinberg wrote articles for this volume: A. I. Braude (ed.), *Istoriya evreiskogo naroda*, xi: *Istoriya evreev v Rossii* (Moscow, 1914). Frenk's article (pp. 352–89) was titled 'Vnutrennii byt evreev v Pol'she i Litve v XVII i XVIII vv.'

'Polish' Jews and more as one of a Jewish community with a distinctive political fate. Through that fate, the community had evolved into a historical subject, one that was not merely a local variant of a uniform Jewish narrative.

In this way, Frenk's view of the history of Jews in Poland clearly differed from Zionist interpretations such as that of Shaul Pinhas Rabinowitz (1845–1910), who was active in Warsaw at the same time. Yet Frenk's views also contrasted with the thinking of scholars engaged in the beginnings of a Polish Jewish historiography in the Polish language.[23] Striking is the recurrent formula of 'the Jews in Poland'.[24] This subject made explicit the contrast with Jewries in other cultural and national contexts, and implicitly marked a divergence from the concept of the 'Polish Jew'. He did not construct a chronology according to the watersheds of Polish history, but rather of Jews in Poland. Here his view differed from the perspective of his prominent contemporary Mojżesz Schorr (1874–1941), who explicitly called for a Jewish history separate from that of Poland, but who framed that history in terms of major turning points in the Polish historical chronicle. Of course, the greatest contrast was with the attitude of authors who encouraged acculturation, such as Hilary Nussbaum, who interpreted the history of Polish Jewry as a process of gradual adoption of Polish culture and Polish patriotism; such writers consequently formulated their ideas and published in the Polish language.[25]

Frenk's most ambitious monograph, his comprehensive work on the neighbourly ties between Christian burghers and Jews in the Middle Ages and early modern period, was written in Hebrew.[26] It was based on Jewish and Polish source material and scholarly literature, and describes the hard-fought disputes over settlement and trade law, especially in the eighteenth century. The work's appendix contains extensive source material in Polish. In contrast with his numerous popularizations of history, Frenk did not include anecdotal matter. Instead, along with published sources such as pamphlets and decrees, he added official source material, rabbinical opinions, and the records of the Opatów community, which he personally copied and then passed on to the library of the Great Synagogue on Tłomackie Street in Warsaw. On the basis of these records, he also wrote an ambitious scholarly history of the legal institution of usufruct.[27] None of his studies published in Yiddish is marked by such extended use of critical historical methods. Although the majority of these works are annotated with references, as a rule they

---

[23] F. Guesnet, 'Geschichte im Kontext: Entwicklungsbedingungen der jüdischen Historiographie im polnischen Sprachraum im 19. Jahrhundert', in U. Wyrwa (ed.), *Judentum und Historismus: Zur Entstehung der jüdischen Geschichtswissenschaft in Europa* (Frankfurt am Main and New York, 2003), 143.

[24] On this, see Frenk, *Di geshikhte fun yidn in poyln*; id., *Yehudei polin beyemei milḥamot napolion*; id., *Letoldot hayehudim bepolin* (Warsaw, 1912); id., 'Vnutrennii byt evreev v Pol'she i Litve'; id., *Ha'ironim vehayehudim bepolin*.

[25] On Hilary Nussbaum (1820–95), see Guesnet, *Polnische Juden im 19. Jahrhundert*, passim; id., 'Geschichte im Kontext', 131–46.   [26] Frenk, *Ha'ironim vehayehudim bepolin*.

[27] Frenk, 'Letoldot haḥazakah'. See also Guesnet, *Polnische Juden im 19. Jahrhundert*, 218–22.

comprise a mélange of genres and are often embellished with anecdotes or dramatized forms of historical presentation. No doubt the non-scholarly textual elements
were meant to entertain the reader or were selected to render the historical description more vivid. A basic reason for this principle of style and structure was the fact
that Frenk's materials were as a rule first published in daily or weekly papers. In his
view, the loss of scientific exactness and rigour must have been compensated for by
the possibility of making historical matters that were to some extent complex more
understandable to a broad Jewish readership. Examples of such 'adding a dash of
spice' to the historical description are present in his short Hebrew monograph on
the Napoleonic wars, where several hasidic legends are reproduced to this ostensible end.[28] By contrast, the description of the 1905 Alfonsn pogrom is styled as a
melodrama that steps boldly into the realm of kitsch. One should, however, still
note the uniqueness of this narrative: for many decades, Frenk's study was the only
monograph of any kind dealing with this politically extremely explosive topic.[29]

It is evident that Frenk viewed Hebrew, resurrected in his day as an everyday
vernacular, as the language of an educated Jewish class, a *Bildungsbürgertum* that
had yet to be solidly established. This was a view that fitted into cultural Zionism.
Correspondingly, his works in Yiddish might be seen to a significant degree as
texts that popularized knowledge and the criteria for knowledge. In contrast to
numerous early agitators in the Jewish Social Democratic movement, Yiddish for
Frenk was actually his mother tongue and home language. Yet he shared the view
of Social Democratic activists that Yiddish should function more as the vehicle for
a popular mass education than as an instrument of linguistic self-assurance and
identity, let alone as the nucleus for cultural renewal. In his eyes, that latter task
was reserved for Hebrew.

In this context, Frenk's role as a translator is significant. Beyond potential pecu-
niary considerations, his motive for translating works by Bolesław Prus (1847–
1912), Eliza Orzeszkowa (1842–1910), and Henryk Sienkiewicz (1846–1916) was
to familiarize Jewish readers with these immensely popular Polish authors.[30] It is
worth noting that Frenk actually translated the novel *Mirtala* by Orzeszkowa
twice: once into Yiddish, shortly before he joined the editorial staff at *Hatsefirah* in
1911, and again in 1923 into Hebrew.[31] The novel describes the persecution and

---

[28] Frenk, *Yehudei polin beyemei milḥamot napolion*. At the beginning of this study, Frenk reproduces
the anecdote (without indicating any source) published by August Wilkoński in 1841 about the Jews of
Schwersenz who greeted Napoleon: see: F. Guesnet, 'The Turkish Cavalry in Swarzędz; or, Jewish
Political Culture at the Borderlines of Modern History', *Yearbook of the Simon Dubnow Institute*, 6
(2007), 229–30.   [29] Frenk, *Der alfonsn-pogrom in varshe*.

[30] *Min hatsir el hatsir* (Warsaw, 1923), Frenk's translation into Hebrew of the best-selling travelogue
by Sven Hedin (1865–1932), *From Pole to Pole*, also combined his educational objectives with the
means of earning his living.

[31] E. Orzeszkowa, *Mirtala: roman fun original iberzetst fun e. n. frenk* (Warsaw, 1911); ead.,
Mirtalah: sipur miyemei galut roma (Warsaw, [1923]). The original edition appeared in 1886 in Warsaw
in Polish under the title *Mirtala*.

dispersal of the Jews by the Romans after the destruction of the Temple in 70 CE. The first translation was also an expression of admiration for the Polish author, who had recently died, and whose empathy in dealing with Jewish themes Frenk emphasized. In evaluating her achievement, Frenk was able to inform his readers about the historical background to Orzeszkowa's personal engagement with these matters: 'At the time of her first marriage, the uprising [of 1863] broke out in Poland, an event which awakened so many beautiful hopes in the hearts of all Poles, and which ended so sadly.' It led to organic work, in the framework of which 'the better spirits endeavoured to be active in all strata of the population, and to raise up the moral, economic, and intellectual condition of the country'.[32] Orzeszkowa regarded her task as being to provide an authentic description of the lives of men and women, aristocrats and the poor, Christians and Jews, in equal measure. It was, Frenk wrote, the greatest challenge for the Polish nobility to become better acquainted with the living conditions of the Jews, 'strangers in their ways of life, language, religion, and culture'.[33] Frenk stressed her journalistic activity at the time of the 1881–2 pogroms, and the novel *Mirtala* was a product of that involvement. As Frenk explains it, the pogroms, and the institution of strict censorship that made it impossible to discuss their underlying causes, motivated Orzeszkowa to write this story: although set in a foreign land and distant time, it contained 'so many similarities with today and current events': 'You see pogroms, you see who makes them, who leads them, who instigates them, who become the victims. You see it all.'[34] In other literary works, Frenk writes—for example in the story 'Ogniwa' ('Elements')—Orzeszkowa also attacked antisemitism, which intensified in the final decades of the nineteenth century and was difficult to combat because of censorship. Frenk stressed that translation into Yiddish would also provide 'the broader strata of the Jewish people with insights into the history of the Second Temple period, as well as of recent eras and the present'.[35]

This formulation of Frenk's, which appears at the end of his introduction to *Mirtala*, illustrates his impetus to educate about the past. He argues that an understanding of history would make possible new insights into one's own past, would show the dynamism of the present, and would reveal the potential of humanistic positions. In summary, it appears that Frenk viewed Yiddish as a medium for popularizing comprehensive knowledge on the history of the Jews in general and Polish Jewry in particular. Parallel with this, he wrote extensive studies in Hebrew. To the extent that Hebrew was the language of the more scholarly works he composed, Frenk accorded it the function of a future cultural language of a Polish Jewry conscious of the past and living in Poland. His translations provided a bridge for conveying important artistic and literary views, especially from the Polish language community, and transposing them into the Jewish community.

[32] E. N. Frenk, introduction to Orzeszkowa, *Mirtala* (1911), p. ii.
[33] Ibid., p. iv.   [34] Ibid., pp. vi–vii.   [35] Ibid., p. viii.

HASIDIC LEGENDS

Throughout his life, Frenk endeavoured to collect, edit, and popularize the textual foundations of hasidism and the orally transmitted legends about the lives of leading hasidic rabbis. As early as 1895, in his Hebrew volume of stories *Miḥayei haḥasidim bepolin* ('From the Life of the Hasidim in Poland'), he described the everyday life of hasidic circles in provincial Poland. In a detailed review, Benjamin Segel, who later distinguished himself with a series of ethnographic studies on east European Jewish life, praised the great documentary value of this description, so true to life. Frenk narrates the adventures of a young hasid who turns away from the leader of his hasidic community, the *tsadik*, because he feels he is not being properly treated, after the *tsadik* has arranged an engagement for him with a woman to whom he is not attracted. After further negative experiences with another hasidic leader, the hero of the tale returns to his former *tsadik*. Significantly, he is not drawn to the Enlightenment, as might have been in keeping with a widespread topos in writings by east European maskilim towards the end of the nineteenth century.[36]

Frenk took a comparable literary approach in his *Yitsḥak me'ir beyaldutav* ('The Childhood of Yitzhak Meir'). Taking as a basis an account of the childhood of the Gerer Rebbe Yitzhak Meir Alter (1798–1866), he treats his readers to richly detailed descriptions of hasidic children's education and hasidic religious customs and holidays. Likewise, his selection and translation of legends from the central text of Jewish medieval mysticism, the Zohar, which he translated from Aramaic to Hebrew, also served as a way of portraying hasidic traditions.[37] His collection of hasidic stories titled *Agadot ḥasidim: levenei hane'urim vele'am* ('Legends of the Hasidim, for Youth and the People') was a set of texts in simple Hebrew, consisting of anecdotes about hasidic leaders, the *tsadikim*. These short pieces, presented by Frenk without commentary, are in the style of simple folk tales, and evidently were intended to represent and convey a core of Polish Jewish tradition.[38] Frenk's significance in this sphere of activity was principally to collect and edit oral narrative traditions of Polish Jewry. Unfortunately, the central part he played in establishing the modern state of knowledge of the history and form of the hasidic movement in eastern Europe has still not been properly acknowledged in the now extensive body of research on the history of hasidism.

[36] Frenk, *Miḥayei haḥasidim bepolin*. On this, see Benjamin W. Segel in *Izraelita*, 1897, no. 10, p. 96. In this review, Segel bemoaned Heinrich Graetz's prejudiced assessment of Hasidism and Simon Dubnow's narrow perspective, which was largely concerned with external developments.

[37] Frenk, *Yitsḥak me'ir beyaldutav*; id., *Agadot hazohar*, 2 vols. (Warsaw, 1923). These texts were unfortunately not available to me when this essay was being written.

[38] Frenk, *Agadot ḥasidim*. For this collection, Frenk drew some of the material from *Miḥayei haḥasidim bepolin*, which was also the source of some of the anecdotes in his work on the fate of the Jews in the Napoleonic wars, *Yehudei polin beyemei milḥamot napolion*.

HISTORICAL TREATISES

Frenk's historical works show a very varied character. In their diversity, they reflect his work as a historian and provide insight into the broad array of genres characteristic of his work. It is clear that Frenk succeeded in developing an analysis of Jewish history and contemporary history in Poland independent of the grand political narratives of his time.

Frenk's boldness in addressing explosive topics was singular. For decades, he was the only author to write about the eruption of violence against the Jewish criminal underworld by Jewish artisans and workers in May 1905. The fury of these attacks continued for three days, targeting in particular Jewish brothels, their owners, and the prostitutes employed there. There were many injured and some deaths, including men among the ranks of the protesting workers. The security authorities took action only after some hesitation, and then only half-heartedly. This notable example of internal Jewish violence was soon eclipsed by the events of the revolution of 1905 and the uprising against tsarist Russian rule in Poland. The Social Democratic organization in the Jewish workers' movement, the Bund, sought, for that reason, to take credit for the militant approach adopted by the aggressors, if not necessarily for the deaths of the procurers, claiming that Social Democratic agitation had sparked the outburst.[39] As a striking event in contemporary Warsaw history, the violent attacks must have fascinated Frenk and challenged his imagination. He presented the 'pogrom' in the form of a dramatized historical narrative in Yiddish,[40] contrasting the external events during the attacks as seen through the eyes of an active participant, Haim, nicknamed Hosh, with a description of the personal fate of the protagonist, via a rolling series of rapid flashbacks. The narrative flow is accelerated by the author's decision to omit introductions or explanations. The approximate unity of time and place gives an impression of theatre, which is strengthened by the choreography of the main characters and the enraged masses. The dramatic high point of the historical tale is the plundering of a middle-class house and the storming of a brothel, which ends in the death of the protagonist and his sister, who worked there as a prostitute. In his narrative, Frenk chose to forgo any direct evaluation of the events. But it becomes quite clear that the violent actions of the workers and artisans had their roots in the cruel social and economic situation that had led to the misery and lack of independence of the male workers, and to prostitution among the women. In describing these conditions, the text is infused with a powerful sense of accusation. Moreover, Frenk leaves us in no doubt that the violence was guided politically by trained agitators. There is no direct judgement of their moral legitimacy, but through the death of Haim and his sister Blumele, that legitimacy is at least called into

[39] For further literature on these events, see F. Guesnet, 'A *Tuml* in the *Shtetl*: Khayim Betsalel Grinberg's *Di khevre-kedishe sude*', *Polin*, 16 (2003), 93–106.

[40] Frenk, *Der alfonsn-pogrom in varshe*.

question. By contrast, the moral integrity of the workers and artisans is beyond any doubt; this is underscored by religious metaphors.

The short narrative is divided into two sections, first following the external events of the plundering of the house of a middle-class family, and then describing the assault on the brothel. The narrative linking of external events with the protagonist's reflections, feelings, and memories is accomplished by very brief stylistic shifts into what seem like 'streams of consciousness'. The tale's ending today seems overly melodramatic, and the metaphors in some passages appear exaggerated or simplistic: the 'burning eyes' of the workers, the 'lacklustre eyes' of the prostitutes, pieces of furniture that, 'like the previous order of things', must now be smashed to bits: 'What do they need all this for? This table, this mirror? What is this?', Yosele shouts, as he lifts up a dressing table and hurls it to the ground. 'It's a solid one too!', he cries, when he sees that the table has not been broken. Haim then shouts in rage: 'Solid, yeah, solid! It's no more solid than the whole previous order of things, a system that makes shameless animals out of the children of the proletariat!'[41]

The fact that Haim himself is partially responsible for his sister's death shows that Frenk, who had been a member of Proletariat, had distanced himself from the more violent forms of social protest. Notwithstanding this, the contemporary historical narrative underscores the moral responsibility of the establishment and of the authorities, sympathizing openly with the victims of the unjust political and economic order. This literary reworking of events in Warsaw's Jewish history, a kind of docu-novella, represents but a brief excursion by Frenk into the field of literature, although in the publications of his later years, the literary dimension did accompany the historical in his work as a collector and translator of oral narrative traditions, and especially as a translator of Polish literature.

The first extensive historical monograph by Frenk was *Di geshikhte fun yidn in poyln biz tsum yor 1907* ('The History of Jews in Poland to the Year 1907'), published in 1910.[42] Probably one of the first, perhaps even the very first, popular account in Yiddish of Jewish history in the Polish lands, this book does not offer any scholarly apparatus. It covers the history of the Jewish presence on Polish soil from its beginnings in the medieval period, explains the crucial relevance of privileges, autonomous communities, and representative bodies, as well as the opposition of burghers and clergy to their settlement. Frenk emphasizes the role of Poland as a centre of Jewish erudition and observance, and as home to the mystical movement of hasidism. Berek Joselewicz is presented as an example of the bond between Jews and the Polish Commonwealth. Writing about the early nineteenth century, Frenk recognizes the honest endeavour by 'better Poles' (82) to improve the status of Jews in Poland, but he also emphasizes the lack of influence of followers of the Jewish Enlightenment. He notes that the abolition of the *kahal* (communal leadership), initiated by the maskilim, and its replacement by the synagogue

---

[41] Frenk, *Der alfonsn-pogrom in varshe*, 15–16.

[42] Subsequent page references to this work are given in the text in parentheses.

supervisory board brought nothing but a relabelling of the traditional relations of power and domination: 'The Polish Jews regarded the laws limiting their rights with a certain indifference' (84). They would continue to collect funds to allow intercession (*shtadlanut*) and effectively obstruct any new legal restrictions: '[Between 1807] and 1847, the year when bribery ceased to avail and even the Polish Jews had to supply a certain number of men to the military, just the intercession to prevent the implementation of Jewish conscription cost the Jews one million zlotys annually' (85). He devoted his final chapter to a very frank description of political developments from the emancipation of the Jews in Congress Poland up to 1907. It is notable that here Frenk mentions the Polish–Jewish brotherhood of 1861, but not the uprising of January 1863. He sketches an unusually positive description of the partial emancipation in 1862: 'With the coming of civil equality in 1862, a new world full of light opened. The Jews quickly began to utilize its advantages, and settled in those localities where to date they had not been permitted to live, establishing large new business enterprises there' (91). The assimilationist Jews were, Frenk notes, so 'intoxicated' by emancipation that they readily closed the doors of the Rabbinical School in Warsaw, established in 1826 (92). At the same time, emancipation led to a situation in which traditional Jewish dress and language again began to spread with a new confidence. The economic situation was developing to their advantage, and hasidism achieved a new, unprecedented level of strength. However, antisemitism was also on the rise, gaining in intensity from the late 1870s. Its adherents sought in particular to remove Jews from their traditional functions as traders by setting up co-operatives, although, as Frenk notes, 'confederations and associations alone were unable to do the Jews any serious harm, since for most people, ideas played no role in matters of purchase and sale' (93). In an effort to maintain the favour of the masses, a number of non-Jewish political currents sponsored the creation of co-operatives: 'Such associations are now being established in every town and village; their aim is to drive Jews out of business. These co-operatives are also acting to spread antisemitism in those strata of the population that earlier were indifferent to it' (94). Although the law on associations introduced in 1906 had permitted Jews to establish societies and associations, some of which had a clear political orientation, these were now prohibited. Frenk notes that Jewish credit unions were of special importance: 'In Warsaw and other Polish cities, special associations for the mutual granting of credit have been established. These are very useful for the Jewish people, since the general economic situation demands that favourable credit be available' (95).

With this perspective, Frenk brought his monograph on the history of the Jews in Poland into the immediate present for his readers. The description of the nineteenth century is conspicuously limited to the history of Jews in the Polish Kingdom. While there are some references to Lithuania and Belarus, in particular regarding the development of the hasidic movement, he does not deal with the Galician or Great Polish dimension of the Polish Jewish legacy of the early modern period, thus significantly reducing the scope of his analysis. The description of the nineteenth century and the most recent past focuses on political rather than on intellectual and religious aspects; in addition, Frenk attaches importance to the development of economic conditions. He excludes, doubtless because of censorship, a description of the repressive dimension of domestic policy in the late tsarist era. Yet he does not in any way gloss over the situation. Frenk is candid, and the significant role of the co-operatives in the inter-ethnic struggle for influence and as a basic dimension of antisemitic policy was seldom so clearly spelled out in that era. His narrative is always anchored in contemporary reality, and his effort to relate political developments to the personal horizon of his readership's experience is clearly manifest. At the same time, he avoids ideological commitments, whether religious or political, but sees Polish Jewry as a historical and political entity, to which he wishes to provide an awareness of its historical roots by means of a comprehensive historical narrative.[43]

The source material for this monograph was clearly the most recent academic literature. Frenk held the communal structure, the development of the regional assemblies, and the comprehensive legal autonomy of Polish Jewry in high regard. He undoubtedly derived his views from insights in works by Schorr, Dubnow, Zbigniew Pazdro, and others. But by this juncture, Frenk had also gathered and evaluated a large body of documentation by himself, and integrated it into his research.[44] This becomes clear in his descriptions of the community life of Jews in Poland in the seventeenth and eighteenth centuries, a sketch that synthesizes contemporary research at a high level of scholarship. Here he includes extensive source materials of his own, in addition to the available literature. Frenk also, as mentioned above, took part in the ambitious project to compile a multi-volume world history of the Jewish people from an east European perspective. This was a project to which almost all leading west European Jewish historians of that time contributed, but it was interrupted by the Great War.[45]

Immediately after the war, Frenk published a second monograph, whose central argument reads like a contemporary commentary on the situation of Polish Jewry in the newly restored Polish state. In *Ha'ironim vehayehudim bepolin* ('The

---

[43] If we consider this monograph and the writings of other historians from before the First World War, such as Bałaban and Schorr, Samuel Kassow's claim that 'the field [of Polish Jewish history] had already begun but was still largely uncharted territory' seems at least debatable: see Kassow, *Who Will Write Our History?*, 52.

[44] On this, see M. Dold, '"Eine Frage der nationalen und staatsbürgerlichen Ehre...": Mayer Bałaban und die jüdische Wissenschaft in Warschau', in M. Dmitrieva and H. Petersen (eds.), *Jüdische Kultur(en) im Neuen Europa* (Leipzig, 2004), 180–97, *passim*; and Guesnet, 'Geschichte im Kontext', 136–9. Frenk's own works on Polish Jewish history that were based on archival and other source materials and equipped with a scholarly apparatus, and that were already in print by this time, included in particular articles which had appeared in various periodicals, such as the short essay on the era of reform in the Noblemen's Republic: 'Di "yidnfrage" in poyln in ponyatovskis tsaytn', *Hoyz-fraynd*, 5 (1908), 165–75, and 'Letoldot haḥazakah'. Unfortunately, the latter was not available to me at the time of this writing.   [45] Frenk, 'Vnutrennii byt evreev v Pol'she i Litve'.

Burghers and the Jews in Poland'), published in Warsaw in 1921 in Hebrew, Frenk focuses on the lines of conflict between the Jews and Christian burghers, calling his monograph a 'historical narrative'.[46] On the basis of scholarly literature in Polish, the records of the *kahal* of Opatów mentioned earlier, and rabbinical responsa (*she'elot uteshuvot*), Frenk describes the conflict between Christian and Jewish town-dwellers as a leitmotif of Jewish and non-Jewish urban cohabitation in the Middle Ages and the early modern era. This conflict had emerged with the rise of economic competition between Christian and Jewish merchants in the first period of their settlement in medieval Poland. The conflict was contained by a range of royal privileges and legislation, but was also manifested in religious hatred (3–7). Here the intermediate position of the Jews between the nobility and the burghers was an important factor. Frenk viewed the non-Jewish legislation and the Jewish communal statutes, such as the Kraków Communal Regulations,[47] with their rules on modest behaviour in public, as a reaction to this tension (7–13). His description makes it clear that the differing interests of the nobility and the burghers turned the latter into opponents of the Jews when it came to legal status (35–39). Using the example of the Opatów community, Frenk describes the complex relationship between the noble owner of the town and the Jewish residents: the financial interests of the owner on the one hand, and the need for protection among the Jews on the other. These circumstances placed the owner in a highly advantageous position, forcing the community to provide additional regular 'gifts' to the proprietor over and above agreed-upon levies and taxes (44).[48]

Frenk illustrates the scope of autonomy of Jewish communities by means of the Ordinances of the Town of Łask, issued by Count Teofil Załuski in 1790, and argues that they facilitated oppression of the lower strata of the Jewish population by the community board (58–62, and appendix 1, 137–42). The subsequent description concentrates increasingly on the situation of the Jews in Warsaw, in particular their efforts to revoke the banishment of 1527. In this context, Frenk points once again to the great importance of Jewish co-operation with the nobility, within the framework of which Jewish businessmen were permitted to stay in the *jurydyki*, the noble enclaves in the Polish capital (68–72). The final part of the exposition deals with the debates on reform for the Jews in the Four Year Sejm (Sejm Czteroletni, 1788–92), the partitions of Poland, the quashing of the Kościuszko uprising, and the establishment of Russian rule over Warsaw and Poland. Specifically in his concluding chapters, Frenk stresses the great importance of

[46] Subsequent page references to this work are given in the text in parentheses.

[47] For his descriptions of the situation in Kraków, Frenk cited the works of Majer Bałaban, e.g. at *Ha'ironim vehayehudim bepolin*, 21, and used the collection of source materials published by M. Bersohn, *Dyplomataryusz dotyczący Żydów w dawnej Polsce na źródłach archiwalnych osnuty (1388–1782)* (Warsaw, 1910).

[48] This same Opatów record book is also the documentary basis of a study published seventy years later: G. D. Hundert, *The Jews in a Polish Private Town: The Case of Opatów in the Eighteenth Century* (Baltimore, 1992).

political efforts by Polish Jews to better their legal situation, and here he deals in detail with the institution of *shtadlanut* practised in this connection. His focus is thus on the political strategies of Jews and their options for articulating and in part advancing their own interests (122–3).[49] At the same time, he emphasizes their readiness, in a time of national danger—the Kościuszko uprising—to fight for the freedom of Warsaw and the Polish Commonwealth. Here Frenk reiterates a veritable topos of Polish Jewish history, yet supplements it with the romantic observation that it was specifically the ordinary Jewish masses who supported Polish independence (129).

Frenk demonstrated his strong interest in difficult topics in Polish Jewish history by writing a series of articles on conversion to Christianity. These appeared initially in *Hatsefirah* in Hebrew and then as a monograph in Yiddish, entitled *Meshumodim in poyln in 19tn yorhundert* ('Converts in Poland in the Nineteenth Century').[50] Frenk prefaces a description of three spectacular conversions of prominent Jews with a short summary of the broader conditions which at the beginning of the nineteenth century were responsible for a clear rise in the number of conversions, though the numbers remained comparatively small. At the end of the eighteenth century there had been only isolated instances, such as that of the false messiah Jacob Frank (6), but changes in the relations between, in particular, the nobility and Jewish middlemen led to a rise in the numbers of conversions in the nineteenth century. Up to that time, converts had been considered 'scum who bathed in Jewish blood', since they vilified Jews, received gifts from their new fellow Christians for this slander, and were in some cases elevated to the nobility (12). In the nineteenth century, however, Jews faced a new, sustained process of displacement from a central sphere of their gainful employment—the production and distribution of alcohol. This was in the hands of the nobility, who through the partition of Poland had been stripped of their status and sources of income (16–20).[51] Now the members of an educated Jewish elite successful in business and influenced by the Enlightenment chose the path of conversion to advance their careers and rise in society. Frenk substantiated this basic thesis with concrete examples, such as that of the banker Samuel Frankel (1773–1833), who relocated in 1798 from Breslau to Warsaw, under Prussian rule since 1796, in order to build up a banking house. He succeeded in this endeavour by relying on close co-operation with the Jewish business elite and through marriage to Atalia Zbytkower (1776–1850), a daughter of the leading Jewish entrepreneur of the day in Warsaw, Shmuel

[49] See F. Guesnet, 'Politik der Vormoderne — Shtadlanut am Vorabend der polnischen Teilungen', *Yearbook of the Simon Dubnow Institute*, 1 (2002), 235–55.

[50] Subsequent page references to this work are given in the text in parentheses. On this topic, see T. Endelman, 'Jewish Converts in Nineteenth-Century Warsaw: A Quantitative Analysis', *Jewish Social Studies*, 4, no. 1 (1997), 28–59.

[51] On this complex, see J. Hensel, 'Polnische Adelsnation und jüdische Vermittler, 1815–1830: Über den vergeblichen Versuch einer Judenemanzipation in einer nicht emanzipierten Gesellschaft', *Forschungen zur osteuropäischen Geschichte*, 23 (1983), 7–227.

Zbytkower (d. 1801; p. 21). Interesting in Frenk's description is his decidedly negative evaluation of German Jewish migrants to Warsaw, among them the third wife
of Zbytkower, Judita Jakubowiczowa (1749–1829), whom he describes as a spouse
devoid of conscience or principles who brutally oppressed her hasidic husband (25,
32). While Frankel distanced himself totally from the Jewish community after his
baptism, Frenk noted a strong tendency among Frankel's children (and those of
other converts) to marry the offspring of other converted families (36–7). The second example is provided by a follower of the Jewish Haskalah and secretary of the
Jewish Committee (Komitet Starozakonnych) set up in 1825, Stanisław Ezechiel
Hoge (1791–1860), whose role in the struggle against hasidism was of special interest to Frenk (72–9).[52] The last example concerns the case of one of the most successful Polish entrepreneurs of the nineteenth century, Leopold Kronenberg
(1812–78, converted 1846), whose great importance for economic innovation in
Congress Poland, intensive co-operation with Jewish businessmen, and relatively
responsible attitudes about social policy made it difficult to evaluate him in a purely
negative light. Frenk sums up Kronenberg's conservative political engagement,
as a result of which Kronenberg chose not to support a resolute struggle against
antisemitism:

Kronenberg never openly opposed antisemitism. But he didn't need to. His very existence
and activity kept the Jew-haters in check. In practical terms, he controlled all the economic
and financial institutions in the country . . . For many, he embodied the proof of just
how useful Jews could be for the country—because all his life, Kronenberg was seen as a
Jew. (136)

In his many-faceted descriptions of three cases of successful converts contributing positively in various spheres of social life, Frenk undoubtedly undercut popular notions of their depravity. But because of his position and his close ties with
kelal yisra'el, Frenk's description here ran little danger of being misinterpreted as a
veiled plea for conversion. He offered a description of Polish Jewish history in the
nineteenth century that was aware of the problem, and rejected simplistic answers
and interpretations. It was a presentation marked by a strong, independent sense of
judgement.

CONCLUSION

With his copious research as a historian, Ezriel Natan Frenk avoided being placed
in the context of the great political and ideological narratives of his era. Despite his
obvious support for the revitalization of Hebrew as the language of a new Jewish
renaissance, it would be going too far to associate him with cultural Zionism.
Frenk's patriotism was committed to *kelal yisra'el* in the form in which it had

---

[52] See M. Wodziński, *Haskalah and Hasidism in the Kingdom of Poland: A History of Conflict*, trans.
S. Cozens (Oxford, 2005), 83–8; and the notes in G. Dynner, 'Pogranicza Haskali', *Kwartalnik Historii
Żydów*, 222 (2007), 239.

crystallized over the centuries in conflict and co-operation in the Polish Common-wealth. Unmistakable is the pride he felt in the political and cultural achievements of Polish Jewry in the early modern period. Also clear is his respect for historical Poland, which provided the framework, shaped by religious and political tolerance, within which this singular community had evolved. Nonetheless, he was blind neither to the social and cultural divide between Jews and Poles, nor to the antag-onisms within Polish Jewry. On both accounts, Frenk's attitude was highly origi-nal. He acknowledged the exceptional degree of Jewish autonomy in the Polish Commonwealth, but did not refrain from emphasizing the long struggles of Jewish communities to maintain it, often against Christian resistance. Did he conceive of his task as a historian as the building of bridges to Polish culture, as, if we accept the assumption of Samuel Kassow, the leading historians of the inter-war period would do?[53] Certainly, in the sense that Frenk conveyed an exceptionally strong claim for the special relationship of the Polish Commonwealth to Jewish history. Also, the fact that Frenk translated so many Polish literary works into Yiddish and Hebrew is a relevant indicator of his vision of the relationship between Jews and their Polish neighbours. He clearly hoped to enhance mutual understanding, and thus allow for more than uncomprehending cohabitation. Nevertheless, his ideal remained a self-conscious, proud, and visible Polish Jewish community. His understanding of this community was one of great diversity. In contrast to many other historians of his epoch, he explored in analytical depth the social, political, and religious fault lines within Polish Jewry. It is evident that he felt a close bond with vernacular forms of expression of hasidic piety and hasidic community life. His efforts over decades to document and specify the characteristics of this culture represent possibly his most important—and to date little-recognized—achievement. Bound up to such a degree with vernacular forms of Polish Jewish folk culture, he felt unable to embrace a Reform-oriented variant of Jewish cul-ture, or one geared centrally to acculturation. The dire situation of Jewish artisans and workers echoes through a series of his works, though he did not reduce these human beings to mere variables in some predestined course of history, as in a Marxist reading of history. Likewise, in his biographical studies on conversion, he investigated the individual dimension in the crossing of borderlines between Jewish and Christian society, and which factors enhanced or reduced the perme-ability of these separate cultures. In his resolute avoidance of non-Jewish lan-guages for his publications, one can also see how he felt beholden to a Polish Jewry deeply aware of its past. At a happy remove, he looked on at the futility of both the specific exertions and the ideological constructions of the assimilationists, whose failure he describes with a certain touch of schadenfreude. Was this position in keeping with some tacit desire on his part for Jews to remain isolated from Polish society? In Frenk's case, such an assessment would certainly be short-sighted. His extensive work as a translator into Yiddish and Hebrew by itself stands out as a

[53] Kassow, *Who Will Write Our History?*, 50.

clear indicator of his readiness to translate literary works, in particular, from the surrounding society, rendering them accessible to Jews who were not proficient in literary Polish.

However, there are no indications that Frenk endeavoured in any appreciable way to make the Polish- or Russian speaking environment more familiar with Jewish legends, literature, or history. Quite clearly, he did not regard this as his task. Rather, it may be suspected that, in his numerous translations, he was concerned with fostering greater Jewish participation in Polish culture. This transfer of culture exclusively in one direction corresponds neither to any intention of isolation on his part nor to an impetus for a comprehensive transparency of cultures, with a high degree of permeability between their contiguous membranes. To some extent, he sought what may be termed a 'semi-permeable' or 'selectively permeable' boundary between the Jewish and Polish worlds.

Moreover, Frenk most certainly cannot be classified within the Rankean tradition of historical science. Only a few of his works fulfil the exacting criterion that is a core element of scientific description, namely the detailed documentation of facts and insights as a foundation for a specific argumentation. One notable modern exception is his description of the conflict between Christian and Jewish burghers, highly fascinating as a study in socio-historical terms. However, Frenk generally appeared as a kind of fatherly storyteller—one whom his readers, for better or worse, had to trust. It is not surprising that this approach, precisely at the time of the first major flowering of historiography in Poland in the inter-war period, was subjected to harsh critique by younger historians such as Jakub Szacki.[54] To a greater extent perhaps than most other authors of his era, Frenk valued the dimension of Jewish political action and the concrete ability to act—and in this he is possibly comparable only to antisemitic authors on the other side. To that extent, his creativity also represents an apotheosis of east European Jewry, itself highly differentiated in political terms. It is hardly conceivable outside the context of a metropolis like Warsaw, which offered an array of different political, religious, and cultural options. It appears that Frenk underestimated the obligation of loyalty within the political movements unfolding at the time. This might explain why they withheld their recognition from him, despite his self-sacrificing activity and engagement. But the fact that Frenk is today almost completely forgotten is attributable above all to one overriding factor within the historical sciences: the strong tendency of the subsequent generation of scholars to dissociate themselves from his approach; members of this later group were more beholden to strict scientific standards, and were unwilling to accept him as their predecessor. This article, which is unable to close the numerous gaps in knowledge and documentation that

---

[54] It would be far too short-sighted to reduce Frenk's historiographical relevance to that of a 'resource' for finding documents and source materials that have been lost to posterity as a result of the destruction of archives during the Second World War. See e.g. Niger and Shatzky (eds.), *Leksikon fun der nayer yidisher literatur*, viii. 520.

still confront us, is intended to point out the importance of this singular and fascinating figure in Polish Jewish historiography.

Translated from the German by Bill Templer

S. A. An-sky—Dialogic Writer

BRIAN HOROWITZ

IN HIS FICTION An-sky inscribes the 'other'. However, rather than treating non-Jews, Russians, or Ukrainians, An-sky devotes most of his fiction to depicting fellow Jews. In his world Jews are multifarious. Portraying the religious and the secular, revolutionaries and nationalists, young and old, rich and poor, women, men, children, and even their animals, An-sky emphasizes Jewish diversity. The key feature of An-sky's fiction is its 'dialogic' character. Refraining from imposing his world view, he gives his protagonists opportunities to present their vision of the world. Although such views often contradict the author's own position, An-sky is committed to a faithful depiction of the 'other' among Jews themselves.

*

In the final sentence of his ground-breaking introduction to a collection of An-sky's stories in English translation, David Roskies expresses this evaluation: 'It would have pleased him to know that besides the riveting—and downright inspirational—story of his life, he had also left behind a literary legacy of varied and formidable proportions.'[1] However, apart from Roskies's own essay on An-sky's life and a few articles written primarily in An-sky's own time, there have been only a handful of serious studies of his 'formidable' literary legacy.[2] Since he wrote over fifteen stories, a novel, and two novellas in a career that spanned more than three decades, it is no exaggeration to assert that An-sky the creative writer deserves more critical attention.

The lack of interest in An-sky's fiction can be explained in part by the fact that, from his multifaceted career, scholars have concentrated on the 'usable past', i.e.

---

[1] D. Roskies, 'Introduction', in S. Ansky, *The Dybbuk and Other Writings*, ed. D. Roskies (New York, 1992), p. xxxvi.

[2] The studies that I allude to are M. Krutikov, 'The Russian Jew as a Modern Hero: Identity Construction in An-sky's Writings'; G. Safran, 'An-sky in 1892: The Jew and the Petersburg Myth'; and my own 'Spiritual and Physical Strength in An-sky's Literary Imagination'. All three articles are to be found in G. Safran and S. J. Zipperstein (eds.), *The Worlds of S. An-sky: A Russian Jewish Intellectual at the Turn of the Century* (Palo Alto, Calif., 2007), 119–36, 53–82, and 103–18, respectively. For an illuminating new biography of An-sky, see G. Safran, *Wandering Soul: The Dybbuk's Creator, S. An-sky* (Cambridge, Mass., 2010).

those aspects that can be adapted to enhance or rebuild modern Jewry.[3] First of all, his ethnographical efforts have interested scholars, while his famous play, *The Dybbuk*, has gained wide renown in part as a medium for recovering memories about the *shtetl* for contemporary audiences. Even his biography (at least, as it has been interpreted by David Roskies)—the story of an Orthodox Jew who became a cosmopolitan revolutionary, but 'returned'—has caught the attention of those who want to find in the past a model of a cultural *ba'al teshuvah*, a prodigal son who reunites with his people.[4]

We have not found an equivalent interest in his fiction, by far the greater part of which was originally written in Russian. Perhaps one can blame An-sky himself. It is hard to imagine who today would identify with the subjects of his stories. In the 1890s he described self-loathing Jews, revolutionaries attacking Orthodox Jewry, and impoverished Jewish tutors and teachers who naively hoped for a world without discrimination. Not only do these figures and problems not resonate well today, but they seem time-bound to the crisis years of late tsarist Russia.

But perhaps scholarly indifference to his fiction may have another cause, the low status of Russian Jewish literature. Before the revolutions of 1917, Russian Jewish literature—literature written by and about Jews in the Russian language—was considered inferior in quality. In fact, Russian Jewish literature was supposed to disappear. Its critics predicted that its writers would ultimately either fully join Russian literature or adopt the Yiddish and Hebrew languages.[5] In fact at the end of the nineteenth century Russian Jewish literature was thought of as existing only as a political mouthpiece to describe Jewish life in order to win the sympathy of non-Jews for the cause of Jewish liberation.[6] An-sky was assigned a place in a group that included such writers as David Aizman, Semen Yushkevich, and Rashel Khin. Together they were classified as *bytopisateli*, observers of daily life.[7]

It seems possible now to dispute some of these claims about Russian Jewish fiction (in particular that this literature has little aesthetic value). I want to reclaim An-sky's reputation largely because his creative writing repudiates the political function. It is occupied less with eliciting sympathy and more with revealing the diversity of and conflict in Jewish life during the last quarter of the nineteenth century. Furthermore, his fiction helps us understand An-sky's intellectual development. While he may not be a genius on the level of Osip Mandelshtam or Isaac

---

[3] See D. G. Roskies, *The Jewish Search for a Usable Past* (Bloomington, Ind., 1999), esp. ch. 1.

[4] See 'S. Ansky (1863–1920): Poet, Ethnographer, Dramatist, Social Activist', *Jewish Heritage Online Magazine*, <http://jhom.com/personalities/ansky/index.htm>, accessed 5 Nov. 2009.

[5] A salient expression of this view can be found in S. Chernikhovsky's entry on Russian Jewish literature, 'Russko-evreiskaya khudozhestvennaya literatura', in *Evreiskaya entsiklopediya: Svod znanii o evreistve i ego kul'ture v proshlom i nastoyashchem*, 16 vols. (St Petersburg, 1907–13), xiii. 641–2.

[6] V. Lvov-Rogachevsky, *A History of Russian Jewish Literature*, ed. and trans. A. Levin (Ann Arbor, 1979), 113.

[7] E. Bronshtein, 'Bytopisateli evreiskoi massy (S. A. An-skii)', *Knizhki Voskhoda*, 1905, no. 10, pp. 105–29.

Babel, his dialogic approach gives us inimitable depictions of Jews in specific times and places.

*

An-sky's stories feature the 'dialogic' method made famous by Mikhail Bakhtin in his analysis of Dostoevsky's novels. According to Bakhtin,

The plurality of independent and unmerged voices and consciousnesses and the genuine polyphony of full-valued voices are in fact characteristics of Dostoevsky's novels. It is not a multitude of characters and fates within a unified objective world, illuminated by the author's unified consciousness that unfolds in his works, but precisely the plurality of equal consciousnesses and their worlds, which are combined here into the unity of a given event, while at the same time retaining the unmergedness. In the author's creative plan, Dostoevsky's principal heroes are indeed not only objects of the author's word, but subjects of their own directly significant word [*neposredstvenno znachashchee slovo*] as well. Therefore the hero's word is here by no means limited to its usual functions of characterization and plot development, but neither does it serve as the expression of the author's own ideological position (as in Byron, for example).[8]

An-sky's fictional writing reveals the kind of polyphony described above. In his stories and novels he gives individual characters distinct voices and ideological independence. He presents ideas that diverge from or even contradict his own views. Since the author identifies with more than one character or viewpoint, many of his stories, plays, and novels conclude on a note of indeterminacy, leaving tensions unresolved.

Undoubtedly this assertion might strike one as curious. After all, if An-sky was known for anything at all, it was for his strong opinions. When he advocated socialism, he was a passionate advocate; as a representative of Jewish nationalism you could hardly find a more dedicated zealot. The same can be said for his advocacy of assimilation, pacifism, hasidism, and Zionism.[9] How then, one might ask, could An-sky be a dialogic writer when he represented ideological preferences? Looking at his ideological affinities, however, one cannot deny his contradictions. A dedicated revolutionary, he also supported Simon Dubnow's Folkspartey, and later Zionism, which rejected revolutionary struggle. It was in his fiction, however, that he gave full voice to ideological diversity, refraining from offering a final pronouncement on any of the big ideas. Fiction provided the space where he could try out, weigh, and compare ideas.

I separate An-sky's œuvre into three periods: an early period in Russia when he began writing short stories, a middle period in the emigration, which is characterized by the use of longer genres, such as the novella and novel, and a final period when he returned to Russia and published the novella *In a New Way* (*V novom rusle*). By 1906, he had stopped writing fiction, concentrating instead on the study

[8] M. Bakhtin, *Problems of Dostoevsky's Poetics*, trans. R. W. Rotsel (Ann Arbor, 1973), 4.

[9] See Horowitz, 'Spiritual and Physical Strength in An-sky's Literary Imagination'.

of Jewish ethnography, leading the first Jewish Ethnographic Expedition (1912). This chronological framework is useful for illuminating the close relationship between his biography and the larger historical context.

*

An-sky was born as Shloyme-Zanvl Rappoport in Vitebsk province (now in Belarus) in 1863, and as a young man he embraced the change that affected many Jewish youths at the time. A description of him is found in the memoirs of Hayim Zhitlowski, the socialist and spokesman for Jewish territorialism, who was his childhood friend. Zhitlowski recounts that the two did not feel anger or prejudice towards the Jewish religion, but expressed enthusiasm for a new cosmopolitanism that was then just coming to life:

> For us (An-sky and me) there was no contrast, such as Jewish and non-Jewish, but a contrast between 'old' people, ideas, ways of thinking and living and 'new' people with new ideas, new strengths, and a striving to higher, more noble, more conscious ways of life. In this regard, there was no difference between Jew and non-Jew. School and *ḥeder* were equally cast away, synagogue and church equally hated, [Dmitry] Pisarev and [Moses Leib] Lilienblum equally beloved and cherished, because both stormed the old fortress with revolutionary drive.[10]

After a period as a tutor of Jewish children in Liozno in Belarus, An-sky fled to the south of Russia, to Ekaterinoslav in the Ukraine's Donbass–Dnieper mining region, himself becoming a miner.[11] The movement in space was paralleled by an ideological shift. He accepted as an uncompromising moral truth that the intelligentsia owed a debt to the lower classes, agreeing too with the idea, as articulated by Petr Lavrov (with its romantic overtones), that the individual was the decisive agent of history.[12] Despite close contact with the Jewish Bund, An-sky rejected the economic determinism characteristic of the Marxism that was a part of the Bund's ideology.

These political ideas clearly shaped An-sky's early attempts at fiction writing. His first published story, 'A Family History' ('Istoriya odnogo semeistva'; 1884), is a good example.[13] Describing a poor family of four daughters, the author inter-

---

[10] Dr H. Zhitlowski, *Zikhroynes fun mayn lebn*, i (New York, 1935), 18. Here and throughout, translations are mine unless noted otherwise.

[11] G. Safran, 'Timeline: Semyon Akimovich An-sky/Shloyme-Zanvl Rappoport', in Safran and Zipperstein (eds.), *Worlds of S. An-sky*, p. xvii.

[12] J. P. Scanlan, 'Introduction', in P. L. Lavrov, *Historical Letters*, ed. and trans. J. P. Scanlan (Berkeley, 1967), 10–12.

[13] Although most critics consider 'A Family History' to be An-sky's first published story, there are good reasons not to accept this claim and to categorize it as a piece of juvenilia, despite the fact that it appeared in *Voskhod*, 1884, nos. 9–12, the leading Jewish journal in Russia and at this time the only one published in Russian. One should also know that the story was originally written in Russian and translated by An-sky himself into Yiddish for possible publication in a Yiddish journal. While the

weaves the plot lines to depict the hopelessness of life for the poor and powerless. One tells about Chiena, who, having become a maid, was raped by her employer. She wants to turn to prostitution, but even that fails when she discovers that she has become pregnant. Another sister, Sora, loses everything when a wall falls on her husband in the workplace, leaving her without a breadwinner. As a result, she becomes a wet nurse for a wealthy family, while her son is undernourished.[14] The injustice of the situation is deepened by the fact that her husband's employer refuses to provide a pension, although he knew about the risk posed by the wall.

The description of the dreary town and of the family's poverty is conventional in Haskalah literature. What makes An-sky's treatment different is that, in contrast to maskilim who satirized the situation, An-sky introduces a strong class consciousness, accusing the wealthy of persecuting the poor.[15] In his treatment of poverty and hopelessness one can notice the influence of Russian authors of the time, such as Nikolay Nekrasov, Vsevolod Krestovsky, and Gleb Uspensky.

In 'At the Auction (a Tale)' ('Na torgakh (rasskaz)'), written in my view shortly before 1890, An-sky protrays what is conventionally called 'Jewish self-hate'.[16] The story takes place in a nondescript village inn the night before a local auction of sheep, and then during the auction. Using their monopoly power to set the price, Jewish traders agree among themselves, paying off anyone who would dare to undercut them. Although the peasants realize that they have been cheated, they are unable to interfere. However, when leaving the town, the Jews are pelted with rocks. The story ends with two traders admitting that the peasants had the right to take revenge.

By portraying the Jewish merchants in this way, An-sky upholds the view that Jews exploit the peasantry. Although such an image buttressed the claims of anti-semites, it was typical of radical writers to revile Jewish businessmen. Nonetheless, it is striking that the story's message concurs with the spirit of the government's so-called May Laws of 1882, which had the intention of removing Jews from the countryside to protect the peasantry.

At about the same time as 'At the Auction' was written, An-sky began 'Mendel Turk' ('Mendl-Turok').[17] In this story An-sky shifted his narrative mode, offering

---

manuscript was passing back and forth, an unknown person sent it to *Voskhod*, where it was retranslated into Russian from the Yiddish and then published anonymously. An-sky himself did not know that it had been published until some time after it appeared.

[14] S. An-sky, 'Istoriya odnogo semeistva', *Voskhod*, 1884, no. 9, p. 126.   [15] Ibid. 132.

[16] Although it is difficult to trace any publication of 'Na torgakh' earlier than that in S. An-sky, *Sobranie sochinenii*, 5 vols. (St Petersburg, 1909–11), v. 103–64, it is my belief that it was written earlier. I base my view on the stylistics (language, literary conventions), theme, and treatment.

[17] Although there was a manuscript version of the story already written in 1892, it was published only in 1902. Gabriella Safran has written about the early version: 'In the 1892 manuscript version of the story, the narrator runs into Mendel 10 years later, after both of them have immigrated to Paris. Although at first Mendel is appalled by what seems to him the degeneracy of Parisian life (he especially dislikes the bare-breasted statue symbolizing the French republic at the Place de la République), he quickly reconciles himself to his new surroundings, takes a job in a factory, and begins to learn French.

a positive image of Jews. Placing the story in an unspecified town in Belarus during the Russo-Turkish War (1878–80), the narrative focuses on Mendel, a hasidic schoolteacher, who assures everyone that the Turks will win, despite the overwhelming evidence to the contrary. Although the story seems to mock hasidism, since Mendel's convictions are shown to have no basis in reality, An-sky treats Mendel with sympathy. The first-person narrator, a maskil who resembles An-sky himself, gives this initial description of Mendel:

For some reason I pictured him as a beastly-looking old man. Actually, he turned out to be young, 27–28 years old, tall and thin with fine features and a small sharp beard. Deep, large black eyes and sharp furrows on his forehead gave his face a particularly serious expression. A velvet yarmulke and fine peyes curled in a spiral that fell from his ears provided, as it were, a suitable frame for his face.[18]

Besides registering an attraction towards Mendel, the narrator also expresses sympathy for the hasidic way of life. He feels nostalgia for the traditions that he once experienced. On his way to the local synagogue to see for himself how the hasidim debate politics, the narrator recalls his own childhood:

Mincha was over. Part of the congregation hurried home to finish the obligatory third sabbath meal and quickly return to synagogue. Others remained. They, quiet and satisfied, walked in deep meditation, up and down the synagogue, holding their hands behind their backs and softly singing a tune . . . The congregation dreamt. Everyone's mood was soft and sublime. The tavern, the shop, business affairs large and small—now all this flew off somewhere far away. In various corners a Jewish tune could be heard, not too loudly, and sporadically, 'Bim-bam-bam', into which each injected his own dream . . . Now someone was astute enough to ask, and even beg, Borekh or Zarekh, who was a famous singer in our synagogue:
'Zarekh! "Say" something!'
Zarekh did not need to be asked twice. Staying where he was, he began to sing a 'piece' from the Rosh Hashanah or Yom Kippur prayers, at first softly and then more and more loudly. Gradually others began to join in and everyone started singing. And for a long, long time beneath the high arches of the synagogue that were lost in darkness there resounded synagogue singing that was at times indistinct, at times victorious, and at times infinitely despairing.[19]

The sentiments of the narrator clearly parallel An-sky's own perspective in his

Within a year and a half, he has become fluent in French and stays up nights reading Marx, Lassalle, and Proudhon; a couple of years later, the narrator finds out that Mendel has moved to London and become a labor organizer and an admired orator. This ending reveals the author's faith in the radical ideals of self-transformation. All it takes is removal from the shtetl and a thorough immersion in radical theory for Mendel to become a different person, one who stands tall and commands the respect of a crowd. The narrator recognizes that Mendel has suffered to remake himself, but he has succeeded. The shtetl Mendel "the Turk", who saw no reason why he should identify with Russians, has taken up the cause of the international worker. In its published form, the story carries no such clear ideological message': Safran, 'An-sky in 1892', 75.

[18] S. An-sky, 'Mendl-Turok', in *Sobranie sochinenii*, i. 17.   [19] Ibid. 31.

memoirs, where he expresses nostalgia for the emotional warmth of the Orthodox Jewish milieu abandoned long before.[20]

In a display of honesty, An-sky has the hasid Mendel express the reasons why he cannot interact socially with non-Jews. Instead of blaming religious differences, Mendel attributes the cleft between himself and his Russian neighbours purely to social antipathy. His acute evaluation entirely contradicts the image of a hasid as largely ignorant of external society:

'What could be the connection between me and them? I mean in general, setting aside the fact that I am a Jew and they are Christians . . . Well, let me give you an example, one that is not abstract at all, you yourself . . . I think you won't be offended by my frankness. To tell you the truth, I look at you as . . . a goy. A Jew who shaves, eats *treyf*, openly breaks the sabbath laws, what is there to say!—this Jew is already not a Jew! Nonetheless, I have some connection with you, I can talk to you, I understand you and you understand me. Why? Because you also have a spiritual life. Whether it is the same or different, whether it is true or false—the point is that you have one. Well, what kind of connection can I have with "them"? "With whom?", I ask you. With the *muzhik* whose life begins in the pigsty and ends in the tavern? Or with the aristocrats who do not know anything and do not want to know more than a fine lunch, pretty clothing, and—excuse me—a lovely *nekevah*, a female? My God, they are as foreign to me as that table over there!

'On the other hand', he went on, more slowly and with a light, ironic smile on his lips, 'on the other hand, I fully understand that "they" too cannot consider me an especially close relative. What kind of person am I, after all, if my name is Mendl and not Ivan, if I don't eat pork, and if I wear a long frock coat! Certainly I am worse than the worst!'[21]

Although at first glance the story appears to recount the awakening of provincial Jews to modern politics either as a parody or perhaps in a pseudo-documentary mode, by the end we realize that we have been shown a hasid's inner psychology. An-sky gives full voice and ideological independence to Mendl, permitting him to defend his views and therefore win the reader's sympathy. Although Mendl's self-conscious candidness seems unrealistic (would a hasid open up to a maskil?), one cannot help noticing the absence of authorial criticism of the hasidim. In fact, the lack of disparaging comments jars with the conventional maskilic treatment of the hasidism and in An-sky's case contradicts his own experience. After all, An-sky was forced to leave Vitebsk and later Liozna by religious Jews who accused him of apostasy and threatened him with forced military service.[22]

---

[20] An-sky's memoirs can be found in Yiddish as *Zikhroynes*, in Sh. An-sky, *Gezamlte shriftn*, 15 vols. (Vilna, Warsaw, and New York, 1920–), vols. x–xi; see also L. S. Dawidowicz (ed.), *The Golden Tradition: Jewish Life and Thought in Eastern Europe* (Syracuse, NY, 1996), 306–11. In these memoirs he expresses his regard for *The Sins of Youth* (*Ḥatot ne'urim*), the influential autobiography in which Moses Leib Lilienblum, a committed maskil, describes his nostalgia for the Lithuanian religious community of his youth. See M. L. Lilienblum, *Ḥatot ne'urim* (Vienna, 1876).

[21] An-sky, 'Mendl-Turok', in *Sobranie sochinenii*, i. 47.

[22] An-sky, 'Zikhroynes', in *Gezamlte shriftn*, x. 18.

It should be noted that such positive treatment of religious Jews has to be recognized as the first of its kind in the Russian language. While Grigory Bogrov did describe religious Jews in *Zapiski russkogo evreya* (1871–3), as did Lev Levanda in a number of his stories, they were always shown as tragically flawed, perhaps even downright detrimental to the cause of enlightenment. Such political goals are foreign to this story.

In his story of 1900 'In a Jewish Family (a Sketch)' ('V evreiskoi sem´e (ocherk)'), An-sky again withheld criticism of religious Jews.[23] Treating a middle-class family, albeit one that is barely holding on to its petit-bourgeois position, he begins *in medias res* by describing a sabbath weekend. As it happens, Borekh, the father, is able this week to return home from his job in the logging industry. In addition, the cast features Leibka, Borekh's son; Malka, his wife and Leibka's mother; and Hana, Leibka's godmother who doubles as maid. We also encounter Ivan, a Russian servant; the local *melamed*; and even the family cat.

The story begins on a Thursday, which incidentally falls on a Rosh Hodesh sometime in early spring about a month before Passover. The narrator provides detail about how Jews prepare for the sabbath, explaining as if to those unacquainted with Jewish rituals (Russian readers?) the rules of what is not permitted on this day. He explains, for example, that a woman is not allowed to cut her nails on Thursdays, because the new nails would begin to grow on the sabbath. The female members of the family discuss at length which hen to slaughter now and which to save for Passover. With such details, An-sky gives us in Russian a rare anthropological portrait of a religiously observant Jewish family.

Although Borekh has a relatively well-paid job, we learn that the family is failing economically, since he is not paid regularly. Moreover, an earlier attempt to open a shop failed when a fire broke out, causing Borekh to lose his investment. Thus, despite the fact that they own their own house, Malka, his wife, has to borrow money for necessities. The question of how much money Borekh has brought home that weekend raises suspense in the first part of the story.

Its second part concerns the family's response to the *melamed*'s beating of Leibka, the son. Although at first the parents react angrily, they calm down when the teacher explains his reasons. However, a civil war breaks out when Hana, Leibka's adopted mother (the parents sold Leibka to Hana once when he was very ill, in order to fool the angel of death), refuses to forgive the teacher and demands that Leibka attend a different *ḥeder*. This part ends with Borekh and Malka threatening to fire Hana.

The next and last scene is short. On Saturday night, the loan shark visits Borekh and demands payment, 53 roubles, or he will pursue his case in court, which will force him to sell his home. The story ends with Borekh and Malka, unable to think of a way out, turning to Hana. 'All the family's hopes were turned to Hana, capable Hana. Hana can do it, Hana will save us.'[24]

---

[23] S. An-sky, 'V evreiskoi sem´e (ocherk)', *Russkoe bogatstvo*, 1900, no. 6, pp. 125–63.
[24] Ibid. 163.

Although An-sky retains a proper, conventional political perspective, condemning the loan shark and showing Hana, the representative of the working class, as the family's saviour, he nonetheless creates characters that have their own viewpoint. They express ideas that one can recognize as legitimate and justified, although they diverge from An-sky's own viewpoint. For example, An-sky gives the teacher an opportunity to exonerate himself of blame for beating Leibka:

'Sit down and listen carefully', replied the old man, more softly now. 'On Thursday it was Reysh-khoydesh. After lunch I let them out, but told them nonetheless to come back to the *heder* and silently study Gemara [Talmud]. I do not like it when children act silly. After lunch I felt like picking up the Zohar [a book of kabbalah] that I had left in the *heder*. I went to the *heder*. I approached the house and I heard noise coming from the yard. I immediately guessed that they were playing. I entered the room and saw that the books were lying open on the table, but no one was there. I set off for the yard and I heard them in the barn. I approached the barn, looked through a crack, and what do you think I saw?'

He leaned a bit towards Borekh, put his hand on his knee, and spoke slowly and expressively:

'My pupils were in the barn and a whole group of Christian boys were with them holding hands and dancing in a circle around an empty barrel on which a girl of 7 or 8 was lying and she was singing a Russian song . . . Well? What do you say about that? Should I have given them a pat on their heads?'[25]

Although in real life presumably An-sky would condemn the *melamed*, it is impossible to know his position from the story itself. The parents and grandmother take the *melamed*'s side, while Hana and Ivan remain adamant that a 'crime' has been committed. Ivan's commitment, however, is suspect, since the author tells us that he sided with Hana only because she gives him food. In fact, he was of the view that schools existed only 'to whip boys'.[26] Although one feels that Hana is right, one also understands that the *melamed* can justify his behaviour. According to the values of the community, the boys deserve a beating for playing with non-Jewish boys and dancing around a barrel; the scene implies eroticism and resembles the worshipping of the Golden Calf. For that crime in the Bible, one recalls, Moses had his enemies put to death.

It is remarkable that the reader confronts multiple points of view. Regarding the beating, the family's indebtedness, whether to fire Hana, and what to do about the loan shark, each character makes his own convincing case without, it seems, authorial interference or the author's clear identification with any single character.

Another surprise is that the author depicts traditional Jewish practice with sympathy and nostalgia. Although the context—the Russian language of the story and the appearance of footnotes to explain Jewish practices to non-Jews—leads one to think that the author is not a religious Jew, An-sky portrays Jewish rituals positively. In one scene Borekh returns with Leibka from synagogue on Friday night.

---

[25] Ibid. 149.   [26] Ibid. 152.

The author describes the scene: 'Borekh, pacing around the room, placed his hands behind him and began to hum the song "Sholem Aleichem", in which are greeted the "ministering angels, messengers of the Most High, of the Supreme King of Kings". Then he sang, but now in a different key, the song "Who can find a good wife? for she is more valuable than a pearl".'[27]

Although his creative writing at this time still reveals a political tendentiousness, An-sky not only gives individual characters viewpoints that diverge from his own, but convincingly serves as their mouthpiece so that the reader does not know exactly where the author stands.

*

In 1889, An-sky took up what he believed was an invitation from the writer Gleb Uspensky to come to St Petersburg.[28] Hired by *Russkoe bogatstvo*, the leading progressive journal in Russia, and of which Vladimir Korolenko and Nikolay Mikhailovsky were editors, An-sky was nonetheless unable to secure a legal permit to live in the city. According to Gabriella Safran, having been jailed once, An-sky grew weary of evading the police and sought to emigrate, in part to seek out his love, Masha Reines, Hayim Zhitlowski's cousin, who lived in Bern in Switzerland.[29] However, when he confessed his love, she rejected his advances. Having considered returning to Russia, he nevertheless continued on to Paris, where he worked at odd jobs, including bookbinding, before being hired as the personal secretary of Petr Lavrov, the famous radical philosopher and leader of the Russian socialists in emigration. Writing for socialist journals and giving talks in a number of European cities, An-sky struck up a friendship with the Socialist Revolutionary leader Viktor Chernov, who was planning to incite revolution in the Russian countryside. For his part, An-sky hoped to create a Jewish division in the Socialist Revolutionary Party as an alternative to the Bund.

In emigration, An-sky attempted longer genres, writing the novella *The First Crack: A Novella (from the 1870s) (Pervaya bresh': Povest' (iz epokhi 70-kh godov))*, and the novel *Pioneers (Pionery)*. In this period, he also wrote some of his finest short stories, including 'Behind a Mask' ('Pod maskoi') and 'Go and Talk to a Goy' ('Pogovorit' s goem').

It goes without saying that the early years of the twentieth century were tumultuous, especially for Jews in France. From the beginning of the Dreyfus trial in 1894, continuing with the endless controversies that erupted in response to Émile Zola's open letter to the president of France, *J'accuse*, and then the reversal of Dreyfus's conviction, there was clearly much to ponder. Moreover, the year 1897 was a watershed. The Bund announced its establishment as a political party and the Zionists, under the leadership of Theodor Herzl, held their first international congress. However, judging by An-sky's fiction one would hardly notice anything was occurring at all. Instead of dealing with these issues, An-sky returned to the

[27] An-sky, 'V evreiskoi sem'e (ocherk)', 140.   [28] Safran, 'An-sky in 1892', 57.
[29] Safran, 'Timeline', p. xix.

time of his youth in the 1870s and to a place that resembled Vitebsk, or perhaps a similar town in the Russian Pale of Settlement.

An-sky fixed his sights on this particular time and place in Jewish history because he believed that it held enormous significance as the pressure point between the old and new. In the 1870s, the resistance to religious Judaism as a way of life, which had earlier been practised by a small number of maskilim, took on enormous proportions. Literally thousands of young men and women left the faith and way of life of their parents. The result was an enormous change in Jewish society, one that had explosive consequences. In the introduction to *The First Crack*, An-sky writes:

It was at the end of the 1870s, that time when the Enlightenment movement captivated broad sections of the Jewish intelligentsia. It was a fantastic time, but in many ways a deeply tragic time too. A wide gap broke through the bedrock of the religious and cultural foundations of Judaism. A whole generation of intellectuals, having thrown off their religious chains, ran towards the light, to a new life. That burst of energy was not commensurate with the individual's strength or external conditions. The brave leap across a millennium cost Judaism dearly. This purely destructive movement placed what would seem to be the whole existence of Judaism on a single card, without replacing it with a new national creativity. It left behind an entire generation of crippled and mutilated people who had left one shore but not arrived at the other. But this burst of energy was also beautiful in its expanse. It was a forceful and bold burst of energy from a people who had awoken to political life.[30]

Pointing out that the radical insurgency paradoxically grew out of the institution that lay at the heart of the Jewish religion, the yeshiva, An-sky noted that boys there became acquainted with secular literature and Western ideas which led them beyond the borders of Jewish life, even to apostasy. In *The First Crack*, An-sky dealt with these issues, contrasting the main character, Itsikovich, who is depicted as weak-willed and dull, with the perception of his strength by the Jewish community:

The young people were on the teacher's side. The heartbeat of young girls speeded up. A fine, sweet dream carried them far away from the dirty marketplace, from the daily grind with its infinite grey background. In contrast, old women expressed the darkest suppositions about the teacher, frightening one another, sighing, despairingly shaking their heads and repeating in a whisper: 'The hour of the Messiah!' And in the evening during dinner in many homes the men were brought into the discussion, and together with dissatisfied exclamations and distressed sighs, phrases were uttered such as 'one has to do something!' . . . 'we cannot leave it as it is!' . . . 'we must speak with the rabbi!' and so on.[31]

The thin plot involves the competing influences on Itsikovich's decision about his future. On the one side, the local priest and government officials ask the teacher to convert to Russian Orthodox Christianity, offering blandishments such as entrance to a university and monetary rewards. When the Jewish community becomes aware of this tactic, the elders come to Itsikovich and promise him an

[30] S. An-sky, *Pervaya bresh´: Povest´ (iz epokhi 70-kh godov)*, in *Sobranie sochinenii*, ii. 18.
[31] Ibid. 37–8.

honoured place in the community, hinting at a very favourable marriage. For a few days Itsikovich walks in the village in the traditional caftan and is celebrated by the traditionalists. However, the victory does not last long, because Itsikovich disappears from the town entirely after permitting himself to be baptized. As in earlier stories, one cannot be certain where exactly the author stands vis-à-vis the plot or the main character.

In his story 'Behind a Mask', An-sky brilliantly exploited the dialogic approach. Recounting the lives of a group of fiery maskilim who 'starve' for the sake of the Haskalah, An-sky describes how they conceive of a plan to save their lives. Krants, the group's leader, should go to Bobiltseve and lie to Hillel's parents, telling them that their son is a star pupil in the yeshiva. If Krants succeeds, they reason, Hillel's parents will send money. At the same time Krants will find work in Bobiltseve as a tutor, earning an income and having opportunities to undercut the religious piety of his students. Although the plan works perfectly, Krants, having become used to freedom from religious ritual and work, becomes frustrated with his new situation and gradually lowers his guard, smoking on the sabbath and making blasphemous remarks. Hillel's mother, Krayne, grows suspicious and finally decides to take a trip to check on her son. In 'V' (Volozhin?) she discovers the truth. Returning to Bobiltseve, she confronts Krants. Prepared for the meeting, Krants counterattacks by threatening that if she harms him in any way, he will order Hillel to convert to Christianity. The next few days pass quietly, but a few days later, while Krants is packing to leave, Krayne comes to him and confesses to having planned to poison him. When Krants objects that she would have been sent to Siberia, Krayne merely laughs and tells him that no one would have cared about his death. In the end, Krayne's full-blown insanity and Krants's exit from the town occur simultaneously.

David Roskies is right that the story depicts the tragic consequences of the break in Jewish society in the 1870s for both the parents and the children. Morally the story reflects an antinomy. Neither character actually offers a positive model. Neither Krayne, the suspicious mother, nor her untalented husband who spends his days in Talmud study have answers for next generation. But at the same time, neither do the maskilim. Although the young boys dream of a new world of equality and justice, in fact they are slothful and ineffective; no one knows about or is affected by their existence. An-sky shows that at this time in Jewish history both generations were tragically isolated, antagonized, and incapable of compromise. Moreover, both were morally corrupt. Convinced that the justice of their cause gave them the right to use people as a means towards an end, both groups inflicted unnecessary harm on themselves most of all.

In his celebrated novel *Pioneers*, An-sky takes up the same milieu, portraying the young intellectuals who simultaneously embraced the Haskalah and Russian culture. In contrast to earlier works An-sky depicts the young men positively, emphasizing their optimism and the salutary effect of their actions on themselves and those around them. Treating once again a circle of young Jewish intellectuals who have flocked from small towns to the town of 'M', An-sky creates a novel of atmosphere, where action is subordinated to discussions about the big questions of Jewish life: what is the Haskalah? what will become of breaking from traditional Judaism? what kind of education is the best one for achieving integration? and how should one live—for oneself alone or for one's neighbour?

The intellectuals, in some cases boys of 15 or 16, live in a house on the outskirts of town, which is symbolic of their outsider status vis-à-vis the traditional community, but provides the central location of the action. They are depicted as serious about studying and acquiring knowledge that will permit them to take entrance exams to become externs at the university, and therefore to get their university diplomas. The young men are not cynical or angry, nor are they dispirited or listless. Led by Mirkin, who organizes the group for the members' mutual benefit (the more educated give lessons to the newcomers), the boys share their scant wealth by dividing up the tutoring, their primary source of income.

The novel is unique in that An-sky faithfully transmits the debates of the maskilim of the 1870s and 1880s. Having little patience for Judaism and the traditional way of life, the young men focus on debating whether the Haskalah is valuable or should be thrown over in favour of cosmopolitan individualism and full Russification. They argue about whether Dostoevsky and Pushkin are better than Peretz Smolenskin and Moses Leib Lilienblum, and whether one should keep kosher or not (as one boy says about eating pork, 'My mind allows it, but my heart doesn't'). An-sky also presents the views of the older generation of maskilim. One of the fathers encourages the boys to respect the Talmud:

You are perhaps smart and educated, but without knowledge of Talmud something is lacking . . . A person who studies Talmud has in addition to his five senses yet another that does not have a particular name, but is expressed in the sensitivity, vivaciousness, and subtlety of thought, in the speed of understanding . . . Just like many of your comrades, you do not have this sixth sense! . . . Everything you do comes out coarse somehow![32]

Allowing each character to present fully his own point of view, nonetheless An-sky lets the reader realize that the smartest individuals in the group value the idealism of Judaism and the education that they received in the *heder*. At the same time their hero, bar none, is Pisarev. But still the members debate, each making his own evaluation. One prefers Mikhailovsky, another Smolenskin, while yet another sings the praise of Nikolay Chernyshevsky and his famous novel *Chto delat'*: "'That book", Tsivershtein erupted in a strange manner . . . "If you placed the whole of literature on one side of the scales, Pushkin, Pisarev, Mikhailovsky, and Dostoevsky, everyone, and on the other side this book alone—it would outweigh them!"'[33] Although one would expect the narrator's irony to slip in, An-sky holds back. A portrait of conflicting points of view is left unresolved.

[32] S. An-sky, *Pionery*, in *Sobranie sochinenii*, iii. 182.   [33] Ibid. 126

In his novel An-sky does not leave out the subject of gender. The narrator shows that the intellectuals adopted the prejudices of their parents, considering that a woman could never be a man's equal. Moreover, any talk of love or feelings was entirely condemned as inappropriate. Yet even this taboo started to change. An acquaintance with a Russian girl, Olga, awakens erotic feelings and emotional warmth in Mirkin, who realizes the stupidity of treating women as subordinates. The view that women are entitled to free choice, just as men are, motivates the group to help a young Jewish woman, Beryasheva, to run from home to escape a prearranged marriage.

The success triggers a utopian epiphany in Mirkin:

For Mirkin Beryasheva's escape gradually ceased looking like a singular event and appeared to him as a huge victory of light over darkness, Haskalah over conservatism, freedom over coercion. Yes! The end of the old world is coming! It cannot endure these more and more powerful, decisive, and lethal blows. Yesterday the dark 'wall' that for ages separated the Jewish people from the rest of the world, life, light, and knowledge was unassailable, now it has become completely unstable. Large holes have been made in it and it is finally ready to fall! The time is not far off! People, all the people are beginning to think clearly and rationally, rejecting their religious and habitual prejudices. They will begin to live by healthy and useful work, create for themselves friendly relations endowed with mutual trust and understanding. And there will be no distinctions between Jews and other people, between those with privilege and without, the strong and the weak. Everyone will be equals and become brothers. Everyone will study and work. Yeshivas, *ḥeders*, and other institutions of ignorance will disappear. High schools and universities will be filled with students. Young people will devote free time to serious reading and scholarly endeavours and will forget about vulgar courting, will not waste valuable time on the useless play of writing poetry . . . A great epoch, unique in the history of the world, has arrived. The break occurred only a few decades ago. Suddenly, in a blinding light, 'Truth', great and immutable, appeared to those wandering in the deep darkness. And everything in humanity that is rational and vivacious went towards it as to a new testament that promised to revive the world. And it was carried like the sacred tablets to the furthest corners of the world and in the name of 'Truth' a holy and merciless war was declared on the entire old world! Victory is near![34]

In this inner monologue composed of a litany of hopes and convictions, one can see the mindset of the revolutionary Jewish youth of the 1880s. Mirkin uses revolutionary vocabulary—'a holy and merciless war', 'a new Bible', 'a new epoch', 'victory'. Emboldened, Mirkin decides to change his plans and leave without taking the qualifying exams for the university, and also decides to forgo a relationship with Olga. Instead he leaves for Mstislavl, deep in the Pale of Settlement, where he will continue the work of spreading the Haskalah.

Pioneers resembles the works in Russian literature that it self-consciously mentions, those by Pisarev, Mikhailovsky, and Chernyshevsky. The boys dedicate their lives to the cause, to be useful to society and bring enlightenment to them-

---

[34] An-sky, *Pionery*, 221–2.

selves and others.[35] Clearly the novel has a biographical subtext. In his youth An-sky was, like Mirkin, ready to sacrifice his own happiness in the struggle for progress.

Since An-sky reveals his ideological preference for Mirkin, *Pioneers* is not really a dialogic novel. Nonetheless, it bears some of the characteristics of the dialogic form. The novel is built upon the conversations and views of the main characters, who, while not extremely dissimilar from one another, present different ideas of what the Haskalah is and should be. An-sky does present one positive ideological rival to Mirkin, Ular's father, and depicts the traditionalist viewpoint, although admittedly giving it short shrift. One possible way to understand the author's open sympathy with Mirkin is to employ intertextuality and recall the critical treatment of the maskilim in his other works. It is possible to view the sympathy for the maskilim in *Pioneers* as part of the author's internal dialogue regarding the Haskalah.

*

An-sky returned to Russia on 31 December 1905, thanks to the government's amnesty for political prisoners. Although his views had changed a great deal during the fourteen years of emigration, An-sky threw his support behind his old comrades, the Socialist Revolutionaries. Despite the outbreak of pogroms against Jews in October and November, An-sky held to his belief that Jews had no other choice but to continue the fight. He was especially incensed by a series of articles that Simon Dubnow published in late 1905, claiming that the revolution of 1905 was less like 1848 and more like 1648, the Khmelnytsky uprising, and 1881–2, the years of pogroms.[36] Emphasizing that Jews were singled out for pogroms because they were Jews, Dubnow claimed that it was time for Jews to confront the truth: assimilation did not ameliorate the Jew's low civil status. Instead of fighting for an illusion—equal rights in a cosmopolitan, democratic state—Russia's Jews should devote themselves 'to the security and development of the people as a whole as a cultural-historical indivisible unit'.[37]

An-sky viewed the pogroms of October 1905 not as a symbol of the Russian people's complicity, but, just as in 1881–2, as a provocation by the conservative elite to deflect popular discontent. Revolutionaries were not blind to national concerns, but those interests had to yield to the defence of all the minorities. By forming self-defence militias, for example, Jewish revolutionaries resisted properly. The failure to stop pogroms was not a sign of the revolutionaries' moral decline, but merely a reflection of the inequality of forces in the present struggle.[38]

---

[35] Nowhere does An-sky mention terror (he was apparently not in favour of terror): G. Safran, 'Zrelishche krovoprolitiya: S. An-skii na granitsakh', in O. V. Budnitsky (ed.), *Mirovoi krizis 1914–1920 godov i sud'ba vostochnoevropeiskogo evreistva* (Moscow, 2005), 302–17.

[36] S. Dubnov [Dubnow], 'Uroki strashnykh dnei', *Voskhod*, 1905, nos. 47–8, p. 9.   [37] Ibid. 2.

[38] S. An-sky, '"Uroki strashnykh vekov" (Po povodu stat'i S. M. Dubnova "Uroki strashnykh dnei")', *Voskhod*, 1906, no. 8, pp. 8–9.

Debates over 1905 played a significant role in the creation of *In a New Way: A Novella* (*V novom rusle: Povest´*).[39] In this short novel An-sky explored the conflict between loyalty to the Jewish cause and commitment to the larger revolution. Choosing as his subject the Bund organization in 'N', a Belarusian town, during a few days in the summer of 1905, he focuses on Basya, a young girl from a working-class family who is a member of the Bund's central committee.[40] Tracing her experiences and inner consciousness, An-sky stuctures his story loosely, giving other characters opportunities to present competing viewpoints.

On one level the plot pivots on a mystery: someone has killed a tsarist police officer, which will likely attract the government's revenge. However, the main bulk of the story is occupied with discussions in which various characters argue about why revolution is needed, whether Jews should fight for Jewish rights or for general rights, and whether Russians and Jews can really join arms in a common struggle.

Using the dialogic method, An-sky presents multifarious perspectives. Not announcing where he stands himself, the author has Basya present the view that, despite appearances to the contrary, all revolutionaries are joined by an invisible thread that cannot be broken. The thread is the knowledge that only through unity can the revolution win and give Jews their basic rights:

Dozens of individual little 'clubs' exist in a state of permanent enmity and hatred of each other. Nonetheless, they are always together and cannot separate. Something sharply divides them and simultaneously unites them. It seems that the parties and fractions, circles and groups that compete with and antagonize each other are nothing other than splinters of a broken whole, splinters that complete their orbit on the same latitude. Although at first glance one only sees broken and disordered confusion, in fact the great labour of creating the people's future idea is already taking place, the all-encompassing idea, the synthesis of a new life—universal and national—is being formed.[41]

At the same time that An-sky gives Basya this perspective, he also lets another character express the opposite viewpoint. Dovid, a fellow Bund leader from a wealthy family, doubts that true unity can ever be achieved. People's egoism and their ambitions and basic cultural differences prevent harmony from enduring:

Does the worker, no matter how much he earns, share his earnings with the starving man? Doesn't the skilled worker treat the unskilled with disdain? Doesn't there exist among the

---

[39] The novel was first published in Yiddish as *In shtrom: ertselung fun der yidisher revolutsyonerer bavegung*, in *Der fraynd*, 1907, no. 2, republished as *In shtrom: ertselung*, in An-sky, *Gezamlte shriftn*, vol. ix. The Russian version appeared as *V novom rusle (povest´)*, in *Novye veyaniya: Pervyi evreiskii sbornik* (Moscow, 1907), 88–286, and also in his *Sobranie sochinenii*, iv. 33–212.

[40] Jonathan Frankel writes that 'the town was clearly modeled on Vitebsk, which An-sky knew well from his school days and in which he spent lengthy stays in 1906–7'. He also notes that this novel, in contrast to others written on the same theme, focused on 'the excitement, the euphoria, of the heady days when the revolution gained momentum from day to day' and not on the pogroms of October. J. Frankel, '"Youth in Revolt": An-sky's *In shtrom* and the Instant Fictionalization of 1905', in Safran and Zipperstein (eds.), *Worlds of S. An-sky*, 140, 155.

[41] S. An-sky, *V novom rusle (povest´)*, in *Sobranie sochinenii*, iv. 97.

workers a division between 'higher' and 'lower' and isn't it drawn in a very sharp way? Doesn't a worker who has read a dozen political booklets already strut around and act pretentious in front of one who hasn't read them? Don't you know that among conscious workers, those fine fighters, petty arguments break out, huge fights go on for the party's leadership roles and honours, and some show their envy, while others reveal a desire to command, give orders, and shout at their comrades? In your view isn't all of this an example of bourgeois habits? Therefore I say to you: the workers do not have the right to demand from the intelligentsia what they wouldn't demand from themselves.[42]

If the author himself does not answer, the novel's plot does resolve some of these questions. An-sky shows us that the traditional Jews, the parents' generation, lend support to the Bund. The father of one of the members of the Bund, a pious scribe, perceives the Bundists as veritable saviours. The narrator announces:

The entire society, young and old, has given its assent and considers the Bundists the community's legitimate leaders. A unity among generations and groups is achieved according to the values and interests of the whole. As much as they were able to do so, the young people took up the work of bringing order to our disordered life, took the fate of the old neighbourhood into their hands, guarded its interests and its human dignity. The neighbourhood, sick and exhausted, acknowledged the power of the children over itself, started to feel pride for them, repeated their words, felt joy for their joys, depair over their woes. Gradually the neighbourhood began to absorb the profound belief in a bright future.[43]

While An-sky shows respect for the Bund, he also portrays the self-destructive and narrow-minded attitudes of the leaders, who are driven by petty concerns, foremost among them vanity. For example, An-sky presents the leader Sender, who envies Russians their physical strength and strong character, while Dovid, intellectual, pretentious, and boastful, has little respect for the working masses.[44] Another leader, Barkanov, makes the claim that all the 'loyal' Jewish intellectuals are prepared to run off and assume positions in the larger Russian radical parties at the first opportunity.[45] Basya, the only person in touch with the problems of actual workers, defers to her educated colleagues and takes her orders from them.

While the leaders are preoccupied with interpersonal conflicts, they neglect to resolve the murder that has endangered the community. By not turning the murderer over to the authorities, they are indirectly responsible for the pogrom that is about to occur. Although the murderer's identity is finally exposed at the story's end (it turns out that it is Gersheon, a pacifist and member of the Politburo, who did it as an act of personal revenge for the murder of his sister and blinding of his father), it is too late to save the community. The final paragraph describes the

---

[42] Ibid. 120.   [43] Ibid. 208.   [44] Ibid. 170–1.

[45] 'The Jewish intellectual seeks a great and expanded role and cannot be satisfied with modest and long-drawn-out work. I know comrades who went over to the "Party" and the Socialist Revolutionaries not for reasons of principle, but because they felt crowded in the Bund. What really is the interest in occupying yourself with the proletariat of a small nation of six million, when you can play a role in a nation of one hundred and forty?': ibid. 152.

sound of beating hooves; the Cossacks have arrived to begin a pogrom that will presumably cause the deaths of many Jews.

What does the ending mean? Should one interpret it as an acknowledgement that the counter-revolution will succeed in destroying Jewish communal unity, or will the Jewish community enter a new period of harmony? It is impossible to say which interpretation is more accurate, since one can argue both convincingly. Although *In a New Way* can be interpreted as a reproach to the authorities for using violence unlawfully, An-sky also blames the revolutionaries. He shows that the causes of the failure of the revolution lie in the Jews themselves; they follow personal urges rather than fulfilling collective needs.

In a New Way reflects An-sky's biography in closely tracing his initial support for the revolution and subsequent criticism of the failures of 1905. However, it is also true that An-sky judiciously presented the viewpoints of the Bundists, the Jewish street, and the Orthodox community, permitting each a full hearing.

After publishing *In a New Way*, An-sky stopped writing fiction. It is perhaps clear that, now back in Russia, he had a different idea of where his contributions could be most effective. Turning to the study of Jewish folklore, he organized the Jewish Ethnographic Expedition, which began work in 1912.[46] The collection of artefacts—among them stories, legends, works of art, manuscripts, and transcribed and recorded music—that he acquired during these years served as the basis for the first Jewish museum in Russia. Just before the First World War, he wrote *The Dybbuk*, which was intended to be performed by the Moscow Art Theatre.[47]

During the war, An-sky volunteered to distribute aid to Jewish war victims on both sides of the conflict. It was very dangerous work because many of the areas he visited were in the direct line of fire. Moreover, he had the unpleasant job of collecting money, knocking at the doors of the Jewish magnates of Kiev, St Petersburg, Odessa, and Moscow.[48] After the Bolsheviks disbanded the Constituent Assembly in January 1918, in which An-sky was supposed to serve as a representative of the Socialist Revolutionaries, a warrant was put out for his arrest. Dressed as a priest, he fled Russia for Vilna, where he resided until 1919.[49] Then he moved to Warsaw, where he died outside the city at a health resort in 1920 at the age of 57.

*

[46] A. Rechtman, *Yidishe etnografye un folklor* (Buenos Aires, 1958), 11–34.

[47] The revolutions of 1917 prevented this, and it was ultimately first performed in Yiddish and was never performed by Stanislavsky's famous troupe. S. Wolitz, 'Inscribing An-sky's *Dybbuk* in Russian and Jewish Letters', in Safran and Zipperstein (eds.), *Worlds of S. An-sky*, 164–202.

[48] Sh. An-sky, *Der yidisher khurbn fun poyln, galitsye un bukovine fun togbukh 1914–17*, in *Gezamlte shriftn*, vols. iv–vi.

[49] He was in a sense chased away from Vilna by a pogrom that occurred in the city in 1919 and in which his close friend, the playwright A. Vayter (pseudonym; real name Isaac-Mayer Devenishsky), was killed.

How should one ultimately evaluate An-sky's fiction in connection with the 'other'? It is impossible to accept the view that he was a mere observer of reality, since his fiction is richer than that. By shaping his stories in order to make the characters confront one another in ideological battle, An-sky, like Dostoevsky in Bakhtin's interpretation, provides a broad space for these debates. Firm in their ideological positions, the characters are permitted to develop their view to its final conclusion. At times it even seems as though the hand of the author had been lifted and the characters able to act freely according to their own 'will'.

From An-sky's dialogic fiction, we learn a great deal about the inner life of Jewish revolutionaries, older maskilim, and traditionalists, and especially their relations with one another. In addition, his sympathetic and extensive treatment of traditional Jews is unprecedented in Russian-language fiction. An-sky's fiction opens the readers' eyes to the great cleft in Russian Jewry that opened up in the 1870s. Moreover, at a time when Russian Jewry seemed to be disintegrating, the Haskalah as an ideology, a challenge to Jewry, and a way of life comes under intense scrutiny. Thus, although he does not offer a solution to the problems of Russian Jewry, his fiction does provide a clear analysis. For example, Mikhail Krutikov has observed that in An-sky's stories and novels we encounter in its earliest form the revolutionary type that would take power over Russia's Jews in Soviet times.[50]

How did An-sky discover the dialogic approach? Although he might have imitated Dostoevsky (though I have no documentary evidence to support such an assertion), An-sky likely came to use polyphony thanks to ideological and emotional contradictions that were unique to him alone. Although he yearned for a unity that would overcome difference, his knowledge of reality gained from experience told him of diversity. Honing a narrative method that permitted him an insider's viewpoint, he put respect for diversity to use in his fiction, perceiving the multifarious, contradictory, and incongruous dimensions of the 'other' in Russian Jewry at the end of the nineteenth and beginning of the twentieth centuries.

---

[50] Professor Krutikov brilliantly shows that An-sky was able to create characters which outlived their creator. According to Krutikov, the author's open-mindedness and his keen interest in signs of the future enabled him to identify and portray certain types that later became the leaders of Russian Jewry. While An-sky's more traditionalist contemporaries were focused on the core elements of Jewish life, he creatively explored its periphery. According to Krutikov, his best characters are not 'organic'; they are artificially constructed out of heterogeneous, sometimes conflicting, elements. He does not depict life according to certain pre-existing schemes and concepts, but attempts to create new ones out of raw material. This makes his characters dynamic and open to the future. Krutikov, 'Russian Jew as a Modern Hero', 123.

Between Judaism and the West

The Making of a Modern Jewish Poet in Uri Zvi Greenberg's 'Memoirs (from the Book of Wanderings)'

KARIN NEUBURGER

ON THE TRACK OF A BURIED STORY

URI ZVI GREENBERG (1897–1981), who wrote 'Memoirs (from the Book of Wanderings)' in 1912, had very good reasons not to publish this story.[1] To publish it would have meant exposing himself excessively on a number of different levels, some of which he was probably aware of, and some of which might only be apparent, retrospectively, to an outside observer. First, this story delivers a harsh critique of traditional Judaism, which is depicted as a social system that denies the Jewish people a dignified existence, and instead subordinates the individual as well as the collective to its rigid doctrines, by preaching 'submission' and a humbling of the spirit (p. 281). Although this argument was not a novelty in a society that had already been infused with Enlightenment ideas and where Zionist thought had acquired a crucial influence,[2] it certainly could have engendered tremendous tension between the young author and his family and community, who are the representatives of this submissive Judaism in the story. And indeed, the 15-year-old Greenberg, the son of a rabbi and a scion of prestigious hasidic families,[3] who still observed the strictly Orthodox dress code,[4] was dependent on his parents and relatives, at least in the financial sense, so that any overt expression of opposition to their way of life might have made things quite difficult for him. Second, the story reveals the author's powerlessness to liberate the Jewish youth who is both protagonist and narrator of the

---

[1] 'Memoirs (from the Book of Wanderings)' ('Zikhroynes (oys dem vander-album)') was first printed in Greenberg's collected works in Yiddish: U. Z. Greenberg, *Gezamlte verk*, i: *1912–1921*, ed. C. Shmeruk (Jerusalem, 1979), 279–90. I shall refer to the story as 'Memoirs' for short, and subsequent page references to it are given in the text in parentheses.

[2] See I. Bartal, 'Teguvot lemoderniyut bemizraḥ eiropah: haskalah, ortodoksiyah, le'umiyut', in S. Almog, J. Reinharz, and A. Shapira (eds.), *Tsiyonut vedat* (Jerusalem, 1994), 31–2.

[3] D. Miron, *Akdamut le'u. ts. grinberg* (Jerusalem, 2002), 10.

[4] M. Ravitch, *Mayn leksikon* (Montreal, 1958), 58.

story. Greenberg intended this youth to represent the 'new' Jew, a free Jew, who by virtue of his independent status would not only refuse to submit to the people of Europe or assimilate into their culture, but would also demonstrate his superiority to the point that, as in a messianic vision of the future days to come, they would choose to cleave to him and his own people (p. 284). However, the youth's quest for freedom ultimately ends with his return to the bosom of his family. He is compelled to return and take his place in the synagogue of the Jewish *shtetl*, as one of its own sons, and to bury his wish for freedom deep in his heart. Or rather, as at the end of the story in which the young narrator is revealed to be a poet, to express this wish in the metaphorical guise of poems addressed to a secret loved one.

However, beyond a sense of personal defeat that Greenberg may have experienced in realizing that he could find no other ending to his story, he may also have made the decision to bury it because the ending he chose was incommensurate with the existential necessity of leaving the *shtetl*, as evidenced in the mass migration of millions of Jews who left eastern Europe for the West.[5] This historical movement was a response not only to the harsh pogroms,[6] but also to the far-reaching transformations that the Jewish communities of eastern Europe were undergoing.[7] In the poetry he composed either while at work on 'Memoirs' or shortly after, and which was published in a variety of literary venues,[8] Greenberg ostensibly responds to the necessity of accommodating to Western culture. This early poetry suppresses all signs of Jewishness, and therefore also conceals the strained relationship the poet maintained both with Orthodox Judaism and with Western culture, which is so pronounced in the story under discussion. This was achieved by moving the focus of events from the external social and historical landscape into interior psychological terrain. The focus on feeling engendered an image of a speaker, depicted as a Romantic or 'sentimental'[9] adolescent youth, who is preoccupied

[5] See e.g. S. E. Aschheim, 'The Ambivalent Heritage: Liberal Jews and the Ostjuden, 1880–1914', in id., *Brothers and Strangers: The East European Jew in German and German Jewish Consciousness, 1800–1923* (Madison, 1982), 37: 'Although statistics are not complete, we know that a large proportion of the 2,750,000 Eastern Jewish immigrants who left Europe for overseas lands between 1880 and 1914 passed through Germany.'

[6] As is well known, in the final decades of the nineteenth century and the early twentieth century the Jews of eastern Europe, Russia, Poland, and also Galicia, where Greenberg lived, were victims of harsh pogroms, which became one of the major causes of Jewish migration to the West. See Aschheim, 'Ambivalent Heritage', 32; B. Harshav, 'Hamahapekhah hayehudit hamodernit: kavim lehavanatah', *Alpayim*, 23 (2002), 16.

[7] See e.g. H. Haumann, *A History of East European Jews* (Budapest and New York, 2002), 99 ff.; E. Lederhendler, *Hahagirah lema'arav vela'olam heḥadash: sheluḥoteiha shel yahadut mizraḥ eiropah, Le'an? Zeramim ḥadashim bekerev yehudei mizraḥ-eiropah*, unit 5 (Ra'anana, 2006).

[8] For example in the journals *Senunit, Hashilo'aḥ, Ha'olam, Hatsefirah*, and *Ha'aḥdut*.

[9] I prefer to enclose this term in quotation marks. It has a certain disparaging connotation and was coined by the New Criticism school in reference to lyrical-romantic poetry which was considered to be void of authentic feeling. See M. R. Amiran, 'The Use of "Sentimentality" as a Critical Term in New Criticism in English', MA thesis (Hebrew University of Jerusalem, 1969). Studies devoted to

with both personal and universal emotions, which are perceived as ahistorical. In other words, it engendered a voice marked by political and cultural naivety. While such a figure is indeed reflected in the poems' speaker, it was identified by the readership with the creator of this poetry, that is, with the poet Uri Zvi Greenberg.[10]

This modus operandi was very effective, as suggested also in studies devoted to Greenberg's early poetry.[11] It released the young poet from engaging in a political discussion which could have encumbered him and revealed his helplessness in face of historical reality. It also prepared the ground for Greenberg's acceptance within the milieu of local poets,[12] who supported the publication of his early works, which seemed to emulate the neo-Romantic spirit and style of their own writing. However, when one reads the poetry Greenberg wrote early in his career against the background of 'Memoirs', it appears to betray the same existential dilemma that motivates this story. One might say that Greenberg's life is an extension of his story: he himself becomes the youth who lives within the east European Jewish community and uses his poetry to express his hidden wish for another, freer and more dignified, type of existence. In other words, while the tension between submissive Orthodoxy and liberated existence is treated openly in 'Memoirs', in Greenberg's early poetry the same tension is expressed by establishing distance between political and cultural reality and poetic fiction. This tension appears therefore only in occulted form in the early poems.

The problematic nature of 'Memoirs', therefore, from the perspective of the young Greenberg, would seem to reside in the very issue which awakens the attention of the contemporary reader, that is, in the story's presentation of the cultural and political space in which Greenberg worked and in which his lyrical discourse took shape. This presentation, of course, is subjective. Greenberg presents this space and the existential questions it produced from a very particular perspective and in a manner that served his own personal intentions and aspirations. This can be seen, for example, in the way the narrative focuses almost exclusively on the story of the Jewish youth, but does not present a broad and complex portrait of the social texture of the *shtetl* in which the plot takes place. Yet, this does not mean that the manner in which the cultural and political realm is presented in 'Memoirs' is devoid of objective features. Not only is it possible to recognize certain patterns employed here in the writings of other authors and thinkers of that generation, but also, and chiefly, the presentation of the cultural and political milieu in 'Memoirs' exceeds

Greenberg's early poetry often use this term to characterize works that do indeed contain 'sentimental' features, but that—for reasons which I shall elaborate below—do not deserve this designation.

[10] I shall address the problematic nature of this identification below.

[11] H. Hever, *Uri tsevi grinberg bimelot lo shemonim: ta'arukhah beveit hasefarim hale'umi veha'universita'i, ulam berman* (Jerusalem, 1977), 8–9; A. Novershtern, 'Hama'avar el ha'ekspresiyonizm bizirat uri tsevi grinberg. Hapo'emah "Mefisto": gilgulei emdot vedovrim', *Hasifrut*, 35–6 (1986), 127; Miron, *Akdamut le'u. ts. grinberg*, 13–14; H. Barzel, *Ekspresiyonizm nevu'i: uri tsevi grinberg, yitshak lamdan, matityahu shoham* (Benei Berak, 2004), 51.

[12] See Hever, *Uri tsevi grinberg bimelot lo shemonim*, 9–10.

the intentions of the author because of its inherent artistic character.[13] In writing 'Memoirs' Greenberg fabricated a poetic structure that, perforce, laid bare the cultural and political mechanisms characteristic of the historical sphere in which he was active. In order to identify these mechanisms, two complementary tacks must be taken: the story must be read with a focus on its poetic structure, while this structure should be elucidated through the cultural and political context in which the story is located.[14] It goes without saying that 'Memoirs' is particularly open to this sort of interpretative reading. This openness has to do with the work's immaturity,[15] as evidenced in the simple and unsophisticated fabrication of the story, which can be explained either by the young artist's lack of awareness or his lack of expertise and skill. In any event, the story's poetic structure is fairly exposed, and is therefore readily available for the type of interpretative reading I wish to present below.

MESSIANIC INTENTIONS AND CULTURAL–POLITICAL CONDITIONING: THE MACRO-STRUCTURE OF 'MEMOIRS'

As suggested above, Greenberg's story incorporates a sort of messianic vision of the end of days. During the night-time vigil of the holiday of Shavuot, after the congregation of worshippers and learners in the synagogue have fallen asleep, the youth stands alone and recites to himself the verse from the *piyut* (liturgical poem) 'Akdamut'[16] which describes the redemption of the people of Israel and the acts of conversion of the gentiles who desire to take part in this redemption (p. 284). However, the young narrator's expectation that the vision will materialize is not fulfilled. His dream is shattered to pieces when confronted with the reality in which power relations between Jews and gentiles are the exact inverse of what he dreams for. Therefore, he is left with no choice but to shut his eyes once in a while and conjure up the vision ignited by the language of the liturgy: 'And as I close my eyelids, memories [*zikhroynes*] long quenched now awaken' (p. 285).

[13] The distinction between the explicitly stated or intentional meaning of a work of literature and the meaning immanent in its poetics was formulated by W. K. Wimsatt Jr. and M. C. Beardsley in their article 'The Intentional Fallacy', in W. K. Wimsatt, *The Verbal Icon: Studies in the Meaning of Poetry* (Lexington, Ky., 1954), 3–20. Ruth HaCohen develops this distinction in the context of the story of the Golden Calf (Exod. 32: 21–5), and demonstrates its crucial importance in her own act of interpretation. See R. HaCohen, 'Sounds of Revelation: Aesthetic-Political Theology in Schoenberg's *Moses und Aron*', *Modernist Cultures*, 1 (2005), 110–12: <http://www.js-modcult.bham.ac.uk/>.

[14] I am grateful to Prof. Hanan Hever for his comments concerning the importance of the second interpretative strategy.

[15] The inferior aesthetic value of the work in question was also perhaps the reason that, in addition to its being buried by its author, most students of Greenberg's early poetry have overlooked it. I have found a reference to 'Memoirs' only in Hillel Barzel's *Ekspresiyonizm nevu'i*, 80–2, who views the story as 'bordering on mysticism', and emphasizes its experiential aspect in his discussion.

[16] This *piyut*, which was composed by Rabbi Meir, son of Rabbi Yitshak of Worms, following the massacre of Jews during the medieval crusades, is customarily recited in the communities of Ashkenaz before the Torah reading on Shavuot.

The centrality of this passage within 'Memoirs' is signalled not only through its use of the first word of the work's title (*zikhroynes*), but also because of its midpoint location within the story, in the second of its three chapters. Moreover, this is the passage in which the plot climaxes and takes its most fateful turn. For it is here that the youth finally learns that he is powerless to overcome the gap between vision and reality. In the following, the process of interiorization will be continued, so that by the end of the story the vision becomes a dream buried deep in the heart of the young narrator. I shall return later to the process of interiorization, but at this point in the discussion I wish to note that this process should not be taken to mean self-reconciliation. In other words, at the end of the story the tension between vision and reality is not resolved. On the contrary, this tension is actually heightened, for the narrator declares not only that he has not relinquished the vision, but that he has merely suspended its realization with the hope that he may one day find the strength to bring about the redemption whose seed is carried in his heart.[17] In addition, the distance between vision and reality is magnified because the macro-structure of the work is oriented towards an ending that contradicts the story's actual closure.[18]

Each of the story's three chapters recounts the youth's experiences during one of the Jewish holidays: Lag Ba'omer, Shavuot, and the Days of Awe. Just as in the passage cited from the second chapter, the narrator's messianic vision is presented as anchored in the Jewish tradition (signified by the *piyut* 'Akdamut'). The overall plot is encased within the framework of this tradition—for the purpose of either breaking it or at least deviating from it. In the narrative section mentioned above, this deviation is alluded to in the way the youth separates himself from the congregation: only after the other worshippers in the synagogue fall asleep, only when he finds himself alone, can the narrator surrender to his wish and conjure up his vision in his mind. It should be noted that the holidays in question follow one another chronologically in the Hebrew calendar; however, they are not consecutive, for the story skips over two significant dates in the calendar: 17 Tamuz and Tisha Be'av, the two fast days that fall between Shavuot and the High Holidays. These ritual dates are meant to orient the hearts and minds of the Jewish people towards the destruction of its Temple and to its exilic existence. Greenberg, then, has omitted from the story the calendar dates that are incommensurate with the

[17] We can infer from this that the topic of messianism in general, and the figure of the Messiah as an object of identification in particular, appear as foundational elements of Greenberg's art from the very beginning. This issue is important because it demonstrates that even Greenberg's early work should be considered as bearing theological and political significance. Beyond this, it attests to the uniformity of Greenberg's œuvre, which has indeed been doubted by different scholars. However, this issue requires greater elaboration, which cannot be adequately undertaken in the current framework.

[18] As I shall show below, this heightening of tension towards the end of the story is commensurate with Greenberg's self-perception as a poet, because, like the narrator in 'Memoirs', he sees the bridging of the gap between his messianic vision and political reality as his chief mission as a poet. He therefore seeks to bring it into sharp relief, and thus amplify the potency of his poetry, which is nourished by the tension created by this gap.

hope for a free existence, a hope he wishes to bestow upon the youthful narrator, and even beyond him, as our discussion has shown, upon the entire nation of Israel. In other words, Greenberg has drawn in his story a linear time-continuum that points directly towards the fulfilment of the vision, towards the redemption that will occur during the Days of Awe, the most important period in the Hebrew calendar. However, upon this linear movement a circular one is superimposed. This is tied to the fact that the vision of the narrator colonizes his whole being, so that he ignores the unique and complex contents of the calendar dates that are still part of his experience, until it appears as if they had one sole purpose: to remind humanity and the Jewish people of its own destiny—to strive for a free existence, unhampered by external factors, or in other words to strive for selfhood. Therefore, instead of delineating a time progression through transitions from one calendar date to the next, the story *repeats* the very same process with each account of the next festival, in each of the three chapters: the narrator's attempt to realize the holiday's purpose and define his selfhood, his failure at this task, his renewed attempt, and so on. Moreover, the tremendous emphasis on the notion of selfhood results in isolating this idea from any specific context, so that it figures as an abstract notion of universal selfhood, and not as Jewish selfhood.

At first glance, the narrator's vision might appear simply to have been inverted: rather than the gentiles joining the Jewish people, the Jews are obliged to relinquish their identity and join the modern Western culture that espouses the belief in man as a universal being. Yet, if this were so, the movement of the narrator would have stopped, that is he would have found his rightful place in the framework of Western culture represented by nature. Instead he wanders from the beginning to the end of the story between *shtetl* and nature, between East and West, between Judaism and Western culture, without being able to take up permanent residence at either pole of his existence. This is to say that the story's movement in time and space is likewise circular. Accordingly, the narrator oscillates incessantly between worlds or between one compulsion and another: the compulsion to leave the *shtetl* and become integrated into the life of modern Western society, on the one hand, and the compulsion to return again and again to the *shtetl*, because such integration is impossible.

Unlike the way in which it is presented in the story, the return of the narrator to his *shtetl* is not determined only by his inability to bridge the gap between his vision and reality; it seems, rather, that his peregrinations, his repeated departure from and return to the *shtetl*, are a product of a certain kind of rootlessness. Moreover, the narrator's meandering between Judaism and Western culture illustrates how the modern Jewish person's rootlessness is articulated as a dynamic between assimilation and dissimilation. Shulamit Volkov has alerted us to this dynamic, and to the way in which German Jews in the second decade of the twentieth century began to become aware of it[19]—that is, at the very same time our story

[19] See S. Volkov, 'The Dynamics of Dissimilation', in J. Reinharz and W. Schatzberg (eds.), *The*

was written. However, when writing this story Greenberg was living neither in Berlin nor in Frankfurt, but rather in Lviv in Galicia. Nor is he the descendant of assimilating Jews who feels a need to go back and connect to his Jewish roots that are revealed to him in the figure of the east European Jew.[20] On the contrary, he himself was an *Ostjude*. His point of departure was therefore different from that of west European Jews. This difference can be seen chiefly in the fact that Greenberg harboured no nostalgic longings for traditional east European Jewry as the embodiment of the original Judaism, but rather regarded it as an obstacle that needed to be overcome on the path to liberated Jewish existence. However, this difference does not mean that modern Western culture should be regarded as something external to Greenberg. This perception is indeed part of the rhetorical strategy deployed in the story 'Memoirs', but other dimensions of the narrative indicate that the cultural and political reality was more complex.

AN ENTITY WITH NO SOURCE: THE MICRO-STRUCTURE OF 'MEMOIRS'

The very first paragraphs of the story provide the reader with a sensuous grasp of the existential circumstances of the narrator in 'Memoirs' and of the dynamic between assimilation and dissimilation. The reader is invited to observe the way in which the narrator constitutes his identity:

As a group, we leave the dingy room, which has been blackened by smoke. Leibke, our assistant teacher with the chestnut eyes, is proudly leading the gang. We follow him slowly . . . the lowly booths with their small and crooked roofs made of half-rotted wood vanish behind us. A light, cool breeze rushes up at us, stroking our pale and tormented faces, tousling our variously coloured sidelocks, something whispers in our ears, as if hoping to reveal to us the secrets of the clear streams gurgling inside a cloistered cave . . . And it feels as though our ribcages expand as we go forth . . . the mouth is wide open, inhaling all the delicate scents of freer and brighter open spaces . . . they penetrate deep into the heart, wander into deep and hidden chambers of the body, find the young soul and pamper it so gently, so kindly . . . and it feels so, so free. (p. 279)

In its description of a Lag Ba'omer outing of east European Jewish youths, under the supervision of an assistant teacher, the narrative space is cloven in two. At one end the space of the Jewish *shtetl* is represented as a sort of dark prison, 'rotten' and 'lowly'. At the other end, in opposition to the *shtetl*, stands the space of nature,

Jewish Response to German Culture: From the Enlightenment to the Second World War (Hanover, NH, and London, 1985), 195–211, esp. 200 and 210–11. Indeed, the Jewish German thinkers who display this awareness, such as Franz Rosenzweig (b. 1886), Walther Benjamin (b. 1892), and Gershom Scholem (b. 1897), were contemporaries of Greenberg, who was born in 1897.

[20] See e.g. S. E. Aschheim, 'Assimilation and its Impossible Discontents: The Case of Moritz Goldstein', in id., *In Times of Crisis: Essays on European Culture, Germans, and Jews* (Madison, 2001), 66; Aschheim, *Brothers and Strangers*, p. xvii.

described as open, 'sun-swept', 'fragrant', and 'pure'. As such, it represents the culture of the gentiles (pp. 281, 282).

The association between nature and the culture of the gentiles, which rested on the opposition between the *shtetl* and nature and which is part of a long and distinguished tradition in modern Jewish literature,[21] requires an explanation that also touches upon the nature of the relationship forged here with the culture of the West. This is a twofold relationship: it situates the Jewish 'I'—represented in the cited passage by the group of youths on their Lag Ba'omer outing—both as external to modern Western culture and as intrinsic to it at one and the same time.[22] It is intrinsic to it, based as it is on the model of the free man first formulated during the final three decades of the eighteenth century in the context of the Sturm and Drang movement in Germany,[23] and which, along with other influences in the European sphere, led to far-reaching cultural developments, a 'radical shift of values . . . which has affected thought, feeling and action in the Western world'.[24] This was the 'Romantic revolution' that located man at the centre of Western culture, defined as a being who is independent of any external factor, who exists in and of himself alone, and who operates autonomously; defined, in brief, as 'the self'.[25]

In the second decade of the twentieth century, this model had already been received in the Western world, and even beyond, within east European cultures. The young Greenberg could therefore have been exposed to it not only by way of German literature or any other 'foreign' Western literature, but also through the literature in his own mother tongue, Yiddish, or alternatively through Hebrew poetry, and its most outstanding exponent at the time, Hayim Nahman Bialik. At the same time, while writing 'Memoirs', Greenberg was forced to treat this model as if it were external to Jewish culture, as if it were up to him to transfer it single-handedly from Western culture.

The term 'transference' (German *Übertragung*) used here to describe Greenberg's

---

[21] It may be sufficient to mention here S. Y. Abramovich's *The Book of the Beggars*, H. N. Bialik's *Behind the Fence*, and S. Y. Agnon's *Simple Story*.

[22] This is dissimilar to the image of the east European Jews in the eyes of German Jews, for example. On the problematic nature of this image, see Y. Weiss, *Etniyut ve'ezraḥut: yehudei germaniyah veyehudei polin, 1933–1940* (Jerusalem, 2000), 35. For the similar status of German Jews vis-à-vis German culture, see S. E. Aschheim, 'German History and German Jewry: Junctions, Boundaries, and Interdependencies', in id., *In Times of Crisis*, 86–92.

[23] According to the literature of the Sturm und Drang movement, free existence is embodied in nature, and a person who bonds with nature becomes a partner to this free existence. Compare *Deutsche Naturlyrik vom Barock bis zur Gegenwart*, ed. G. E. Grimm (Stuttgart, 1995), 504, regarding Goethe's conception of nature, and K. O. Conrady, 'Zur Bedeutung von Goethes Lyrik im Sturm und Drang', in W. Hinck (ed.), *Sturm und Drang* (Frankfurt am Main, 1989), 100–1, regarding the conception of nature held by the Sturm und Drang movement in general.

[24] See I. Berlin, *The Roots of Romanticism*, ed. H. Hardy (Princeton, 1999), 5–6, 11.

[25] See M. Foucault, *The Order of Things: An Archaeology of the Human Sciences* (London and New York, 2002), p. xxiv; D. E. Wellbery, *The Specular Moment: Goethe's Early Lyric and the Beginnings of Romanticism* (Stanford, Calif., 1996), 3–26.

action in 'Memoirs' requires explanation. I have borrowed it from David E. Wellbery, who coined it in the course of reading the poetry of the young Goethe.[26] In this context, the term signifies the pattern of action pursued by a subject in constituting himself as an autonomous being. To sketch the outline of this pattern of action, we may address the philosophical writings of Johann Gottlieb Fichte.[27] Reference to Fichte's philosophy is very useful here, since it allows us to observe schematically the poetic manoeuvre that Greenberg accomplishes in 'Memoirs' in order to construct the character of the narrator as a modern Jew, and thus present it in a clear and lucid form. But it also entails a certain danger, for this clarity involves a certain simplification and elides the cultural and political context which endows matters with their specific meanings.[28] The elucidation of the scheme can therefore serve only as a preliminary to the reading of 'Memoirs'.

The central concept in Fichte's thought is that of *Ichheit* ('I-ness'), or also *Selbstbewußtsein* ('self-awareness/consciousness'). This concept signifies the autonomous being and subjectivity of the self, which underlies any conscious act. The existence of this subject, Fichte explains, assumes some kind of inner identity, 'something that is always equal to itself, is always one, and is always the same'. This identity can be expressed in the following formula: 'I = I, I am I'.[29]

It should be said that Fichte's formula does not represent a static state, but rather an action that occurs in the consciousness of the I who posits itself as a self. The selfhood of the I is dependent on its ability to ascertain that it is indeed identical to itself. To do so it must split itself in two. It must posit itself as an other in relation to itself (I $\neq$ I), for only when it turns itself into an object of self-contemplation can it determine anything about itself. However, this split is only an intermediate step. The I must go back and eliminate the distinction between subject and object, between the I and the other, in order to recognize its identity with itself (I = I). To do so, it is not enough to mend the split created in the self. The I must subvert this split and retreat back into the origin of the I whose unity and self-identity always was and still is. This movement from the unity of the I to its splitting, and back to the original I, the self, is what Wellbery calls 'transference'.

It is important to point out for the sake of our discussion that, according to this outlook, autonomy equals originality. This is why Greenberg could not simply imitate the works of other poets and present the I of the narrator in 'Memoirs' as a fait accompli. For all imitation proceeds from an awareness of a prior original, and therefore it undermines the autonomy of whoever has engaged in it. In other words, the subject may be thought of as autonomous only if it can prove that it is creating itself *ex nihilo*, when it proves that none other than itself is at the source of its being.

---

[26] Wellbery, *Specular Moment*, 182.

[27] This turn to Fichte's philosophy also follows Wellbery, ibid. 57–9.

[28] I am grateful to Ruth HaCohen for refining this point in discussions we held together.

[29] J. G. Fichte, 'Grundlage der gesamten Wissenschaftslehre' (1794, 1802), in *Fichtes Werke*, ed. I. H. Fichte, i (Berlin, 1971), 94: '*Ich = Ich*; Ich bin Ich'.

Therefore, when Greenberg seeks to establish an autonomous subject he cannot mimic the aforementioned act of transference by means of which the Western poets constituted their identities. On the contrary, he supposedly had to invent it, and thus demonstrate his originality in respect to the notion of subjectivity offered by Western culture. This became possible only by transforming the tension that he experienced in relation to Western culture into the foundation of his art. In other words, Greenberg had to posit Western culture as one side of that very same split I which needs to be subverted in order to return to the I that is identical to itself: to the self.

The particularity of this self in relation to the self established by Western culture is reflected through his Jewish identity. But to claim originality for the Jewish self Greenberg had to extricate himself from traditional Judaism, since the latter contained no notion of an autonomous subject. Therefore he posits traditional Judaism as the second side of the split I, which must be subverted in order to accomplish selfhood. This is how the I becomes identified with traditional Judaism, while the other is equated with Western culture, whereas the I that strives for selfhood attempts to unite the two.

Such a union will indeed be produced in the later sections of 'Memoirs', which opens, as will be recalled, in a description of a Lag Ba'omer outing, entailing a spatial split that places the squalid *shtetl* on one side and pristine nature on the other. In the subsequent paragraphs, this split will be further underscored when the initially implicit connection between nature (Western culture) and freedom on the one hand, and the *shtetl* (Orthodox Judaism) and servitude on the other, is made explicit. The youths leave the *shtetl* happy and high-spirited. They breathe in the fresh air and revel in the sense of freedom. But soon they discover that this freedom has only been granted in small measure. They discover that Orthodox Judaism in fact separates them from nature and deprives them of a true experience of freedom.

In the course of their outing the youths encounter a hill that faces them 'with impudence and pride' (p. 279).[30] They desire to climb it despite the absolute prohibition of the teacher, the representative of Jewish tradition, a prohibition that contains allusions to the story of the Tower of Babel (Gen. 11: 1–9) and the story of the rebels (Num. 14: 39–45). However, the youths are not willing to accept the yoke of the Torah, and instead of obeying the teacher, who functions here as a sort of divine emissary, they heed only their own 'boiling blood'[31] and climb to the top of the hill to try and touch the clouds:

[30] Although the description of the situation suggests that the youths climbed only a hill (from the top of it they can still hear the voice of their teacher coming from the foot), Greenberg chose to use the Yiddish word *barg*, 'mountain', probably in order to convey the viewpoint of the narrator and his comrades as well as to suggest the narrator's high aspirations.

[31] This expression is remarkable. Here it is used inconspicuously, in an almost perfunctory way, the way it is used in Greenberg's early poems. It indicates the violent aspect of the I that is coming into being here. This aspect will be at the centre of the poetry Greenberg will write a few years later.

. . . what then? . . . Today, on Lag Ba'omer, also unfree? . . . Oh, no, no . . . let him beat us later . . . let us just live today . . . Leibke is so wicked! We climb, scrape ourselves . . . continue to ascend higher and higher. Soon, soon at the top . . . we breathe . . . the blood boils . . . the tiny hearts expand and beat hard . . . a hot panic spreads over the bodies . . . here, very soon, in a bit . . . just a bit, now it's over and done with, up in the heights, so very near the clouds. (p. 280)

This episode and its representation play a decisive role in the movement the narrative text undertakes, which, as I have argued, is marked by the notion of selfhood and therefore strives to unite the I with the other. To accomplish this, Greenberg presents the youths' ascent to the summit neither as a sin nor as an act that detracts from their Jewishness. On the contrary, the story makes clear that it is in the very act of transgressing the boundary set by tradition that they realize their natural right for freedom, the actual physical need to bond with nature. They thus prove their loyalty to Jewish tradition, which maintains that the holiday of Lag Ba'omer contains the essence of the experience of freedom for every Jew (p. 280). Yet this conception of Lag Ba'omer and of the youths' actions as a realization of the spirit of this holiday poses a simultaneous challenge to traditional Judaism and to Western culture. On the one hand, the narrative implies that, by ignoring the imperative to experience freedom in an unmediated way,[32] Orthodox Judaism loses its force as a true embodiment of Jewish tradition, while the youths who act in the spirit of Lag Ba'omer and honour this imperative substitute their own actions for tradition's authority, and prove that they are the proponents of the true, which is to say, the original Jewish tradition. This is the tradition of the dissidents,[33] of the builders of the Tower of Babel,[34] of the rebels who ascended the mountain, and of Bar-Kokhba's followers, whose victory should not only be *remembered* on Lag Ba'omer, but be *re-enacted* in deed. Therefore, the description of the youths as compelled by Jewish tradition to conquer the hill that belongs to the realm of nature undermines both the ostensible originality of gentile culture, that is, its position within the source that is nature,[35] and also its position as a source in respect of the Jewish self that is forged by this act.

[32] The Jewish culture of remembrance does indeed 'give presence' to an event, but in doing so marks it undoubtedly as a historical event, i.e. distances it from the present as an event that occurred in the past.

[33] Rebellion against any kind of authority represented by a father figure, both in the sense of a biological father and in the sense of the heavenly father, is a central and essential element of the Romantic tradition: see Berlin, *Roots of Romanticism*, 97.

[34] This tradition is also invoked in Sturm und Drang literature as a symbol of the rebellion and independence of the autonomous subject. See Wellbery, *Specular Moment*, 127–8. It should be noted that Wellbery deals with the topos of the builders of the Tower of Babel in the context of his discussion of the sexually charged dimensions of the autonomous subject, who is identified with the phallus (ibid.). In Greenberg's work, too, where the self is engendered at the top of the hill, these sexual overtones also appear. However, unlike later phases of his work, here they are still quite muted.

[35] See n. 20 above.

Our discussion of the macro-structure of the story has already demonstrated that aspiring to selfhood leads to a blurring of the outlines of Jewish identity. Now we see that this has to do with the need to establish the primacy of Judaism in relation to Western culture, because it obliges Greenberg to broaden the compass of Judaism and make it a universal phenomenon, and even subject it to radical reform. First of all, to pronounce the element of rebellion as a cultural impulse stemming from Judaism is essentially to present the builders of the Tower of Babel as Jews, and not as mere humans, as they are described in the biblical text. Second, it should be noted that the rebels who climb the hill in 'Memoirs' are not punished. Moreover, even when atop the hill, as near to heaven as possible, the youths do not encounter God, nor any another character or power who might have punished them for their apostasy. On the contrary, they are full of mirth, and even ridicule their assistant teacher, who stands at the foot of the hill and implores them to come down:

And later, when we were already at the top, we looked down all smiles—down below, by the foot of the hill, we saw Leibke standing alone, like a shepherd whose sheep have absconded . . . we remember our bows and arrows, others are reminded of the Lag Ba'omer boxes tied to their waists with rope. We scan the open spaces, like soldiers in combat searching for a target to aim at . . . suddenly a shot sped out from among the gang. From the bottom a deep voice booms at us: *Sheygetses, sheygetses!* Such are the deeds they do! . . . Leibke's delicate hand waved up to us, threatening—we burst out laughing. (p. 280)

Thus the biblical story of the rebels is presented as a story that is at odds with reality, as a story that was distorted by the interests of the oppressive Orthodox establishment, and that is here being retold in its true rendition. However, the act of Judaizing the pre-Jewish protagonists of the biblical story and of rewriting the story of the rebels does not achieve its purpose. It proves inadequate to support a claim of Judaism's primacy in respect to Western culture, but rather demonstrates the equivalence of the two. For in pronouncing the element of rebellion whose function it is to challenge the social and religious hierarchy, which is to challenge the transcendent status of God, there is nothing really new. Its purpose is to grant to the I identified here with the gang of youths the virtue of liberty that renders it a self, an autonomous subject, ungoverned by any external force. Therefore, the tack taken by Greenberg in the context of Jewish culture is not unlike the tack taken by the Sturm and Drang movement when, in the context of German Christian bourgeois culture some 140 years earlier, it rebelled against the church establishment and its conception of the divine. One need only recall Goethe's famous poem 'Prometheus', which dramatizes this rebellion in the context of Greek culture, and clarifies that the aspiration for selfhood does not conform to the Olympian understanding of divinity.[36]

Yet, even if the tack Greenberg takes is similar in principle to Goethe's, the two authors differ in fundamental ways. Goethe expanded the boundaries of his

[36] Wellbery, *Specular Moment*, 294.

cultural world and thus not only established himself as a young poet, but also affirmed his identity as a member of the majority culture, which as such, and by virtue of its self-definition as a universal culture, could assimilate foreign cultural elements.[37] As a member of a minority, on the other hand, Greenberg's very attempt to stretch the boundaries of his culture and encompass universality risked the loss of his own identity in relation to members of the majority culture, and so, by attempting this he was pulling the carpet from under his own feet. In the face of this danger, 'Memoirs' offers two possible responses: to retreat to the *shtetl*, which serves as a refuge from danger, on the one hand; or, on the other hand, to contend stubbornly with the challenge posed by modern Western culture, while simultaneously attempting to undermine the majority culture, and even overcome it. The first response is that of the gang of youths whom the narrator joins on their outing. While amusing themselves in play on the hilltop, they observe the setting sun and realize it is time to go back to the *shtetl* to take part in the *hilulah*[38] that is to take place at the synagogue during the evening prayer of Lag Ba'omer. We infer from this that the youths, who as full accomplices to the forbidden ascent had become, along with the youthful narrator, emblems of an independent Judaism, have now reverted to being representatives of the culture of the *shtetl*. Therefore these youths are presented as viewing nature and *shtetl* as two separate realms, and as willing to return to the *shtetl* and turn their backs on nature and all it signifies. For them, the act of rebellion was no more than a prank. Therefore the young narrator, who opts for the second response, sees them as 'naive' children (p. 281), while he perceives himself as fully comprehending the meaning of the revolt against the culture of the *shtetl* and profoundly senses the rift it has engendered. He recoils from his mates,[39] and when they begin their descent from the hill he turns to look towards the sun setting in the west; in this scene he finds the image of his selfhood, a being whose essence is its union of *shtetl* and nature, of Orthodox Judaism and Western culture. This union is achieved poetically through the metaphorical representation of the sunset that permits the fusion of both foundational aspects of the narrator's being: 'See far below, yonder, yonder, at the corner of the firmament spreading out such a beautiful *hilulah* illuminated by thousands of shining and gleaming lights . . . is it not more beautiful than the one in the *beit midrash*, which Hirshl the beadle is preparing with the youths out of simple coloured paper?' (p. 280).

[37] For example various elements of ancient Greek culture. Later, Goethe and Schiller were both to express their reservations about this approach. See Ulrich Gaier's discussion of the character of Helena in *Faust*: U. Gaier, *Fausts Modernität: Essays* (Stuttgart, 2000).

[38] A *hilulah* is an ecstatic celebration on the anniversary of the death of a saint. On Lag Ba'omer the *hilulah* revolves around the person of Rabbi Shimon bar Yohai and is celebrated with a festive bonfire, also called a *hilulah*. In the text quoted below, the word *hilulah* also refers to paper decorations in the synagogue that imitated the form of a bonfire.

[39] Here we encounter the same element in which the I is isolated and becomes singular, a motif already encountered in the passage mentioned earlier where the narrator secludes himself in order to devote himself to his vision of redemption.

The narrator's description of the sunset sets up an equation that sums up the act of transference taking place at this moment: unlike the other youths, the narrator perceives the setting sun not only as a natural phenomenon but as a *hilulah*. Furthermore, he sees it as the source of all *hilulah* bonfires, while he regards the *hilulah* performed in the synagogue as a shabby imitation of the original. Moreover, this original *hilulah* is not really the sun. It is rather the *hilulah* itself: it is made of the light of all the mysteries that Rabbi Shimon bar Yohai (Rashbi) revealed to his students on the day he died, on Lag Ba'omer.[40] In other words, when the narrator notices the *hilulah* on the western horizon he sees sunlight that is pregnant with meanings, that carries within it the source of light, or mystery. Essentially, it is the person of Rashbi, who dispersed the great light when he died, that is figured in the light of this setting sun. Here he is portrayed as the founder of an autonomous Jewish culture, which fuses together the mystery and the light (p. 280).

This act of transference also subverts the two foundational elements that make up the world of the narrator. It subverts Orthodox Judaism, the Judaism of the *shtetl*, which is presented here as a cultural system that is indeed rich in meaning, but once severed from its connection to nature has lost its vitality; it also undermines the Western culture that is now in decline, so it seems,[41] because although it maintains its connection with nature, it has not preserved its meaning, its inner mystery. Moreover, because of its intrinsic qualities, this act of transference does not achieve its goal.[42] It does not lead to the desired union with the origin of being represented here through the metaphor of the sun's *hilulah* setting on the horizon. The lack of an origin is signified in the text in several ways. First, the moment he connects with his 'true' origin, with the image of his selfhood, the narrator becomes severed from what had hitherto appeared to be the natural source of his life, the culture of the *shtetl*. Greenberg underscores this when he describes the narrator at this moment mentally rejecting the possibility of returning to the *shtetl* and, further, as feeling 'as if someone wanted to tear him out of his mother's arms' (p. 280).[43]

---

[40] E. Kitov, *The Book of our Heritage: The Jewish Year and its Days of Significance*, iii: *Iyar–Elul*, trans. N. Bulman (New York, 1970), 37.

[41] It should be noted that Oswald Spengler published the first volume of his book *The Decline of the West* only in 1919: O. Spengler, *Der Untergang des Abendlandes: Umrisse einer Morphologie der Weltgeschichte*, i (Munich, 1919). Even if Greenberg read this book when it came out, it would be inaccurate to say that his outlook was especially influenced by it: see Miron, *Akdamut le'u. ts. grinberg*, 50. It appears, rather, that Greenberg's views in this regard were in the spirit of the times, since many intellectuals in the German cultural sphere held such views in the early twentieth century.

[42] The self that is created through the connection of the I to the other is not sustainable. It collapses the moment it is created, since the moment the I undermines the rift between it and its other, the I's identity becomes determined as the other. But this mutual identification entails a loss of identity. Once it attains its origin, the I loses itself in its other, as the other loses itself in the I. In this process they neutralize not only one another, but also the existence of the self. At the end of the process of transference, therefore, what emerges is a void and not a self.

[43] It should be noted that the appearance of the mother figure in this context is not coincidental at all, and there is a close connection between this representation of the mother as a source that has been

Second, it should be noted that the image of the narrator's selfhood, i.e. the figure that is positioned at the origin, is seen by him only at a great temporal remove (the time of Rashbi) and spatial remove (the horizon). In other words, he can only experience his selfhood through an intermediary, without himself becoming a self, i.e. without truly attaining his own origin. Third, the self by means of which the youth—through his own reflection in it—experiences himself as having arrived at his own source, seems to be undermined. It vanishes in front of the youth's eyes and leaves a void.[44] In the following narrative section this process is represented concretely as an evacuation of the world, which is swallowed up by the night: 'A wondrous hand spread out a canopy, enveloped everything, and swallowed the entire surroundings with the calm of night.'[45]

ANALOGOUS STATES AND THE DEVELOPMENT OF ORDERS[46]

This moment, whose impact on the narrator's existential condition is the topic of this essay, is the constitutive experience that defines his entire being. This is the point to which the entire narrative leads, and around which the plot will revolve until the end of the story, while the youth never ceases from trying to relive it, hoping to achieve the impossible and bridge the abyss that has opened up between him and his origin. In this respect, the story describes the existential plight of modern man, of the man whom Michel Foucault described as a 'being without origin':

Paradoxically, the original, in man, does not herald the time of his birth, or the most ancient kernel of his experience: it links him to that which does not have the same time as himself; and it sets free in him everything that is not contemporaneous with him; it indicates ceaselessly, and in an ever-renewed proliferation, that things began long before him, and that for this very reason, and since his experience is wholly constituted and limited by things, no one can ever assign him an origin. Now, this impossibility itself has two aspects: on the one hand, it signifies that the origin of things is always pushed further back, since it goes back to a calendar upon which man does not figure; but, on the other hand, it signifies that man . . . is the being without origin, who has 'neither country nor date', whose birth is never accessible because it never took 'place'.[47]

abandoned and the understanding of the autonomous subject as was formulated in German literature and culture towards the end of the eighteenth century; see Wellbery, *Specular Moment*, 104.

[44] See n. 42 above.

[45] 'Everything' here, of course, does not refer to the entire world, for the narrator stays at the top of the hill, and later finds his way back to the town. 'Everything' is the narrator's self, which includes within it his I and his other and unites the two. The self is what disappears while the I and the other continue to exist separately from one another.

[46] This poetic dimension will be developed in Greenberg's later works, and especially in his long poem *Mephisto*, while here, in the short story 'Memoirs', it is indeed clearly intimated, but it stands in tension with Greenberg's desire to tell a story with a linear plot development. I therefore limit myself to a brief presentation of it, which will be elaborated in a future discussion.

[47] Foucault, *Order of Things*, 361.

At first, that is, while still appearing to him in the form of the *hilulah* on the western horizon, his origin is positioned in an analogous relation to the narrator, who is reflected in this image and identifies with it, but never was nor ever will be identical to it. Moreover, the moment his origin becomes a point of reference, through which the narrator narrates his being, this 'analogousness' characterizes the narrator's attitude to everything surrounding him, not only in the dimension of time, which Foucault explicitly addresses in the foregoing citation, but beyond that, within every other plane of his existence. Therefore, this phenomenon is given various expressions in the poetics of 'Memoirs'. I shall here treat only one of these expressions—the circular structure, which characterizes the movement of the narrator in time and in space. This movement is produced out of the youth's repeated attempts to attain his origin.[48] Poetically speaking, the significance of these attempts is that the story is constructed as a concatenation of analogous acts of transference, so that in principle one could continue to string out an infinite chain of them, exposing the fact that the origin is in essence unattainable. In other words, the narrator has no possibility of creating a permanent or sustainable union between the two elemental components of his being, *shtetl* and nature, Judaism and Western culture. Furthermore, since neither of the two can serve the youth as his origin, since he is granted no possibility of remaining either in the world of the *shtetl* or in the space identified with modern Western society,[49] he is condemned to oscillate between the two as between two parallel entities which are as distant from each other as the youth is from his origin.

IMPOSSIBLE INTERIORIZATION:
ON THE CONDITION OF MINOR LITERATURE

The very fact of being 'a being without origin' signifies that the narrator belongs to modern Western culture. However, since, once having joined this culture, he is obliged, as explained above, to posit it as the other in relation to his I, he is only free to move around at its margins and is unable to penetrate its inner spaces. This is apparent in the process of interiorization which I indicated above. This process is necessitated by the I's fervent search for its origin,[50] since every attempt to attain the origin requires an even deeper penetration into the world of the I, in order to arrive at its original unity. Or, to employ the rhetoric of 'Memoirs', the process of

[48] At a later place in the discussion quoted above, Foucault points out that repetition is the central characteristic of modern man's search for his origin: *Order of Things*, 364.

[49] It is important to note that, upon his discovery of the origin, the space of Western society overlaps with that of the origin itself, for the sun that sets in the west is the figure of Rashbi. By the same token, this space is closed off to the narrator once the origin disappears. As soon as the sun sets, he must return to the *shtetl*. This provides an illustration to the argument above concerning exteriority/interiority or belonging/not-belonging to Western culture: see pp. 151–2 above.

[50] See also Foucault, *Order of Things*, 363–4.

interiorization is required because every failure of the narrator's attempt to realize his vision lays bare the gap between vision and reality even more starkly, until he has no choice but to relinquish temporarily its actual realization and to bury the vision deep in his heart. This process reaches its climax in the third and final chapter of the story. The subject of this chapter, which takes place during the Days of Awe, is a sort of repentance on the narrator's part, through which he restores his faith in his own vision. This occurs when he leaves the *shtetl* again to behold the spectacular sight of the setting sun, now appearing to him in the form of a bride:

> Near the bank, at the foot of the small hills of alabaster-grey, the sun stood orphaned, ringed by blonde braids, as a bride might plait her hair. She began—like a holy bride—to curtsy and bow, modestly cleansing herself in the small gilded clouds of sundown on the new year's eve . . . and it seemed that from very distant heights the horizon bowed down to the far edge of the fields, and from there, appearing as a face, the heavenly saintly bride was to descend, escorted by nimble little angels with silvery wings . . .
>
> I wished to wait for this. But my heart was encircled by a trembling fear— (p. 288)

The setting sun in the form of a bride locates the metaphor semantically[51] in the inner world of the narrator, within the psychological realm, and not in the socio-political realm. However, the analogy between this scene and the narrator's confrontation with the setting sun in the first chapter of the story charges even this image too with its inherent political meanings.[52] The bride does not have the power to expunge Rashbi from memory, nor, certainly, to elide the fact that her image is positioned at midpoint between *shtetl* and nature, between Judaism and Western culture. In other words, the discourse of love here embroidered serves at the very most as camouflage for the socio-political meanings associated with the metaphor of the sunset, but cannot eliminate them.

This point is doubly valid in regard to Greenberg's early poetry. This body of work depends on the story 'Memoirs,' which, as I have argued, describes the making of the narrator as a poet.[53] Thus, for example, the first poem that Greenberg wrote in Hebrew is a lyrical elaboration of the first meeting between the narrator standing on the mountain top and the setting sun:

[51] For the semantic structure of the metaphor, see B. Hrushovski, 'Torat hametaforah vehabidyon hashiri', *Hasifrut*, 34 (1985), 71–99. This article explains that metaphor must be seen as a dynamic system which is based on the combination of different frames of reference that are signified in or alluded to in the poetic text.

[52] The analogical dimension of a metaphor that is constructed out of semantic material associated with at least two frames of reference (see previous note) will be fully exploited by Greenberg in his later works, that is, to the point that the metaphor is voided of any specific meaning, and by virtue of this signifies the emptiness of the modern man's experience. For further discussion of this issue, see my analysis of the metaphoric structure of *Mephisto* in K. Neuburger, 'Einleitung', in U. Z. Greenberg, *Mephisto*, ed. A. Noor (Munich, 2007), 32–5.

[53] 'Memoirs' is not an autobiographical story, although it is certainly not unrelated to Greenberg's biographical reality. Its significance, therefore, is not due to its being a faithful representation of Greenberg's young life, but because it presents the poetic myth which underlies Greenberg's poetry.

The path leads . . .

The path leads my feet to the plain
Up above a wondrous hand strews stars
My heart is in ferment, my eye yearns
For the sacred majesty of a setting sun

In the distance a crimson gold light seeps out
From the luminous glow, miraculous, at the edge of the blazing West—
Something creeps in, secret, hesitant
Like the wail of a man in the silent expanse

The edges deepen—the bounds of the firmament
The limitless reaches catch the bonfire's blaze
All is silent around . . . so enchanting and fine
The world of Yah is enshrined in poetry[54]

This poem bears witness to its source. It directly quotes from 'Memoirs' the image of a 'wondrous hand', which also appears there in conjunction with the verb 'to strew'; and it recycles the image of darkness spreading to drown everything in silence: 'All is silent around . . .'.[55] At the same time, as in the scene from the third chapter of the story, the lyrical version contains no allusions to the cultural or political meanings of the scene depicted. Even if the word 'bonfire' in the final stanza contains such an allusion, a reader unequipped with the information in 'Memoirs' would not be able to understand the sunset as a metaphor for a *hilulah*. Moreover, such a reader has no way of apprehending the acute political and existential meanings of this metaphor. On the contrary, the sunset appears in this poem as a universal symbol of life's temporality in this world. As such, this poetic image is unremarkable and seems empty and pedestrian.[56] However, when the poem is read against the background of the story, it becomes clear that this vacuity, which is a general characteristic of other early poems by Greenberg, is expressive of the existential state not only of someone who has become a 'being without origin' (such is the state of any individual in modern society), but even more so of someone who, despite having become a 'being without origin', cannot genuinely belong to this society of individuals. This can be inferred from the fact that in the context of the poem 'The path leads . . .' the sunset cannot be understood merely as a universal symbol but must be interpreted in and of itself as a metaphor whose import is particular, and which subverts the universal meaning of the symbol without obviating it. Paradoxically, the vacuous and plain linguistic figure of the sunset

---

[54] U. Z. Greenberg, *Kol ketavav*, iv, ed. D. Miron (Jerusalem, 1992), 9.

[55] See the passage from the story quoted on p. 163 above.

[56] For the same reason, the speaker's effusions of emotion in viewing the sunset are incomprehensible, and also create an 'empty' impression. This observation regarding the vacuousness and banality of emotion in Greenberg's early poetry has led to the characterization of this poetry as sentimental or as the juvenile lyricisms of an inexperienced youth.

is revealed in the space of oscillation that the narrator occupies in 'Memoirs': the space of oscillation between the universal and the particular, between the psychological and the political, and between the interior and the exterior. Therefore the vacuity that characterizes Greenberg's early poetry bears a political meaning—the political meaning borne by a minor literature.[57] It appears that Greenberg himself was sensible of this when he chose to underscore this vacuousness in different ways, and to turn it during the early years of his activity as a poet into the focus of his poetic strivings.[58]

Translated from the Hebrew by Ilana Goldberg

[57] According to the definition proposed by Deleuze and Guattari: see G. Deleuze and F. Guattari, *Kafka: Toward a Minor Literature*, trans. D. Polan (Minneapolis and London, 1986). My own focus here is on the second of the three characteristics identified by Deleuze and Guattari in their definition of a 'minor literature'. The two other characteristics also exist, to my mind, in Greenberg's story, but that argument would require more detailed elaboration.

[58] See K. Neuburger, 'Shirat uri tsevi grinberg bezikatah lesifrut germaniyah uletarbutah', Ph.D. thesis (Hebrew University of Jerusalem, 2007).

Between State Loyalty and National Identity

Electoral Behaviour in Inter-War Poland

JEFFREY S. KOPSTEIN and JASON WITTENBERG

RECENT HISTORIOGRAPHY has painted a complex and nuanced picture of the relationship among ethnic groups in inter-war Poland. Rather than study discrete ethnic groups as cohabiting solitudes, a new generation of historians maintains it is no longer plausible or even possible to tell the story of Poland without reference to ethnically non-Polish citizens. Especially evocative have been memoirs that focus on particular towns. Shimon Redlich's scholarly memoir of his native Brzeżany, Eva Hoffman's riveting study of Brańsk, and Norman Salsitz's panorama of his childhood in Kolbuszowa all provide us with first-hand accounts of the multitude of ways in which ethnic groups interacted and collectively experienced the economic and political tribulations of the inter-war Republic.[1] Padraic Kenney elegantly formulates the general point in referring to the role of Jews in Poland's national identity, a point just as readily made for Ukrainians, Germans, and Belarusians: 'they were not simply "also there" in the space that became modern Poland; they have been imbricated in the Polish national construction from the very beginning'.[2]

In this chapter we examine the political consequences of ethnic cohabitation: did the encounter between Poles, Ukrainians, Jews, Germans, and Belarusians induce political moderation, or lead to political polarization? The memoir literature offers one point of entrance to this question, but rich as it is, it is ultimately anecdotal in nature. After all, which reality represents the 'true' Poland? Brzeżany,

For research support we thank the National Council for Eurasian and East European Research and the National Science Foundation (SES-0217499).

[1] S. Redlich, *Together and Apart in Brzezany: Poles, Jews, and Ukrainians, 1919–1945* (Bloomington, Ind., 2002); E. Hoffman, *Shtetl: The Life and Death of a Small Town and the World of the Polish Jews* (Boston and New York, 1997), esp. 159–200; N. Salsitz, *A Jewish Boyhood in Poland: Remembering Kolbuszowa* (Syracuse, NY, 1992).

[2] P. Kenney, 'After the Blank Spots are Filled: Recent Perspectives on Modern Poland', *Journal of Modern History*, 79 (2007), 139.

where according to Redlich 'there was never a pogrom-like atmosphere' before the war?[3] Or Brańsk, where Hoffman notes the steadily increasing influence of the Endecja? Obviously they both represent different facets of an intricate political mosaic. We seek to explore that mosaic by investigating the relationship between local ethnic demographics and electoral behaviour for Poland as a whole. We are particularly interested in how the propensity of different groups to support parties advocating ethnic co-operation (or conflict) varies with their degree of local demographic dominance. For example, did ethnic Poles' preference for the right increase as they came into greater contact with the minorities? Were the minorities more or less likely to support moderate 'Polish' parties when they lived among Poles? The answers to these and similar questions allow us to isolate conditions under which moderate political parties, and by extension moderate politics, were most likely to thrive.

The chapter proceeds as follows. We first describe the data on which our analysis is based. Ours is not the first foray into the political behaviour of Poland's ethnic groups.[4] Like these prior studies, ours relies on the published results of the 1921 census and the 1922 and 1928 elections to the Sejm.[5] However, our data set is far more encompassing, comprising roughly 3,500 communities for which we have collected census and electoral data. Next we describe our method, which draws on recent advances in ecological inference. Ecological inference permits more accu-

---

[3] Redlich, *Together and Apart in Brzezany*, 53.

[4] The list of works discussing this at a general level is long. One early study of Warsaw is L. Hass, *Wybory warszawskie, 1918–1926: Postawy polityczne mieszkańców Warszawy w świetle wyników głosowania do ciał przedstawicielskich* (Warsaw, 1972), an excellent treatment of Warsaw's ethnic vote using the city's districts. Also on Warsaw's Jews, see A. S. Zuckerman, 'Division and Cohesion in the Process of Modernization: A Comparison of the Jewish Communities of Vienna and Warsaw during the 1920s', in S. Volkov (ed.), *Deutsche Juden und die Moderne* (Munich, 1994). Zuckerman's work re-estimates Hass's data. Using local elections Daniel Blatman estimates Jewish support for the Bund in 'The Bund in Poland, 1935–1939', *Polin*, 9 (1996), 58–82. More general treatments are S. Horak, *Poland and her National Minorities, 1919–1939* (New York, 1961); A. Polonsky, *Politics in Independent Poland, 1921–1939: The Crisis of Constitutional Government* (Oxford, 1972); J. Holzer, *Mozaika polityczna Drugiej Rzeczypospolitej* (Warsaw, 1974); A. Chojnowski, *Koncepcje polityki narodowościowej rządów polskich w latach 1921–1939* (Wrocław, 1979); E. Mendelsohn, *The Jews of East Central Europe between the World Wars* (Bloomington, Ind., 1983), 11–84; on Jews, see also J. Marcus, *Social and Political History of the Jews in Poland, 1919–1939* (Berlin, 1983), esp. 263–91. Two careful treatments of the Ukrainain experience (concentrating primarily on the Kresy) are C. Schenke, *Nationalstaat und nationale Frage: Polen und die Ukrainer, 1921–1939* (Hamburg, 2004), esp. 36–56 and 109–36, and W. Benecke, *Die Ostgebeiete der Zweiten Polnischen Republik: Staatsmacht und öffentliche Ordnung in einer Minderheitenregion, 1918–1939* (Cologne, 1999).

[5] The census was published in fifteen volumes throughout the 1920s, one for each voivodeship, by the Main Statistical Office (Główny Urząd Statystyczny) under the general title *Skorowidz miejscowości Rzeczypospolitej Polskiej* (Warsaw, 1923–6). Electoral results appeared in two separate publications, *Statistique des élections à la Diète et au Sénat effectuées le 5 et le 12 Novembre 1922* (Warsaw, 1926) and *Statystyka wyborów do Sejmu i Senatu odbytych w dniu 4 i 11 marca 1928 roku* (Warsaw, 1930).

rate estimates of group support for political parties in a wider variety of contexts than is possible with older, aggregate data analysis approaches. After the methods section we present and discuss our estimates of who voted for whom in the 1922 and 1928 national parliamentary elections.

DATA

Both the census and electoral data have limitations. Poland's census of 1921 was a bold exercise for a very young country. Enumerators attempted to count every single person in the country and classify them with respect to nationality, religion, and socio-economic status. Ultimately results for the community (*gmina*) level were published only for nationality and religion. Socio-economic variables were published at the district (*powiat*) level. The census authorities published fifteen volumes of these data, one for each voivodeship, and then presented them by regions that reflected the historical divisions of Poland: Western, Central (Congress), Southern (Habsburg Galicia), and Eastern (Russian Poland, the Kresy).

The results revealed an ethnically diverse country in which ethnic Poles constituted only about two-thirds of the total population. Communities range from being nearly 100 per cent ethnically Polish to 100 per cent ethnically Jewish, Ukrainian, German, and Belarusian, with the vast majority occupying a place between these extremes. However, as Jerzy Tomaszewski has shown in a number of studies, the results seriously undercount the number of Ukrainians.[6] His solution, the one we adopt in this chapter, is to infer ethnicity from religious affiliation. Roman Catholics, for example, are assumed to be Poles, Greek Catholics are assumed to be Ukrainians, and self-declared Jews by religious affiliation are considered to be Jews. This solution is imperfect for a number of reasons. It leaves out the not insignificant number of Protestant Poles, fails to differentiate between Orthodox residents in the Kresy who may have been either Ukrainians or Belarusians (or possibly ethnically Polish), and does not acknowledge the significant number of Jews in Galicia who classified themselves as Polish by nationality. We compensate for these limitations by excluding settlements with high numbers of Protestants and focusing (mostly) on Central Poland, the Kresy, and Galicia.[7]

The 1922 and 1928 electoral data were also collected at the *gmina* level, but were published only for communities with at least 500 eligible voters. This does not

---

[6] Tomaszewski's re-estimations of the census are to be found in J. Tomaszewski, *Ojczyzna nie tylko Polaków: Mniejszości narodowe w Polsce w latach 1918–1939* (Warsaw, 1985), 50. An alternative for Galicia in about 1939 would be to use the less precise study by V. Kubijovyč, *Ethnic Groups of the South-Western Ukraine (Halyčyna–Galicia), 1.1.1939: National Statistics and Ethnographic Map* (Wiesbaden, 1983).

[7] A second census was held in 1931 but cannot be used because the *gmina*-level results were never published. The unpublished materials appear not to have survived the war and have never been located by the Main Statistical Office in Warsaw.

pose a problem for matching with the census data, but it does mean that we cannot analyse the electoral behaviour of a number of small rural estate settlements (*obszary dworskie*). This reduces the total population considered in our analysis by approximately one-third, a matter less serious for considering the Jewish vote because Jews tended to live in larger communities, but it does exclude some rural Ukrainians. Nevertheless, even with these considerations there are over 3,500 communities for which we have some electoral and ethno-demographic data. The data set provides an unprecedented view of inter-war Poland's ethnic and political diversity.

METHODS

Our goal in this chapter is to estimate the proportion of a social group voting for a particular party (or group of parties) using census and electoral data available only at the community (*gmina*) level. This poses a statistical problem. Our ultimate quantity of interest is an unobserved quantity: the proportion of a group of individuals voting for a party. We observe, however, only the aggregated geographical distribution of the social group and the electoral results. Historians and political scientists have usually solved this problem by examining the results from ethnically homogeneous areas. It is easy to discern, for example, how many Jews voted for a given party in a village that is 100 per cent Jewish. Considering areas where there are no minorities, by contrast, allows us to absolve the minorities from responsibility for whatever parties get elected in those areas. There is a limit, however, to the usefulness of such aggregate analysis. In mixed areas the proportion of each group that supports a given party cannot be 'read off' from the raw census and electoral data.

We use recently developed ecological inference techniques to estimate group preferences for political parties. The best of these methods combines deterministic information about the possible values of the quantity of interest (in this case the fraction of a particular social group in a locality that could hypothetically have supported a given party or bloc) with a statistical model of what the most likely values of that quantity are within that range of possibilities. For example, if there were a municipality with a population that was 90 per cent Jewish and the communist party received 5 per cent of the vote, then we know that at most 5.5 per cent (5/90) of the Jews there could have voted communist, and possibly none at all (if all the support for the communists came from non-Jews). The range of possible Jewish support for the communists is [0,5.5]. The goal of ecological inference is to estimate where in that range the actual level of support is most likely to be. We employ the model presented by Ori Rosen and colleagues, which yields consistent estimates when there are more than two parties or social groups.[8]

[8] See O. Rosen et al., 'Bayesian and Frequentist Inference for Ecological Inference: The R × C Case', *Statistica Neerlandica*, 55 (2001), 134–56. All estimates were computed using R 2.5.1 software.

Our analysis of group political behaviour focuses on Central and Eastern Poland in 1922 and the South in 1928. There are two reasons for this. First, they are the most usable results from each election. The 1922 Ukrainian boycott in Galicia and known administrative pressure in the East in 1928 render these less reliable than the 1922 Eastern and 1928 Southern results.[9] Second, estimating each group's support for each bloc requires a large amount of non-missing data, and our method works best when there are at least some people from each ethnic group in each settlement. Both Central and Eastern Poland in 1922 and the South in 1928 (but not the West in either year) have enough observations to permit distinct analyses of majority and minority Polish settlements. Even then there are not enough data to permit a separate estimate of group support for the communists in 1922.

In both 1922 and 1928 we exploit data on the number of eligible voters to estimate voter turnout for each group. Turnout is important because it is a measure of integration into the political system, as indicated most dramatically by the 1922 Ukrainian boycott. We might expect the minorities, Ukrainians and Belarusians especially, to have a lower turnout than Poles. One methodological consequence of including turnout is that our numbers on group support for different political blocs represent estimates of the fraction of eligible voters rather than actual voters supporting a political bloc. Such estimates may be somewhat unorthodox, but they also provide a more realistic picture of the distribution of political preferences in society.

THE ELECTION OF 1922

Poland's constitution of 1921 called for a strong parliament and weak presidency. Historians generally acknowledge that this institutional outcome represented a victory for National Democrats, who expected to outperform the non-revolutionary left and especially Józef Piłsudski in any non-plebiscitary national election. The highly proportional voting rules induced twenty-two parties to run on the state list and dozens of other parties to compete on the regional lists.

The presence of so many parties, some with very similar platforms, permits the grouping of them into blocs. The main parties within each bloc are listed in the Appendix. Even where historians disagree on details, they do agree on the general contours of the country's party system in 1922.[10] On the right, the National

See J. Wittenberg et al., 'ei.RxC: Hierarchical Multinomial-Dirichlet Ecological Inference Model for $R \times C$ Tables' (2007), in K. Imai, G. King, and O. Lau, *Zelig: Everyone's Statistical Software*, <http://gking.harvard.edu/zelig>.

[9] Most Galician Ukrainian parties boycotted the 1922 election as a protest against the creation of a Polish national state on Ukrainian territory. In many locations violators of the boycott risked social sanction and physical violence.

[10] Our categorization of parties is based on the above-mentioned general works (see n. 4) along with the important analysis of the party platforms and press which appeared in A. Bełcikowska, *Stronnictwa i związki polityczne w Polsce: Charakterystyki, dane historyczne, programy, rezolucje, organizacje partyjne, prasa, przywódcy* (Warsaw, 1925).

Democrats teamed up with various Christian Democratic parties to run as the Christian Alliance of National Unity (Chrześcijański Związek Jedności Narodowej; Chjena). On nationality questions, although their practice was frequently quite pragmatic, the electoral position of the National Democrats was clearly one of assimilation for the country's Slav minorities and discrimination against Poland's Jews and Germans. They viewed the country's security as threatened primarily by ethnic competition in urban areas. In the centre of the spectrum came the peasantist Piast, the working-class National Workers' Party, and the Polish Centre. It is appropriate to mention at this point that, on nationality questions, the position of the centre parties did not deviate a great deal from that of the parties on the right. Assimilation and discrimination remained the tools of choice. Even so, the emphasis in the campaigns of the two groups differed sharply, with the right stressing the peril the country faced from the sea of prospective minority members in the Sejm.

'Polish' parties on the left wing of the political spectrum opted for some version of accommodation with the national minorities that would today be characterized as 'multiculturalism'. Although there was some discussion of 'federation', such talk remained highly theoretical. In practice, the issues were far more mundane: funding for schools, the mandating of days of rest, and various employment quotas in public administration and universities. The main parties on the non-revolutionary left consisted of the Polish Socialist Party (Polska Partia Socjalistyczna; PPS), which attempted to attract working-class voters and the urban intelligentsia of ethnic Poles, but also voters from among the country's minorities. 'Liberation' (Wyzwolenie), a left-of-centre party whose message was pitched at land-hungry peasants, also advocated accommodation with non-ethnic Poles. In practice, Poland's national minorities could choose to vote either for parties on the left or for parties running under ethnic banners.

Most of the German and a large number of Jewish, Belarusian, and Ukrainian parties ran in 1922 under an umbrella Bloc of National Minorities, with the understanding that the seats would be split up among them once the results of the election were known. Some of the Jewish parties (such as the East and West Galician Zionists—the Jewish National Union—the Bund, and Po'alei Tsiyon) and the pro-Polish Ukrainian Khliboroby chose to run on their own. Since our analysis focuses in part on the extent to which Poland's ethnic minorities would vote for non-ethnic parties and the local demographic conditions under which this might occur, we group all these parties together under the category 'ethnic'.[11]

At the extreme left of the political spectrum was the Communist Party of Poland, which, although illegal, managed to run in 1922 on a state list as the openly named Communist Union of Urban and Rural Proletariat. The communists attempted to attract votes both from the working class and from the country's

---

[11] Merging all ethnic parties together does not permit a more finely grained analysis of the impact of Polish presence on Jewish and Ukrainian support for different kinds of Jewish and Ukrainian parties, but—as we shall see below—this does not affect our analysis.

ethnic minorities, to whom it promised a future of non-ethnically based solidari-
ties. It favoured a communist revolution, the creation of a Soviet Poland, and the
rights of the country's minorities to the kind of autonomy that was evolving within
the new Soviet state. In voivodeships with large Ukrainian and Belarusian populations, the communists had their own ethnically based communist organizations
which were tenuously tied to the larger Polish organization. State authorities
regarded all of these organizations as traitorous and irredentist.

In the end the right was the big winner in 1922. It received 29 per cent of the
overall vote, compared with 22 per cent for the parties of the centre and 23 per cent
for those of the non-revolutionary left, 22 per cent for the parties of the minorities,
and a minuscule 1 per cent for the communists.

Table 1 shows the results for 1922 for Central and Eastern Poland (Congress
and the Kresy). The table is broken up into three sets of estimates, one for the full
sample of settlements, one for the sub-sample of communities where Roman
Catholics lived in a clear minority, comprising less than 40 per cent of the local
population, and one where Roman Catholics were a clear majority, exceeding 60
per cent. The interior of each cell represents the estimated percentage of the eligible voters of the relevant group supporting the corresponding bloc. To minimize
the effect of invalid votes we exclude those relatively few settlements where more
than 2 per cent of the votes were declared invalid.

We begin our analysis with turnout. As noted above, voter participation is an
excellent indicator of integration into the political system. We report non-voting
(100 minus turnout) in the last column of the table. Why should the rate of
Orthodox non-participation (50 per cent) be nearly twice that of Roman Catholics
(27 per cent) and three times that of Jews (17 per cent) in Central and Eastern Poland
as a whole? Some of these non-voters were undoubtedly Orthodox Ukrainians who
were supporting the Ukrainian boycott.[12] But there are other reasons to expect a
lower turnout of Belarusians. They were concentrated in the poorest region of the
new state, were far more illiterate than Jews, Poles, or Galician Ukrainians, and had
the least experience in self-government.[13] It is little wonder that so many stayed
away.

If we now consider areas where minorities dominated (the middle set of estimates in the table) together with areas where Roman Catholics dominated (the bottom set), the most striking difference is that for all groups significantly fewer voters
in primarily Polish settlements stayed home. Where Poles constitute the local
majority, turnout rises to 72 per cent for both Catholics and Orthodox, and an
astounding 94 per cent for Jews. Scholars consider the 1922 election to be largely
free of the irregularities that occurred in 1928. Nevertheless, it is known that the

---

[12] Our estimate using a sample of over 1,000 settlements in Galicia shows that 89% of Uniates did
not vote.

[13] For literacy data, see J. Rothschild, *East Central Europe between the Two World Wars* (Seattle,
1974), 44.

Table 1. The 1922 Sejm election: ethnic group voting in majority- and minority-dominant communities in Central and Eastern Poland (estimated % of eligible voters)

	Left	Centre	Minorities	Right	Other	Not voting
Full sample (N = 287)						
Roman Catholic	30 (24,35)[a]	19 (15,22)	5 (2,7)	19 (15,23)	0	27 (24,29)
Orthodox	16 (12,21)	0	30 (25,35)	1 (0,2)	3 (2,4)	50 (47,52)
Jewish	0	2 (1,4)	68 (63,73)	9 (6,12)	5 (2,8)	17 (11,21)
Communities with 2–40% of pop. Roman Catholic (N = 173)						
Roman Catholic	5 (1,13)	15 (11,19)	14 (2,34)	14 (8,22)	8 (3,14)	44 (30,55)
Orthodox	19 (15,24)	1 (0,2)	29 (24,34)	2 (1,4)	2 (1,3)	47 (43,50)
Jewish	1 (0,2)	1 (0,2)	65 (59,72)	8 (5,11)	4 (2,6)	20 (14,26)
Communities with at least 60% of pop. Roman Catholic (N = 80)						
Roman Catholic	33 (24,41)	17 (12,23)	2 (1,3)	20 (15,25)	1 (1,1)	28 (25,32)
Orthodox	14 (1,43)	8 (1,35)	45 (31,62)	2 (0,10)	3 (1,4)	28 (5,47)
Jewish	27 (1,94)	11 (1,56)	47 (3,68)	7 (0,34)	2 (1,4)	6 (2,11)

[a] Figures in parentheses are 95% confidence intervals.

Sources: Authors' computations from data available in *Skorowidz miejscowości Rzeczypospolitej Polskiej* (Warsaw, 1923–6) and *Statistique des élections à la Diète et au Sénat effectuées le 5 et le 12 Novembre 1922* (Warsaw, 1926).

Constituent Assembly (elected in 1919) did not wish to empower the Eastern territories and indeed had postponed the national parliamentary elections.[14] A generous interpretation of the high non-participation rates in minority areas is that the Polish state lacked the administrative capacity to manage elections in these border areas. A less generous view would be that the state was finding ways to keep these voters, even the Poles among them, at home.

Turnout rates are also key to interpreting differences in voter choice as we move from minority-dominated areas (middle section of table) to Polish-dominated areas (bottom section). The most significant differences are the increase in support for the left (PPS and 'Liberation') and to a lesser extent the centre. For example, support for the left rises from 5 to 33 per cent among Poles, and, though the estimates are far more uncertain, from 1 to 27 per cent among the Jews. The most straightforward interpretation of this is that the voters from the increased turnout went to the left and centre. Such a view would fit well with our 'less generous' interpretation of the reason for low turnouts because the right, the dominant force in the Constituent Assembly, would have been keen on reducing support for the left, its principal political opposition. It is also true that both the PPS and Chjena were aiming at urban voters (Polish support for the right also rises modestly, from 14 to 20 per cent). Cities were the site of both ethnic tolerance and hostility, of both

[14] See e.g. Rothschild, *East Central Europe between the Two World Wars*, 48.

accommodation and perceived threat. The parties of the minorities seem to have benefited the most from the increase in Orthodox turnout. We speculate that the Orthodox, who on the whole were less willing than Jews to assimilate politically, preferred their own parties to 'Polish' ones when they dwelt as a local minority.[15]

THE ELECTION OF 1928

The election of 1928 was far more controversial than the exercise of 1922. It was held after the 1926 coup with the intention of securing Piłsudski's supporters a parliamentary majority.[16] The vehicle for this majority would be the Non-Partisan Bloc for Co-operation with the Government (Bezpartyjny Blok Współpracy z Rządem; BBWR).

The BBWR was an odd organization. It was run primarily by state officials. Whereas political parties at this point in European history generally attempted to mobilize voters through mass organizations at the grass roots, the BBWR was in some ways a throwback to earlier parties of local notables. It espoused a general and vague ideology of state and bureaucratic rectitude but was clearly an anti-parliamentary parliamentary party and did not wish the population to remain active in politics once the election results were in.[17] Timothy Snyder, in his study of Volhynia, characterizes the BBWR as an attempt from above to reconstruct the political 'centre' in Poland. In this he is probably correct: the BBWR tried to attract support across social classes and ethnic groups, but in doing so, it was required to remain far more ambiguous on its plans for ethnic accommodation than parties of the non-revolutionary and revolutionary left such as the PPS and the various communist parties.[18]

Both archival records and the data themselves demonstrate the huge advantage of authoritarian incumbency enjoyed by the BBWR. In the run-up to the election, local officials wrote regular reports on the activities of opposition parties and the measures taken to increase the BBWR's strength, which was understood to be

[15] One seemingly puzzling result is the 7–9% of Jews who are estimated to have voted for the right. We suspect this to be a consequence of aggregation bias rather than actual voting behaviour. If the fraction of Poles supporting the right is highly correlated with the proportion of Jews in the community, then our method may attribute some of that support to Jews rather than Poles. Aggregation bias is a well-known phenomenon and serves to underscore the importance of having some theoretical expectation of how groups ought to be voting. A similar interpretation can be given to the 14% of Catholics estimated to have supported minority parties in minority-dominated settlements. If the presence of Poles caused increases in the proportion of minorities voting for minority parties, then some support for these parties might be inaccurately attributed to Catholics. It is also possible these Catholics were in fact ethnically Belarusian or Ukrainian.

[16] J. Rothschild, *Piłsudski's Coup d'État* (New York, 1966), 311–28.

[17] A. Chojnowski, *Piłsudczycy u władzy: Dzieje Bezpartyjnego Bloku Współpracy z Rządem* (Wrocław, 1986).

[18] T. Snyder, *Sketches from a Secret War: A Polish Artist's Mission to Liberate Soviet Ukraine* (New Haven, 2005), 64–74.

rooted not in civil society but in the state.[19] The data on the elections themselves
reveal a number of settlements, especially in the Eastern territories, where large
numbers of ballots were invalidated.[20] Yet, the modicum of administrative pressure applied in selected areas does not entitle us to characterize the election as
entirely fraudulent. The internal reports of the Ministry of Internal Affairs make
this clear enough. So do the results. Not only did the BBWR not secure its parliamentary majority, the right still managed to win a respectable (if much smaller)
number of votes, and the big winners were the parties of the left, mainly the non-
revolutionary left but also the numerous communist parties, divided along ethnic
and doctrinal lines, which, although illegal, still managed to run under a series of
easily decipherable cover names. Several, such as the Ukrainian Sel-Rob, ran on
state lists. Others ran on the regional lists with names referring to some combination of 'workers and peasants'. In total the BBWR received 24 per cent of the vote,
the right won 16 per cent, the non-revolutionary left took 28 per cent, the Bloc of
National Minorities won 19 per cent, and the various communist and pro-Soviet
ethnic parties captured 8 per cent.

Of course, Poland itself had changed in important ways in the years between
1922 and 1928, which in some respects makes the later election more interesting.
Most importantly, the coup had broken the parliamentary deadlock that existed
between the right and the left, which could not be broken without the participation
in some way of the country's national minorities—a clear taboo from the first election until the May events. As noted, the BBWR attempted to attract the votes of
the country's minorities through policies of moderation and accommodation. In
its view, these groups had little interest in the raucous democracy of the pre-
Sanacja era, since that had proved to benefit primarily the demagogic National
Democrats. Instead, if they could be incorporated through a 'state party', the irredentist threat to Poland from abroad could be attenuated and the country could
return to a normal path of development. This new orientation, however, continued
to compete with the non-revolutionary left (which had always advocated accommodation) among Poles and with the ethnic parties among the country's national
minorities.

Table 2 breaks down the overall vote by ethnic group. As in 1922, we divide the
results into two sub-samples of Polish-dominant and minority-dominant communities. However, we now present results from the South (though we shall introduce some results from the Centre and East), and estimate support for a slightly

[19] Archiwum Akt Nowych, Warsaw (hereafter AAN), Ministerstwo Spraw Wewnętrznych (MSW),
1/849/1-200; AAN, MSW, 1029 and 1079.

[20] The total number of invalidated ballots was 320,142 out of 11,728,360. The corrected numbers,
along with a detailed report on the conduct of the election, can be found in 'Udział ugrupowań wywro-
towych w wyborach do ciał ustawodawczych w Polsce w roku 1928', in AAN, MSW, 1186. This report
concentrates especially on the threat posed by the numerous communist parties, which were characterized as campaigning hard for a heavy turnout in minority areas, and on the steps taken to reduce
turnout where they were expected to perform well.

Table 2. The 1928 Sejm election: ethnic group voting in majority- and minority-dominant communities in the South (Galicia) (estimated % of eligible voters)

	Communist	Left	Pro-govt.	Minorities	Right	Other	Not voting
Full sample (N = 1,080)							
Roman Catholic	0	22 (19,24)[a]	33 (28,37)	6 (3,9)	14 (12,17)	0	24 (21,27)
Uniate	8 (7,9)	0	15 (13,16)	49 (47,51)	0	9 (8,10)	20 (18,21)
Jewish	3 (1,4)	1 (0,1)	18 (13,24)	52 (46,59)	1 (1,3)	3 (1,5)	22 (17,28)
Communities with 2–40% of pop. Roman Catholic (N = 814)							
Roman Catholic	1 (0,3)	14 (11,17)	36 (28,43)	14 (4,23)	10 (8,12)	1 (0,3)	24 (15,33)
Uniate	8 (7,9)	0	14 (12,16)	48 (45,51)	0	9 (7,10)	21 (19,23)
Jewish	3 (1,5)	2 (1,5)	16 (12,21)	49 (43,55)	2 (0,3)	3 (1,4)	26 (18,32)
Communities with at least 60% of pop. Roman Catholic (N = 117)							
Roman Catholic	1 (1,2)	25 (19,31)	30 (22,38)	5 (1,10)	14 (12,17)	1 (1,2)	23 (18,28)
Uniate	7 (2,12)	1 (0,6)	20 (2,41)	50 (33,66)	2 (0,9)	7 (2,12)	12 (3,28)
Jewish	5 (1,13)	20 (1,56)	25 (1,81)	33 (2,64)	2 (1,5)	5 (1,14)	9 (3,19)

[a] Figures in parentheses are 95% confidence intervals.

Sources: Authors' computations from data available in *Skorowidz miejscowości Rzeczypospolitej Polskiej* (Warsaw, 1923–6) and *Statystyka wyborów do Sejmu i Senatu odbytych w dniu 4 i 11 marca 1928 roku* (Warsaw, 1930).

different set of blocs. Our potentially most controversial decision is to move the Piast from the centre to the right part of the Polish spectrum (see Appendix). This reflects the disintegration of the Polish centre after 1923, the party's own movement on nationality questions during its time in government together with the National Democrats before the 1926 coup, and its campaign statements on nationality issues printed in its own newspaper, *Piast*, in the run-up to the 1928 election.[21] The centre has now been redesignated 'pro-government' to reflect the attempt by the BBWR to capture this space. We also now provide separate estimates of communist support.[22]

How successful was the BBWR in its efforts at political integration? Judging by voter participation, the Sanacja's goal of politically integrating the country's minorities was partially successful. Whereas in 1922 only 11 per cent of Ukrainian Uniates were estimated to have voted, by 1928, without a boycott, the proportion increased to 80 per cent (i.e. 20 per cent not turning out). Jewish (and Polish) turnout was largely unchanged from 1922, at roughly 75 per cent. Not shown in the table, however, is the continued relatively low turnout of Orthodox Ukrainians and Belarusians, at just over 53 per cent.

The real plan for the integration of Poland's minorities, however, was to have them vote for the BBWR. Our estimates (the top set in the table) suggest that this was also partially achieved: 15 per cent of Greek Catholics (Uniates) and 18 per

[21] Based on analysis of each issue of the paper during the three months before the election.
[22] The communist parties are listed in AAN, MSW, 1186, pp. 1–20.

cent of Jews voted for pro-government parties, which included either the BBWR or its allies.[23] At the same time, however, the anti-system and pro-Soviet communists clearly made inroads among the country's minorities. Support for the communists was 8 per cent among Uniates and, though not shown in the table, 29 per cent among the Orthodox. Jewish communist voting remained very low, never exceeding 5 per cent.[24] Poles also strongly supported the BBWR, at 33 per cent.[25]

To what extent were these results conditioned by ethnic demography at the local level? Despite the inclusion of the communist bloc and the geographical shift from the Centre and East to the South, the differences between Polish-dominated and minority-dominated areas in 1928 are qualitatively similar to those from 1922. As before, the proportion not voting is lower in Polish areas, though this applies only to minorities. Likewise, as before both the ethnically tolerant left and the right performed better among Poles in ethnically Polish communities (25 and 14 per cent, respectively) than among Poles in minority areas (14 and 10 per cent). The contrast with 1922 is that the divergences between the two types of areas are less stark, and, because Polish turnout does not vary, are less easily ascribed to a 'suppressed' leftist vote in minority areas. Rather, the left was simply more popular among Poles in Polish areas. The 'flattening out' of ethnic Polish political support across different types of communities (relative to 1922) is indicative of a nationalization of Polish politics, a point we return to in the Conclusion.

The story for the minorities is necessarily more speculative owing to the paucity of data in Polish-dominated settlements and concomitant wide confidence intervals around estimates for the Jews. However, our limited data do suggest that, as in 1922, increased turnout among Jews and Ukrainians in Polish-dominated areas redounded to the benefit of the moderate left and, as the newly reconstituted centre in 1928, the pro-government bloc. In the case of Jews, support for pro-government parties was greater in Polish-dominated areas (25 per cent, as against 16 per cent in minority-dominated areas), as was support for the left (20 per cent, versus only 2 per cent in minority-dominated areas). For Uniates there was a more moderate contrast in pro-government support (20 per cent and 14 per cent, correspondingly). The popularity among the minorities of the moderate 'Polish' parties, the BBWR in particular, is consistent with the idea that by 1928 substantial proportions of both Jews and Ukrainians viewed Piłsudski as a protector against the pathology of National Democracy. In the case of the Jews the combined proportion of the vote in Polish-dominated areas for the BBWR and the left exceeded that of the vote for the minority parties, indicating a degree of political assimilation to the Polish state

[23] In Central and Eastern Poland, where administrative pressure was more severe, 25% of Jews and 17% of Orthodox are estimated to have supported the BBWR.

[24] This finding buttresses our earlier research on Jewish support for communism, which was based on *powiat*-level data. See J. S. Kopstein and J. Wittenberg, 'Who Voted Communist? Reconsidering the Social Bases of Radicalism in Interwar Poland', *Slavic Review*, 62 (2003), 87–109.

[25] In Central and Eastern Poland the BBWR only attracted 12% support among Poles. This is not surprising, given that Piłsudski's original political base was in Galicia.

project that has gone largely unsubstantiated, if not unnoticed, in the literature on inter-war Poland. It was in these communities that the BBWR and parties of the tolerant Polish left could successfully compete with Jewish parties for the Jewish vote.[26]

CONCLUSION

What were the political consequences of the local encounter between Poles and the minorities? There are two ways to interpret our finding that in both 1922 and 1928 voter turnout and support for moderate parties reached their peak in Polish-dominated settlements. On the positive side, it is a sign that both Poles and the minorities in these areas felt a stake in the success of the new system, and is thus indicative of an increasingly integrated polity. On the negative side, it serves as a stark reminder of the new state's administrative incapacity and fear of the minority vote. Clearly the state had some way to go to properly incorporate minority-dominated regions into the political system.[27]

If we consider trends between 1922 and 1928, our principal finding is that for Poles electoral behaviour became increasingly independent of local ethnic demography. This is true of voter turnout, which increased sharply in minority-dominated areas, and of support for the left. We attribute the closing of the gap between Polish-dominated and minority-dominated areas to an ongoing regional homogenization of politics. This was occurring at the level of the state, which had increased its presence in minority areas in the intervening six years, but also at the level of party politics.[28]

Perhaps our most interesting results concern the nature of the Sanacja regime and its impact on Poland's ethnic minorities. Judging from the increase in voter turnout across ethnic groups, Piłsudski and his followers successfully integrated the country's minorities into political life.[29] Of course, minority parties did not lose their dominant place among Jews, Ukrainians, and Belarusians, but the ability of the BBWR to attract voters apart from Poles in 1928 indicates that the

[26] The confidence intervals in the Jewish vote for the left and the BBWR in Polish settlements are large. However, the vote percentages and the confidence intervals across blocs indicate that the vote totals could rise or fall between these two categories, which supports the present point.

[27] We recognize that not just contact, but quality of contact, may influence political behaviour. The memoir literature illustrates how the complex relationships between Poles, Jews, Belarusians, and Ukrainians coloured everyday life: see, for example, Redlich, *Together and Apart in Brzezany*, 44–76. Alas, we lack the data to explore this more systematically. Moreover, apart from noting that certain parties directed their appeals either to urban or to rural voters, we have not conditioned any of our results on the socio-economic structure of Poland's districts and regions, and acknowledge that this might alter our conclusions.

[28] See Paczkowski's analysis of the inter-war press, in which even local editions of party newspapers were expected to hew closely to the national line. A. Paczkowski, *Prasa Drugiej Rzeczypospolitej, 1918–1939* (Warsaw, 1971), 26–33.

[29] The exception remained the Belarusians, only 53% of whom we estimate to have voted in 1928.

regime made headway, especially among Jews and Ukrainians who lived in Polish-dominated regions. Again, a reasonable interpretation of this is that, since the BBWR was so closely associated with the state, it would perform better in those areas where the state infrastructure was most developed.

Even in 1928 the Polish state was less articulated in minority than in Polish communities.[30] At the same time, Jewish willingness to back the BBWR as well as other 'Polish' parties in Polish-majority settlements opens the tantalizing possibility that for Jews, the prospect of political assimilation was real and not simply theoretical. Polish political culture was not unattractive to Jews, and if the country had been afforded more time, even with widespread political intolerance in the ethnically Polish population, perhaps this political assimilation would have deepened.

Even with the Sanacja's modest success, its strength was undercut, at least in part, by the growing popularity of pro-Soviet communist parties, which explicitly traded on their ethnic universalism. The communists gained among otherwise passive and non-voting Belarusians and even among the highly nationalist Galician Ukrainians, a success that did not vary with changing ethnic balance. Just as politics for ethnic Poles was becoming increasingly 'nationalized', for Belarusians and Ukrainians homogeneous communist support across both Polish- and minority-dominated areas reflected an incipient 'internationalization', at least on the extreme left.

APPENDIX
Party Blocs in 1922 and 1928

1922

Right: Christian Alliance of National Unity (Chjena) (National Democrats, Christian Democrats, and Christian National Party); National Union of the State; Polish Conservatives.

Centre: Polish Peasant Party (Piast); Polish Centre; Bourgeois Centre; National Workers' Party.

Non-revolutionary left: 'Liberation' (Polskie Stronnictwo Ludowe 'Wyzwolenie'); Polish Socialist Party (Polska Partia Socjalistyczna; PPS); People's Councils; Peasant Party—Left Wing; Association for the Protection of Labour; Independent Socialists of Poland; Independent Socialists of Eastern Galicia; Union of Polish Women.

Communist: Communist Union of Urban and Rural Proletariat; Communist Party of Upper Silesia.

Minorities lists: Bloc of National Minorities; Committee of the Unified Jewish National Party; Jewish National Union; Jewish Democratic National Bloc; Khliboroby (pro-Polish Ukrainians); General Jewish Workers' Federation of

---

[30] Schencke, *Nationalstaat und nationale Frage*, 309–21.

Poland (Bund); Po'alei Tsiyon; Jewish National Unity Party; Committee of Independent Ukrainian Peasants; Agrarian Party of Ukrainian Peasants.

1928

Right: Catholic National List (Endecja); Polish Peasant Party (Piast); Monarchist Organization.

Pro-government: Non-Partisan Bloc for Co-operation with the Government (Bezpartyjny Blok Współpracy z Rządem; BBWR); Peasant Association; National State Bloc of Labour.

Non-revolutionary left: Polish Socialist Party (Polska Partia Socjalistyczna; PPS); 'Liberation' (Polskie Stronnictwo Ludowe 'Wyzwolenie'); Peasant Party (Stronnictwo Chłopskie).

Communist and pro-Soviet: Union of Workers and Peasants; Peasant Self-Help; Ukrainian Socialist Union and Peasants and Workers; Sel-Rob Left; Bloc of Workers and Peasants; PPS-Left; Ukrainian Party of Labour; Belarusian Union of Peasants and Workers; Cultural Union of Belarusian Workers; Belarusian Economic Union of Poland; General Belarusian Populist List; List for the Struggle of Workers and Peasants.

Minorities lists: Bloc of National Minorities; Ukrainian National Union; Ruthenian List; General Jewish National Federation in Małopolska; General Jewish National Bloc; 'For the Ukrainian Cause'; Electoral Bloc of the Ukrainian Socialist Party of Peasants and Workers; General Jewish Workers' Federation (Bund); Po'alei Tsiyon.

Failed Integration

Jews and the Beginning of the Communist Movement in Poland

PIOTR WRÓBEL

ONE OF THE MOST persistent and powerful elements of antisemitism, particularly in eastern Europe, is the concept of a communist–Jewish conspiracy, or 'Judaeo-communism' (*żydokomuna*). According to this theory, a natural and close link exists between Jews and communism; indeed, it is alleged that the political movement was invented, developed, and led by the Jews throughout the nineteenth and twentieth centuries. Many supporters of this belief use it to explain or even justify antisemitism and demand a collective Jewish apology for communism and its crimes.[1] Those who question the concept are frequently answered with a historical argument: the Polish communist movement in general and the inter-war Communist Party of Poland (Komunistyczna Partia Polski; KPP) in particular were numerically dominated and politically controlled by the Jews.

STATISTICS

It is true that Jews constituted a significant part of the KPP membership and that, in the party leadership, 'the Poles most frequently formed a minority'.[2] However, exact numbers and proportions are difficult to establish. The party operated deep underground, especially during the Polish–Soviet war of 1919–20, and the authorities of the KPP (until 1925, the Communist Workers' Party of Poland: Komunistyczna Partia Robotnicza Polski; KPRP) did not maintain regular statistical reports until the second half of 1923. Subsequent reports for the years 1926 and 1929 also contain incomplete data.[3]

---

[1] J. Schatz, 'Jews and the Communist Movement in Interwar Poland', in J. Frankel (ed.), *Dark Times, Dire Decisions: Jews and Communism* (Oxford, 2004), 13.

[2] H. Cimek, *Komuniści, Polska, Stalin, 1918–1939* (Białystok, 1990), 7.

[3] F. Świetlikowa, 'Liczebność okręgowych organizacji KPP w latach 1919–1937', *Z pola walki*, 50 (1970), 183; G. Simoncini, 'Ethnic and Social Diversity in the Membership of the Communist Party of Poland, 1918–1938', *Nationalities Papers*, 22, suppl. 1 (1994), 59.

The KPP was only one part of the communist movement in Poland. There was fluidity of membership between it and the Communist Party of Western Belarus (Komunistyczna Partia Zachodniej Białorusi; KPZB), the Communist Party of Western Ukraine (Komunistyczna Partia Zachodniej Ukrainy; KPZU), the three youth organizations of these parties, and the Polish-based International Organization of Help for the Revolutionaries (Międzynarodowa Organizacja Pomocy Rewolucjonistom; MOPR). Six communist parties were active in Poland in the early 1920s: the KPRP, KPZB, KPZU, Kombund, Po'alei Tsiyon Left, and the Communist Party of Upper Silesia (Komunistyczna Partia Górnego Śląska).

According to Jaff Schatz, 'the proportion of Jews in the KPP was never lower than 22 percent countrywide, reaching a peak of 35 percent (in 1930) . . . the level of Jewish members of the Communist movement then dropped to no more than 24 percent for the remainder of the decade'.[4] Schatz claims further that the percentage of Jewish members in the KPZU and KPZB was similar to that of the KPP; however, in the youth movements it ranged between 31 and 51 per cent, while 'in 1932, out of 6,000 members of the MOPR, about 90 percent were Jews'.[5] Other experts cite similar figures. Moshe Mishkinsky argues that Jews constituted about 20 per cent of the KPRP membership by the end of 1923, with a higher proportion in the Union of Communist Youth in Poland (Związek Młodzieży Komunistycznej w Polsce; ZMKwP). Julia Brun-Zejmis writes: 'The average presence of Jews in the KPP was estimated at 22 percent to 26 percent as compared to 33 percent for ethnic Poles. In particular, the Party's leadership was believed to contain a considerable number of Jews.' Similarly, Gabriele Simoncini claims that Jews made up a quarter of party members and a greater component of the KPP leadership.[6]

By contrast, most specialists recall that, during the Second Party Congress in 1923, out of sixty-nine delegates, fourteen identified themselves as being 'of Jewish origin' and seven others as Jews.[7] In addition, the delegates to the congress presented basic statistical reports about their districts (*okręgi*), confirming that party authorities were not certain about the exact number of members and that Jews usually formed a large group in district organizations.[8]

[4] Schatz, 'Jews and the Communist Movement', 20.   [5] Ibid.

[6] M. Mishkinsky, 'The Communist Party of Poland and the Jews', in Y. Gutman et al. (eds.), *The Jews of Poland between Two World Wars* (Hanover, NH, 1989), 62; J. Brun-Zejmis, 'National Self-Denial and Marxist Ideology: The Origin of the Communist Movement in Poland and the Jewish Question, 1918–1923', *Nationalities Papers*, 22, suppl. 1 (1994), 29; Simoncini, 'Ethnic and Social Diversity', 60.

[7] Mishkinsky, 'Communist Party of Poland and the Jews', 64; H. Cimek and L. Kieszczyński, *Komunistyczna Partia Polski, 1918–1938* (Warsaw, 1984), 79; *II Zjazd Komunistycznej Partii Robotniczej Polski (19. IX. – 2. X. 1923): Protokoły obrad i uchwały*, ed. G. Iwański, H. Malinowski, and F. Świetlikowa (Warsaw, 1968), 310.

[8] A delegate from Warsaw and Warsaw suburbs said: 'The number of members during the last two years: 1,200; those who regularly pay fees: 800, including 350 Jews, 100 women. 58 party cells, 18 [communist] fractions [in the trade unions] (10 in Jewish unions, 8 in general unions). Communist youth: 250, including 160 Jews. The young people help a lot. The number of people that we can mobi-

Party leaders were fully aware of the 'Jewish statistical problem'. In 1925, during the Third Party Congress, Gerszon Dua-Bogen, a member of the Central Jewish Bureau (Centralne Biuro Żydowskie; CBŻ), said (in Yiddish): 'It's a fact that, up to now, the percentage of Jews in our party is disproportionately large in comparison to the comrades of Polish nationality.'[9] In 1930, during the Fifth Congress of the KPP, its secretary general, Julian Leński-Leszczyński, provided basic information about the growth of the party, claiming that it had 7,000 members, as well as some 5,000 in the Communist Youth Association (Komunistyczny Związek Młodzieży; KZM). He complained about a large 'fluidity' of membership and a 'bad structure' due to the growing number of Jews: 'In this respect, the KZM looks the worse, since the percentage of Jews there reaches 50 per cent, of Poles only 20 per cent, and the rest—Ukrainians and Belarusians.'[10] Yet, the numbers given by the congress delegates did not look that 'bad', particularly in central Poland. A delegate from the Warsaw Suburban district (Warszawa Podmiejska) reported that there were 121 cells with 706 members in his area, including 169 Jews.[11]

IDENTITIES

Jewish members of the KPP did not form a monolithic or homogeneous body and can be divided into several groups. The most numerous, particularly among ordinary members, were 'Jewish Jews' (*yidishe yidn*), coming from a traditional, Yiddish-speaking, working-class milieu. In the leadership and in the apparatus, the assimilated 'non-Jewish Jews' (*goyishe yidn*) prevailed. They came to the party from middle- or upper-class families, and their communist involvement completed their Polonization. As they frequently violated Jewish law, many traditional Jews considered them 'worse than gentiles'. Often, their national self-denial and rebellion against Jewish tradition constituted a more important motivation than their hatred of social injustice. Moreover, a nebulous transitional group existed, composed of 'universalists' who believed in 'a single humanity' and who left the Jewish milieu, acculturating but not assimilating into Polish culture. Finally, there were the Litvaks and Russian-assimilated Jews.[12]

---

lize for larger actions: up to 3,000. Manifestations and marches attract up to 12,000 workers.' A delegate from eastern Galicia claimed that Ukrainians constituted 75% of the district members; Jews and Poles made up the rest. The Kielce–Radom delegate estimated that Jews constituted about 20% of all the members in his district. In the Ciechanów district, Jews made up 40%; in the Łomża–Siedlce district, all the cells were 'exclusively Jewish'; and, in the Brest-Litovsk district, Jews constituted about 70% of the members. See *II Zjazd Komunistycznej Partii Robotniczej Polski*, 82–96.

[9] Archiwum Akt Nowych, Warsaw (hereafter AAN), KPP, 158/I-3, vol. 4, 'III Zjazd', p. 204.

[10] AAN, KPP, 158/I-5, vol. 1, 'V Zjazd — Seria główna', pp. 75–6.

[11] AAN, KPP, 158/I-5, vol. 3, 'V Zjazd', p. 110.

[12] Schatz, 'Jews and the Communist Movement', 26; Brun-Zejmis, 'National Self-Denial and Marxist Ideology', 29.

Questions remain. Did the Jews dominate the party politically? Did they manage to incorporate specifically Jewish goals into the party programme and activities? Did they create a 'Jewish atmosphere' in the party? Or, as this essay argues,
was their situation in the party ambiguous? Following this latter view, I maintain
that Jewish national aspirations were restricted; access to communism was usually
an act of rebellion against and rejection of Jewish cultural and national background;
antisemites were not rare among communists; the attitude of the party leadership
towards Jews was vague and contradictory; and—most important—an attempt to
integrate 'Jewish Jews' into the movement failed.

THE BEGINNING OF THE JEWISH
REVOLUTIONARY MOVEMENT

The ambiguous identity of Jews within the KPP was determined by historical
experience. Jews in Poland first became involved with politics in the 1870s, originally in the western Russian areas (or the central and eastern lands of the former
Polish–Lithuanian Commonwealth), economically one of the most developed
parts of the empire, where newly established capitalism contributed to a ruthless
economic system. In the 1860s Jews who were sentenced for political crimes constituted only 3 per cent of all political prisoners in Russia. In the 1870s the number
rose to 7 per cent and was rapidly increasing. The Jews, persecuted and exploited,
began to join revolutionary groups and organized themselves. In the 1870s the
Jewish tobacco and textile workers in Vilna and Białystok arranged the first strikes,
and in the 1880s brush-makers, tailors, printers, and hosiery and textile workers
from Vilna, Białystok, and Minsk formed the first illegal trade unions. Marxist
groups attracted Jewish students, and the intelligentsia began to co-operate with
the workers. By 1890 the Jewish socialist Vilna-Grupe was established. In 1892 the
Vilna Jewish Social Democrats held their first May Day rallies, and in 1893 they
began to publish underground pamphlets and discussed long-term programmes.
In 1894 and 1895 the first conferences of the Jewish Social Democrats took place.
By the mid-1890s the Jewish Social Democrats had evolved into a significant
movement and were ready to organize a Marxist party. In 1897, at a founding con-
gress in Vilna, representatives of the Jewish Social Democrats from Vilna,
Warsaw, Białystok, Minsk, and Vitebsk established the General Jewish Workers'
Union of Lithuania, Poland, and Russia (Algemeyner Yidisher Arbeter Bund in
Lite, Poyln un Rusland), known as the Bund.[13]

[13] B. K. Johnpoll, *The Politics of Futility: The General Jewish Workers Bund of Poland, 1917–1943*
(Ithaca, NY, 1967), 22–4; S. Lambroza, 'Jewish Self-Defence during the Russian Pogroms of 1903–
1906', *Jewish Journal of Sociology*, 23 (1981), 123, 124; A. Litvak, *Geklibene shriftn* (New York, 1945),
162; E. Mendelsohn, 'Die jüdische Arbeiterbewegung in Osteuropa', in M. Brocke (ed.), *Beter und
Rebellen: Aus 1000 Jahren Judentum in Polen* (Frankfurt am Main, 1983), *passim*; J. Bunzl,
Klassenkampf in der Diaspora: Zur Geschichte der jüdischen Arbeiterbewegung (Vienna, 1975), 48–61; E.
Mendelsohn, *Class Struggle in the Pale: The Formative Years of the Jewish Workers' Movement in Tsarist*

THE BUND, THE RUSSIAN SOCIAL DEMOCRACY, AND THE NATIONAL ISSUE

The creation of the Bund paralleled the unification of the Russian Social Democratic Workers' Party (RSDRP). In its first months, the Bund devoted most of its energy to the formation of the RSDRP and prepared its founding congress in 1898. The Bund apparatus became the basis of the Russian party network and its largest autonomous segment. In addition to workers, the ranks of the Bund swelled with Jewish students from middle-class families attracted by the romantic revolutionary atmosphere in the party and disappointed with their situation in Russia. In 1905 the Bund had about 35,000 members.[14]

The founding congress of the Bund proceeded in Russian and was dominated by Russian-assimilated Jews. The Jewish Social Democracy came on the scene when the Jewish intelligentsia was still fascinated with Russian culture. Initially, Bund leaders devoted little time to the Jewish national problem; Jewish issues were considered only a matter of tactics, and Yiddish was used for practical reasons. However, an influx of young people from Jewish districts changed the profile of the party. After the pogroms of 1903, the Bund began to organize its self-defence and demanded that the Russian Social Democracy be a federation of national parties. Nonetheless, the 1898 founding congress of the Russian Social Democracy accepted a motion that the Bund 'enters the Party as an autonomous organization independent only in questions which specifically concern the Jewish proletariat'.[15]

Gradually, the national issue became increasingly important in party debates. The 1901 congress of the Bund placed the national problem at the top of its agenda, adopted a fully-fledged national programme, declared that Jews should be recognized as a nation and receive 'national-cultural autonomy', called for Russia

Russia (Cambridge, 1970), 17–48; Hersch Mendel (Hersz Sztokfisz), *Erinnerungen eines jüdischen Revolutionärs* (Berlin, 1979), 17–19; B. Orlov, 'A Statistical Analysis of Jewish Participation in the Russian Revolutionary Movement of the 1870s', *Slavic and Soviet Series*, 4, nos. 1–2 (1979), 320.

[14] Johnpoll, *Politics of Futility*, 24–6; Bunzl, *Klassenkampf in der Diaspora*, 61–7; A. L. Patkin, *The Origins of the Russian-Jewish Labour Movement* (Melbourne and London, 1947), 143–4; Litvak, *Geklibene shriftn*, 164; P. Schwartz, 'Revolutionary Activities of the Jewish Labour Bund in the Czarist Army', *YIVO Annual of Jewish Social Science*, 13 (1965), 229–31; J. L. H. Keep, *The Rise of Social Democracy in Russia* (Oxford, 1963), 44–52; E. Goldhagen, 'The Ethnic Consciousness of Early Russian Jewish Socialists', *Judaism*, 23 (1974), 481.

[15] Quotation from Y. Peled, *Class and Ethnicity in the Pale: The Political Economy of Jewish Workers' Nationalism in Late Imperial Russia* (London, 1989), 50; Johnpoll, *Politics of Futility*, 24–7; Bunzl, *Klassenkampf in der Diaspora*, 58–78; L. Bloom, 'The Bund and the Zionist Movement in the Early Years', *Judaism*, 33 (1984), 479; Lambroza, 'Jewish Self-Defence', 123–4; C. B. Sherman, *Bund, Galuth Nationalism, Yiddishism* (New York, 1958), 8; J. Frankel, *Prophecy and Politics: Socialism, Nationalism and the Russian Jews, 1826–1917* (Cambridge, 1981), 171; J. Kancewicz, *Polska Partia Socjalistyczna w latach 1892–1896* (Warsaw, 1984), 120; C. Abramsky, 'The Jewish Labour Movement: Some Historiographical Problems', *Soviet Jewish Affairs*, 1 (1971), 47; U. Ihnatowski, *Historyya Belarusi* (Minsk, 1926), 195.

to be reorganized as a democratic multinational republic based on the principle of national-cultural autonomy, and stated that the Bund should have the status of a separate national social-democratic party within the federal structure of the RSDRP. A faction claimed that the Bund should develop a Jewish national consciousness.[16] Nonetheless, the leadership of the Russian Social Democracy was against the 1901 resolutions and reminded the Bund that it had autonomy within the RSDRP only with regard to specifically Jewish issues. Many people came to the Bund from the general Russian Social Democracy, which had many Jewish members; their withdrawal from the RSDRP could have been dangerous to this party. At times, a newly established Bund group drew most of its members from an already existing local RSDRP cell. At the 1903 Brussels congress of the RSDRP, the Bund demanded to be regarded as the sole representative of the Jewish proletariat in Russia, asked again for the RSDRP to be rebuilt into a federal party, and stated that Yiddish should be one of the official languages in the future democratic Russian federation and that Jews should enjoy 'national-cultural autonomy'. Lenin and the Russian delegates rejected this and called the Bund 'opportunistic, nationalistic, and separatist'. Since the Bund's delegates were less numerous than the Russians, the motion was defeated. In response, the Bund left the RSDRP, whose leadership became hostile towards the Jewish party.[17]

THE BUND AND THE POLISH REVOLUTIONARY LEFT

The Polish Socialist Party (Polska Partia Socjalistyczna; PPS), established in 1892, opposed the Bund's aspiration to represent all of Russia's Jewish workers. In addition, the PPS accused the Jewish Social Democrats of activities leading to Russification of the lands of the former Polish–Lithuanian Commonwealth.[18] The PPS, theoretically a Marxist party, united social and national goals and aimed to rebuild Poland as a democratic republic. The PPS tried to be active in all parts of the former Commonwealth and hoped to persuade all its ethnic groups to contribute to its revival. Some Jewish Social Democratic groups joined the PPS or co-operated with it.[19] The establishment and activities of the Bund became a serious

---

[16] Peled, *Class and Ethnicity in the Pale*, i, 51–3; Patkin, *Origins of the Russian-Jewish Labour Movement*, 145.

[17] Peled, *Class and Ethnicity in the Pale*, 62; Patkin, *Origins of the Russian-Jewish Labour Movement*, 145; Johnpoll, *Politics of Futility*, 27–30; Bunzl, *Klassenkampf in der Diaspora*, 58; Sherman, *Bund, Galuth Nationalism, Yiddishism*, 9.

[18] J. Jurkiewicz, *Rozwój polskiej myśli politycznej na Litwie i Białorusi w latach 1905–1922* (Poznań, 1983), 31.

[19] M. Mishkinsky, 'Polish Socialism and the Jewish Question on the Eve of the Establishment of the Polish Socialist Party (PPS) and Social Democracy of the Kingdom of Poland (SDKP)', *Polin*, 5 (1990), 263–5; J. Kancewicz, 'Działalność organizacji warszawskiej PPS w latach 1894–1896', in S. Kalabiński and R. Kołodziejczyk (eds.), *Warszawa popowstaniowa, 1864–1918*, ii (Warsaw, 1969), 67–77; H. Piasecki, *Żydowska organizacja PPS, 1893–1907* (Wrocław, 1978), 14–19.

obstacle in this context. The PPS believed that a future Poland would control the regions of Vilna, Białystok, Minsk, and Vitebsk after an anticipated fall of the tsarist empire. The PPS tried to prevent the establishment of other socialist parties there and to act as the sole representative of workers in the lands of partitioned Poland.[20]

In this way, the aspirations of the Bund and the PPS were in conflict, even though Jews participated in the Polish socialist movement from its beginning and Polish socialist leaders had always been aware of the Jewish question. Jews were active in the 'First' or 'Great Proletariat' during 1882–6 and, after 1888, in the 'Second Proletariat'. Both of these parties tried to influence and co-operate with Jewish socialist groups in Poland.[21] Most Polish socialists of this era were influenced by Marx's *On the Jewish Question* and claimed that Jews were not a separate nation and should assimilate. The leaders of the Polish socialists, of both Polish and Jewish origin, claimed that all workers in the Polish territories must act together, and rejected national programmes, including the Jewish one. Ludwik Waryński and other leaders of the 'Proletariats' did not ponder the nationality issue and assumed an attitude that its critics called 'national nihilism'. In 1891 the Second Congress of the Socialist International in Brussels called for a union between Jewish and non-Jewish proletarians. The Polish socialists translated the original French expression 'union avec' into the more emphatic 'zlanie się' (fusion) and called for Jews to join Polish socialist parties both as individuals and as organizations. Russian socialists shared this approach.[22]

The Polish socialists were concerned not only with the problem of Jewish 'separateness' but also with the Russification of Poland. The fall of the anti-Russian uprising in 1863 was followed by repressions against Poles. The Poles became second-class subjects of the empire; consequently, they considered resistance against Russification not only a matter of national survival but also a defence of decent life. At that time, thousands of Litvaks, Jews from historical Lithuania, moved to central Poland. Both ethnic Poles and Polish Jews watched their appearance with apprehension. The Litvaks had families and extended connections in Russia and were a competitive threat to Polish businessmen. Usually more

[20] Piasecki, *Żydowska organizacja PPS*, 39; Mendelsohn, *Class Struggle in the Pale*, 33; Mishkinsky, 'Polish Socialism and the Jewish Question', 264; Peled, *Class and Ethnicity in the Pale*, 53, 56.

[21] B. Mark, 'Proletariat żydowski w przededniu rewolucji 1905 roku', *Biuletyn Żydowskiego Instytutu Historycznego*, 13–14 (1955), 23–7; L. Baumgarten, 'Pierwsze kółko żydowskiej młodzieży rewolucyjnej w Warszawie', *Biuletyn Żydowskiego Instytutu Historycznego*, 63 (1967), 65–8; Piasecki, *Żydowska organizacja PPS*, 14, 15.

[22] Mishkinsky, 'Polish Socialism and the Jewish Question', 258; M. Śliwa, 'Kwestia żydowska w polskiej myśli socjalistycznej', in F. Kiryk (ed.), *Żydzi w Małopolsce: Studia z dziejów osadnictwa i życia społecznego* (Przemyśl, 1991), 275; L. Blit, *The Origins of Polish Socialism: The History and Ideas of the First Polish Socialist Party, 1878–1886* (Cambridge, 1971), 45; H. J. Tobias, *The Jewish Bund in Russia from its Origins to 1905* (Stanford, Calif., 1972), 65; J. Holzer, 'Polish Political Parties and Antisemitism', *Polin*, 8 (1994), 194; AAN, Julian Brun — Spuścizna, 186/III-16, MS 'Kwestia narodowa w rewolucji i kontrrewolucji', p. 39.

assimilated than the Polish Jews, they did not speak Polish, but spoke a different dialect of Yiddish at home and Russian in public. Sometimes the Litvaks pretended not to know Yiddish, thinking it was more prestigious to speak only Russian. The Poles were unhappy about this spread of Russian language and culture and considered the 'Jewish question' a part of Polish–Russian antagonism.[23]

The danger of Russification was especially clear in historical Lithuania, where Poles had been losing ground since the 1820s. Józef Piłsudski, the leader of the Polish–Lithuanian PPS branch, tried to draw the Jewish Social Democrats away from their co-operation with Russians and to win Jews over to the Polish party. In most cases, this was impossible, and Piłsudski bitterly criticized the Jewish Social Democrats for the Russification of Lithuania and for 'economism', concentration on economic demands and neglect of politics or, in other words, refusing to participate in the fight for an independent Poland.[24] During May Day celebrations in 1892, the Russian-speaking leaders of the Vilna-Grupe declared: 'We are Jews and Russian subjects.'[25] The PPS resented this 'Russophile' stand. In June 1893, during its first congress in Vilna, the PPS made an appeal to the Grupe, arguing that its pro-Russian attitude was disadvantageous to both Polish and Jewish interests. Joining the Russian movement would lead to the Russification of Jews, claimed the Poles, who also attempted to persuade Lithuanian and Russian Social Democrats active in Lithuania to recognize the supremacy of the PPS.[26]

THE WAR BETWEEN THE BUND AND THE PPS

The PPS also tried to co-operate with the Jewish Social Democrats in Warsaw, but in the mid-1890s the co-operation turned into competition. As far back as the early 1890s, a group of Jewish Social Democrats had come from Vilna to Warsaw to persuade the Jews that were co-operating with the PPS to break off this connection and to join the Jewish Social Democratic movement. The PPS countered and created its own Jewish Organization (Żydowska Organizacja PPS) in 1893. The agitators from Vilna were more fluent in Yiddish, produced superior propaganda materials, had been better prepared to work with Jews, and competed successfully

[23] M. Nietyksza, *Rozwój miast i aglomeracji miejsko-przemysłowych w Królestwie Polskim, 1865–1914* (Warsaw, 1986), 210–14; O. von Zwiedineck, 'Die Litwaki', *Neue jüdische Monatshefte*, 10 June 1918; B. Singer, *Moje Nalewki* (Warsaw, 1959), 38, 47; S. Asch, *Three Cities*, trans. W. and E. Muir (London, 1933), 284; *Dzień* (Warsaw), 21 Aug. 1909; S. Hirszhorn, *Historja Żydów w Polsce od Sejmu Czteroletniego do wojny europejskiej, 1788–1914* (Warsaw, 1921), 247; Mishkinsky, 'Polish Socialism and the Jewish Question', 250–60; *Głos Żydowski* (Warsaw), 29 Apr. 1906.

[24] U. Haustein, *Sozialismus und nationale Frage in Polen: Die Entwicklung der sozialistischen Bewegung in Kongresspolen von 1875 bis 1900 unter Berücksichtigung der Polnischen Sozialistischen Partei, PPS* (Cologne, 1969), 340; Śliwa, 'Kwestia żydowska w polskiej myśli socjalistycznej', 276.

[25] Mishkinsky, 'Polish Socialism and the Jewish Question', 265; Kancewicz, *Polska Partia Socjalistyczna*, 404; J. S. Hertz, 'The Bund's Nationality Program and its Critics in the Russian, Polish and Austrian Socialist Movements', *YIVO Annual of Jewish Social Science*, 14 (1969), 53.

[26] Jurkiewicz, *Rozwój polskiej myśli politycznej*, 32.

with the PPS in the Jewish field.[27] One of the first brochures printed by the Bund accused the PPS of waging a war against the Jewish Social Democrats. The Bund did not invite the PPS to the founding congress of the RSDRP in 1898. The Third Congress of the Bund in 1899 decided to oppose the PPS. Increasing numbers of Bundist activists from Vilna and Russia proper arrived in Warsaw and central Poland to develop Bundist groups, which became larger than the PPS Jewish Organization. In eastern Poland and Lithuania, the Bund was several times larger than the entire PPS.[28] Bundist propaganda accused Polish socialists of not being real revolutionaries fighting for socialism, instead referring to them as nationalists aiming to reconstruct a Polish multinational state and 'leading the workers into a trap of bourgeois politics'. As a proof, the Jewish Social Democrats pointed to the fact that the PPS did not agree to allow Jews to have their own socialist organization. The Bund emphasized that it alone represented the Jewish proletariat and rejected the right of Polish parties to represent the Jews.[29]

The PPS accused the Bund of bourgeois, nationalistic, and separatist tendencies, and of creating an anti-Polish attitude in the RSDRP and depicting the PPS as chauvinistic in the international socialist arena. The PPS believed that a restoration of Poland would solve the Jewish problem automatically because Jews would be equal citizens within a Polish democratic republic. The PPS leaders believed that cultural-national autonomy was important only in feudal or authoritarian countries. In a fully democratic country, such as the United States, even the Bund did not suggest cultural autonomy, argued the Polish socialists. They claimed to have strong support among Polish Jews, while the Bund consisted exclusively of Litvaks. Initially, some Polish socialists identified the Bund with a branch of Zionism. The PPS also condemned the Bund for co-operating with the Social Democracy of the Kingdom of Poland and Lithuania (Socjal-Demokracja Królestwa Polskiego i Litwy; SDKPiL), organized in 1893 by a group of Polish socialists who opposed the programme of the PPS, believed that the workers' revolution would automatically solve the national question, and opposed the rebuilding of an independent Polish state as dangerous to the international socialist movement. They opted for a Polish autonomous republic within the future Socialist Federation of Russia. This and a

---

[27] Johnpoll, *Politics of Futility*, 38; Piasecki, *Żydowska organizacja PPS*, 19–23; *Robotnik Litewski* (Vilna), 2 (Mar. 1897), 80; L. Wasilewski, *Zarys dziejów Polskiej Partii Socjalistycznej w związku z historią socjalizmu polskiego w trzech zaborach i na emigracji* (Warsaw, c.1920), 58–9; *Głos Żydowski* (Warsaw), 29 Apr. 1906; Kancewicz, *Polska Partia Socjalistyczna*, 120–1; J. Holzer, 'Relations between Polish and Jewish Left Wing Groups in Interwar Poland', in C. Abramsky, M. Jachimczyk, and A. Polonsky (eds.), *The Jews in Poland* (Oxford, 1986), 140.

[28] A. Żarnowska, *Geneza rozłamu w Polskiej Partii Socjalistycznej, 1904–1906* (Warsaw, 1965), 40; Keep, *Rise of Social Democracy in Russia*, 44.

[29] Johnpoll, *Politics of Futility*, 26–7; Bunzl, *Klassenkampf in der Diaspora*, 92–3; *Źródła do dziejów klasy robotniczej na ziemiach polskich*, ed. N. Gąsiorowska-Grabowska, iii/1 (Warsaw, 1968), 37, 77–8, 86; Piasecki, *Żydowska organizacja PPS*, 73; P. Samuś, 'The Jewish Community in the Political Life of Łódź in the Years 1865–1914', *Polin*, 6 (1991), 95, 96.

common hostility towards the PPS made co-operation between the Bund and the SDKPiL easier. They jointly organized the United Committee of the Red Cross to aid political prisoners. Yet, there were also tensions between them. The SDKPiL opposed the Bundist claim to exclusive representation of the Jewish proletariat. Most SDKPiL leaders, including Rosa Luxemburg, disliked Jewish 'separatism' and represented 'national nihilism'.[30]

Tensions between the PPS and the Bund eased when, after the 1906 split in the PPS, the radical PPS Left abandoned its anti-Bundist position. The relationship had begun improving during the 1905 Russian revolution, which the Bundists had entered with optimism and enthusiasm, believing that the revolution predicted by Marxism had finally arrived. They fought with exceptional devotion and suffered large casualties during clashes with the Russian army and police. But although the Bund, the SDKPiL, and the PPS did manage to co-operate in some towns, such co-operation was frequently lacking. Typically, each tried to lead the fighting in 'its' territories.[31]

THE 1905 REVOLUTION

During the revolution, the Bund reached its zenith, counting about 35,000 members in the Russian empire, including some 16,000 in Poland and historical Lithuania.[32] After the defeat of the revolution, the party went through a crisis, lost most of its members and control over trade unions, and faced new competition from the freshly established Po'alei Tsiyon party. Factions within the Bund fiercely discussed its relationship with the Russian Social Democracy. In 1912 the Bund became a section of the Mensheviks, who recognized the idea of a federated

---

[30] Hertz, 'Bund's Nationality Program', 60; Wasilewski, *Zarys dziejów PPS*, 59, 82–111, 169; V. Medem, *The Life and Soul of a Legendary Jewish Socialist*, trans. S. A. Portnoy (New York, 1979), 260, 484, 485; Johnpoll, *Politics of Futility*, 27; Tobias, *Jewish Bund in Russia*, 72; Bunzl, *Klassenkampf in der Diaspora*, 93; Piasecki, *Żydowska organizacja PPS*, 58; L. Wasilewski, *Die Judenfrage in Kongress-Polen* (Vienna, 1915), 21; Śliwa, 'Kwestia żydowska w polskiej myśli socjalistycznej', 276–81; J. Nusbaum-Hilarowicz, *Pamiętniki przyrodnika: Autobiografja* (Lwów, n.d.), 33; AAN, Julian Brun — Spuścizna, 186/III-16, 'Kwestia narodowa w rewolucji i kontrrewolucji', p. 25.

[31] Śliwa, 'Kwestia żydowska w polskiej myśli socjalistycznej', 277–8; D. Blatman, 'The Bund in Poland, 1935–1939', *Polin*, 9 (1996), 71, 72; Archiwum Miasta Stołecznego Warszawy (hereafter AMSW), Zarząd Oberpolicmajstra Warszawskiego, file no. 12; Samuś, 'Jewish Community in the Political Life of Łódź', 97–9; Tobias, *Jewish Bund in Russia*, 298; H. J. Tobias and C. E. Woodhouse, 'Revolutionary Optimism and the Practice of Revolution: The Jewish Bund in 1905', *Jewish Social Studies*, 47 (1985), 136; Wasilewski, *Zarys dziejów PPS*, 159, 160; Johnpoll, *Politics of Futility*, 32; Bunzl, *Klassenkampf in der Diaspora*, 96, 97; Mendel, *Erinnerungen eines jüdischen Revolutionärs*, 27–32; H. Piasecki, 'Żydowska klasa robotnicza w rewolucji 1905 roku', *Biuletyn Żydowskiego Instytutu Historycznego*, 98 (1976), 42; U. Głowacka-Maksymiuk, 'PPS i Bund w latach rewolucji 1905–1907 roku na terenie guberni siedleckiej', *Rocznik Mazowiecki*, 6 (1976), 207–13; B. Mark, 'Udział proletariatu żydowskiego w czerwcowym powstaniu łódzkim i w walkach solidarnościowych', *Biuletyn Żydowskiego Instytutu Historycznego*, 23 (1957), 34–6.

[32] Piasecki, *Żydowska organizacja PPS*, 228, 229.

organization. During the 1910 congress of the Bund, only 609 members were represented and only nine local groups survived. Most of them were in the former Polish territories.[33]

The decline of the Bund was paralleled by a crisis in the PPS, whose national minorities experts still claimed that the Jews were not a nation but a 'medieval relic', that Yiddish was a jargon, and that a programme of national-cultural autonomy was a utopian idea. The PPS paid less attention to the Jewish issue after the 1905 revolution, after which its party programme vaguely explained that all citizens of a future democratic Poland would have equal rights, and that national minorities would enjoy special prerogatives and be able to maintain educational systems in their own languages.[34] In historical Lithuania, the PPS almost ceased to exist.[35] The Bund–PPS conflict eased but there was no co-operation. The 1910 conference of the Bund stated that an independent Poland would not offer improved status for Jews. 'The Polish bourgeoisie, if it gets power, plans to oppress the other minorities', claimed the Bund leadership, who concluded that neither a free Poland nor a Jewish state in Palestine but a federal Russia would be the desired future. Relations between the PPS Left and the SDKPiL were difficult as well; the parties could not find a common language, particularly over the national question.[36] The Bund began to intensify its activities in 1911, but was closely watched and infiltrated by the tsarist secret police. The SDKPiL and the PPS Left also experienced a revival in 1912, and explored a possible unification. However, international events delayed these plans.[37]

THE FIRST WORLD WAR

The outbreak of the First World War paralysed the socialist organizations and revealed their weaknesses. The PPS and the Polish socialists of Galicia formed a coalition with several non-socialist parties to fight for an independent Poland in alliance with the Central Powers. Some members of the PPS Left and SDKPiL supported this policy, but most of their comrades opposed it. In Warsaw, the Bund, the PPS Left, and the SDKPiL distributed anti-war leaflets, condemned the war, and called upon workers to organize a general strike. On 2 August 1914

[33] Johnpoll, *Politics of Futility*, 33–5; Piasecki, *Żydowska organizacja PPS*, 201–11; Bunzl, *Klassenkampf in der Diaspora*, 101; Mendel, *Erinnerungen eines jüdischen Revolutionärs*, 32–94; AMSW, Zarząd Oberpolicmajstra Warszawskiego, file no. 20, 'Działalność rewolucyjna 1911–1914'; *Royter pinkes. Tsu der geshikhte fun der yidisher arbeter-bavegung un sotsyalistishe shtrebungen bay yidn* (Warsaw, 1921), 131, 132; Ihnatowski, *Historyya Belarusi*, 217; V. Biržiška, *Praeities pabiros: rinkinys straipsnių iš Lietuvos praeities* (Brooklyn, NY, 1960), 316–23, 345–51.

[34] Śliwa, 'Kwestia żydowska w polskiej myśli socjalistycznej', 282, 283; W. Jodko-Narkiewicz (Wroński), *Objaśnienie programu Polskiej Partyi Socyalistycznej* (Kraków, 1913), 120.

[35] Jurkiewicz, *Rozwój polskiej myśli politycznej*, 40.

[36] Quotation from Johnpoll, *Politics of Futility*, 35; Medem, *Life and Soul of a Legendary Jewish Socialist*, 484–7; G. Simoncini, *The Communist Party of Poland, 1918–1929: A Study in Political Ideology* (Lewiston, NY, 1993), 13. [37] Simoncini, *Communist Party of Poland*, 14.

the representatives of these three parties met in Warsaw, after which they issued a joint manifesto against the war and elected a common Inter-Party Workers' Council. Yet the organization was loose and its members disagreed on basic matters: should they suspend the class struggle and fight against German militarism? and should they co-operate with the 'citizens' committees' established for charitable and self-governing purposes? After 30 March 1915, when the Russian authorities granted local self-government to the former Congress Poland, the conflict escalated, and in October of that year the Warsaw leadership of the SDKPiL, which rejected any co-operation with the self-governing body, recalled its representatives from the Inter-Party Council, which disintegrated.[38]

In 1915 the split between the socialist parties was growing. The PPS was ready to participate in the war, while the PPS Left and the Main Committee of the SDKPiL wanted to end the war and reconstruct the Second International. The Warsaw SDKPiL moved towards the Leninist position that the international conflict should evolve into a civil war, which would lead to the fall of capitalism and the triumph of socialism. The Bund was divided and faced another challenge. It became obvious that Bundist groups in central Poland would be isolated from the Bund in Russia proper by the Russian–German front. By November 1914 the Central Committee of the Bund in St Petersburg appointed the Warsaw Committee of the Bund Organizations in Poland. This was de facto the beginning of the Bund in Poland as a separate organization. In August 1915 the Germans took Warsaw, and communication between the Polish and the Russian Bund became difficult. Without oppression from Russia, the lives of Jews achieved German standards. Jewish educational, cultural, political, social, and economic institutions mushroomed. Initially, the Jewish population's attitude towards the Germans was friendly. Later, though, the situation of the entire population worsened as a result of the Germans' merciless economic exploitation of the occupied territories.[39]

The Bund underwent a period of organizational explosion in the Polish territories occupied by Germany, but party leaders were still divided on the issue of Polish independence. On 5 November 1916 the German and Austrian emperors proclaimed the establishment of a Polish Kingdom, a political manoeuvre that was supposed to encourage the local population to support the German–Austrian war effort. The PPS supported the idea of a Polish state allied with Germany and Austria, the PPS Left mostly ignored the event, while the SDKPiL attacked the proclamation. Yet, the turn of events prompted a rapprochement between the PPS Left and the SDKPiL. They wanted to fight for a revolution and a democratic Russia. Independence was considered unrealistic and unnecessary. The Bund, in

[38] M. K. Dziewanowski, 'World War I and the Marxist Movement of Poland', *American Slavic and East European Review*, 12 (1953), 72–4; Simoncini, *Communist Party of Poland*, 14–15; A. Czubiński, *Komunistyczna Partia Polski (1918–1938): Zarys historii* (Warsaw, 1985), 12.

[39] S. Dzierzbicki, *Pamiętniki z lat wojny, 1915–1918* (Warsaw, 1983), 63; F. Golczewski, *Polnisch-jüdische Beziehungen, 1881–1922: Eine Studie zur Geschichte des Antisemitismus in Osteuropa* (Wiesbaden, 1981), 130–3; I. J. Singer, *Blood Harvest* (London, n.d.), 73–6.

turn, issued a statement opposing the creation of Poland without approval from the working class. In June 1917, after the March Revolution in Russia and during a plenum of the St Petersburg Soviet, one of the most important Bundist leaders, Henryk Erlich, proposed a resolution calling for Polish independence. Most Bundist participants at this meeting agreed to support the resolution only if assurances would first be given that in a future Poland the rights of all national minorities would be protected and Jews would enjoy cultural autonomy. The Bundists did not welcome the division of their party into two organizations, Russian and Polish, and were lukewarm about Poland's independence. The PPS, by contrast, did not want to accept any conditions, claiming that Jews were indifferent to the independence of Poland. When, in 1916, the Bund had appealed to all socialists to form an electoral bloc for the first municipal elections in Congress Poland, the PPS refused. The Bund then formed an electoral bloc with PPS Left. The SDKPiL, hostile to the idea of independence, went to the polls alone.[40]

THE RUSSIAN REVOLUTION

The Russian Revolution divided the Bund. The organization was placed ideologically between the Bolsheviks and the Mensheviks. The Bund's leadership condemned the revolution of November 1917 as a coup and a conspiracy against a real revolution. According to Erlich, the Bolshevik government was not a true workers' government and the Bolshevik system was not socialism. Yet numerous Bundists supported the Bolsheviks. The revolution of November 1917 initiated the disappearance of the Bund in Russia. One faction of the party joined the Bolsheviks; another part, which opposed them, ceased to exist in 1921.[41]

The Russian Revolution also divided the Polish left. The PPS accepted with satisfaction the manifesto of the Russian Provisional Government of 30 March 1917, which promised to respect Poland's independence, and the subsequent proclamation of the Petrograd Soviet that confirmed Poland's right to self-determination. The SDKPiL leaders opted for Poland as a part of the Russian revolutionary republic; they were against an independent Polish state, and in this respect went further than Lenin, who, for tactical reasons, supported the principle of self-determination and called the SDKPiL position a 'strange and monstrous error'. The PPS Left hesitated. After the March Revolution, the organizations of the Polish radical left grew quickly in Russia. The SDKPiL, with about 5,000 members, moved towards the Bolsheviks, while the PPS Left, about 3,000 strong, preferred to co-operate with the Mensheviks.[42]

[40] Johnpoll, *Politics of Futility*, 46–52; J. Holzer, *Polska Partia Socjalistyczna w latach 1917–1919* (Warsaw, 1962), 34, 134; M. K. Dziewanowski, 'The Foundation of the Communist Party of Poland', *American Slavic and East European Review*, 11 (1952), 82–3; Simoncini, *Communist Party of Poland*, 15–16. [41] Johnpoll, *Politics of Futility*, 54–64.

[42] Simoncini, *Communist Party of Poland*, 15–17; Czubiński, *Komunistyczna Partia Polski*, 14–16; T. Teslar, *Czerwona gwiazda: Prawda o Sowietach i komuniźmie* (Warsaw, 1928), 62–86.

The success of the Bolsheviks in November 1917 strengthened the inflexible internationalist position of the SDKPiL and the left wing of the PPS Left. Now they had no understanding about national programmes, promoted the unification of their parties and the merger of the Polish revolutionary movement with the Bolsheviks, and joined their ranks in Russia. The core of the PPS Left, however, was afraid of the Bolshevik determination to subordinate all groups to their control and continued to co-operate with the Bund, which, to the SDKPiL, was a nationalist party ready to compromise with the bourgeoisie. In late 1917, in German- and Austrian-occupied Polish territories, the radical left was limited to small groups which lacked strong leadership, were unable to organize significant activities, and were outside the mainstream of politics. In 1918 these groups became more active and attracted new members. Many SDKPiL and PPS Left leaders returned from Russia to Poland and discussed the unification of Polish revolutionary forces.[43]

THE LAST WEEKS OF THE FIRST WORLD WAR

In early November 1918, when the collapse of the Central Powers was certain, the SDKPiL issued a proclamation titled 'To the Toiling People of Towns and Villages'. It called for the formation of councils of workers', peasants', and soldiers' deputies, for the establishment of the Red Guard, and for placing 'all power in the hands of the people'. Poland, like most of Europe, had entered a post-war economic crisis, and it seemed that masses of unemployed angry people were ready for a revolution. On 5 November 1918 the first workers' council was formed in Lublin; soon, hundreds of councils appeared in other parts of Poland. On 11 November the SDKPiL, the PPS Left, and the Council of Trade Unions organized the Warsaw Council. At the same time, though, an overwhelming majority of Poles supported the idea of independence. Hence, an efficient central government, led by Piłsudski, was established in Warsaw. The quickly growing Polish army disarmed the Red Guards. The PPS, which rejected the prospect of a Bolshevik revolution and supported the convocation of the Constituent Assembly, joined and dominated most of the councils. The Warsaw government issued a series of popular decrees that introduced the eight-hour working day, state inspection of factories, protection of labour, and obligatory insurance against accidents, illness, and unemployment. The spectre of revolution was dimming in Poland.[44]

Nonetheless, the radical left was determined to fight. A re-establishment of a Polish 'bourgeois' state was opposed to leftist ideology and plans. Radical leaders, immersed in Marxism, could not understand how it was possible for independent Poland to re-establish itself. They explained its emergence as a consequence of the imperialistic plans of the Entente, rejected the new nominally socialist government

---

[43] Dziewanowski, 'Foundation of the Communist Party of Poland', 85–7; Simoncini, *Communist Party of Poland*, 17–18.

[44] Dziewanowski, 'Foundation of the Communist Party of Poland', 106–12.

of Poland, counted on Bolshevik help, and grew drunk with the pan-European revolutionary atmosphere: on 4 November the Austrian Communist Party was founded, on 21 November the Hungarian communist parties, and on 18 December the German. The Polish left started negotiating its unification, and on 15–16 November the SDKPiL held a conference to prepare for unification with the PPS Left, which gradually assumed an ultra-radical position, especially after some party groups went over to the PPS to protest the Bolshevik policies of the leadership and in support of free Poland. In late October, the PPS Left conference condemned all 'illusions connected with creating an independent Polish State' and decided to unite with the SDKPiL. The PPS Left broke with its traditionally good relations with the Bund, now considered a 'petit-bourgeois nationalist' and 'reformist' party, even though both radical parties protested the growing anti-Jewish violence, which, in their opinion, constituted a reactionary attempt to channel mass revolutionary energy into xenophobic nationalism. Ideological and theoretical subtleties became less important in the face of epochal events; instead, practical action was favoured. At the grass-roots level, the unification of the two Polish radical leftist parties had begun even before their leaders made formal decisions.[45]

THE 'UNITY CONGRESS' AND A NEW PARTY

On 16 December 1918 the 'Unity Congress', the Twelfth Congress of the PPS Left and the National Conference of the SDKPiL working in tandem in Warsaw, formed the Communist Workers' Party of Poland (KPRP; initially the phrase 'United SDKPiL and PPS Left' was added under the new name) and outlined its programme, the so-called Political Platform (Platforma polityczna). It criticized the Second International for opportunism, predicted an imminent revolution ('the World War leads to world revolution') and an inevitable downfall of the Polish state, rejected self-determination as impossible under capitalism and unnecessary under socialism, stuck to the old 'national nihilism' position, and called upon the masses to unite and fight for power against the parties that supported nationalism, opportunism, and social peace, such as the PPS and the Bund. Lenin criticized this ultra-radical position at the Eighth Conference of the Bolshevik Party in March 1919, later addressing his book *'Left Wing' Communism: An Infantile Disorder*, published in June 1920, to the Polish communists. The Soviet leaders considered the KPRP's hostile attitude towards the Polish state a tactical mistake. Moreover, the First Congress of the KPRP adopted a short 'Protest Resolution against Anti-Jewish Pogroms' ('Uchwała protestacyjna przeciwko pogromom antyżydowskim').[46]

---

[45] Ibid. 112–15; Simoncini, *Communist Party of Poland*, 19–21; AAN, Julian Brun — Spuścizna, 186/III-16, 'Kwestia narodowa w rewolucji i kontrrewolucji', p. 171; H. Walecki, *Wybór pism*, ii (Warsaw, 1967), 152; Cimek and Kieszczyński, *Komunistyczna Partia Polski*, 15.

[46] Dziewanowski, 'Foundation of the Communist Party of Poland', 115–21; M. K. Dziewanowski, *The Communist Party of Poland: An Outline of History* (Cambridge, Mass., 1959), 78; Czubiński,

The new party was full of revolutionary enthusiasm, energy, and optimism, but it had no clear plan for immediate activities. Polish communists believed that they were in the middle of a European revolution and that its victory would solve all problems. The KPRP adopted the platform of the SDKPiL. In some towns, the PPS Left did not exist and local SDKPiL groups assumed a new name. The programme was weak with regard to strategic political questions and inadequate in the new post-war situation. It completely rejected Polish national tradition and did not accept the worker–peasant alliance. It was not clear about specific forms of the dictatorship of the proletariat, future borders, and peasant, church, and intelligentsia issues. The practical organizational decisions were frequently sketchy and general because the party's founders believed that in three months its second congress would meet and explain all the issues.[47]

The national question was one of the weakest parts of this revolutionary utopianism. This was a serious problem because the party soon became multinational. Initially, it was active only in the former Congress Poland, where Jews formed a large part of the proletariat. The situation of Jewish workers was particularly grim after the war. Like others, Jews suffered from the economic crisis, but Poland's revival offered no consolation for them. On the contrary, they faced a wave of anti-Jewish violence. As a consequence, political life among Jews revived. Numerous Jews, particularly the young and the poor, grew interested in communism; many Jewish organizations leaned to the left. The KPRP in Russia sent messengers to Poland to instruct the Polish leadership to deal with the Jewish issue. Some Polish activists believed that Polish and Jewish workers' organizations and trade unions should be separate. Yet the party leadership did not change its 'national nihilism' attitude towards the Jewish problem, and emphasized that dealing with national issues would weaken the class struggle.[48]

The First Congress of the KPRP elected its Central Committee of twelve members—six each from the SDKPiL and the PPS Left.[49] Four were of Jewish back-

Komunistyczna Partia Polski, 23–8; *KPP: Uchwały i rezolucje*, i, ed. T. Daniszewski (Warsaw, 1953), 54; Cimek, *Komuniści, Polska, Stalin*, 9–19; Cimek and Kieszczyński, *Komunistyczna Partia Polski*, 18.

[47] Simoncini, *Communist Party of Poland*, 21–4; Czubiński, *Komunistyczna Partia Polski*, 19–31; M. Grinberg, 'Komuniści polscy wobec wojny polsko-radzieckiej, 1919–1920', Ph.D. thesis (Wyższa Szkoła Nauk Społecznych przy KC PZPR, Warsaw, 1962), 32–8; E. Horoch, *Komunistyczna Partia Polski w województwie lubelskim w latach 1918–1938* (Lublin, 1993), 23; J. A. Reguła, *Historia Komunistycznej Partii Polski* (Warsaw, 1934), 35; Cimek and Kieszczyński, *Komunistyczna Partia Polski*, 62.

[48] Archiwum Żydowskiego Instytutu Historycznego, Warsaw (hereafter AŻIH), Ruch Robotniczy, 253, 'Działalność KPP w masach żydowskich', report of Aleksander Zatorski, p. 1; M. Zalcman, *Als Mosche Kommunist war: Die Lebensgeschichte eines jüdischen Arbeiters in Polen und in der Sovjetunion unter Stalin* (Darmstadt, 1982), 36; AAN, ZHP przy KC PZPR, 397/I-1, Centralny Komitet Wykonawczy grup KPRP w Rosji. Protokoły posiedzeń, 1, pp. 52–3, and AAN, KC PZPR, Teczki osobowe, 101: Saul Amsterdam, p. 9; Cimek, *Komuniści, Polska, Stalin*, 23.

[49] SDKPiL was represented by Franciszek Fiedler, Franciszek Grzelszczak-Grzegorzewski, Władysław Kowalski, Szczepan Rybacki, Henryk Stein-Domski, and Adolf Zalberg-Piotrowski, and

ground, but came from the Polish-assimilated milieu. Some were similar to Adolf Warski-Warszawski, who joined the party's Central Committee in February 1919 and was portrayed by Pinkus Minc, another revolutionary, in the following way: 'Although a Jew by birth, he was completely assimilated and gave the impression of being a typical old Polish revolutionary intellectual of bourgeois background. Warski's wife was a Pole from an aristocratic family, and in his home she maintained her old aristocratic ways.'[50]

In 1918 and 1919 the newly established party had between 5,000 and 10,000 members, and a large group of sympathizers and collaborators existed as well. Most of the people linked to the KPRP lived in Warsaw, Łódź, and the Dąbrowa mining region, bordering on Silesia. The KPRP leadership did not really know how many people belonged to the party because no systematic statistics were compiled under the conditions of strict conspiracy until the second half of 1923. It is also unclear how many Jews were in this party that, after its foundation, was predominantly ethnically Polish and limited to the former Congress Kingdom.[51] Some Jewish groups existed in the KPRP before its unification with the Kombund and the factions of Po'alei Tsiyon and the United Jewish Socialist Workers' Party (Fareynikte Yidishe Sotsyalistishe Arbeter Partey). Even though these groups were not numerous, they frequently brought together people who did not speak Polish. Separate but parallel Polish- and Yiddish-speaking party cells existed in several towns.[52]

The 1918 Statute of the KPRP stipulated (in article 28) that

To deal with political and social issues specific to the Jewish and German workers' movement and in order to serve the special needs of this movement, special organs exist in the central committee, district committees, and regional committees: bureaus of the Jewish section and German bureaus, elected during the national, district, or regional conferences of the Jewish and German party members. These elections have to be endorsed by the appropriate party committees. These bureaus work under the direct supervision of the appropriate party authorities and accordingly under the regulations accepted by the central committee.[53]

---

the PPS Left by Józef Ciszewski, Maksymilian Horwitz (Henryk Walecki), Henryk Iwiński, Maria Koszutska (Wera Kostrzewa), Stefan Królikowski, and Wacław Wróblewski. See Cimek and Kieszczyński, *Komunistyczna Partia Polski*, 16, or F. Świetlikowa, 'Centralne instancje partyjne KPP w latach 1918–1939', *Z pola walki*, 48 (1969), 140.

[50] P. Minc, *The History of a False Illusion: Memoirs on the Communist Movements in Poland (1918– 1938)*, trans. R. Michaels (Lewiston, NY, 2002), 71–2.

[51] AAN, KPP, 1157, 'Odpisy dokumentów KPP — materiały KC 1918–1925', p. 11; Świetlikowa, 'Liczebność okręgowych organizacji KPP', 183–4; J. Ławnik, *Represje policyjne wobec ruchu robotniczego, 1918–1939* (Warsaw, 1979), 135; AŻIH, Ruch Robotniczy, 253, *Głos Komunistyczny*, no. 1 (Dec. 1921), 1.

[52] B. Wachowska, *Łódzka organizacja KPP w latach 1918–1926* (Łódź, 1981), 233; Cimek and Kieszczyński, *Komunistyczna Partia Polski*, 65; AŻIH, Ruch Robotniczy, 253, *Głos Komunistyczny*, no. 1 (Dec. 1921), 3.

[53] AAN, KPP, 1157, 'Odpisy dokumentów KPP — materiały KC 1918–1925', p. 6.

THE JEWISH DEPARTMENT

The Jewish Department (Wydział Żydowski) was formed in early 1919 but initially was not very active. The party leadership did emphasize the importance of a campaign against antisemitism but, simultaneously, was committed to centralization. It initially opposed any organizational autonomy for categories of party members, varied in its attitude towards Jews, kept 'a low profile about the activities "on the Jewish street"', and 'was careful not to emphasize the uniqueness of Jewish problems'.[54] In 1920 a new edition of a booklet, *Antysemityzm a robotnicy* ('Antisemitism and the Workers'), was published in Warsaw. Its author, Julian Marchlewski, one of the most prominent veterans and ideologues of the SDKPiL and a major Polish communist leader in Soviet Russia, argued that Polish workers had already rejected antisemitism. He opposed Yiddish, supported assimilation, and described antisemitism and 'Jewish nationalism' as two opposite but negative phenomena.[55]

The Jewish Department (composed of Bernard Cukierwar, Eksztejn, Israel Gajst, Symche Segalewicz, Abram Wajcblum (Karolski), and Henryk Zatorski) did not include any important party leaders, was located in the overwhelmingly Jewish Muranów district of Warsaw, and concentrated its work there to such an extent that, among party members, it was associated with that neighbourhood. The Jewish cells which joined the KPRP as a part of the SDKPiL were few and small. Frequently, they gathered together partially assimilated Jewish workers and were relatively well integrated into the party. Members discussed whether the Jewish nation would survive or would assimilate completely after the revolution. Initially, the KPRP was predominantly ethnically Polish, but at least half of the Central Committee members were of Jewish origin. The Jewish Department formed Jewish divisions in the district and regional committees. Yet, in autumn 1920, the Jewish Department was almost completely destroyed as a result of police activity. Many activists emigrated from Poland or surrendered their party cards. In May 1921 the Jewish Department, according to one of its reports, had 'contacts' in forty-nine towns and cities.[56]

[54] Brun-Zejmis, 'National Self-Denial and Marxist Ideology', 45.

[55] Mishkinsky, 'Communist Party of Poland and the Jews', 68.

[56] In Warsaw and the Warsaw party district, eleven 'points' (*punkty*): Warsaw, Mińsk, Pruszków, Żelechów, Żyrardów, Grodzisk, Skierniewice, Grójec, Wyszków, Nowy Dwór, and Zakroczym; in Łódź and the Łódź district, seven points: Łódź, Pabianice, Aleksandrów, Ozorków, Kalisz, Piotrków, and Częstochowa; in the Białystok district, seven points: Białystok, Zabłudów, Horodok, Wołkowysk, Krynki, Słonim, and Baranowicze; in the Brest-Litovsk district, six points: Brześć, Kobryń, Wysokie Litewskie, Pińsk, Terespol, and Kowel; plus points in Radom, Kielce, Skarżysko, Szydłowiec, Siedlce, Łuków, Międzyrzecz, Lublin, Chełm, Zamość, Włocławek, Kutno, Dąbrowa Górnicza, Sosnowiec, Będzin, Kraków, the Kraków suburbs, and Lwów. See Świetlikowa, 'Centralne instancje partyjne KPP', 140, 145; AŻIH, Ruch Robotniczy, 253, 'Działalność KPP w masach żydowskich', report of Aleksander Zatorski, pp. 5 and 20; AŻIH, Ruch Robotniczy, 245, excerpts from *Głos*

The same report, for the period from August 1920 to May 1921, complained that the Jewish Department had no venues at which to reach the Jewish workers. Owing to police operations, it did not have clubs or meeting facilities and was unable to organize its own demonstrations. It tried, therefore, to make use of events arranged by the Bund and Po'alei Tsiyon and to infiltrate their trade unions, whose leaders counteracted them. This was understandable, said the report, but unfortunately 'our own comrades' saw these activities as a manifestation of Jewish separatism and liquidated or opposed the Jewish sections in their regions.[57]

The shape of the Jewish Department reflected the general situation of the KPRP between 1918 and 1920. The party was growing slowly because of police persecutions and its own policies, the latter being difficult for most Poles to understand. To emphasize its contemptuous attitude towards bourgeois Poland and its institutions, the KPRP boycotted the first parliamentary elections in February 1919. In the first week of 1919, the government introduced a state of emergency and arrested many people involved in strikes, workers' councils, and anti-state activities. The KPRP ignored a governmental decree of mid-January that required all associations to register with administrative authorities within a month. In February 1919 the KPRP went underground and was treated as a subversive organization. By January 1919 the Polish police considered the KPRP an agency of the Bolshevik government, believed in a special link between communism and the Jews, and looked for communist cells particularly carefully within Jewish organizations. Police repressions were especially hard during the most dangerous moments of the Polish–Soviet war, when the KPRP joined the Soviet-established revolutionary committees in regions occupied by the Red Army, and after its retreat from Poland in September–October 1920. The party lost about half its members and almost disintegrated. Many people, including the party leaders, moved abroad. The KPRP, one of the smallest sections of the Comintern, lost the independence it had had in 1919–20, when, because of the Polish–Soviet war, it had almost no contact with Moscow. Now it relied on Soviet help and, in consequence, had to accept Comintern ideological guidance and decisions in the selection of the KPRP leaders.[58]

Komunistyczny, nos. 3–4 (1921–2), 1; AAN, ZHP przy KC PZPR, KPP, 1157, 'Odpisy dokumentów KPP — materiały KC 1918–1925', pp. 6–7, and Centralne Biuro Żydowskie, 158/X-2, vol. 8, 'Sprawozdanie Centralnego Wydziału Żydowskiego za okres sierpień 1920–maj 1921', pp. 1–2; Karolski (Abram Wajcblum), 'Bolączki roboty żydowskiej KPRP i jak je usuwać', *Nowy Przegląd*, 3, no. 13 (Dec. 1924), repr. in *Nowy Przegląd: Reedycja*, ii (Warsaw, 1959), 202; Horoch, *Komunistyczna Partia Polski w województwie lubelskim*, 23.

[57] AAN, ZHP przy KC PZPR, KPP, Centralne Biuro Żydowskie, 158/X-2, vol. 8, 'Sprawozdanie Centralnego Wydziału Żydowskiego za okres sierpień 1920–maj 1921', p. 1.

[58] AAN, MSW, Wydział Bezpieczeństwa, 1196, 'Sprawozdanie z działalności Biura Wywiadowczego o ruchu bolszewickim, szpiegostwie, PPS, ruchu żydowskim i innych. Styczeń 1919', p. 1; Czubiński, *Komunistyczna Partia Polski*, 65, 72; J. B. de Weydenthal, *The Communists of Poland: An Historical Outline* (Stanford, Calif., 1978), 10–16; Simoncini, *Communist Party of Poland*, 73; Horoch, *Komunistyczna Partia Polski w województwie lubelskim*, 30–4; Dziewanowski, *Communist Party of Poland*, 80–3.

THE PARTY RECONSTRUCTION AND THE SECOND CONGRESS (SEPTEMBER–OCTOBER 1923)

From early 1921, the KPRP leadership and the Comintern discussed new strategies. The era of revolutionary communism was over and the vision of rapid and immediate transformation had disappeared. The Polish state survived; the Polish economy recovered; and the revolution in Hungary, Germany, and generally in the West had failed. It became obvious that the party needed new tactics to replace the old broad and unclear programme. The Second Party Conference in February 1921 determined that poor peasants and the working intelligentsia should be considered a part of the revolutionary forces. In April 1922 the Third Party Conference accepted the tactic of the united front, discussed the party's agrarian policy, and began to change its national policy. The Central Committee was asked to organize a German department and to reach out towards those Jewish trade unionists who did not speak Polish.

A new party leadership, led by Maria Koszutska (Wera Kostrzewa) and Maksymilian Horwitz (Henryk Walecki) from the former PPS Left and Adolf Warszawski (Warski) from the SDKPiL—the 'Three Ws'—prevailed over the old-line leftist radicals, 'moved to the right', and accepted the Comintern line of a united front with other political parties of the left, such as the PPS and the Polish Peasant Party 'Liberation' (Polskie Stronnictwo Ludowe 'Wyzwolenie'). The KPRP turned towards a 'political NEP' and fought not only for the future revolution but also for better conditions for workers within the existing political system. Pressed by the Comintern, the party accepted the right to self-determination for national minorities. In November 1922 the KPRP established a legal organization, the Union of the Proletariat of the Town and Country (Związek Proletariatu Miast i Wsi), to participate in the parliamentary elections. In spite of severe repression, the Union obtained 132,000 votes. The KPRP abandoned its negation of the Polish state and accepted the possibility of a two-stage revolution: first, a worker–peasant government established during parliamentary elections, and then a proletarian revolution and dictatorship. The party was growing again, to a large extent through an influx of splinter groups from other organizations. In 1922–3 the membership reached somewhere between 4,000 and 7,000. The turbulent events of late 1923, inflation, widespread strikes, a workers' rebellion in Kraków, and a new revolutionary wave outside Poland brought the KPRP fresh members and opportunities. In autumn 1923 Polish communist leaders and the Comintern were convinced that a new wave of revolutionary events in Germany would come soon to trigger the next step of the world revolution.[59]

[59] Simoncini, *Communist Party of Poland*, 77–9, 103–7; Weydenthal, *Communists of Poland*, 7, 15; *II Zjazd Komunistycznej Partii Robotniczej Polski*, 5–9; Reguła, *Historia Komunistycznej Partii Polski*, 54; Cimek, *Komuniści, Polska, Stalin*, 32–6; Czubiński, *Komunistyczna Partia Polski*, 76–86, 101; Cimek and Kieszczyński, *Komunistyczna Partia Polski*, 35, 70–2; Dziewanowski, *Communist Party of Poland*, 99–101; *KPP: Uchwały i rezolucje*, i. 172.

To define a new strategy in this decisive moment, particularly with regard to the agrarian problem, the united front, the national question, and a new party's role, its Second Congress was organized in Bolshevo near Moscow in September–October 1923. Strongly pressed by the Comintern and skilfully run by the Three Ws, the KPRP officially rejected the 'Luxemburgist' national strategy and accepted the Leninist slogan of self-determination.[60]

The congress tried to resolve the situation of the Communist Party of Eastern Galicia (Komunistyczna Partia Galicji Wschodniej; KPGW). Established in 1919 in the West Ukrainian People's Republic, which was later conquered by Poland, the party was forced by the Soviets to join the KPRP in 1921 as an autonomous territorial branch of the Polish party. This compromise, rejected by many Polish and Ukrainian communists, was slightly changed during the Second Congress when the KPGW was transformed into the Communist Party of Western Ukraine, which was more independent but still associated with the KPRP and directed and financed by Soviet Ukraine. Similar status was granted to the Communist Party of Western Belarus. These changes were to emphasize that the eastern territories of Poland, populated mostly by Ukrainians and Belarusians, had the right to secede and to join the Ukrainian and Belarusian Soviet Republics. On the other hand, the Communist Party of Upper Silesia, established in December 1918, had been incorporated into the KPRP in 1922. Finally, the new party line accepted the existence of independent Poland, postulated its democratization, and defined the KPRP as the representative of the entire Polish nation and the champion of Poland's political and economic independence.[61]

The congress discussed the peasant issue, previously essentially ignored, and criticized the old party policies which did not treat the peasant as a potential revolutionary force.[62] The congress reorganized and reformed the party's organizational structure and leadership, which initially were quite provisional. The founding congress had established a Party Council (Rada Partyjna) and elected a twelve-member Central Committee, the party's highest policy-making body, divided equally between the former SDKPiL and PPS Left leaders. This leadership functioned on a majority-vote basis and was deliberative rather than operational. In the spring of 1919 a secretariat was established to take care of administrative issues. In 1920, during the Polish–Soviet war, the party's organizational structure fell into disarray. The Central Committee moved to Berlin and then to the Free City of Danzig. A conflict arose between party leaders residing

[60] AAN, Julian Brun — Spuścizna, 186/III-16, 'Kwestia narodowa w rewolucji i kontrrewolucji', p. 180; *II Zjazd Komunistycznej Partii Robotniczej Polski*, 19–48; Cimek, *Komuniści, Polska, Stalin*, 36–40.

[61] Simoncini, *Communist Party of Poland*, 41–4; Cimek, *Komuniści, Polska, Stalin*, 31–40; Cimek and Kieszczyński, *Komunistyczna Partia Polski*, 81–3; Dziewanowski, *Communist Party of Poland*, 105; *II Zjazd Komunistycznej Partii Robotniczej Polski*, 18, 67–9, 128–33.

[62] Simoncini, *Communist Party of Poland*, 57; Cimek and Kieszczyński, *Komunistyczna Partia Polski*, 80; Dziewanowski, *Communist Party of Poland*, 103.

abroad and those in the country, and the Central Committee consulted with both the Comintern and the Polish Bureau of the Bolshevik Party.[63]

The Second Congress introduced the well-defined Comintern principles into the party's organizational structure. Individual cells were united in an area committee (*komitet dzielnicowy*), which was a part of a district committee (*komitet okręgowy*), which, in turn, belonged to one of sixteen regional committees (*komitet obwodowy*). The newly established political bureau was supposed to execute the Central Committee's decisions, and the organizational bureau took over some responsibilities of the Central Committee's secretariat. Several important issues were taken care of by vertical departments (*wydziały*) supervised and directed by the Central Committee. In its first year, the party established departments for workers' council affairs, trade unions, agriculture, the army, Jews, culture and education, and technical matters. Later, it added departments for prisons, cooperatives, youth, women, and Germans.[64]

At its conclusion, the congress elected a new nineteen-person Central Committee, headed again by the Three Ws—Warski, Walecki, Wera Kostrzewa—the representatives of the 'majority'. The congress was a boost to the party, even though it was still internally divided. A group of radicals, led by Julian Leszczyński, Izaak Gordin (Aleksander Lenowicz), Henryk Stein-Domski, Zofia Unszlicht, Stanisław Martens (Skulski), and Saul Amsterdam, opposed the new strategy, calling it opportunistic and defensive. They rejected the Polish state, the two-stage revolution, the united front, and the 'Leninist' policy of national self-determination. The political victory of the Three Ws was not, however, complete. The blueprint for the post-revolution future was still vague: after the millennium, Poland would become part of a 'Federation of Free Worker–Peasant Republics of Europe'.[65]

THE JEWISH REVOLUTIONARY LEFT ENTERS THE PARTY

The correction of the national policy of the KPRP, introduced during the Second and the Third National Party Conferences and during the Second Congress, improved conditions for 'Jewish work' in the party. In 1921 this had had to be rebuilt from scratch, but it became increasingly important as a growing number of individual Jews and splinters from other Jewish parties joined the KPRP. Moreover, the Bund and Po'alei Tsiyon controlled several trade unions that the KPRP wanted to take over. The Third National Party Conference in February 1921 strengthened the autonomy of the Jewish Department and elected its new leaders (Pinkus Bukshorn, Gerszon Dua-Bogen, Pinkus Fiszel-Prawin, Aron

[63] Weydenthal, *Communists of Poland*, 7–14; Simoncini, *Communist Party of Poland*, 31–3.

[64] Simoncini, *Communist Party of Poland*, 36–7; Czubiński, *Komunistyczna Partia Polski*, 104.

[65] Cimek, *Komuniści, Polska, Stalin*, 37–43; Weydenthal, *Communists of Poland*, 18–19; Czubiński, *Komunistyczna Partia Polski*, 91.

Lewartowski, and Henryk Zatorski). It was supposed to concentrate on propaganda in Yiddish and on the struggle against Jewish nationalism and clericalism. According to the statute of the Jewish Department, it was crucial that all its activities be undertaken in the name of the entire party under strict control of its leaders. The statute accepted the possibility that separate Jewish local cells might be formed for 'linguistic reasons', but those cells had to belong to regular party district organizations. All districts would have Jewish departments, which were supposed to send Jewish instructors to the local units. The highest authorities of the Jewish semi-autonomous structure were to be national Jewish conferences. Between them, plenary meetings of the Jewish Department were supposed to take place. Routine work would be conducted by the department's secretariat. Its members (between five and seven persons), elected during a national conference, would be responsible for organizational matters, publications, trade unions, cultural activities, and youth.[66]

As early as November 1918, about 180 people left the Warsaw organization of the Po'alei Tsiyon party, led by a member of its central committee. During the last years of the war, Po'alei Tsiyon became much more radical but still supported the idea of an independent Poland. The dissenters were against this. Most of them joined the KPRP, and were followed by other party members outside Warsaw. In 1921 a second split in Po'alei Tsiyon took place and a relatively large group, led by Amsterdam, Alfred Lampe, and Lewartowski, joined the KPRP.[67]

A much larger group came to the KPRP from the Bund. In 1918 the Bund supported the independence of Poland but demanded cultural autonomy for the Jews. It was suspicious of the PPS and refused Piłsudski's invitation to consult with him unless all minorities in Poland were granted national autonomy. When anti-Jewish violence started in the territories controlled by Poland, the Bund accused the PPS of not taking a strong stand against antisemitism and asked the Socialist International for help.[68]

By December 1918, at the Second Conference of the Polish Bund, a powerful radical left wing had appeared and was able to take control of the party's youth organization, Tsukunft. From the Third Conference in April 1919, the left wing controlled the party. The division within the Bund deepened during the first

---

[66] Simoncini, *Communist Party of Poland*, 38–9; Świetlikowa, 'Centralne instancje partyjne KPP', 145; AAN, KPP, Centralne Biuro Żydowskie, 158/X-2, vol. 5, 'Projekt Statutu Wydziału Żydowskiego przy KC KPRP', pp. 1–3; AŻIH, Ruch Robotniczy, 253, *Głos Komunistyczny*, no. 1 (Dec. 1921), 2.

[67] AŻIH, Ruch Robotniczy, 253, 'Działalność KPP w masach żydowskich', report of Szymon Zachariasz, pp. 10–12; AAN, ZHP przy KC PZPR, Żydowska Robotnicza Organizacja Poale-Syjon, 29/1, pp. 1–37.

[68] Johnpoll, *Politics of Futility*, 69–75; A. Brumberg, 'The Bund and the Polish Socialist Party in the late 1930s', in Gutman et al. (eds.), *Jews of Poland between Two World Wars*, 76, 81; Śliwa, 'Kwestia żydowska w polskiej myśli socjalistycznej', 284–5; A. Polonsky, *Politics in Independent Poland, 1921–1939* (Oxford, 1972), 95.

elections to the Polish parliament in January 1919. The left wing believed in an imminent victory of world revolutions and, encouraged by the KPRP, opposed parliamentary democracy and supported Bolshevik ideology, Soviet power, and the dictatorship of the proletariat. Radicals were against participation in the elections, took control over the party, and fought against the centre and the right wing. This struggle almost paralysed the party for the next four years. The Bund did not participate in the first parliamentary election in 1919, fought against the PPS in the councils of workers' delegates, and opposed the war with Soviet Russia, which caused Polish police retaliation and further alienation from the PPS. In some regions of the reborn Polish state, such as the Vilna or the Białystok provinces, the Bund considered itself more Russian than Polish. From 1919 the leftist Bund leadership attempted to join the Comintern, but this proved to be impossible. The KPRP denounced the Bund as a nationalistic party that was trying to monopolize revolutionary activities among the Jews. In fact, the Bund, probably twice as large as the KPRP, did constitute a dangerous competitor. The Comintern set conditions for those parties wanting to join: a purge of 'reformists' from the party, an ideological purge, and organizational centralization. The Bund leadership refused to accept any of the conditions. As a consequence of this stalemate, whole Bund groups switched to the KPRP, and the Comintern sent its agents to Poland to split the Bund. In 1921 the Kombund Fraktsye was created and, in 1922, it was re-formed into the Jewish Communist Workers' Bund of Poland (Yidish Komunist Arbeter Bund fun Poyln). The Kombund had between 2,000 and 3,500 members (about one-fourth of the Bund), concentrated mostly in Warsaw, Łódź, and Kraków. It established itself as a separate party, created a contact committee with the KPRP, and having accepted the conditions of the Comintern, entered the KPRP as an independent section. The KPRP, however, was against the establishment of a second communist party in Poland with an almost identical programme, and pressed for unification. In addition, some Kombund members still kept in touch with the Bund. In late 1922, when members started returning from the Kombund to the Bund, most of the Kombund, led by Aleksander Minc, Abe Pflug, and Grynberg, joined the KPRP. The radical part of the Tsukunft (Komtsukunft), which made up about 80 per cent of its members (about 3,500 people in sixty-five groups, according to Szymon Zachariasz), was incorporated into the Communist Association of Polish Youth (Komunistyczny Związek Młodzieży Polskiej; KZMP).[69] Later, in the last weeks of 1924, another small group left the

[69] Johnpoll, *Politics of Futility*, 82–120; A. Bełcikowska, *Stronnictwa i związki polityczne w Polsce: Charakterystyki, dane historyczne, programy, rezolucje, organizacje partyjne, prasa, przywódcy* (Warsaw, 1925), 884–6; J. Tomicki, 'The General Union of Jewish Workers (Bund) in Poland, 1918–1939', *Acta Poloniae Historica*, 45 (1982), 100–3; S. Kassow, 'Jewish Communal Politics in Transition: The Vilna Kehile, 1919–1920', *YIVO Annual*, 20 (1991), 70–2; P. Wróbel, 'Na równi pochyłej. Żydzi Białegostoku w latach 1918–1939: demografia, ekonomika, dezintegracja, konflikty z Polakami', *Przegląd Historyczny*, 79 (1988), 280, 281; AŻIH, Ruch Robotniczy, 253, 'Działalność KPP w masach żydowskich', report of Szymon Zachariasz, 26 Mar. 1963, pp. 1–16, report of Henryk Zołotow, p. 2,

Bund for the KPRP.[70] After the 1922 unification, according to the Polish police, the KPRP became the most influential party among Jewish factory workers.[71]

The unification of the Kombund and the KPRP was preceded by time-consuming negotiations at the local and central levels, accompanied by angry attacks from the Bund. When the Kombund was accepted as a member of the Comintern, it promised to unite with the KPRP. Yet no deadline was accepted and the Kombund did not rush with unification procedures. It wanted a real unification with, and not simply incorporation into, the KPRP. Some Kombund leaders asked for a status given later to the communist parties of Western Ukraine and Western Belarus. Some demanded the exclusive right to decide about Jewish matters in the united party and asked the KPRP to give the Kombund the status of a separate KPRP district. Some were simply against unification. From the beginning, the political supremacy of the Polish partner was obvious. A Central Jewish Bureau (Centralne Biuro Żydowskie, CBŻ—or, according to the official terminology, the Central Bureau of the Jewish Sections, Centralne Biuro Sekcji Żydowskich) was supposed to have been elected by members of the Kombund groups transferred to the KPRP. Such elections had never taken place. Instead, Kombund district leaders had simply been appointed to the bureau. In turn, the KPRP leaders complained that the former Kombund, together with former Po'alei Tsiyon and Fareynikte activists, did not want to share control of the Jewish Culture League (Kulturlige) with members of the KPRP.[72]

The Jewish Department gained importance during unification negotiations with the Kombund.[73] In March 1922 the Second All-Polish Jewish Conference took place. 'Jewish work' became more intensive, even though the police had arrested many Jewish activists. The Kombund wanted to be an autonomous section in the KPRP but eventually a compromise was accepted: in addition to the Jewish Department, the Central Jewish Bureau was established, as noted above. It was supposed to co-ordinate a parallel network of Jewish boards on various levels of the territorial committees, specialize in Yiddish propaganda, and take care of specifically Jewish issues.[74]

---

and report of Aleksander Zatorski, pp. 3–6; AAN, ZHP przy KC PZPR, Teczki osobowe, 101: Saul Amsterdam, p. 10; AAN, KPP, Centralne Biuro Żydowskie, 158/X-2, vol. 9, 'Sprawozdanie Wydziału Żydowskiego, 1. III. 1922', p. 4; G. Iwański, 'Żydowski Komunistyczny Związek Robotniczy Kombund w Polsce, 1921–1923', *Z pola walki*, 68 (1974), 44–66.

[70] AAN, KPP, Centralne Biuro Żydowskie, 158/X-2, vol. 12, 'Styczeń 1925', p. 2.

[71] AAN, MSW, 1185, 'Historia KPP od II Zjazdu do lat kryzysu 1923–1925: Sytuacja w okresie 1930–1933', p. 66.

[72] AAN, KPP, Centralne Biuro Żydowskie, 158/X-2, vol. 9, 'Sprawozdanie Wydziału Żydowskiego, 1. III. 1922', pp. 1–4; AŻIH, Ruch Robotniczy, 253, 'Działalność KPP w masach żydowskich', report of Szymon Zachariasz, 26 Mar. 1963, pp. 1–17.

[73] Simoncini, *Communist Party of Poland*, 38–9.

[74] AŻIH, Ruch Robotniczy, 245, *Głos Komunistyczny*, no. 3 (June 1922) and no. 4 (Aug. 1922), and 253, 'Działalność KPP w masach żydowskich', report of Szymon Zachariasz, 26 Mar. 1963, p. 10.

Somewhat earlier, in 1921, Fareynikte split into three factions. The Unification Faction (Frakcja Połączeniowa), led by Izaak Gordin, Israel Gajst, and Wigdor Fryszman, joined the KPRP; another group moved to the Bund; and a small group tried unsuccessfully to save the old party.[75]

The Jewish secessionists were not the only newcomers to the KPRP. It was joined also by two groups from the PPS: the PPS Opozycja, led by Adam Landy and Tadeusz Żarski, in 1919; and a splinter faction headed by Stanisław Łańcucki and Jerzy Czeszejko-Sochacki in 1921. In 1919 the peasant leader and Sejm deputy Tomasz Dąbal joined the party, followed by a small group of activists from the Polish Peasant Party 'Liberation'. In 1920 the Communist Party of Eastern Galicia was incorporated into the KPRP. Yet all of them were much smaller than the Kombund, whose members formed a significant part of the KPRP.

THE SECOND CONGRESS AND THE JEWISH ISSUE

The Second Congress of the KPRP also discussed the Jewish issue, even though this topic was marginalized and overshadowed by the problems of national minorities in the borderlands. From the Soviet point of view, Ukrainians and Belarusians were much more important than Jews, leaving aside the fact that Soviet leaders were frequently not sure if Jews constituted a separate nation. Grigory Zinovev, of Jewish background himself, the chairman of the executive committee of the Comintern and a full member of the Bolshevik Politburo, opened the congress and devoted about half of his long speech to the national issue. Only a few sentences concerned Jews specifically. Zinovev expressed surprise about the Jewish problem of the KPRP:

We have heard about the results of your elections [of 1922] and we learned that, in Poland, the Jews do not vote for the communists. It means that there is an essential error here. I have purposely taken a nationality not too popular in Poland—apparently even among communists. But we deal here with political struggle and not with personal likes or dislikes. With us, before the November Revolution, the Jews in Ukraine voted for the Bolsheviks; in fact, they voted for them in masses, even though the Bolsheviks had been considered a Russian party, etc. And it cannot be otherwise. Why would a nationality, persecuted and attacked, not be defended by the workers' class? I know very well that there is a Jewish bourgeoisie, Jewish workers, and the Jewish lower middle class, but the Jewish workers and lower middle class, if we apply the proper policy, will be with us at the very moment when they realize that we have definitely broken with antisemitism; that we offer a solution to the national question that cannot be offered by any party. Exactly these tactics caused the Jewish lower middle class in Ukraine to support us to a large degree.[76]

Only three congress delegates, all from the Central Jewish Bureau, devoted significant parts of their speeches specifically to the Jewish issue; some participants felt that

[75] AŻIH, Ruch Robotniczy, 245, *Głos Komunistyczny*, no. 1 (Dec. 1921); AAN, KPP, Centralne Biuro Żydowskie, 158/X-2, vol. 9, 'Sprawozdanie Wydziału Żydowskiego, 1. III. 1922', p. 1.
[76] *II Zjazd Komunistycznej Partii Robotniczej Polski*, 29–30.

it had been ignored during the debates.[77] Several languages were used at the congress, but only one delegate, Aron Lewartowski, formerly of Po'ale Tsiyon, spoke in Yiddish (though he, too, ignored the Jewish problem).[78] Saul Amsterdam, also from Po'alei Tsiyon, depicted the KPRP Jewish work as a great success.[79] Yet Izaak Gordin (Aleksander Lenowicz), originally from Fareynikte, was more cautious:

> I want to touch on an important issue—the attitude of various party organizations to Jewish work. As for the Central Committee, it pays proper attention to Jewish work. But in the districts, the comrades neglect the work among the Jews. [Our] influence among the Jewish workers is sometimes larger than among the Polish workers. We have to accustom our own comrades to the fact that Jewish work is a part of the general work.[80]

Gordin emphasized that Jews were important to the revolution and that its success could be threatened by a lack of fraternal relations between Jewish and Polish workers. He described situations when, during a communist rally, Polish workers did not defend Jewish workers attacked by the crowd. He also recalled cases of anti-Jewish prejudice among party members and was supported by another delegate in postulating that the struggle against antisemitism should be the party's priority.[81] Pinkus Bukshorn, a former activist of Fareynikte, also complained: '[Our] struggle against antisemitism is weak. Antisemitic trends exist even in the party. In Łódź, a case of scandalous behaviour on the part of a trade union official, sent by the trade union sector, took place. Some comrades don't understand how important this matter is. The district functionary wanted to establish an exterritorial Jewish district.'[82] Bukshorn, supported by two other delegates, strongly argued against the existence of separate Jewish and Polish trade unions and insisted that these unions should be united, even though some party officials were opposed, claiming that it pushed many Polish workers out of the movement.[83]

When the KPRP leadership accused East Galician Ukrainian communists of nationalism, one of them answered: 'Scornful words about "little Jews" in the party, spoken by some of you, and similar nice things, oblige you to look for nationalism among yourselves.'[84] Another delegate warned that the party should prepare itself because, certainly, Polish nationalists would present the coming German revolution as a 'Jewish intrigue'.[85]

The congress's final resolution on the national issue, 'For Our and Your Freedom' ('Za Naszą i Waszą Wolność'), reflected the way in which the Jewish issue had been dealt with during the debates. Out of seven pages, devoted mostly to Ukrainian and Belarusian issues, the Jewish problem received only several general, declaratory sentences.[86] Finally, the congress elected a new Central Committee of

---

[77] Ibid. 210.   [78] Ibid. 224.   [79] Ibid. 110–11.   [80] Ibid. 100.

[81] Simoncini, *Communist Party of Poland*, 39, 121; *II Zjazd Komunistycznej Partii Robotniczej Polski*, 345–7.   [82] *II Zjazd Komunistycznej Partii Robotniczej Polski*, 114.

[83] Ibid. 399–404.   [84] Ibid. 133.   [85] Ibid. 224.

[86] 'The Polish bourgeoisie applies a no less licentious [than to other nationalities] policy of national, economic, legal, and religious oppression towards the German and Jewish minorities. The unbridling of

the KPRP. Out of its sixteen members, seven were of Jewish background, as were three out of eight deputy members.[87]

After the Second Congress, the Central Jewish Bureau tried to broaden its activities beyond propaganda and activity within the Jewish trade unions. The bureau regretted that it had no real influence among the poor non-proletarian masses (*biedota*) and the supporters of clericalism within the Jewish intelligentsia, controlled mostly by the Bund, as well as the Zionists. The bureau contemplated establishing cultural and educational institutions, which—like the Bund and the Zionists—would influence the Jewish social groups reluctant to accept the KPRP leadership. In November 1923 'Jewish work' was undertaken in new regions; messengers from the bureau travelled across the country. Yet Jewish communist 'work' developed mostly in Warsaw, Łódź, and central Poland. The bureau had no contact with Galicia.[88] In December 1923 the bureau started preparing a national Jewish conference and district pre-conferences. Some local activists were afraid that an influx of poor non-proletarians could make the party profile less clear. Also, provincial leaders emphasized that Polish workers should be educated about the Jews.[89] In early 1924 the bureau sent its representatives to participate in the Jewish school week (organized by the Bund), tried to strengthen its influence in the trade unions, and fought against religious communities. District conferences of the Jewish sector took place in several provinces, but an attempt to organize the badly needed national conference failed through lack of funds. Everywhere, the bureau had to work hard to convince the former Bund and Po'alei Tsiyon activists that their fight for autonomy within the KPRP was utopian and 'of petit bourgeois, bourgeois, and nationalistic character'.[90]

antisemitism, which is supposed to divert the attention of the Polish working classes from those responsible for the poverty and misfortune of the working people, not only hits the Jewish population, but also hampers the struggle of Polish workers and peasants for their own class liberation. The Polish proletariat has to demand the elimination of all the anti-Jewish limitations in the administration, the judiciary, and education. It demands for the Jewish masses a complete freedom in cultural development, liquidation of the ghetto supported by the government, abolition of the religious *ḥeders*, introduction of state and municipal secular schools with Yiddish as the language of instruction, unlimited access for the Jews to public schools, the right to use their mother tongue in the administration and the courts': ibid. 574.

[87] The Central Committee members were Maria Koszutska, Władysław Stein-Krajewski, Maksymilian Horwitz-Walecki, Adolf Warszawski, Jerzy Czeszejko-Sochacki, Wacław Wróblewski, Franciszek Grzelszczak-Grzegorzewski, Osip Kriłyk, Franciszek Fiedler, Julian Brun, Ludwik Szabatowski, Aleksander Danieluk-Stefański, Saul Amsterdam, Roman Jabłonowski, Henryk Bitner, and Stanisław Martens. The deputy members were Mieczysław Bernstein, Tomasz Dąbal, Tadeusz Żarski, Adolf Langer (Ostap Dłuski), Leon Purman, Szczepan Rybacki, Józef Paszta, and Jan Hempel. See *II Zjazd Komunistycznej Partii Robotniczej Polski*, 302, 306; Świetlikowa, 'Centralne instancje partyjne KPP', 141.

[88] AAN, KPP, Centralne Biuro Żydowskie, 158/X-2, vol. 10, 'Sprawozdanie Centralnego Biura Sekcji Żydowskich za listopad 1923', pp. 1–3.   [89] Ibid. 4–5.

[90] AAN, KPP, Centralne Biuro Żydowskie, 158/X-2, vol. 11, 'Sprawozdanie Centralnego Biura Żydowskiego: Styczeń 1924', and 'Sprawozdanie Centralnego Biura Żydowskiego za marzec [1924]', pp. 1–3.

FACTIONAL STRUGGLE AND A CRISIS IN THE PARTY

In 1924 it became obvious that rebellions in Germany and Poland the year before were not the beginning of a European revolutionary upheaval but its epilogue. Disappointment and bitterness within the KPRP, which had not managed to establish a united front, fuelled support for the radicals. After Lenin's death in January 1924, Polish communists watched the battles in the Bolshevik Party and warned its leaders that the fight against Trotsky could split the Russian and the world revolutionary movement. This Polish 'intervention' provoked a negative reaction from the Comintern. Stalin angrily reprimanded the KPRP's Central Committee for interfering in Soviet domestic affairs and accused the Three Ws leadership of disruptive activities in the international communist movement and of defending 'right-wing' German communists and the 'opportunistic faction' among the Bolsheviks. Stalin's intervention solidified the opposition within the KPRP. Closely linked to Stalin and his supporters in the Bolshevik Party, it attacked the Three Ws and linked their alleged mistakes and weakness to their former membership in PPS Left, or the Bund, or Po'alei Tsiyon. The opposition followed a new line of the Comintern, which held that the united front should be created 'from below' and that the socialists were counter-revolutionaries.

In 1924 the Comintern became more autocratic. It considered any disagreement with it to be an anti-Soviet activity. Polish communists residing in Moscow accused the KPRP leadership of incompetence and asked the Comintern to intervene. The Fifth Congress of the Comintern in June–July 1924 drastically limited the concept of the united front strategy and the concept of the worker–peasant government, condemned the Polish 'opportunistic' party leadership, and replaced it with a new central committee, headed by Julian Leński and his 'minority' group. The new leaders claimed that the tense situation in Poland could result in a civil war and revolution and tried to spread a general strike to the entire country. The Three Ws and their supporters vigorously attacked this position.[91]

The internal party conflicts were resolved during the Third Congress of the KPRP in January–February 1925 in Minsk in Belarus. This 'Congress of Bolshevization' adopted the Soviet party's organizational model, criticized the political line of the Second Congress and the Three Ws for alleged opportunism, limited the latter's political influence, placed the party under the close supervision of the Comintern, and pushed the KPRP towards an ultra-left position. Ignoring the economic stabilization of Poland in 1924, clearly recognized by most party leaders, the Soviets pushed the KPRP to prepare itself for a revolution, to infiltrate the army, and to gather arms and create self-defence units. A significant part of the congress debates was devoted to questions linked to this uprising: how to start it and how to mobilize the masses. Here, the leaders emphasized the importance of

---

[91] Simoncini, *Communist Party of Poland*, 127–32; *II Zjazd Komunistycznej Partii Robotniczej Polski*, 10; Weydenthal, *Communists of Poland*, 19–21; Cimek, *Komuniści, Polska, Stalin*, 44–5.

engaging the peasants and of minorities issues. Yet those taking part in the discussions were unable to agree on many issues, especially on the peasant question and the issue of dictatorship of the proletariat versus a peasant–worker government. Some of the mutual accusations exchanged by members of party factions during the debates were offensive or sounded like denunciations. Warski, the leader of the 'majority' faction, delivered a humiliating self-critique,[92] and the congress accepted a resolution condemning the Three Ws' leadership.[93] The party changed its name to the Communist Party of Poland (Komunistyczna Partia Polski; KPP). Special resolutions were devoted to the agrarian question and to the fight against oppression of national minorities, whose right to self-determination and separation from Poland was confirmed; however, this right did not apply to Jews and Germans.[94] The party leadership claimed that it had re-established branches in several districts that had been suspended after 1921. According to the official congress report, the KPP had fifteen districts (*okręgi*) with 6,074 members.[95]

After the Third Congress, the KPP leaders went so far to the revolutionary left that even some members of the Comintern opposed the new strategy. Some KPP leaders, in turn, criticized the allegedly too moderate line of the Comintern. The militant attitude of the new KPP leadership intensified the anti-communist operations of the police. The unrealistic interpretation of the situation in Poland contributed to the party's growing isolation, as it entered a crisis, lost many members, and was losing the struggle with the police. One theory suggested that the circumstances were due to an increasing infiltration of the party by police agents, which was answered with armed actions against provocateurs, bordering on terror. Many communists were confused and afraid to share their opinions with party comrades. In mid-1925, a new Polish commission of the Comintern, now in full control of the KPP, condemned the ultra-leftist leadership, dismissed it, and restored the old leaders.[96]

Yet by the end of 1925, Poland's worsening economic situation and the weakening of its international situation after the Locarno Treaty, as well as the emergence of a leftist opposition in the PPS and the Polish Peasant Party 'Liberation', gave the KPP leaders new hope. They disagreed, however, on many crucial issues concerning trade unions, a united front, Polish independence, possible secessions of Western Ukraine and Western Belarus, the peasant question, and the attitude to the parties of the centre and the right. Vast differences in strategic, tactical, and

[92] AAN, KPP, 158/I-3, vol. 8, 'III Zjazd', p. 227.

[93] AAN, KPP, 158/I-3, vol. 9, 'III Zjazd', pp. 7–9.

[94] AAN, KPP, 158/I-3, vol. 3, 'III Zjazd', pp. 158–64, 168–9, and vol. 1, 'III Zjazd', pp. 38–122; Simoncini, *Communist Party of Poland*, 132–48; Cimek, *Komuniści, Polska, Stalin*, 46–7.

[95] The members were divided among the districts in the following way: Warsaw, 798; Łódź, 285; Zagłębie, 308; Częstochowa, 209; Kielce–Radom, 214; Lublin, 100; Włocławek, 100; Płock, 18; Ciechanów, 137; Siedlce–Łomża, 246; Kraków, 72; Silesia, 177; Poznań, 29; Western Ukraine, 1,712; Western Belarus, 869; in prisons, 750; employees of central institutions, 50. AAN, KPP, 158/I-3, vol. 1, 'III Zjazd', p. 37.   [96] Weydenthal, *Communists of Poland*, 22.

ideological matters contributed to the further decline of the KPP. In early 1926 it had dwindled to the point where it had only about 1,200 members (not counting the KPZU and the KPZB).[97]

THE 'MAY ERROR'

One of the most significant disagreements within the KPP leadership concerned Piłsudski and his intentions. Was he a fascist to be resisted, or a former socialist popular among workers, who should be supported as a democrat fighting against fascism? The Comintern shared this indecision and sometimes compared Piłsudski to Kerensky. In May 1926 the communists, surprised by the coup, urged workers to support Piłsudski, organized rallies in Warsaw, and tried to mobilize the people and contact other leftist parties. They even thought about forming a 'workers' battalion'.[98]

Initially after the coup, the KPP Central Committee was divided, even though by 16 May 1926 Stalin was calling support for the Marshal a mistake. Piłsudski restored order quickly and assumed a political course which was far from the communists' expectations. The May events occurred so quickly that the party had no chance to exploit an allegedly potentially revolutionary situation. In June, during a plenary meeting of the KPP Central Committee, it accepted the concept of the 'May error', holding that the party's support for the Piłsudski coup had been a mistake, but this did not prevent a major dispute over the reasons for this 'mistake'.[99] In the meantime, Piłsudski was consolidating his power and the KPP grew increasingly hostile towards his government, declaring it a fascist dictatorship and bitterly attacking it during subsequent plenary meetings of the KPP leadership.[100] The Comintern announced that the entire KPP Central Committee was responsible for the opportunistic conduct during the coup, but no personnel changes were introduced, probably because of conflicts within the Bolshevik Party. Angry factional conflicts continued in the KPP for years. The 'minority', 'national Bolsheviks' to their enemies, claimed that the leaders of the 'majority', whom they accused of 'Menshevism', were responsible for the 'May mistake' and that the party should abandon the 'Second Congress line'. Both factions fought at every level of the party for control over its institutions. The 'minority', more radical, aggressive, and pro-Soviet, demanded the removal of the 'majority', more conciliatory and less radical, from the party. The infighting and general confusion were strengthened by the fact that Poland's economic situation stabilized in 1926.

[97] Simoncini, *Communist Party of Poland*, 148–61.
[98] Ibid. 161–72; Weydenthal, *Communists of Poland*, 23; Cimek, *Komuniści, Polska, Stalin*, 65.
[99] AAN, KPP, 158/III, vol. 11, 'Plenum czerwcowe KC — Materiały dla Sekcji Polskiej MK', pp. 2–11.
[100] AAN, KPP, 158/III, vol. 12, 'Plenum wrześniowe KC', p. 2; vol. 13, 'Plenum wrześniowe', vol. 2, pp. 16, 133–5; vol. 14, 'Plenum wrześniowe, aneks', pp. 41–6.

Factional interests took over party plans and priorities.[101] The party entered a long period of crisis and was controlled increasingly tightly by the Comintern, which manipulated the factional conflicts.

'JEWISH WORK' DURING THE PARTY CRISIS

Radical changes at the top of the party apparatus affected the work of the Central Jewish Bureau. Harassed by police, involved in constant struggle with other Jewish parties (particularly the Zionists and the Bund), and pressed by the quarrelling party factions, it worked under very difficult conditions, changing its composition four times between November 1924 and April 1925.[102] It was ordered to implement the decisions of the Fourth Congress of the Comintern, which meant, among other things, 'the Bolshevization of Jewish work'. 'Murdziel' (Muranów dzielnica), an autonomous Jewish unit of the KPP structure in Warsaw, was deprived of its autonomy and was re-formed into a regular territorial unit. To achieve this, several Jewish cells were transferred from Murdziel to other districts of Warsaw. This was supposed to reverse the 'ghetto' trend, by which Jews from other districts of Warsaw belonged to Jewish organizations in Murdziel. In addition, attempts were made to end Jewish 'separatism in trade union and educational work'.[103]

Some territorial Jewish sections, however, did not want to follow the instructions sent from the party's Central Committee. The Jewish bureau in Częstochowa refused to co-operate and stopped paying its membership fees. In Łódź, the local bureau intended to participate in the Bund-organized sixth anniversary of the Tsukunft's activities. Special messengers were sent to Łódź by the Central Committee to intervene. They were told in Łódź that the KPP Jewish work in that city did not go beyond the anticlerical and anti-Zionist campaign, and that the Bund and the Tsukunft constituted the only centre of Jewish revolutionary activities in Łódź.[104]

The 1925 congress discussion on minorities showed again that the 'subjugated nations'—Ukrainians, Belarusians, and Lithuanians—were more important from the party point of view than the 'dispersed' (*rozsiane*) nationalities, Jews and Germans.[105] Some delegates believed that a revolutionary uprising would soon start in the Eastern Borderlands (Kresy).[106] According to the party line, only the

[101] Simoncini, *Communist Party of Poland*, 172–93; Weydenthal, *Communists of Poland*, 24.

[102] AAN, KPP, Centralne Biuro Żydowskie, 158/X-2, vol. 1, 'Sprawozdanie Centralnego Biura Żydowskiego za luty 1925', p. 6, and 'Protokół Posiedzenia Plenarnego dn. 16. IV. 25', p. 1.

[103] AAN, KPP, Centralne Biuro Żydowskie, 158/X-2, vol. 1, 'Protokół Posiedzenia Plenarnego dn. 16. IV. 25', pp. 1–2; AAN, MSW, 1158, 'Odpisy dokumentów KPP, materiały KC 1926–1928', p. 228.

[104] AAN, KPP, Centralne Biuro Żydowskie, 158/X-2, vol. 1, 'Protokół Posiedzenia Plenarnego dn. 16. IV. 25', p. 2.

[105] This terminology alone suggested the party's attitude towards these nations. AAN, KPP, 158/I-3, vol. 12, 'Tezy w kwestii narodowościowej', p. 399.

[106] AAN, KPP, 158/I-3, vol. 3, 'III Zjazd', pp. 36–7.

revolution could bring freedom to these, and every minority activist was destined to be a communist. This applied also to the Jews, who were deprived of the rights of citizenship, exploited economically, suppressed politically and nationally, and kept in a ghetto. The 'Theses on National Minorities' and the final resolution of the congress demanded that Jews receive full citizenship and national equality, complete freedom in cultural development, recognition of Yiddish in the administration and the judiciary, establishment of state schools with Yiddish as the language of instruction, and free access of their youths to the general educational networks.[107] To achieve this, the KPP would have to fight not only with the Polish bourgeoisie, but also with some Jewish parties, especially Zionists, who allegedly diverted the attention of the Jewish masses from the 'real' causes of their misfortune and propagated the utopian belief that concentrating the Jews in Palestine would solve their problem. Thus, the 'Theses' maintained that Zionism and its close ally, Jewish clericalism, were collaborators with British imperialism; and that the party should react by fighting energetically against 'autonomism' propagated by the Jewish 'social-nationalists', the Bund and Po'alei Tsiyon, who were enemies of the Jewish masses. 'Autonomism' was, according to the 'Theses', a utopian and reactionary movement and one of the main enemies of class solidarity. This is also why Jewish communists fought against the Jewish religious communities (*kehilot*), the strongholds of obscurantism and ignorance, and against Jewish educational institutions. The participation of the Bund and Po'alei Tsiyon in the *kehilot* was considered direct proof of their true character, promoting nationalist social conciliation and nationalist separatism. The separatist and national tendencies of the Bund and Po'alei Tsiyon were strengthened by the antisemitic threat, a dangerous enemy of the entire working class. Antisemitism on the one hand, and Bundist separatism on the other, were the main reasons why it was impossible to unite Polish and Jewish trade unions. The Jewish part of the 'Theses on National Minorities' concluded as follows:

Within the Communist Party, we have to strive to achieve the closest unification of Jewish workers with Polish workers. Our goal should be to create homogeneous party cells, gathering all the workers working in a factory. In those places where linguistic problems—especially underground—force us to establish separate Polish and Jewish cells, we have to strive to link these cells within homogeneous party districts as soon as possible.[108]

By contrast with the situation in relation to Ukrainian and Belarusian issues, during the 1925 congress there was no major disagreement on Jewish issues, which appeared only marginally. Party policy was expressed in the form of ready slogans and declarations, especially concerning the need for an intensive fight against antisemitism. Dmitry Manuilsky, who represented the Bolshevik leadership at the congress, did not mention Jews in his speech titled 'The Communist Party of

[107] AAN, KPP, 158/I-3, vol. 9, 'III Zjazd', pp. 28–9.
[108] AAN, KPP, 158/I-3, vol. 12, 'Tezy w kwestii narodowościowej', pp. 399–412.

Poland and the National Question'.[109] Some delegates called Zionism a Jewish National Democracy (*żydowska endecja*). Yet Warski called the Zionists the most powerful Jewish organization in Poland and warned that only an organization with deep and extensive influence among the Jewish masses would be in a position to fight effectively against Zionism. He also claimed that the party was losing its fight against Jewish clericalism, was unable to eliminate the influences of the Bund and Po'alei Tsiyon, and had not been able to unite Polish and Jewish trade unions.[110] Dua-Bogen, from the Central Jewish Bureau, complained that the Jewish resolution of the Second Congress had been not realized and that Jewish workers were still isolated from their Polish comrades. He postulated that the Central Jewish Bureau should have a wider field of action than the other sections (*wydziały*) of the Central Committee because it dealt with more complicated and diverse matters. He refuted accusations that a strong Jewish bureau would constitute an autonomous Jewish unit within the party.[111]

To deal with these and similar problems, a plenary meeting of the Central Jewish Bureau (the 'second Jewish consultation': *druga narada żydowska*) was held on 16 April 1925. The meeting was stormy. Some delegates argued bitterly: Jewish work had almost ceased; in Warsaw, Jewish cells had been isolated in the party; in the Secretariat of the Central Jewish Bureau, there were comrades who not only did not do anything for Jewish work but also tried to stop it; the best comrades had not been appointed to the bureau because they did not accept the new party line; and the plenum should express its lack of confidence in the secretariat. Some defended the secretariat: it was ineffective because of frequent changes in the bureau; the changes, in turn, were necessary and the reorganization of Jewish work was of crucial importance; the bureau could not concentrate exclusively on Jewish work because it would lead to a ghetto situation. Some delegates claimed that the Central Jewish Bureau was of larger calibre than other departments of the Central Committee and should be elected and not appointed.[112]

Several months later, however, the issues discussed in April were still unresolved. The division of Murdziel among the neighbouring party districts failed. The Central Jewish Bureau still fought against the Bund, trying to sabotage its school organizations and to infiltrate its trade unions, leading to 'brotherly struggle' in the unions. Co-ordinating the work of Polish and Jewish comrades was still a problem. 'Jewish work' in Warsaw was mostly limited to propaganda and was barely visible in the provinces, and it did not reach the poorest of the Jewish population. The bureau also attacked the 'Polish–Jewish agreement' (*ugoda*) between the Jewish Parliamentary Club and the government of Władysław Grabski. Grabski was responsible, in the eyes of the Jewish communists, for the pauperiza-

---

[109] AAN, KPP, 158/I-3, vol. 4, 'III Zjazd', pp. 72–82.
[110] AAN, KPP, 158/I-3, vol. 1, 'III Zjazd', pp. 69–70.
[111] AAN, KPP, 158/I-3, vol. 4, 'III Zjazd', pp. 204–6.
[112] Ibid. 2–4; AAN, MSW, 1158, 'Odpisy dokumentów KPP, materiały KC 1926–1928', p. 228.

tion of the Jewish masses. Instead of collaborating with the government, claimed the Central Jewish Bureau, Jewish organizations should follow the KPP leadership and fight against exploitation by taxes, and for an eight-hour working day, welfare for the unemployed, and access to work in the administration and state institutions.[113] 'Our most serious shortcoming', stated the protocol of a plenary meeting of the bureau held at the end of 1925, was the 'unsatisfactory struggle against Zionism and Jewish clericalism'. 'The same applies to the struggle of our entire Party against antisemitism.' The plenum also condemned those who criticized the bureau: these were former Bundists who had 'conducted conspicuous Bundist work under the banners of the KPRP', co-operated with 'militant Jewish nationalism', and, in doing so, hindered a 'crystallization of a clear Bolshevik line in our party'.[114]

After May 1926 the entire party was dominated by the issue of the Piłsudski coup. 'Jewish work' was far from the party's priorities, and the KPP leadership became very cautious after the 'May error' and did not want to tackle difficult issues. During the Fourth Congress of the KPP in 1927, Pinkus Minc said: 'It is a fact that our Jewish work has weakened recently. In the organizations that gather together broad Jewish masses, we don't work, being afraid of making mistakes.'[115] Responding to the issue of 'Jewish separatism', Minc asked: 'Why don't you talk about special assignments of Polish workers within Jewish work? I believe that there is a certain separatism among us [in the KPP], shown by Polish comrades towards Jewish work, and this is why we should fight both separatisms—Jewish and Polish.'[116]

FAILED INTEGRATION

Marxists have always believed that the unity of workers' movements was crucial to the success of a social revolution and the establishment of the dictatorship of the proletariat. Yet this unity was never achieved. Among the most important phenomena that contributed to this fiasco was the so-called national question. Marxists underestimated and misunderstood the importance of national divisions and identities. The 'Jewish issue', in turn, constituted a serious and special problem within the national question. A significant Jewish contribution to the establishment and development of Marxist movements cannot be denied. Paradoxically, however, Marxist parties always had difficulties integrating the Jewish 'working

---

[113] AAN, KPP, Centralne Biuro Żydowskie, 158/X-2, vol. 12, 'Sprawozdanie Centralnego Biura Żydowskiego za luty 1925', pp. 6–17, and 'Sprawozdanie Centralnego Biura Żydowskiego za lipiec, sierpień i wrzesień 1925', pp. 17–22; AAN, MSW, 1158, 'Odpisy dokumentów KPP, materiały KC 1926–1928', pp. 161–2: 'W sprawie sytuacji i zadań partii w środowisku żydowskim'.

[114] AAN, KPP, Centralne Biuro Żydowskie, 158/X-2, vol. 1, 'Sprawozdanie z plenarnego posiedzenia Centralnego Biura żydowskiej sekcji, 14 [month illegible but date later than Jewish New Year] 1925', pp. 5–12.

[115] AAN, KPP, 158/I-4, vol. 11, 'IV Zjazd', p. 126.   [116] Ibid. 125.

masses'. 'Red assimilation' had its limits. Although there were numerous acculturated Jews among socialists and communists, most Jews, especially those who did
not want to abandon their national traditions and identity, had serious difficulties
with integration into socialist and communist parties. The Jewish experience in the
Polish communist movement in general and in the KPP in particular is a good
illustration of this problem.

The leaders of the Polish radical left had always been afraid that their organiza-
tions would be categorized as Jewish and, consequently, would be unpopular among
Poles. Frequently, the leaders themselves believed in the Judaeo-communist myth,
were hostile to any form of Jewish autonomy, and constantly looked for evidence of
'Jewish separatism'. Some leaders were simply antisemitic. In the KPP, every member coming from the Bund or Po'alei Tsiyon or Fareynikte was suspected of holding
Jewish nationalistic tendencies, even by former comrades from these organizations.
The party leadership and the Central Jewish Bureau fought against Jewish tradition
and culture but were unable to break the barrier between the Poles and the Jews.
The amalgamation of the Polish and Jewish communist cells progressed slowly. A
police report from 1928, describing the communist movement in the Warsaw
province, cited a number of Polish and Jewish cells in particular towns, and concluded: 'The fact should be emphasized that there is no harmony between Polish
and Jewish organizations.'[117] The Jewish communist activists were unable to
explain why the KPP influence on the poorest Jewish social strata was limited, why
Jewish communist cells were particularly prone to factional conflicts, and why
Warsaw's Murdziel problem could not be solved.[118] The old Polish–Jewish conflict
proved to be stronger than internationalist slogans, especially because they were
used in communist propaganda but were not applied to inter-party relations.
The Jews could not dominate the Polish communist movement because most
of them were not able to integrate into it and remained strangers even among the
internationalists.

---

[117] AAN, Urząd Wojewódzki Warszawski. Wydział Bezpieczeństwa, 276/II-4, 'Stan organizacyjny
i struktura organizacji komunistycznych w województwie warszawskim: Sprawozdania', pp. 8–15.
[118] AAN, KPP, 158/I-5, vol. 3, 'V Zjazd', pp. 35–8, 101.

The Jewel in the Yiddish Crown

Who Will Occupy the Chair in Yiddish at the University of Vilnius?

KALMAN WEISER

WITH THE SIGNING OF THE notorious Molotov–Ribbentrop Non-Aggression Pact of late August 1939, the Nazis and Soviets secretly divided Finland, Estonia, Latvia, Lithuania, Poland, and Romania into spheres of influence. The following month, Germany conquered the western section of Poland and the Soviet Union occupied its eastern part, annexing some of its regions to the Belarusian and Ukrainian Soviet Socialist Republics.

Caught between the German 'hammer' and the Bolshevik 'sickle', tiny Lithuania remained neutral, hoping to maintain good relations with both titans. For Jewish refugees fleeing occupied Poland, it represented virtually the only escape route to the free world by late that year. In mid-September 1939, the Soviets issued an ultimatum to Lithuania: in return for agreeing to the presence of Soviet military bases and a standing Soviet force on its soil, Lithuania would retain its independence. To sweeten the deal, the Soviets retreated from Vilna (or Vilnius, as it is known in Lithuanian) after a forty-day occupation and awarded it to the Baltic republic in late October.[1] Under Russian rule prior to the First World War and Polish rule in the inter-war period, the contested multi-ethnic city was now in the hands of the Lithuanians, who regarded it as their historic capital.

In an atmosphere of intense anxiety, the administration of YIVO, the Jewish Scientific Institute, found itself confronted with the dilemma of whether to continue or to suspend its operations for the duration of the war. Founded in 1925, the fledgling institute came into existence in order to serve as a national university, language academy, and library for a stateless Yiddish-speaking Jewry at a time before Jewish studies was widely recognized in academia. Headquartered in Vilna, it had branches and support groups throughout the world. It found its primary supporters, however, among the impoverished Jewish masses of non-Soviet eastern

---

[1] D. Levin, *The Lesser of Two Evils: East European Jewry under Soviet Rule, 1939–1941*, trans. N. Greenwood (Philadelphia and Jerusalem, 1995), 198–217.

Europe, especially in eastern Poland and the Baltic States, who eagerly contributed data and material for its collections and research. Its mission was to apply the latest techniques in the social sciences to gather information about and study objectively their language (to whose standardization it made major contributions), history, psychology, economics, and culture. At the same time, it endeavoured to disseminate its work through its publications and exhibitions both to the broader world and specifically to the objects of its study in order to improve their present-day conditions and help them build a secularized, Yiddish-speaking future.[2]

The war had effectively cut off YIVO from its primary material and cultural basis, the more than three-million-strong Jewish community of Poland. Communications with the outside world were impaired, and much of YIVO's academic and administrative leadership was not to be found in Lithuania. In particular, the philologist and newspaper editor Zalmen Reyzen, a pillar of YIVO, had been arrested in September, along with other important Jewish cultural figures, for reasons then unclear.[3] The institute's guiding spirit and co-founder, the internationally renowned scholar Max Weinreich, was in Copenhagen with his elder son Uriel, en route to an international linguistics conference in Brussels, when the war broke out.

At the same time, Vilna became home to an unprecedented concentration of creative forces, members of the cultural, political, and religious elites of Polish Jewry. In all, more than 14,000 Polish Jews, most intending to continue on to Japan and the western hemisphere, gathered in Vilna between the outbreak of war and June 1940. The presence of these refugees, coupled with the absorption of tens of thousands of other Jews fleeing war and depredations, most of them Yiddish-speakers, made possible a cultural efflorescence. The departure of the Soviets, who had banned the Yiddish press and pursued individuals and organizations deemed dangerous to its interests, opened new vistas for Jewish culture in more tolerant Lithuania. Lithuanian Jewry had been separated from its Polish brethren throughout most of the inter-war period owing to the absence of diplomatic relations between the two lands. Now it received these refugees generously and was eager to benefit from their creative and organizational talents.[4]

After much deliberation, the provisional administration of YIVO, a mixture of old and newly co-opted members, decided to continue its publications and scholarly

[2] On the history of YIVO prior to the Second World War, see C. E. Kuznitz, 'The Origins of Jewish Scholarship and the YIVO Institute for Jewish Research', Ph.D. diss. (Stanford University, 2000) as well as her overview of the institute in G. D. Hundert (ed.), *The YIVO Encyclopedia of Jews in Eastern Europe*, 2 vols. (New Haven, 2008), ii. 2090–6; Y. Shatski, 'Finf un tsvantsik yor yivo', in *Shatski-bukh*, ed. Y. Lifshits (New York and Buenos Aires, 1958), 303–17; also, Lucy Dawidowicz's memoir, *From That Place and Time: A Memoir, 1938–1947* (New York, 1989).

[3] D. Levin, 'The Jews of Vilna under Soviet Rule, 19 September–28 October 1939', *Polin*, 9 (1996), 117.

[4] See e.g. M. Mandelman, 'In freyd un leyd tsvishn litvishe yidn (fun 1938 biz 1940)', in M. Sudarsky et al. (eds.), *Lite*, i (New York, 1951), 1333–58; Levin, *Lesser of Two Evils*, 200.

work as much as possible, as well as to undertake new activities. Most conspicuous was a plan for the establishment of a state-funded chair in Yiddish language and literature. The creation of this chair in Vilna, the unofficial capital of secular Yiddish culture, was a long-cherished dream of the Yiddishist movement. In the eyes of Yiddishists, who sought to make Yiddish language and culture the focal point of secularized Jewish life and identity, the establishment of a chair announced definitively that Yiddish high culture was as valid and venerable as any other European high culture. It represented official recognition for an idiom whose supporters still struggled for its acceptance among Jews and non-Jews alike as a legitimate and full-fledged language, let alone a national one. Such public recognition for Yiddish was inconceivable in inter-war Poland, whose government was openly hostile towards Yiddish and the ideals of cultural autonomy for the Jews espoused by most of YIVO's supporters, despite having signed an international treaty to protect the cultural rights of national minorities after the First World War.[5]

Yet, the proposal to create a chair was cause more for acrimonious debates among Yiddishists than for collective rejoicing. Given the highly politicized and factious nature of inter-war Jewish society, this should come as little surprise despite YIVO's avowed goal of remaining above party politics beyond commitment to the research and propagation of the Yiddish language and a secular Jewish culture expressed in it. The case of the chair reflects as much personal rivalries and antagonisms as it does differing perspectives among Yiddishists on the very value and viability of secular Yiddish culture at a moment that was widely understood to represent a crossroads in Jewish history. Beyond this, it offers an opportunity to examine relationships between Jews and their neighbours in eastern Europe in this tense period and to consider contemporary Yiddishists' own evaluations of prospects for extraterritorial national cultural autonomy for Jews in differing political environments.

BACKGROUND

For centuries, Lithuania was linked with Poland in a dynastic union as part of the medieval Polish–Lithuanian Commonwealth. Its ruling nobility was ethnically Polish or Polonized, while the majority of the rural population was made up of Lithuanian-speaking or, in some places, Belarusian-speaking peasants. Yiddish-speaking Jews, and to a lesser extent Poles, were the dominant group in urban settings. More than a century of tsarist rule following the partitions of Poland in the late eighteenth century established a Russian bureaucracy and military. Russification policies introduced in response to the failed 1863 Polish insurrection against tsarist rule severely restricted the use of local languages but neither

---

[5] On the Polish state's attitude towards Yiddish and Jewish cultural autonomy, see J. Żyndul, *Państwo w państwie? Autonomia narodowo-kulturalna w Europie Środkowowschodniej w XX wieku* (Warsaw, 2000).

eliminated the prestige of Polish on the territory of the former Commonwealth nor eradicated the Lithuanian language. By the late nineteenth century, the latter was used mainly by peasants but was also cultivated and championed as a national language by a thin stratum of intellectuals eager for the restoration of Lithuanian autonomy, if not sovereignty. Lithuanian was seldom learned by Jews since they saw no socio-economic or cultural attraction in mastering an overwhelmingly rural tongue, let alone making it one's own. The same can be said about Belarusian, a language then commonly considered a peasant dialect of Russian. In fact, the Jews of the Kresy (the former eastern borderlands of the Polish–Lithuanian Commonwealth, corresponding to much of modern-day Lithuania, Belarus, and Ukraine) were among the least acculturated in eastern Europe, even if they had undergone a large degree of secularization by the end of the First World War, and the most supportive of Jewish nationalism.[6] In an atmosphere where no local nationality or culture dominated, Jews exhibited a strong attachment to Jewish languages—both Yiddish, their traditional vernacular in the region, and Hebrew, their holy language—and culture, both traditionally religious and modern. In addition to these languages, they may have acquired (and even adopted as their dominant language) Polish, German, or, most frequently, Russian, for reasons of prestige, pragmatism, and genuine appreciation of the depth and breadth of their literary cultures, but usually identified themselves as belonging to the Jewish people.[7]

To the chagrin of Lithuanian nationalists, Vilna, located in the north-west of the tsarist empire, was hardly populated by ethnic Lithuanians. It was essentially Polish and Jewish at the end of the First World War and its hinterlands were populated mainly by Belarusian peasants. After Poles (45 per cent), Jews made up the second largest group (37 per cent) in the city. The rest of its population of approximately 200,000 before the Second World War consisted of Lithuanians (10 per cent), Belarusians (5 per cent), and Russians (2 per cent).[8] Building on previous co-operation in elections to the 1906 Russian Duma and a relatively weak tradition of antisemitic violence among Lithuanians, Lithuanian leaders hoped to cultivate Jews as an ally after the First World War in order to secure international recognition for Vilna as a Lithuanian, and not Polish or Soviet, city. Lithuanian Jews generally did not identify culturally or politically with the Poles and feared the kind of antisemitism that erupted as a pogrom when Poland took control of Vilna in 1920. Despite disproportionate Jewish membership in communist organizations (according to one estimate, one-third of all Communist Party members in

---

[6] E. Mendelsohn, *On Modern Jewish Politics* (New York, 1993), 40–4.

[7] On the languages and cultures of the groups inhabiting the Kresy and their relationship to the tsarist regime, see T. R. Weeks, *Nation and State in Late Imperial Russia: Nationalism and Russification on the Western Frontier, 1863–1914* (DeKalb, Ill., 1996). On Jewish attitudes towards Lithuanian and other languages of the region, see A. Lieven, *The Baltic Revolution: Estonia, Latvia, Lithuania and the Path to Independence* (New Haven, 1993), 146–7.

[8] Levin, 'Jews of Vilna under Soviet Rule', 108.

Lithuania by the end of the inter-war period were Jews),[9] most Jews would also be wary of the Bolsheviks' hostility towards capitalism, religion, and all non-Soviet political ideologies. Jews' considerable weight—demographic, economic, and political (including ties to Jewish communities abroad, especially the United States)—also made them useful. Moreover, in keeping with Wilsonian notions of self-determination and the need to demonstrate the viability of an independent state, it would make a favourable impression on the victorious West to support national minority rights. At the 1919 Paris Peace Conference, Jewish delegations enthusiastically received Lithuanian pledges for national cultural autonomy for Lithuanians, Jews, Poles, and Belarusians alike.[10]

The support of Jews and other minorities ceased to be crucial, however, once Lithuanian independence was internationally recognized and Jewish numbers proved to be far smaller than anticipated. During negotiations regarding Lithuania's future it was assumed that Jews made up about 13 per cent of the Lithuanian population.[11] As a result of emigration, the mass deportation of some 120,000 Lithuanian Jews to Russia during the First World War, and, above all, the annexation of the disputed Vilna district by Poland in 1920, the number of Jews in independent Lithuania dropped to about 155,000.[12] The official 1923 census of Lithuania (excluding Vilna) revealed slightly over 2 million inhabitants, of which 81.7 per cent were Lithuanian, 7.6 per cent Jews, 4.1 per cent Germans, 3.0 per cent Poles, and 2.3 per cent Belarusians.[13]

The country was thus ethnically and linguistically quite homogeneous when deprived of the Vilna region. Extensive promises for Jewish autonomy were largely fulfilled in the state's first years but never enshrined in the Lithuanian constitution. They were, however, severely curtailed in the early 1920s. Increasingly nationalist political circles, seeing no need to create a federation of nationalities rather than a nation state, felt little motivation to accede to minority demands and gradually undid provisions for national cultural autonomy. They sought to Lithuanize the country linguistically and culturally and opposed the creation of a 'state within a state' by minorities.[14]

By 1924, the Ministry of Jewish Affairs was discontinued, as was the legal recognition of many Jewish institutions, including the right of organized Jewish

---

[9] E. Mendelsohn, *The Jews of East Central Europe between the World Wars* (Bloomington, Ind., 1983), 227.

[10] S. Sužiedėlis, 'The Historical Sources for Antisemitism in Lithuania and Jewish–Lithuanian Relations during the 1930s', in A. Nikžentaitis, S. Schreiner, and D. Staliūnas (eds.), *The Vanished World of Lithuanian Jews* (Amsterdam and New York, 2004), 123–4.

[11] Mendelsohn, *Jews of East Central Europe*, 223–4.

[12] D. Levin, 'Lithuania', in Hundert (ed.), *YIVO Encyclopedia of Jews in Eastern Europe*, i. 1071.

[13] Š. Liekis, *A State within a State? Jewish Autonomy in Lithuania, 1918–1925* (Vilnius, 2003), 82.

[14] On Lithuanian state policy towards its Jewish citizens, see Liekis, *State within a State*, and L. Truska, 'Antisemitism in the Interwar Republic of Lithuania: Focus on the 1930s', *Jews in Russia and Eastern Europe*, 54–5 (2005), 54–90.

communities (*kehilot*) to tax their members for both religious and secular purposes, including education and social welfare. The state treasury continued, however, to cover the salaries of rabbis, as it did the clergymen of other religions. Such measures undermined the ability of Jews to organize and administer their own cultural affairs as well as encouraging them to identify, as in western Europe, as citizens belonging to a religious community rather than as members of a linguistically and culturally distinct national minority. The government also stipulated that businesses close on Sundays and on Catholic and state holidays. This measure was clearly harmful to Jews, especially those who did not work on Saturdays, the Jewish sabbath, and could therefore only work five days a week. Further, citizens could no longer address the government in any language other than the official one, and it was mandated that signs, notices, and posters in public places, as well as business records, be in Lithuanian.[15]

Lithuania followed patterns similar to those in Poland and elsewhere in the region, where concerted efforts were made to 'nationalize' society and promote the interests of the dominant ethnic group in their 'own country'.[16] Jews and Poles, who previously owned much of the land, were drastically affected by policies intended to redress historical injustices done to the Lithuanian people and to reinforce the Lithuanian cultural character of the land. Such measures included encouraging peasant migration to the cities. Anatol Lievin observes:

The result, by the middle 1930s, was a virtual social revolution, with the creation of a Lithuanian urban middle class, and a graduate workforce, where none had existed before. In 1897, only 11.5 per cent of the population of towns was Lithuanian. By the 1930s, this had risen to more than 50 per cent. This led however to a typically 'Third-World' phenomenon: thousands of semi-educated young people and aspiring petty-bourgeois dependent upon an economy too weak to provide the jobs to which they aspired.[17]

The emerging ethnic Lithuanian urban middle class saw economic competitors in Jews, who long dominated commerce and artisanry as well as being prominent in

---

[15] M. Greenbaum, *The Jews of Lithuania: A History of a Remarkable Community, 1316–1945* (Jerusalem, 1995), 254; Truska, 'Antisemitism in the Interwar Republic of Lithuania', 62–4.

[16] Political scientist Sammy Smooha describes such a political system as an 'ethnic democracy', 'a system which combines the extension of civil and political rights to individuals and some collective rights to minorities, with institutionalization of majority control over the state. Driven by ethnic nationalism, the state is identified with a "core ethnic nation", not with its citizens. The state practices a policy of creating a homogenous nation-state, a state of and for a particular ethnic nation, and acts to promote the language, culture, numerical majority, economic well-being, and political interests of this group. Although enjoying citizenship and voting rights, the minorities are treated as second-class citizens, feared as a threat, excluded from the national power structure, and placed under some control. At the same time, the minorities are allowed to conduct a democratic and peaceful struggle that yields incremental improvement in their status': S. Smooha, 'Ethnic Democracy: Israel as an Archetype', *Israel Studies*, 2, no. 2 (1997), 199–200. For a critique of Smooha's model, particularly as it applies to Israel, see A. Ghanem, N. Rouhana, and O. Yiftachel, 'Questioning "Ethnic Democracy": A Response to Sammy Smooha', *Israel Studies*, 3, no. 2 (1998), 253–66.   [17] Lieven, *Baltic Revolution*, 144–5.

educated classes and the professions. Increasingly difficult economic straits and government policies directly and indirectly favouring ethnic Lithuanians over minorities also narrowed Jewish educational (particularly at the post-secondary level) and occupational horizons. The Jewish share in commerce, industry, and the professions, as well as in the composition of university student bodies, declined sharply between the beginning and end of the inter-war period even though it remained large. Responding to worsening conditions and often motivated by Zionist sentiments, between 1928 and 1936 some 12,690 Jews emigrated. They found new homes in South Africa, Palestine, and elsewhere, thereby decreasing the Jewish percentage of the population.[18]

Despite its conception of Lithuania as a nation state justly practising legitimate ethnic favouritism, the right-wing authoritarian regime that came to power in Lithuania following a coup d'état in 1926 never attempted to undo Jewish emancipation. On the contrary, it opposed antisemitic violence and permitted remaining institutions of Jewish cultural autonomy—schools and co-operative banks—to continue. While Jewish culture was foreign to Lithuanians and most Jews were equally alien to Lithuanian culture,[19] they were usually considered the most loyal national minority since they harboured no irredentist yearnings or identification with a mother state which threatened Lithuania. In contrast, the Polish and German minorities were viewed with suspicion and hostility: the Poles because of

---

[18] Mendelsohn, *Jews of East Central Europe*, 225.

[19] On what the Vilna native and Lithuanian poet Tomas Venclova describes as the 'spiritual isolation' prevalent between Lithuanians and Jews and their mutual ignorance despite centuries of cohabitation, see his famous essay 'Jews and Lithuanians' in his *Forms of Hope: Essays* (Riverdale-on-Hudson, NY, 1999). There he comments: 'We, Lithuanians, knew not a little about Polish culture and something about German and Russian cultures, but we hadn't the slightest idea about Jewish culture which was unfolding in our country in front of our eyes. The religion, language, alphabet, and customs turned out to be too great a barrier. The Jewish community was understood as an exotic enclave spiritually unrelated to us. It is clear that this was a grave mistake. The Jews, also, knew little about Lithuanian traditions and culture. Those who assimilated usually adopted Russian, or sometimes German. Two national renaissances—Lithuanian and Jewish—blossomed simultaneously and contiguously, but in different dimensions . . . The first cautious attempts to overcome this impenetrable barrier, to become acquainted with one another's cultural potential, occurred in the interwar period. The Jews took the initiative' (pp. 46–7). The Israeli historian Mordechai Zalkin notes the tendency in Jewish historiography to focus on Jews' relations with the Polish aristocracy or Russian officialdom in Lithuania and to ignore some five centuries of Jewish–Lithuanian relations prior to the Holocaust. In his survey of Lithuanian scholarship he applauds the recent engagement by current Lithuanian scholars with painful topics and with the complexity of Lithuanian–Jewish relations: M. Zalkin, 'Lita'im veyehudim: he'arah arukah beshulei hama'amar', *Iyunim betekumat yisra'el*, 14 (2004), 471–8. In contrast, he laments the tendency in Jewish historiography and both Israeli and Jewish collective consciousness to view the entirety of Jewish–Lithuanian relations through the prism of the Holocaust and to prefer the 'classic dichotomous narrative of "bad versus good" to a more nuanced and chronologically encompassing picture' (p. 478). His annotated Hebrew translation of Venclova's essay ('Yehudim velita'im', *Iyunim betekumat yisra'el*, 14 (2004), 461–71) is meant to challenge this image and inspire further research among Jewish scholars.

the Polish seizure of Vilna and the historical danger posed to Lithuanian national identity by Polish language and culture, the language of the nobility on whose land Lithuanian peasants toiled for centuries; the Germans because the Lithuanian annexation of the Klaipėda (Memel) region represented a bone of contention. The region, which was under German rule prior to the First World War, had a large German population and became a focus of Nazi attention in the 1930s.

Jewish ignorance of Lithuanian and preference for Russian as a language of high culture and lingua franca were sources of great irritation for Lithuanians, especially right-wing nationalists, who viewed it as a sign of disrespect for Lithuanian culture and disloyalty to the state. In the estimation of many Lithuanians, including the president Antanas Smetona, it was preferable for Jews to use their own languages amongst themselves and Lithuanian for interactions outside their community.[20] The government provided more than 90 per cent of the budget of the Jewish elementary school system, which functioned in Hebrew and Yiddish. As official state schools, Jewish elementary schools were under the supervision of the Ministry of Education.[21] State secondary schools and universities functioned only in Lithuanian, however, obliging Jews themselves to fund secondary institutions in Hebrew and Yiddish for children who wished to continue their education in these languages. The diplomas of the schools were, however, recognized by the state, and state moneys were available here too, making up one-third to one-fourth of the total budget of Jewish secondary schools. Over twenty years, the Jewish schools educated about 90 per cent of Jewish children.[22]

Three school systems competed for dominance among Lithuanian Jews, a factor undermining the fulfilment of cultural autonomy from within. Despite the fact that Yiddish was the mother tongue of nearly all Lithuanian Jews, secular Yiddish schools drew only 15–20 per cent of students in the inter-war period.[23] Yiddish schools suffered from widespread association, especially in the early state years when they were largely run by the pro-Soviet Kulturlige, with anti-religious, anti-traditional, left-leaning tendencies. They were consequently harassed by Lithuanian officials.[24] They continued to be avoided by parents even after the Kulturlige was outlawed in 1924 and the schools had come under the auspices mainly of the bourgeois nationalist Folkists. Instead of studying in their mother tongue, most Jewish children attended the Hebrew-language schools of the secular Zionist Tarbut system (75 per cent of Jewish schoolchildren in 1928), which encouraged emigration to Palestine, or those of the Orthodox Yavneh system,

[20] Sužiedėlis, 'Historical Sources for Antisemitism', 129.

[21] Truska, 'Antisemitism in the Interwar Republic of Lithuania', 63; Mendelsohn, *Jews of East Central Europe*, 217–25.   [22] Levin, 'Lithuania', 1072–3.

[23] 'Lithuania can serve as a prominent example of the possibility of a chasm between a milieu that is 100% Yiddish-Jewish and a Yiddish school, which occupied only a corner in the Jewish milieu (apart from the first years, only 15–20% of Jewish children studied in the modern secular Yiddish schools)': Y. Mark, 'Beit hasefer ha'idi belita ha'atsma'it', in N. Goren et al. (eds.), *Yahadut lita*, ii (Tel Aviv, 1972), 169.   [24] Ibid. 167, 169.

which functioned in Hebrew or in both Hebrew and Yiddish.[25] The success these school systems achieved in providing a high-quality, modern education is made all the more remarkable by the fact that the movement to revive Hebrew as a spoken language was only a few decades old and faced the significant challenge of overcoming the linguistic practices of a culturally homogeneous Jewish community generally sharing a common mother tongue.[26]

While parents often had little knowledge of Lithuanian prior to the First World War, children became comfortable with the language of the land as a result of its mandatory instruction in all schools. Familiarity with Lithuanian increased over time, especially after 1926, as the government demanded more hours for Lithuanian in Jewish schools and the expanded teaching of general subject matter in that language.[27] Towards the end of the inter-war period, in fact, increasing numbers of Jewish students began attending Lithuanian-language rather than Jewish-language schools, whose numbers were being reduced by the state. This made sense as familiarity with Lithuanian language and culture grew and the utility of Lithuanian as the state language (and the undesirability of Russian, Polish, and German), as well as the failure to implement national cultural autonomy, became apparent. If before the 1930s Jewish attendance in Lithuanian schools was rare, by the school year 1935/6 20.3 per cent of Jewish students (3,483) attended them.[28] Had the Second World War not erupted, it is likely that this trend would have intensified with time. Nonetheless, despite the triumph of Hebrew-language education and changing government policies, inter-war Lithuanian Jewry remained overwhelmingly Yiddish-speaking, showing significantly less linguistic assimilation than the much larger Polish Jewry (to be discussed below) on the eve of the Second World War.[29]

Prior to the inter-war period, Lithuania experienced little anti-Jewish unrest, and modern, especially racial, antisemitism was not widely known. Certainly, Lithuanian–Jewish encounters were not necessarily cordial, and mutual stereo-

[25] Y. Iram, 'The Persistence of Jewish Ethnic Identity: The Educational Experience in Inter-War Poland and Lithuania, 1919–1939', *History of Education*, 14 (1985), 279.

[26] In Palestine, where the Jewish population was more linguistically heterogeneous, the force of entrenched linguistic habit and resistance from older and more traditional elements posed less of an obstacle to speaking Hebrew as an everyday language among young Zionist immigrants living in new communities outside traditional areas of Jewish residence. On the revival of Hebrew in Palestine as a vernacular and as a language of modern education, see J. Myhill, *Language in Jewish Society: Towards a New Understanding* (Clevedon, 2004), 73–97. On the question of using Hebrew as a medium of instruction in the Zionist 'reformed *ḥeder*' (*ḥeder metukan*) in late imperial Russia, see S. J. Zipperstein, *Imagining Russian Jewry: Memory, History, Identity* (Seattle, 1999), 49 ff.

[27] Mark, 'Beit hasefer ha'idi belita ha'atsma'it', 169.

[28] D. Lapits, 'Haḥinukh ha'ivri vehatenuah ha'ivrit belita ha'atsma'it', in Goren et al. (eds.), *Yahadut lita*, ii. 117.

[29] On issues of schooling and linguistic acculturation, see G. Bacon, 'National Revival, Ongoing Acculturation—Jewish Education in Interwar Poland', *Jahrbuch des Simon-Dubnow-Instituts*, 1 (2002), 71–92.

types, suspicions, and feelings of alienation prevailed in relations between the groups. Jews were, however, accepted as a natural part of the landscape, a peculiar group of neither natives nor foreigners who performed needed, if distasteful, economic and other functions. Building on traditional Christian Judaeophobia and associations of Jews with Bolshevism widespread in Europe, antisemitic incidents and agitation grew in the inter-war period, especially as a result of economic conflict between ethnic communities. Lithuanian–Jewish relations deteriorated most significantly in the late 1930s. Fascination with fascism, biological racism, and extreme nationalist ideologies took hold here too.

Unfortunately, despite condemnations of antisemitism and the low tolerance of violence against Jews expressed by nationalist President Antanas Smetona's government, anti-Jewish attitudes increased among nearly all strata of Lithuanian society. Anti-Jewish rhetoric became less restrained and street-level violence increased, including beatings of Jews and the destruction or vandalizing of Jewish property. Calls for racial segregation (including the establishment of 'ghetto benches' for Jewish students, a measure which had aroused condemnation earlier in the Lithuanian press as an example of Polish bigotry when introduced at the Polish-controlled Stefan Batory University in Vilna) and for the removal of Jews from society were also heard from more radical elements. Still, the tone of antisemitism was far less strident here and its violent manifestations less common and significantly less extensive than in neighbouring Poland between the world wars.[30]

VILNA IN LITHUANIAN HANDS

Lithuanian–Jewish relations took a turn for the worse after the Soviet invasion of Poland in September 1939 and the sealing of a mutual defence pact between Lithuania and the Soviet Union on 11 October. Soviet forces seized Vilna on 19 September and continued to occupy the city until late October. Though aware of the repressive nature of the Soviet regime, even those Jews whose interests and values conflicted most with communism, such as factory owners, Orthodox, Bundists, and Zionists, understandably preferred the lesser of the two evils— Soviet rule—to being overrun by the implacably antisemitic Nazis. Indeed, many rank-and-file Jews, not to mention those genuinely committed to communism or sympathetic to the Soviets, did not conceal their enthusiasm for the arrival of forces that would hopefully guarantee their physical safety even if they also deprived them of political, cultural, and economic freedom.

Since they could not side with the Nazis, Jews were considered relatively reliable by the Soviets. Moreover, as a consequence of the prestige of Russian in the

[30] J. Tauber, 'Antisemitismus in den baltischen Staaten in der Zwischenkriegszeit am Beispiel Litauens', *Zeitschrift für Osmitteleuropa-Forschung*, 54 (2005), 25–34; Sužiedėlis, 'Historical Sources for Antisemitism', 120–46; Levin, 'Lithuania', 1073; Truska, 'Antisemitism in the Interwar Republic of Lithuania', 65.

period before the First World War, when the Vilna region still belonged to the tsarist empire, many Jews, especially intellectuals and those in the upper classes, spoke Russian as a native or second language. This facilitated communication and co-operation with the new occupiers, as well as making Jews useful in administrative and other positions requiring linguistic competence and literacy. During their six-week occupation of Vilna, the Soviets lifted discriminatory Polish measures affecting Jews and elevated many to unprecedented positions of authority and influence over non-Jews. Such observations tended to reinforce for Poles and Lithuanians, for whom the Russian language was associated with the suppression of national cultures and the crushing of aspirations for independence, the already strong linking of Jews, a formerly subordinate group in the political hierarchy, with Bolsheviks.

Many Jews, whether or not previously active as communists, acted in the name of Soviet authority in occupied Vilna. Others, however, were arrested and deported no differently from members of other national groups who were judged harmful to the interests of the regime. Nor were Jews the only ones to benefit from Soviet rule: members of all national communities found employment in the Soviet apparatus. The general uncertainty of the times, the disruption of normal life and livelihoods, and resentment over the influx of refugees undoubtedly also contributed to the heightening of tensions between ethnic groups.[31]

Even the handing over of Vilna to the Lithuanians at the end of October, the one positive aspect of the Soviet–Lithuanian pact from a Lithuanian perspective, inflamed inter-ethnic tensions. Lithuanian joy over the annexation of their ancient capital was 'adulterated by anguish at the surrender to the rule of Russia, from whose yoke Lithuania had freed itself only twenty years earlier and whose image in Lithuania was decidedly unfavourable'.[32] The announcement of a disadvantageous exchange rate for the Polish currency, which was to be removed from circulation, sparked a rapid inflation and rumours circulated that Jews were hoarding flour. Meanwhile, local Poles protested against the 'Lithuanian occupation' of the city, while Jews formed a large contingent at unruly pro-Soviet gatherings. Violent confrontation between Poles and Jews followed, as well as with Lithuanian police and military arriving from Kaunas who were unfamiliar with local conditions. Within seventy-two hours of the Lithuanian military's entry into Vilna on 28 October 1939, bloody riots erupted against Jews in Vilna and several other towns in the region.[33] The pogrom was fuelled, if not triggered, by the widespread identification of Jews, whose numbers had swelled with refugees from Poland and elsewhere, with the despised Bolsheviks.

[31] On this period, see Š. Liekis, 'Jewish–Polish Relations and the Lithuanian Authorities in Vilna, 1939–1940', *Polin*, 19 (2007), 521–36; M. Wierzbicki, 'Polish–Jewish Relations in Vilna and the Region of Western Vilna under Soviet Occupation, 1939–1941', *Polin*, 19 (2007), 487–516.

[32] A. Shochat, 'Jews, Lithuanians and Russians, 1939–1941', in B. Vago and G. L. Mosses (eds.), *Jews and Non-Jews in Eastern Europe, 1918–1945* (New Brunswick, NJ, 1974), 304.

[33] Sužiedėlis, 'Historical Sources for Antisemitism', 141.

Public order was soon restored, however, by the Lithuanian authorities with the help of Red Army soldiers. Further, Vilna benefited from the general economic prosperity of the period, to which Russian soldiers' purchases added and the presence of refugee consumers, including large numbers of refugee Jews and Poles arriving from Poland, contributed. Since not only urban businessmen, Jewish and non-Jewish, but also Lithuanian rural farmers benefited from these conditions, agitation to trade only with 'one's own' national group diminished and public displays of anti-Jewish sentiment subsided.[34] Significantly, the absorption of so many Jews from the Vilna region and beyond increased the proportion of Jews in the general population, raising it from around 153,000 (6.4 per cent) to 241,600 (8.4 per cent).[35] These Jews were communally and culturally very active, accounting for more than one-third of organizations in the Vilna area.[36] As at the end of the First World War, the Jews' numbers and their cultural and economic prominence made them consequential to Lithuanian officials.

The Lithuanian authorities undoubtedly sought to have Jews on their side rather than on that of rival Poles. It was expected that Polish nationalists could never reconcile themselves to Lithuanian control over the city. Jewish nationalists, on the other hand, could make peace with this, as their loyalty would be to whichever state offered them the opportunity to pursue their own national aims. (Indeed, many Vilna Jews supported Lithuanian control of the city after the First World War, arousing Polish hostility.) Further, seeking to Lithuanize the city, Lithuanian officials preferred that Jews in Vilna, few of whom knew Lithuanian but many of whom—especially the refugees from central Poland—spoke Polish as their primary language, use Yiddish in public life. Certainly, it was preferable that Jews speak and develop their culture in languages of their own rather than make use of those of Lithuania's hostile neighbours, Poland and Soviet Russia. While it was desirable for Jews to master Lithuanian and to integrate, it was not a serious consideration that they be assimilated into Lithuanian society, as was hoped of Poles who were long-term residents of the Vilna area. These Poles were seen as renegade Lithuanians whose Polonization over generations had to be reversed. In contrast, Polish refugees from 'ethnic' Poland, also numbering in the thousands, were considered an obstacle to the Lithuanization of the city and were consequently to be deported.[37]

THE CHAIR IN YIDDISH

Given these circumstances, it is not surprising that Lithuanian officials, especially liberal intellectuals, evinced great sympathy for Jewish culture. The idea of creating a chair in Yiddish was revived—one of three university positions (of which

---

[34] Shochat, 'Jews, Lithuanians and Russians', 304–5.
[35] Š. Liekis, *1939: The Year that Changed Everything in Lithuania's History* (Amsterdam and New York, 2010), 214.   [36] Liekis, *State within a State*, 223.
[37] Liekis, 'Jewish–Polish Relations and the Lithuanian Authorities in Vilna', 533.

only one, a chair in Semitics at the University of Kaunas, was realized) in Jewish studies proposed in the 'golden years' when Jewish autonomy was fully intact.[38] The initiative to create a chair in Yiddish issued, however, from outside both Lithuanian and Lithuanian-Jewish circles proper. Instead, it was a refugee from Warsaw, Noah Prylucki, and his colleagues in the Diaspora nationalist Folkspartay who first pursued the matter with Lithuanian academics. In addition to leading the small bourgeois party in Poland, Prylucki was a prominent journalist and a prolific, if idiosyncratic, autodidact scholar of Yiddish literature, theatre, and linguistics. The championing of Yiddish was his *raison d'être* and he condemned its abandonment in a secular age as tantamount to national suicide for the Jews. Though he, like many, was frustrated by the failure of Jewish nationalist politics in the interwar period to achieve its stated aims, Prylucki remained committed throughout his life to winning state support for Yiddish cultural institutions. He understood that this was essential in order to ensure that the pursuit of higher culture and socio economic mobility did not entail the replacement of Yiddish with the dominant languages of non-Jewish society.

In Poland, promised state support for schools in Jewish languages, the foundation of the Folkists' vision of Jewish national cultural autonomy, was scarcely forthcoming. Jewish secular schools necessarily functioned as private institutions reliant on funding from political parties and charitable organizations, especially those of American Jewry, to keep afloat, since impoverished parents had difficulty paying even meagre tuition fees. Moreover, these institutions, especially those of the Yiddishist Tsisho[39] network, were frequently harassed by the state for left-leaning and suspected pro-Soviet ideological tendencies. Nor were Jewish parents, particularly the traditionally religious majority, necessarily in favour of their educational goals. Economic obstacles, the instability of these schools, and the relative disadvantage they conferred in a Polish-speaking society made Yiddishist and Hebraist schools an attractive option only to relatively small circles of the ideologically committed. They were most popular in the Kresy (including the Vilna region), where Polonization proceeded least rapidly because of the multi-ethnic make-up of the population and the lack of a Polish majority in the region. Since universal primary education was required by law, most Jewish children in interwar Poland received their elementary school education in free Polish-language state schools. The minority of Jews who went on to higher education, particularly those who hoped to gain admission to a Polish university, typically studied in private Polish-language Jewish secondary schools, since it was notoriously difficult

---

[38] <http://litvakai.mch.mii.lt/the_past/education.htm>. Simon Dubnow was invited to occupy a chair in Jewish history within the planned department of Jewish studies at the University of Kaunas in 1922 but refused the position: V. Dohrn, 'State and Minorities: The First Lithuanian Republic and S. M. Dubnov's Concept of Cultural Autonomy', in Nikžentaitis, Schreiner, and Staliūnas (eds.), *Vanished World of Lithuanian Jews*, 163–4.

[39] A Yiddish acronym for Central Jewish School Organization; it was aligned most prominently, although not exclusively, with Jewish socialist parties, especially the Bund.

for Jews to obtain admission to state-run ones. The cumulative effect, readily observable even within the brief existence of the Second Polish Republic, was rapidly increasing linguistic Polonization of the generation coming of age in the inter-war period. This situation naturally presented a major dilemma for Yiddishists, who were alarmed by the linguistic 'defection' of Jews and the emergence of a specifically Polish-language Jewish cultural sphere: newspapers, schools, theatre, youth groups, and political organizations all functioning in Polish but oriented towards a Jewish constituency.[40]

Though he arrived almost penniless as a refugee from Warsaw in early October 1939, Prylucki was optimistic about the horizons Vilna offered for the propagation of secular Yiddish culture. He almost immediately became involved in cultural activities in Vilna and enjoyed the companionship of long-time colleagues as well as of promising young talents such as the young Vilna poets Shmerke Kaczerginski, Chaim Grade, and Avrom Sutzkever.[41] He refused to succumb to pessimism and inertia in the face of a tragedy of historic if yet unknown proportions that had befallen Polish Jewry, reminding his YIVO colleagues that 'The war has not destroyed us. We must work with what is available. We owe much to the Kaunas Friends [of YIVO Society] for their help and for making YIVO respectable in the eyes of the authorities.'[42] He called for the expansion of YIVO's activities beyond its pre-war academic agenda to include more popular educational undertakings and to draw as much as possible upon the abundance of refugee talents, including his own. Aside from delivering popular academic lectures (such as one honouring Y. L. Peretz on the twenty-fifth anniversary of his death, at the University of Vilnius, formerly in the inter-war period the Polish Stefan Batory University), Prylucki prepared to give lectures on Yiddish grammar to teachers and organized a historical commission funded by the Joint Distribution Committee to document Nazi persecution of Jews.[43]

Prylucki optimistically viewed the present occupation as the chance to build cultural institutions much in the same way that he and other Yiddishists had taken advantage of the chaos and destruction of the First World War to begin the first network of legal secular schools with Yiddish as their language of instruction. That war had resulted in an influx of Yiddish-speaking refugees, including thousands of children, into Warsaw. During their occupation of Poland and Lithuania in the First World War, the German authorities not only lifted discriminatory tsarist regulations in the name of basic equality, peace, and stability among different

---

[40] For more on Polonization among Jews and the Yiddishist response to it, see K. Weiser, 'The Yiddishist Ideology of Noah Prylucki', *Polin*, 21 (2009), 363–400.

[41] H.-D. Kats, 'Kapitelekh yidish: a merkverdike froy', *Forverts*, 17 Mar. 2000.

[42] 'Protokol fun der ferter shlus zitsung, zuntik dem 10tn detsember 1939', pp. 35–42: YIVO Archives, New York, RG 1.1, box 31, folder 631.

[43] M. Balberyszski, *Shtarker fun ayzn* (Tel Aviv, 1967), 88, 118; H. Kruk, *Togbukh fun vilner geto* (New York, 1961), 535 n. 425.

nationalities there, but required all children, regardless of origins and sex, to enrol in primary schools teaching in their 'mother tongue'. For practical reasons they made use of Yiddish in official proclamations, implicitly recognizing it as being on a par with other languages, and permitted the functioning of Yiddish secular schools alongside those using other languages suppressed by the tsarist regime.[44] Thus, for Yiddishists, the suffering engendered by the First World War was at least in part compensated for by the political and cultural gains it yielded.

Similar enthusiasm for Lithuanian rule of Vilna in the early days of the Second World War was expressed by Max Weinreich, the guiding spirit of YIVO. From Copenhagen, Weinreich relied on erratic mail delivery to relay news and information between colleagues in YIVO's branches in Kaunas, Vilna, Paris, and New York in order to help co-ordinate the activity of the institute worldwide. Fearing for Weinreich's personal safety and the future of YIVO as a research institution, Naftali Feinerman, the director of its American subsidiary Amopteyl (Amerikaner opteyl, American Division), urged him to come to New York for at least the duration of the war. Weinreich, however, was eager to return, if possible, to YIVO's headquarters in Vilna and to his family and friends. Conditions under independent Lithuanian rule, he expected, would be far better for YIVO and Yiddish culture than in Poland, since in Lithuania 'there is no assimilation'.[45] There, in contrast with Poland, where most children attended Polish-language state schools, state support for schools functioning in Jewish languages existed throughout the interwar period. Consequently, Weinreich argued, Yiddish schools could grow there and their staff would necessarily turn to YIVO for guidance in questions of language and pedagogy. This would justify the need for YIVO's *aspirantur* and *proaspirantur* programmes, which prepared researchers, teachers, and social workers. Instead of losing a generation in the long struggle with 'demonic forces' (*sitreakhre*; here, Polonization), as Weinreich feared had occurred in Poland in the 1920s and 1930s, the dream of a self-sustaining, multi-generational intellectual and academic culture seemed possible in Lithuania. 'If Vilna does not became a backroom of Russia, it can again became a mother city in Israel—not only for Lithuanian Jews' but for Jews arriving from elsewhere too.[46] As long as there was no Soviet intervention in Lithuania's domestic affairs, he wrote, 'YIVO is saved, then my place is in Vilna'. Otherwise, 'we must think about saving the collections and people by transporting them to America and ending the European period of YIVO's history'.[47] He recognized, however, that establishing YIVO's headquarters in America would be an uphill battle. In his evaluation, American Jewry

---

[44] On this period, see Z. Szajkowski, 'The Struggle for Yiddish During World War I', *Leo Baeck Institute Year Book*, 9 (1964), 131–58. See also the works of Chaim Szlomo Kazdan, *Fun kheyder biz tsisho* (Mexico City, 1956) and *Di geshikhte fun yidishn shulvezn in umophengikn poyln* (Mexico City, 1947).

[45] Letter from Max Weinreich to Naftali Feinerman, 14 Oct. 1939: YIVO Archives, RG 584, box 30, folder 293b.   [46] Ibid.   [47] Ibid.

showed far less commitment to Yiddish and appreciation of YIVO's mission than the Jews in Yiddish's eastern European heartland.[48]

Without consulting Weinreich or other YIVO colleagues, Noah Prylucki seized the moment in the name of Yiddish culture. In late 1939 he approached Professor Mykolas Biržiška, a historian of Lithuanian culture and literature with friendly ties to Jewish cultural circles, about the possibility of creating a Yiddish chair. Prylucki had first met him during a visit to Kaunas in the 1920s. This time Prylucki was accompanied by Majer Balberyszski, a Lithuanian Folkist colleague who enjoyed cordial relations with Biržiška and his family, and was supported in his endeavours by the Kaunas Friends of YIVO Society.[49] Prylucki did not inform the YIVO administration in Vilna, which, unlike the Kaunas society, had no legal status yet in Lithuania, of these meetings.

A signatory of Lithuanian independence in 1918, the liberal Biržiška was elected rector of the Vytautas Magnus University in Kaunas in 1940.[50] He was an admirer of Jewish culture who participated in the founding of a Department of Semitics in Kaunas in the 1930s and sent salutations to the first YIVO conference in Vilna in 1929.[51] Maintaining, like his brother Vaclovas, also a professor, close contact with the leaders of the Lithuanian Jewish community prior to the Second World War, he founded the Lithuanian–Jewish Friendship Association.[52] According to the Jewish writer Daniel Tsharni, he even knew Yiddish and read the Yiddish press fluently while sitting in cafés.[53] Not surprisingly, then, he pronounced himself in favour of a project for a chair in Yiddish language and literature and offered to assist in directing a proposal for its establishment to the proper audience.

The proposed position would be established in Vilna, where the Humanities Faculty of the Vytautas Magnus University was to be transferred from Kaunas.[54]

---

[48] Urging the Amopteyl to expand its activities in preparation for whatever might lie ahead, he wrote, 'Now we must at least reckon with the possibility that for years to come, the few tens of our own people must stand at the foreposts. American Jews are not yet ready. We know that. But you, our people, must be ready to take over the [YIVO] mission': letter from Max Weinreich to Naftali Feinerman, 25 Sept. 1939: YIVO Archives, RG 584, box 30, folder 293b. 'Who can honestly say that Jewish America cannot live without YIVO?', he later wrote in the American Yiddish daily *Forverts*: M. Vaynraykh, 'Der yidisher visnshaftlekher institut hot zikh "bazetst" in amerike biz di milkhome vet fariber', *Forverts*, 11 Jan. 1942. Weinreich, like a number of his colleagues in Vilna and New York, expressed deep pessimism by the early 1940s over the future of YIVO and of Yiddish in America—a language in a 'state of disintegration' in the mouths of American-born speakers unaccustomed to speaking it outside the home: M. Vaynraykh, 'Vegn englishe elementn in unzer kulturshprakh', *Yidishe shprakh*, 1, no. 2 (1941), 34.   [49] Balberyszski, *Shtarker fun ayzn*, 79.

[50] J. Šukys, *'And I burned with shame': The Testimony of Ona Šimaitė, Righteous among the Nations. A Letter to Isaac Nachman Steinberg* (Jerusalem, 2007), 38.

[51] I. Lempertas, 'Užmiršta jidiš puoselėtoja: Nojaus Priluckio katedra Vilniaus universitete', in L. Lempertienė (ed.), *Vilniaus žydų intelektualinis gyvenimas iki Antrojo pasaulinio karo* (Vilnius, 2004), 185; Mandelman, 'In freyd un leyd tsvishn litvishe yidn', 1335 n.

[52] A. Tory, *Surviving the Holocaust: The Kovno Ghetto Diary* (Cambridge, Mass., 1990), 317.

[53] D. Tsharni, 'In kovner lite in 1933', in Sudarsky et al. (eds.), *Lite*, i. 1326.

[54] T. Venclova, 'Four Centuries of Enlightenment: A Historic View of the University of Vilnius,

According to Prylucki, who subsequently explained the nature of their meeting to YIVO's temporary administration, Biržiška maintained that the greatest impediment to the endeavour was funding: it was doubtful that the Lithuanian state would provide financial support in the early years of the chair. He suggested involving Chaim Nachman Shapiro, the Professor of Semitics in Kaunas, in negotiations, since Shapiro took an interest in Yiddish culture. Prylucki, however, was eager to keep the matter from him. Biržiška interpreted this as an indication of anticipated opposition on the part of local Hebraists to the plan.[55] Prylucki and the Folkists feared Zionist opposition and wanted to avoid a combined Hebrew–Yiddish chair. Also, they were eager to secure the position for an ideological Yiddishist who accepted the orthographic system for Yiddish which YIVO had elaborated and propagated in collaboration with the Tsisho network of Yiddish schools in Poland. The position should not be awarded to a scholar not committed in his personal life to the growth and vitality of Yiddish culture since, in Prylucki's words, 'The chair is a national and political position.'[56] He reported to his YIVO colleagues that a candidate would need neither a special linguistics diploma nor Lithuanian citizenship, since the Lithuanian authorities would be willing to appoint a lector rather than a professor to teach.[57] Such conditions made Prylucki, a Polish citizen lacking formal linguistics training, a viable candidate for the position.

Prylucki's enthusiasm for the proposed chair and the expansion of YIVO's activities was matched only by Zelig Kalmanowicz's pessimism. When war broke out, Kalmanowicz fled to neighbouring Latvia to escape the Soviets. Out of a sense of obligation to colleagues, he returned to Vilna once the Red Army had departed and grudgingly accepted appointment by the Lithuanian authorities as YIVO's superintendent (*kurator*), since he was the only remaining member of the YIVO executive who was a Lithuanian citizen.

A one-time Folkist in Lithuania and like Prylucki also a member of YIVO's philological section, Kalmanowicz had come to despair of the prospects for independent Jewish cultural life in eastern Europe long before the German invasion of Poland. In his analysis, secular Yiddish culture, with its offerings of literature and theatre, was ultimately insufficient to sustain Jewish identity in the post-Emancipation era.[58] Since Jews did not possess a self-sufficient economy, they

1579–1979', *Lithuanian Quarterly Journal of Arts and Sciences*, 27, no. 1 (Summer 1981): <http://www.lituanus.org/1981_2/81_2_01.htm>.

[55] These concerns were later put to rest by a subsequent YIVO delegation to Biržiška not including Prylucki; it assured him that Yiddishists and Hebraists were capable of co operation, as evidenced by YIVO's good relations with the Hebrew University in Jerusalem. 'Barikht vegn dem bazukh fun der delegatsye fun yivo bay prof' birzhishko vegn dem inyen katedre far yidisher shprakh un literatur baym vilner universitet', undated: YIVO Archives, RG 1.1, box 31, folder 633.

[56] 'Protokol fun der zitsung fun der tsaytvayliker farvaltung fun yivo, vilne, dem 27tn yanuar 1940', p. 19: YIVO Archives, RG 1.1, box 31, folder 631.   [57] Ibid.

[58] As he put matters to the historian Lucy Dawidowicz, then a young *aspirant* studying at YIVO in 1938–9, 'What kind of movement can it be whose program is to read a Yiddish book and to go to the Yiddish theater once in a while?': Dawidowicz, *From That Place and Time*, 100.

would always need to know the language of the land. The Jews in Poland were linguistically assimilating despite pauperization and widespread antisemitism. The Marxist Yiddish culture offered in the Soviet Union, divorced as it was from its roots in the Hebrew language and religious tradition, was destructive of Jewish national uniqueness. In contrast with Prylucki, who never tired of demanding state support for Yiddish culture in the name of basic justice, Kalmanowicz became convinced by the 1930s that the Jews could not rely on such appeals and on navigating political channels. Only the socio-economic concentration of the Jews in a territory of their own and the embracing of the entirety of their cultural legacy could impede assimilation and guarantee Jewish national survival. Though not a Zionist, he increasingly leaned in this direction, maintaining that only the Zionists had correctly evaluated the dangers of Diaspora life.[59] On the eve of the Second World War he considered settling in Palestine, where his only son lived and where, he later announced to the YIVO executive in frustration, he could have found 'an excellent position'.[60]

'The head and heart of YIVO is gone', Kalmanowicz lamented to his colleagues in January 1940, referring to Zalmen Reyzen's arrest. 'How can YIVO live without him?'[61] In Kalmanowicz's gloomy appraisal, it was hopeless to carry on YIVO's activities as before, let alone expand them to include new ones, some of which, such as courses aimed at a popular audience, he felt were not in consonance with YIVO's academic mission. He enumerated a number of formal obstacles to YIVO's operations, including a paucity of funding arriving from abroad and delays in formalizing YIVO's legal status with the Lithuanian authorities—all obstacles that his more optimistic colleagues rejected as temporary inconveniences. Deploring the grievous events that had befallen Polish Jewry since the outbreak of war in 1939, he urged that all activities beyond the cataloguing of inventory be transferred to New York, the site of the Amopteyl. Such a move was firmly rejected by the Folkists, Bundists, and other parties alike represented in YIVO's provisional administration. They objected that it would signal to the world the shifting of Yiddish high culture from its centre to its periphery and the demise of eastern European Jewry. From the vantage point of eastern European Jewish intellectuals and communal activists, America was a culturally underdeveloped Jewish colony despite the presence of many talented individuals ideologically committed to Yiddish.[62] In America, as Bundist Gershon Pludermakher put matters succinctly, 'the Yiddish movement is

[59] J. Karlip, 'At the Crossroads between War and Genocide: A Reassessment of Jewish Ideology in 1940', *Jewish Social Studies*, 11, no. 2 (2005), 170–201.

[60] 'Protokol fun der zitsung fun der tsaytvayliker farvaltung fun yivo, 10tn marts 1940', p. 19: YIVO Archives, RG 1.1, box 31, folder 631.

[61] 'Protokol fun der zitsung fun der tsaytvayliker farvaltung fun yivo, vilne, dem 27tn yanuar 1940', p. 13: YIVO Archives, RG 1.1, box 31, folder 631.

[62] Nina Warnke notes of Sholem Aleichem, 'Whereas he acknowledged the benefits of political freedom and economic opportunity for Jews in America, he continuously mocked in his writings the low level of the immigrants' culture and the shallowness of their values': N. Warnke, 'Of Plays and

not faring well'.[63] To these kinds of objections, Kalmanowicz, who had fled Lithuania to escape the Soviets at the outbreak of the war, affirmed his commitment to work on behalf of Jewish culture in Vilna despite his lack of hope for its future: 'Reyzen was optimistic. He remained, and was arrested. I was pessimistic. I ran away and I am standing here now. I don't approve of Jewish life here but I work and I want there to be a Jewish life.'[64]

A YIVO delegation comprising Kalmanowicz, the lawyer and Yiddish philologist Pinkhas Kohn, and the community activist Vladimir (David) Kaplan-Kaplanski visited Biržiška on 16 January 1940 and presented him with a memorandum prepared by Weinreich regarding the chair.[65] Prylucki, feeling deliberately excluded from YIVO affairs, made clear to the YIVO administration his dissatisfaction that he had not been informed of the delegation's mission. Kohn, irritated by Prylucki's protests, retorted at the same meeting that the delegation had used at least 80 per cent of its time with the professor to correct what he described as 'fundamental errors' made by Prylucki in what was a private initiative rather than a meeting authorized by YIVO.[66]

Regardless of this squabbling, the writer Vincas Krėvė-Mickevičius, Professor of Slavonic Languages and Literatures and a former dean of the Humanities Faculty, announced to the YIVO delegation that the university faculty supported their initiative. He recommended, however, that YIVO hold out for a proper chair rather than a lector position as had been suggested.[67] Showing their support for YIVO and its endeavours, a group of Lithuanian professors from the Humanities Faculty of the University of Vilnius headed by Biržiška visited YIVO in April 1940 to acquaint themselves with the institute's contents and to view an exhibition honouring the writer Peretz.[68] Biržiška also participated in a radio presentation in honour of Peretz to which the historian Simon Dubnow, the head of the Jewish community Dr Jacob Wygodzki, and others contributed.[69]

The matter of nominating a candidate for the position for approval by the university was entrusted by YIVO to Max Weinreich as secretary of its philological

Politics: Sholem Aleichem's First Visit to America', *YIVO Annual*, 20 (1991), 251. Similarly, Chone Shmeruk notes the degradation of eastern European Jewish 'aristocrats' in the USA: C. Shmeruk, 'Sholem Aleichem and America', *YIVO Annual*, 20 (1991), 227. On the feelings of eastern European Jewish intellectuals and political figures regarding America, see also M. Brown, *The Israeli–American Connection: Its Roots in the Yishuv, 1914–1945* (Detroit, 1996).

[63] 'Protokol fun der zitsung fun der tsaytvayliker farvaltung fun yivo, vilne, dem 27tn yanuar 1940', pp. 23–4: YIVO Archives, RG 1.1, box 31, folder 631.

[64] 'Protokol fun der driter zitsung, zuntik dem 10tn detsember, 1939, 11 a zeyger f'm', p. 33: YIVO Archives, RG 1.1, box 31, folder 631.   [65] Lempertas, 'Užmiršta jidiš puoselėtoja', 186.

[66] 'Protokol fun der zitsung fun der tsaytvayliker farvaltung fun yivo, vilne, dem 27tn yanuar 1940', p. 20: YIVO Archives, RG 1.1, box 31, folder 631.

[67] Lempertas, 'Užmiršta jidiš puoselėtoja', 187.

[68] 'Profesorn fun vilner universitet oyf der perets-oysshtelung yivo', YIVO Archives, RG 584, box 30, folder 293; Mandelman, 'In freyd un leyd tsvishn litvishe yidn', 1349.

[69] D. Levin, 'Tsvishn hamer un serp', *Yivo-bleter*, 46 (1975), 85.

section. From Copenhagen Weinreich conducted (most likely sometime in February) a referendum by telegraph among the section's members Shmuel Niger, Yude Yofe, and Yudel Mark, all residents of New York City. They unanimously approved his nomination of Kalmanowicz for the chair. Kalmanowicz categorically refused, however, leaving Weinreich to nominate himself. Prylucki, who had for years aspired to an academic position, denounced the referendum as tendentious and illegitimate. Not only had Weinreich unilaterally nominated candidates and presented no alternatives, he protested, Weinreich had also failed to present him, a founding member of the philological section and the initiator of the chair, with the referendum in time for him to participate.[70]

Always quick to defend his honour, Prylucki threatened to leave YIVO over this insult and offered an angry critique of the institute. He decried it as a cliquish den of inertia and academic protectionism. Weinreich and Kalmanowicz, both of whom possessed doctorates, discouraged independent scholarly initiative and were reluctant to permit outsiders, the refugees from Poland, to work. Prylucki alleged that Weinreich had nominated Kalmanowicz solely in order to prevent Prylucki's appointment. However, Kalmanowicz's disparaging attitude towards Yiddishism, his commitment to Jewish scholarship notwithstanding, made him an unaccept-able candidate.[71] (This evaluation was shared by other members of the provisional administration and by Kalmanowicz himself.) When Kalmanowicz refused the nomination, Prylucki continued, Weinreich nominated himself in order to block Prylucki's ambitions (this charge, as indicated by Kalmanowicz's correspondence with Max Weinreich, proved in fact to be true).[72] He further argued that Weinreich could not be relied upon to return in time for the coming academic year beginning in the autumn since he had committed himself to going to New York until after the summer on YIVO business. Waiting for Weinreich, Prylucki warned, meant forfeiting the chair.[73]

YIVO's provisional administration, which was dominated by Bundists, upheld Weinreich's candidacy since he enjoyed near-universal respect for his scholarly contributions. That Weinreich was himself a supporter of the Bund does not seem to have played a significant role. While recognizing that Prylucki had been unjustly slighted by the referendum, the administration faulted him and his Folkist col-

---

[70] 'Protokol fun der zitsung fun der tsaytvayliker farvaltung fun yivo, vilne, dem 27tn yanuar 1940', pp. 16–21: YIVO Archives, RG 1.1, box 31, folder 631; 'Zitsung fun der tsaytvayliker farvaltung fun yivo, 10tn marts 1940', pp. 3–5: ibid.

[71] David Kaplan-Kaplanski, for example, expressed his disapproval of Kalmanowicz as a candidate for the proposed chair in Yiddish at the University of Vilnius with these words: 'It's not possible for him to occupy the post because his talk resounds in my ears about Jews not being a people and Yiddish not surviving': 'Protokol fun der zitsung fun der tsaytvayliker farvaltung fun yivo, 10tn marts 1940', p. 15: YIVO Archives, RG 1.1, box 31, folder 631.

[72] Letter from Kalmanowicz to Weinreich, undated: YIVO Archives, RG 584, box 30, folder 293b.

[73] 'Protokol fun der zitsung fun der tsaytvayliker farvaltung fun yivo, 10tn marts 1940', pp. 15–17, 21: YIVO Archives, RG 1.1, box 31, folder 631.

leagues for conducting what amounted to private and therefore potentially harmful negotiations with Professor Biržiška. It urged him to put the needs of the institute above all private interests and personal ambitions and to accept nomination as Weinreich's replacement in case he was unable to return to Vilna.[74]

Though he was pessimistic about the chair and the Yiddishist aspirations it embodied, Kalmanowicz did not refrain from raising objections to Prylucki's candidacy. Indeed, he was Prylucki's most severe critic in YIVO. Kalmanowicz, who harboured quite hostile feelings towards Prylucki, denounced him without restraint as a 'simple collector', an autodidact lacking 'the minimal scholarly qualifications' to edit the philological section's journal *Yidish far ale*.[75] He was even more explicit about Prylucki's shortcomings in a personal letter written in late 1938 to linguist Yudel Mark, who had resided in the United States since the mid-1930s. Kalmanowicz complained that *Yidish far ale* had fallen into the hands of Prylucki, who 'destroys Yiddish in his own way'. 'Poor *mame-loshn* [mother tongue] has the misfortune that such a scholarly graphomaniac has latched on to it and occupies its top position, driving away every expert and letting in the defect [*felenish*] of sickly egotism.' He maintained that Max Weinreich and Zalmen Reyzen concurred with him in this assessment and in the need to deprive Prylucki of the editorship of the journal.[76] Indeed, correspondence from 1938 between the philological section and Prylucki regarding the journal suggests that colleagues sought to deprive Prylucki of the final say in editorial matters of the journal but nevertheless depended on his labours.[77]

Apart from his scholarly objections, Kalmanowicz doubtless objected to Prylucki's apparent flirtation with the Soviets, expressed in his affiliation with the Kaunas *Folksblat*, a formerly Folkist newspaper which had fallen into communist hands in 1938.[78] While Kalmanowicz's hostility to communism was hardly con-

---

[74] 'Protokol fun der zitsung fun der tsaytvayliker farvaltung fun yivo, 1otn marts 1940': YIVO Archives, RG 1.1, box 31, folder 631; undated, handwritten note in name of Central Administration of YIVO: YIVO Archives, RG 1.1, box 31, folder 633.

[75] 'Zitsung fun der tsaytvayliker farvaltung fun yivo, 1otn marts 1940', pp. 18–19: YIVO Archives, RG 1.1, box 31, folder 631.

[76] Letter from Kalmanowicz to Mark, 8 Dec. 1938: YIVO Archives, RG 540, box 9, folder 161.

[77] Letter from YIVO Vilna to Prylucki (signature cut off), 4 Apr. 1938: YIVO Archives, RG 1.1 box 3, folder 65. Prylucki, for his part, protested that the articles were sent to him late and without any prior corrections: Noah Prylucki to YIVO, unspecified addressee, 1 Jan. 1939: ibid.

[78] Y. Gar, 'Di kovner togtsaytung "folksblat"', in Ch. Leikowicz (ed.), *Lite*, ii (Tel Aviv, 1965), 419–39. Gar suggests that those who worked on the communist *Folksblat* were either convinced communists or opportunists who understood that the Soviets were soon to take over Lithuania and wished to advance their careers. Remembering Prylucki on the twenty-fifth anniversary of his death in the Polish communist *Folksshtime*, the writer Shloyme Belis recalls that Prylucki sympathized ideologically with the *Folksblat*, which Belis describes as a 'progressive' newspaper that had many enemies. Upon his request, Prylucki joined the circle of 'Friends of the *Folksblat*' in 1939 in Vilna. Belis does not, however, explain the nature of this organization's activities. Sh. Belis, 'Dos gantse lebn farn mame-loshn', *Folksshtime*, 13 Aug. 1966.

cealed, he kept silent on his antipathy towards individuals with pro-Soviet sympathies during YIVO meetings. In a letter to the Amopteyl in New York dated January 1940, however, he complained bitterly of those in YIVO 'whose heart has remained in the East [Soviet Union]' and who had the audacity to remain in YIVO even after the Soviets had, he correctly assumed, murdered Zalmen Reyzen.[79]

In contrast to Kalmanowicz's reserve, Bundists in the provisional administration reacted openly to the tactics of the Kaunas *Folksblat*. The Bundist pedagogues Shloyme Mendelson, also a former Folkist, and Shloyme Gilinski objected to the affiliation of Prylucki and unspecified others in YIVO with the newspaper. They pointed out that the *Folksblat* condemned the current YIVO administration as the 'liquidators' of YIVO and denounced socialists in general as sell-outs and the lackeys of British Prime Minister Chamberlain.[80] Nonetheless, the Bundists were willing to support Prylucki as a replacement for Weinreich, since his attitude towards Yiddish, unlike Kalmanowicz's, was in accord with Yiddishist ideology. Resisting entreaties from colleagues, Prylucki, whose pride had been injured, demonstratively quit all YIVO activities in March 1940 and refused to be considered as a candidate for the chair.[81] Reporting in early June 1940 on the recent activity of YIVO as outlined by Kalmanowicz, the *Folksblat* opined dismissively, 'Whether this work satisfies the broad classes of the Jewish population interested in cultural work and whether there aren't more important areas and more necessary ones than research about the archive of the miracle workers from Grätz, Karlin hasidism, Yeshivat Hokhmei Lublin and the like—that is a separate question.'[82]

Negotiations between YIVO and Lithuanian academics continued without Prylucki and culminated in a plan to establish a lector position rather than a chair in Yiddish at the University of Vilnius. Funding would have to be provided by the Lithuanian Jewish community in advance for the first three years.[83] Max Weinreich, who arrived in America in March 1940, was proposed for the position and he was expected to return after the summer to accept it.

YIVO UNDER SOVIET RULE

These plans, however, never came to fruition. The Red Army re-entered Lithuania in mid-June 1940 and annexed it as the sixteenth Soviet Socialist Republic in August. Even then, however, departure from Lithuania via the Soviet

---

[79] Letter from Kalmanowicz to Amopteyl, 1 Jan. 1940, excerpted in Z. Szajkowski (ed.), *Der yivo un zayne grinder: katalog fun der oysshtelung tsum 50-yorikn yoyvl fun yidishn visnshaftlekhn institut* (New York, 1975), 56.

[80] 'Protokol fun oysfir-byuro', fragment, date unspecified, pp. 32–3: YIVO Archives, RG 1.1, box 31, folder 629.

[81] 'Protokol fun der zitsung fun der tsaytvayliker farvaltung fun yivo, 10tn marts 1940', p. 21: YIVO Archives, RG 1.1, box 31, folder 631.

[82] 'Vos tut der "yivo" in milkhome tsayt?', *Folksblat*, 7 June 1940.

[83] S., 'An intervyu mit profesor noyekh prilutski', *Morgn-frayhayt*, 15 Dec. 1940.

Union remained possible for those with the requisite wherewithal, connections, and luck.[84]

The immediate imposition of Soviet nationalities policy on the tiny Baltic republic, as in other territories annexed by the Soviets since the outbreak of the Second World War (eastern Poland, the Baltic lands, Bessarabia, and northern Bukovina), meant the hasty and radical overhaul of schools in accordance with Soviet ideology and goals. The Soviet constitution assured Jews, like other national minorities, the right to education in their 'mother tongue'. It held out the promise of state-supported Yiddish culture that Poland had demonstratively refused to provide and whose institutions it had even actively undermined during the preceding twenty years. In contrast with the Jews of Poland, the largest part of Jewish pupils in independent Lithuania was already enrolled in state-supported Jewish schools before the outbreak of the war. Now, virtually overnight, the secular Hebrew and religious schools in which the vast majority of Lithuanian Jewish children studied were closed or transformed into state-run secular Yiddish schools. Books and school personnel were 'imported' from elsewhere in the Soviet Union to complement pre-existing cadres of Jewish pedagogues, including those previously active in Hebrew and religious schools who needed to be 're-educated' and sometimes coerced to teach Soviet curricula in Yiddish. The Soviets revived the plan for a state-funded Yiddish chair at the University of Vilnius. At the same time, they eliminated the position for Hebrew there, along with many others.

From mid-August until the end of 1940, YIVO underwent a 'process of purging and reorganization', ridding it of Bundists and Zionists and virtually anyone else judged ideologically unsuitable.[85] Archivist Moyshe Lerer, a committed Marxist friendly with Prylucki,[86] was made YIVO's curator, displacing Kalmanowicz, who eked out a living thereafter as a copy-editor.[87] In an article titled 'The "YIVO" too is finally dragged out of the swamp', the Vilna *Togblat* reported on 16 August 1940 that the institute had been delivered from corrupt oligarchic control and 'returned' to its rightful owners—the working Jewish masses:[88]

YIVO, which was built with dedication by the folk masses, was cynically controlled by a small group of people who transformed the institute into a 'political' clique [*klayzl*]. At the head of the institute stood people who related cynically to the interests, sufferings, and struggles of the folk masses and their language. The institute was transformed into a fortress behind which avowed Zionists and Bundists barricaded themselves. United, they exploited the institute as a nest of protectionism and personal careers, on the one hand, and

---

[84] Levin, *Lesser of Two Evils*, 198–217; Dawidowicz, *From That Place and Time*, 215. Mordkhe Tsanin, himself a refuge in Vilna at this time, depicts frantic attempts to secure visas and permission to exit Soviet Lithuania in his wartime memoirs, *Grenetsn biz tsum himl* (Tel Aviv, 1969).

[85] Levin, 'Tsvishn hamer un serp', 86; Sh. Kaczerginski, *Tsvishn hamer un serp: tsu der geshikhte fun der likvidatsye fun der yidisher kultur in sovetn-rusland* (Buenos Aires, 1950), 20, 28.

[86] Balberyszski, *Shtarker fun ayzn*, 103.   [87] Kaczerginski, *Tsvishn hamer un serp*, 28.

[88] Levin, 'Tsvishn hamer un serp', 88–91; Yisroel Lempert (Izraelis Lempertas), 'Der goyrl fun yivo in historishn iberbrokh (1939–1941)', *Yivo-bleter*, NS, 3 (1997), 9–42.

struggle against the communist party and its friends, on the other. People were not allowed in the institute who could raise the institute to an appropriate level with their academic qualifications . . . Having the complete protection of all prior reactionary regimes, the 'activists' of YIVO were destroyers of every fertile plan made for the sake of Yiddish culture. Thus, these people buried the plan for a Yiddish chair at the University of Vilnius and one of the chief schemers from the Yiddish Scientific Institute travelled around preaching the dark purpose of Yiddish.[89]

In its first two decades, the Soviet Union had created an 'elaborate machinery of Jewish national districts in the Far East (Birobidzhan), Ukraine, and Crimea, soviets, kolkhozes, educational and scientific institutions, courts and police stations, periodicals and publishing houses, Party, trade-union, and Komsomol cells, and more'. Yiddish institutions, including schools of different levels and teacher-training colleges, were still in expansion in the early 1930s.[90] Indeed, hundreds of Yiddish educational institutions had been established in the Soviet Union in the 1920s and 1930s. To the dismay of many parents, however, by the end of the 1920s they were drained of national content and denied connections to 'reactionary' Hebrew and traditional culture. Further, by 1939, if not sooner, they were being systematically restricted to the point of disappearance as a result of both state Russification policy and parents' preference for Russian schools, which enjoyed better conditions and could better prepare students for admission to Russophone institutions of higher learning.[91] Whereas in 1926 almost 73 per cent of Soviet Jews reported that Yiddish was their native language, in 1939 this figure had declined to 41 per cent. At the same time, the number of Jews declaring Russian as their native language more than doubled.[92] Whether or not these statistics are accurate, they certainly reflect the fact that Soviet Jews had internalized the message that Yiddish was marginal in the eyes of the authorities and that their future lay in the Russian language.

A similar pattern quickly emerged in Soviet-occupied Poland. Despite the extensive 'Yiddishization' of the Jewish educational system there in late 1939, a reduction in the number of Yiddish schools became noticeable after only a few months. This was accompanied by increased enrolments in schools that used Russian or other languages as it become clear to parents that higher and vocational education was not available in Yiddish and that the state discouraged Yiddish-language education, which was in any case rendered more difficult by a lack of teachers and materials.

In contrast, in Soviet Lithuania, in the evaluation of historian Dov Levin, 'Jewish education seemed to be holding its own; there were almost no indications of real infringements, at least on the surface'. In the short term at least, plans to eliminate Jewish education were not evident here. Jewish educators were under-

[89] 'Oykh der "yivo" vert endlekh aroysgetsoygn fun zumf', *Togblat*, 16 Aug. 1940; L. Ran, *Ash fun yerushalayim de'lite* (New York, 1959), 176–9.

[90] G. Estraikh, *Soviet Yiddish: Language Planning and Linguistic Development* (Oxford, 1999), 62–3.

[91] Levin, *Lesser of Two Evils*, 89–95; A. Zeltser, 'Soviet Yiddish-Language Schools', in Hundert (ed.), *YIVO Encyclopedia of Jews in Eastern Europe*, ii. 1791.   [92] Estraikh, *Soviet Yiddish*, 97.

standably worried, however, that this situation, as elsewhere in the annexed territories, would follow the model set by Jewish educational institutions in older Soviet areas but at an accelerated pace and thus not endure long.[93]

For Prylucki, who despaired over the future of Yiddish in Poland and likely even more so in America after a disappointing visit there in the 1920s,[94] the prospect of mandatory Yiddish schools and state-sponsored cultural life was very attractive. Through coercive measures Yiddish-based cultural autonomy—an impossibility elsewhere—could become a reality, even if its future was uncertain. Moreover, Prylucki was granted by the Soviet authorities the recognition as a scholar which he craved and was denied by many of his colleagues, most notably Weinreich and Kalmanowicz. In August 1940 he was nominated by YIVO as its candidate for the coveted Yiddish chair, as well as appointed chief lector for Yiddish language and culture at state teachers' courses initiated through the Bureau for Minorities of the Communist Party in Lithuania—a clear endorsement of his acceptability to Soviet authorities.[95] These courses served to prepare teachers previously employed in the now liquidated Tarbut Hebrew and Yavneh religious schools to teach in Yiddish communist schools, which banned Hebrew and combated religion.[96] (Some Hebraist teachers, however, preferred to teach in Russian—an affront to Lithuanians—rather than promote Yiddish.[97]) The following month he was provided the means to publish these lectures under the title *Yidishe fonetik: elementar kurs far lerer un aleynlerner* ('Yiddish Phonetics: Elementary Course for Teachers and Independent Learners'), as well as his research about Yiddish theatre, *Farvos iz dos yidishe teater azoy shpet oyfgekumen?* ('Why did the Yiddish Theatre Arise So Late?'). This study was first published in the literary anthology *Untervegs*, which appeared with an appropriate Marxist introduction celebrating Soviet rule. It included new works by a number of renowned writers (among them Chaim Grade, Avrom Sutzkever, Yisroel Rabon, and Y. Y. Trunk) who found themselves in Vilna and with whom the senior Prylucki cultivated close relationships of mentorship and camaraderie. His research was recognized by the Senate of the Soviet Lithuanian University in Vilnius. Though lacking formal training as a philologist, he was routinely referred to in official Soviet documents as 'Professor' even before his appointment in October 1940 on a one-year contract as docent to the newly founded Chair in Yiddish Language and Culture.[98]

[93] Levin, *Lesser of Two Evils*, 89–95, 111.

[94] See Weiser, 'Yiddishist Ideology of Noah Prylucki'.

[95] Letter from M. Lerer to Prof. Mykolas Biržiška, 20 Aug. 1940: Lietuvos Centrinis Valstybės Archyvas, Vilnius (hereafter LCVA), f. R856, ap. 2, b. 1123, Noachas Priluckis, Vilnius University Papers. A letter from the editor of the 'Vilnius daily [Yiddish] newspaper' to the rector certified that Prylucki was a specialist in his field and 'has always been friendly to the USSR': letter to Rector of Vilnius University, 24 Aug. 1940, ibid.

[96] Y. Gar, 'Be'ol hakibush hasoviyeti', in Goren et al. (eds.), *Yahadut lita*, ii. 374.

[97] Shochat, 'Jews, Lithuanians and Russians', 309.

[98] Lempert, 'Der goyrl fun yivo in historishn iberbrokh', 21; letter from N. Prylucki to Vilnius

In an interview with an unidentified reporter published in the New York City communist daily *Morgn-frayhayt* in December 1940 (likely a reprint from the Soviet Yiddish press), Prylucki expressed his gratitude to the Soviet authorities. He noted that a 'completely equal chair in Yiddish language and literature could only come into existence when the "rays of the five-pointed red star rose over Lithuania"'. He explained that he would teach three main courses (a special Yiddish language course, history of the Yiddish language, and history of Yiddish literature) plus six special courses (phonetic characteristics of the Yiddish language, history of the Jewish people, history of Yiddish theatre, Yiddish folklore, history of Jewish art, and history of Jewish folk humour) over the course of eight semesters. Additionally, he intended to offer a course every semester on a special topic. He had already begun that semester to teach phonetic characteristics of the Yiddish language (focusing on stylistics and poetics) and history of the Yiddish language, as well as holding lectures twice weekly about Y. L. Peretz. In addition to his courses, Yiddish students would also study Lithuanian language, Marxism-Leninism, and introduction to language research, among other general courses required of all students in the Philology Department.[99] Thirty-five students were enrolled and more than one hundred hailing from throughout the Soviet Union were projected for the future.[100]

In order to emphasize the academic level of YIVO and to co-ordinate scholarly activity with the chair, Prylucki was also appointed director of YIVO on 1 January 1941 by Professor Krėvė-Mickevičius, who headed the Academy of Sciences of Soviet Lithuania following a brief stint as Lithuanian foreign minister the preceding summer. Prylucki worked feverishly to maintain YIVO's operations with a diminished staff. The Sovietized YIVO, now exclusively a research institution, was soon integrated into the Academy of Sciences of the Soviet Lithuanian Republic. Renamed the Institute for Jewish Culture, it was thus parallel to the Institute for Polish Culture among the Lithuanian institutes for linguistics, history, and ethnography.[101] Eager to publish new scholarly works, Prylucki undertook contacts with scholars throughout the Soviet Union.[102]

His public enthusiasm for the Soviets notwithstanding, Prylucki was well aware of the oppressive nature of the Soviet regime. Moreover, according to journalist Mordkhe Tsanin, a fellow refugee from Poland, he bore no illusion that Yiddish schools would continue there beyond the duration of the war. Commenting on the situation, he made clear his awareness of his role as an instrument of a policy that

University Humanities Faculty, 3 Apr. 1941: LCVA, f. R856, ap. 2, b. 1123, Noachas Priluckis, Vilnius University Papers.

[99] S., 'An intervyu mit profesor noyekh prilutski'.

[100] Lempertas, 'Užmiršta jidiš puoselėtoja',189.

[101] Levin, 'Tsvishn hamer un serp', 88–91; Lempert, 'Der goyrl fun yivo in historishn iberbrokh'; Lempertas, 'Užmiršta jidiš puoselėtoja', 190. On Vincas Krėvė-Mickevičius's political career, see A. E. Senn, *Lithuania 1940: Revolution from Above* (Amsterdam and New York, 2007), 139 ff.

[102] Kh. Beyder, 'Noyekh prilutskis briv tsu arn gurshteyn', *Di pen*, 32 (1997), 41–5.

promoted Yiddish temporarily in order to accelerate Sovietization of the Jewish population. Coercing teachers to replace Hebrew with Yiddish in the classroom, he acknowledged, would not assure the long-term future of Yiddish: 'The Soviet authority will not allow a Jewish school system in Vilna. It will want to have the Jewish children in Russian schools. So, who asks the former Hebrew teachers to give declarations for me, Noah Prylucki, that in teaching Hebrew to Jewish children they were ideationally misled by Zionist capitalism . . .?'[103]

Nonetheless, convinced that the Soviets would defeat the Nazis quickly,[104] Prylucki preferred to take his chances as a professor among the Soviets than attempt escape to America. In integrationist America, where immigrant acculturation was an ideal and nationalist politics were foreign to the political system, the tenets of national cultural autonomy had little meaning and even less opportunity to be realized. 'I've seen Jewish life in America,' he explained to Balberyszski, 'and it's no place for me. Should I live from Cahan's handouts?' The Cahan he spoke of was, of course, Abraham Cahan, the powerful editor of the New York daily *Forverts* and Yiddish cultural tsar, who advocated the Americanization of his readers and the gradual disappearance of Yiddish in America. Being a 60-year-old refugee in America meant being reduced to dependence, economic and otherwise, on American Jewish patricians, especially the autocratic Cahan, who had little interest in encouraging Yiddish scholarship and 'serious' literature without a socialist message.[105] For Prylucki, a self-styled Jewish aristocrat who had devoted his life to the cause of Yiddish and cultural autonomy, the impossibility of politics as he knew it in America and the lack of enthusiasm for Yiddish culture among the children of eastern European immigrants were surely unattractive. Moreover, the challenge of immigrant adjustment and the loss of personal prestige, influence, and perhaps even purpose in life were likely too much to contemplate.

He applied for Soviet citizenship, presumably to facilitate his integration into the new order and demonstrate his loyalty to the new masters of the land. Once he had received citizenship, he requested that he be treated on a par with other university docents with regard to salary and privileges.[106]

Though Prylucki reportedly considered *Das Kapital* to be the 'best *shund* novel' he had ever read,[107] when the Soviets took control of Vilna he was willing to enlist himself in their service in return for benefits for himself and Yiddish culture beyond the crucial protection of life and limb. 'In no other land will I have such opportunities for my scholarly work as in the Soviet Union', he explained to

---

[103] Tsanin, *Grenetsn biz tsum himl*, 13–14.

[104] A. Sutzkever, *Vilner geto, 1941–1944* (Paris, 1946), 3.

[105] On Cahan and his policies in *Forverts*, see I. Howe, *World of our Fathers* (New York, 1989); E. D. Kellman, 'The Newspaper Novel in the Jewish Daily *Forward*: Fiction as Entertainment and Serious Literature', diss. (Columbia University, 2000).

[106] Levin, 'Tsvishn hamer un serp', 89; letter from N. Prylucki to University of Vilnius Humanities Faculty, 3 Apr. 1941: LCVA, f. R856, ap. 2, b. 1123, Noachas Priluckis, Vilnius University Papers.

[107] Interview between the author and Mordkhe Tsanin, Tel Aviv, 4 July 1999.

Balberyszski, who urged that he join him in fleeing Lithuania. In contrast with Bundists and Zionists, Prylucki maintained, Folkists had no reason to fear political repression from the Soviets. Theirs was the only bourgeois party to join 'the popular front together with the Communists' against fascism. When questioned about the fate of their pro-Soviet colleagues Reyzen and Joseph Czernichow, who had been arrested during the initial Soviet occupation in the autumn of 1939, he suggested that they had been arrested because they constituted a political danger to the Soviets: the former for anti-Soviet statements in *Der tog*, the Vilna daily which he edited, and the latter for publishing his memoirs as a lawyer defending clients charged with 'counter-revolution and speculation' in the early Soviet period.[108]

In trying to assess why Prylucki, given his own vehement anti-Soviet pronouncements in preceding years, remained relatively calm in the situation, it is difficult to determine whether he was an optimist making the best of a horrendous situation or was in wilful, if cynical, collusion with the Soviets. Or maybe he was a combination of both. According to Tsanin, Prylucki focused on his scholarly work, insulating himself with 'dialectical calm' from the conflagration engulfing the world. He was convinced that the war between Nazis and Soviets was an ineluctable process in the Hegelian scheme of history.[109]

It is not wholly clear why Prylucki was acceptable to the Soviets, especially considering that he equated the Soviet Union with Nazi Germany in articles critical of the Soviet persecution of intellectual and ideological heresy published throughout the 1930s.[110] Perhaps it was because, as Prylucki himself explained to a friend, the Folkists, unlike Zionists and Bundists, had never been significant ideological opponents or rivals of the Bolsheviks. Perhaps it was because Prylucki, frustrated by his treatment and the direction of YIVO, had expressed pro-Soviet sympathies by working in the Kaunas *Folksblat*.

Quite likely, the Soviets, beyond intending to use Yiddish as a means for ideological indoctrination, wished to make a favourable impression on the annexed Jewish population by supporting Jewish culture, at least its secular Yiddish dimension. More than Poles or Ukrainians, who saw their states dismantled by Soviet imperialism, Jews could be relied on to support the Soviet regime, particularly when their only alternative was the Nazis. Prylucki, arguably the most qualified Yiddish scholar remaining in Vilna after the arrest of Zalmen Reyzen and in the

---

[108] Y. Tshernikhov, *In revtribunal: zikhroynes fun a farteydiker* (Vilna, 1932); H. Abramowicz, *Profiles of a Lost World: Memoirs of East European Jewish Life before World War II*, ed. D. Abramowicz and J. Shandler, trans. E. Z. Dobin (Detroit, 1999), 286. Balberyszski attributes the following statement to Prylucki: 'The Bolsheviks are applying repressions against the Bundists because Lenin and Stalin were already combating the Bund as a counter-revolutionary, Menshevik movement. The Bund has been dangerous for them for decades because it agitates among workers and speaks in the name of socialism. They combat Zionism, on the other hand, as a reactionary, pro-English movement': Balberyszski, *Shtarker fun ayzn*, 105.　　　　[109] Tsanin, *Grenetsn biz tsum himl*, 13.

[110] N. Prilutski, 'Notitsn on politik', *Der moment*, 18 Oct. 1931; *Der moment*, 27 May 1932, 29 May 1932; 'Oy, doles, doles! . . .', *Der moment*, 25 Aug. 1933.

absence of his rival Max Weinreich, was willing to co-operate as a public figure in return for the fulfilment of his ideal of state-supported Yiddish culture (albeit under Soviet aegis with all its ideological strictures) and the opportunity to continue his own scholarly work. As he explained to Soviet Lithuanian university officials, an academic career was out of the question for him in Poland, where a publicly funded university position in Yiddish was an impossibility.[111]

He reported to his Lithuanian Folkist colleague Balberyszski on several occasions that he derived great moral and intellectual satisfaction from his work and was convinced that his students were extraordinarily pleased with him. His wife Paula, who had previously expressed the hope that he would one day occupy the chair in Yiddish philology at a Yiddish university in Vilna,[112] was proud of his academic success but lacked his equanimity and worried about the stability of the political situation.[113]

His students at the University of Vilnius were, however, allegedly disappointed by his failure to adhere to Marxist ideology in his teaching and interpretations of literature. Unbeknownst to him, Prylucki was to be replaced in the coming academic year 1941/2. Despite Stalinist purges that decimated Yiddish and other national cultures, an institute for Jewish literature and folklore still functioned as part of the Belarusian Academy of Sciences (the Institute for Jewish Culture of the Ukrainian Academy of Sciences was closed in 1936).[114]

A new school year did not come, however. After the Germans conquered Lithuania in the summer of 1941, Prylucki suffered, as did his bitter opponent Kalmanowicz, the same gruesome fate at Nazi hands as millions of other Jews, most of them Yiddish-speakers. More specifically, Prylucki was dismissed from his university position along with eight other Jewish professors on 27 June 1941[115] and arrested by the Gestapo on 28 July 1941. His familiarity with YIVO collections and his expertise in the field of Old Yiddish literature and book publishing were

---

[111] 'Anketa': LCVA, f. R856, ap. 2, b. 1123, Noachas Priluckis, Vilnius University Papers.

[112] M. K-ski (Magnus Krinski), 'Di yoyvl-fayerung fun noyekh prilutski', *Der moment*, 8 May 1931; 'Banket lekoved noyekh prilutski', *Der moment*, 10 May 1931.

[113] M. Balberyszski, 'Di yidishe katedre baym vilner universitet', *Driter oystralish-yidisher almanakh* (1967), 382–3.

[114] On the basis of a conversation in the Warsaw ghetto with Rabbi Kurlianczik, who supervised the chair as Commissar for Cultural Affairs in Lithuania, Balberyszski maintains that the Soviets intended to replace Prylucki with a more politically reliable scholar from Minsk or Kiev in the next academic year. His interpretations, to the disappointment of students, were often contrary to the Marxist line. Balberyszski does not mention the name of Prylucki's replacement: Balberyszki, 'Di yidishe katedre baym vilner universitet', 382–3. On the history and activity of Soviet Jewish research institutes, see A. Greenbaum, *Jewish Scholarship and Scholarly Institutions in Soviet Russia, 1918–1953* (Jerusalem, 1978); R. Peltz and M. W. Kiel, 'Di Yiddish-Imperye: The Dashed Hopes for a Yiddish Cultural Empire in the Soviet Union', in I. T. Kreindler (ed.), *Sociolinguistic Perspectives on Soviet National Languages: Their Past, Present and Future* (Berlin, 1985), 277–309.

[115] Declaration signed by M. Biržiška, 27 June 1941: LCVA, f. R856, ap. 2, b. 1123, Noachas Priluckis, Vilnius University Papers.

yoked into service by the notorious Rosenbergstab (Einsatzstab Reichsleiter Rosenberg), whose task was to ransack Judaica collections throughout Europe and to send their contents to the Institut zur Erforschung der Judenfrage in Frankfurt. He and Eliyohu Yankev Goldshmidt, a Yiddish journalist and director of the Ansky Jewish Ethnographic Museum in Vilna, were transported daily from their cell in a Gestapo prison to the city's famed Strashun Judaica library, where they were forced to compile lists of incunabula in preparation for their shipment to Germany. On 12 August 1941, the nearly 60-year-old Prylucki, infirm after repeated beatings and abuse, was 'liquidated' by his captors. Goldshmidt died in his cell.[116] Zelig Kalmanowicz was charged with similar work, also sorting through the pillaged contents of Vilna libraries and preparing selected volumes for shipment to Germany. With the liquidation of the Vilna ghetto, Kalmanowicz was deported in September 1943 to labour camps in Estonia. He never returned, succumbing to hunger and disease in 1944.[117]

CONCLUDING THOUGHTS

Given the native sympathies among Jews for Yiddish and the extremely low degree of acculturation in Lithuania, both Prylucki and Weinreich held high hopes for the development there of the Yiddish language and a secular culture expressed in it. What could not be achieved in Poland or America, they reasoned, could be achieved there. True, 'assimilation', as Weinreich pointed out, was far less advanced among Jews in inter-war Lithuania than in Poland and government support for Jewish culture was real. Jews and Lithuanians remained throughout the inter-war period largely ignorant of each other's cultures and socialized to a great extent in distinct, ethnically defined circles. Lithuanian was, however, gaining in status and utility among Jews, and some Jews, admittedly still a small minority, had begun to integrate into Lithuanian society and culture. Support for Jewish cultural autonomy, at least its linguistic dimension, existed among Lithuanian officials as long as such a policy was beneficial to the Lithuanian state. Initially, to the satisfaction of the Jewish minority, the state encouraged the perpetuation of de facto ethnic social and occupational segregation through support for a parallel Jewish-language educational system. Both state financial and popular Jewish support indeed existed for schools teaching in Jewish languages in independent Lithuania. But this support was declining by the 1930s, as the state desired the Lithuanization of its population and the Lithuanian public grew more hostile to a 'foreign' presence in its midst. As a population that could not be assimilated or was

[116] L. Beder and M. Yelin, 'Di letste yorn fun noyekh prilutskin', *Sovetish heymland* (Mar. 1965), 146–8; D. E. Fishman, *Embers Plucked from the Fire: The Rescue of Jewish Cultural Treasures in Vilna* (New York, 1996), 4; Sh. Katsherginski, *Khurbn vilne* (New York, 1947), 203–4; Sutzkever, *Vilner geto*, 108.

[117] Dawidowicz, *From That Place and Time*, 271; Z. Kalmanovitsh, 'A Diary of the Nazi Ghetto in Vilna', *YIVO Annual of Jewish Social Science*, 8 (1953), 9.

not considered suitable for assimilation, Jews were being progressively pushed out of the economy. They were seen as competitors by Lithuanians entering their traditional occupational niches and other sectors of the economy in which Lithuanians were not previously well represented.

Kalmanowicz was perhaps more far-sighted in his evaluation than Weinreich and Prylucki. He understood that without state support for a fully functioning educational system and opportunities to exercise one's professional life in Yiddish, modern Yiddish culture as promoted by YIVO and its supporters could likely not withstand competition from the dominant language of society. In the absence of universities that functioned in Jewish languages and the possibility to communicate with or serve the state in these languages, a glass ceiling would necessarily exist for Yiddish-speakers. It is probable that young Jews here, as elsewhere in eastern Europe, who did not wish to be confined to a shrinking Jewish economic sector functioning in Yiddish would increasingly have sought opportunities—educational, cultural, and professional—available only in the official language of the land. Quite possibly, Lithuanian would eventually have replaced Russian as the dominant language of the more educated Jewish classes, leaving Yiddish as the language of Jews with fewer aspirations outside their community or beyond ethnic economic niches. These arguments, of course, presume that such opportunities would remain accessible to Jews and not be severely restricted or reduced to the point of irrelevance.

In order for a modern high culture in Yiddish to flourish, Jewish children needed to attend a multi-level Yiddish-language educational system that would help prepare them to consume, appreciate, and produce literature, theatre, and scholarship—all in Yiddish. Otherwise, Yiddish high culture would likely remain the domain of dilettantes, autodidacts, or scholars and artists trained in other fields.[118] Yet, despite the fact that Yiddish was the native language of virtually all Lithuanian Jews and supported a ramified network of cultural institutions such as newspapers, theatres, schools, etc., unified support did not exist among them for their mother tongue as the dominant language of education. Indeed, most Jewish children received their education in Hebrew, a language suited to making a life for oneself in the Zionist Yishuv in Palestine but not widely spoken as a daily language in the Diaspora—not even among Jews in Lithuania. To achieve the Yiddishization of the educational system, the attitudes of Jewish society towards a secular Yiddish school system would have to change.

Weinreich and Kalmanowicz, who had in tandem successfully and insultingly blocked Prylucki's career ambitions, were bitter opponents of communism.

---

[118] Cecile Kuznitz refers to this complex of cultural consumption and production as the 'cycle of Yiddish culture' and develops it in her work. I thank her for providing me with a copy of her unpublished lecture 'The People and the Book: YIVO and the Economy of Jewish Knowledge, 1925–1939', delivered at the University of Maryland Jewish Book Conference, 28 Oct. 2002, and with excerpts from her forthcoming book about the history of YIVO.

Prylucki, in contrast, was more pliant than his academic rivals. Indeed, he was willing to compromise many of his democratic ideals in what appears to have been a Faustian accord with the Soviets. For one year, Prylucki's academic fortunes rose along with the Soviet red star over Vilna. He was hardly a convinced communist and well aware of the nature of Soviet politics. Of course, once the Soviets had seized control of Lithuania, he possessed few options. Certainly, from Prylucki's perspective, coercing Jewish children who already knew Yiddish to attend communist Yiddish schools was preferable to enrolling them in communist schools functioning in non-Jewish languages, since language was for him the core of identity.

In retrospect, it appears that the Soviets saw promoting Yiddish in newly annexed territories as a temporary tactical step, something Prylucki seems to have anticipated. In the short run, Yiddish could be made the exclusive language of Jewish society and new vistas opened for its secular cultural development. In the long run, however, it seems that Yiddishist aspirations would ultimately be frustrated here too. Indeed, a combination of Jewish desires for socio-economic mobility and Soviet Russification policy, not to mention the antisemitism of the period following the Second World War that discouraged public manifestations of Jewish identity, yielded the eventual Russification of Jews throughout the Soviet sphere.

Remarkably, Yiddish schools were created for child survivors of the Holocaust in post-war Soviet Lithuania. Jewish pedagogues and sympathetic Red Army and party officials convincingly argued that it was dangerous to enrol Jewish children in schools of any other local nationalities owing to the antisemitism that prevailed among these groups. These schools, however, like those in the Jewish autonomous region of Birobidzhan, were closed by the early 1950s under charges of encouraging nationalistic tendencies and through lack of parental support for under-funded schools that did not convey practical benefit in Soviet society.[119] Of course, the imprisonment and, all too often, murder in the early 1950s of many Yiddish writers and cultural figures hastened the ultimate decline of modern Yiddish culture in the Soviet Union, where nearly three million Jews continued to live until the final years of that regime.

In post-war Poland, the communist government, hoping to revive cultural life among the pathetic remnant of Polish Jewry (most of whom emigrated by 1951), briefly granted Jews quasi-autonomy in cultural matters. Financial support from the West, especially from the Joint Distribution Committee, helped establish a variety of institutions, including publishing houses, theatres, and schools. Some of these schools functioned in Hebrew or Polish but most taught in Yiddish. Despite the propaganda benefits and Western moneys derived by the regime from such a policy, the Polish government too closed nearly all Jewish schools by the mid-

---

[119] Zeltser, 'Soviet Yiddish-Language Schools', 1791; D. Levin, 'Haperek ha'aḥaron shel batei hasefer hayehudiyim hamamlakhtiyim beverit hamo'atsot', in B. Pinkus (ed.), *Yahadut mizraḥ-eiropah bein sho'ah letekumah, 1944–1948* (Sedeh Boker, 1987), 88–106.

1950s (only one was still in operation in 1968) and refused the Joint Distribution Committee permission to continue its activity. A Yiddish press and theatre (which employed many actors with no prior knowledge of Yiddish) continued to function into the 1980s but very few individuals remained culturally active in Yiddish and it ceased to be the dominant language of a Jewish community officially numbering around 10,000 after the forced emigration of 1968.[120]

Having thrown in his lot with the Soviets, Noah Prylucki was spared the fate of colleagues such as Max Weinreich and Yudel Mark, who were active in YIVO after the Second World War in New York. Safe in America, they necessarily watched from afar, powerless during the destruction of a civilization they cherished and the gradual attrition of its survivors. In the post-war era they witnessed the realization of perhaps Prylucki's greatest fear—not only the failure of national cultural autonomy but the decline of Yiddish as a vehicle of modern, secular culture and of Yiddishism as a viable ideology in eastern Europe and beyond.

[120] F. Bergman, 'Yiddish in Poland after 1945', in G. Estraikh and M. Krutikov (eds.), *Yiddish and the Left* (Oxford, 2001), 167–74.

Rites of Violence?

The Pogroms of Summer 1941

KAI STRUVE

IN THE FIRST DAYS and weeks after the German attack on the Soviet Union on 22 June 1941, a wave of violence against the Jews by the indigenous Christian population erupted in the territories between the Baltic and Black seas occupied by the German forces. These same areas had been occupied by the Soviets in September 1939 and June 1940.[1] In many localities, the violence was closely bound up with activities by German police personnel bent on 'establishing and maintaining security' in the area. Those police actions likewise primarily targeted Jews.

Researchers have long recognized that pogroms took place in Lithuania, the Ukrainian territories, northern Bukovina, and Bessarabia. However, with the publication of Jan Tomasz Gross's controversial study in 2000 on the Jedwabne pogrom of north-eastern Poland on 10 July 1941, followed by other works, it became known that a large number of pogroms had occurred in Soviet-occupied areas populated mainly by Poles, between Łomża and Białystok.[2]

In the vehement debate sparked by Gross's study, two principal questions were at the forefront of controversy: was the hatred manifested in the pogrom due to an especially close Jewish collaboration with the Soviets and a widespread pro-Soviet

[1] On 17 September 1939, sixteen days after the German attack on Poland, the Red Army marched into eastern Poland. In mid-June 1940, it occupied Lithuania, Latvia, and Estonia, which even as early as October 1939 had been forced to consent to the construction of Soviet military bases on their soil. Finally, in late June and early July 1940, the Red Army occupied northern Bukovina and Bessarabia, which had belonged to Romania in the inter-war years.

[2] J. T. Gross, *Sąsiedzi: Historia zagłady żydowskiego miasteczka* (Sejny, 2000); English version, *Neighbors: The Destruction of the Jewish Community in Jedwabne, Poland* (Princeton, 2001). Knowledge of violence against Jews in north-eastern Poland in the summer of 1941 was significantly expanded through the publication in 2002 of the results of research carried out by the Instytut Pamięci Narodowej, in P. Machcewicz and K. Persak (eds.), *Wokół Jedwabnego* (Warsaw, 2002), vol. i: *Studia*, vol. ii: *Dokumenty*. See esp. E. Dmitrów, 'Oddziały operacyjne niemieckiej Policji Bezpieczeństwa i Służby Bezpieczeństwa a początek zagłady Żydów w Łomżyńskiem i na Białostocczyźnie latem 1941 roku', ibid. i. 273–351, and A. Żbikowski, 'Pogromy i mordy ludności żydowskiej w Łomżyńskiem i na Białostocczyźnie latem 1941 roku w świetle relacji ocalałych Żydów i dokumentów sądowych', ibid. i. 159–271. See also A. Żbikowski, *U genezy Jedwabnego: Żydzi na kresach północno-wschodnich II Rzeczypospolitej, wrzesień 1939–lipiec 1941* (Warsaw, 2006).

attitude among the Jews there in the twenty-one months of Soviet occupation, or was it attributable to antisemitic stereotypes? And what was the role of the Germans in the pogrom in Jedwabne, and more generally in relation to the local perpetrators?[3] Conflicts arose around similar questions that had long been controversial in other regions as well, but whose discussion had been less intense.[4]

Relying on the now extensive and richly documented studies on pogroms in the Polish areas, and comparing these with events in Lithuania and the territories in eastern Poland that had a Ukrainian majority,[5] the present chapter explores the different contexts that generated violence in the summer of 1941 in the occupied territories, contexts that mutually reinforced each other.

THE GERMAN CONTEXT

The beginning of the war against the Soviet Union was associated with a qualitative change in the German 'war against the Jews', in Lucy Dawidowicz's words. It marked the start of a new stage of escalation, which in subsequent months would lead to the beginning of the systematic murder of Jews in the newly occupied territories, and ultimately to the attempt to annihilate all Jews under German rule.[6] One central factor at work in this escalation was the fact that, in the German view, a very different significance attached to Jews in this war compared to all the wars that Germany had waged in the past. Jews were considered to be agents of Bolshevism, and Soviet rule was regarded as rule by Jews. Despite the anti-Jewish

[3] On the Jedwabne controversy, see A. Polonsky and J. B. Michlic (eds.), *The Neighbors Respond: The Controversy over the Jedwabne Massacre in Poland* (Princeton, 2004).

[4] See e.g. P. Friedman, 'Ukrainian–Jewish Relations during the Nazi Occupation', *YIVO Annual of Jewish Social Science*, 12 (1958/9), 259–96; Y. Bilinsky, 'Methodological Problems and Philosophical Issues in the Study of Jewish–Ukrainian Relations during the Second World War', in P. J. Potichnyj and H. Aster (eds.), *Ukrainian–Jewish Relations in Historical Perspective* (Edmonton, 1988), 373–407; A. Weiss, 'Jewish–Ukrainian Relations in Western Ukraine during the Holocaust', ibid. 409–20; A. Eidintas, *Jews, Lithuanians, and the Holocaust* (Vilnius, 2003), 336–447. For a balanced discussion of the problem of Ukrainian collaboration, see F. Golczewski, 'Shades of Grey: Reflections on Jewish–Ukrainian and German–Ukrainian Relations in Galicia', in R. Brandon and W. Lower (eds.), *The Shoah in Ukraine: History, Testimony, Memorialization* (Bloomington, Ind., 2008), 114–55.

[5] On the other regions, here not considered in detail, see V. Solonari, 'Patterns of Violence: The Local Population and the Mass Murder of Jews in Bessarabia and Northern Bukovina, July–August 1941', *Kritika: Explorations in Russian and Eurasian History*, 8 (2007), 749–87. On Latvia, see A. Ezergailis, *The Holocaust in Latvia, 1941–1944: The Missing Center* (Riga, 1996); A. Angrick and P. Klein, *Die 'Endlösung' in Riga: Ausbeutung und Vernichtung, 1941–1944* (Darmstadt, 2006), 76–90. On Estonia, see R. B. Birn, *Die Sicherheitspolizei in Estland, 1941–1944: Eine Studie zur Kollaboration im Osten* (Paderborn, 2006), 159–71. In Estonia there was no pogrom-like violence. The stereotypical equating of Jews and communists appears to have been a comparatively weak phenomenon there.

[6] Admittedly, German policy towards Jews had increasingly been tending to genocide since the occupation of Poland in September 1939: see C. R. Browning, with contributions by J. Matthäus, *The Origins of the Final Solution: The Evolution of Nazi Jewish Policy, September 1939–March 1942* (Lincoln, Nebr., 2004).

excesses which took place in 1939 during the campaign in Poland, at that juncture it was Polish elites who were regarded as the real threat and adversary; consequently, it was the latter who became the principal targets of the 'cleansing operations' carried out by SS and police units.[7] In this connection, Klaus-Michael Mallmann notes:

Now [in the war against the Soviet Union] it was a matter of destroying the main enemy, defined in racial terms: 'Jewish Bolshevism'. The assertion of this essential identity made possible the constant reinterpretation and interchange of both terms. Right from the start, that altered the significance of the Jewish population. Now it was no longer, as it was in Poland, a despised population. Rather, it was considered an agent and creator, the biological substrate of the Soviet system. It was only this fusion of the two central images of the enemy—the Jews and communism—their mutual overlapping, interpenetration, and strengthening, which triggered that dynamism which would lead to genocide.[8]

Thus Jews were regarded from the war's outset as real or potential agents of resistance, and their liquidation was deemed a (prophylactic) measure to ensure security.[9] Such an interpretation of the role of Jews in the Soviet Union and in the communist movement as a whole not only decisively shaped the thinking of the top echelon of the Nazi regime, the SS, and the police, but was also widespread in the Wehrmacht command and in broad sections of the population.[10] It guided the activities of the SS and police units which were charged with maintaining security in the occupied areas. These were primarily the *Einsatzgruppen* (special-operations units) of the Security Police and Security Service, along with battalions of uniformed regular police, the so-called Ordnungspolizei (Order Police), as well as Waffen-SS units of the Kommandostab Reichsführer-SS.[11] In addition, in the

---

[7] On the war with Poland in 1939, see A. B. Rossino, *Hitler Strikes Poland: Blitzkrieg, Ideology, and Atrocity* (Lawrence, Kan., 2003). On crimes by the Wehrmacht in this war, see J. Böhler, *Auftakt zum Vernichtungskrieg: Die Wehrmacht in Polen, 1939* (Frankfurt am Main, 2006). On the activities of the *Einsatzgruppen* in 1939, see also K.-M. Mallmann, J. Böhler, and J. Matthäus (eds.), *Einsatzgruppen in Polen: Darstellung und Dokumentation* (Darmstadt, 2008).

[8] K.-M. Mallmann, 'Die Türöffner der "Endlösung": Zur Genesis des Genozids', in G. Paul and K.-M. Mallmann (eds.), *Die Gestapo im Zweiten Weltkrieg: 'Heimatfront' und besetztes Europa* (Darmstadt, 2000), 443–4.

[9] Ibid. 445. See also J. Matthäus, 'Controlled Escalation: Himmler's Men in the Summer of 1941 and the Holocaust in the Occupied Soviet Territories', *Holocaust and Genocide Studies*, 21 (2007), 218–42.

[10] On the image of 'Jewish Bolshevism' and Soviet rule as Jewish rule in 1941 and thereafter in National Socialist propaganda, see W. Meyer zu Uptrup, *Kampf gegen die 'jüdische Weltverschwörung': Propaganda und Antisemitismus der Nationalsozialisten, 1919 bis 1945* (Berlin, 2003), 373–93. On the association of anti-Bolshevism and antisemitism in the Soviet Union as perceived by the leadership echelon of the Wehrmacht, see J. Hürter, *Hitlers Heerführer: Die deutschen Oberbefehlshaber im Krieg gegen die Sowjetunion, 1941/42* (Munich, 2006), 514–17, and J. Förster, 'Zum Rußlandbild der Militärs, 1941–1945', in H.-E. Volkmann (ed.), *Das Rußlandbild im Dritten Reich* (Cologne, 1994), 141–63.

[11] The most extensive studies are on the *Einsatzgruppen*. Among these, see H. Krausnick and H.-H. Wilhelm, *Die Truppe des Weltanschauungskrieges: Die Einsatzgruppen der Sicherheitspolizei und des SD,*

areas bordering the Generalgouvernement and the German Reich in East Prussia, further mobile units of the Security Police who had been dispatched there were active on the ground.[12]

The officers of the *Einsatzgruppen* had been briefed on their assigned tasks by Reinhard Heydrich at a discussion in Berlin on 17 June 1941. The basic roles of the *Einsatzgruppen* and other police units in the newly occupied territories were to ensure security, gather intelligence, and combat opponents of the German occupation, who as a rule were to be executed.[13]

One special assignment of the *Einsatzgruppen* was to instigate pogroms in these newly occupied territories immediately after the front passed through the area. That task emerged as central in the first written instruction given to the *Einsatzgruppen*, sent by Heydrich on 29 June 1941, with reference to the earlier briefing of 17 June. It stated explicitly:

The self-cleansing endeavours of anti-communist or anti-Jewish circles in the territories which will soon be occupied are not to be hindered. On the contrary: they should be actively instigated, but without leaving any trace, intensified where necessary, and guided onto the right path—though without these local 'self-defence circles' later being able to point to any orders or political assurances given to them.[14]

The order may reflect experience gained in the first days of the offensive, especially with regard to the pogrom in Kaunas that commenced on 23 June and was intensified after the intervention of the commander of Einsatzgruppe A, Franz Walter Stahlecker, who arrived there on 24 June.[15] At a meeting of several SS and police commanders in East Prussia on 28 June, the day before the above order was sent, Himmler apparently voiced the criticism that no pogroms had yet taken place in

1938–1942 (Stuttgart, 1981); R. Ogorreck, *Die Einsatzgruppen und die 'Genesis der Endlösung'* (Berlin, 1996); see also *Die Einsatzgruppen in der besetzten Sowjetunion, 1941/42: Die Tätigkeits- und Lageberichte des Chefs der Sicherheitspolizei und des SD*, ed. P. Klein (Berlin, 1997). A detailed study on the activities of the police battalions is W. Curilla, *Die deutsche Ordnungspolizei und der Holocaust im Baltikum und in Weißrussland, 1941–1944* (Paderborn, 2006). See also M. Cüppers, *Wegbereiter der Shoah: Die Waffen-SS, der Kommandostab Reichsführer-SS und die Judenvernichtung, 1939–1945* (Darmstadt, 2005).

[12] Żbikowski, *U genezy Jedwabnego*, 189–91; Dmitrów, 'Oddziały operacyjne', 284–92; A. B. Rossino, 'Polish "Neighbours" and German Invaders: Anti-Jewish Violence in the Białystok District during the Opening Weeks of Operation Barbarossa', *Polin*, 16 (2003), 431–52.

[13] What was discussed at this meeting can only be approximately reconstructed from post-war testimony and later documents: see Ogorreck, *Die Einsatzgruppen*, 47–94.

[14] *Die Einsatzgruppen*, ed. Klein, 319.

[15] On the Kaunas pogrom, see C. Dieckmann, 'Lithuania in Summer 1941: The German Invasion and the Kaunas Pogrom', in E. Barkan, E. A. Cole, and K. Struve (eds.), *Shared History—Divided Memory: Jews and Others in Soviet-Occupied Poland, 1939–1941* (Leipzig, 2007), 355–85; C. Dieckmann and S. Sužiedėlis, *The Persecution and Mass Murder of Lithuanian Jews during Summer and Fall 1941* (Vilnius, 2006) 120–36; T. Szarota, *U progu zagłady: Zajścia antyżydowskie i pogromy w okupowanej Europie* (Warsaw, 2000), 199–266.

the neighbouring district of Białystok.[16] Alexander Rossino views this as the background to the decision to deploy further *Einsatzkommando* units in the General-gouvernement on 30 June; these units immediately set off for Białystok and Lviv (Lwów). Operating in the rear areas, they were ordered to take over the tasks of the *Einsatzgruppen* which were moving in behind the rapid advance of the Wehrmacht.[17]

In Operational Order No. 2 to commanders of the *Einsatzgruppen*, sent on 1 July, Heydrich re-emphasized the assigned prime target of *Einsatzgruppen* operations: 'It goes without saying that the cleansing operations must primarily be directed at the Bolsheviks and the Jews.'[18] But how to deal with the Polish population in the newly occupied territories was clearly less self-evident; it is likely that this was the reason for the communication. In contrast with September 1939, when the Polish elites had been the principal target of Security Police operations, Heydrich explained that here the Polish population would, 'on the basis of their experience, be both anti-communist and anti-Jewish' and thus be ready to co-operate. For that reason, Heydrich continued, it was also 'self-evident' 'that Poles with such convictions should not be included in the cleansing operations, especially since they are important as potential initiators (though with limited scope, in keeping with the local situation) in connection with pogroms and as informants'.[19]

This somewhat laboriously worded formulation meant that Poles, in contrast to 'Bolsheviks and Jews', should not become a primary focus of executions; their readiness to co-operate should not be endangered.[20] This differed from the situation in 1939. Heydrich did not mention Lithuanians and Ukrainians here because there was no doubt among his subordinates that they mostly supported the German invasion as liberation from Bolshevism.

In the first few weeks of the occupation, the *Einsatzkommando* units did not

---

[16] Rossino, 'Polish "Neighbours" and German Invaders', 443.

[17] Ibid. 444–6; D. Pohl, *Nationalsozialistische Judenverfolgung in Ostgalizien, 1941–1944: Organisation und Durchführung eines staatlichen Massenverbrechens* (Munich, 1996), 53–4.

[18] Here he sets out the actual task of the *Einsatzgruppen* in far clearer terms than in a communication to the Higher SS and Police Leader in the East, dated 2 July 1941, which he defined as a summary of his instructions to the *Einsatzgruppen*. It contains an oft-cited, relatively detailed list of groups of people to be executed, mainly Soviet party functionaries, state officials, and persons active in the resistance. It mentions 'Jews in positions in the party apparatus and government' among these many groups, but only as if incidentally, and therefore somewhat misleadingly. On this, see Ogorreck, *Die Einsatzgruppen*, 102–3; the document is printed in *Die Einsatzgruppen*, ed. Klein, 323–8.

[19] *Die Einsatzgruppen*, ed. Klein, 320.

[20] Heydrich gave this clarification evidently as a reaction to a communication from the 17th Army Supreme Command, stationed near Lviv; see also Ereignismeldungen UdSSR des Chefs der Sicherheitspolizei und des SD, no. 10, 2 July 1941: Bundesarchiv Berlin, R 58/214, fos. 52–3. On various slightly differing interpretations of this order, see Żbikowski, *U genezy Jedwabnego*, 169–71. Hannes Heer interprets this, not very convincingly, as evidence that the 17th Army and its commander Carl Heinrich von Stülpnagel played an active role in instigating pogroms: see H. Heer, 'Einübung in den Holocaust: Lemberg, Juni/Juli 1941', *Zeitschrift für Geschichtswissenschaft*, 49 (2001), 414–15.

engage in totally indiscriminate attacks on the Jewish population as a whole. At this juncture, it was largely males of an age appropriate for military service who were executed. But even they became a target for summary executions only gradually. As a rule, local militias were assigned the task of rounding up sympathizers or collaborators with Soviet rule; these units had arisen either spontaneously or under the influence of nationalist organizations.[21] The *Einsatzkommandos* wanted to utilize local knowledge about individuals who worked closely with the Soviets. The Germans and their local helpers concurred that Jews were the primary group in which supporters of the Soviet regime should be sought, and that a substantial segment of Jews were communists, in particular members of the Jewish intelligentsia. Since from the German viewpoint Jews were perceived as a general threat to security, and were on the whole deemed 'undesirable', it was only natural to interpret the task of executing communists rather broadly and, with regard to Jews, to extend the executions beyond the circle of true active supporters of Soviet rule. As will be shown, this attitude also characterized the indigenous nationalist organizations that were co-operating with the Germans at the war's outset. Without proactive local support, the relatively weak German forces on the ground, who usually had no reliable information about local relations, would hardly have been in a position to carry out the 'cleansing operations'.

Documentation exists for the north-eastern Polish regions on how, in numerous localities, the Jewish population or a part of it was seized and brought to the market square, along with non-Jewish communists or collaborators with the Soviet occupiers. In Andrzej Żbikowski's words, veritable 'spectacles of terror' were organized.[22] Those who had been rounded up were maltreated; in some localities, Jewish inhabitants were forced to march in procession, where they were symbolically identified with the Soviet occupation and derided. On a number of occasions, these processions ended in pogrom-type violence, but only in two towns, Radziłów and Jedwabne, did these result in mass murders on 7 and 10 July 1941 that were clearly intended to liquidate all the Jewish inhabitants.

Edmund Dmitrów suspects that the core contingent among the local pogrom perpetrators had received concrete instructions for their attempt to kill all Jewish residents from an *Einsatzkommando* unit of the Security Police in Ciechanów active in the region; they were given instructions on the preferred method to be used, namely herding Jews into the synagogue or some other building, and then setting it ablaze. This would mean that at least one of Heydrich's mobile killing units attempted to exterminate entire Jewish communities before the escalation to this level took place on a larger scale in late July and early August 1941 during the operations of SS troops in the Pripyat marshes.[23] However, there is as yet no

[21] On the mechanisms of formation of militias in the north-eastern Polish areas, see Żbikowski, *U genezy Jedwabnego*, 226–7; see also below.

[22] Żbikowski, *U genezy Jedwabnego*, 224; see also Dmitrów, 'Oddziały operacyjne', 340–3.

[23] Dmitrów, 'Oddziały operacyjne', 336–9, 344–6. On the killings in the Pripyat marshes, see Cüppers, *Wegbereiter der Shoah*.

incontrovertible proof of this. In his study, Gross suggested that there had been a relatively greater initiative by indigenous pogrom perpetrators, and that fewer specific instructions had been passed on from the Germans.[24]

Frequently, however, only a selection was made from those who had been rounded up or arrested; they were then executed, either immediately or after several days, generally outside the locality. Though carried out by the Gestapo, these executions often also involved the participation of locals; in some places Jews were beaten to death. These actions indicate that the entire Jewish population was branded with suspicion of having supported the Soviet regime. By contrast, in the non-Jewish population, the only people executed had indeed been working with the Soviets, or at least were strongly suspected of such collaboration. In a number of places, the punishment meted out to them was less severe than that which Jews received. Non-Jews were frequently only beaten or otherwise maltreated, or put behind bars, while Jews in most cases were killed.[25]

The *Einsatzkommando* units apparently expected that by means of these pogroms a part of their assigned tasks in security maintenance would be advanced. But propaganda purposes were also meant to be served through the staging of public spectacles of hatred for Jews. These were linked with reports about crimes committed against prisoners in the jails of the Soviet occupiers in the final days before the German forces rolled in. The intention was to legitimize both the war against the Soviet Union and a harsh anti-Jewish policy.[26]

Along with the somewhat strategic activities of the German police units (primarily the Security Police), there were also a large number of spontaneous violent actions and cases of maltreatment of Jews by German police personnel and Wehrmacht soldiers.[27] One well-known example is the pogrom in Białystok on 27 June 1941 instigated by Police Battalion 309 belonging to the Wehrmacht's 221st Security Division, which reportedly took the lives of more than 2,000 Jews, including 700–800 who were locked in the city's main synagogue and then burned to death.[28] By means of this and other violent actions, the Germans were broadcasting

---

[24] Andrzej Żbikowski also agrees with such an interpretation: *U genezy Jedwabnego*, 230–1.

[25] Żbikowski, 'Pogromy i mordy ludności żydowskiej', *passim*; id., *U genezy Jedwabnego*, 219–27. Although detailed research has not been carried out, Dieter Pohl assumes there was a similar pattern in eastern Galicia: see Pohl, *Nationalsozialistische Judenverfolgung*, 71. On Volhynia, see S. Spector, *The Holocaust of the Volhynian Jews, 1941–1944* (Jerusalem, 1990), 72–6.

[26] On the murder of the prisoners, see below. On propagandistic purposes, see B. Musial, *'Konterrevolutionäre Elemente sind zu erschießen': Die Brutalisierung des deutsch-sowjetischen Krieges im Sommer 1941* (Munich, 2000), 200–9; Dmitrów, 'Oddziały operacyjne', 304–5.

[27] The sources, for the most part memoirs of surviving Jews, often do not permit us to distinguish whether police or Wehrmacht units were responsible for maltreatment, the burning of synagogues, the desecration of Torah scrolls, or similar actions. For that reason, it also cannot always be established if these were spontaneous excesses or intentional repression. For the example of north-eastern Poland, see Żbikowski, *U genezy Jedwabnego*, 223–4.

[28] P. Longerich, *Politik der Vernichtung: Eine Gesamtdarstellung der nationalsozialistischen Judenverfolgung* (Munich, 1998), 345–8.

a clear message: Jews no longer enjoyed protection. The Germans thus, by their example, encouraged the local population to pillage and engage in anti-Jewish violence.[29]

THE EAST-CENTRAL EUROPEAN NATIONAL CONTEXT

For the Poles and the Baltic nations, the partitioning of the east-central European territory between Germany and the Soviet Union as part of the Hitler–Stalin Pact and the beginning of the Second World War in September 1939 marked a national catastrophe. These nations lost their independence, which had been only recently won or regained in 1918. However, these events, seen from the viewpoint of the Ukrainian national movement, were more ambiguous. On the one hand, Ukrainian nationalists considered the Soviet occupation a new form of foreign domination: Ukrainian national institutions that had been built up by the efforts of the national movement over several decades were now dissolved, and politically active Ukrainians were now threatened by persecution in the areas of Poland occupied by the Soviets; a large number lost their lives as a result. On the other hand, with the renewed partition of Poland, the political situation was in a state of flux. There now appeared to be prospects for the realization of a project that had failed after the First World War: the establishment of a Ukrainian nation state, on the side of Germany, in the context of a German–Soviet war now expected in the near future. For Ukrainians, Lithuanians, Latvians, and Estonians, hope of gaining or regaining independence was associated with Germany. After their territories had been occupied, many people from these nations, especially the political elites, had fled to the German sphere of power. There they set about organizing for the struggle against Soviet occupation. This was accompanied by a marginalization of the more moderate political forces among them.[30]

For the Ukrainians, the radical nationalist Orhanizatsiya Ukrayinskykh Natsionalistiv (Organization of Ukrainian Nationalists; OUN) became the dominant force. Since the 1930s it had been fighting for Ukrainian independence using terror tactics, and was primarily based in eastern Galicia.[31] In February 1940 a wing of younger, more radical activists, generally called the OUN-B, after its leader Stepan Bandera, split off from the main body. On the whole, the OUN-B

---

[29] In individual instances, however, units of the Wehrmacht or the field police did also prohibit pogrom-like violence: see Żbikowski, *U genezy Jedwabnego*, 225.

[30] K. Kangeris, 'Kollaboration vor der Kollaboration? Die baltischen Emigranten und ihre "Befreiungskomitees" in Deutschland, 1940/1941', in W. Röhr (ed.), *Okkupation und Kollaboration (1938–1945): Beiträge zu Konzepten und Praxis der Kollaboration in der deutschen Okkupationspolitik* (Berlin, 1994), 165–90; R. Torzecki, *Polacy i Ukraińcy: Sprawa ukraińska w czasie II wojny światowej na terenie II Rzeczypospolitej* (Warsaw, 1993), 44–68.

[31] R. Wysocki, *Organizacja Ukraińskich Nacjonalistów w Polsce w latach 1929–1939: Geneza, struktura, program, ideologia* (Lublin, 2003); F. Bruder, *'Den ukrainischen Staat erkämpfen oder sterben!' Die Organisation Ukrainischer Nationalisten (OUN), 1929–1948* (Berlin, 2007); J. A. Armstrong, *Ukrainian Nationalism* (New York, 1963).

represented active OUN members inside the Generalgouvernement and in the underground of eastern Galicia.[32]

In November 1940 Lithuanian emigrants in Berlin founded the Lietuvių Aktyvistų Frontas (Front of Lithuanian Activists; LAF), whose aim was to re-establish Lithuanian independence. They and the OUN were bound to National Socialist Germany by a folkish-nationalist ideology and the conception of a state organized along authoritarian lines. Guidelines for members of the LAF, put forward in Berlin on 10 May 1941, not only blamed Jews for the loss of Lithuanian independence, but also asserted that communism was rooted in Judaism.[33] Hence, the struggle for Lithuanian independence became a struggle against the Jews as well. Thus, in a flyer distributed by the Lithuanian underground, the LAF called for the liberation of Lithuania 'not only from the slavery of the Asiatic Bolsheviks', but also from the 'long-standing Jewish yoke'.[34] In a call for insurrection distributed in the spring of 1941, the LAF hoped that the outbreak of the anticipated German–Soviet war could be used to 'drive out the Jews along with the Red Russians'.[35]

By the spring of 1941, the writings of the LAF contained threats to murder Jews. In March 1941, for example, in an appeal addressed to the Lithuanian people, the LAF called upon Jews to leave the country, so that later on there would not be any 'unnecessary victims'. Another passage stated that all Lithuanian communists and other 'traitors', who after liberation would immediately be imprisoned, would only be forgiven 'if they are really able to prove that they have liquidated a Jew'.[36]

The OUN, by contrast, produced no known official declarations with comparably clear calls for violence against Jews during the period before the beginning of the German–Soviet war.[37] However, the equating of communist rule with domination

---

[32] Armstrong, *Ukrainian Nationalism*, 26–72.

[33] S. Gasparaitis, '"Verrätern wird nur dann vergeben, wenn sie wirklich beweisen können, dass sie mindestens einen Juden liquidiert haben": Die "Front Litauischer Aktivisten" (LAF) und die anti-sowjetischen Aufstände 1941', *Zeitschrift für Geschichtswissenschaft*, 49 (2001), 893.

[34] Ibid. 894.

[35] Quoted in M. MacQueen, 'The Context of Mass Destruction: Agents and Prerequisites of the Holocaust in Lithuania', *Holocaust and Genocide Studies*, 12 (1998), 34.

[36] The authenticity of the last quotation is, however, controversial. It is contained in only one of the two extant copies of the flyer in the archives, and was presumably added in this case when copies smuggled from the German Reich into Lithuania were being duplicated: see Dieckmann, 'Lithuania in Summer 1941', 372–3. Along with the LAF, whose members were largely supporters of the dictatorial president Smetona, the paramilitary organization Geležinis Vilkas (Iron Wolf) of the former prime minister Augustinas Voldemaras, which espoused a radical anti-Bolshevist and antisemitic line, also enjoyed support from the Germans. See MacQueen, 'Context of Mass Destruction', 29–32.

[37] However, even in the 1930s there had been attacks on Jews in Poland by the OUN. They regarded Jews as people co-operating with the Poles and a foreign element which exploited Ukrainians economically and participated in their political oppression. See Bruder, *'Den ukrainischen Staat erkämpfen oder sterben!'*, 99–101.

by Jews was also widespread among Ukrainians, and such feelings intensified during the Soviet occupation of 1939–41.[38] Even before the German attack on the Soviet Union, radical OUN nationalists, especially of the Bandera faction, were characterized by their high degree of readiness to use violence and terror to achieve a nation state in which Ukrainians would predominate, and ultimately constitute a nationally homogeneous population. In eastern Europe too the world view of radical nationalists had taken on a profoundly Darwinian character, seeing nations as biological units engaged in a permanent struggle for survival.[39]

The OUN considered Russians, Poles, and Jews as the main opposition standing in the way of realizing a national utopia. These opponents were to be ousted from all positions of power, and ultimately from the nation state envisaged by the OUN, which was conceived of as a *natsiokratiya*, a 'natiocracy'.[40] However, in the spring of 1941 and also later, during the war, OUN-B leaders at various times stated that their arch-enemy was Moscow, and that the struggle against the Jews should not divert them from the prime necessity: Ukrainian independence had to be fought for principally against rule by Moscow. The resolutions of the Second Congress of the OUN-B in April 1941 even contained a warning to avoid pogroms against Jews 'in the time of insurgency', in order to avoid diverting attention from the 'real originators of evil', the 'Muscovite–Bolshevik regime'. The warning stated: 'The OUN strives against the Jews as a pillar of support for the Muscovite–Bolshevik regime, but at the same time makes clear to the masses that Moscow is the main enemy.'[41] Jews were declared to be adversaries, but were only of secondary importance. In this programmatic statement, the OUN-B's world view clearly differed from that of the Nazi regime, despite the stereotypical view of Jews expressed in it. In National Socialist ideology, behind 'Moscow' stood the real enemy, namely the Jews.[42] This difference nevertheless did not hinder the radical Ukrainian nationalists from exploiting the opportunity that arose after the beginning of the German–Soviet war

[38] C. Mick, '"Only the Jews do not waver . . .": L'viv under Soviet Occupation', in Barkan, Cole, and Struve (eds.), *Shared History—Divided Memory*, 245–62. A detailed study of the extended history of the stereotypical equating of 'Jewish' and 'communist' as exemplified in Poland is J. B. Michlic, *Poland's Threatening Other: The Image of the Jew from 1880 to the Present* (Lincoln, Nebr., 2006). See also A. Pufelska, *Die 'Judäo-Kommune': Ein Feindbild in Polen. Das polnische Selbstverständnis im Schatten des Antisemitismus, 1939–1948* (Paderborn, 2007).

[39] For the Ukrainians, see e.g. Bruder, *'Den ukrainischen Staat erkämpfen oder sterben!'*, 34–52; A. Weiner, *Making Sense of War: The Second World War and the Fate of the Bolshevik Revolution* (Princeton, 2001), 239–44. On the roots of such notions in the nineteenth century, see B. Porter, *When Nationalism Began to Hate: Imagining Modern Politics in Nineteenth-Century Poland* (New York, 2000).

[40] The title of a book by a programmatic ideological forerunner of the OUN, Mykola Stsiborsky, *Natsiokratiya* (Paris, 1935). 'Ethnocracy' might be a more contemporary term. After the split in the OUN at the beginning of 1940, Stsiborsky remained loyal to the Melnyk faction. He was shot in September 1941 in Zhytomyr, apparently as part of the feud between the two OUN factions.

[41] Quoted in Bruder, *'Den ukrainischen Staat erkämpfen oder sterben!'*, 124.

[42] J. Herf, *The Jewish Enemy: Nazi Propaganda during World War II and the Holocaust* (Cambridge, Mass., 2006).

to advance their goal regarding the Jews: to subdue them and, ultimately, remove them from their national territory.

In guidelines issued in May 1941 for the behaviour of OUN activists, the OUN-B listed 'clearing hostile elements from the terrain' among its objectives and tasks, declaring that 'at a time of chaos and confusion, liquidation of undesirable Polish, Muscovite, and Jewish activists is permitted, especially supporters of Bolshevik–Muscovite imperialism'.[43] After 22 June, this instruction was apparently interpreted quite broadly, when the Germans encouraged the policy and provided latitude for its implementation—even if supposedly there were no further general orders from the OUN-B leaders for initiating pogroms and intentional acts of violence against Jews.[44] Local militias, culled from the underground structures of the OUN in areas under Soviet occupation, and sometimes assisted by the OUN organizational units known as *pokhidni hrupy*, 'field groups', which after the outbreak of war started to move eastwards from the Generalgouvernement, were integrated into the 'cleansing operations' by the Germans in various places in the manner sketched above, or undertook such actions independently.[45]

There is to date no extensive study on anti-Jewish violence in the summer of 1941 in eastern Poland's largely Ukrainian areas of eastern Galicia and Volhynia, or in Lithuania.[46] By contrast, very detailed studies exist for the predominantly Polish regions. Andrzej Żbikowski has established that there were forty-two localities in which violence was perpetrated against Jews by the local populations between 22 June and mid-September 1941 in the regions of Łomża and Białystok, and twenty-five other such localities in other parts of 'Western Belarus', as the Soviets called the territory annexed to Belarus in 1939.[47]

[43] Quoted in K. C. Berkhoff and M. Carynnyk, 'The Organization of Ukrainian Nationalists and its Attitude toward Germans and Jews: Iaroslav Stets'ko's 1941 *Zhyttiepys*', *Harvard Ukrainian Studies*, 23, nos. 3–4 (1999), 153.

[44] However, there are two leaflets signed by Ivan Klymiv, who headed the OUN-B underground in the Soviet-occupied territories, that were distributed in Lviv and other localities after the Soviet retreat. They contained among other instructions the following: 'People! Know this! Moscow, Poland, the Hungarians, and the Jews—these are your enemies. Destroy them.' Another leaflet, also signed by Klymiv, declared: 'I am introducing mass (ethnic and national) responsibility for crimes against the Ukrainian state and the Ukrainian army.' See *Ukrayins'ke derzhavotvorennya: Akt 30 chervnya 1941. Zbirnyk dokumentiv i materialiv*, ed. O. Dzyuban (Lviv, 2001), 129, 131.

[45] F. Grelka, *Die ukrainische Nationalbewegung unter deutscher Besatzungsherrschaft 1918 und 1941/42* (Wiesbaden, 2005), 241–4, 276–86. However, Volodymyr Vyatrovych rejects the notion that the OUN was responsible for excessive anti-Jewish violence: see V. Vyatrovych, *Stavlennya OUN do yevreyiv: Formuvannya pozytsiyi na tli katastrofy* (Lviv, 2006). For an excellent critique of this book, see T. Kurylo and I. Khymka [J.-P. Himka], 'Yak OUN stavylasya do yevreyiv? Rozdumy nad knyzhkoyu Volodymyra V"yatrovycha', *Ukrayina Moderna*, 13 (2008), 252–65.

[46] But see, on eastern Galicia, Pohl, *Nationalsozialistische Judenverfolgung*, 54–67; T. Sandkühler, *'Endlösung' in Galizien: Der Judenmord in Ostpolen und Rettungsinitiativen von Berthold Beitz, 1941–1944* (Bonn, 1996), 110–22; on Volhynia, Spector, *Holocaust of the Volhynian Jews*, 64–79. See also Musial, *'Konterrevolutionäre Elemente sind zu erschießen'*, 175–91.

[47] Żbikowski, *U genezy Jedwabnego*, 213.

To date, when it comes to the far less investigated western Ukraine, there have been only initial attempts to piece together a quantitative picture of the pogroms, and these have arrived at quite different findings. The figures for eastern Galicia and Volhynia range from thirty-five to more than 140 pogroms, with the number of victims estimated at from 12,000 to 35,000 thousand.[48] In the case of Lithuania, Dov Levin assumes that violence against Jews occurred in at least forty places even before Wehrmacht units arrived.[49] In Kaunas and other cities, violence escalated as the German SS and police units moved in, with the latter encouraging Lithuanian groups of insurgents and militia members, here generally termed 'partisans', to engage in further violence.[50]

One factor that considerably heightened the mood of pogrom in eastern Galicia after the German occupation was the discovery of the corpses of prisoners who had been murdered by the NKVD before the Soviets left. Crimes against prisoners in jails were perpetrated in many places before the Soviets retreated. In eastern Galicia their number was especially large.[51] A substantial portion of the prisoners had been arrested and interned only in the final weeks leading up to the outbreak of the German–Soviet war, or even after that conflict had started. Against the backdrop of increasing tension in the Soviet Union's relations with Germany, and with OUN activities being launched from the Generalgouvernement, the Soviet security organs initiated an operation against Ukrainian nationalists in early April 1941. In this context there was also a 'cleansing operation' on 22 May 1941, in which

[48] See A. Żbikowski, 'Lokalne pogromy Żydów w czerwcu i lipcu 1941 roku na wschodnich rubieżach II Rzeczypospolitej', *Biuletyn Żydowskiego Instytutu Historycznego*, 162–3 (1992), 12–13; A. Weiss, 'The Holocaust and the Ukrainian Victims', in M. Berenbaum (ed.), *A Mosaic of Victims: Non-Jews Persecuted and Murdered by the Nazis* (New York, 1990), 110; A. Kruglov, 'Pogromy v vostochnoi Galitsii letom 1941 g.: Organizatory, uchastniki, masshtaby i posledstviya', in *Voina na unichtozhenie: Natsistskaya politika genotsida na territorii Vostochnoi Evropy. Materialy mezhdunarodnoi nauchnoi konferentsii* (Moscow, 2010). See also D. Pohl, 'Anti-Jewish Pogroms in Western Ukraine: A Research Agenda', in Barkan, Cole, and Struve (eds.), *Shared History—Divided Memory*, 305–13.

[49] D. Levin, 'On the Relations between the Baltic Peoples and their Jewish Neighbors before, during and after World War II', *Holocaust and Genocide Studies*, 5 (1990), 56. Christoph Dieckmann and Saulius Sužiedėlis do not consider this an exaggerated estimate: see Dieckmann and Sužiedėlis, *Persecution and Mass Murder of Lithuanian Jews*, 104.

[50] For details of the events in Kaunas, see n. 15 above. As examples of events in the province, see the sketches on the district of Utena and the Jurbarkas locality in Dieckmann and Sužiedėlis, *Persecution and Mass Murder of Lithuanian Jews*, 157–70.

[51] Grzegorz Hryciuk gives the figure of at least 8,700 murdered prisoners in western Ukraine and 700 in Belarus, in his 'Victims 1939–1941: Soviet Repressions in Eastern Poland', in Barkan, Cole, and Struve (eds.), *Shared History—Divided Memory*, 183. Other estimates are much higher. Thus, Krzysztof Popiński suspects that in eastern Poland, 20,000–24,000 prisoners were murdered; Bogdan Musial thinks the total might have been 30,000 victims. See K. Popiński, 'Ewakuacja więzień kresowych w czerwcu 1941 r. na podstawie dokumentacji "Memoriału" i Archiwum Wschodniego', in A. Skrzypek et al. (eds.), *Zbrodnicza ewakuacja więzień i aresztów NKWD na Kresach Wschodnich II Rzeczypospolitej w czerwcu–lipcu 1941 roku* (Warsaw, 1997), 71–114; Musial, *'Konterrevolutionäre Elemente sind zu erschießen'*, 135–8.

some 11,000 people were transported into the interior of the Soviet Union. Similar mass deportations befell the population of the Baltic States on 14 June 1941, and the Polish population of Western Belarus on 19–20 June.[52]

Pogroms did not erupt in every locality where bodies of prisoners were discovered.[53] However, in many places where murdered inmates had been found, the prisons were at the centre of the pogroms. Jews were snatched from the streets by Ukrainian militias or were dragged from their homes and hauled off to prison, being subjected to abuse and maltreatment on the way. In the prisons, Jews were forced to retrieve the bodies of prisoners from mass graves and wash them, and in some places also pulled carts bringing corpses for burial in cemeteries. These were public rituals of expiation, during which allegedly guilty individuals were put on public display.[54] Exhumation and retrieval of the corpses was accompanied by numerous acts of maltreatment and murder.[55] However, systematic shooting of Jews by the *Einsatzgruppen* did not begin in Lviv until after 2 July 1941, the day the public violence came to an end. Mass shootings there and in other localities were declared to be 'revenge' for murders perpetrated by the NKVD.[56] In Zolochiv, Jews rounded up by the Ukrainian militia for retrieving the bodies of murdered prisoners in the local NKVD prison were killed by the SS Division 'Wiking'.[57] In other towns, such as Drohobych, Jews who were compelled to retrieve and prepare bodies for burial were subsequently murdered by the Ukrainian militia.[58]

In analysing Lithuanian examples, Siegfried Gasparaitis interprets the violence

[52] S. Ciesielski, G. Hryciuk, and A. Srebrakowski, *Masowe deportacje ludności w Związku Radzieckim* (Toruń, 2004), 262–70. On crimes committed by the NKVD in western Ukraine, see also O. Romaniv and I. Fedushchak, *Zakhidnoukrayins'ka trahediya, 1941* (Lviv, 2002).

[53] Pohl, *Nationalsozialistische Judenverfolgung*, 55; Friedman, 'Ukrainian–Jewish Relations during the Nazi Occupation', 274–5; M. Carynnyk, 'The Palace on the Ikva: Dubne, September 18th, 1939, and June 24th, 1941', in Barkan, Cole, and Struve (eds.), *Shared History–Divided Memory*, 263–301. For an attempt to visualize the connection between Soviet prisons and pogroms in western Ukraine on maps, see Brandon and Lower (eds.), *Shoah in Ukraine*, 93, 137.

[54] For short descriptions of the pogroms in Lviv, Sambir, Kolomyya, Zolochiv, Dobromyl, Boryslav, Berezhany, and Drohobych, see Musial, *'Konterrevolutionäre Elemente sind zu erschießen'*, 175–91. However, Musial does not address the question of the role of the OUN. On Zolochiv, with an interpretation somewhat different from that of Musial, see B. Boll, 'Złoczów, July 1941: The Wehrmacht and the Beginning of the Holocaust in Galicia. From a Criticism of Photographs to a Revision of the Past', in O. Bartov, A. Grossman, and M. Nolan (eds.), *Crimes of War: Guilt and Denial in the Twentieth Century* (New York, 2002), 61–99.

[55] For a detailed description of the maltreatment and killing of Jews in the Zamarstyniv prison in Lviv, see I. Khymka [J.-P. Himka], 'Dostovirnist' svidchennya: Relyatsiya Ruzi Vagner pro l'vivs'kyi pohrom vlitku 1941 r.', *Holokost i suchasnist'*, 2 (4) (2008), 43–79.

[56] Pohl, *Nationalsozialistische Judenverfolgung*, 69.

[57] Boll, 'Złoczów'. See also M. Tsarynnyk [Carynnyk], 'Zolochiv movchyt'', *Krytyka*, 2005, no. 10, pp. 14–17.

[58] Musial, *'Konterrevolutionäre Elemente sind zu erschießen'*, 189–90. Apparently the same occurred in Kremenets.

as 'stagings of a national revival'.[59] Against the backdrop of equating Jews with the Soviet regime, violence against Jews symbolized the victory of the Lithuanian nation over an opponent that had stripped it of its independence, and had spread fear and terror among Lithuanians actively struggling for the national cause. Here and in other regions the violent excesses thus celebrated the restoration of a legiti-mate order—a national order—that favoured one's own nation over that of the Jews. The situation of the Jews and their attitudes and behaviour in the period of Soviet occupation remain controversial. However, it seems clear that the pur-ported pro-Soviet position attributed to Jews rested on a stereotypical perception of them, a perception which admittedly had some basis in reality, not only because of individual cases of pro-Soviet activity by Jews, but also because, in the status hierarchies of the various population groups, Jews experienced a relative rise under the Soviet occupation regime. While in the pre-war period they had in practical terms only been second-class citizens, and had in many cases suffered discrimina-tion, they now enjoyed equality and were given access to positions in the adminis-tration or education system that had previously been largely closed to them. At the same time, Poles and Lithuanians forfeited their relatively privileged positions.[60] Through the 'rites of violence' in the pogroms, the improved status of Jews was now revoked by force. Jews were punished for having overstepped the set bound-ary, and were pushed back into the subordinate social space which, from the per-spective of the pogrom perpetrators, was all that they deserved.[61]

The motif of celebrating the 'triumph of the nation' after a phase of defeat, cri-sis, and suffering was probably all the more powerful for the Ukrainians and Lithuanians in the first few days after 22 June 1941, when national governments had been established in Kaunas and Lviv and had declared their claims to inde-pendent states, because it was not yet evident that Berlin would not accede to their aspirations to independence and statehood.[62] This 'rebirth of the nation', cele-brated with excessive violence, was to be of a nation without Jews.

The 'self-cleansing' demanded by the Germans and aspired to by the indige-nous nationalists took on a comprehensive meaning, signifying the 'cleansing' of one's own nation, envisaged as a homogeneous community on its own territory. The violence marked not only revenge for suffering under the year of Soviet rule,

---

[59] Gasparaitis, '"Verrätern wird nur dann vergeben . . ."', 901.

[60] On the situation of the Jews under the Soviet occupation, see the survey of the scholarly debate in K. Struve, 'Geschichte und Gedächtnis: Polen und Juden unter sowjetischer Herrschaft, 1939–1941', *Jahrbuch des Simon-Dubnow-Instituts*, 7 (2008), 459–530.

[61] Roger Petersen explains the pogroms of summer 1941 in Lithuania and eastern Poland as caused by a feeling of resentment at the changes in group status in the period of Soviet occupation: R. D. Petersen, *Understanding Ethnic Violence: Fear, Hatred, and Resentment in Twentieth-Century Eastern Europe* (Cambridge, 2002), 95–136. For an excellent analysis of pogrom violence as public ritual, see W. W. Hagen, 'The Moral Economy of Ethnic Violence: The Pogrom in Lwów, November 1918', in R. C. Blobaum (ed.), *Antisemitism and its Opponents in Modern Poland* (Ithaca, NY, 2005), 124–47.

[62] Grelka, *Die ukrainische Nationalbewegung*, 256–76.

but was also a part of the realization of a national utopia. Jews were not just victimized because they were equated with Bolshevism, but were also victims of efforts to implement the 'purity' of the nation on its own territory.

In contrast with eastern Galicia and Lithuania, in the predominantly Polish areas there were no nationalist organizations collaborating with the Germans. Nonetheless, here too in numerous localities violence flared up against Jews. People well known as nationalists often played a central role.[63] However, most of the pogrom-like excesses in the initial days had a comparatively lower level of violence than later pogroms.[64] Pogroms that cost the lives of many victims—the most bloody were in Radziłów and Jedwabne—occurred relatively late, as part of a wave of violent actions many of which were directly connected with the 'cleansing operations' of the German Security Police.[65] In the Polish areas, the element of national triumph was lacking. Moreover, the local militia units had initially not been integrated into the machinery of the German 'cleansing operations' to the same extent as in Lithuania and the predominantly Ukrainian areas, since the national organizations which functioned as an intermediary authority were not present.

THE CONTEXT OF FOLK CULTURE

There appears to have been a third context for violence. It took effect in the summer of 1941, and was rooted in patterns of folk culture associated with older Christian imagery of the Jews.

Polish folklore studies and cultural anthropology have established the ambivalent concepts that existed about Jews in Polish folk culture and in the vernacular peasant culture of the eastern border regions. Characteristic of peasant culture was a sharp distinction between 'the alien' and 'one's own'. Using the terms *orbis interior* and *orbis exterior*, the cultural anthropologist Ludwik Stomma describes this key dichotomy in the world view of the peasant.[66] In this context, Jews appeared as representatives of the alien, threatening, external world, the *orbis exterior*. Traditionally, they not only had a central mediating function as tradesmen and innkeepers in the sphere of everyday peasant life, but were also believed to possess magical powers and functions of mediation with the world beyond. Jews were predestined for such a role not only as representatives of what was 'foreign' and alien in the everyday world of the peasant, but also by the place they held in Christian mythology, which was seen as a powerful shaping force of the vernacular peasant view of the world. On the one hand, Jews were considered the murderers of Christ.

[63] Żbikowski, *U genezy Jedwabnego*, 228–9.

[64] But apparently one exception was the locality of Szczuczyn, where during a pogrom on 27 June it is possible that more than 300 Jews were murdered: see Żbikowski, 'Pogromy i mordy ludności żydowskiej', 172–8. Edmund Dmitrów suspects that a small mobile unit of the *Einsatzgruppen* from Allenstein was involved: see Dmitrów, 'Oddziały operacyjne', 344.

[65] On the different phases of the wave of pogroms, see Żbikowski, *U genezy Jedwabnego*, 239–41.

[66] L. Stomma, *Antropologia kultury wsi polskiej XIX w.* (Warsaw, 1986).

For that reason, they were deemed damned as a people, and had been dispersed among the nations as their just punishment. On the other, they were also participants in and witnesses of the Passion, and were thus also the living proof of the eternal truth of the Gospel.[67]

In their routine contacts, Jews and Christian peasants maintained a precarious balance that under normal conditions was largely stable. In times of crisis, however, the image of the Jew in folk culture sustained at its core a high potential for violence. Moral obligations towards Jews were not the same as obligations towards members of the *orbis interior*.[68] Plunder, destruction, and violence could be triggered simply if the impression arose that Jews were no longer under the protection of a higher authority.[69]

In times of crisis, Jews as representatives of the *orbis exterior* were viewed in the eyes of the peasant population as the authors of evil. Frequently ignited by the spark of rumours about 'ritual murders', the pogroms were real ritual murders.[70] In the interpretative patterns of folk culture, pogroms might have been able to 'restore the order of the world'. In times in which the *orbis exterior* became a threat and destabilized the balance of the *orbis interior*, aggression was directed towards Jews as representatives of the *orbis exterior*. The terror and local tensions that the interval of Soviet occupation had brought into the local communities were deflected into violence against Jews, and all the more so because Soviet rule, widely interpreted as tantamount to 'Jewish rule', was also associated in folk culture with an overstepping of the traditional boundaries set for Jews. These now had to be restored by violent means. Even when plunder and material motives played a major role in the violence,[71] they only assumed legitimacy by means of this same context of just punishment for the transgression of boundaries.

In such large-scale atrocities as took place in Radziłów and Jedwabne, a further element of the image of the Jews, as moulded by Christian traditions in folk culture, may have been involved. When the Germans attacked the Soviet Union on 22 June 1941, a message began to spread: not only did the Jews no longer enjoy any protection, but they would all be murdered once the Germans arrived.[72] In the

---

[67] Alina Cała sums up this ambivalent place occupied by the Jews in folk culture by noting that they were simultaneously considered 'holy' and 'damned': see A. Cała, *Wizerunek Żyda w polskiej kulturze ludowej* (Warsaw, 1992), 178.

[68] See also J. Tokarska-Bakir, 'Żydzi u Kolberga', *Res Publica Nowa*, 1999, nos. 7–8, pp. 30–8.

[69] Thus, in the spring of 1898 in central Galicia, there was a wave of pogroms, although largely limited to plunder and destruction, after the rumour had spread that for a limited time it was permitted to attack and beat Jews and plunder their inns and shops because they had tried to assassinate the emperor. See F. Golczewski, *Polnisch-jüdische Beziehungen, 1881–1922: Eine Studie zur Geschichte des Antisemitismus in Osteuropa* (Wiesbaden, 1981), 60–84.

[70] M. Horkheimer and T. W. Adorno, *Dialektik der Aufklärung: Philosophische Fragmente* (Frankfurt am Main, 1988), 180; Cała, *Wizerunek Żyda w polskiej kulturze ludowej*, 147–52.

[71] Żbikowski, *U genezy Jedwabnego*, 227–8.

[72] Such rumours were reported from the localities of Wasiłków and Zabłudów: see Żbikowski, 'Pogromy i mordy ludności żydowskiej', 208–9.

interpretative patterns of Christian folk culture, the murder of the Jews could become in a sense part of the cosmic, apocalyptic event through which the divine order that the Jews had violated would be restored. That violation had occurred not only during the period of the Soviet occupation, but in a fundamental way through their role in the Passion of Christ. Punishing the Jews for their transgression of the boundaries set for them in the period of Soviet occupation could reflect to a certain extent the absolute punishment for the absolute crime, the murder of the Son of God. That is how the simpler strata in the Polish population apparently interpreted the Holocaust.[73] Such an interpretation may also have played a role earlier on, during the violence in the summer of 1941.

CONCLUSION

Violence against Jews in the summer of 1941 sprang from various contexts which, in this complex of events, can be seen in a sense as overlapping layers of causation. The concrete significance attributable to the respective contexts varied from locality to locality. In play were, first, the German occupation and the German persecution of the Jews, culminating in the Holocaust; second, the radical nationalisms that had arisen in the region itself, which had their roots in the nineteenth century and had gained momentum especially in the inter-war period; and, third, the images of Jews shaped by Christian traditions and passed on through generations in folk culture.

The element knitting together these different contexts, and orienting them to violence against Jews, was the equating of Jews with the Soviet regime. This phenomenon had a shaping influence on the German perception of the Soviet Union and the communist movement, and was the driving force behind the escalation of German violence against Jews in the first days and weeks of the German–Soviet conflict. Violence emanating from indigenous nationalist circles should likewise be interpreted to a significant extent as a reaction to, and—from the standpoint of the perpetrators—a punishment for, the Jews and their alleged collaboration in the period of communist rule.

Another factor at work in this context was the somewhat strategic calculations of the radical nationalist organizations. They wished to utilize the favourable opportunity afforded by the German invasion in order to press on towards their goal of a homogeneous nation on their own national territory. The pogroms thus served them as a violent instrument for achieving the long-term goal of the 'ethnic cleansing' of their territory with regard to the Jews.

[73] On the basis of field research conducted in villages to the east and south-east of Warsaw in the 1970s and 1980s: see Cała, *Wizerunek Żyda w polskiej kulturze ludowej*, 152. On the possible importance of the image of Jews in folk cultures for the pogroms of summer 1941, see also W. W. Hagen, 'A "Potent, Devilish Mixture" of Motives: Explanatory Strategy and Assignment of Meaning in Jan Gross's *Neighbors*', *Slavic Review*, 61 (2002), 474–5.

However, in the pogroms one might also discern a catalytic element of older origin: the perception of the Jew in local folk culture as the paradigmatic 'foreigner', the 'other'. As such, Jews could then easily be identified with external threats to the peasant world, especially when those threats were manifested in a formation hostile to Christian culture, as in the case of the Bolshevik regime. Also in connection with this element, the motif of punishment of the Jews for ostensibly overstepping the boundaries of the social space permitted to them in the period of Soviet rule played a significant role.

Thus, in the violence that transpired in the summer of 1941, we find a certain overlapping of the basic elements of the image of the Jews prevalent in the Christian majority society, elements which sprang from different times and situations. First there was the biological-racial, Manichaean world view of the Nazis, in which Jews embodied absolute evil, and which ultimately culminated in the utopian project of removing evil from the world by eliminating the Jews. Second, there was the surge of an ever more radical nationalism in eastern Europe, characterized by a more limited mission in relation to Jews and other nationalities, namely to achieve clear predominance and, if possible, a high degree of ethnic homogeneity in the hoped-for national territory. Here Jews were seen mostly as an obstacle and a competitor on the way towards that aim. Finally, there was the image of the Jew as representative of the 'alien' passed down in folk culture and to a great extent shaped by elements of traditional Christian anti-Jewish animus.

Translated from the German by Bill Templer

Nusekh poyln?

Communism, Publishing, and Paths to Polishness among the Jewish Parents of 16 Ujazdowskie Avenue

KAREN AUERBACH

IN JULY 1959, the Marxist philosopher Emil Adler sat down at his desk in Warsaw and addressed a handwritten letter to his only son, Marian, who was approaching his twelfth birthday. As Emil remembered his son's birth in the aftermath of the Holocaust, his thoughts turned to his own childhood in a traditional Jewish home in early twentieth-century Galicia and to the chasm which separated his young son from the vanished world of Emil's pre-war family. Despite the handful of Hebrew grammar books interspersed among the Polish literature and works of political ideology on the family's bookshelves,[1] despite Emil's insistence on retaining his non-Polish-sounding surname and passing it on to his children, his post-war family's distance from the Jewish past had created a blank spot that separated his son Marian and daughter Halina from the way of life which had defined Emil's pre-war childhood.

On Emil's own twelfth birthday nearly half a century earlier, his father had begun to prepare him for the bar mitzvah ceremony. Now, with the traditional Jewish marker of his son Marian's adulthood looming just a year away, Emil began to rethink the spirit in which he and his wife Genia were raising their children, who did not have any understanding of the Jewish traditions which had linked Emil and Genia to their own parents and grandparents.

The words which came to Emil Adler on his son's birthday in Warsaw of 1959 maintained an atheist's rejection of Emil's childhood faith but seek nevertheless to

---

The phrase *nusekh poyln*, which can be translated as 'Polish style', is taken from the title of a chapter in Hersh Smolar's memoir *Oyf der letster pozitsye mit der letster hofenung* (Tel Aviv, 1982). The chapter describes the reaction of the Jewish communal leadership in Poland to the revelations in 1956 of the murder of Soviet Yiddish writers and other persecutions of Soviet Jews.

[1] The Adler family was required to compile a list of all the books they brought with them when they emigrated from Poland in 1968. This list is located in the Adler family papers.

fill in those blank spots. Underlying the letter's sentiments are the ambiguities and ambivalence of a Communist Party member of Jewish background in post-Holocaust Poland, whose longing for his vanished childhood home and murdered family was intertwined with recollections of the traditional Jewish world which he had long since left behind.

From the first sentences of the letter which Emil addressed 'To Marian' on 29 July 1959, the father seeks to connect his son to the memory of Emil's pre-war family. The father initially hesitates, however, to emphasize the specifically Jewish past that eventually emerges as his reason for writing. At first he describes only his 'first meeting' with his son twelve years earlier, in a hospital on Warsaw's right bank, where he was able to pick out the infant Marian from the sea of newborns because 'you were so similar to my father'.

He continues: 'On that day, 29 July, you were a few hours, perhaps a dozen hours, into the first year of your life. Today, 29 July, you have already reached [begun] the thirteenth year.[2] Today you are a few hours, a dozen hours into your thirteenth year.'

Then Emil Adler, a pre-war communist who was a founding editor of Marxist-Leninist literature for the party's post-war publishing house Książka i Wiedza (Book and Knowledge),[3] broaches his main reason for writing. In a four-page letter, he tries to make up for the previous twelve years in which Jewishness had meant for his son Marian only a sign of difference, a vague understanding of where his parents came from, and why they had lost so much in wartime.[4] Emil writes:

13—this number is treated differently by various nations. Some consider it to be an unlucky rite of passage, some—otherwise; in any case, it is not possible to experience one's thirteenth year with indifference. For Jewish children, for example, an interesting date is [that of entering] the thirteenth year of life. For them, in the thirteenth year a new period of life begins. By new, I mean here mature, more serious.

I will describe to you how this was with me. My parents were believing people, believing Jews, and they raised me in the Jewish tradition. According to this tradition, the age of childhood ends with the twelfth year.

For twelve years the father takes upon himself all the sins arising from the behaviour of the child (a son!—a girl, that is another matter), and when the boy reaches his thirteenth year, the father brings a prayer to God and says 'barukh sheptarani', which means 'blessed

[2] In Polish, when an individual reaches his birthday, the expression is literally to 'finish the year'. For example, when Marian turned 12, the expression would have been to 'finish the twelfth year', and therefore begin his thirteenth year. This seems to be the basis for Emil's reference to his son 'reaching the thirteenth year' on his son's twelfth birthday. It is unclear, however, whether Emil's letter on Marian's twelfth birthday is connected to the Polish expression of Marian's 'finishing his twelfth year' and beginning the thirteenth, or to the Jewish custom by which the father sometimes begins preparing the son for the bar mitzvah after he turns 12.

[3] Książka i Wiedza was the name of the publishing house formed by the absorption in 1948 of the Polish Socialist Party's publishing house Wiedza by the Communist Party's publishing house Książka.

[4] This characterization of Marian Adler's childhood understanding of his Jewish background is based on an extensive interview with Marian Adler, Göttingen, 2–3 Dec. 2006.

are you who liberated me', and so he withdraws from responsibility for his son. The boy receives the liturgical vestments,[5] the so-called 'tefillin' (boxes made of leather, containing the basic prayer written on parchment),[6] which he puts on daily from now until the end of his life for the morning prayer, and takes part in fasts (very difficult and rigorous among Jews) and in other rituals. The rituals are like rituals always are; every religion has its own and for as long as they are believed in, they exert influence.

Emil continues with a passage that refers to his own struggle to make his Jewish past relevant to his secular world view, despite his childhood loss of faith and eventual turn to communism. He emphasizes to Marian a humanistic interpretation of Judaism which he judges to be compatible not only with his own atheism and political ideology, but also with the secular nature of his son's upbringing:

This is how it was with me. Then came education, knowledge, and all of these fairy tales and myths were cast off into a corner. But one thing in all of this is worthy of attention, and this is why I have described these things to you. Remember that I experienced my thirteenth birthday very deeply!

I think to myself, dear little son, that you are raised in a secular spirit, without any superstitious formulas. But I also think that from the various traditions, we should keep from the discarded myths that which is true and sensible in them. In this case, I believe that this sensible thing is the feeling of *responsibility*[7] which should accompany a 13-year-old. On those days, when I went through them, when the thirteenth year of life began there was a feeling that a new period was beginning in my life, when I would be responsible for myself. At that time I saw this responsibility, through the eyes of an incomprehending boy, first of all as responsibility towards God. But on a daily basis it meant responsibility for actions concerning people, and in reality, when I was 13 years old, I already felt serious, adult, in short— responsible. You should think about this, reflect on how your greater maturity and responsibility will manifest itself from this moment on. This will be responsibility not towards God, but—significantly more difficult—towards people . . . It is not the Lord God [*Pan Bóg*] who will judge your results, but people.[8]

Despite the nostalgic and philosophic references to the traditional Jewish world of his youth, Emil refers to Marian in closing not only as his son and friend, but also as his 'comrade'.

Forty-seven years later, living in Göttingen in Germany, with his German wife but still longing for Poland, Marian Adler did not recall receiving the letter which his father had written to him as he began his thirteenth year of life. In 2006, a decade after his father's death, Marian still had not looked through the piles of letters, papers, and photographs that his parents had left behind, a hesitancy that he shared with others of his generation who had grown up as neighbours at 16 Ujazdowskie Avenue. Even as an adult, Marian did not realize after reading this letter that his father expressed these sentiments in order to explain the preparations for a bar mitzvah which he would not have.

---

[5] This is a literal translation of the Polish *szaty liturgiczne*.
[6] The explanation here is Adler's, in the original.   [7] This word is underlined in the original.
[8] Adler family papers: letter from Emil Adler to Marian Adler, 29 July 1959.

At age 12, and at age 59, Marian did not have any frame of reference for understanding his father's intentions. Although Marian had been aware of his Jewish identity from early childhood, neither the thoroughly secular home in which he and his sister were raised nor their education in Polish schools provided markers for understanding the substance of that identity, its connection with religious traditions, or the rituals and practices of their parents' pre-war Jewish homes.

This absence created the very barrier against the past that Emil himself had cautioned his wife in 1946 not to erect.[9] For the children's generation, it was a barrier not only against the Jewish substance of their families' history and of their own identities, but also against a full understanding of their parents' lives and world view.

THE JEWISH FAMILIES OF 16 UJAZDOWSKIE AVENUE

Emil Adler, his wife Genia, and their children were among ten Jewish families who were neighbours in an apartment building in Warsaw after the Second World War, at 16 Ujazdowskie Avenue in the city centre. The concentration of ten families of Jewish background, making up nearly half of the residents in a building with just twenty-three apartments, resulted from the clustering of Jewish employees, including Emil Adler, in the Polish Communist Party's post-war publishing house, which had been assigned the building for its use. Employees of other publishing institutions moved into the apartment house after it came under the jurisdiction of an umbrella publishing co-operative.

The involvement of Jewish families at 16 Ujazdowskie Avenue in press and publishing institutions in post-war Poland developed in part from pre-war political and publishing activities. Eight of the nineteen parents of Jewish background at 16 Ujazdowskie Avenue had been Communist Party members before the Second World War; another three became members of the reconstructed party at the end of the war; and one was a member of the communist youth organization in prewar Łódź but did not join the post-war party in Poland. Of the ten families, members of five of them had been involved in illegal publishing and propaganda activities of the pre-war Communist Party of Poland.

The post-war lives of the Jewish parents at 16 Ujazdowskie Avenue are replete with contradictions. The majority of them were internationalists, yet through their publishing work they were immersed in the Polish word and in Polish culture.

---

[9] In July 1946 Emil wrote to his wife Genia about his childhood in Brody: 'Everything else is already passing, but loneliness leads one to dwell on various things: thoughts have come back about my brothers, my parents—categorically, my dear little one, one should not allow oneself to be cut off from such experiences.' Adler's letter went on to describe a vacation his mother had taken him on when he was 4 years old and a photograph that was taken during the trip: 'always, when we looked at this picture, we remembered the events [of the trip], which remain in my memory in all their detail . . . Not even one photo! I am certain that if I went to Brody I would find a few pictures there. I am thinking seriously about a trip there—all the more so because it is necessary to sell my home': Adler family papers: letter from Emil to Genia, Ciechocinek, 24 July 1946, pp. 1–2. It was only in 1968, shortly before the Adlers emigrated from Poland, that Emil made his only post-war trip to his childhood home in Brody.

They were distanced from post-war Jewish institutions, yet they lived in a building where nearly half of their neighbours were of Jewish background. Despite the parents' integration into Polish culture both before and after the Second World War, and despite their internationalism, their association with communism prevented their social integration; one resident of 16 Ujazdowskie Avenue who moved there in the 1970s and whose father was a pre-war communist referred to his parents' social circles as the 'Jewish communist intellectual ghetto'. It was only in the generation of the children that the parents' cultural integration, and in some cases the parents' ideology, led to social integration among the families that remained in Poland after the emigration wave of 1968–70.

Jewish life in Poland after the Holocaust is often depicted as a history of antisemitism and emigration, and these are undoubtedly essential and continuous factors in post-war Polish Jewish life. Yet antisemitism and emigration do not comprise the whole picture. A third element is essential to the narrative, that of integration. Despite the drastically reduced size of the Jewish population after the Holocaust, the early post-war pogroms, and antisemitic politics that prompted periodic waves of Jewish emigration, remnants of Polish Jewry continued to live, work, and educate their children in Poland. The case of the families of 16 Ujazdowskie Avenue underscores how these contradictory forces of integration, on the one hand, and antisemitism and emigration, on the other, coexisted and interacted in Poland after the Holocaust.

From early on in post-war Poland, the stereotype of 'Jewish dominance' in the Polish communist regime significantly affected the Jewish families of 16 Ujazdowskie Avenue. Their marginalization, partly resulting from the marginalization of the Książka i Wiedza publishing house within the party, had begun by the end of the first post-war decade. For the parents who had been party members before the war, the revelations and political upheavals of 1956 were a turning point in both their political disillusionment and the place of the Jewish past within their family lives.

Emil Adler's letter to his son of July 1959, with its ruminations on the Jewish past, hints at the significance of the year 1956 and its aftermath in the post-war paths of a generation of Jews in Poland, particularly the minority who were communists. For the first post-war decade, Emil Adler and other pre-war communists, Jewish and non-Jewish, had placed their faith in a government they expected would realize the utopian political ideals of radical equality and internationalism for which they had been imprisoned in pre-war Poland.

Yet Marian Adler's twelfth birthday came less than three years after a tumultuous period of political upheaval in communist eastern Europe and the Soviet Union, from Moscow to Warsaw to Budapest, which left some pre-war communists struggling with the gap between their ideology and the repressive post-war political reality of Stalinist Poland. Adler was himself a Stalinist, having attended a party school in the Soviet Union in 1950 with other Marxist philosophers, and among his personal papers are newspaper clippings of typically praise-filled poems in Yiddish and Polish about Stalin.[10] For Emil Adler and other Jews who had been communists before the war, the open resurgence of nationalist and antisemitic sentiments in the Polish Communist Party and within some segments of Polish society in the wake of the political events of 1956 intensified their questioning of the possibility of realizing their political ideals. The years immediately following 1956 were a particularly difficult transitional period, when political faith was challenged, social circles and families were disrupted by emigration, and the possibility of full integration into post-war Polish society was called into question.

The events of 1956 and their aftermath exposed the contradictions in the life paths of Polish Jewish communists. Before the Second World War, their internationalist ideology had promised the possibility of becoming full members of modern Europe at a time when the political states established on the embers of the former empires of east-central Europe were increasingly defining themselves according to the principles of ethnic nationalism. In the early years after the Second World War, these individuals placed their hopes in an ideology that they had hoped would prevail over nationalism and would create a new society that could include them as equal members. Jews and non-Jews alike who were building the communist government continued in the first post-war decade to maintain faith in the possibility of transforming the surrounding society. Opposition to the communist government among the Polish masses, anti-Jewish violence in the early aftermath of the Holocaust, and the continued strength of the Catholic Church in post-war Poland were explained as part of the 'reaction' which was expected and predetermined by the historical process. Socialist propaganda and education, communists believed, would allow human nature to transcend these national and religious divisions.[11] The work of the residents at 16 Ujazdowskie Avenue in the party publishing house and other publishing institutions was intended to spread this ideology.

Neither Emil Adler nor the other residents of Jewish background at 16 Ujazdowskie Avenue publicly voiced disillusionment either in 1956 or in the following decade. Among the building's ten Jewish families, only the Sławny family's departure from Poland in 1956 and 1957 can be understood as a clear expression of political disillusionment, although the parents had never been members of the post-war Polish Communist Party.[12]

---

[10] Curriculum vitae and newspaper clippings, Adler family papers.

[11] András Kovács describes a similar viewpoint among the minority of Jews in post-war Hungary who became communists: 'They believed that it [communism] would create a society where there would be no "Jewish problem" and no antisemitism. Joining the Communist party, they thought, would assure them of an integration into society superior even to that which they had attempted to achieve before the war because the Communist programme sought to change not only the life of the Jews but the entire society': A. Kovács, 'Changes in Jewish Identity in Modern Hungary', in J. Webber (ed.), *Jewish Identities in the New Europe* (London, 1994), 155.

[12] Władysław Sławny was a member of the Union of Communist Youth in pre-war Łódź and was a photographer for leftist Polish newspapers in France in the 1930s, but he never joined the post-war Polish Communist Party.

Adler's letter to his son in 1959, however, provides a glimpse of a certain shift in mindset from that of the early post-war years regarding the Jewish past. His reaction to the political upheavals of 1956 included a reconsideration of what he had sacrificed as a Jew for a party and a government that was gradually pushing him and his peers to the margins even then, while playing on nationalist sentiments to gain popular legitimacy. In 1956, the dissonance between the party's propaganda of equality and the continued stigma of one's Jewish background even within the party itself pointed to the system's broader falsification of reality and of the ideals it purported to support. By that year, it was already becoming evident to some Jewish survivors in post-war Poland, both communist and non-communist, that what those of Jewish background had left behind both before and after the Second World War in exchange for full membership in surrounding society had not had the desired effect. It was as if the bargain of Jewish emancipation had been entered into once again, and had not been upheld.

Among those who remained in Poland, the seeds of questioning grew into full bloom in 1967 and 1968, when the party's antisemitic propaganda accusing Jews of disloyalty towards Poland underscored the bankruptcy of the communist political system. Yet the path from political questioning in the mid-1950s to open disillusionment during the 'anti-Zionist' campaign of 1967–8 was not a course set in 1956. In the wake of the political upheavals of October 1956 and their aftermath, eventual denunciations of antisemitism made by Polish intellectuals and Premier Józef Cyrankiewicz nourished the hopes of Jews still seeking to become full members of Polish society. For those assimilating Jews who did not follow the emigration wave to Israel and the West between 1956 and 1960, remaining in Poland meant maintaining faith that the promise of integration would still be fulfilled, even as they were reminded from within and without that their Jewish background shaped their lives in ways that distinguished their families from their non-Jewish neighbours.

THE POLITICAL AND THE PERSONAL BEFORE AND AFTER 1956

From the beginning of the post-war period, Jewish Communist Party members in Poland had been split into two general groups: those who were active on the 'Jewish street', and those who had no formal association with the Jewish political and cultural institutions of People's Poland. Both groups had remained in Poland after the Second World War believing that socialism would eradicate the so-called Jewish problem. Even in the first post-war decade, however, the boundaries between the two groups were always somewhat blurred by overlapping social networks and common pre-war activities.

Both circles grappled with contradictions between their world view and their everyday lives, although the nature of these contradictions differed between them.

On the one hand, communists active on the Jewish street followed the party line in condemning 'Jewish nationalism' and avoiding reference to the Jews as a nation. Yet they emphasized the importance of sustaining Jewish culture, particularly in Yiddish, lamented the weak knowledge of Yiddish among their children, and grappled with the question of intermarriage among their children's generation. For these individuals, an unresolved tension within their world view was the question whether complete absorption into surrounding society, and the implications of this absorption for future generations, would be or was intended to be the long-term result of communist policy towards the Jews.

On the other hand, communists such as those among the Jewish families at 16 Ujazdowskie Avenue who avoided formal association with Jewish institutions saw absorption into surrounding society as an ideal that was integrally connected with their political ideology, even as most of them continued to be isolated in their own social circles from non-Jews. Their lives were characterized by another contradiction: despite their internationalist ideology, communists of Jewish background emphasized the ideal of 'perfect Polish' and usually identified their nationality as Polish on official forms. The identification with Polishness was not only a compromise with the present realities. It can be seen as an unspoken, and contradictory, goal underlying their communist ideology, which developed in the inter-war period when ethnic nationalism and antisemitism narrowed the political options for Jews who sought to become full members of the society in which they lived.

The emigration wave of 1956–60, expressions of antisemitism, and the political upheavals in the second half of the 1950s affected not only Jews who belonged to circles that sought to ensure the continuation of Jewish institutional and cultural life, but also those who had left behind these connections in order to seek full integration into post-war Polish society. Émigrés to Israel after 1956 included communist leaders of provincial branches of the Social-Cultural Association of Jews in Poland (Towarzystwo Społeczno-Kulturalne Żydów w Polsce) as well as communists of Jewish background who had no connections with Jewish institutions.

Furthermore, the boundaries between Jews active on the Jewish street and those cut off from Jewish institutional life became blurred even further among those who remained in Poland, as communists of Jewish background who lost their positions within government institutions and the military found refuge in work co-operatives of the Social-Cultural Association. At the same time, members of both groups were beginning to question their political faith as a result of Khrushchev's speech revealing Stalin's crimes, expressions of antisemitism in Poland after 1956, the Doctors' Plot just before Stalin's death, or a combination of these phenomena.

*

After the political upheavals of October 1956 in Poland, Tola Sławna, who had survived the Second World War in France, packed up her family's belongings from her apartment on the fourth floor of 16 Ujazdowskie Avenue and took the train from Warsaw to Paris with her two sons, Janek and Franek. She refused to return to Poland. That year, her young school-age sons had heard schoolyard taunts and other antisemitic expressions in Poland. One incident that stood out in the memory of the elder Sławny brother, Franek, was an anti-Jewish comment at a May Day rally in 1956. Aside from the Jewish issue, the political repressions which Tola had lived through for six years in Stalinist Poland had convinced her that her family's future belonged in France, rather than in Poland, the country of her birth. Her sons, who had arrived in Warsaw in 1950 speaking only French, now remembered how to speak only Polish upon their return six years later to France, which was the land of their own birth. They now had to relearn their native tongue all over again.[13]

Tola's husband Władysław remained in Poland for another year after his wife and sons left for France. He travelled to the Soviet Union, Yugoslavia, East Germany, and Holland, taking advantage of the freer political atmosphere to photograph everyday life in those countries for the respected Polish photo-weekly *Świat*, where he remained photography editor. In December 1957, however, he received permission to travel to France for a one-year stay.[14] He never returned to Poland.

Of the ten Jewish families that lived at 16 Ujazdowskie Avenue in post-war Warsaw, the Sławnys were the only ones to leave Poland between 1956 and 1960, but all of the families were affected by the waves of Jewish emigration and repatriation in those years. Siblings and cousins of two residents of the building emigrated, while at least one parent in at least seven of the ten families travelled to Israel in 1957 and 1958 to visit relatives whom they had not seen for a decade or more. When Stanisława Kruc and Stefania Fedecka visited the Jewish state in the same period, they brought with them their young children,[15] who had their first contact with an openly Jewish society. Stefan,[16] Fedecka's only child, recalled the embarrassment he felt during his visit to Israel at being the only one among his male cousins who was uncircumcised.[17] At the same time, the wave of repatriation from the Soviet Union connected at least three Jewish families at 16 Ujazdowskie Avenue to the cities and communities of their pre-war lives.

The political upheavals of 1956 and their aftermath impacted each of the families at 16 Ujazdowskie Avenue to varying degrees, resulting in changes on three levels: as Poles living in a society emerging from the repressive Stalinist years; for at least one parent in the majority of the families, as pre-war Communist Party members or sympathizers coming to grips with the reality of the post-war system

[13] Interview with Janek and Franek Sławny, Paris, 13 Mar. 2007.

[14] Archiwum Instytutu Pamięci Narodowej (hereafter AIPN), BU, 1358/5137: 'Władysław Sławny, Akta Osobowe Cudzoziemca', p. 3.

[15] AIPN, BU 1368/633: 'Stanisława Kruc, Akta Osobowe Cudzoziemca', document dated 18 Mar. 1957; and interview with Stefan F., Paris, 15 Mar. 2007.

[16] At his request, I have not used the surname of Stefania Fedecka's son, which he takes from his father.   [17] Interview with Stefan F., Paris, 15 Mar. 2007.

which they had helped to create; and as Jews at a time when resurgent Polish nationalism led to expressions of antisemitism in both the party and some segments of Polish society. On all three levels, the families' Jewish background was an important factor in shaping the ways in which the changes affected them as well as their responses to these developments. It was in 1956 and the years immediately afterwards that the freer political atmosphere in Poland allowed some of the parents at 16 Ujazdowskie Avenue to give greater expression to their Jewish background, to varying degrees as an organic part of their family lives. These expressions took place in the personal sphere even as political disillusionment was growing in several of the parents who were long-time communists and whose Jewish background had contributed to the shaping of their political ideology.

For those residents of 16 Ujazdowskie Avenue who had been communists before the war, the events of 1956 affected them first and foremost as committed political activists who had dedicated both their pre-war lives and the first post-war decade to publishing and propaganda work in support of the Communist Party. Khrushchev's 'secret speech' to the Twentieth Party Congress of the Communist Party of the Soviet Union in February 1956, denouncing the crimes of the Stalinist years, sent shock waves through the staff at Książka i Wiedza. Because the publishing house's editors and directors had privileged access to information from abroad, they read about the revelations early on, while the Polish government was still grappling with the problem of how to respond before publishing news about the Twentieth Party Congress in the Polish newspapers.

Among the Jewish parents from 16 Ujazdowskie Avenue, two, Stefan Bergman and Józef Tyszelman, both founding directors of Książka i Wiedza after the war, were still employed in top posts at the publishing house in 1956. Their post-war neighbour Genia Adler, who had met her husband Emil while working for Książka i Wiedza in 1946 and who had not been a party member before the war, also continued to work at the publishing house as an editor and translator.[18] Barbara H., who was editor-in-chief from 1946 to 1950 but had joined the party only towards the end of the Second World War in Moscow, had moved on to a position as assistant editor at the Polish literary journal *Twórczość* before returning to Książka i Wiedza in October 1958 for five months.[19]

Stefan Bergman and Józef Tyszelman, both pre-war Communist Party members, were particularly involved in Książka i Wiedza's discussions of the political upheavals in 1956. Minutes of meetings of the publishing house's party cell

[18] Another resident of 16 Ujazdowskie Avenue, Ignacy Kruc, was director of the economic department and plenipotentiary for the main governing board of Książka i Wiedza from 3 Nov. 1947 to 31 Oct. 1951. He was then transferred to the Central Office of Publishers (Centralny Urząd Wydawnictw). Kruc began working in the Supreme Office of the Inspectorate (Najwyższa Izba Kontroli) in January 1958 and was working there as senior inspector for state control when he submitted his papers for emigration in August 1969. See the archive of Książka i Wiedza, Warsaw, personnel file of Ignacy Kruc; and AIPN, BU 1368/632.

[19] Archive of Książka i Wiedza, personnel file of Barbara H., unnumbered.

portray the employees' attempts to confront the corrupt political reality which
their ideology had created.

Stefan Bergman later recalled the impact of the revelations of those years. In his
speeches recorded in the minutes of meetings of the party cell at Książka i Wiedza
in 1956 and 1957, he cautiously criticized the political reality of communist Poland
yet expressed his continued commitment to communist ideology. He later recalled, however, that the start of his political disillusionment began earlier, before
the Twentieth Party Congress. He seemed never to lose faith in his political ideology, but concluded that the ideology had not been and could not be realized
through revolution.

One might attribute the gap between his later recollections and the substance of
his speeches in 1956 and 1957 to hindsight. However, it is just as likely that what
he said openly in 1956 and 1957 reflected the caution of an individual who had
spent six years in Stalinist camps before the Second World War, whose wife had
spent nearly a decade in those camps, and who had lost a sister and friends to the
Stalinist purges. He understood the danger of criticism during periods of political
change and knew well how quickly political winds could change. Both the indirect
references in the minutes and correspondence to strong criticism of the political
situation in the Soviet Union and Poland by Książka i Wiedza editors at the party
cell meeting on 22 March 1956, and Bergman's later reflections, indicate that his
disillusionment began before the events of that year. When he was asked in an
interview in 1992 at what point he began to 'come to his senses', he replied: 'Not
long before the Twentieth Congress, in the years 1954–5. Personally I did not
belong to the pioneers of the new currents; however, even though the entire pan-
theon of young academics in Poland took to criticizing our reality, I did not take
part in this, but I experienced a lot and I contemplated.' In that interview,
Bergman recalled that immediately after the Second World War, despite his family's suffering as a result of his and his wife's imprisonment in the Stalinist camps,
'I still considered myself fundamentally a communist'. About his dedication to the
communist movement for almost all of his adult life, Bergman said:

I did not regret it . . . after all, we believed that we were fighting for the realization of the
best desires of humanity and that our road was the most just. The transformation of that
which was called communism into something completely the opposite, into totalitarianism,
and even into one of the worst incarnations of totalitarianism—this was a process, and those
like me believed for many years that these were only temporary 'distortions'.[20]

---

[20] Interview with Stefan Bergman by Borys Weil for Deutsche Welle radio, 17 Aug. 1992.
Published in translation from Russian by Bergman's nephew Szymon Rudnicki and daughter Zosia
Zarębska in *Kwartalnik Historii Żydów*, Sept. 2004, no. 3 (211), 414.

FAMILY LIFE, GENERATIONS, AND THE JEWISH PAST AT 16 UJAZDOWSKIE AVENUE

In 1959, after the political upheavals began in Poland, Stefan Bergman's ageing mother died. Paulina Bergman, born Pesia, was buried in the cemetery at Powązki, which had been transformed after the Second World War from a tsarist-era military burial ground into a non-denominational cemetery where many communist dignitaries were buried. The simple stone placed on her grave read, in Polish: 'Mother. Grandmother. Comrade.'

The absence of Jewish ritual at the burial was typical of life-cycle events among the Jewish families at 16 Ujazdowskie Avenue in post-war Warsaw. None of the children in the families recalled in their childhood or teenage years in Warsaw any weddings, funerals, or births characterized by Jewish customs. Nor did they report any Jewish holidays celebrated in the home, even in a secular manner. Even in the Bergman-Rudnicka family, where Jewishness was more openly expressed than among their neighbours, domestic life was marked mainly by the absence of rituals rooted in the past. In the Bergman and the Tyszelman families, no second-generation member recalled their parents sitting shivah, reciting Kaddish, or lighting *yortsayt* candles on the anniversary of the deaths of their grandmothers, who were the only surviving grandparents among the Jewish families at 16 Ujazdowskie Avenue. None of the second-generation members of any of the families report visiting cemeteries on All Saints' Day as children. Aside from the Bergman and Tyszelman families, such rituals would have been difficult to observe, since there were few graves of parents and siblings to visit, and the dates to commemorate the anniversary of those murdered during the Holocaust were mostly unknown. The absence of graves as a result of the anonymity of wartime deaths in itself signified a difference between them and most of their non-Jewish neighbours.

Among the Jewish families at 16 Ujazdowskie Avenue, therefore, life-cycle events were characteristically different from those of most other Polish families not because of the presence of Jewish ritual, but because of the very absence of ritual. Among most other Poles, in contrast, despite the secularization of everyday life and culture which the communist system sought to impose on Polish society, politics had not erased the influence of Catholic identity, and religious elements continued to shape family life even in secular families. Name days, connected with Catholic saints, were celebrated more often than birthdays, and individuals continued to visit graves on All Saints' Day and Easter Sunday. Extended families, regardless of religious observance, still gathered at Christmas and Easter.

To be sure, certain aspects of integration in pre-war Poland were present among Polonized Jewish families in the post-war period as well. As in pre-war Poland, many of the Polonized Jewish families at 16 Ujazdowskie Avenue and in other homes of Jewish communist families had Christmas trees for their children, although sometimes with a red star at the top. Many of the families gathered during *wigilia*, Christmas Eve dinner, with their few surviving relatives or with close friends, also of Jewish background.

The more ideological families at 16 Ujazdowskie Avenue also created new family rituals through the celebration of political holidays. Among the seven families in the building in which at least one parent was an ideological communist, the parents were connected by a shared political faith that replaced religious rituals of family life. May Day became an annual holiday celebrated communally, at least in the first post-war decade. Photographs from the 1950s, for example, show the Adler and Bergman families attending the May Day parades together with other employees from Książka i Wiedza.[21] The shared bonds were first and foremost ideological. Neither the Jewish nor the non-Jewish families from the 'front' of 16 Ujazdowskie Avenue had a part in the informal bonds shared by neighbours in the *oficyna*, the back part of the building around the courtyard, many of whom attended the nearby Church of St Aleksander on Plac Trzech Krzyży (Three Crosses Square).[22]

Despite the absence of Jewish rituals associated with life-cycle events and most holidays, however, indications of the families' Jewish background were not entirely absent from their homes, and the Jewish past continued to be present on the margins and under the surface of their parents' post-war lives. In a letter written to her husband Emil just after Christmas 1959, for example, Genia Adler wrote that she and Aleksandra Bergman had attended the Jewish theatre in Warsaw two nights in a row for a performance of the Yiddish classic *Green Fields*,[23] perhaps responding to their longing for their murdered families at a time when most Polish families were celebrating Christmas together. Stefan Bergman, his sister Luba Rudnicka, and their mother Paulina sometimes spoke Yiddish with one another and with Stefan's wife Aleksandra. Just upstairs from them at 16 Ujazdowskie Avenue, Samuel Neftalin sang in Yiddish while shaving, to his wife Nina's dismay,[24] but Nina and her sons nevertheless gave Samuel a Hebrew book for a birthday present when the two boys, Jurek and Piotr, were still young.[25] Easter was not a family occasion for the Jewish families, but both Bernard Kruc and Liliana Tyszelman, as well as other members of their generation of Jewish families who were not residents of 16 Ujazdowskie Avenue, recalled that their parents sometimes had matzah in their homes around that time.[26] Only as adults did Liliana, Bernard, and others of the generation of survivors' children at 16 Ujazdowskie Avenue understand the

---

[21] e.g. photograph located in the Adler family papers.

[22] Interview with Wojciech Chodorowski, Warsaw, 14 Feb. 2007. Chodorowski's family lived in the *oficyna* at 16 Ujazdowskie Avenue before the Second World War, and he and his mother returned to the same apartment immediately after war's end. Chodorowski and his wife were still living there in 2007.　　　[23] Adler family papers: letter from Genia Adler to Emil Adler, 27 Dec. 1959.

[24] Interview with Jurek Neftalin, Warsaw, 14–15 Nov. 2006.

[25] Interview with Piotr Sztuczyński, Warsaw, 10 Nov., 20 Nov., and 24 Nov. 2006.

[26] Telephone interview with Bernard Kruc, 8 July 2007, and interview with Liliana Tyszelman, Warsaw, 1 Dec. 2006.

connection between their parents' peculiar Easter-time ritual of obtaining matzah for the home and the Jewish holiday of Passover.

The transformation of home life among the Jewish families at 16 Ujazdowskie Avenue resulted partly from the ideology of at least one parent in seven of the ten families as well as the secularizing policies of People's Poland. These changes in family life were one aspect of the intrusion of political ideology into private life in post-war Poland, an impact that was strongest among pre-war communists, whose politicization of their private lives before the Second World War was now officially sanctioned and supported by education and government policy. Whereas other families in post-war Poland, both Jewish and non-Jewish, often sought to limit the imposition of politics on their private lives, ideological communists embraced the erosion of barriers between political and private spheres, at least initially. This transformation of family life was even more significant among Jewish communist parents compared with their non-Jewish communist comrades, because of the destruction of extended pre-war families and communities during the Holocaust as well as the stigma associated with Jewish expression in the post-war political conditions.

Throughout the children's early years in the first post-war decade, the blurring of the political and the personal was particularly evident in the strong connections between work and private life, beginning with the very setting of their families' everyday lives. Apartments were sometimes allocated to institutions or government agencies for their employees, as at 16 Ujazdowskie Avenue, so work colleagues became neighbours as well, and the very nature of their relatively privileged material surroundings was often dependent on a parent's political connections.

In highly ideological institutions such as Książka i Wiedza, where parents in five of the ten families at 16 Ujazdowskie Avenue worked for longer or shorter periods in post-war Poland, the personal and the political were even further intertwined. Parents who believed in communist ideology shaped their families' lives according to the tenets of their secular faith. Among Jewish survivors starting life anew, political comrades became both social circle and family in the early post-war period, connections that were often maintained for decades, disrupted only by the waves of emigration of 1956–60 and 1968–70.

The strong connections between personal and political life among the majority of the Jewish families at 16 Ujazdowskie Avenue meant that shifts in political winds affected their home lives to an even greater degree than among other Jewish families in post-war Poland. As individuals of Jewish background, meanwhile, antisemitism during periods of political upheaval underscored the gap between political ideology and reality in a way that affected them more personally than non-Jewish families. The political and the personal were therefore inextricably linked among communist Jewish families when it came to shifts in how both parents and children related to their Jewish background.

In 1956, the parents' generation at 16 Ujazdowskie Avenue was reacting to the political upheavals on both the personal and political levels just as their children, most of them born during or just after the Second World War, were reaching an age when they were beginning to understand and question their surroundings. Their parents' political questioning and the greater openness with which they were able to express themselves in 1956, on Jewish issues among others, coincided with the children beginning to develop their own world views.

Among Jewish families in post-war Warsaw where the parents were pre-war communists, the intrusion of political ideology into the families' homes took place at the same time as the parents were beginning a gradual process of political disillusionment in the 1950s and 1960s. The continued marginalization of their parents as Jews in the decade after 1956 in a political system whose slogans asserted equality regardless of religious or national background undermined the politicized aspects of their home lives and the suppression to greater or lesser degree of their Jewish background. Among communist parents, meanwhile, final proof in 1967 and 1968 of the bankruptcy of a political system to which they had committed much of their adult lives led some of them to return to connections with their Jewish background and with the Jewish institutions of post-war Poland.[27]

'THEY STOLE FROM ME MY HOLY TOPIC': THE 1968 EVENTS AT KSIĄŻKA I WIEDZA

In the same year as the anti-Zionist campaign was reaching its height, 1968, the Polish United Workers' Party (Polska Zjednoczona Partia Robotnicza; PZPR) was marking the fiftieth anniversary of the founding of the Communist Party of Poland. A dispute between Książka i Wiedza and the Jewish Historical Institute (Żydowski Instytut Historyczny; ŻIH) in that year over the publication of materials commemorating Jewish participation in the Communist Party's history underscores the marginalization of Jews in the previous decade in the leadership of the party publishing house.

For more than two years, researchers at the Jewish Historical Institute had been collecting materials for a volume about the role of Jews in both the Communist Party of Poland and the international communist movement. In 1968, however, in a letter sent to the Centre for the History of the Party, to the State Academic Publishing House (Państwowe Wydawnictwo Naukowe), and to other institutions, the director of the Jewish Historical Institute, Artur Eisenbach, complained that Książka i Wiedza had not responded to requests to publish either a series of volumes about Jews in the communist movement or a second manuscript about help

---

[27] At 16 Ujazdowskie Avenue, parents remaining in Poland who became involved in Jewish institutions in the 1970s, 1980s, and 1990s included Stefan Bergman, Józef Tyszelman, Stefania Fedecka, and Salomea Falk. Nina Sztuczyńska and Samuel Neftalin attended vacation retreats organized by the Social-Cultural Association of Jews in Poland outside Warsaw with their grandchildren. Barbara and Janina H. remained completely distanced from Jewish communal life. Aleksandra Bergman never gave up her party membership, which allowed her to maintain access to archives for her research on Belarusian history.

given to Jews by Poles during the Second World War. Furthermore, Eisenbach wrote, the Jewish Historical Institute had been working for several years with the Centre for the History of the Party of the Central Committee of the PZPR to collect documents about the history of the 'revolutionary workers' movement' in Jewish circles in Poland.[28]

The April 1968 letter prompted an angry response three months later from the main governing board of Książka i Wiedza. Stanisław Macheta, acting on behalf of the board, wrote that in 1961 the Jewish Historical Institute had submitted to Juliusz Burgin, president of Książka i Wiedza at that time, a volume of documents about help given to Jews by Poles during the Second World War, but that the current directors of the publishing house did not have documentation as to why the book had not been published.[29] Regarding the volumes about the revolutionary workers' movement among Jews in Poland, Macheta noted that 'the governing board of KiW [Książka i Wiedza] cannot give any clear explanations, since nothing is known about such proposals or manuscripts coming to our publishing house'. Pointing out that Eisenbach had sent his letter of complaint to 'various institutions' but not to Książka i Wiedza itself, Macheta wrote that such behaviour 'provokes sharp opposition, since it does not follow normal procedures and, in the specific post-March situation in Poland, it contains elements of political insinuation'.[30]

The political nature of the dispute must be seen in the context of changes in the leadership of Książka i Wiedza in the first half of the 1960s. In the twelve years after 1956, Jewish residents of 16 Ujazdowskie Avenue had been marginalized within the publishing house as part of a gradual elimination of Jews from leadership positions in certain Polish publishing institutions in the 1960s, culminating in the 1968 anti-Jewish campaign. Stefan Bergman and Józef Tyszelman, both residents of 16 Ujazdowskie Avenue and among the publishing house's founding

---

[28] Archiwum Żydowskiego Instytutu Historycznego, Warsaw (hereafter AŻIH), Sekretariat ŻIH, korespondencja przychodząca i wychodząca za 1968, unnumbered: letter from Artur Eisenbach, 6 Apr. 1968. See also AŻIH, Sekretariat ŻIH, korespondencja przychodząca i wychodząca za 1967, unnumbered: letter from Artur Eisenbach to T. Daniszewski, 1967. Although the letter does not bear an exact date, it refers to a meeting with the Centre for the History of the Party on 14 October 1967.

[29] Burgin, who according to Adler's son was an old friend and distant relative of Emil Adler, was a pre-war communist and, like Bergman and Tyszelman, a founding director of Książka i Wiedza after the war; he was its president until 1963. More than a decade before Macheta's letter, Burgin had written in a 1957 article in *Przegląd Kulturalny* about the wave of Jews emigrating from Poland in that period: 'The exodus is a fact containing a frightful charge against our people's authority, our party, and all of us. The preponderant part of the Jews who remained after the Hitlerite slaughters have reached the conclusion that in the conditions that prevail after twelve years of the people's authority, they are unable to work, breathe, and live.' *Przegląd Kulturalny*, 1957, no. 6.

[30] AŻIH, Sekretariat ŻIH, korespondencja przychodząca i wychodząca za 1968, unnumbered: letter from S. Macheta to Artur Eisenbach, 27 July 1968. A copy of the letter is also located in the Archiwum Akt Nowych, Warsaw (hereafter AAN), KC PZPR, 237/VIII-1110, pp. 45–7. See also AAN, KC PZPR, 237/VIII-1110, p. 44: letter from Stanisław Wroński to Ryszard Paciorkowski, member of the Council of Książka i Wiedza, 28 July 1968.

directors after the war, were removed from their positions of authority in 1963, just as Stanisław Wroński connected with the 'partisan' grouping associated with Mieczysław Moczar within the PZPR, became director of the publishing house.[31] The grouping around Moczar within the party was responsible for increased surveillance of Jews throughout the 1960s, and in 1968 Wroński, still director of Książka i Wiedza, also became a member of the Central Committee of the PZPR. Wroński's ascent to the directorship of Książka i Wiedza was decided at the same meeting at which the removal of Józef Tyszelman and another Jewish colleague from their leadership positions was voted on, although there is no available documentation directly explaining why they lost their posts, and its new leadership might have protected at least one lower-level employee from dismissal.

Another Jewish resident of 16 Ujazdowskie Avenue, Ernest Falk, a pre-war communist from Stanisławów who was a top administrator in the umbrella publishing institution RSW-Prasa, was fired in 1964 following accusations that he and other employees used official cars for private business, a dismissal which he appealed to the courts.[32] The fate of the Jewish residents of 16 Ujazdowskie

---

[31] Josef Banas, in his book on the 1968 events and the subsequent emigration, has this to say about Wroński: 'Wroński, who during the war served with a Soviet guerrilla detachment in Eastern Poland, was later considered to be a liaison man between the Soviet authorities and the "police faction" in Poland. Even after Moczar's disgrace he managed to keep his ministerial post, and though later dismissed for non-political reasons, he is still a member of the party's Central Committee.' (The book was published in 1979.) Banas also notes that, in 1971, Wroński, who was Minister of Culture and Art at the time, co-authored with Maria Zwolakowa a book titled *Polacy — Żydzi, 1939–45*, which was 'designed to provide documentary proof of the assistance rendered by Poles to their persecuted brethren during the years of the German occupation. The authors put the number of Polish Jews who managed to survive the Nazi rule at 500,000. This is probably an exaggerated figure, unless it includes all those who had been deported to Russia—only part of whom managed to return to Poland.' Banas later adds: 'when he gave the inflated figure of Jewish survivors of the Holocaust, he was presumably not aware of the implication of his exaggeration: even if we reduce his estimate, the number of survivors would still run into six figures'. J. Banas, *The Scapegoats: The Exodus of the Remnants of Polish Jewry*, trans. T. Szafar, ed. L. Kochan (London, 1979), 53–4. Jerzy Eisler, in his comprehensive study of the 1968 events, notes that Wroński was among the twelve partisan commanders of the People's Guard (Gwardia Ludowa), including Mieczysław Moczar, who were interviewed for the 1961 book *Ludzie, fakty, refleksje*. Eisler notes, however, that not all of those interviewed were 'Moczar people': J. Eisler, *Polski rok 1968* (Warsaw, 2006), 23. The People's Guard was the communist partisan underground in Poland during the Second World War; communists who spent the war years in Poland had conflicts from the earliest post-war years with those who were in the Soviet Union during the war.

[32] AAN, KC PZPR, VII/21, pp. 488–95, report dated 8 May 1964. The report details accusations against three employees of RSW-Prasa regarding the sale of cars at reduced cost, and accusations against six other employees, including Falk, for using RSW-Prasa cars for private needs. At the time, Falk was a member of the main governing board of RSW-Prasa and director of the Department for Organization and Employment. The report noted that he had been a member of the Communist Party of Poland since 1929, and from 1952 to 1953 was a member of the RSW-Prasa executive and lecturer in party training for the party cell of RSW-Prasa's main governing body. A subsequent report, dated 3 June 1964, noted that Falk and a second employee, Jan Głowacki, were fired immediately and that both had appealed their dismissals to the court. The results of that court appeal are not known. AAN, KC PZPR, VII/21, pp. 496–8.

Avenue in the mid-1960s at publishing institutions they had helped to found in early post-war Poland supports the argument that the 1968 events were part of a longer process of marginalization of Jews, whose beginning can be dated to at least 1956.

*

The fiftieth anniversary of the Communist Party of Poland, taking place as the anti-Jewish campaign was reaching a culmination in 1968, also coincided with the fiftieth anniversary of the Książka i Wiedza publishing house, which saw itself as the continuation of the pre-war Communist Party of Poland's underground press. A commemorative volume issued for the publishing house's anniversary detailed its history and included ten essays of reminiscences, apparently none of them from among the institution's post-war founding editors and directors. The section on the post-war period detailed what Książka i Wiedza had published but did not refer to any individual editors or other employees.[33]

The political turmoil clearly had an impact on the publishing house in 1968. In addition to the dispute with the Jewish Historical Institute and the omissions from its commemorative volume, Książka i Wiedza was mobilized in distributing pamphlets and other publications as part of the anti-Jewish propaganda campaign.[34]

Yet in that same year, a new volume of Polish translations of the works of Marx, Lenin, and Engels named Stefan Bergman as its translator and editor for the first time, which Bergman's elder daughter Zosia took as a sign of support for him among some of the publishing house's employees and as their protest against the anti-Jewish campaign.[35] Furthermore, in the 1968 commemorative volume, the last essay, written by Zygmunt Trawiński, cited a poem that was probably a statement more about 1968 than about the pre-war period which was the focus of the essay. The poem, largely unrelated to the rest of the reminiscence, was written by the pre-war communist Jan Hempel, a board member of the pre-war publishing house Książka. Trawiński's essay, which notes that the poem was sung to the melody of the Polish Christmas carol 'Wśród nocnej ciszy' ('In the stillness of the night'), cited the following excerpt:

> I am a Polish freethinker,
> I know—as the Lord our Saviour taught.
> I would write about Christianity,

---

[33] T. Bujnowska, Z. Słowik, and T. Weintraub (eds.), *Książka i Wiedza: Przeszłość i teraźniejszość, 1918–1968* (Warsaw, 1968). The volume's introductory note from the publishing house is dated November 1968.

[34] AAN, KC PZPR, 237/VIII-1110, pp. 1, 6, 9, 10, 18–21, 26–8.

[35] Interview with Zosia Zarębska, 12 July and 2 Aug. 2004. A letter from Emil Adler to his wife Genia in 1946 referred to the party leadership's decision not to publish either Adler's or Bergman's names in the translations of these works, although Emil did not explain why. Adler family papers: letter from Emil to Genia, 4 June 1946.

> Which arose in a Jewish state,
> I would publish it in a book.
> I would write—I give you my word of honour,
> But Karl Kautsky beat me to it,[36]
> The cursed Germans beat me to it,
> They stole from me my holy topic,
> In their thick volume.[37]

A decade later, when the publishing house issued a slim volume to mark its six-tieth anniversary in 1978, its tone had changed, as signalled in the introductory section, titled 'In the Service of the Nation [*naród*] and the Party', using a word for 'nation' that has an ethnic connotation, rather than *państwo*, which refers more neutrally to the state. The section included the following characterization of the publishing house's history, colouring its communist roots with national goals:

The long-time activity of the publishing house encompasses a period of great historical events, Poland's regaining of independence, the quickened rhythm of political life, and profound crises deciding the future of the nation. It is possible to state with complete certainty that throughout these sixty years—despite obstacles and difficulties, and also at times its own shortcomings and stumblings—the publishing house has accompanied the nation [*naród*], the working class, the party, served with dedication and benefited them. From the moment of independence it has served the nation, spreading as far as possible progressive ideas, the newest political thought and scientific theory about social development. Its publishing and bookselling activity, inspired and directed by the party, made possible the goals most beneficial to the nation and the methods of realizing them, it was active in revolution-izing in the inter-war years, and in People's Poland it was mobilized to rebuild national life. With the printed word it fought for the good of the nation, for creating the best conditions for its development.[38]

*

In June 1968, in the middle of the dispute between the Jewish Historical Institute and Książka i Wiedza, Artur Eisenbach resigned from his short-lived role as direc-tor of the institute in that trying year. Among the specific reasons for his resigna-tion, Eisenbach cited false accusations against the institute about its alleged involvement in a German edition of materials from the Ringelblum archives, pre-sumably of an anti-Polish nature, as Eisenbach had referred to in previous letters; the decision of the professional committee of the PZPR at the Polish Academy of Sciences to suspend Eisenbach's rights as a party member; and the government's removal of materials from the institute's museum and archives to deposit in other institutions. 'In this situation, when I cannot defend ŻIH and the collective of

---

[36] Probably a reference to Kautsky's *Are the Jews a Race?* (New York, 1926), a translation of the sec-ond German edition.

[37] Z. Trawiński, 'Mój jubileusz', in Bujnowska, Słowik, and Weintraub (eds.), *Książka i Wiedza*, 116.   [38] J. Gajewski (ed.), '*Książka i Wiedza*': *Sześćdziesiąt lat działalności* (Warsaw, 1978).

employees against baseless accusations, or protect the institute against the dismemberment and dispersal of the materials it possesses which were collected with such great difficulty, I resign as of today from the position of director as well as from my other functions in ŻIH.'[39]

The following February, an employee of the Polish Ministry of Internal Affairs sent a detailed report to Premier Władysław Gomułka summarizing the emigration wave from Poland in the wake of the March events of 1968. The report estimated the total number of 'individuals of Jewish nationality' employed in government ministries, publishing houses, and other media institutions, and tracked the number of individuals in leading positions who had emigrated in the wake of the March events, from government officials to doctors and engineers, to professors, physicists, writers, and editors.[40]

Among those departing in 1968 were eighty-eight Jews who had held leading positions in publishing, television, and radio. Seven of those emigrants had been employed in the small circles of Yiddish newspapers and publishers, but the vast majority had been top editors and administrators in Polish media institutions.

The emigrants listed among editors and administrators in media institutions included five top employees from a publishing house that had once held a special place within the post-war Polish communist government, Książka i Wiedza. Five individuals had vacated top positions in the publishing house in 1968 in order to leave Poland during the emigration wave: two editors, a historian, a journalist, and an economist. In addition, Mieczysław Orlański, who had spoken out at the Książka i Wiedza party cell meeting in 1956 cited earlier, left Poland in the post-1968 wave, his son, Marek Orleański,[41] having been among the seventy-three students at the University of Warsaw who were arrested on 21 March 1968 in connection with the student protests.[42]

A GERMAN WINDOW ON WARSAW: EMIL ADLER
BEFORE AND AFTER 1968

By 1970, only four of the ten Jewish families who had lived at 16 Ujazdowskie Avenue in post-war Warsaw remained fully in Poland, while two other families were split between Poland and emigration. Three of the five Książka i Wiedza families remained in Warsaw. The Adlers, meanwhile, who had moved to Plac Narutowicza in the early 1950s and had lived there for more than a decade before their emigration from Poland in 1968, left first for Vienna in 1968 before settling

---

[39] AŻIH, Sekretariat ŻIH, korespondencja przychodząca i wychodząca za 1968, unnumbered: letter from Artur Eisenbach to the main governing board of the Jewish Historical Institute, 19 June 1968.

[40] AIPN, MSW II, 4524, pp. 1–308. In the television and radio industry, for example, the report noted that 700 out of 3,500 employees were of 'Jewish nationality'.

[41] The reason for the different spelling of the father's and son's surnames is unclear.

[42] Twelve of the arrested students were the children of employees of Polish press, publishing, and radio institutions.

permanently in Göttingen, where they lived out their lives in a home across the street from the Goethe Institute. Genia, a survivor of Auschwitz, found solace among her young German colleagues in the publishing house where she worked, despite frequent nightmares and depression, while Emil taught at the university and continued to write about Herder. They became lay leaders of the local synagogue, and Emil began reading a passage each day from a small Hebrew Bible.[43]

In post-war Poland, Adler's writings had echoed with the traditions of nineteenth-century German Jewish thought, which clung to the rationalist and humanist ideals of the German Enlightenment even after many Germans themselves had begun to imbue these ideals with Romantic nationalism. Adler grappled in his writings with the relationship between the state and the individual, between religion and state, and between the nation and religion.[44] Just as these preoccupations among German Jewish thinkers had been rooted in the German Jewish experience of a gradual and tumultuous process of emancipation in the nineteenth century, a similar focus by Adler can be seen as rooted in the twentieth-century experiences of Polish Jews, and of European Jews more broadly, in the inter-war period and during the Second World War. And just as 'German Jews probably had stronger ties to nineteenth-century German liberalism than most other segments of the German population, because their legal equality and acceptance in German society depended to a large extent on the success of liberal politics', as Michael Brenner argued about German Jewish thinkers,[45] communists of Jewish background who

[43] Interview with Halina Adler-Bramley, Sharon, Massachusetts, 7 Jan. 2007.

[44] For example, in the section of his *Herder i Oświecenie niemieckie* just preceding the extract that I quote later, Adler writes: 'Divinity humanized does not at all pretend to any kind of lofty isolation in the world. On the contrary, let us recall that it was Herder's and Goethe's triumph to discover yet more evidence of the unity of man with nature and to contribute to the laicization of thought. In the face of anthropocentric tendencies flowing from Christian doctrine and erecting a barrier between man and the rest of nature, the Spinozistic thought that brought God to the world also prompted an examination of man against the background of the general correctness of nature': E. Adler, *Herder i Oświecenie niemieckie* (Warszawa, 1965), 356. In a review article published four years earlier, Adler wrote: 'An interesting stage in the development of Goethe's views on the religious problem is his Strassburg dissertation, not preserved . . . The author [of the book which Adler is reviewing] recalls that Goethe took up in the book the conflict between the state and the Church in the matter of establishing [an official] religious cult in the state. Goethe believed that this activity was the obligation of the state and that clerics should be obedient in this to the state. Despite the fact that this was how matters actually stood . . . it was not desirable for the state to present religion so brutally as being exclusively a matter for the government, with the omission of faith and conscience. So at the moment when a broad attempt was made to accept a practice justified by theory, religion was unmasked as something entirely formal, as a thing of very problematic content. Each ruler could determine the content for himself, and so it was not a generally binding content. It is obvious that such a viewpoint, because of the fact that it separated the public character of religion from the private, content from form, was considered to be anti-religious': E. Adler, 'Spinozyzm a spór o "Prometeusza"', *Studia Filozoficzne*, 25 (1961), 202. The essay is a review of E. Braemer, *Goethes Prometheus und die Grundpositionen des Sturm und Drang* (Weimar, 1959).

[45] M. Brenner, *The Renaissance of Jewish Culture in Weimar Germany* (New Haven, 1996), 38.

remained in Poland after the war had more invested than others in a post-war political system that sought to weaken Polish ethnic nationalism and Catholic religious identity, which were a barrier to the integration of Jews and other minorities into the Polish state, nation, and society.

In 1965, however, while still living in Poland, Adler published a book about Herder and the German Enlightenment in which he argues that Herder's embrace of the 'national idea' does not necessarily exclude faith in universalism. Adler's work was issued that year not by Książka i Wiedza, the publishing house he had helped to found, but by the State Academic Publishing House. The subject that Adler chose to analyse reflects the political questioning of a pre-war communist who was clearly struggling with both the question of Jewish integration and a flagging faith in internationalism. Later, while living in Göttingen, Emil pencilled in an entry 'Jews' in the book's table of contents. He probably made this addition around the time of the fall of communism in Poland in 1989, a year which was written in pencil elsewhere in the book; perhaps Emil hoped to republish the work in an uncensored version in a free Poland. The passage to which the added entry refers describes Herder's analysis of German Jews' struggle for emancipation from the mid-eighteenth century through the nineteenth century. Herder, Adler wrote in the mid-1960s while still living in Poland, argues that a state's treatment of its Jews is a barometer of the country's broader ideals, and that a state that does not find a place for its Jews is discredited in the eyes of all its residents. One can find significance in the fact that, although Emil pencilled 'Jews' into the table of contents only in 1989, the analysis which the entry points to was present even in 1965. In the passage, Adler wrote:

The idea of humanity, despite its universal foundations, does not exclude, but rather establishes the simultaneous development of the national idea, whose foremost proponent in the German Enlightenment . . . was Herder.

An argument in favour of the practical and political role of the idea of humanity is its application to the Jewish problem . . . Herder's final conclusion [in 'Bekehrung der Juden', 1802] is this: for Jews, Palestine should be those countries in which they live and work. 'All laws that treat Jews worse than cattle do not encourage in them the least trust and in this manner every day, every hour, defame them in the eyes of all, are testimony to the unremitting barbarism of this state, which tolerates such laws from barbaric times', writes Herder, not leaving the slightest doubt about what kind of state is first and foremost concerned. The style of debate recalls in a lively way his full polemical passion derived from the Sturm und Drang period. 'Who, when reading the philosophical writings of Spinoza, Mendelssohn, Herz, would arrive at the thought that Jews wrote them?' The community of culture, Herder adds, unites people of all times, countries and nations.

Let us remember that this was written at a time when in Germany edicts discriminatory towards Jews were still in place, and Mendelssohn . . . as a young boy was helpless before the Rosenthal Gate of Berlin (the only one through which Jews were allowed to enter the city), because he did not have money to pay the humiliating Jewish tax.[46]

[46] Adler, *Herder i Oświecenie niemieckie*, 356–7.

Although the book addresses nineteenth-century Germany, Adler might have been writing indirectly about the national idea both in twentieth-century Poland and in Jewish thought more broadly. When read in light of his letter to his son on Marian's twelfth birthday six years earlier, the passage can be seen as reflecting Adler's own personal struggle to integrate his identification with his Jewish past into his political faith in universalism and sense of belonging to Poland at a time when Jews in post-war Poland were already feeling alienated by their increasing marginalization. In Adler's work about Herder and in his other writings from the 1960s, one can catch a glimpse of the various stages of his thought: both the figurative *heder* boy reading Spinoza for the first time, beginning to question his childhood faith; and a disillusioned Marxist who had placed his faith in man, only to be disappointed.[47]

[47] See e.g. Adler's 'Spinozyzm a spór o "Prometeusza"', which includes the following passage: 'It might seem strange that precisely the philosophy of Spinoza was for Herder (and for Goethe) a source of such deep humanistic inspiration, because such direct conclusions did not arise from Spinoza's system. Not only opponents of the thinker, but also his adherents saw this. Heine, responding to the accusation of atheism, which ". . . only stupidity and envy could attribute to the science of Spinoza", added, "Rather than saying that Spinoza renounces God, it would be possible to say that he renounces man"': Adler, 'Spinozyzm a spór o "Prometeusza"', 202.

Changing Images of 'the Jews' in Polish Literature and Culture 1980–2000

DOROTA GLOWACKA

I have never felt here other than like a stranger.

W.J.[1]

Strangeness and proximity are my destiny.

BOŻENA KEFF[2]

'POLAND: WHAT HAVE I TO DO WITH THEE?'[3]

IN *Poland's Threatening Other*,[4] Joanna Michlic argues that representations of Jews have played a central, though mostly negative, role in the construction of the Polish national narrative. Having emerged at the end of the nineteenth century around a heroic, martyrological ideal, that narrative was strengthened by the exclusion of the Jewish other, who was perceived as a threat to national unity and security. Polish national myth, focused on the struggle for liberation from the yoke of the foreign oppressor, has always depended on the antisemitic topos to forge a sense of cultural, linguistic, and historical cohesion.

It is unsurprising that a similar idiom of the Jewish menace has resurfaced in post-communist Poland, and that it has been instrumentalized to help redefine the country's national identity against global capital, the European Union, shifting political alliances, and the influx of 'Western' values and cultural ideals. There is no doubt that, since 1989, Poland has embarked on the process of democratization, accelerated by its accession to the European Union in 2004. At the same time, a deeply conservative Catholic faction has continued to shape public opinion, affecting a wide spectrum of political and social phenomena, from electoral outcomes

---

[1] From a conversation with a Polish Jew and Holocaust survivor, Poznań, summer 2008.

[2] B. Keff, *Utwór o Matce i Ojczyźnie* (Kraków, 2008), 72.

[3] The title of this section is an allusion to R. F. Scharf's book *Poland, What Have I to Do with Thee . . .: Essays without Prejudice* (London, 1997).

[4] J. B. Michlic, *Poland's Threatening Other: The Image of the Jew from 1880 to the Present* (Lincoln, Nebr., 2006).

and allocation of public funds, to debates about high-school curricula and places of commemoration. With astonishing predictability, conservative agendas have been coupled with negative representations of Jews. As social anthropologist Joanna Tokarska-Bakir asserts, 'Without a reference to this enemy, the Polish national-Catholic community would either fall apart or become marginalized. It is anti-semitism that maintains the illusion of its existence, unity, and power.'[5] In the absence of an identifiable political oppressor (such as the Soviet evil) in post-communist Poland to legitimize the nation's struggle for liberation, the national narrative has depended on a phantasm of the powerful, threatening other in order to uphold its integrity and cohesiveness. Since negative stereotyping of the Jewish other helps maintain a cohesive body politic, it is often peddled as a form of ardent patriotism.

Although recent polls indicate that Jews are no longer the least-liked ethnic group in Poland,[6] the negative valorization of Jewishness continues to be deeply entrenched in the Polish consciousness. As Leszek Kołakowski remarked, 'the Jew' functions in the Polish language as 'an abstract negative symbol',[7] and the word is still invoked in everyday speech in invective or as a term of abuse, during street brawls, at the marketplace, and in electoral campaigns.

Michlic concludes her book on a hopeful note, observing that the paradigm of the menacing Jewish other has been gradually losing its currency in the new, post-communist reality. The recent emergence in Poland of positive valuations of Jewishness has coincided with the proliferation of interest in Jewish topics, as reflected in scholarship, literature, and cultural events, while the vanished Jewish world has become symbolic of the Polish national narrative's lost or forgotten difference.[8] These efforts to overcome historical amnesia are especially poignant when they bear upon the subject of the Holocaust, including the difficult issue of Polish complicity in the suffering of Polish Jews. It is likely that fascination with the forgotten Jewish other is a positive indication that Poles are beginning to engage more seriously in the work of mourning and to overcome what Anna Zeidler-Janiszewska describes as 'the dysfunction of Polish collective memory in the face of the truth about the Holocaust'.[9] In that case, is the openness to the

---

[5] J. Tokarska-Bakir, *Legendy o krwi: Antropologia przesądu* (Warsaw, 2008), 50–1.

[6] According to the recent study *Sympatia i niechęć do innych narodów* (Warsaw, 2007), conducted by the Centrum Badania Opinii Społecznej, the antipathy towards Jews in Poland has been surpassed by negative attitudes towards Turks, Romanians, the Roma, and Arabs. See <http://www.cbos.pl/SPISKOM.POL/2007/K_144_07.PDF>, accessed 20 Aug. 2010.

[7] Quoted in Tokarska-Bakir, *Legendy o krwi*, 43.

[8] D. Krawczyńska and G. Wołowiec argue that the recognition of the inadequacy of the monolithic national narrative has been one of the landmarks in recent cultural debates in Poland. See D. Krawczyńska and G. Wołowiec, 'Fazy i sposoby pisania o Zagładzie', in A. Brodzka-Wald, D. Krawczyńska, and J. Leociak (eds.), *Literatura Polska wobec Zagłady* (Warsaw, 2000), 27.

[9] A. Zeidler-Janiszewska, foreword to ead. (ed.), *Memory of the Shoah: Contemporary Representations* (= *Kultura Współczesna: Teoria, interpretacja, praktyka*, 38) (2003), 7–9.

excluded, often dark pages of history indicative of a gradual transformation of the Polish national narrative? Or is the interest in Jewishness only a symptom of historical and cultural nostalgia, of a superficial 'settling the scores' that does not lead to a change in the status quo? Further, if a new Polish national narrative is indeed emerging, is it going to be receptive to a larger question of difference and, as such, open to a vision of a pluralistic, multi-ethnic Poland?

In this study, I engage with these questions through the lens of literature, which has recently emerged in Poland as a powerful vehicle for remembering Polish Jews. Not only does this literature reflect important political and cultural changes, but it has also been an influential factor in shaping attitudes towards Jews, thus contributing to social, cultural, and political transformations in Poland. I shall discuss several works by Polish authors of Jewish origin, whose sense of identity has been defined by their Jewish heritage and family legacy of the Holocaust. I shall then juxtapose these self-portraits of Polish Jews with some recent works by non-Jewish Polish writers. Do these perceptions, on what still appear to be two sides of the divide along the axis of ethnic belonging, converge and speak to each other, or is there a discrepancy between them that needs to be accounted for?[10]

This starting point is justified if we consider that one of the most frequently noted characteristics of Polish literature that has commemorated the tragedy of Polish Jewry during the Holocaust is a rift between the voices of Jewish victims and those of empathetic Polish witnesses. As the late Jan Błoński observed, owing to the difference of perspectives, caused by the incommensurability of wartime experiences between the two groups, 'Polish literature speaks, from cruel necessity, in two voices'.[11] This *dwugłos* (double voice) could already be painfully heard in works created during the war. As Władysław Szlengel, the poet of the Warsaw ghetto, wrote shortly before his death in April 1943, 'Your death and our death | are two different deaths.'[12] Throughout the post-war decades, this doubling was tragically amplified by what has been frequently referred to as the 'competition of martyrologies' between Jewish and Polish victims of the Nazi regime. As a result, the vast majority of Polish war literature did not even mention the Jewish fate, which was consistent with the communist campaign of 'organized forgetting'. On the other hand, some literary testimonies to Jewish suffering by sympathetic Polish witnesses emerged in literature even during the war, including Jan Karski's diary *Story of a Secret State* (in which he described his visits to the Warsaw ghetto and to one of the Nazi camps), Czesław Miłosz's emblematic poem 'Campo di Fiori',

---

[10] I realize that this division may appear problematic, even unhelpful, in the eyes of those who would like to move beyond such classifications, and who argue that, as long as these authors 'bear witness' it does not and should not matter whether they are descendants of Holocaust survivors: we are now equally heirs to the memory of the Holocaust. I find the distinction relevant, however, since, for the most part, contemporary Polish writers of Jewish descent have been reluctant to abandon these identity-based categorizations.

[11] Quoted in Krawczyńska and Wołowiec, 'Fazy i sposoby pisania o Zagładzie', 14.

[12] W. Szlengel, *Co czytałem umarłym: Wiersze getta warszawskiego* (Warsaw, 1979), 105.

Jerzy Andrzejewski's novella *Wielki Tydzień* (about the Warsaw ghetto uprising), and Zofia Nałkowska's reflections on the Nazi atrocities entitled *Medaliony*.[13]

It is significant that, in contrast to earlier accounts of survival in Nazi concentration camps, the books about the Holocaust that have recently drawn the most attention in Poland speak of survival on the 'Aryan side', such as memoirs by Władysław Szpilman, Joanna Wiszniewicz, Michał Głowiński, Kurt Lewin, and Maria Szelestowska.[14] This includes a belated interest in Israeli writer Ida Fink's short stories, which received only a lukewarm reception in Poland when they first appeared in print in 1987.[15] All these literary autobiographies focus on the intertwining of Polish and Jewish fates, and although they do not disguise the hostility and distrust between Christian Poles and Jews, they also underscore the courage of righteous Poles who helped their authors remain alive.[16] The popularity in Poland of Holocaust literature that focuses on survival on the 'Aryan side' must be attributed to more than the box-office success of Roman Polanski's film version of Szpilman's memoir. Occurring at a time of social and cultural transformations, this shift of attention towards accounts that focus on the coexistence of Poles and Jews under the Nazi occupation, on the stories of friendship and betrayal, compassion and indifference, indicates a desire to integrate the stories of Jewish survival into the narrative of the Polish struggle against the German invader. The interweaving of Polish and Jewish experiences during the war also resonates with Polish efforts to foreground the history of the Polish rescue of Jews, most recently augmented by the belated international recognition of Irena Sendlerowa.[17] Although divided perceptions of the Jewish other and conflicted memories of the Second World War have not been overcome in the 'new' Poland, a number of recent literary works signal a rapprochement.

Bringing together Jewish and non-Jewish fates has always been the landmark of Hanna Krall's literary reportages, which should be mentioned separately as a sui generis phenomenon in contemporary Polish literature. Krall, most of whose family members perished in Majdanek, also survived the war on the 'Aryan side', although she has been reluctant to relate the story of her own sur-

[13] J. Karski, *Story of a Secret State* (Boston, Mass., 1944), Polish version *Tajne Państwo: Opowieść o polskim podziemiu* (Warsaw, 2004); C. Miłosz, *Poezje zebrane* (Warsaw, 1957); J. Andrzejewski, *Wielki Tydzień* (1945; Warsaw, 1993); and Z. Nałkowska, *Medaliony* (1946; Wrocław, 2003).

[14] W. Szpilman, *Pianista: Warszawskie wspomnienia, 1939–1945* (1946; Kraków, 2001); J. Wiszniewicz, *A jednak czasem miewam sny: Historia pewnej samotności Joannie Wiszniewicz opowiedziana* (Warsaw, 1996); M. Głowiński, *Czarne sezony* (Warsaw, 1998); K. Lewin, *Przeżyłem: Saga Świętego Jura spisana w roku 1946 przez syna rabina Lwowa* (Warsaw, 2006); and M. Szelestowska, *Lubię żyć* (Warsaw, 2000).

[15] I. Fink, *Skrawek czasu* (London, 1987).

[16] The stories of survival on the 'Aryan side' have been recently documented in historical and sociological studies, such as M. Melchior, *Zagłada a tożsamość: Polscy Żydzi ocaleni 'na aryjskich papierach'* (Warsaw, 2004), and G. S. Paulsson, *Secret City: The Hidden Jews of Warsaw, 1940–1945* (New Haven, 2002).

[17] Irena Sendlerowa is credited with saving more than 2,200 Jewish children. See A. Mieszkowska, *Matka dzieci Holocaustu: Historia Ireny Sendlerowej* (Warsaw, 2005).

vival.[18] Starting in 1977 with a fictionalized interview with Marek Edelman, one of the leaders of the Warsaw ghetto uprising, entitled *Zdążyć przed Panem Bogiem* ('To Steal a March on God'), she has laboured to bring back Polish Jews from the brink of oblivion. By recounting their life stories, culminating in their tragic fate during the Holocaust, Krall forces open dominant Polish narratives of the war, allowing forgotten Jewish voices to come alive.[19] Rather than singling out the tragedy of the extermination of Polish Jews, Krall recounts their fate as inseparable from Polish history and as indelibly etched in familiar Polish landscapes. Krall's writing is thus unique in its attempt to re-invite the Jewish memory back into the cultural and historical space from which it has been expelled—not only by the tragedy of extermination but also by centuries of negative perceptions of Jews in Poland as foreigners and hostile others.

Although Krall's writings merit special attention, I shall focus on texts that belong to what I would like to call the 'mythic genre', even if they vary significantly in terms of thematic scope and the authors' backgrounds (some of these writers are little known, while others are established literary figures; some live in Poland, while others emigrated and now live abroad). All of them, however, draw on the literary conventions of dream, allegory, fable, and myth in order to question received cultural and linguistic norms. By proposing the category of the 'mythic genre', which traverses conventional genres of literature, I hope to capture these writers' quests for innovative forms of expression that break away from the sanctioned ways of talking about biography, autobiography, and history. In order to convey meanings that verge on the inexpressible, they must find new idioms and creative ways of using the Polish language. I shall argue that these novel forms of writing about 'the Jewish other' harbour a positive, transformative potential.

PORTRAITS OF (JEWISH) WRITERS AS YOUNG (POLISH) MEN AND WOMEN[20]

The texts by Polish Jewish writers under consideration here are Roman Gren's *Krajobraz z dzieckiem* ('Landscape with a Child'), Ewa Kuryluk's *Goldi*,[21] and

---

[18] A number of indirect autobiographical references can be found in almost all of Krall's texts, especially in *Sublokatorka* (Kraków, 1985). The novel appeared in English as *The Subtenant: To Outwit God* (Evanston, Ill., 1992).

[19] H. Krall, *Zdążyć przed Panem Bogiem* (Kraków, 1977). Krall's works that document Jewish fates include *Taniec na cudzym weselu* (Warsaw, 1993), *Dowody na istnienie* (Poznań, 1995), *Tam już nie ma żadnej rzeki* (Kraków, 1998), *Wyjątkowo długa linia* (Kraków, 2005), and *Król kier znów na wylocie* (Warsaw, 2006).

[20] This subtitle is a reference to James Joyce's Bildungsroman *A Portrait of the Artist as a Young Man*. I am alluding here to the themes of self-discovery and self-transformation, which were coupled in Joyce's novel with inventive narrative techniques.

[21] R. Gren, *Krajobraz z dzieckiem* (Warsaw, 1996); E. Kuryluk, *Goldi: Apoteoza zwierzaczkowatości* (Warsaw, 2005).

Bożena Keff's *Utwór o Matce i Ojczyźnie* ('A Poem about the Mother and the Fatherland'). All written by children of survivors, they can be interpreted as the second-generation survivors' response to the new political climate in post-communist Poland. A complex problematic of identity formation traverses these accounts as the authors struggle to plait together often incommensurate strains of Polish and Jewish cultural identities. Similar to the accounts by first-generation survivors, these texts are permeated with an affective ambivalence of love and emotional attachment, and hate and fear with respect to Poland and ethnic Poles.[22] Unlike some second-generation authors who have written more traditional memoirs,[23] the three authors discussed here lend a poetic and allegorical dimension to their exploration of the questions of belonging and identity.

Roman Gren left Poland with his parents in 1968, as part of the so-called March emigration. His novel *Landscape with a Child* offers a glimpse into the reality of growing up as a child of Holocaust survivors, from the viewpoint of a young boy who was shielded by his parents from knowledge of his Jewish roots. The dream-like form of the account allows the author to convey the atmosphere of childhood fears and confused memories. As Gren explains, he first felt the urge to tell his story when, as an adult living in France, he had a dream about his time as a Polish boy scout, in which he was terrified to see Polish eagles fly off the buttons of his beloved scout uniform. In the novel, Gren describes a household pervaded with a sense of mystery and secrecy, announced in the opening scene by the arrival of a parcel with Jaffa oranges, the origin of which the parents refuse to disclose. Any references to the past and to certain places, such as the inscription 'Jerusalem' on a key-chain, cause panic, especially in his mother, 'behind whom stood a terrifying, unrevealed nightmare'.[24] The boy senses that his family is 'different': in his home, even the Christmas tree seems 'threatened and insecure, while it is so stable and safe in their [Christian] houses',[25] and the walls are not adorned with the pictures of Jesus and the saints which, in the homes of his Catholic friends, impose order and security. The boy's apartment exudes an aura of unreality and rootlessness, and even the words exchanged by family members sound as if they were unhinged from the objects they refer to: 'Everything was told in a half-whisper, and strangely accented words barely held on to the things they were describing.'[26] The sense of mystery and unreality, and the child protagonist's dream-like escapades, evoke the atmosphere of Bruno Schulz's *Sklepy cynamonowe* ('Cinnamon Shops'), possibly as a homage to the memory of this best-known Polish Jewish writer, tragically murdered in 1942.[27]

Despite the secrecy, the good neighbours 'know': the boy is taunted by his playmates, who say that it was Jews like him who killed Jesus. In an attempt to fit in, he

---

[22] For fascinating reflections on this ambiguity, see also S. Krajewski, *Poland and the Jews: Reflections of a Polish Polish Jew* (Kraków, 2005), and Scharf, *Poland, What Have I to Do with Thee . . .*

[23] See e.g. A. Tuszyńska, *Rodzinna historia lęku* (Kraków, 2005), and H. Dasko, *Dworzec Gdański: Historia niedokończona* (Kraków, 2008).   [24] Gren, *Krajobraz z dzieckiem*, 28.

[25] Ibid. 21.   [26] Ibid.   [27] B. Schulz, *Sklepy cynamonowe* (1933; Warsaw, 1991).

interiorizes antisemitic attitudes and views himself through the eyes of Catholic children, with hidden shame and self-disgust (he pretends to say Catholic prayers and accuses himself of being a 'usurer'). And despite his parents' efforts to protect him from the truth about his origins, the boy discovers it when he finds hidden photographs of murdered family members, among which is a picture of a child whose name was Awram and to whom he bears an uncanny resemblance. In 1968, the parents' desperate strategies to assimilate and to conceal their roots (as if they were still living on the 'Aryan side') prove fruitless: his father loses his job, and their Polish neighbours no longer conceal their hostility (a woman selling newspapers in a little kiosk refuses to renew the boy's magazine subscription, and a beggar in front of the church spits in his path). Gren ends his account with a scene of the family awaiting their imminent departure from Poland: 'We are leaving!'

Against the background of this traumatic displacement, Gren searches for the meaning of the term 'Polish Jew', even if he never mentions this expression, as if it were forbidden, unpleasant, or too painful to evoke. Young Gren's yearning for Polishness, for a family genealogy that would let him situate his sad little life within the trajectory of national heroes and patriotic uprisings, is heart-wrenching. For instance, he longs for an uncle who is an uhlan or a member of the 303 Flying Squadron, and for a father who fought in the 1944 Warsaw Uprising. The little boy's nightmare of being surrounded by hate at the eagerly awaited boy scouts camp and being stripped of the eagles on the buttons of his uniform is a powerful metaphor of a Polish Jew's conflicted self-perception and fractured identity, compounded by an overwhelming affective burden of his unrequited, frustrated love for Poland.

Like Gren's oneiric memoir, Ewa Kuryluk's *Goldi* offers a poetic account of growing up in a household full of secrets. Kuryluk is a well-known artist, art historian, and writer, whose father, Karol, was a prominent Polish intellectual—the editor of the pre-war journal *Sygnały* and then, after the war, of *Odrodzenie* (from which he was fired for political reasons). He was also the president of the State Academic Publishing House (Państwowe Wydawnictwo Naukowe; PWN), the institution directly involved in the scandal, in 1967–8, surrounding the editors' decision to include the entry 'Nazi death camps' (as distinct from 'Nazi concentration camps') in a new edition of the encyclopedia, which contained a reference to the fact that 99 per cent of those who perished there were Jews. Indirectly, then, Kuryluk's memoir adds another chapter to the saga of the PWN editorship and speaks to Henryk Grynberg's *Memorbuch* (2000), in which the writer pays tribute to the former president of PWN, Adam Bromberg, who also fell victim to the antisemitic repressions of the 1960s.[28]

Unknown to Kuryluk, her mother was Jewish, and she survived the war hidden in Lviv by her husband, Kuryluk's father, who later received a posthumous award of Righteous among the Nations. Her mother, a talented pianist, suffered from

---

[28] See H. Grynberg, *Memorbuch* (Warsaw, 2000).

schizophrenia, most likely triggered by the wartime trauma, as did her brother, Piotr, who fell ill after their father's death and spent most of his adult life in a mental institution in Tworki. Kuryluk's reminiscences focus on loving relations between family members, which veil the tragedy as if it were in a soft cocoon, making the pain bearable.[29] In the author's playful phrase, the book is 'an apotheosis of little animals', written in the form of an animal fable, which features hamster Goldi as its protagonist. Throughout the novel, the author engages in an imaginary conversation with her father, who died of a heart attack in 1967, at the time when the placards 'PWN out!' and 'Hands off the Polish nation's suffering!' were a common sight during street demonstrations. It was only after her mother's death in 2001 that Kuryluk found the photographs of her grandparents Paulina and Hirsch Kohany, hidden in one of her mother's shoes, which she had tucked away in a closet. The incomprehensible fragments of history emerge gradually from the shelter of Kuryluk's animal fable, intertwined with revelations about the author's Jewish ancestry, and they loom as barely perceptible yet recognizable traces. For instance, the parents react with shock when little Ewa repeats the word 'Madagascar',[30] overheard in day care, and her brother instinctively panics when, on a walk in the mountains, the family encounters a group of Austrian tourists with an aggressive German shepherd dog.

The warm, moving humour of the account allows Kuryluk to reckon with family ghosts, which are always in cahoots with the demons of Polish history. She is trying to confront the taboo of Jewishness and to pass on some of the stories that her mother could not even bear to remember. As if respectful of her mother's silence and her desire to remain in the closet as a Jew, not once does Kuryluk write the word *Żyd* ('Jew'), although she conveys its pejorative connotations that persist among the family's neighbours and colleagues. Describing her father's rejoinder to an antisemitic innuendo, she comments: '"It does not concern us. After all, we are not . . .". I use the ellipsis because we do not use expletives on Frascati Street.'[31] The exceptions to Kuryluk's good-natured humour are passages in which she condemns the callousness of psychiatrists who were treating her mother and brother,

---

[29] Kuryluk has been accused of sentimentality by some critics (unjustly, in my view). For reviews of Kuryluk's book, see e.g. A. Sabor, 'Kanarkowe niebo: Rodzinne opowieści Ewy Kuryluk', *Tygodnik Powszechny*, 17 July 2005; J. Juryś, 'Torba chomika Goldi', *Zeszyty Literackie*, 13 Sept. 2005; M. Radziwon, 'Goldi, Kuryluk, Ewa', *Gazeta Wyborcza*, 19 Dec. 2004.

[30] 'Madagascar' is an allusion to a pre-war antisemitic slogan 'Żydzi na Madagaskar!' ('Jews to Madagascar!'), coined by the ethno-nationalist National Democracy Party (Endecja) and the National Radical Camp (Obóz Narodowo-Radykalny). It referred to a plan to deport 70,000 Polish Jews, and eventually the entire Jewish population of Poland, to the island of Madagascar in order to establish a Jewish colony there. The plan was the initiative of the French colonial minister Marius Moutet, and it was discussed with the Polish government in 1937. According to the plan, France would cede the island to Poland, and it would become a Polish oversees territory. The 'Madagascar Plan' to deport all the Jews of Europe to the island was later proposed by the Nazi Franz Rademacher in 1940.

[31] Kuryluk, *Goldi*, 67.

and she speaks bitterly of the betrayal by family friends who, after 1967, crossed the street to avoid greeting her.

In 2005, in conjunction with the publication of her book, Kuryluk created an installation entitled *Tabuś* ('Taboo'), which was first exhibited in its entirety during the Jewish Culture Festival in Kraków. 'Tabuś' also makes an appearance in *Goldi*: it is the name of a little marmot from one of her mother's tales, who lives in the mountains, a survivor of an avalanche. Both of the courageous and wise rodents incarnate the family history of perpetual secrecy and alienation, as well as the author's struggle to define who she is vis-à-vis conflicted memory and history. But perhaps hamster Goldi, the only confidant of Kuryluk's father, also bears a family resemblance to the famous mole from Miłosz's poem 'Biedny chrześcijanin patrzy na ghetto' ('A Poor Christian Looks at the Ghetto'). Miłosz's mole toils underground: 'Slowly, boring a tunnel, a guardian mole makes his way | . . . | He touches buried bodies, counts them, pushes on.'[32] The guardian of memory, the mole burrows beneath the parts of history that Poles have consciously remembered and acknowledged. Yet, as the literary critic Jan Błoński pointed out, this buried knowledge causes them to experience 'a sense of guilt, which we do not want to admit'.[33] Like Miłosz's mole, Goldi is an unwitting witness, the role that Kuryluk also assumes as if despite herself, perhaps because her parents refused to do so. She imagines her mother saying: 'Fate appointed me to be a witness to history. But I copped out and did not say a word.'[34] Kuryluk's family legacy is her Jewish difference, which condemned the family to pariah status and cast them out beyond the pale of humanity in post-war Poland. Yet she is also the daughter of a Righteous among the Nations, with a claim to the proudest part of Polish wartime history. Writing at the beginning of the twenty-first century, she is searching for a way to include both of these chapters of Polish history in the same history book.

My last example of a recent Polish Jewish voice, Bożena Keff's *A Poem about the Mother and the Fatherland*, is vastly different in tenor, although, as in the previous two examples, the author is trying to work through emotional investments that both bind her to her 'fatherland' and alienate her from it. Central to this exploration is a reflection on the author's difficult, suffocating relationship with her mother, a Holocaust survivor, whom she calls 'a monster'. Indeed, Keff's text is unprecedented in its emotional assault on the sanctity of her mother's Holocaust experience.[35] The

---

[32] Quoted in J. Błoński, *Biedni Polacy patrzą na getto* (Kraków, 1996), 27. An English translation of the entire poem is at <http://nobelprize.org/nobel_prizes/literature/laureates/1980/milosz-poems -4-e.html>, accessed 23 Sept. 2008.

[33] Błoński, *Biedni Polacy patrzą na getto*, 17.   [34] Kuryluk, *Goldi*, 146.

[35] During the war, Keff's mother escaped from Lviv to the east of Russia. Her entire family was executed in a nearby forest when the Germans entered Lviv. The author's father, also a Holocaust survivor, committed suicide when she was 6 years old. As the author explains in an interview, in her approach to the subject of the Holocaust, she was directly inspired by the graphic novel *Maus*, in which A. Spiegelman offers an unflattering portrayal of his father, a Holocaust survivor. See K. Bielas, 'Nielegalny plik', interview with Bożena Umińska-Keff, *Gazeta Wyborcza*, 27 May 2008, p. 2.

narrator's iconoclastic tone targets a double taboo: the piety of Holocaust memory and the sacredness of the mother figure. In the Polish tradition, the mother has been elevated to a mythic status, and, in the words of Maria Janion, 'The mother and the Fatherland are equally sacred, and they are one and the same.'[36]

Memory of the Holocaust, which is Keff's mother's sole point of reference (as if she were 'belching a corpse'),[37] is an onus that her daughter is unable to bear. The mother, the sole survivor of her family, burdens her daughter with an incessant deluge of memories, in stark contrast to the weighty silences of the parents in *A Landscape with a Child* and *Goldi*. Defying her mother's demand that she become a memorial candle, the protagonist blasphemously screams at her mother: 'You hyena, go f— yourself!'[38] Yet the mother's memory of horror returns to the daughter as a recurrent nightmare. In her dream, she is holding a bloodied, screaming creature: 'perhaps a child . . . it wriggles, it jerks its bloodied tufts of hair'.[39] The creature embodies a bleeding, painful memory that has been bequeathed to her against her will. This is sick, wounded memory, which destroys both the mother and the daughter like a mortal disease, 'a cursed infection'.[40]

The rage and anguish that define the narrator's relationship with her mother are also directed at her 'fatherland'. She is exasperated with 'this dreadful country, this mad antisemitic country!' whose citizens 'do not understand their own history and have no identity . . . The other must be a Jew and hatch schemes in the basement.'[41] The last poem of the volume is a bitter satire entitled 'Pieśń z przychodni lekarskiej' ('Song from the Waiting Room at the Doctor's Surgery'), in which the narrator quotes a litany of antisemitic beliefs, commonly expressed by 'the people': 'If there weren't that many of them, if they didn't rule over us | This country would look different. | Would our pensions be so ridiculous? Would we have unemployment?'[42]

A Poem gives a chilling portrayal of Keff's self-perception as a Polish Jewish woman, intensely alienated from her surroundings on both personal and collective levels: 'It feels strange everywhere, like with your own mother.'[43] Just as her

---

[36] M. Janion and I. Filipiak, 'Zmagania z Matką i Ojczyzną', in Keff, *Utwór o Matce i Ojczyźnie*, 94.

[37] Keff, *Utwór o Matce i Ojczyźnie*, 9.

[38] Ibid. 39. In the Jewish tradition, the anniversary of the death of loved ones is commemorated by lighting small *yortsayt* or 'memorial' candles. The candles burn for twenty-four hours, symbolizing the flame of life and the unity of body and soul. The term 'memorial candles' in reference to the second generation of Holocaust survivors was coined by Dina Wardi, in her book *Memorial Candles: Children of the Holocaust*, trans. Naomi Goldblum (London, 1992). Wardi was one of the first psychoanalysts in Israel to use group therapy in the treatment of children of Holocaust survivors. Wardi writes, 'in most of the survivors' families, one of the children is designated as a "memorial candle" for all the relatives who perished in the Holocaust, and he is given the burden of participating in his parents' emotional world to a much greater extent than are his brothers or sisters' (p. 6). For the second generation, the metaphor of the memorial candle symbolizes both the emotional burden of the parents' memory and hope for the future.   [39] Keff, *Utwór o Matce i Ojczyźnie*, 35.   [40] Ibid. 17.

[41] Ibid. 31–2.   [42] Ibid. 77.

[43] Ibid. 33. The author's conflicted sense of identity has been reflected in the changes to her family

mother's Holocaust narrative leaves the poet 'empty' and excluded from the Jewish experience of suffering, she also feels alienated from the Polish martyrological narrative. In that sense, the two are parallel, as the narrator is stripped of any historical context by which to define her identity. She returns empty-handed from her poetic excursions in search of who she is: over-saturated with the mother's horror stories yet devoid of genealogy and self-knowledge.

While Kuryluk drew on the convention of animal fable in order to blunt the pain of family history, Keff buffers the rawness of her emotions by resorting to the ancient form of Greek theatre, although its pathos is continually undermined by irony and dark, venomous humour. The narrative passages alternate with choir sequences, which express a lament over the emotional and communicational gulf between the two women, as well as between the two genealogies, Polish and Jewish, in which the author has not been able to anchor herself. The myth of Persephone and Demeter is the organizing leitmotif of the narration: Keff–Persephone is condemned to sojourn in the realm of death, always only half alive. Keff also borrows abundantly from other sources: Aztec mythology, the history of slavery in America, and popular culture, thus seeking a universalizing and distancing effect that would temper the impact of harrowing memories. Interestingly, with the exception of one reference to Psalm 137,[44] she never draws on Jewish lore and Judaism or on the Catholic tradition, as if trying to separate herself from any markers of tribal belonging—Jewishness on the one hand and Polishness on the other.

Keff's is a bleak and unnerving reflection, written at the time when the rise of right-wing ideologies in Poland threatened to turn back the clock on democratic gains, including the prospects of Christian–Jewish reconciliation. And yet the mythic character of Persephone, with whom the narrator identifies, is also Kore (and she calls herself Kora, Korusia, or Usia), the goddess of the harvest, hope, and rebirth. Thus, the blasphemous cornucopia that she offers in her poems does not necessarily cancel out the possibility of renewal and a more hopeful future. Although she does not foresee a swift change, in the poem 'Szkic manifestu' ('A Sketch of a Manifesto') she pleads for a world in which differences and otherness will be celebrated rather than hounded down: 'To give oneself, one's history, other species, and the Earth a chance | and to include instead of exclude one another | to multiply the four colours of skin and the two sexes, to abolish otherness.'[45]

The three authors I have presented in this section offer a powerful and disconcerting commentary on the situation and self-perception of Polish Jews, either liv-

---

name. Her father, Henryk Keff, an officer in the Polish army, was forced to change the family name to Umiński in 1947. In the 1980s, however, the author started using the surname Keff to sign her literary works. Some of her other publications appeared under the name Bożena Umińska, e.g. *Postać z cieniem: Portrety Żydówek w polskiej literaturze od końca XIX wieku do 1939 roku* (Warsaw, 2001).

[44] 'I sat on the shores of the Babylon waste | not weeping and not strumming my musical instruments and I did not remember | because what would I remember?': Keff, *Utwór o Matce i Ojczyźnie*, 18.   [45] Ibid. 77.

ing in Poland (as does Keff) or living abroad and returning to the mother country (Gren and Kuryluk). By turning to non-Jewish writers, all of whom can also be situated within the mythic genre, I shall trace the affinities as well as the dissonances between the images of Jews that emerge from these portrayals. I shall consider four recent works within this stream: Paweł Huelle's *Weiser Dawidek*, Maciej Karpiński's *Cud purymowy* ('The Purim Miracle'), Marian Pankowski's *Była Żydówka, nie ma Żydówki* ('There Was a Jewess, There Is No Jewess'), and Mariusz Sieniewicz's *Żydówek nie obsługujemy* ('We Do Not Serve Jewesses Here').[46]

THE MAGICIAN OF OLIWA AND THE (MIRACULOUS) TRANSFORMATION OF THE JEWISH OTHER

Huelle's novel, first published in 1987, was acclaimed as a turning point in the literature of emergent 'new' Poland. Hailed by Polish literary critics as the most important literary event of the 1980s, it was translated into several languages and made into a film. The events described in the novel take place in the summer of 1957, in Oliwa (near Gdańsk), although the narrative also reaches forward, into the early 1980s. The protagonist is a boy about whom no facts can be ascertained: he is said to be Jewish, although he has no parents and lives with a Jewish tailor, possibly his grandfather. Although he was born in 1945, the boy's small stature, large dark eyes, and slightly hunched back conjure a familiar image of a Jewish child who has survived the war in hiding. Weiser appears to be fearful and withdrawn, yet conspicuous in his 'funny' outfits. Thus, the description of Weiser might be said to conform to a stereotypical projection of the physiognomy and general 'look' of the Jewish other. He is also compared to a rare species of butterfly and to the plant *Arnica montana*, both of which have been found in Oliwa outside their natural, mountainous habitat, indicating his outsider status.

At the beginning of the novel, Weiser seems to embody a cliché of Jewish self-effacement, physical weakness, victimization, and cowardice, as verbalized in Weiser's classmates' antisemitic name-calling. Yet, these negative perceptions of the Jewish boy are swiftly struck down in Huelle's novel: all of a sudden, Weiser displays unusual physical prowess and athletic skills when he single-handedly defeats a hoodlum soccer team. The circumstances of this tour de force are telling if we consider that antisemitic graffiti frequently appear in Poland in the context of

---

[46] P. Huelle, *Weiser Dawidek* (Gdańsk, 1987); M. Karpiński, *Cud purymowy; Miss mokrego podkoszulka* (Warsaw, 2004); M. Pankowski, *Była Żydówka, nie ma Żydówki* (Warsaw, 2008); and M. Sieniewicz, *Żydówek nie obsługujemy* (Warsaw, 2005). Other well-known Polish authors who have explored the subject of the Holocaust and the theme of Jewishness in the 'mythic' convention are P. Szewc, in *Zagłada* (Warsaw, 1987) and *Zmierzchy i poranki* (Kraków, 2000), and M. Bieńczyk, in *Tworki* (Warsaw, 1999). For an extensive discussion of these works, see A. Molisak, 'Figures of Memory: Polish Holocaust Literature', in D. Glowacka and J. Zylinska (eds.), *Imaginary Neighbors: Mediating Polish–Jewish Relations after the Holocaust* (Lincoln, Nebr., 2007), 205–22.

soccer turf wars. In the course of the novel, Weiser undergoes a transformation from a social pariah into a character of mythic stature, endowed with the extraordinary powers of a magician: he can tame wild animals, levitate, speak in tongues, step on burning coals, and produce powerful explosions. Being in the company of Weiser, says the narrator, 'made your flesh creep and an electric shock run the length of our bodies'.[47] Weiser becomes the leader of a group of boys (the etymology of his German surname implies wisdom, knowledge, and guidance), who fall under his spell and unconditionally follow his orders. Weiser's magical abilities and charisma are possibly an allusion to the character of Yasha Mazur from Isaac Bashevis Singer's *The Magician of Lublin*, which is the only thread that connects the ephemeral character of Weiser to the reality of Singer's *shtetl*.

For the boys, Weiser brings relief from the boredom of an uneventful summer, made worse by unrelenting heat and a mysterious plague, which has turned their favourite beach into a smelly mess of fish carcasses. At the end of the novel, following his last spectacular explosion, Weiser disappears into a tunnel, never to be found again. Yet, the memory of the Jewish boy has been inscribed in the landscape of Oliwa, indelibly transforming familiar sights. For the narrator, Weiser 'implanted an idea of himself quite imperceptibly',[48] intruding into even the most intimate spheres of his life. Weiser stands for a deep wound of memory, symbolized in a throbbing scar on the adult narrator's heel, where Weiser once shot him with a gun. Indeed, the memory of Weiser is like Achilles' heel: a weakness that will not allow the narrator to reassemble his world according to known co-ordinates. Weiser's visitations in his nightmares, reminiscent of traumatic repetition compulsion, mark the narrator's repeated efforts to work through the loss of his Jewish friend, which in turn symbolizes mourning for the Jews who have left a gaping absence in the Polish post-war landscape. With his life history of communist indoctrination, on the one hand, and the Catholic teaching of contempt for the Jews on the other, the narrator is incapable of verbalizing this experience. The unclaimed past returns, however, even as it remains elusive and incomprehensible.

If we consider *Weiser Dawidek* to present an allegory of the spiritual and ideological wasteland of the post-war communist Poland, the Jewish boy becomes emblematic of the desire for a different order: 'The longing for change was firing up our souls, stifled as they were by deadly boredom. Suddenly we realized that only Weiser could provide us with that change.'[49] Not unlike a magus himself, Huelle transforms the image of the Jew from a figure of abjection into a symbol of positive change. This transformation is shown to depend on the exposure of the self-enclosed community, with its prejudices, small-town habits, and narrow-minded beliefs, to the part of history from which Weiser has come. Although Huelle's novel is oriented towards 'the light at the end of the tunnel' (the tunnel of history and memory in which Weiser has disappeared), the author realizes that a

---

[47] P. Huelle, *Who Was David Weiser?*, trans. A. Lloyd-Jones (London, 1991), 21.
[48] Ibid. 55.   [49] Ibid. 88.

real change in the Polish ways of thinking will take a long time to occur. Perhaps that is why the novel ends in the future tense: the narrator will always be trying to find out who Weiser was, calling to him to 'come out'.[50]

Jerzy Jarzębski recognizes in Weiser a composite of characteristics that make up a positive image of the Polish Jew: wisdom, efficiency, goodness, and a unique sense of humour; such is the 'Jewish genius' that has been exiled from Polish culture yet which continues to haunt it as absence, a nagging lack.[51] Yet a number of critics who have praised Huelle's innovative approach have discussed the book's achievements without a single reference to the writer's use of the symbolic Jew, as if it were simply natural in Polish culture that it is the Jewish other who functions as an emblem of difference.[52] Krzysztof Gajewski even proposes the interpretation of Weiser as a Christ figure; but although his analysis of Huelle's reliance on biblical symbolism is compelling, the critic fails to mention Weiser's Jewish roots and is unreflective about the danger of Christianizing the novel's subtle references to Jewishness.[53] Such contrasts in the novel's interpretative frameworks, despite its uniformly positive reception, indicate significant differences in Polish literary critics' sensitivity to Jewish contexts.

A similar desire for a positive transformation of the closed Polish community animates a novella by Maciej Karpiński, entitled *The Purim Miracle*. Karpiński tells a story of an ordinary Pole, Jan Kochanowski, who lives an average life in one of the 'concrete human anthills' in Łódź.[54] Kochanowski is also possessed with an average Polish urge to blame all his failures on the Jews; in revenge, he stealthily draws a Star of David hanging on a gallows on the wall of the elevator, and is very vocal at demonstrations against the closure of his factory (where placards stating 'We will not give the factory into the hands of the foreigners' and an effigy of deputy prime minister Leszek Balcerowicz with a Star of David are paraded). One day, Kochanowski learns that he has inherited a fortune from a close relative in the United States, who is *not* descended from the most distinguished Polish Renaissance poet but from the Cohen family (Kochanowski's parents, as it turns out, legally changed their family name in 1954). In the course of the story, Kochanowski (albeit initially motivated by greed) transfigures into a Cohen, discovering in the process that his wife is also Jewish, but that she has never dared to reveal her identity in a household 'full of antisemites'. Their son Heniek embraces the new family identity and breaks with his former friends, the fans of the soccer

---

[50] Huelle, *Who Was David Weiser?*, 214.   [51] J. Jarzębski, on the cover of *Weiser Dawidek*.

[52] See e.g. T. Mizerkiewicz, '*Weiser Dawidek* i współczesne doświadczenie mityczne', *Polonistyka*, 1999, no. 1, pp. 18–23, or S. Gromadzki, '*Weiser Dawidek* jako powieść-poszukiwanie czyli o paradoksie książki nienapisanej', *Przegląd Humanistyczny*, 1999, no. 1, pp. 103–20. On the other hand, for an excellent discussion of Weiser as allegory of the Jewish other, see H. Gosk, 'Ja — inny — obcy: *Weiser Dawidek* Pawła Huelle', in M. Dąbrowski and H. Gosk (eds.), *Czytane na nowo: Polska proza XX wieku a współczesne orientacje w badaniach ltierackich* (Warsaw, 2004), 184–92.

[53] K. Gajewski, '*Weiser Dawidek* jako opis doświadczenia religijnego', *Teksty Drugie*, 2004, nos. 1–2, pp. 291–305.   [54] Karpiński, *Cud purymowy*, 6.

club Polonia, with whom he used to chant 'Legia — Żydzi' ('the Legia team are Jews'), and starts dating the daughter of Kochanowski's formerly despised Jewish neighbour, Mr Holzman. The story culminates in the festivities of Purim and Kochanowski's joyous hasidic dance around the table, even though he has just learnt that he is not entitled to the inheritance, after all.

Joanna Zylinska reads this utopian social satire as a parable of the transformation of the Polish exclusionary model of neighbourliness, in which the parameters of one's neighbourhood are secured by eliminating the other, into a space of hospitality, in which one welcomes the other into one's home.[55] In Karpiński's story, such unconditional hospitality is literally grounded in the discovery of a Jew within him, a Jew who has lived in his Polish household all along, albeit unnoticed and perceived only as a menacing void. Embracing the Jew within himself becomes a symbolic healing force: it positively transforms the Kochanowski family, provides an alternative to empty religious rituals, and leads to a more genuine exploration of their spiritual needs. It also paves the way for the new generation—the offspring of the Kochanowski and Holzman families—to form promising alliances based on the acceptance of difference. As Zylinska has noted, the allusion to Jan Kochanowski, the author of the famous *Threnodies* written after the death of his beloved daughter, can be read as an invitation to engage in the work of mourning, even if Karpiński himself is silent about the tragic fate of the Polish Jews.[56]

The elegiac tone is deliberate, however, in a recently published novella by Marian Pankowski, entitled *There Was a Jewess, There Is No Jewess*. Chronologically speaking, the author, who was an inmate of Nazi concentration camps, can be said to belong to an earlier generation than the other writers discussed here. On the other hand, although he has been publishing for decades, it is only in the last few years that his books have gained recognition and critical acclaim in Poland. Pankowski uses a mixture of genres: legend, fairy tale, dramatic re-enactment, and childlike black and white illustrations (by Jakub Julian Ziółkowski) to recount the story of Fajga, the sole survivor from a small Polish town. In Belgium, where the writer emigrated after the war, Pankowski married Regina Fern, who had survived in Warsaw on 'Aryan' papers and later participated in the Warsaw Uprising of 1944. The book is dedicated to her memory, while Fajga's ordeal is loosely based on his wife's experiences. The author's biography was intertwined with the fate of his Jewish neighbours: in interviews, he often speaks of the shock of returning to his home town of Sanok and noticing the gaping absence of Jews. He recites the names of the Jews of Sanok mournfully, wishing to give testimony to their disappearance: 'I can see them bent over our land, in their black frocks, the actors

---

[55] J. Zylinska, '"Who Is My Neighbor?" Ethics under Duress', in Glowacka and Zylinska (eds.), *Imaginary Neighbors*, 276–8.

[56] J. Zylinska, unpublished presentation at the Jewish Book Fair, London, 6 Feb. 2008. A line from Kochanowski's best-known elegy from the *Threnodies* series, 'You have caused terrible absence in this house of mine', is repeated in the novella several times. In the absence of Jewish neighbours in Kochanowski's Warsaw, this apparently casual repetition rings with a note of mourning.

gathered for the last Kaddish . . . I can see . . . Fire is consuming the registry of the inhabitants of the town they have orphaned. Four thousand healthy, living Jews—up in smoke!'[57] Pankowski's sorrowful attention to the tragic fate of Polish Jews is unique among the non-Jewish writers, although, like the other authors discussed here, he also experiments with the mythic genre and with different registers of the Polish language to perform the rites of mourning.

As in his previous books, in which he reckoned with other subjects that had remained closeted in Polish consciousness (homosexuality, paedophilia, dogmatic Roman Catholic religiosity), Pankowski is fearless in his portrayal of antisemitic prejudices, citing popular folk depictions of Jews as impure vermin, devilish snakes, or lascivious cats.[58] These beliefs are revealed through the prism of Fajga's experiences, as throughout the war she was hunted down by both Germans and Poles (including a group of children who set a trap to catch her), although she also recalls the kindly neighbours who saved her life. Pankowski has no illusions that Jews have always been perceived in Poland as strangers and branded with a mark of absolute otherness, which has not been purified 'even by the smoke from the crematoria'.[59] He concludes his recollection with a bitterly ironic declaration on behalf of Poles: 'We, the inhabitants of the European Land of Nowhere, are jealous of your primacy in the martyrology of nations, and this is why we are unable to comprehend the immensity of Jewish suffering.'[60]

A more ambiguous exploration of the self–other dynamic in the politically and emotionally fraught Polish Jewish contexts is the title story from Mariusz Sieniewicz's book *We Do Not Serve Jewesses Here*. In the country where the word *Żyd* is never neutral, where it is always uttered with a certain hesitation or in a lowered voice, and invariably marks and transforms the context in which it is used, such a title is in itself provocative, even transgressive.[61] Unlike Karpiński's good-

---

[57] Pankowski, *Była Żydówka, nie ma Żydówki*, 6–8.

[58] Referring to his disregard for national taboos and his relentless efforts to draw attention to 'certain sick distortions of our national and religious imagination', which, for decades, have made him unpopular both in Poland and in the Polish émigré community, Pankowski refers to himself as 'a Jew' of Polish literature, and recalls being rebuked by prominent literary critic Jan Kott for writing 'against the literary currents'. See J. Zalesiński, 'Myśleć nie na klęczkach', interview with Marian Pankowski, *Dziennik Bałtycki*, 18 Nov. 2008; K. Janowska, 'Marian Pankowski: "W literaturze jestem Żydem"', *Gazeta Wyborcza*, 25 Dec. 2007; G. Janowicz, 'Pan pisze wbrew nurtowi!', *Mrówkojad*, no. 15 (Dec. 2007). In 2008, Pankowski received the prestigious Gdynia Literary Award for his novel *Ostatni zlot aniołów*, while his novel *Rudolf* became a leading text in the burgeoning Polish gay movement.

[59] Pankowski, *Była Żydówka, nie ma Żydówki*, 29.

[60] Ibid. 66. Pankowski borrows the phrase 'the Land of Nowhere' in reference to Poland from Alfred Jarry's *Ubu le roi*.

[61] In interviews and at book promotions, Sieniewicz was often taken to task for his iconoclastic use of the term 'Jewess'. He had to dispel the suspicion, among others, that the intent of the book was antisemitic. For reviews of the book, see e.g. J. Sobolewska, 'Dopaść innego', *Przekrój*, 2005, no. 20, p. 80; M. Larek, 'Tej Pani nie obsługiwałem?!', *Czas Kultury*, 2005, no. 5, pp. 165–7. See also interviews with Sieniewicz, e.g. F. Onichimowski, 'Rozmowa z pisarzem Mariuszem Sieniewiczem', *Gazeta Olsztyńska*, 23 Dec. 2005, and R. Ostaszewski, 'Każdy bywa Żydówką', *Tygodnik Powszechny*, 22 May 2005.

natured satire, Sieniewicz's parable of contemporary Poland is a mordant social critique. Its male narrator is nauseated by the banality of life and tormented by an inner 'dwarf' that has turned him into 'a dead herring of everydayness'.[62] Yearning for change, he immerses himself in a hallucinatory dream sequence, in which, in the most banal of circumstances—while paying for his purchases at a supermarket—he suddenly discovers that he has metamorphosed into a Jewess. At first, he reacts with disbelief: 'Shit, what's this? You—a Jewess? F— shit, impossible! Once again, with repulsion . . . a Star of David on my sleeve! What a piece of crap!'[63] Thus, unexpectedly, the narrator is thrust onto 'the mine of strangeness', which explodes the world as he has always known it. As a 'Jewess', he can find no recourse in his love for Poland, which he initially professes with a paraphrase of a well-known popular patriotic verse: 'But I love her truly! I believe in a Poland we have won with our blood!'[64] The narrator, alias a Jewess, is pelted with food and consumer objects, while the supermarket crowd shouts slogans: 'Shame! Christ-killers! Away with perverts! A woman and her family, not whores and feminisms!'[65] which bring to mind the electoral platform of the ultra-conservative party Liga Polskich Rodzin (League of Polish Families). The protagonist is locked up in a freezer (which is a rather disconcerting, inverted symbol of a crematorium oven), beaten, and raped, and barely escapes summary execution by a nebulous Gestapo/communist special squad. In the end, however, he/she emerges victorious and radiantly transformed by this experience: 'The whip of epochs snaps in two. The supermarket plunges into an abyss.'[66] Untouched by a crowd of skinheads and unmoved by the vicinity of the Lake of the Umpteenth National Uprising, he/she celebrates her regained freedom and her 'difference' at a lesbian orgy. As in Karpiński's story, Sieniewicz's phantasmagoria ends with a festival; albeit surreal, it is indicative of the yearning for collective rituals of purification, marked with a sign of difference: a Jewish holiday, a lesbian orgy . . .

Stripped of the comfort of his identity as it has been forged, in his own words, in the crucible of the Great Consortium of Man and the Great Consortium of Polishness, denuded to his bare life (and quite literally naked), the narrator descends into the depths of otherness at the crossroads of race and gender.[67] Sieniewicz offers a disturbing version of the Hegelian judgement of history: it is always the other that becomes sacrificed on history's slaughter-bench: 'The axe of history, old but robust, is hanging over your head, ready as usual to chop to pieces the uncharred bones of all those aliens.'[68] Terrifying and funny to the point of intense discomfort, the story is a macabre fantasy, in which Franz Kafka (from 'The Metamorphosis') meets Witold Gombrowicz (the famous 'grimace' from *Ferdydurke* is conjoined with the most grotesque gambol of the Polish patriots in

---

[62] Sieniewicz, *Żydówek nie obsługujemy*, 188.

[63] Ibid. 191.   [64] Ibid. 193.   [65] Ibid. 195–6.   [66] Ibid. 227.

[67] In *Postać z cieniem*, Umińska (Keff) draws attention to the persistent feminization of the trope of the Jew as the menacing other.   [68] Sieniewicz, *Żydówek nie obsługujemy*, 198.

Trans-Atlantyk).[69] Sieniewicz's peculiar form of *littérature engagée* pitches the grotesque against the socio-political real, in which right-wing conservatism breeds antisemitism, sexism, xenophobia, and homophobia—all the ancient prejudices, now combined with rapacious consumerism.

Sieniewicz's outrageous allegory can be read as a paradigmatic Pole's confrontation with the Polish narrative's repressed forces, of which its antisemitic topos is the most pronounced psychotic symptom. As in Huelle's novel, in the suffocating atmosphere of commodified patriotism, the topos of the Jewess stands for a possibility of disruption and renewal of the national myth, which, up until now, has been stocked with nothing but calcified values and empty, nostalgic versions of history. Like Keff's idolatrous ode to her monstrous mother, Sieniewicz's 'Postmodernismus macht frei' (in his own chilling phrase) defies taboos, destroys the boundaries of decorum that, six decades after the Holocaust and despite the success of works such as Benigni's film *Life is Beautiful* or Spiegelman's *Maus*, are still not easily overstepped in Poland and cannot be overstepped without the consequences of seriously transforming the dynamic of the entire discourse about the Jewish other. The similarity of acerbic tone and language registers in Keff and Sieniewicz is not coincidental if we consider that both writers are responding to the political reality of the shift to the right under the Kaczyński brothers' conservative government (2005–7), and neither writer gives much reason to be overly optimistic about 'identity politics *à la polonaise*'.[70] Keff does not hesitate to write in her 'Song from the Waiting Room at the Doctor's Surgery', repeating the slogans made popular by the right-wing organization Młodzież Wszechpolska (All-Polish Youth), 'Jews are fags! And Jewesses are dykes! And feminists are jews!'[71] As Agnieszka Graff explains, the association, noted by both writers, between Jewishness and homosexuality (which is still widely perceived in Poland to be a sexual perversion or illness) has recently become an entrenched and commonly accepted cultural code. Both of these recent texts thus make it clear that, in new political contexts, the Jewish other, yet again, functions as the cipher of unwanted difference, and it has been deployed to promote conservative agendas. Generally speaking, the ambience of these works is starkly different from that of the works written only a few years earlier, such as Gren's and Kuryluk's, on the side of Polish Jewish authors, in which the pain of exclusion does not prohibit positive emotional attitudes towards Poland, or Huelle's, Karpiński's, and Pankowski's, which offer idealized and unambiguous images of Jewishness by sympathetic Poles. What these works make clear, however, is that in the new political and social reality, 'different words, different images, different associations, and different forms of collective identity are urgently needed'.[72]

---

[69] F. Kafka, 'The Metamorphosis', in id., *The Complete Stories* (New York, 1971), 89–139; W. Gombrowicz, *Ferdydurke* (Paris, 1969) and *Trans-Atlantyk* (Kraków, 1986).

[70] A. Graff, *Rykoszetem: Rzecz o płci, seksualności i narodzie* (Warsaw, 2008), 141.

[71] Keff, *Utwór o Matce i Ojczyźnie*, 77. The capitalization follows that of the Polish 'Żydzi pedały! I Żydówy lesby, i feministki żydzianki!'   [72] Graff, *Rykoszetem*, 142.

'IN THE CAUSE OF AN OTHER': TOWARDS A NEW POLITICS OF REPRESENTATION

The writers who explore what I have called the 'mythic genre' have been searching for altogether different means of expressing the relation with otherness. They are acutely aware of the need for an alternative language, freed from the burden of antisemitic stereotypes. As Joanna Tokarska-Bakir avers, these stereotypes are inscribed in the fabric of the Polish language in the form of linguistic fossils and dead metaphors, whose forgotten roots reach deeply into the centuries of prejudice.[73] Tokarska-Bakir demonstrates that linguistic acts of negative valuation of the Jewish other occur 'naturally' and are not registered by language users since they stem from sources that may not be consciously grasped and acknowledged. To confirm this with an example from one of the texts discussed above, in *The Purim Miracle*, Heniek (before his transformation into a Jew) cannot explain to his mother why he and his friends yell at the players of Legia, 'Jew, Jew, all of Poland is ashamed of you.' All he can say is that they do it because 'it rhymes'.[74] Even if, on the surface, these hate words seem meaningless to the speakers, the language draws on the wealth of historical tradition and long-established social practices. Thus any change in the entrenched attitudes and habits requires a conscious struggle within the Polish language, the language that has produced the stultifying stereotypes in which the Jewish other has remained trapped. When Keff and Sieniewicz discard political correctness in order to provoke and tear down taboos, they expose the narrow-mindedness and the lethal power of the ossified expressions that have become so deeply ingrained in Polish ways of thinking.

The change called for by Graff requires a radical upheaval in the very fabric of language as well as in narrative patterns, and in this respect the mythic genre harbours more potential than traditional forms of writing. Innovative literary topographies make it possible to forge an alternative place of encounter in which Jews and non-Jews, in Poland and in the Diaspora, can enter into a conversation. For both Jewish and non-Jewish writers, the mythic forms also offer a degree of freedom from personal and national histories and from the confines of national, ethnic, and gender identity categories. Despite the difference in perspectives and life experiences, these writers meet within the Polish language, in the discursive space where they strive to bridge the seemingly intraversable divide that has marked their respective Polish and Jewish historical and cultural memories. They wrestle with the mother tongue and in some cases even abuse it, but at the site of this encounter, they ask that Polish readers of their works, in their turn, assume responsibility for the legacy of harmful representations of Jews in Polish history and culture. Przemysław Czapliński, a representative of a new, progressive generation of scholars, posits that such 'penance of reading' is imperative for Polish memory after the

---

[73] Tokarska-Bakir, *Legendy o krwi*, 47.
[74] Karpiński, *Cud purymowy*, 15: 'Żydzi, Żydzi, cała Polska się was wstydzi.'

Holocaust. In the face of the Polish failure to offer compassion to Jewish victims, assuming collective responsibility through the experience of reading amounts to atoning for the 'crime embedded in the deepest sources of memory'.[75] Engaging in the rituals of reading and reflection forces the readers to re-engage memory along different axes of belonging—multiple rather than exclusionary. The task of literature is to reflect these changes but also, perhaps more importantly, to forge positive re-significations of 'the Jew' in new Polish contexts and to reclaim it from negative and hostile linguistic uses. This is where, against the old, stale language of contempt and hatred, there emerges a way of representing the other in the idiom that entails not merely tolerance of difference but also a recognition of the other's fundamental belonging and contribution to 'my' culture and tradition.

When the protagonist of Sieniewicz's story becomes a Jewess, the narrator comments: 'The stranger got you. You carried him inside for years, and he nourished himself on you, preyed on you, only to show his true face now.'[76] In her book *Strangers to Ourselves*, the French philosopher Julia Kristeva shows that, within the Western paradigm of otherness, the intrusion of the other into the familiar is a source of fear, which turns into rage and hatred against those whom we perceive as strangers.[77] Kristeva enjoins us to embrace the stranger within and, by respecting our own constitutive foreignness, to reconceptualize otherness so that we may welcome strangers in our midst instead of 'hounding' them.[78] In the medium of literature, Sieniewicz and the other writers discussed here engage in a transvaluation of the very conception of otherness. They propose that the other, traditionally conceived as a threat to the integrity of 'the same', be it an individual or a group, must become recognized as constitutive of who we are in the first place. Respect for difference and the acknowledgement of its positive value is then a precondition of respect we have for ourselves and for our own community. In Poland, such a radical shift in the way otherness is construed would lead to a realization that it is not just the Jews who are wounded by negative representations, but that this kind of language also causes irreparable harm to 'us', to the entire Polish community. The encounter with the other that escapes known explanatory frameworks and detonates (not unlike Weiser's explosions) the existing order of things calls for a different sensibility, which does not allow for assimilating otherness to the structures of existing knowledge. Such engagement, which shifts otherness from hostile to positive contexts, also has the effect of evicting us from familiar surroundings, from the comfort of our own home, in order to welcome the other, who, as we now recognize, has always lived in our house.

The transvaluation of otherness, therefore, must not be synonymous with neutralizing particular differences, the Jewish difference in this case. The danger of the innovative mythic genre is that universalizing the Jewish other and exploring it

---

[75] P. Czapliński, 'Recovering the Holocaust', in Zeidler-Janiszewska (ed.), *Memory of the Shoah*, 77.

[76] Sieniewicz, *Żydówek nie obsługujemy*, 192.

[77] J. Kristeva, *Strangers to Ourselves*, trans. L. S. Roudiez (New York, 1991).   [78] Ibid. 191.

as a metaphor for difference in general may dissolve its historical and cultural specificity. It is crucial that the rich history of Polish Jews does not disappear from view even before it truly becomes a part of Polish national history. Sieniewicz is not unaware of this danger when he pokes fun at the commercial exploitation of difference and the commodification of historical contexts.[79] The emerging new conceptions and innovative idioms must remain welded to the physical locations and historical frameworks from which to remember and engage with the Jewish other, both those in the past, and those in the present when we reconstitute the past. Here Kuryluk's descriptions of the family's Warsaw apartment on Frascati Street and Huelle's Oliwa anchor this memory in specific spatio-temporal parameters, in contrast to Sieniewicz's more generic 'supermarket' or Keff's 'waiting room at the doctor's surgery'. If such concrete locations are lacking, the second, third, and ensuing generations of witnesses might be left with nothing but a vague, nostalgic memory of the vanished Jewish other.

With these caveats in mind, it can be argued that innovative literature has a transformative potential not only in the cultural but also in the social and political realms, in so far as it can bring about a radical change in how otherness is conceptualized and expressed. The poet Paul Celan, a Holocaust survivor, wrote that a unique gift, a hope of literature had always been 'to speak in the cause of the *strange* . . . to speak *in the cause of an Other*—who knows, perhaps in the cause of a *wholly Other*'. For Celan, literature is a path on which we travel towards this 'wholly other', so that this distant otherness can become 'a quite near other', a neighbour.[80] The mythic genre is a discursive territory for linguistic and narrative exploration, in which different voices call forth to one another, address each other, and signal the incommunicable experiences of loss, trauma, and betrayal across the chasm of national, cultural, and generational divides. As such, it offers a unique opportunity to open up a space of dialogue and to work towards new cross-cultural configurations.

Although 'the Jewish other' still commonly functions in today's Poland as a cipher of conservative ethno-nationalism, and negative perceptions continue to be deeply entrenched and normalized in the Polish cultural imaginary, one can conclude on a hopeful note nevertheless. Paradoxically, perhaps, in recent years representations of Jews have also acquired opposite, positive connotations and have begun to function as a symbol of democratic hope in the country and of Polish society's opening up to pluralistic, more welcoming forms of being with others in the world. Perhaps because 'the Jew', the perpetual foreigner, has always been the force that disrupts the continuity and cohesiveness of the national myth, 'the Jew' has also become the expression of the desire to open up the boundaries of the

---

[79] For a discussion of cultural nostalgia on the example of the Jewish district of Kazimierz in Kraków, see E. Lehrer, 'Bearing False Witness? "Vicarious" Jewish Identity and the Politics of Affinity', in Głowacka and Zylinska (eds.), *Imaginary Neighbors*, 274–300.

[80] P. Celan, 'The Meridian', in *Selected Poems and Prose of Paul Celan*, trans. J. Felstiner (New York, 2001), 408.

nation, to guide it (like Weiser) towards a future in which the communal 'we' is in constant flux. The fact that, at present, extreme forms of ethno-nationalism and prejudice so conspicuously clash in Poland with new, pluralistic, and positive conceptions of the Jewish other is a sign that the labour of mourning and the hard work of coming to terms with the centuries of hostility and contempt have only just begun.

PART II

New Views

Ogee Arcades in the Synagogue Architecture of Volhynia and Podolia in the Seventeenth and Eighteenth Centuries

SERGEY R. KRAVTSOV

THE SEVENTEENTH CENTURY was a period of transition in style for architecture in the Polish–Lithuanian Commonwealth. Step by step, the remnants of Gothic, Renaissance, and the regional version of Mannerism were replaced by Baroque architectural forms. The new style was imported by monastic orders, initially by the Jesuits, whose churches in Poland took on Italian patterns as early as the end of the sixteenth century. Baroque was massively adopted by monastic builders and guild masons. Nevertheless, Gothic forms survived in the south-eastern borderlands of Volhynia, Ruthenia, and Podolia well into the eighteenth century.[1]

The provincial, multi-ethnic, and multi-religious character of local cities surfaced in the heterogeneity of their sacred building. The builders—mainly Roman Catholics—adjusted architectural means not only to the demands of the dominant Roman Catholic Church, but also to the needs of their Orthodox Christian, Greek Catholic, Armenian, and Jewish Rabbanite and Karaite clients. Owing to the considerable growth of Jewish communities in the first half of the seventeenth century, their striving for a place in the urban landscape resulted in a novel design of synagogue.

In the present chapter, I wish to discuss a particular decorative shape, an ogee arch, in regional architecture.[2] It appears in two diverse arrangements: as an arcade composed of blind ogee arches in parapet and interior walls, and as a decoration of

---

[1] S. R. Kravtsov, 'Gothic Survival in Synagogue Architecture of the 17th and 18th Centuries in Volhynia, Ruthenia and Podolia', *Architectura: Zeitschrift für Geschichte der Baukunst / Journal of the History of Architecture*, 35 (2005), 69–94.

[2] See F. Woodman, 'Ogee', in J. Turner (ed.), *The Dictionary of Art*, 34 vols. (New York, 1996), xxiv. 368. The ogee arch was a common form in early Indian architecture. From India this motif passed into Chinese and Western art, probably through small, portable decorative objects, and was employed freely in Islamic art. It remained a minor decorative device in Europe until the mid-thirteenth century, when it was adopted at San Marco in Venice, as well as in Gothic structures in France. It was in England, however, that the ogee became the most fashionable; from there it spread to Germany, Bohemia, and France. The history of the ogee in Russian architecture extends back to

Catholic church belfries. The parapet wall was a typical element of Mannerist architecture in Poland, also traceable in Jewish sacred building to the Old Synagogue in the Kazimierz suburb of Kraków, dating from 1570, and in a broader architectural context to the parapet walls of fortress buildings. The ogee decoration of belfries was applied to a very limited group of monuments in the region. The ogee arch was rare in Baroque architecture, though popular in Volhynian monuments in the first half of the seventeenth century. Its application and meaning in local context are deserving of special attention, as it crosses the boundaries of religious and ethnic communities.

Monuments bearing ogee arcades from that period are located in a comparatively small area limited to the towns of Lutsk, Olyka, and Klevan.[3] Edifices exhibiting this feature include the Gate Tower of Lutsk Castle (its original ogee arcade was lost in the nineteenth century), an Orthodox church, a town gate, two synagogues, and belfries of Roman Catholic churches. In addition, the motif is found in several later monuments beyond this region of Ukraine.

The oldest monument in this group is probably the Gate Tower of the Upper Castle in Lutsk (Figure 1). It is a brick structure of five tiers, the beginnings of which are quite vaguely dated to the reign of Prince Liubartas of Galicia-Volhynia (died c.1385). The bottom tier of the tower is a Gothic brickwork structure. The uppermost one, which deteriorated and was disassembled in 1890 and was then reconstructed in its allegedly original form in 1970–4, was decorated with a blind ogee arcade. In 1862–3 this arcade was documented by the engineer O. Peske, whose first name is known to us only by its initial (see Figure 2).[4]

This drawing is the only available visual source for the original shape of the top tier; other accessible archival documents are silent about its construction, and archaeological investigation is impossible, since it was dismantled in 1890. The shape of the arcade and crowning battlement visible in Peske's drawing suggests a building date of around 1600. This date is supported by the published catalogue of Ukrainian monuments.[5]

Muscovite monuments of the late fourteenth century. See P. N. Maksimov, 'Rannemoskovskoe zodchestvo', in B. P. Mikhailov (ed.), *Vseobshchaya istoriya arkhitektury*, 2 vols. (Moscow, 1958–63), i. 633. In the nineteenth century some architectural historians suggested that the Russian architecture of that period was influenced by Persia. See A. Choisy, *Histoire de l'architecture*, 2 vols. (Paris, 1899), ii. 61. Another hypothesis points to the forms of Russian wooden architecture as a model for masonry ogee arches. See A. Voyce, 'National Elements in Russian Architecture', *Journal of the Society of Architectural Historians*, 16, no. 2 (1957), 6–16.

[3] Today, Lutsk (Polish Łuck) and Olyka (Polish Ołyka) are located in the Volhynian oblast of the Ukrainian republic, Lutsk being the administrative centre of this oblast, and Klevan (Polish Klewań) is in the Rivne oblast.

[4] B. Kolosok, 'Istoriohrafiya ukriplen' Luts'ka (do 1.09.1939)', *Arkhitekturna spadshchyna Ukrayiny*, 3, pt. 1 (1996), 51, fig. 6. The original drawing is preserved in the Rossiiskii gosudarstvennyi voenno-istoricheskii arkhiv, Moscow.

[5] N. L. Zharikov (ed.), *Pamyatniki gradostroitel'stva i arkhitektury Ukrainskoi SSR*, 4 vols. (Kiev, 1983–6), ii. 49.

Figure 1. Gate Tower, Upper
Castle, Lutsk
Photo by Anton I. Sipos, 2007.
Reproduced with permission

Figure 2. Gate Tower, Upper
Castle, Lutsk
As documented by O. Peske in 1862–3.
Rossiiskii gosudarstvennyi voenno-
istoricheskii arkhiv, Moscow, f. 218,
op. 2, d. 969, fo. 5. Reproduced with
permission

Another monument in this group is the Great Synagogue of Lutsk, built between 1626 and 1629.[6] The circumstances of its construction are clearly specified in the records: the permission issued by King Zygmunt III Vasa on 5 May 1626 allowed for a new synagogue in place of an old one. The document reads:

We, Zygmunt III etc., declare that according to the request submitted to us by . . . the unbelieving Jews of the Rabbanite[7] Congregation of our city of Lutsk, wishing to provide this city with the best defence against hostile incursions and to guard against everyday outbreaks of fire in it in future, have readily given them permission to build their synagogue in stone in the same place where today the old synagogue stands. Herewith we permit them to build it of stone, as large and high as before. But with this our privilege, however, we particularly stipulate that on the top of this synagogue on all four sides they should make sufficient provision for the placement of guns and for defence against enemies, and that they, having procured at their own expense a reliable cannon, should during pagan raids post certain of their own people there for the defence of the city, according to need; and they should be present there along with the local citizens in the case of, God forbid, any violent assault on the city, and should not thwart in any way the city administration in times of danger from enemies.[8]

In 1628 King Zygmunt III confirmed his permission, mentioning that the synagogue was located at a sufficient distance from the Dominican monastery, and that its height did not exceed that of other churches. Thus the king legalized the structure, which otherwise could have been banned by the clergy, for it was built anew, from stone, and in a royal city—at once violating three prohibitions adopted by the Piotrków Synod in 1542.[9]

The overall composition of the synagogue comprises an impressive mass of a prayer hall preceded by a lower western extension including a vestibule and women's area, and a higher tower. Both prayer hall and tower bear parapet walls, which used to be an element of fortification and fire protection. These walls are decorated with blind ogee arcades on the exterior. The interior of the prayer hall is also decorated with an ogee arcade (Figures 3 and 4).

One can make certain judgements about the brickwork of the parapet wall that crowns the mass of the prayer hall and the tower: it was depicted free of plaster in a number of high-quality photographs taken before the Second World War,[10] and some dilapidated unplastered fragments are evident *in situ* even today. This brickwork does not bear signs of overall reconstruction and does not differ in its bond throughout the structure; no differences in brickwork were noticeable even in the

---

[6] M. Bersohn, 'Żydowska bóżnica w mieście Łucku', *Sprawozdania Komisyi do Badania Historyi Sztuki w Polsce*, 5, zesz. 4 (1896), 87–9; M. and K. Piechotka, *Bramy nieba: Bóżnice murowane na ziemiach dawnej Rzeczypospolitej* (Warsaw, 1999), 188.

[7] The document specifies the Rabbanite Jews as opposed to the local Karaites.

[8] Bersohn, 'Żydowska bóżnica w mieście Łucku', 88.

[9] For the text of the synod decree, see M. Bałaban, *Żydzi lwowscy na przełomie XVI i XVII wieku* (Lwów, 1906), 53.

[10] Instytut Sztuki Polskiej Akademii Nauk, Warsaw, photograph collection, nos. 2952, 2954, 18831, 18833, 23503, 6011 B.

Figure 3. Great Synagogue of Lutsk, 1626–9: exterior viewed from the west
Photo by Szymon Zajczyk, 1939. Instytut Sztuki Polskiej Akademii Nauk, photographic
collection, negative no. 18831. Reproduced with permission

Figure 4. Great Synagogue of Lutsk, 1626–9: interior of the prayer hall
Photo by Henryk Poddębski, 1925. Instytut Sztuki Polskiej Akademii Nauk, photographic collection,
negative no. 23516. Reproduced with permission

1950s, when the whole building stood dilapidated after the Second World War.[11] Moreover, investigation by the architects Leonid Maslov and Valeryan Sahaidakivsky proved in 1933 that the prayer hall, the tower, and the lower floor of the western extension were built simultaneously.[12] It is possible to learn from the photographs and the actual monument that the brickwork employs a bond characteristic of the Baroque seventeenth-century masonry of this region, with alternating courses of headers and stretchers, one known in the West as an 'English bond'. The outline of the exterior and interior ogee arches is very similar: convex and concave segments of the ogee curve are connected by a horizontal straight segment that facilitates the execution of this detail in brick. Hence, it is plausible that the whole structure, on both the exterior and the interior, including its ogee arcades, was built in 1626–9, in conformance with the royal permit. Notwithstanding an existing alternative theoretical reconstruction of the original building, exhibited as a model in the Tel Aviv Museum of the Jewish Diaspora,[13] there is no doubt about the authenticity of its ogee elements.

The synagogue of Lutsk exemplifies the type of sacred building called a *bimah-support synagogue*,[14] in which the central piers are close to one another, and in their height do not reach the springing point of the major vaults; they bear a masonry canopy that supports the barrel vaulting on all four sides of the prayer hall. This type originated in late sixteenth-century Poland. In Lutsk, this design scheme included a number of Gothic elements. These were a small ribbed sail vault above the *bimah*, the octagonal central piers, and the blind ogee arcades. All these rendered the Lutsk synagogue more 'retarded' and more related to its locality in its style than its precursor of the same type, the Old Synagogue of Przemyśl, built in 1592.

According to Maria and Kazimierz Piechotka, the ogee arcades of the Lutsk synagogue are analogous to those of the Orthodox Church of the Elevation of the Cross in the same city (Figure 5).

This church belonged to a persecuted Orthodox brotherhood which tried to preserve the Orthodox rite well after the Union of Brest signed in 1596. It was built, in the Piechotkas' opinion, between 1619 and 1622.[15] However, according to

---

[11] R. Metelnytsky, *Deyaki storinky yevreis'koyi zabudovy Luts'ka* (Kiev, 2001), 101–2.

[12] L. Maslov, *Arkhitektura staroho Luts'ka* (Lviv, 1939), 35–6; Metelnytsky, *Deyaki storinky yevreis'koyi zabudovy Luts'ka*, 92–4.

[13] G. Wigoder, *The Story of the Synagogue: A Diaspora Museum Book* (Tel Aviv, 1986), 102. Probably this erroneous reconstruction was inspired by George Loukomski's suggestion about the ogee arcade as a product of some 'late' reconstruction of the seventeenth century. See G. Lukomsky, *Lutskii zamok* (Petrograd, 1917), 15.

[14] M. and K. Piechotka, *Wooden Synagogues* (Warsaw, 1957), 30–3; Piechotka and Piechotka, *Bramy nieba: Bóżnice murowane*, 70–1. Carol H. Krinsky calls this type of synagogue 'four-pillar tabernacle', while Thomas C. Hubka calls it 'clustered-column': C. H. Krinsky, *Synagogues of Europe: Architecture, History, Meaning* (Cambridge, Mass., 1985), 11; T. C. Hubka, *Resplendent Synagogue: Architecture and Worship in an Eighteenth-Century Polish Community* (London, 2003), 67.

[15] Piechotka and Piechotka, *Bramy nieba: Bóżnice murowane*, 189. The Piechotkas mistakenly identify this building as a Roman Catholic church.

Figure 5. Orthodox Church of the Elevation of the Cross, Lutsk, 1634–1640s
Photo by Sergey Kravtsov, 2003

records these dates refer to a temporary wooden church of the brotherhood, which was later replaced by a masonry one.[16] The earliest record of the masonry church dates from January 1634, when a certain Anna Hulewiczówna donated 500 Polish zlotys for its foundations, walls, and ritual objects.[17] According to an archaeological survey conducted by Leonid Kroshchenko and Yevhen Osadchy, the core of this church was built between the second half of the 1630s and the mid-1640s.[18] This survey proved that the church was of English bond brickwork.[19] In 1803 the church burned down, and its ruins were then documented in a drawing made that same year (Figure 6).[20]

The ogee arcade is evident in the northern façade of the apse in this drawing, and hence is an original element of the structure. When the decaying ruins were

[16] B. Kolosok, 'Budivnychi Luts´koho bratstva', *Volyn´*, 1991, no. 1, pp. 33–5.

[17] Ibid.; *Arkhiv Yugo-Zapadnoi Rossii*, pt. 1, vol. vi, *Akty o tserkovno-religioznykh otnosheniyakh v Yugo-Zapadnoi Rusi, 1322–1648 gg.* (Kiev, 1883), 678–80. I would like to express my gratitude to Serhy Yurchenko for his research assistance on the history of this church.

[18] L. Kroshchenko and Ye. Osadchy, 'Do problemy vidtvorennya pervisnoho vyhlyadu oboronnoyi Khrestovozdvyzhens´koyi tserkvy brats´koho monastyrya v m. Luts´ku', in *Fortyfikatsiya Ukrayiny* (Kamyanets-Podilsky, 1993), 37.

[19] I am very grateful to Yevhen Osadchy for this information.

[20] Rossiiskii gosudarstvennyi istoricheskii arkhiv, St Petersburg, f. 1488, op. 1, d. 673, fo. 4.

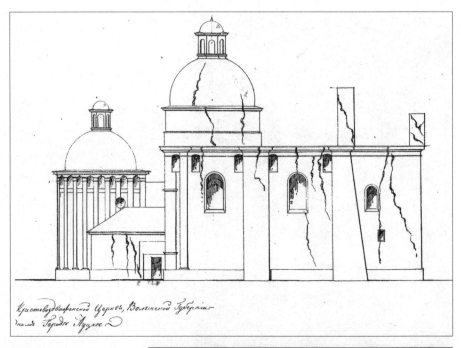

Figure 6. Orthodox
Church of the Elevation of
the Cross, Lutsk

As documented in 1803.
Rossiiskii gosudarstvennyi
istoricheskii arkhiv,
St Petersburg, f. 1488, op. 1,
d. 673, fo. 4. Reproduced with
permission

Figure 7. Lutsk Gate,
Olyka, 1628–1630s
Photo by Sergey Kravtsov,
2003

finally reconstructed in 1888–90, the ogee arcade followed the old pattern.[21] It should be concluded that the Church of the Elevation of the Cross in Lutsk, with its ogee arcade, was built no earlier than 1634, and hence could not have served as a model for the Great Synagogue.

I believe that the Great Synagogue of Lutsk, as well as the Church of the Elevation of the Cross, were modelled on the Gate Tower of the Upper Castle in Lutsk. They 'quoted' its ogee forms in a novel, post-Gothic masonry technique. Apparently, the castle was selected as a model to express a rootedness—a relatedness to the revered source of authority—sought by both the Jewish congregation and the Orthodox brotherhood of Lutsk. By these means the fringe communities intended to state their legitimacy in the cultural landscape.

Another Volhynian monument with an ogee arcade is the Lutsk Gate, formerly called the Klevan Gate, in the town of Olyka, some 40 km from Lutsk (Figure 7). The Ukrainian catalogue of monuments dates that structure to the 1630s.[22] It was one component of new fortifications built after a decree issued in 1628 by the overlord of Olyka, Prince Albrecht Stanisław Radziwiłł (1595–1656), subsequently the chancellor of Lithuania.[23] The gate is crowned by a parapet wall decorated with blind ogee arches alternating with round-headed ones. In addition to these ogees on the parapet wall, there are also two shallow ogee niches on the passage tier of the gate. The outline of the ogee curve is quite similar to those of the Upper Castle, the Great Synagogue, and the Church of the Elevation of the Cross in Lutsk. Till the reconstruction of 2006, the gate consisted of unplastered brickwork, with its stretchers and headers alternating in every course; this type of work is known in the West as 'Flemish bond'. The dark glazed headers produce a 'diamond' chain pattern in the shallow niches, a characteristic of Gothic brickwork in this region. This work produces an impression of genuine survival of the Late Gothic technique and shape. It is unlikely that the Lutsk Gate of Olyka and the Great Synagogue of Lutsk were built by the same group of masons: the diversity of the bonds leaves no room for such a hypothesis. The fact that the ogee arches were executed in diverse masons' techniques indicates that these elements were not a mere craftsman's device, not only a surviving reminiscence of the Gothic, but a meaningful architectural element.

It is plausible that the master builder of the Lutsk Gate of Olyka was the same one dismissed by Radziwiłł in 1635 as 'incapable'. The town overlord called in the Italian architects and Jesuit friars Benedetto Molli and Giovanni Maliverna, accompanied by a master mason, Reinhold Beffka, to construct a new church in a 'Roman [i.e. Baroque] style'.[24]

Another group of monuments with blind ogee arches consists of Roman Catholic belfries. Apparently, the oldest monument in this collection is the belfry

---

[21] Zharikov (ed.), *Pamyatniki gradostroitel'stva i arkhitektury Ukrainskoi SSR*, ii. 53.

[22] Ibid. 79–80.

[23] T. J. Stecki, 'Radziwiłłowska Ołyka', *Przegląd Powszechny*, 15 (1887), 39–42.

[24] M. Brykowska, 'Urbanistyka i architektura Ołyki w XVI–XVII wieku', in A. Sulimierska and A. Szmelter (eds.), *Studium Urbis: Charisteria Teresiae Zarębska Anno Iubilaei Oblata* (Warsaw, 2003), 46–7.

Figure 8. Belfry of the Jesuit
monastery, Lutsk

Photo by Sergey Kravtsov, 2003

of the Jesuit monastery in Lutsk (Figure 8),[25] which was part of the Lutsk Trinity
Cathedral from 1539.

After the destruction of the cathedral by fire in 1781, its belfry was incorporated
into the ensemble of the Jesuit monastery, designed by the Italian architect and
Jesuit friar Giacomo Briano (1589–1649) in 1616[26] and completed in 1640.[27] There
is no documentary evidence by which to judge whether the belfry, which was
apparently renovated at that time, bore the remnants of older, original Gothic ogee
niches, acquired them during that renovation, or was remodelled in a later period.

However, there is a consensus of opinion that the Lutsk Jesuit belfry probably
served as a model for the similar, though more Baroque-featured, belfries of the
Trinity Church in Olyka,[28] built in 1635–40 (Figure 9), and the Dominican
monastery in the not very distant Ruthenian town of Pidkamin, built in about 1704
(Figure 10).[29]

[25] Zharikov (ed.), *Pamyatniki gradostroitel´stva i arkhitektury Ukrainskoi SSR*, ii. 52–3.

[26] J. Paszenda, 'Biografia architekta Giacomo Briano', *Biuletyn Historii Sztuki*, 1973, no. 1, pp. 11–12.

[27] *S. Orgelbranda encyklopedja powszechna*, 28 vols. (Warsaw, 1859–68), xvii. 673.

[28] Zharikov (ed.), *Pamyatniki gradostroitel´stva i arkhitektury Ukrainskoi SSR*, iii. 110–11;
Brykowska, 'Urbanistyka i architektura Ołyki', 48.

[29] Zharikov (ed.), *Pamyatniki gradostroitel´stva i arkhitektury Ukrainskoi SSR*, iii. 81–3. The Polish
name of Pidkamin is Podkamień.

Figure 9. Belfry of the Trinity Church, Olyka, 1635–40.

Photo by Sergey Kravtsov, 2003

Figure 10. Belfry of the Dominican monastery, Pidkamin, *c*.1704

Photo by Ilja van de Pavert, 2007. Reproduced with permission

The belfry of the Trinity Church in Olyka includes four round-headed openings for bells. Its pillars are decorated with narrow niches spanned by ogee arches. The variation of ogee and round-arched shapes is based on the alternation of the void and full, the bell openings and the pillar decoration. In this motif, the Lutsk Gate of Olyka and the belfry are similar.

At least one attempt to explain the origins and meaning of the ogee arcades of Volhynia was made in the past. Tadeusz Mańkowski suggested that the ogee forms of Lutsk and Olyka were an Oriental motif combined with a Gothic building technique.[30] He believed that the element derived from a 'Persian arch', a product of Armenian builders active in Moldavia, Ruthenia, and Volhynia; Lutsk was one of the extreme northern Armenian colonies in these lands.[31] While sharing the hypothesis of an Oriental expression, I do not agree with two points of Mańkowski's theory of Armenian authorship. First, the known ogee arcades of the Armenian Cathedral in Lviv, the alleged precursors to those of Lutsk, date from as early as the second half of the fourteenth century.[32] Hence, the chronological gap between the Lviv and Lutsk monuments is very wide, spanning many generations of masons. Second, the Armenian Church of St Stephen in Lutsk, where the signs of relatedness to Lviv would have been discerned in the first place, lacked ogee elements.[33]

The hypothesis of reconstruction of an older Lutsk belfry, which initially could have contained Gothic elements, is realistic. The flamboyant phase of the dying Gothic style reached Volhynia in the early sixteenth century: an ogee arch was used in the Epiphany (Bohoyavlenska) Church in Ostroh, built between 1515 and 1539, though this was a single arch and not an arcade.[34] However, while reconstruction of the Lutsk belfry could help to clarify the provenance of a single monument, it cannot explain a series of similar monuments. I would argue that the blind ogee arches of seventeenth-century Volhynia were initially Gothic in their shape and masons' technique, as was the Lutsk Gate of Olyka and, possibly, the Gate Tower of the Lutsk Castle. Soon afterwards their application and meaning underwent two alterations. The first was the replication of the ogee arcade in English bond on the Great Synagogue and the Church of the Elevation of the Cross. The second alteration emerged in the Olyka belfry, where the ogee shape became adjusted to Jesuit architecture.

Whereas in the Great Synagogue and the Church of the Elevation of the Cross the

---

[30] T. Mańkowski, 'Sztuka Ormian lwowskich', *Prace Komisji Historji Sztuki* (Kraków), 6 (1934), 117–18.   [31] Ibid. 118.

[32] Ju. Smirnow, *Katedra Ormiańska we Lwowie: Dzieje Archidiecezji Ormiańskiej Lwowskiej* (Lviv, 2002), 5–16.

[33] O. Oliinyk, 'Tserkva sv. Stepana v Luts'ku', *Pam"yatnyky Ukrayiny*, 1993, no. 1, pp. 33–4.

[34] W. Łuszczkiewicz, 'Ruina Bohojawleńskiej cerkwi w zamku Ostrogskim na Wołyniu', *Sprawozdania Komisji do Badania Historii Sztuki w Polsce*, 3, zesz. 3 (1886), 67–92; S. Jurczenko, 'Niektóre osobliwości ewolucji przestrzennej wołyńskich cerkwi z XVI w.', *Kwartalnik Architektury i Urbanistyki*, 1998, no. 4, p. 310.

ogee arcade became a sign of relatedness to the place, in the Jesuit architecture the ogee arch acquired the meaning of an Oriental, exotic signifier. It is known that Briano, who designed the Jesuit monastery in Lutsk and supervised Jesuit construction in Małopolska, planned to crown the Jesuit church of the Volhynian city of Ostroh with an onion dome, a skyline shape related to the ogee form.[35] Briano's intention was clear: he wanted to make Catholic architecture seem more familiar, and thus attractive, to the local population.[36] By 'local population' he meant members of Greek Catholic and Ukrainian Orthodox congregations, who would be new or potential converts to Catholicism. It is likely that Briano tried to convey the tolerance of the Catholic Church for the tastes of new converts from churches of the Eastern rite.[37]

The formal pattern of the onion dome was borrowed not from Islamic architecture, which was less familiar in Europe, but from Russia, the Orthodox stronghold at that time and the eastern neighbour of the Polish–Lithuanian Commonwealth. For Poland, Moscow was the goal of conquest or dynastic union. It was invaded by Poles several times in the late sixteenth and early seventeenth centuries, and the Polish prince Władysław was elected tsar of Muscovy in 1610; although he did not assume the throne, he continued to style himself Grand Prince of Muscovy until 1634. Russian architecture was accessible to architects active in Volhynia not only via itinerant merchants, or through military and diplomatic relations, but also through professional architectural contacts,[38] Jesuit friars who accompanied Polish troops, and the Jesuit and Carmelite missionaries who saw Moscow on their way from Persia in the first half of the seventeenth century.[39]

The source of the onion-shaped dome and ogee arch in Russian sacred buildings is worthy of separate research. It should be noted, however, that in the early seventeenth century it was already a recognizable sign, the hallmark of Moscow. Most of the Kremlin churches already bore this type of crowning by that time. The impression that Moscow produced on Western visitors was confusing. On the one hand, they were aware of the Italian authorship of the Kremlin buildings. On the other hand, some described Moscow as 'looking like Jerusalem on the exterior and

---

[35] A cross-section of the onion dome forms an ogee curve.

[36] This information was shared by Prof. Dr Richard Bösel in his lecture at the Congress of Ukrainists in Lviv in August 1993. I would like to express my gratitude to him as well as to Dr Andrzej Betlej and Prof. Dr Jerzy Kowalczyk for their help in my research.

[37] Briano's concept was related to a very specific context; its sophistication is liable to mislead the modern researcher. Probably it was for this reason that a photograph of a street scene taken against the background of the Lutsk Jesuit Church was at the beginning of the twenty-first century provided with an erroneous caption: 'A Jewish corner with a touch of the Byzantine'. See A. Kaczyne, *Poyln: Jewish Life in the Old Country*, ed. M. Web (New York, 2001), 19.

[38] I. Grabar, *Arkhitekturni vzayemozv"yazky Ukrayiny z Rosiyeyu* (c.1954), manuscript published by Viktor Vechersky at <http://www.heritage.com.ua/PU/arhitektura/doslidzhenja/index.php?id =26>, accessed 25 Aug. 2010. Grabar's text was written to celebrate the tercentenary of the 'reunion' of Russia and Ukraine, and bears signs of Soviet teleology, which saw the intimacy of Russian and Ukrainian cultures as a good thing.

[39] T. Mańkowski, *Sztuka Islamu w Polsce w XVII i XVIII wieku* (Kraków, 1935), 14–15.

Bethlehem in the interior'.[40] To foreign eyes, the comparison to Jerusalem and Bethlehem would strengthen the Oriental connotations of architectural images in the Russian capital.

The use of ogee arches in Russian architecture was apparent in the so-called *zakomary*[41] and *kokoshniki*[42] long before the seventeenth century. In 1624–5 the Frolovskaya Tower,[43] the ceremonial entrance to the Kremlin, was reconstructed under the guidance of the Scotsman Christopher Galloway, assisted by the Russian architect Bazhen Ogurtsov.[44] The tower gained two new tiers of ogee decoration: a parapet wall and a belfry above the chiming clock. These elements were florid decorative features of the flamboyant Gothic style,[45] and also served as a tribute to the Russian building tradition of ogee toppings. This remarkable architectural development in the very heart of Moscow was an important achievement of the newly elected tsar, Michael Romanov.

In my opinion, the ogee shape found in the Jesuit architecture of Volhynia represented a generalized conception of Oriental style, not a replica of an actual architectural form, as the geometry of the ogee arcades differs greatly in the Moscow and Volhynian monuments. Though the idea of Oriental decoration was rejected in the Ostroh Jesuit project by its benefactress Anna Chodkowiczowa (a fanatically devout Catholic proselyte), it could have been adopted in the Lutsk Jesuit belfry and a number of related structures in the shape of ogee arcades. The patron of Olyka, Albrecht Stanisław Radziwiłł, was likely guided in the choice of architectural decoration by Jesuits, who surrounded him throughout his life.[46]

Later, in the eighteenth century, blind ogee arches appeared in the synagogue of Klevan, a town located about 50 km from Lutsk and 15 km from Olyka (Figure 11).[47] In this monument, the ogee arches on the upper tier of the interior arcades differed from the patterns found in early Lutsk and Olyka, since their outline did not include the horizontal straight segments mentioned above. Nevertheless, these arcades may be considered an offshoot of the respected synagogue of Lutsk.

Another synagogue bearing the ogee arcade in its parapet wall, far from Volhynia, is in the Podolian town of Husyatyn. It is a massive structure with a lofty prayer hall and an extension in the lower vestibule, today crowned with parapet walls (Figure 12).

[40] A. Olearius, *The Voyages and Travells of the Ambassadors Sent by Frederic Duke of Holstein, to the Great Duke of Muscovy and the King of Persia* (London, 1669), quoted in *Rossiya XV–XVII vv. glazami inostrantsev*, ed. Yu. A. Limonov (Leningrad, 1986), 323.

[41] A *zakomara* (plural *zakomary*) is an arched crowning of a church wall which regularly follows the shape of the interior vault. The term derives from the Greek word *kamara*, 'vault'.

[42] *Kokoshniki* are additional decorative arches on top of the vault that form the pyramidal silhouette of the church roof. The term derives from the name of a kind of Russian folk women's headwear.

[43] Frolovskaya Tower was the early name of the Saviour Gate.

[44] A. Voyce, *The Moscow Kremlin: Its History, Architecture and Art Treasures* (London, 1955), 27.

[45] Ibid.

[46] A. Przyboś, 'Radziwiłł Albrecht Stanisław', in *Polski słownik biograficzny*, xxx (Kraków, 1987), 143–8.   [47] Instytut Sztuki Polskiej Akademii Nauk, photograph collection, nos. 2869, 2870.

Figure 11. Great Synagogue, Klevan, eighteenth century

Photo by unknown author, before 1939. Instytut Sztuki Polskiej Akademii Nauk, photographic collection, negative no. 2870. Reproduced with permission

Figure 12. Synagogue, Husyatyn

Photo by unknown author, before 1914. Nationalbibliothek, Vienna, Bildarchiv, negative nr. 191.241 CR. Reproduced with permission

The parapet of the prayer hall is decorated with a blind ogee arcade and with a mihrab-like central niche on the western façade. This parapet wall is crowned with a crenellation composed of acanthus leaves or palmettes, a motif that is repeated above the cornice of the vestibule. The ogee shape of the parapet arcade does not resemble those on Volhynian monuments, as it does not include rectilinear segments between convex and concave curves. In the opinion of Tytus Hevryk, the synagogue in Husyatyn was built in 1654;[48] a different view has been suggested by the Piechotkas, who claim it was built in 1692, when the city was under Turkish rule.[49] Their opinion is based on that of Majer Bałaban, who went through the Polish archives of that period.[50] The later date of construction seems unconvincing when one consults contemporary Turkish sources. Great masses of the Podolian population fled to Volhynia, Ruthenia, Moldova, and Russia from this dangerous borderland occupied by the Turks between 1672 and 1699, and apparently many Podolian Jews were among them. Indeed, there were only two Jews remaining in Husyatyn and paying taxes in 1681.[51] Certainly, the legal status of the Jews improved under Ottoman rule, and they were considered fortunate traitors by the Poles, whose status had worsened.[52] Nevertheless, the economic situation in Podolia deteriorated significantly, improving only with the end of Turkish occupation. In 1721, the Jews of Husyatyn paid a poll tax of 856 zlotys, and in 1765 the Jewish population there had increased to 1,435.[53] Private ownership of Husyatyn passed to Michał Potocki in 1729; this nobleman was involved in a suit brought by the bishop of Kamyanets, Wacław Hieronim Sierakowski (1700–70), against the Jews of Husyatyn, who allegedly built their synagogue on church land.[54] The local Jews lost the case.

It is my opinion that the synagogue of Husyatyn was fundamentally rebuilt between 1699 and 1729, after the Turks had left the city. It was apparently at that time that the pointed windows of the prayer hall were built, since one of them blocked a staircase that had originally led to the fortified parapet.[55] This kind of architecture was not anachronistic in Podolia: the Gothic survived there in sacred buildings as late as 1714, for instance in the Roman Catholic parish church of Skala Podilska.[56] Moreover, the ogee-arched parapet wall of the Husyatyn synagogue could be a product of the reconstruction around 1900, when acanthus-like crenel-

---

[48] T. Hevryk, 'Murovani synahohy v Ukrayini i doslidzhennya yikh', *Pam"yatnyky Ukrayiny*, 1996, no. 2, p. 33.   [49] Piechotka and Piechotka, *Bramy nieba: Bóżnice murowane*, 256.

[50] M. Bałaban, *Yidn in poyln* (Warsaw, 1930), 263–4.

[51] D. Kołodziejczyk, *Podole pod panowaniem tureckim: Ejalet Kamieniecki, 1672–1699* (Warsaw, 1994), 146.   [52] Ibid. 140–1.

[53] *Sefer zikaron husiatyn vehasviva*, ed. A. Becker (Tel Aviv, 1976), 18.

[54] Bałaban, *Yidn in poyln*, 263–4. The city of Kamyanets-Podilsky is called Kamieniec Podolski in Polish.

[55] O. Plamenytska, 'Oboronni khramy Podillya', *Pam"yatnyky Ukrayiny*, 2002, nos. 1–2, pp. 34–5.

[56] S. Jurczenko, 'Krzyżowe kościoły Ukrainy w pierwszej połowie XVII wieku', *Biuletyn Historii Sztuki*, 1995, nos. 3–4, pp. 290–3. The Polish name of this place is Skała nad Zbruczem.

Figure 13. Synagogue, Husyatyn, fragment of watercolour by Napoleon Orda, 1872
National Museum, Kraków. Reproduced with permission

lations were added atop the parapet wall and above the vestibule cornice.[57] The late origins of the ogee arcade may be supported by the drawing by Napoleon Orda from 1872, in which the parapet arcade is depicted as round-headed (see Figure 13). The changes of about 1900 might better be explained in terms of the so-called Moorish style of nineteenth-century synagogue architecture than in terms of Gothic Survival.

It is worthy of note that ogee arcades are present not only in the masonry synagogue architecture of the south-eastern borderland of the former Commonwealth, but also in several wooden synagogues of the late seventeenth and eighteenth centuries. Such arcades decorated the octagonal *bimot* in Hvizdets and Minkivtsi.[58] These arcades, produced in wood, not by guild master masons, are still awaiting comprehensive research.

In conclusion, the blind ogee arcades were a decoration of Mannerist parapet walls, popular throughout the sixteenth to the eighteenth centuries, and as a decoration of niches in belfries of Catholic churches. The ogee arcades, uncommon in

[57] Piechotka and Piechotka, *Bramy nieba: Bóżnice murowane*, 258.

[58] For Hvizdets (Polish Gwoździec), see M. and K. Piechotka, *Bramy nieba: Bóżnice drewniane na ziemiach dawnej Rzeczypospolitej* (Warsaw, 1996), 108, 229, 297; for Minkivtsi, see Natsional'na biblioteka Ukrayiny imeni V. I. Vernads'koho, Kiev, Manuscripts Department, Stefan Taranushchenko Collection, photograph no. 604.

Baroque formal vocabulary, were used in the third and fourth decades of the seventeenth century as a non-classical supplement to the new edifices. Religious minorities, including Jews and Orthodox Christians, as well as the dominant Catholics, employed ogee forms for diverse ends. It is plausible that these architectural devices were intended to convey in built form the relatedness of the local Jewish and Orthodox Christian brethren to the revered centre of authority, the Castle of Lutsk, and hence to express the legality of their presence in the urban landscape. At the same time and in the same region, Jesuit architects employed ogee and onion shapes to express the openness of the Catholic Church towards potential converts. Their works tended towards Oriental, exotic expression, and not only quoted the local Gothic Survival patterns, but were modelled on some generalized concept of the Orient, to which Volhynia was only a gateway.

The Attitude of American Jews and American Diplomacy towards the Bill Banning *Sheḥitah* in Poland in the Second Half of the 1930s

PRZEMYSŁAW RÓŻAŃSKI

POLAND, WHICH REGAINED its independence in 1918, entered the second half of the 1930s weighed down by serious social, economic, and political problems. They included the disastrous impact of the Great Depression on a largely agricultural country, the complex ethnic and religious make-up of the country, and the ongoing political battle between the ruling government camp (the 'obóz piłsudczykowsko-sanacyjny', Sanacja) and the opposition parties, especially those derived from the right-wing National Democratic Party.[1] The political tensions ran even deeper because of the unresolved struggle for power within the ruling camp after the death of Marshal Józef Piłsudski in May 1935. Among his political heirs, there was no single candidate who could measure up to him in terms of authority and thus unite the heterogeneous group of his political epigones. There were other reasons for political instability. Ultimately, the fate of the Second Republic was to be decided not by internal problems but by the international scene, which led to the invasion of Poland by both Nazi and Soviet forces in September 1939.

Among the tensions that arose from the multi-ethnic character of the Polish state, those resulting from the attempts by antisemites to reduce Jewish influence became particularly acute in the 1930s.[2] The death of Piłsudski was a turning point

---

[1] Although the year 1935 is considered to mark the end of the Great Depression in Poland, the biggest strikes in the history of the Second Polish Republic took place in 1936–7. See J. Skodlarski, *Zarys historii gospodarczej Polski* (Warsaw, 2000), 290–1.

[2] For the ethnic composition of the population of Poland, according to the official data of 1931 and corrections made to these, see J. Tomaszewski, *Ojczyzna nie tylko Polaków: Mniejszości narodowe w Polsce w latach 1918–1939* (Warsaw, 1985), 50, table 1. According to the census data of 1931, Poles constituted 69% of the overall population of the Second Polish Republic, while according to Tomaszewski's estimates they made up only 65%. The 1931 census lists 3,113,900 Jews in Poland,

in the growth of hostility towards Jews. Although a radicalization of anti-Jewish attitudes was evident from 1929, the charisma of Piłsudski and his opposition to antisemitism were a major barrier to the development of anti-Jewish campaigns by nationalists under the banner of the Endecja, and even more so within the government Sanacja camp.[3] Foreign observers of the Polish political scene were well aware of the changed atmosphere. Less than a year after the Marshal's death, the American ambassador in Warsaw, John Cudahy, noted: 'During the time that he was in power in Poland he did not permit the anti-Semitic element openly to manifest itself.'[4] However, 'When the Jews no longer were protected by the power and prestige of the Marshal the National Democrats lost no time in intensifying the anti-Semitic propaganda which, while it had not completely disappeared after the *coup d'état* of May 1926, had been carried on in a subdued tone.'[5]

In the second half of the 1930s, in an attempt to win popular support Piłsudski's political heirs adopted to some degree the anti-Jewish radicalism of the political parties rooted in the Endecja. As was noted by Cudahy, the increase in anti-Jewish feelings in Poland also owed something to the example of Nazi Germany.[6] Recent historical works have discerned in the passage or attempted passage of bills clearly harmful to the economic interest of the Jewish minority in Poland a growing official support in some government circles for the antisemitic slogans of the Endecja.[7]

9.8% of the overall population. In 1939 the number of Jews had grown to 3,460,000, but the percentage diminished to 9.7% of the total population: J. Tomaszewski (ed.), *Najnowsze dzieje Żydów w Polsce* (Warsaw, 1993), 159. The *American Jewish Year Book* accepted the 1931 census figure, i.e. 3,113,900, to determine the number of Jews in Poland in 1939. See *American Jewish Year Book* (hereafter *AJYB*), 41 (1939), 585, table 7. *AJYB* estimated the number of Jews in Poland in the first half of the 1920s at some 3.5 million, which would make 12.9% of the overall population. Though accepting the 1921 census figure for the total population of Poland (27,060,163 citizens), *AJYB* considered the number of Jews listed in that census to be significantly understated. This, it was claimed, resulted from methodological imperfections in taking the census (the failure to consider simultaneously both religious and ethnic criteria; for example, Jews often reported the nationality dominant in a given country or region as their own) or from a deliberate lowering of the number of Jews by the administration: *AJYB*, 23 (1921), 329, table 4.

[3] On this issue Jan Tomasz Gross has written: 'But when Marshal Piłsudski died, the Jewish street was plunged into deep mourning, as if it were precisely there, in the Jewish quarters of the towns and villages, that the veterans of the Legions thronged together': J. T. Gross, *Strach: Antysemityzm w Polsce tuż po wojnie. Historia moralnej zapaści* (Kraków, 2008), 255. For more on the subject, see P. Różański, 'Śmierć Józefa Piłsudskiego i jej postrzeganie w Stanach Zjednoczonych a zagadnienie żydowskie w Polsce', *Dzieje Najnowsze*, 2008, no. 4, pp. 146–57.

[4] John Cudahy was a non-career appointee. He received his appointment as ambassador on 13 June 1933, presented his credentials in Warsaw on 6 September 1933, and completed his mission on 23 April 1937. See the Internet site of the US Department of State, <http://history.state.gov/departmenthistory/people/cudahy-john-clarence>, accessed 1 Sept. 2010. For the quotation, see National Archives and Records Administration, Department of State, College Park, Maryland (hereafter NARA, DS), roll 45, no. 860c.4016/451: Warsaw, 1 Apr. 1936, Cudahy to the Secretary of State, subject: 'Increasing anti-Semitism in Poland', p. 3.

[5] Ibid. 4.   [6] Ibid. 3.

[7] S. Rudnicki, *Żydzi w parlamencie II Rzeczypospolitej* (Warsaw, 2004), 385–9; Tomaszewski (ed.),

The bill banning Jewish methods of animal slaughter (*sheḥitah*) was one of these basically anti-Jewish laws. The lobbying associated with the bill and its eventual passage has already been the subject of scholarly research.[8] This chapter is an attempt to describe the attitude of American Jews and of American diplomacy towards this bill, as well as towards other legislative actions by the Polish parliament which reflected the intensification of Polish antisemitism in the second half of the 1930s.

Objections had been raised to *sheḥitah* already before the First World War and attempts to ban it were made in independent Poland in May 1923 and again in 1928 and 1935.[9] The issue was revived in February 1936 on the initiative of Janina Prystorowa, a member of the Sejm who was the wife of Colonel Aleksander Prystor, the Speaker of the Senate and a former prime minister. Jews in Poland and abroad, including the United States, protested vehemently. The Federation of Polish Jews in America, which, since the passage of a critical resolution on the Polish government's policies towards the Jews in June 1931, was no longer on friendly terms with the local Polish embassy, frequently censured the Polish authorities for their treatment of the Jews in Poland.[10] Its views on the policy of the Polish government were set out in a memorandum of 10 March 1936 which was provoked by the proposed bill on *sheḥitah*.[11] The leaders of the federation personally delivered it to Cordell Hull, the Secretary of State. In the view of Benjamin

---

Najnowsze dzieje Żydów w Polsce, 194–9. The support for antisemitism in 'official circles' was noted by the subsequent ambassador of the United States in Warsaw, Anthony J. Drexel Biddle Jr., in one of the reports on the growing antisemitic tendencies in Poland addressed to the Secretary of State: see NARA, DS, roll 45, no. 860c.4016/548: Warsaw, 6 Apr. 1938, Biddle to the Secretary of State, subject: 'Growing official support of anti-Semitic measures in Poland', p. 1. Parts of the first three pages of the document have been published in *Foreign Relations of the United States: Diplomatic Papers, 1938*, ii: *The British Commonwealth, Europe, Near East and Africa* (Washington, DC, 1955), 653–4.

[8] R. Modras, *Kościół katolicki i antysemityzm w Polsce w latach 1933–1939*, trans. W. Turopolski (Kraków, 2004), 237–40; S. Rudnicki, 'Ritual Slaughter as a Political Issue', *Polin*, 7 (1992), 147–60.

[9] In 1878 the Polish League of Animal Protection (Liga Ochrony Zwierząt) in Warsaw protested against *sheḥitah*, and a second protest was connected with the publication of Andrzej Niemojewski's *Dusza żydowska w zwierciadle Talmudu* in 1914. The subsequent attempts at banning or limiting *sheḥitah* in 1928 and 1935 were organized by the Warsaw municipality. See Rudnicki, 'Ritual Slaughter as a Political Issue', 148–9; id., *Żydzi w parlamencie II Rzeczypospolitej*, 386.

[10] For more on the federation, see A. Kapiszewski, 'The Federation of Polish Jews in America in Polish–Jewish Relations during the Interwar Years (1924–1939)', *Polish American Studies*, 56, no. 2 (1999), 47–8, and the memorandum of the Consulate General in New York: Archiwum Akt Nowych, Warsaw (hereafter AAN), Ambasada RP w Waszyngtonie, 2616: 21 Jan. 1930, Mieczysław Marchlewski to the Ambassador of the Polish Republic in Washington, fos. 12–17. The resolution of the federation of 6–7 June 1931 marked the beginning of the end to friendly relations between the Polish embassy in Washington and the Federation of Polish Jews in America. This resolution blamed the Polish government for the difficult economic situation of the Jewish minority in Poland. The text can be found in AAN, Ambasada RP w Waszyngtonie, 2617, fos. 256 ff.

[11] NARA, DS, roll 45, no. 860c.4016/446: 10 Mar. 1936, memorandum submitted by the Federation of Polish Jews in America to his Excellency the Secretary of State, pp. 1–5.

Winter, the federation's president, the bill dealt a severe blow to the way of life of the 3.5-million-strong Jewish minority in Poland. Jews could only consume meat which was slaughtered in the way prescribed by Jewish religious law. Passing the bill would make it impossible for them to eat meat, with deleterious effects on their health. In addition, the bill would deprive of their livelihood thousands of Jewish families, who would join the 'ranks of starving Jews'. Those in this dire position were estimated to make up one-third of the Jews in Poland.[12] It was in order to assist these destitute Jews that a 'group of distinguished American citizens' had attempted to provide material assistance through the American Committee Appeal for the Jews in Poland.[13] According to the federation, the bill violated the treaty guaranteeing the rights of racial, religious, and linguistic minorities signed by Poland on 28 June 1919.[14] The memorandum cited in particular articles 2, 7, and 8 of this treaty, which guaranteed the equality of all citizens before the law, undertook to facilitate the use of native languages other than Polish in courts and offices, and accorded the protection of life and freedom to all inhabitants of Poland, regardless of their social background, ethnicity, language, race, and religion.[15] In addition, article 2 guaranteed the right to 'the free practice, both publicly and privately, of any faith, religion, or belief, providing its practices do not violate public order and decency'.[16] This was interpreted as guaranteeing to Jews the right to practise *sheḥitah*. In addition, by article 1 of the Minority Treaty Poland had agreed to incorporate the resolutions embodied in articles 2–8 into the fundamental laws of the country, while article 109 of the constitution of 17 March 1921 guaranteed to every citizen the right to cultivate his or her own ethnic customs.[17] *Sheḥitah* was a religious practice, and since the Jewish religion was basically synonymous with Jewish nationality, it could be interpreted not only as a religious dogma but also as a component of the Jewish national tradition. A new constitution had been adopted in Poland in April 1935, but articles 99, 109–118, and 120 of the

---

[12] NARA, DS, roll 45, no. 860c.4016/446. 4. [13] Ibid.

[14] Often referred to as the Minority Treaty, it was officially styled the Treaty between the Principal Allied and Associated Powers and Poland (Traktat między Głównymi Mocarstwami Sprzymierzonymi i Stowarzyszonymi a Polską). For its terms, see *Dokumenty z dziejów polskiej polityki zagranicznej, 1918–1939*, i: *1918–1932*, ed. T. Jędruszczak and M. Nowak-Kiełbikowa (Warsaw, 1989), 71–8. [15] Ibid. 72–3.

[16] Ibid. 72. This clause, in a practically unaltered form, is also article 111 of the constitution of 17 March 1921.

[17] NARA, DS, roll 45, no. 860c.4016/446: 10 Mar. 1936, memorandum submitted by the Federation of Polish Jews in America to his Excellency the Secretary of State, p. 2. Article 109 reads: 'Every citizen has a right to preserve his nationality and cultivate his language and national values. Separate laws will assure to minorities in the Polish State the full and free development of their national values through autonomous minority associations of a public-law character within the scope of the associations of general self-government. The state will have the right to control their activities and supplement their financial means': see *Konstytucje Rzeczypospolitej Polskiej*, ed. L. Falandysz (Warsaw, 1998), 390–1.

previous constitution had been incorporated into the new one.[18] The memorandum did not refer directly to the suspension of the Minority Treaty by Józef Beck on 13 September 1934 in a speech made before the League of Nations.[19] It attempted to deal with this by referring instead to Beck's statement on that occasion: 'The interests of the minorities are and will remain protected by the fundamental laws of Poland.'[20] It therefore ignored Beck's explanation that he was suspending this treaty because minority treaties had not obtained general applicability and did not apply to the major powers. The memorandum also stressed the decisive role of the victorious powers, and especially the United States led by President Woodrow Wilson, in the rebirth of the 'free and independent Polish state'.[21] This also made America responsible for the situation of the minorities in Poland, while Poland had a moral debt of gratitude towards the United States. In addition, the federation pointed out the financial, economic, and moral support provided by the American government and by the American nation in the rebuilding of the Polish state and referred to the 'traditional policy' of the US government of protecting persecuted minorities, whether religious or racial.[22]

The memorandum also quoted the opinion of the priest Bronisław Żongołłowicz, Deputy Minister of Religious Cults and Public Education and a professor of canon law at the Stefan Batory University in Vilna, who opposed the bill in the form proposed by Prystorowa.[23] In addition, it cited a telegram addressed to the editor of the *New York Times* of 6 March 1936 which described how a delegation of Polish rabbis had explained to the government that Jews could not consume non-kosher meat. It also referred to the constitution, which guaranteed freedom of belief to all citizens of the Polish Republic.[24]

The federation's memorandum was personally delivered to Cordell Hull on 10 March 1936 by its leaders. Emanuel Celler, who represented Brooklyn and Queens in the US House of Representatives, signed the memorandum and participated in the meeting with the Secretary of State. The next day, an article appeared in the *New York Herald Tribune* repeating the arguments of the memorandum. It claimed that the Secretary of State had listened with interest to the presentation of the Jewish delegates and had promised to 'do whatever seemed wise' after the problem

---

[18] Article 81.2: 'Simultaneously, the law of 17 March 1921 is rescinded . . . with the amendments introduced by the act of 2 August 1926 . . . with the exception of arts. 99, 109–18, and 120.' See *Konstytucje Rzeczypospolitej Polskiej*, ed. Falandysz, 423.

[19] S. Sierpowski, *Mniejszości narodowe jako instrument polityki międzynarodowej, 1919–1939* (Poznań, 1986), 69.

[20] NARA, DS, roll 45, no. 860c.4016/446, 10 Mar. 1936, memorandum submitted by the Federation of Polish Jews in America to his Excellency the Secretary of State, p. 3.   [21] Ibid.

[22] It should be added here that the US financial assistance to Poland referred to by the federation was quite modest throughout the existence of the Second Polish Republic.

[23] The spelling 'von Gollowicz' used in the document is wrong. The authors of the memorandum are almost certainly referring to Fr. Bronisław Żongołłowicz.

[24] NARA, DS, roll 45, no. 860c.4016/446, 10 Mar. 1936, memorandum submitted by the Federation of Polish Jews in America to his Excellency the Secretary of State, p. 4.

had been thoroughly examined.[25] This caused some alarm among Polish diplomats in the United States. On the very same day, Edward Kulikowski, second secretary of the Polish embassy in Washington, met Robert F. Kelley, head of the East European Bureau of the State Department.[26] During the meeting, Kelley read large portions of the federation's memorandum to Kulikowski. Kulikowski emphasized that the bill was an internal Polish matter and that he could not understand why the United States should show any interest in it. This was typical of the reaction of the Polish diplomatic service to any interest shown by other countries in the Jewish issue in Poland. This issue was seen as an international problem only when it was a question of obtaining outside assistance in organizing the resettlement of Polish Jews. On this occasion the concern proved groundless. The US government had no intention of intervening with the Polish authorities on the bill banning *sheḥitah*. Hull's promise to take 'wise' steps had no substance, as was confirmed to Kulikowski by Kelley. In spite of this assurance, however, Kulikowski sought a meeting with William Phillips, the Under Secretary of State at the State Department. That meeting took place a few days after the meeting with Kelley and confirmed his interpretation of the meeting between the federation and Cordell Hull. According to Phillips, the US Department of State had never planned any intervention to oppose the proposed ban on *sheḥitah* in Poland. Hull's meeting with the Jewish delegation and his expression of willingness to consider its views had merely been normal politeness.[27]

In addition to the Federation of Polish Jews in America, the American Jewish Committee (AJC) also intervened on behalf of the Polish Jews, asking ambassador Stanisław Patek, who held the office from 1 January 1933 to 30 April 1936, to convey to Warsaw their concerns over the bill.[28] The AJC was perhaps the most influential Jewish organization in the United States and was made up mostly of affluent and assimilated American Jews of German origin. In his letter to ambassador Patek, Cyrus Adler, the organization's president, objected to the bill's requirement that animals should be stunned before being slaughtered. This, he claimed, violated the ritual requirements for the slaughter of animals accepted by Jews for over two thousand years. The Bible forbade Jews to consume blood, so that meat had to be drained of it before consumption. In order to ensure that this took place, very specific and restrictive requirements had to be met. The animals should be slaughtered exclusively by a trained professional following an established method and with the help of special tools. These *shoḥetim* possessed a detailed knowledge of

[25] NARA, DS, roll 45, no. 860c.4016/447, p. 3: 'Polish Jews Ask Hull Aid on Ritual Slaughter Ban', *New York Herald Tribune*, 11 Mar. 1936.

[26] NARA, DS, roll 45, no. 860c.4016/447, pp. 1–2: 11 Mar. 1936, memorandum of conversation between Mr Edward Kulikowski, Second Secretary, Polish Embassy, and Mr Robert Kelley.

[27] NARA, DS, roll 45, no. 860c.4016/448: 14 Mar. 1936, memorandum of conversation with the Polish Chargé d'Affaires.

[28] On Patek, see AAN, Ambasada RP w Waszyngtonie, [1918] 1919–45, no. 490/I, Dzieje ustrojowe urzędu, pp. 2–3; on the AJC's concerns, NARA, DS, roll 45, no. 860c.4016/453: 9 Mar. 1936, AJC President Cyrus Adler to the Ambassador of Poland Stanisław Patek.

the anatomy and pathology of animals earmarked for slaughter. Adler also rebutted the argument that this method of slaughter was inhumane, pointing out that in 1922 at the Forty-Sixth Annual Convention of the American Humane Association in St Paul, Minnesota, it had been recognized that this was not the case. Similar views had found confirmation in the 'opinions of hundreds of competent non-Jewish experts' from countries 'in all parts of the world'.[29]

Władysław Sokołowski, chargé d'affaires *ad interim* at the Polish embassy, replied to Adler's letter. He claimed that the bill in question was not inspired by the government but was in reality the result of a 'private parliamentary initiative' and had the support of many members of parliament.[30] The Polish government, he claimed, was opposed to any legislation infringing on the freedom of religious practice. It was clear that he was well informed about the progress of the bill and was able to let Adler know about changes to it proposed by the government. These, he argued, would allow *sheḥitah* to be practised by Polish citizens of Jewish, Muslim, and Karaite faiths. On the other hand, the Polish authorities supported those clauses of the bill which would make it possible for Christian consumers to purchase meat that was not slaughtered according to *sheḥitah*. The goal of such a move was economic— to lower the prices of meat consumed by the Christian population of Poland. These facts were clearly set out in the March issue of the *Polish Press Information Bulletin* published by the Polish Information Service, to which he referred the leaders of the AJC.[31] Sokołowski repeated at greater length the arguments contained in this article in a later and much longer letter to Adler.[32] In this he again stated the economic argument for the bill, which—along with the officially enunciated humane considerations—had been the principle guiding the bill's initiator, Janina Prystorowa: 'Its primary purpose was to adjust the abnormal conditions existing at present in the Polish cattle and meat industry, which, in an agricultural country like Poland, have a direct effect on the entire economic situation.'[33]

The Polish authorities claimed that the basic problem caused by *sheḥitah* was that butchers refused to buy whole animals directly from farmers, but took only the forequarters or the hindquarters, as Jews consumed only the forequarters. Farmers suffered losses, as they had to sell animals to wholesalers at a lower price. Wholesalers paid *shoḥetim* approved by rabbis, which further increased the price of meat. Since in the majority of Polish cities meat was the product of *sheḥitah*, the financial burden arising from the raised prices had to be borne by Christian

[29] NARA, DS, roll 45, no. 860c.4016/453: 9 Mar. 1936, AJC President Cyrus Adler to the Ambassador of Poland Stanisław Patek. Adler listed medical authorities in the field of physiology, such as Professor Sir Michael Foster of Cambridge and Professors Virchof and Reymond, 'eminent German physiologists'.

[30] NARA, DS, roll 45, no. 860c.4016/453: Washington, 17 Mar. 1936, Sokołowski to Adler.

[31] NARA, DS, roll 45, no. 860c.4016/443: *Polish Press Information Bulletin*, vol. vi, no. 107, 2 Mar. 1936, pp. 10, 20–2.

[32] NARA, DS, roll 45, no. 860c.4016/453: Polish Embassy, Washington, 24 Mar. 1936, Sokołowski to Adler, pp. 1–4.   [33] Ibid. 1.

consumers.[34] This applied particularly to those cities in which Christians were the main consumers of meat. They bought their meat from the hindquarters of cattle, while Jews bought the forequarters. The price of meat purchased by Christians was much higher than that of kosher meat.[35] In the opinion of the Polish authorities, *sheḥitah* made animal slaughtering practically a Jewish monopoly. In addition, Christians could not find employment in slaughterhouses and with wholesalers because a Christian was not able to slaughter animals according to *sheḥitah*. It was for this reason that the Polish government supported the bill.[36] However, it was willing to introduce amendments to allow Jews and other ethnic and religious minorities to practise their own religious customs, including *sheḥitah*. To support his case, the Polish diplomat quoted the statement made by deputy minister Fr. Bronisław Żongołłowicz, who at the session of the Administrative and Self-Government Commission of the Sejm on 5 March 1936 had stated: 'In order, therefore, that the Constitution should not be violated, the Bill must be amended in such a way as to make it possible for the Jews to perform ritual slaughter of animals for their consumption.'[37] This was what was actually done in the final act, which made the quantity of animals slaughtered according to *sheḥitah* proportionate to the number of Jewish consumers in a given province.

On 18 March, according to Sokołowski's report, the government proposed an amendment to the bill to allow for ritual slaughter in the case of 'citizens of the Jewish, as well as of the Mohamedan and Karaim creeds'. On this occasion, Juliusz Poniatowski, the Minister of Agriculture, argued that completely banning *sheḥitah* would be contrary 'to our spirit of tolerance, to our Constitution and to our previous legislative enactments'.[38] Poniatowski claimed that restricting ritual slaughter to the Jews, Muslims, and Karaites would maintain religious freedom, while also improving conditions in the Polish meat industry.[39] Foreign Minister Józef Beck also commented on the matter. At a meeting with representatives of the World Federation of Polish Jews in London on 22 March, he claimed that the Polish government would remain faithful to the principle of the legal equality of all citizens 'in accordance with the Constitution and with the Polish traditions'.[40] The

---

[34] 'Christian consumers', particularly as used in relation to the Second Polish Republic, is quite a vague term, but without in any way detracting from Greek Catholics, Russian Orthodox, and Protestants, it may be observed that the matter concerned above all Roman Catholics, who constituted the majority of Polish citizens.

[35] NARA, DS, roll 45, no. 860c.4016/453: Polish Embassy, Washington, 24 Mar. 1936, Sokołowski to Adler, p. 1; see also Modras, *Kościół katolicki i antysemityzm w Polsce*, 237–40.

[36] NARA, DS, roll 45, no. 860c.4016/453: Polish Embassy, Washington, 24 Mar. 1936, Sokołowski to Adler, pp. 1–4.

[37] See ibid. 2. For Fr. Żongołłowicz's attitude towards the bill, see Tomaszewski (ed.), *Najnowsze dzieje Żydów w Polsce*, 195. Sokołowski's letter to Adler refers to the Administrative Commission. This should be the Administrative and Self-Government Commission (Komisja Administracyjno-Samorządowa). See Rudnicki, *Żydzi w parlamencie II Rzeczypospolitej*, 386.

[38] See NARA, DS, roll 45, no. 860c.4016/453: Polish Embassy, Washington, 24 Mar. 1936, Sokołowski to Adler, p. 2.   [39] Ibid.   [40] Ibid.

Administrative and Self-Government Commission and the Sejm, in a plenary session, accepted the government's amendments. Sokołowski informed Adler of this in his letter dated 24 March, which was thus sent four days after the bill had been adopted by the Sejm and forwarded to the Senate for approval. In April 1936 the Senate passed the bill, which was to become law at the beginning of the following year. In his correspondence with Adler, Sokołowski supported his statements with information from the *Polish Press Information Bulletin*. He also quoted various other government statements reproduced in that bulletin, including one made by Marian Zyndram Kościałkowski, the prime minister, in his exposé of 17 February 1936. Zyndram Kościałkowski claimed in this that the difficult economic situation in the country was being used by radical parties of the left and the right to advance their political agendas. On the one hand, the ultra-left-wing party, the 'exponents of the Third International',[41] employed the slogans of class struggle, while on the other the nationalistic parties exploited antisemitic resentment and even provoked anti-Jewish riots. He declared that in both cases those who broke the law would be brought to justice. Władysław Raczkiewicz, the Minister of Internal Affairs, spoke in much the same vein. During the discussion of the educational budget, Wojciech Świętosławski, the Minister of Religious Cults and Public Education, warned that he would take appropriate steps to curtail anti-Jewish excesses in the universities.[42] The Minister of Foreign Affairs, Józef Beck, responded to a question from the Łódź MP Jakub Lejb Mincberg regarding government protection of Polish citizens of Jewish faith residing in Germany. He claimed that, by comparison with officials of other countries, Polish diplomats were certainly inferior to none in the performance of their duties, as was shown by the many expressions of appreciation and gratitude received from these Polish citizens. He stressed that his duty was 'the protection and care of the Polish citizens abroad' regardless of their ethnicity or religion.[43]

Sokołowski also quoted the pastoral letter of the Polish primate Cardinal August Hlond of 29 February 1936, in which he condemned antisemitic rhetoric 'imported from abroad as being contrary to the Church ethics', a clear reference to Nazism, as well as Polish political parties which 'propagate anti-Semitism'.[44] But he was quoting Hlond selectively, since the pastoral letter also accepted the economic boycott of Jews, affirming that 'In commercial relations, it is good to put our own before others and to bypass Jewish shops and Jewish stalls in the market, but one must not plunder a Jewish shop, destroy Jewish goods, break their windows, or hurl stones at their houses.'[45]

---

[41] Ibid. 3.   [42] Ibid.   [43] Ibid. 3–4.

[44] Ibid. 4. Sokołowski's letter from which these quotations are taken was written in English; it wrongly dates the pastoral letter 'On Catholic Moral Principles' to 31 March. See the full text of the pastoral letter in *August Kardynał Hlond, Prymas Polski, Dzieła: Nauczanie, 1897–1948*, i, ed. J. Konieczny (Toruń, 2003), 523–36.

[45] *August Kardynał Hlond, Prymas Polski, Dzieła*, i. 530.

The church hierarchy in Poland thus supported the economic boycott, only dissociating itself from the attendant violence. The letter also contained the following statement: 'In a jew[46] also one should respect and love a human being and a neighbour, even if one is not to respect the indescribably tragic nature of that nation which was the guardian of the messianic idea and which produced the Saviour . . . Beware of those who incite anti-Jewish violence. They serve an evil cause.'[47]

Cyrus Adler replied to Sokołowski on 2 April 1936.[48] In response to the claim that Polish farmers could not sell whole animals to wholesalers, he replied that in the United States, and most probably in every other country which observed well-defined rules of hygiene, butchers never bought a whole animal but only a part of it, because they would not be able to sell it quickly enough. In response to the complaint that wholesalers did not employ Christian workers even if they were able to slaughter an animal in accordance with the principles defined by the Jewish religion, he pointed out that *shoḥetim*, according to Jewish religious law, were required to be pious Jews and to be qualified to decide if animals were healthy and fit for consumption.[49] As regards the claim that Christian consumers were subsidizing kosher meat, he pointed out that the hindquarters of the animal were always more expensive because they were considered more tasty and more suitable for consumption. He appreciated the assurances conveyed in the statements by the politicians quoted by Sokołowski, but those assurances were at odds with information received: 'the reports come almost daily of further anti-Jewish disturbances' in Poland.[50] After referring to the great joy of 'all Americans' at the rebirth of the Polish state and recognizing 'the severe trials' Poland had gone through during the war and and in the subsequent struggle to establish its frontiers, he expressed the hope that Poland would keep in mind its difficult history and deal fairly with all its citizens, becoming in this way an example for other nations to follow. He recognized that much of the intolerance resulted from economic hardship, and 'no doubt the severe economic condition of the world was responsible to a great extent'.[51] Yet this could not justify the removal of Jewish employees from public administration and even from the nationalized sectors of industry, where Jews had hitherto been employed. As a result, in those sectors of the national economy where the state was the employer, Polish citizens of Jewish extraction could not successfully seek employment.[52] Because of this, Jews in Poland and the United

---

[46] The capitalization follows that of 'żydzie' in the Polish original.

[47] *August Kardynał Hlond, Prymas Polski, Dzieła*, i. 530.

[48] NARA, DS, roll 45, no. 860c.4016/453: 2 Apr. 1936, Adler to Sokołowski, pp. 1–2.

[49] Ibid. 1. [50] Ibid. 2. [51] Ibid.

[52] Complaints made by Jewish organizations about the dismissal of Jews from municipal and state jobs were recorded from the very beginning of the Second Polish Republic's existence. For example, in January 1919 the trade unions demanded that Jewish employees be dismissed from jobs on the railways. The superiors of the fired employees gave them employment references which stated their diligence in fulfilling their duties, their dismissal being motivated only by their Jewish origin. Here is an example of such a document: 'This is to certify that Szmul Gorowicz was employed as a worker at the

States saw the bill banning *sheḥitah* as part of an anti-Jewish economic policy. Even though this could be in part attributed to the economic crisis, 'nevertheless, I very much fear that the Jews of Poland have had the minimum rather than the maximum of the good fortune and protection which we all hoped they would enjoy'.[53] The results of this policy had 'reduced the Jewish population in Poland to a condition of poverty worse I think than has prevailed at any time during this and a great part of the preceding century'.[54]

Although this last statement could be seen as an exaggeration, it reflected American Jewish alarm at the situation of the Jews in Poland. At the same time, in spite of all the critical remarks, the correspondence between Adler and Sokołowski was conducted in a friendly tone. Nevertheless, at the end of the letter Adler expressed his anxiety that not everyone in the government and in parliament shared the tolerant stance of the Prime Minister, the Minister of Foreign Affairs, and Sokołowski himself. Adler also sent this exchange of letters with Sokołowski to Cordell Hull.[55]

In the end, the law of 20 March 1936 introduced only a partial ban on *sheḥitah*. A total ban was introduced only in provinces where Jews comprised less than 3 per cent of the total population. Even in those provinces—Pomerania, Poznania, and Silesia, the area of which roughly covered the territory of the former Prussian partition— local authorities had the right to allow *sheḥitah* with the approval of the provincial governor.[56] In the remainder of the country, the law restricted *sheḥitah* to a proportion corresponding to that of the 'Jewish, Muslim, and Karaite population inhabiting the respective province'.[57] The law was to come into force on 1 January 1937. The American Jewish Committee found the law completely unacceptable, estimating that the restriction of *sheḥitah* had destroyed the livelihood of some 20,000 Jewish families who had worked in the meat industry. It also estimated that the income of the *kehilot*, which were partly dependent on the sale of kosher meat, had been halved, which severely limited their ability to relieve the ever more widespread impoverishment of the Jewish community. As a result, Polish Jews were now increasingly dependent on the assistance of Jewish charitable organizations abroad.[58]

Brześć factory from 1 November 1917 to 1 January 1919, when he was dismissed because of his Jewish origin, as a consequence of the directive issued by the railway trade unions. Signed by: Director of the Workshops in Brześć.' See Library of Congress, Washington, DC, Manuscript Division, Papers of Henry Morgenthau, reel 29, container 35, Collected Material on Economic Boycott, Warsaw, 5 Aug. 1919, American Mission to Poland, Appendix no. 2; Translation from the Polish of confirmation of discharge. The original of the handwritten document in Polish, with stamps and signatures, along with a translation into English, can be seen at NARA, DS, roll 15, no. 860c.4016, frames 0985, 0987, 0988; quoted in P. Różański, *Stany Zjednoczone wobec kwestii żydowskiej w Polsce, 1918–1921* (Gdańsk, 2007), 157.

[53] NARA, DS, roll 45, no. 860c.4016/453: 2 Apr. 1936, Adler to Sokołowski, p. 2.   [54] Ibid.
[55] NARA, DS, roll 45, no. 860c.4016/453: New York, 17 Apr. 1936, Adler to Hull.
[56] Rudnicki, 'Ritual Slaughter as a Political Issue', 150–1; id., *Żydzi w parlamencie II Rzeczypospolitej*, 387.
[57] Tomaszewski (ed.), *Najnowsze dzieje Żydów w Polsce*, 195.   [58] *AJYB*, 40 (1938), 596.

The controversies surrounding the bill banning *sheḥitah*, and the growth of anti-semitism in general, were carefully observed by John Cudahy, the US ambassador in Poland. In a report titled 'Increasing anti-Semitism in Poland', dated 1 April 1936, he described the ban on *sheḥitah* as one of the main manifestations of this phenomenon.[59] In his opinion, the bill presented to the Sejm on 7 February 1936 by Janina Prystorowa introduced 'a new note of bitterness' into the already far from satisfactory Polish–Jewish relations. Had the bill been accepted in its original form, it would have banned ritual slaughter all over the country. However, in its final form, approved by both houses of parliament, the bill permitted *sheḥitah* 'without restrictions', except in the western provinces of Poland, where Jews made up less than 3 per cent of the total population; here it might render impossible 'the preparation of kosher meats'. In these provinces, local authorities had the right to forbid *sheḥitah* but the Jews were allowed 'to import kosher meat from other parts of Poland'.[60]

Cudahy speculated as to the real motives of those who introduced the bill. Certainly Jews felt that it abrogated the rights which they enjoyed under article 111 of the constitution.[61] Cudahy believed that humanitarian and economic motives,

[59] NARA, DS, roll 45, no. 860c.4016/451: Warsaw, 1 Apr. 1936, Cudahy to the Secretary of State, subject: 'Increasing anti-Semitism in Poland', pp. 1–13. In his report, Cudahy raised, amongst other things, the problem of growing antisemitism in the Polish countryside, as when Jews were evicted from their places in markets where they had traditionally traded. He also mentioned repeated anti-Jewish riots and tried to determine the reasons for such tensions. Cudahy estimated the number of Jews in Poland at some 3.5 million. He sought the beginning of the tension between Poles and Jews in the influx of Russian Jews before the First World War into those Polish lands that later fell within the borders of the Second Republic. He correctly argued that the organized antisemitic campaign was initiated by the Roman Dmowski boycotts and had started in 1912, though this date did not appear in the report. Instead, Cudahy placed the beginnings 'shortly before the World War'. The economic boycott, observed the diplomat, had proved long-lasting and had recently 'become intensified for several reasons'. Among the reasons for Polish antisemitism, Cudahy listed the period of the German occupation during the First World War, when Jews supported the occupiers, and the allegedly pro-Bolshevik attitude of the Jewish population at the time of the Polish–Bolshevik war. Another element of the growing aversion to Jews was the imposition on Poland of the Minority Treaty of 28 June 1919. Polish public opinion laid the blame for that treaty on the Jews, claimed Cudahy, which 'placed it [Poland] in a position of inferiority before the world'. The Great Depression brought about new animosities in Polish–Jewish relations because the general public felt that the Jewish minority was not so painfully affected by it. This, in turn, allegedly made the non-Jewish part of the population jealous and prone to the radical antisemitic solutions proposed and practised in Nazi Germany. In addition, the death of Józef Piłsudski, according to the American diplomat, was a turning point in Polish–Jewish relations, because his regime stemmed the rise of antisemitic attitudes in Poland.

[60] NARA, DS, roll 45, no. 860c.4016/451: Warsaw, 1 Apr. 1936, Cudahy to the Secretary of State, subject: 'Increasing anti-Semitism in Poland', p. 10.

[61] Article 111 reads: 'All citizens are guaranteed freedom of conscience and religion. No citizen can be restricted in laws enjoyed by other citizens because of his faith and religious persuasion. All inhabitants of the Polish State have a right to practise their faith both publicly and privately, and to observe their religion or ritual as long as it does not violate public order or public decency': *Konstytucje Rzeczypospolitej Polskiej*, ed. Falandysz, 391.

including the drive to remove Jews from the meat industry, were less important than the desire of the army to ensure 'reserves of meat in case of war'.[62] This objective appeared 'most plausible' to him, while 'the desire of destroying the monopoly of slaughtering which the Jews in Poland long have enjoyed' should not be seen as the primary goal of the bill.[63] Jews disposed of meat within forty-eight hours, because they had no deep-freeze facilities. Such facilities hardly existed in Poland, even in the three western provinces. Cudahy believed that the goal of the bill was to transfer the meat trade to Polish companies and Polish retailers, while simultaneously cold-storage facilities were built. Meat reserves for a war could only be created once such facilities had been established. This was the main aim of the bill, and ending the dominant Jewish position in the meat trade was only a side effect. There is some basis to Cudahy's speculations. In the spring of 1937 a 'state agricultural and provisions plan' was established to create a supply reserve for the army. Investments were made in the infrastructure with the construction of a large slaughterhouse and processing plant in Gdynia, and the beginnings of a cold-storage facility in Warsaw.[64] The military and the economic goals in fact seemed to complement each other. According to the American ambassador, the takeover of slaughterhouses and wholesale outlets from Jews by the Christian population would allow for the construction of new facilities for processing and storing meat. The desire to exclude Jews from the meat trade was the reason why the authorities did not simply force the Jewish owners of wholesale outlets and meat shops gradually to equip them with appropriate deep-freeze facilities. This would have been a much simpler solution, but it was unacceptable on antisemitic grounds.

Cudahy's report provides an insight into how the problem was viewed, not only by American diplomats, but also by those Poles with whom they came into contact. Cudahy's remarks can also be seen as an answer to Cyrus Adler's argument that in most countries butchers did not buy a whole animal for reasons of hygiene, as they needed to sell all their products quickly. If in the Poland of that time, a poor and underdeveloped country, there existed only a small number of deep-freeze facilities, certainly in a country like the United States such facilities must have been fairly common.

In his report Cudahy also repeated the claim that the Christian population of Poland had been 'compelled to eat kosher meats, for all slaughtering is in the hands of the Jews'.[65] The only exception was in the western provinces, where the percentage of Jews was very low. He also argued that the question of the deep-freeze facilities would not disappear. On the contrary, there would be an increased demand for

---

[62] NARA, DS, roll 45, no. 860c.4016/451: Warsaw, 1 Apr. 1936, Cudahy to the Secretary of State, subject: 'Increasing anti-Semitism in Poland', p. 11.   [63] Ibid.

[64] Skodlarski, *Zarys historii gospodarczej Polski*, 299. The goal was to create grain reserves of 25,000 tons of rye and 27,000 tons of oats, to construct granaries and a modern grain elevator, and to make investments in the food-processing industry.

[65] NARA, DS, roll 45, no. 860c.4016/451: Warsaw, 1 Apr. 1936, Cudahy to the Secretary of State, subject: 'Increasing anti-Semitism in Poland', p. 11.

them.[66] He also commented on the way the debate had strengthened attempts to undermine the economic situation of the Jews: 'A considerable part of the non-Jewish population, which formerly either was not aware of or was indifferent to the fact that it could obtain only kosher meats has been stirred by the lively debate in the Parliament and by the press campaign which accompanied it. It almost certainly will demand non-kosher meats as soon as they become available.'[67]

On the question of the bill, the government, in his view, had adopted a wait-and-see and 'non-committal' attitude.[68] Once the amendments reinstating *sheḥitah* were introduced, the government 'mildly supported' the project. He believed that the Polish authorities considered the introduction of the bill, at least in 1936, inappropriate and backed down only when pressed by the General Staff.[69] To support his hypothesis of the decisive influence of the military, he recalled the fact that for a long time Jews had held a monopoly on the slaughter of farm animals and the Christian population had not objected. The first attempt at banning the ritual slaughter of farm animals had been made as early as 1923.

The bill of March 1936 severely limiting *sheḥitah*, and the proposed amendments to it of 1938, were only two of many attempts to undermine the position of the Jews undertaken after 1935. Among legislation discriminating against Jews were the Bill on the Legal Profession and the Bill on the Production and Trade of Devotional Objects of 1938. The goal of both those acts was the economic advance of ethnic Poles at the expense of citizens of Jewish faith.[70] If we take into account

[66] Interestingly, in his report Cudahy never mentioned importing such installations from abroad but talked about 'constructing' or 'producing' them, suggesting that they would be made domestically. See NARA, DS, roll 45, no. 860c.4016/451: Warsaw, 1 Apr. 1936, Cudahy to the Secretary of State, subject: 'Increasing anti-Semitism in Poland', pp. 11–12.

[67] Ibid. 12.   [68] Ibid.   [69] Ibid.

[70] The Bill on the Production and Trade of Devotional Objects of March 1938 forbade Jews to produce and sell objects of a religious nature. Publicly, the authors of this bill referred to the offence caused to the religious sensitivity of Catholics, but, as with the bill banning *sheḥitah*, their goal was to destroy the monopoly of Jewish craftsmen and merchants in the trade in devotional objects. The bill changing the rules of the legal profession introduced two-stage legal training: two years in a court of law and three years in a barrister's office, prior to taking the Bar examinations. Previously, legal training was limited only to a period of articles at a law firm. The new bill aimed at restricting the number of potential Jewish lawyers, since the courts of law as state institutions were dominated by Poles, who reluctantly hired Jews. On the other hand, however, law offices in Poland were in many cases run by Jews, which in turn made it difficult for Christians to go through the training, as Jews accepted mostly their own co-religionists. Ambassador Biddle presented such an interpretation of the intentions of the lawmakers in his report to the Secretary of State. In line with Polish estimates, he informed Washington that Jews made up 53% of the Polish Bar; he also quoted German data estimating the proportion of Jews at less than 45%. In addition, he considered that the Bill on the Legal Professions 'meets with wide and unquestioned approval in racially Polish circles'. In Biddle's opinion, the only objection raised against the bill was that it did not apply retroactively to already practising lawyers. This would delay the expulsion of Jews from the legal profession. See Modras, *Kościół katolicki i anty-semityzm w Polsce*, 240–2; S. Rudnicki, 'Walka o zmianę ustawy o adwokaturze w II Rzeczypospolitej', *Kwartalnik Historii Żydów*, 201 (2002), 49–61; id., *Żydzi w parlamencie II Rzeczypospolitej*, 388. For Biddle's report to the Secretary of State, see NARA, DS, roll 45, no. 860c.4016/548: Warsaw, 6 Apr.

the frequent antisemitic riots of 1936 and 1937, notably those at Przytyk and Brześć nad Bugiem,[71] the *numerus clausus* restricting the number of Jewish students at Polish universities, the introduction of 'ghetto benches' there, and the attempts of the Polish authorities from September 1936 to facilitate the mass emigration of the Jewish population from Poland, we get a picture of the escalating anti-Jewish campaign in the second half of the 1930s. At the beginning of 1937, the annual report in the *American Jewish Year Book* noted that 'since the death of Marshal Piłsudski, discrimination against the Jews had grown more widespread, physical outbreaks had become more numerous and while anti-Semitism had grown more flagrant, the authorities had apparently become more indulgent to such agitation than the previous government'.[72]

Under these circumstances, it is no surprise that American Jews, not for the first time in the inter-war years, sought to investigate the situation of their Polish co-religionists on the spot. Ambassador Cudahy reported that at the end of March 1936 George Backer, president of the board of the Jewish Telegraphic Agency, and Jacob Landau, its managing director, visited Poland. Both met Cudahy at the American embassy. Backer agreed to give him a copy of his memorandum on their visits, which Cudahy promised to send to the State Department should it prove to be 'of interest'.[73]

1938, Biddle to the Secretary of State, subject: 'Growing official support of anti-Semitic measures in Poland', pp. 3–5.

[71] The fullest monograph on the events at Przytyk, based on broad archival research, is P. Gontarczyk, *Pogrom? Zajścia polsko-żydowskie w Przytyku 9 marca 1936 roku: Mity, fakty, dokumenty* (Biała Podlaska and Pruszków, 2000). However, it is a deeply flawed work. For example, it makes the exaggerated claim that 'the events at Przytyk were the most tragic incident of that type in pre-war Poland and almost immediately became used in a political campaign' (p. 9). The number of deaths that occurred here—two Jews and one Pole—does not bear comparison with the much more tragic incidents which occurred in Lviv, Vilna, and Pinsk in the years 1918–19. Several dozen Jews died in each of those incidents. See P. Różański, 'Pogrom lwowski 22 listopada 1918 roku w świetle zeznań Organizacji Syjonistycznej złożonych przed Komisją Morgenthaua', *Kwartalnik Historii Żydów*, 211 (2004), 347–58; id., 'Wilno, 19–21 kwietnia 1919 roku', *Kwartalnik Historii Żydów*, 217 (2006), 13–34; J. Tomaszewski, 'Pińsk, Saturday 5 April 1919', *Polin*, 1 (1986), 227–51. On the incidents at Brześć nad Bugiem, see W. Śleszyński, *Zajścia antyżydowskie w Brześciu nad Bugiem 13 maja 1937 roku* (Białystok, 2007). See also J. Żyndul, *Zajścia antyżydowskie w Polsce w latach 1935–1937* (Warsaw, 1994).

[72] *AJYB*, 39 (1937), 227. For more on the antisemitic riots at Polish universities, see P. Różański, 'Wystąpienia antyżydowskie na polskich uczelniach wyższych w latach 1936–1937 w raportach ambasady amerykańskiej w Warszawie', *Studia Judaica*, 12 (2009), 207–35. On *numerus clausus* at Polish universities, see H. Haumann, *Historia Żydów w Europie Środkowej i Wschodniej* (Warsaw, 2000), 236–7; M. Kulczykowski, *Żydzi-studenci Uniwersytetu Jagiellońskiego w Drugiej Rzeczypospolitej (1918–1939)* (Kraków, 2004), 439 ff.; Z. Opacki, 'Postawy profesorów Uniwersytetu Stefana Batorego w Wilnie wobec antysemityzmu na uczelni: Marian Zdziechowski i Manfred Kridl', in W. Moskovich and I. Fijałkowska-Janiak (eds.), *Jewish–Polish and Jewish–Russian Contacts* (Jerusalem and Gdańsk, 2003), 88–9.

[73] NARA, DS, roll 45, no. 860c.4016/451: Warsaw, 1 Apr. 1936, Cudahy to the Secretary of State, subject: 'Increasing anti-Semitism in Poland', pp. 12–13.

The next American ambassador in Warsaw, Anthony J. Drexel Biddle Jr., followed attentively the fate of the bill limiting *sheḥitah* and other manifestations of worsening Polish–Jewish relations.[74] After the only partially successful campaign to get rid of *sheḥitah*, those seeking to ban it did not give up, and in February 1938 they proposed amendments to the law that would have practically forbidden it. These amendments were accepted by the Administrative and Self-Government Commission on 22 March 1938 and passed by the Sejm three days later.[75] This last vote rejected government amendments as well as those proposed by the Jewish parliamentary deputy Emil Sommerstein. Biddle pointed this out in a telegram of 29 March addressed to Cordell Hull, the Secretary of State, and also to President Roosevelt. Along with the bill banning ritual slaughter, Biddle mentioned also two other bills reflecting the 'intensification of anti-Semitism in Poland'.[76] These were the law depriving people of citizenship who had lived outside Poland for more than five years, and that limiting Jewish access to the legal profession.[77] These two bills, along with others that never actually became law in Poland, were intended to undermine the economic and political position of the Jewish community. This was well understood by the American ambassador, who had no doubt that, although the drafts of these laws did not mention Jews, they were aimed at them, as was the attempt to ban *sheḥitah*. The attitude of the government was much more ambiguous. In Biddle's view, the amendment to the law on *sheḥitah* had not been initiated by the government. In his opinion, the antisemitic intentions of its drafters were demonstrated by the rapidity with which it was passed in spite of the objections raised by two deputy ministers: the Minister of Religious Cults and Public Education, who believed that the bill was in violation of the constitution, and the Minister of Agriculture, who feared economic unrest because of a fall in meat consumption.[78] According to Biddle, some 2.5 million Jewish consumers required kosher meat. Apart from the Jewish and Ukrainian deputies, only five members of parliament voted against the amended bill.[79] Passage of the bill in the Senate,

[74] Anthony J. Drexel Biddle Jr. was a non-career appointee. He received his appointment as ambassador on 4 May 1937, presented his credentials in Warsaw on 2 June 1937, and completed his mission on 1 December 1943. See the Internet site of the US Department of State, <http://history.state.gov/departmenthistory/people/biddle-anthony-joseph-drexel-jr>, accessed 1 Sept. 2010. For more on Biddle and his activities in Poland, see *Poland and the Coming of the Second World War: The Diplomatic Papers of A. J. Drexel Biddle, Jr., United States Ambassador to Poland, 1937–1939*, ed. P. V. Cannistraro, E. D. Wynot Jr., and T. P. Kovaleff (Columbus, Ohio, 1976), 3–38.

[75] Rudnicki, *Żydzi w parlamencie II Rzeczypospolitej*, 387.

[76] NARA, DS, roll 45, no. 860c.4016/545: Warsaw, 29 Mar. 1938, Biddle to the Secretary of State, headed 'Strictly confidential for the president and secretary'. Sections of the document are published in *Foreign Relations of the United States*, ii. 652.

[77] On the subject of rescinding citizenship, see W. T. Drymmer, 'Zagadnienie żydowskie w Polsce w latach 1935–1939: Wspomnienie z pracy w Ministerstwie Spraw Zagranicznych', *Zeszyty Historyczne* (Paris), 13 (1968), 66; J. Tomaszewski, *Preludium zagłady: Wygnanie Żydów polskich z Niemiec w 1938 r.* (Warsaw, 1993), 75–113.

[78] *Foreign Relations of the United States*, ii. 652.   [79] Ibid.

Biddle pointed out, did not mean it would necessarily become law, as there was a chance that the Senate, which in the past had proved to be 'more liberal' than the lower house on Jewish matters, would under government influence postpone its ratification to the following session.

In the following month Biddle sent a nine-page report (not counting attachments) to Hull describing the intensification of antisemitism in the Polish parliament.[80] He noted the growing support for anti-Jewish measures in Polish 'official circles, particularly in both Houses of the Parliament'.[81] The government, until then relatively immune to the rising antisemitic wave, did not now oppose its manifestations—at least, not openly—and gave in to pressure from the nationalists, who accused the opponents of anti-Jewish measures of yielding to Jewish and foreign influence. The Polish–Jewish tension was manifested in the fact that practically every issue discussed in the Sejm and the Senate provided an occasion for antisemitic rhetoric. Previously the upper house of the Polish parliament had been considered more liberal towards Jews than the Sejm. 'The spokesmen of the Jewish minority' in parliament inevitably responded strongly to manifestations of antisemitism, which by March 1938 had created an inflamed atmosphere.[82]

For Biddle, the course of the budgetary session which ended on 31 March had demonstrated that the civic rights of Jews and their interests were clearly endangered by the increasing wave of antisemitism. As evidence he cited the bills which had been passed which were 'manifestly harmful to Jewish interests' and were directed against their customs and religious beliefs. Among these was the Bill on the Production and Trade of Devotional Objects.[83] This was debated in the Sejm in March 1937 and passed a year later. Those who supported this bill, which forbade Jews from producing and selling religious objects, claimed that they wished to end an affront to Catholic religious sensibilities,[84] but as in the case of the bill banning ritual slaughter their goal was to drive Jewish craftsmen and merchants out of the market in religious objects.[85] Another bill adversely affecting Jews was that passed on 31 March, which took Polish citizenship away from people residing abroad. These were not the only proposals which adversely affected Jews. Parliament had also considered a law banning 'Jewish–Masonic–Communist' activities, reflecting a belief in a conspiracy of Jews, Masons, and Communists, and

[80] NARA, DS, roll 45, no. 860c.4016/548: Warsaw, 6 Apr. 1938, Biddle to the Secretary of State, subject: 'Growing official support of anti-Semitic measures in Poland', partially published in *Foreign Relations of the United States*, ii. 653–4.   [81] *Foreign Relations of the United States*, ii. 653.

[82] Ibid.   [83] Ibid.

[84] Fr. Stefan Downar, who drafted the bill, claimed that 'the production of Christian religious objects by Jews is an affront to Christian sensibilities': see Rudnicki, *Żydzi w parlamencie II Rzeczypospolitej*, 388.

[85] Fr. Downar stated in his speech, 'It is high time that we made efforts to achieve full economic independence of foreign elements, as without that we shall never be economically independent': quoted in Rudnicki, *Żydzi w parlamencie II Rzeczypospolitej*, 388. On the trade in religious objects and the bill banning the production and sale of them by people of other religions, see Modras, *Kościół katolicki i antysemityzm w Polsce*, 240–2.

another excluding Jews from the production and sale of tobacco products, although neither of these was enacted.[86]

Biddle also discussed at length the proposed amendments to the law limiting *sheḥitah*. He recalled that this law had only been passed after an 'acrimonious debate' and had reduced the amount of meat slaughtered in accordance with Jewish law to one-quarter of the amount before its introduction.[87] Nevertheless, even now the meat trade remained mostly 'in the hands of the Jews' and meat slaughtered according to *sheḥitah* was still bought by Christians.[88] The bill of 1936, he claimed, had been intended to make possible the entry of 'racial Poles' into the meat industry in the capacity of butchers, wholesalers, and retailers and had raised protests from Jews who felt threatened with the loss of their 'practical monopoly on this lucrative trade'.[89] While it had ostensibly been motivated by humanitarian considerations, the proposed amendments were clearly anti-Jewish and strictly economic. They were supported by the majority of Polish society, while 'governmental circles on the other hand apparently are not prepared as yet to interfere with the exercise of ritual slaughter as an integral and vital part of the Jewish rite'.[90] The government was, however, aware of public opinion abroad, as the authorities knew that Polish Jews could generate support and sympathy in defence of *sheḥitah*. The Minister of Agriculture was also wary of disrupting the meat industry and was prepared to postpone radical changes until Poles were ready to take over this branch of the economy, which would also require a more thorough investigation of the market and the construction of deep-freeze facilities. In this way Biddle echoed the views of his predecessor, Cudahy. 'Jewish parliamentary and religious circles' had certainly made clear the deleterious consequences the amendments would have on meat consumption. Since most Polish Jews were Orthodox, this threat was not mere words.[91] In his conclusion, Biddle argued that the support of 'Polish official circles' for antisemitic proposals in parliament was a response to popular pressure. The government was not the originator of the tension in Polish–Jewish relations but was rather deferring to the prevailing atmosphere. At the same time, by giving in to the antisemites, the Polish authorities were losing control of the domestic agenda. They were destabilizing the country and undermining efforts to create a positive image of Poland abroad. In effect, the government was no longer 'a brake on the rapidly developing anti-Semitic tendencies and activities' within Polish society.[92]

Obviously the 1936 law on *sheḥitah* and the proposed amendments were motivated by a number of considerations—humane, economic, and political. Above all, they were the result of a desire to eliminate Jews from the process of producing and selling meat, in order to advance Poles economically. In this way the Polish middle

---

[86] *Foreign Relations of the United States*, ii. 654.

[87] NARA, DS, roll 45, no. 860c.4016/548: Warsaw, 6 Apr. 1938, Biddle to the Secretary of State, subject: 'Growing official support of anti-Semitic measures in Poland', p. 6.

[88] Ibid. 6 n.   [89] Ibid. 6.   [90] Ibid. 7.   [91] Ibid.   [92] Ibid. 9.

class would be strengthened.[93] Poland was not, however, the first country to ban *sheḥitah*. Switzerland forbade it as early as 1893, Sweden on 3 August 1928, and Norway on 12 June 1929. A ban on ritual slaughter was introduced in Austria by a law of 25 May 1930, long before the Anschluss in 1938, while the Nazis introduced such a ban in 1933. *Sheḥitah* was also prohibited in some French cities, notably in Lyon and Nice.[94] These precedents did not play a decisive role in the argument over *sheḥitah* in Poland. Moreover, there were many countries in Europe and North America which did permit *sheḥitah*. The supporters of *sheḥitah* in Poland, organized in the Committee for the Protection of Ritual Slaughter (Komitet dla Obrony Uboju Rytualnego), listed seventeen European countries, plus the United States, where the practice of *sheḥitah* did not encounter any difficulties.[95]

While it could be claimed that *sheḥitah* did involve unnecessary suffering to animals, its advocates argued that this was also true of the stunning of an animal before slaughter. In addition, it could hardly be claimed that humanitarian considerations were a major factor in passing the bill, taking into account the backward conditions which prevailed in the Polish countryside in the 1930s and the way animals were treated by Polish or Ukrainian peasants. This treatment violated all humanitarian norms. In addition, as Cyrus Adler had pointed out, the Annual Convention of the American Humane Association had concluded that *sheḥitah* was a humane form of slaughter. The Polish side responded by quoting the findings of other animal protection bodies, such as those of the Congress of the Associations for the Protection of Animals in Brussels in August 1935, at which a resolution was passed which demanded that animals be stunned before slaughter.[96]

In the United States, and particularly among American Jews, the attempt to ban *sheḥitah* was seen as a sign of the growing strength of antisemitism in Polish society. This was also the view of the two American ambassadors in Warsaw during this period. Ambassador Biddle also saw the legislation as the result of the 'Polish official circles' yielding to the anti-Jewish tendencies permeating Polish society. In this respect, their conclusions do not differ in essence from those of Polish historians, who agree that the 1930s, particularly after 1935, were marked by increased Polish–Jewish animosities. Against this background, the 1920s appear in a more favourable light, which was reflected in the better image of the Polish Republic on the international scene.[97] The view of American diplomats that economic and political motives

[93] Rudnicki, *Żydzi w parlamencie II Rzeczypospolitej*, 385–8; id., 'Ritual Slaughter as a Political Issue', 150–1, 156; J. Tomaszewski, 'Społeczność żydowska a Polacy w II Rzeczypospolitej', in E. Grześkowiak-Łuczyk (ed.), *Polska — Polacy — mniejszości narodowe* (Wrocław, 1992), 118; J. Tomaszewski, in id. (ed.), *Najnowsze dzieje Żydów w Polsce*, 194–6.

[94] NARA, DS, roll 45, no. 860c.4016/444: 'The Ritual Slaughter Bill', *Polish Press Information Bulletin*, p. 21.   [95] See Rudnicki, 'Ritual Slaughter as a Political Issue', 152.

[96] NARA, DS, roll 45, no. 860c.4016/444: 'The Ritual Slaughter Bill', *Polish Press Information Bulletin*, p. 21.

[97] For a historian researching how Jewish issues influenced Polish–American relations, it is very interesting to compare the perception of Polish–Jewish relations by two different American ambassa-

lay at the foundation of the bill forbidding *sheḥitah* in 1936 and the amendments two years later is also confirmed by the later findings of historians. Ambassador Cudahy particularly stressed the role of the General Staff in supporting the bill. However, he did not notice another possible political aspect to the bill, namely the attempt by one faction of the Sanacja, led by Janina Prystorowa, the wife of a former prime minister, which had been excluded from power, both to embarrass the government and to win support from the right-wing section of Polish society.[98] Polish public opinion generally supported the ban on *sheḥitah*. The government, however, could not openly support the proposed law because it violated religious freedom and the right of Jewish society to preserve its 'national identity', which were guaranteed by the constitution. At the same time, serious opposition to the proposed law would make the government unpopular with the public. It seems that this may have been the true reason for its initiation.

The amendments to the law passed by the Sejm in March 1938, which completely forbade *sheḥitah*, were never ratified by the Senate. Before they could be debated President Ignacy Mościcki dissolved parliament in September 1938. The next Sejm passed a bill imposing a complete ban on *sheḥitah* to come into force from the end of 1942, but this also was not passed by the Senate.[99] The partition of Czechoslovakia in March 1939 and the growing threat from the Third Reich led the Polish authorities to place anti-Jewish policies in abeyance. The American Jewish Committee emphasized the role of Foreign Minister Beck in putting a halt to antisemitic propaganda, and above all the anti-Jewish activities of members of parliament. According to the annual report in the *American Jewish Year Book* of 1939, legal discrimination against the Jewish population 'clashed' with Beck's foreign policy.[100] In view of the growing threat from Nazi Germany, the authorities of the Second Polish Republic initiated a policy of mobilizing all sectors of society in

dors to Poland: the first one ever, Hugh S. Gibson, and the last one of the two inter-war decades, Drexel Biddle. Both of them paid much attention to Jewish issues in Poland in the reports that they sent to the State Department in Washington. Neither diplomat ever questioned the existence of Polish antisemitism. However, Gibson in his correspondence with the State Department in the years 1919 and 1922 defended the stance taken by the Poles towards the accusations that they organized Jewish pogroms and discriminated against Jews in the rebuilt Polish state. This attitude of the American representative in Poland brought him much trouble from the American Jews led by Louis Marshall. On Gibson's activities in Poland, see M. Weil, *A Pretty Good Club: The Founding Fathers of the U.S. Foreign Service* (New York, 1978), 24–45; P. Różański, 'Hugh Gibson wobec kwestii żydowskiej w Polsce w 1919 roku', *Przegląd Historyczny*, 2004, no. 2, pp. 233–40; id., *Stany Zjednoczone wobec kwestii żydowskiej w Polsce*, 152–5. Hugh S. Gibson was a Foreign Service officer, the first ever Ambassador Extraordinary and Plenipotentiary in the history of Polish–American relations. He presented his credentials in Warsaw to the head of state on 2 May 1919 and completed his mission in Poland on 3 May 1924. See the Internet site of the US Department of State, <http://history.state. gov/departmenthistory/people/gibson-hugh-simons>, accessed 1 Sept. 2010.

[98] Professor Jerzy Tomaszewski has raised this aspect of the bill. See Tomaszewski (ed.), *Najnowsze dzieje Żydów w Polsce*, 194–5.

[99] Ibid. 195–6.   [100] *AJYB*, 41 (1939), 293–4.

preparation for the probable war. It was clear that exacerbating the conflicts with citizens of the Jewish religion on the eve of war would have led to a fragmentation of society, and there was a risk that, in the words of the report, it would have 'plunged the country into a constitutional crisis'.[101] Possibly for the same reason, in May 1939 Prime Minister Felicjan Sławoj Składkowski urged the members of parliament not to create difficulties for the government by proposing anti-Jewish measures. Thus the argument that it was the outbreak of war that prevented the Senate's ratification of the total ban on *sheḥitah* is not justified, as work on the ratification of that bill, as well as of other anti-Jewish laws, was deliberately put on hold a few months before the war started: it was the break-up of Czechoslovakia in March 1939 that led the Senate to halt the process. According to the report in the *American Jewish Year Book*, the course of international events had twice, in spite of everything, protected the legal status of the Jewish minority in Poland: first on 13 September 1938, when the president dissolved parliament in response to the Czechoslovak crisis, and secondly on 15 March 1939, when the German army entered Prague.[102] A total ban on *sheḥitah* was only introduced with the German occupation of Poland.

Translated from the Polish by Aleksandra Hawiger

[101] Ibid. 294.   [102] Ibid.

Imagining Polish Jews

British Perspectives in the Period 1944–1946

MICHAEL FLEMING

THIS CHAPTER ANALYSES the views and actions of British officialdom regarding Polish Jews in the years 1944–6. It considers the positions taken by staff of the British embassy to Poland and experts from the Foreign Office, and examines the perspectives of officials based within the British zone of occupation in Germany. It traces how Polish Jews were imagined in these places and shows how these presuppositions support Tony Kushner's thesis on 'liberal' antisemitism.[1] The marked similarities between British and Polish positions on Jews in the immediate aftermath of the war are explored and the differences, where they emerge, are discussed.

The essay highlights how Polish debates about Jews found echoes within British policy-making circles. It illustrates how Polish nationalist and communist policy prescriptions were comprehended and, perhaps more surprisingly, mirrored in British discussions. I argue that the British understanding of difference was marked by a liberalism which emphasized uniformity rather than plurality, and which conflated volume (number of people) and type (sort of people). This perspective led to a biased understanding of Polish–Jewish relations, with the consequence that stereotypes of both Jews and Poles played a role in official analysis of and commentary on the difficult political situation that unfolded in Poland in the immediate aftermath of the war. I also contend that British 'liberal' understanding of Polish Jews echoes, at different moments, the positions of both Polish nationalists and communists, suggesting that the debate on Polish antisemitism during the immediate post-war period would benefit from a broader analysis in order to interrogate how British (and American) liberalism influenced not only the Polish government-in-exile, but also (if at all) Polish communists during the crucial early post-war years.

I am therefore sketching a geography of engagement, a notion that can be conceptualized in the following way. It deals with how encounters, whether with texts,

---

[1] T. Kushner, *The Holocaust and the Liberal Imagination: A Social and Cultural History* (Oxford, 1994).

ideas, or problematics, are influenced by the places and communities in which they take place and vice versa. This is by no means a novel approach; it echoes David Livingstone's geography of reading that he has recently explored in relation to the reception of Darwin in different places.[2] The geography of engagement analysed here illustrates how British officials, whether based in London, Warsaw, or Berlin, negotiated a landscape dominated by a particular liberal world view. The nodes of this landscape—the Foreign Office, the Control Commission headquarters, and the British embassy to Poland—had an influence on officials' imaginations to such an extent that alternative world views derived from differing national cultures were comprehended instrumentally: that is, by how they affected the British position. Thus British liberalism merged with institutional identification to exclude varying and perhaps problematic perspectives. Place, therefore, is shown, in this instance, to be hierarchically ordered, with ideology derived from social upbringing (liberalism/Britain) merging with function (work/office) to inhibit and even block alternative trajectories of understanding, though, as is shown, the same end point can be reached from different positions.

SHAPING THE BRITISH IMAGINATION

The British conceptualization of Polish Jews was framed in the late nineteenth century and early twentieth century by Jewish migration from Russian Poland. The response of the British parliament found concrete expression in the 1905 Aliens Act, which sought to limit the flow of east European Jews to Britain. While the target of the 1905 act was obvious to all, anti-immigration activists were keen to avoid the charge of antisemitism. For example, William Evans Gordon—a leader of the anti-immigration movement and Tory MP for Stepney from 1900—declared, 'Let there be no mistake about this . . . the moment we allow this agitation to be used as a cloak for religious passion or racial animosity we put ourselves in the wrong.'[3] The path that people such as Gordon were attempting to cut aimed to restrict immigration to Britain on the grounds of social and cultural differences (as well as the real economic concerns of constituents) while promoting the formal equality of successful migrants.[4] Racist and antisemitic discourses were repeatedly

---

[2] D. N. Livingstone, 'Science, Text and Space: Thoughts on the Geography of Reading', *Transactions of the Institute of British Geographers*, 30 (2005), 391–401.

[3] Quoted in D. Feldman, 'Excluding Immigrants, Including Minorities: Britain 1880–1910 and 1948–1970', working paper presented at the workshop 'Paths of Integration: Similarities and Differences in the Settlement Process of Immigrants in Europe, 1880–2000', University of Osnabrück, IMIS, 20–21 June 2003. William Evans Gordon was also a supporter of the Zionist movement and enjoyed productive relationships with Chaim Weizmann, leader of the Zionist Organization and later president of Israel.

[4] See L. P. Gartner, 'Eastern European Jewish Migration', in M. Brenner et al. (eds.), *Two Nations: British and German Jews in Comparative Perspective* (Tübingen, 1999), 117–33. The anti-immigrant British Brothers League was founded in 1901 and made frequent reference to economic concerns.

challenged. Nevertheless, the balancing act between demands to restrict immigration and to extend equality to immigrants was not untroubled, and process (immigration) and person (immigrant) were frequently collapsed in antisemitic statements and actions by the wider public.

Subsequent to the First World War, immigration to Britain was legislated by the 1919 Aliens Act and subsequent Aliens Orders, which were based on the 1914 Aliens Act. The 1914 act was an emergency measure passed in the first few days of the war and endowed the home secretary with the power to decide immigration policy. This discretionary regime survived intact until 1938, when the British government, in response to rising numbers of German Jews arriving following Hitler's ascendancy to the chancellorship, decided to introduce visas for immigrants from Germany and Austria. But even here, as Louise London demonstrates, the Home Office was reluctant to outline policy, preserving the home secretary's discretionary power which allowed him (and the government) to be as restrictive or as compassionate as they chose to be.[5]

The study of British policy towards Jewish immigration during the period of the Second World War has now been firmly established by writers such as Martin Gilbert, David Cesarani, and Tony Kushner.[6] Through Kushner's work, insights into the nature of British 'liberal' antisemitism have been gained. In his book *The Holocaust and the Liberal Imagination* Kushner argues that the demand made by British society for Jews to assimilate or risk being viewed as problematic constitutes a form of antisemitism. The intolerance inherent in British liberalism is also discussed by Cesarani, who maintains that 'the state, society and culture in Britain operated a discourse about Jews that was exclusive and oppressive, that eventuated in and legitimated discrimination'.[7] These authors point to the oppressive face of a liberalism which hierarchically ordered different cultural practices under the rubric of national identity. The political scientist Iris Marion Young covers much the same ground theoretically and discusses the structural and systematic constraints on groups as a result of 'unquestioned norms, habits and symbols' as well as 'in the assumptions underlying institutional rules'.[8] She shows how in well-meaning liberal societies minority groups are subjected to the tyranny of the majority. In the context of Jews in Britain, Geoffrey Alderman argues that Jews had to 'conform to what they felt were Gentile expectations of acceptable Jewish behaviour'.[9]

---

[5] L. London, *Whitehall and the Jews, 1933–1948: British Immigration Policy, Jewish Refugees and the Holocaust* (Cambridge, 2000).

[6] D. Cesarani, *Britain and the Holocaust* (London, 1998); M. Gilbert, *Auschwitz and the Allies* (London, 1991); Kushner, *The Holocaust and the Liberal Imagination*.

[7] D. Cesarani (ed.), *The Making of Modern Anglo-Jewry* (Oxford, 1989), 7.

[8] I. M. Young, *Justice and the Politics of Difference* (Princeton, 1990), 41. See also ead., *Inclusion and Democracy* (Oxford, 2000).

[9] G. Alderman, 'English Jews or Jews of the English Persuasion? Reflections on the Emancipation of Anglo-Jewry', in P. Birnbaum and I. Katznelson (eds.), *Paths of Emancipation: Jews, States, and Citizenship* (Princeton, 1995), esp. 129.

In the following sections I offer a preliminary sketch of three episodes that illustrate how British perceptions of Polish Jews were shaped by British liberalism and institutional instrumentality, and how these perceptions coloured understandings of events unfolding in Poland. The first relates the response of Foreign Office officials and staff at the British embassy to Poland to an alleged secret document of the Polish Government (based in London) reprinted in the Yiddish journal *Der tog* in the spring of 1944. The second examines a series of correspondence between the British embassy in Warsaw, the Foreign Office, and the British Element of the Control Commission in Germany in December 1945 regarding Polish Jewish emigration from Poland. The third discusses the British reaction to the news that an 'Operation Swallow' train had transported Polish Jews rather than ethnic Germans out of Poland in May 1946.

THE *TOG* ARTICLE

In the summer of 1944 staff at the Foreign Office analysed two intercepted messages sent from New York to London regarding an article published in the New York Yiddish daily *Der tog*.[10] Both the sender and the recipient of the telegrams were Jewish activists with interest in Poland. The article that excited such attention was an alleged Polish secret document which, according to Emanuel Nowogrodsky of the Bund in New York, proposed 'that Jews should not be allowed to return to Poland after the war, that their economic positions were now taken by Poles, and that the Polish government should endeavour to find for the Jews a "National Home" somewhere in Eastern Europe'. According to Nowogrodsky, the document was submitted by a Polish government delegate, Zygmunt Berezowski.[11] The Polish government contended throughout 1944 that it knew nothing about the paper and advised officials from the British Foreign Office that the document actually circulated amongst members of the Commission for Foreign Affairs—which, according to Professor Olgierd Górka, an adviser to Interior Minister Władysław Banaczyk, was a private body whose members were of National Democratic leanings (rightist nationalists).[12] The actual story of the document is somewhat different, as the historians Dariusz Stola and Dariusz Libionka have made clear.[13]

[10] National Archives, Kew (hereafter NA), FO 371/39524 (C8119). *Morgn-frayhayt*, a New York Yiddish daily with communist sympathies, in its issue of 7 May 1944 praised *Der tog* for printing the document and provided a detailed commentary on it.

[11] NA, FO 371/39524 (C7711—intercept LON/ULD134824/44).

[12] Berezowski was an important member of the National Democrats and served in the government-in-exile from November 1944 to 1947.

[13] The document was written in August 1943 by Roman Knoll, the director of the Commission for Foreign Affairs of the Delegatura (the Government Delegation for Poland, the secret agency in Poland of the government-in-exile). In other words, the document originated from an organization loyal to, and commanded by, the Polish government-in-exile, and the Commission for Foreign Affairs was not

The Polish government, through the Polish Telegraph Agency, published an official statement, distancing itself from the secret document, that was sent to New York on 10 May and to Jerusalem on 25 May 1944. In this statement the Polish government declared that the document was 'contrary to the policy, rulings, and plans of the Polish government',[14] and emphasized that it had not received any such report.

Nevertheless, experts on Poland at the Foreign Office were asked to comment on the article, largely because the document did give an insight into how part of the Polish political class was thinking about the post-war settlement in relation to Polish Jews, and because the author of the document advocated a position sympathetic to Jewish national aspirations, declaring that 'the Jews are a people and a nation and have a just claim to a territory of their own', but preferably not in Palestine, 'which after all, is much too small, non-indigenous, exotic, and provokes conflicts with the Arab world'.[15] The document also expressed concern that the return of Jews could stimulate antisemitism in Poland.

Robin Hankey, son of Lord Hankey, a Whitehall mandarin knighted in 1939, who was attached to the British embassy to Poland prior to, during, and after the war, analysed the document and wrote a commentary on it. Along with Fred Savery, he was the Foreign Office's Polish expert. Hankey's insights from 4 July 1944 are worth quoting at length:

The Poles have long favoured Zionism as a means of getting rid of their Jews. The document strikes me as rather realistic, but from Eastern Depts point of view we shall not want a flood of Jews directed from Poland to the M.E. [Middle East]

2. In point of fact, most of Poland's Jews lived in the East, & the Soviets carried a great many off & refused to let them go. This is about the only real service the Soviets seem likely to render the Poles. However Poland's plague of Jews (some towns in the east were 80% Jewish) was mainly due to anti-Jewish legislation by the Czarist regime at the end of the last

a 'private body' as Professor Górka maintained. See Archiwum Akt Nowych, Warsaw (hereafter AAN), 202/XIV-9, 135: 'Uwagi o naszej polityce zagranicznej', no. 1 (1943). A copy of Knoll's document can also be found at the Sikorski Institute, London, AIP, A.9, Ie/15. Dariusz Libionka has pointed out that, according to delegate S. Jankowski, the document was supposed to be a private letter to Foreign Minister T. Romer. Libionka argues that Knoll's paper reflected public sentiment in Poland. See D. Libionka, 'Kwestia żydowska w Polsce w ocenie Delegatury Rządu RP i KG ZWZ-AK w latach 1942–1944', in B. Engelking et al. (eds.), *Zagłada Żydów: Pamięć narodowa a pisanie historii w Polsce i we Francji. Wybrane materiały z kolokwium polsko-francuskiego, Lublin, 22–23 stycznia 2004,* forthcoming. I would like to thank Dariusz Libionka for forwarding me a copy of this paper and clarifying the origins of the 'secret' document. See also D. Stola, *Nadzieja i Zagłada: Ignacy Schwarzbart — żydowski przedstawiciel w Radzie Narodowej RP, 1940–1945* (Warsaw, 1995), 229–33. Stola relates that Knoll's document reached London in the summer of 1943 and somehow found its way to Ignacy Schwarzbart, a Jewish representative on the Polish National Council, which was an advisory body to the Polish government-in-exile. Schwarzbart considered Knoll's opinions as bad for Poland, morally inferior, and politically stupid. He demanded that the government act in a decisive way to stem harmful opinions about Jews being articulated by officials of the Delegatura.

[14] NA, FO 371/39524 (Annexe A).　　　　　　　　　[15] NA, FO 371/39524 (C8119).

century, so if the Soviet Govt do stick to their Jews it will only be undoing another Czarist iniquity.

3. This document (if genuine) is interesting confirmation of the view some people express that anti-semitism may be worse & not better after the war. If so the Jewish problem will be a world one, as this document fortunately recognises. Too many people in C. Europe thought before the war there was room in Palestine for everyone. The Poles & Czechs who will go back from Palestine after the war will know well how tiny the place is.[16]

Hankey's evaluation of Polish–Jewish relations as well as his unacknowledged anti-semitism ('plague of Jews', for example) is fairly representative of the understanding and sentiment of the Foreign Office and embassy staff. Two distinct precepts inform Hankey's analysis. The first is that Jews constitute and have constituted a problem for Poles (who are implicitly uniformly gentile: the formulation of the Polish Jew as a sociocultural identity rather than an administrative identity is not posited); here, Polish antisemitism is implied. On the grounds that Polish Jews were removed from Poland, Hankey positively appraises the Soviet deportations of 1940, in which more than 300,000 people were transferred from Soviet-occupied Poland to the Soviet Union, both Jews and non-Jews.

The second precept which guides British thinking is that quantity matters. In other words, the number of Jews in Poland is a crucial variable: for Hankey, the 3 million Polish Jews, just less than 10 per cent of the pre-war population of Poland, constituted a 'plague'. Not only does this have unfortunate resonances with National Socialist sociobiological categories, but Hankey and his audience in the Foreign Office, aware of the pre-war history of migration to Britain and Britain's policy, also uncritically accepted the formulation of assimilation to the majoritarian culture and sociopolitical equality as providing a sound basis for a harmonious society. Since the sociocultural matrix in Poland was, prior to the war, plural and frequently marked by separation, social groups not conforming to the majoritarian culture were by definition problematic.

Tony Kushner's argument regarding Britain's 'liberal' antisemitism refers not just to Britain, but can be extended to British spaces overseas. Thus a Polish tradition of preserving and frequently valuing social and cultural differences is opposed to the British liberal vision in which difference is a temporary aberration en route to sociocultural assimilation to majoritarian norms. In this sense British 'liberal' antisemitism functioned as a prism through which events in Poland were under-stood and problematized—and this affected Polish Jews and non-Jews alike. It is worth noting that British liberal views regarding the necessity of assimilation are not so far from Soviet nationality policy, which endowed minorities with sociopo-litical equality while failing to tolerate sociocultural differences. As Jan Gross has argued, Soviet policy did not accept 'wilful separation from the rest of society . . . Jews could acquire Soviet citizenship, with all the rights and entitlements that went with the honour, but they could not sustain their community life anymore . . .

[16] NA, FO 371/39524 (C8119/7711/55).

they could not be Jews *and* citizens of the state that claimed jurisdiction over them ... it was always an either/or'.[17]

Fred Savery's response to the secret document was more extensive and provides detailed analysis of Polish–Jewish relations over a twenty-five-year period prior to the time of writing in July 1944.[18] His analysis was read by civil servants at the Foreign Office and at the British embassy to Poland who were concerned with the challenges posed by Polish Jews. Like Hankey's, his analysis is framed by the consideration of a 'Jewish problem' and the size of the Jewish population.

He describes how in pre-war Poland 'the Jewish problem was most acute in the smaller provincial towns' and the 'predominance of the Jewish element in the small towns was felt by all Poles to be unfortunate from both a cultural and an economic point of view'. He goes on to assert that Polish officials' 'efforts to clean up and generally to civilise the little towns in their districts ... were constantly confronted by the obstruction of Jewish inhabitants who all too frequently had the majority of the local town council'.[19]

He then proceeds to discuss the economic situation as responsible for breaking the 'curious toleration of one another based on mutual contempt. The Jew despised the Pole for not understanding how to make money fructify; the Polish peasant despised the Jew for not being able to drive the plough or fell timber.' He argues that what 'finally put an end [to this curious toleration] was not so much nationalism on either the Polish or the Jewish side as the economic pressure due to increasing over-population of Poland which in its turn resulted from the closing of the safety valve of emigration when economic crisis set in, principally in the United States'. Savery claims that 'there is no doubt whatever that Poles of all classes have shown sincere fellow feeling with the persecuted Jews and have at their own great risk helped them to escape extermination at the German hands'. He considers that 'owing to [the] vast diminution of the Jewish population the Jewish problem in Poland has ceased to be insoluble ... [and] there is no return to the unhealthy state of things in which the small towns were overwhelmingly Jewish and only the countryside Slav'. Finally he provides a rationale for anti-Jewish sentiment in Poland by asserting that 'very numerous elements of the Jewish proletariat in the east did in fact cooperate at once and very enthusiastically with the Soviet authorities; there is no doubt that in many cases Jews denounced to the Soviet authorities Polish officers who were concealed or disguised officers who may have subsequently lost their lives at Katyn'.[20]

---

[17] J. T. Gross, *Revolution from Abroad: The Soviet Conquest of Poland's Western Ukraine and Western Belorussia* (Princeton, 2002), 142. Polish nationality policy echoed Soviet policy especially during the Stalinist period. However, nationality practice oscillated between tight controls over minority life and more liberal control. See E. Mironowicz, *Polityka narodowościowa PRL* (Białystok, 2000).

[18] NA, FO 371/39524 (C9465).   [19] Ibid.

[20] Ibid. The reaction of Jews to the Soviet invasion of eastern Poland on 17 September 1939 has been much discussed. See A. Żbikowski, 'Jewish Reaction to the Soviet Arrival in the Kresy in September 1939', *Polin*, 13 (2000), 62–72, for a brief overview. Savery's statement regarding Jewish

Though Savery is a more sensitive observer and analyst than Hankey, he still employs stereotypes to make his argument. For example, when he writes of the attempts to 'civilise the little towns', he reveals disdain for Jewish cultural achievements in the eastern *shtetl*s. This is not because he is ignorant of Jewish life in that area (he had travelled extensively through Poland over a number of years), but rather because Jewish culture is viewed to be inherently problematic and inferior because it does not conform to the majoritarian culture. The British imagination of majority–minority relations exercises a controlling and in the final analysis deciding function in both the perception and understanding of societal phenomena and relationships.

One of Savery's readers at the Foreign Office, a Mr Walker, followed up Savery's analysis on 29 July 1944 with a brief note. He wrote: 'I think the Jewish population of Poland will tend to look towards the USSR—Jews always do, and that may cause difficulties with the native Poles . . . There is no remedy.'[21] While the view that Jews were inherently pro-communist may not have been that of Savery, it certainly found a constituency within the Foreign Office and beyond. Indeed, the tension between imaginations of Jews as being either quintessential communists or capitalists, so familiar in the antisemitic literature and propaganda of the period, was reproduced, albeit in a more carefully worded and restrained fashion, in the Foreign Office.

EMIGRATION OF POLISH JEWS

The power of the Foreign Office's prejudicial analytical model is clearly demonstrated in a series of exchanges between the British embassy in Warsaw, the Foreign Office, and the Control Commission for Germany (British Element)

collaboration with the Soviets is too generalized and his assertion regarding Katyn is especially questionable. Nevertheless, the view that Jews welcomed the Red Army in September 1939 was fairly common within the British government. On 6 May 1940, in the midst of the Pritt affair (see below), Mr Harrison at the War Office wrote a secret and personal note to Mr Makins at the Foreign Office, asserting that 'The Jews' behaviour in Poland during the Russian advance must clearly have caused a feeling of animosity in Army circles which I think is justified': NA, FO 371/24481/109.

More generally, the relationship between Polish Jews and the Soviet Union as understood by the British was influenced by stereotypes of Jews, as this extract from a report of 14 February 1940 by Mr Russell of the Foreign Office to his superiors makes clear: 'A large percentage of the population of Lwów is of Jewish blood. So far they have not suffered under the Bolsheviks on racial grounds, but their acquisitive instincts are sadly offended by Soviet principles. While despising the barbarian illiteracy of the Soviet officials, they still prefer the latter to their Nazi counterparts. One of the former directors of the Hotel Bristol, a Jew both by race and profession, remarked to me one day, when we were discussing the fate of Jews under Hitler on the one hand, and under the Bolsheviks under the other: "Der eine tötet ohne weiteres die Fische. Die anderen lassen langsam das Wasser heraus"; i.e., "The former kills the fish without more ado, the latter slowly lets the water out"': NA, FO 372/24471/185, 'Memorandum on Conditions in the Soviet-Occupied Areas of Polish Ukraine'.

[21] NA, FO 371/39524 (C9465/7711/55).

(CCG (BE)) during December 1945. Both Foreign Office officials in London and those seconded to the CCG (BE) in Berlin were becoming increasingly concerned about Jewish emigration from Poland.

On 5 December 1945, Hilary Young of the Political Division of CCG (BE) in Berlin wrote to Robin Hankey regarding the movement of Jews from Poland into Berlin, stating, 'It does rather look as if this may be part of an organised plan to increase the number of Jewish DPs in Germany, while at the same time a propaganda campaign is laid on to work up increased sympathy for their plight.'[22]

Hankey replied on 18 December 1945:

I have discussed with the Ambassador the question of whether anything can be done to stop the present exodus but we do not think anything can be done. It is not so much a matter of the Polish Government's policy, though they do give passports to Jews to leave the country in isolated cases (especially where the recipients pay adequately for these facilities) but most of the movement is spontaneous and is due to the fact that twentyfive million Poles dislike Jews.[23]

While antisemitism in Poland in the immediate post-war period existed and was more violent than in the inter-war period,[24] branding the entire Polish population as antisemitic was incorrect. The assertion, however, was not challenged by other officials at the Foreign Office. Indeed, Hankey's superior, ambassador Victor Cavendish-Bentinck, expressed the view that 'the Poles [were] as antisemitic as they were 25 years ago' in a note sent to the Foreign Office on the same day.[25] Consequently, the manipulation of the Jewish issue by the Provisional Government of National Unity (Tymczasowy Rząd Jedności Narodowej) based in Warsaw, which was still engaged in both a real war against former Home Army soldiers in Poland and a propaganda war against the Polish government-in-exile based in London, was either not fully discerned, or ignored.[26] The Foreign Office assumptions about Polish antisemitism disarmed and neutralized the British response to what we now understand as Provisional Government of National Unity propaganda regarding antisemitic outrages in Poland (to be clear, the practice of blaming antisemitic violence and actions on 'reactionaries') and its not so covert war against Home Army successor groups and those remaining loyal to (though not controlled by) the London-based Polish government. Indeed, British officials were beginning to rationalize alleged Polish antisemitism through the use of the Jewish communist–Jewish capitalist identities, as is illustrated in Hankey's letter to Charles Baxter at the Foreign Office of 8 December 1945:

---

[22] NA, FO 688/31/3.

[23] Ibid. A report sent from the British consulate in Katowice dated 5 October 1945 to the British embassy in Warsaw provided details of the movement of Jews out of Poland.

[24] J. Michlic-Coren, 'Anti-Jewish Violence in Poland, 1918–1939 and 1945–1947', *Polin*, 13 (2000), 34–61. See also D. Engel, 'Patterns of Anti-Jewish Violence in Poland, 1944–1946', *Yad Vashem Studies*, 26 (1998), 43–85.   [25] NA, FO 371/57684, WR15.

[26] On 8 February 1945, the London Polish government ordered that all military resistance to the Polish communists should cease. It did not.

Quite a lot of Jews are at present leaving Poland. They are moved to leave partly by the anti-semitism which still exists here (encouraged by the number of Jews employed by the Secret Police and in the Government offices), and partly by the fact that Poland is no longer an easy country to start or run a private business . . . Many leave without passports via Prague, or via Stettin and Berlin.

Hankey notes that there are 'not many Jews in Poland at all'. He continues, 'The Polish government encourages Jews to leave and on occasion even gives them passports valid for one crossing only of the Polish frontier.'[27]

For while British officials at the embassy in Warsaw and at the Foreign Office in London were aware of violence against Jews and the murder of them (in 1945, according to the bulletin of the Central Committee of Jews in Poland (Centralny Komitet Żydów w Polsce), 353 Jews were murdered in Poland), they remained blinded to the actual circumstances of these killings.[28] In other words, alleged Jewish fidelity to the communist project, coupled with perceived inherent Polish antisemitism, 'explained' murder and violence. The British ambassador to Poland, Cavendish-Bentinck, rejected the Provisional Government of National Unity's assertion that these killings were inspired by reactionary groups in contact with General Anders in Italy and with the former émigré government in London,[29] and instead pointed to widespread antisemitism and the fact that Jews occupied positions in government and security forces.[30] However, he was able to find agreement with the US ambassador to Poland and London members of the Provisional Government of National Unity, Mr Stańczyk and Mr Mikołajczyk, that 'the Jews are not in such physical danger here that they need to leave Poland en masse for their safety'.[31] Nevertheless, many Polish Jews were deciding to leave, and insecurity as well as Zionist ideology were strong motivating factors. By June 1946, the Bundist newspaper *Unzere shtime* was concerned about the movement of Jews out of Poland and accused 'the Zionists of spreading and sowing despair and weakness among the Jewish masses purposely'.[32] If the goal was to stem the movement, it

---

[27] NA, FO 688/31/3. Hankey's statement regarding private business, while largely true—in the immediate post-war period legal private enterprise was difficult—should be understood in relation to his earlier pronouncements on Jewish business. In December 1943, Hankey gave his opinion on the US proposal to license the transmission of foreign exchange in order to rescue 70,000 Romanian Jews. He stated: 'I suspect the real object of the scheme is financial—Jews in Europe getting into dollars while there is yet time': NA, FO 371/36747.   [28] AAN, 201/24/78.

[29] AAN, 201/24/136: 2 May 1946, President Bierut on the situation of Jews in Poland during a meeting with Dr Tenenbaum, President of the American Federation of Polish Jews.

[30] NA, FO 371/57684, WR15. Through 1945 and 1946 the British ambassador's assessment of the Jewish situation was consistent. In a letter dated 17 September 1945, ambassador Cavendish-Bentinck advised C. W. Baxter at the Foreign Office that 'There is no doubt that the Jews in the country have been virtually exterminated. They are never to be seen in Warsaw except a few who have come back and entered the higher ranks of Government administration': NA, FO 688/31/3.

[31] NA, FO 371/57684, WR96.

[32] *Unzere shtime*, 4 June 1946, quoted in Y. Bauer, *Flight and Rescue: Brichah* (New York, 1970), 150.

failed. A month later, in Kielce, a pogrom claimed forty-two Jewish lives and per-suaded many to leave the country.

The shred of underlying commonality between the views of the Provisional Government of National Unity and the British is the fact that both saw visible minorities as problematic. In the universe of the Provisional Government of National Unity, the outrages allegedly committed by the National Armed Forces (Narodowe Siły Zbrojne) confirmed its view that assimilation through socio-economic and political measures was called for. In both world views, the actual vic-tims of violence and murder—frequently ordinary people on the transport net-work—became less important than what their victimhood was seen to represent.

Consequently, as social unrest in Poland unfolded through 1945–6, the British reaction to the slaying of Jews and the various forms of violence committed against them was muted by the acceptance of stereotypes of both Poles and Jews. This clouded the assessment of what Anna Prażmowska has described as civil war and Jan Gross describes as 'a time of banditry and rampant violence almost on the scale of civil war'. As Gross goes on to point out, 'given the general level of disorder at the time, and that many of the victims were killed not as Jews but as targets of political violence or armed robbery, only a fraction of [the killings] can be attrib-uted to antisemitism', but he cautions that 'one must be aware of the circumstances of each episode: robbers often chose their targets on the basis of ethnicity'.[33]

Furthermore, since many officials both at the Foreign Office in London and at the British embassy in Warsaw had engaged with the Pritt affair in 1940, the claims of the Provisional Government of National Unity regarding reactionary elements, though rejected by the ambassador, did find some resonance in London and were not so readily dismissed.[34] The alleged antisemitism of the Polish government in

---

[33] A. J. Prażmowska, *Civil War in Poland, 1942–1948* (London, 2004); J. Gross, 'Stereotypes of Polish–Jewish Relations after the War: The Special Commission of the Central Committee of Polish Jews', *Polin*, 13 (2000), 196. This is not to say that the British did not know what was happening in Poland throughout 1945. Reports from Poland were received via the Polish government based in London (which remained the Polish government recognized by the British until 5 July 1945). However, much of the information given to the British was dismissed as being exaggeration, especially in relation to NKVD arrests, deportations, rapes, and theft: NA, HS 4/319, note of 17 Mar. 1945. The British also had suspicions about some informers: NA, FO 688/31/26. Nevertheless, a report submit-ted by Lt. Col. Boughey in March 1945 did provide a basis for the Polish reports to be treated more sympathetically. Boughey wrote, 'The Russian secret police is very strong and it's estimated that there are as many as 80,000 agents scattered throughout Poland as against the number of 30,000 Gestapo': NA, HS 4/319, Reports from Poland December 1940–July 1945. Furthermore, given the co-operation of British and Polish intelligence services during the war and the generally high standard of material forwarded by the Poles to Britain, the frequent incredulity expressed by the British regarding Soviet operations in Poland in 1944 and 1945 requires further exploration. See *Intelligence Co-operation between Poland and Great Britain during World War II*, ii: *Documents*, ed. J. S. Ciechanowski (Warsaw, 2005).

[34] D. N. Pritt, MP, wrote to R. A. Butler, MP, at the Foreign Office on 2 April 1940 regarding anti-semitism in the Polish army based in France. Following an investigation, Mr Makins of the Foreign Office concluded that 'It seems quite on the cards that anti-Semitism is in fact quite rife in the Polish

London and its armed forces undermined its views at the international level subsequent to British and American transference of legal recognition to the Warsaw government on 5 July 1945.

Though the Provisional Government of National Unity used the accusation of antisemitism as a political weapon against its enemies—mainly individuals and organizations either loyal to the London-based government-in-exile or those simply resisting a de facto communist takeover—it remained an unreliable propaganda tool subsequent to the Kraków pogrom of 1945 and especially the 1946 pogrom in Kielce. For while the antisemitism of factions linked to the Polish government in London was believable to the British, and the Provisional Government of National Unity's Jewish policy echoed to a degree the policy operative in the United Kingdom (assimilation), the general stereotype of Polish antisemitism challenged the assertions of the Warsaw government that it was limited to pro-Western Poles.

However, the antisemitism imagined by the British was not the kind articulated in the universalistic declarations of the Provisional Government of National Unity. As British 'liberal' antisemitism remained unproblematized, Polish 'communist' antisemitism, at least on a formal level, was neither seen nor discussed.[35] Only those who were most affected by it voiced grievances—those Jews who did not wish to be 'forcibly' assimilated.[36]

By January 1946 the strategy of the Polish government in Warsaw regarding Polish Jews was increasingly transparent. Early that month Jewish representatives from Po'alei Tsiyon Left (Adolf Berman) and the Bund (Michał Szuldonfrei) participated in discussions at the ninth session of the National Home Council (Krajowa Rada Narodowa) in which they declared fidelity to the government line and focused upon the problem of antisemitism.[37] On 3 January 1946, the bulletin

Army, but in this particular case [an antisemitic speech by a Polish army captain] some allowance must be made for the mess-room exuberance of a Polish officer.' Butler replied to Pritt on 27 July 1940, declaring that 'there had undoubtedly been a certain amount of anti-Semitic feeling in the Army. No reports here so far reached us of any active persecution' and referring Pritt to the official Polish government position. Pritt was not satisfied. By 5 August 1940 General Sikorski was trying to end the scandal and declared that any soldier who took up arms for Poland was a Pole regardless of race or religion, and that the military authorities would take active care that these orders would be observed. However, the description of an antisemitic speech as 'mess-room exuberance' is indicative of British toleration of anti-Jewish prejudice. NA, FO 371/24481/89, 92, 104, 109, 110.

[35] The Polish president Bolesław Bierut discussed the situation of Jews with the British ambassador Cavendish-Bentinck on 25 August 1945. Bierut confirmed that Jews would enjoy the privileges granted to them under the 1921 constitution: NA, FO 688/34.

[36] See Kushner's essay on the merits of comparing antisemitisms: T. Kushner, 'Comparing Anti-Semitisms: A Useful Exercise?', in Brenner et al. (eds.), *Two Nations*, 91–110.

[37] Adolf Berman was the younger brother of Jakub Berman, one of the triumvirate of post-war leaders of Poland. Adolf emigrated to Israel in 1950 and became a member of the Knesset. For an excellent analysis of the complex identities—intellectual, European, Marxist, Jewish—and relationships of the period 1918–68, see M. Shore, *Caviar and Ashes: A Warsaw Generation's Life and Death in Marxism, 1918–1968* (London, 2006).

of the Central Committee of Jews in Poland informed its readers of the committee's policy line, which was endorsed by the government.[38] The bulletin of 26 January quoted Prime Minister Edward Osóbka-Morawski reiterating the government position of helping Jews rebuild their workplaces in Poland and assisting legal voluntary emigration.[39]

Later, on 29 April, at the plenary session of the National Home Council, Prime Minister Osóbka-Morawski defined the Polish government position, affirming the 'full equality of all citizens regardless of race, nationality and creed' and stating that 'all citizens without exception are entitled to full care from the side of the state and equal rights and equal obligations towards the state'. The prime minister also stated that 'the government will not, however, stop the emigration of those Jews who will wish to leave Poland. In the face of the tragedy suffered by the Jewish nation, Jews who wish it should have their national aspirations in Palestine facilitated.'[40]

The Polish government created a number of organizations to help Polish Jews rebuild their lives in Poland, such as the Office of the Government Commissar Relating to the Productivization of the Jewish Populace (Biuro Komisarza Rządu dla Spraw Produktywizacji Ludności Żydowskiej), and fostered forums for Jewish perspectives to emerge, such as the Central Committee of Jews in Poland. Nevertheless, the limits of these efforts, predicated upon integration of Jews as citizens rather than as Jews to the majoritarian culture (assimilation), were acutely felt by those Jews hostile to the assimilation model pursued under the rubric of building socialism. This included Rabbi David Kahane, whose complaints against Jewish communists were clearly heard by British officialdom, while his implied protest against assimilation was not.[41]

OPERATION SWALLOW: TRAIN 165

'Operation Swallow' was the arrangement made between Britain and Poland to displace 1.5 million ethnic Germans from Poland, mainly from the 'Recovered Territories' to the British zone of occupation in Germany in 1946. The operation, to take place under the rubric of the agreement made at Potsdam in August 1945 and more specific instructions of 14 February 1946, was to remove ethnic Germans by rail and sea to Germany.[42] Following a suggestion from the Soviets, the British sent liaison missions to embarkation points at Szczecin and Kaławsk. Here, their

---

[38] AAN, 201/24/2.   [39] AAN, 201/24/26.   [40] AAN, 201/24/123.

[41] Rabbi Kahane declared upon meeting representatives from Britain and the United States on 16 February 1946 that those Jews in the government should not be regarded as part of the Jewish community. Minutes of the meeting were taken by Mr Russell of the Foreign Office: NA, FO 688/34. Indeed, the sentiment was mutual. After the Kielce pogrom, Jakub Berman is said to have told Rabbi Kahane, 'If you think I am a Jew you are mistaken. My father and my mother were Jews and it so happens that I am working for my ideal in Warsaw': quoted in Bauer, *Flight and Rescue*, 114.

[42] NA, FO 1052/324/20A. This document defines the routes and protocols of the population transfer/expulsion.

tasks were to ensure that the requirements made in the February protocol, derived from the Potsdam agreement, were being satisfied.

On 19 May 1946, a train with 2,028 people on board—train 165—arrived at the Mariental reception point in the British zone of occupation in Germany. Of those 2,028, only fifty-six people were deemed to be genuine 'Swallows'—that is, ethnic Germans to be removed from Poland under the British–Polish agreement. The rest were Polish Jews. According to a report submitted by Captain F. Garner the following month, 'these Jews were well fed and dressed and in actual fact were not expellees, but volunteers for the American Zone and were surprised to learn on arrival that they were going to be treated as normal refugees'.[43]

The British authorities were very concerned by the arrival of a Swallow train carrying Jews rather than ethnic Germans. These concerns were heightened by the arrival of a second train at Mariental on 6 July, carrying 1,700 Jews. British enquiries about this second train discovered that the travellers had paid $30, had visas for the United States, and were expecting to catch a ship from Le Havre to the United States the following day. Nevertheless, the occupants of the second train were 'despatched under ordinary dispersal arrangements for Swallow, as nothing could be proved that they were not genuine German although there is good reason to believe that many of the papers were forged'.[44] In response to the arrival of these two trains, Brigadier A. G. Kenchington, chief of the Prisoners of War and Displaced Persons Division, wrote to the Department Chief of Staff (Policy) of the CCG (BE) on 16 July, stating: 'There has been much evidence in the past to suggest that there is a powerful Jewish Underground organisation working in Europe to effect the emigration of Jews from the Continent.'[45] A week later, on 23 July 1946, Major General George Erskine distributed a note to the headquarters of CCG (BE), stating that 'We have received several unconfirmed reports from POLAND that papers showing GERMAN nationality are being given to POLISH Jews to induce them to leave POLAND.'[46] The assumption here was that the Polish government was giving them papers with German nationality, whereas the forging of documents was well within the capabilities of the Jews themselves.[47] By underestimating the agency of the Polish Jews, the British fell back on the notion of Polish antisemitism and the assumed Polish desire to see Jews emigrate, and consequently increased the pressure on the Polish Foreign Ministry rather than improving surveillance at the departure points of Szczecin and Kaławsk.

The British, despite their enquiries, did not become aware of the degree to

---

[43] NA, FO 1032/836, 'Report on train No 165'. Bauer, *Flight and Rescue*, 122, points out that those Jews departing Poland under the auspices of the organized Berihah sold their last possessions in Poland and sometimes bought a new suit or converted money into gold pieces or rings. The evidence in Garner's report would indicate that train 165 was used by Berihah, though I cannot confirm this.

[44] NA, FO 1032/836.   [45] NA, FO 1032/836 (134B).

[46] NA, FO 1032/836 (12A).   [47] Bauer, *Flight and Rescue*, 25.

which Operation Swallow facilitated the movement of Jews out of Poland to the British zone of occupation in Germany, though there was a degree of knowledge that Polish Jews were leaving Poland as German expellees.[48] Indeed, during spring and summer 1946, members of Berihah—the clandestine Jewish organization directing Jewish emigration from east to central Europe—managed to include an average of 200 Jews on Swallow trains leaving Szczecin for the British zone, though occasionally nearly the whole train was occupied by Polish Jews.[49]

British understanding of the flight of Polish Jews from Poland oscillated between emphasizing a clandestine Jewish plan of which they had little concrete evidence, and highlighting 'rationales' of the Polish government to assist Jews to leave Poland, with, the British thought, the Polish government extending tacit support to the emigrants. Though the British never found out about the Berihah organization, their sense that at least some of the movement out of Poland was organized was correct. The Polish government, especially the Ministry of Foreign Affairs, did not approve of illegal emigration and tried to regulate the movement. However, its efforts were compromised by a secret arrangement made between officials at the Defence Ministry and Berihah activists to facilitate Jewish emigration from Poland.[50]

Following the arrival of train 165, British enquiries revealed that the travellers were collected at Warsaw and had paid between $500 and $600. Though this figure remains unsubstantiated, and has to be questioned in light of the alleged $30 fee charged to those on the second train, the fact that the transportation was well organized cannot be questioned.[51] Indeed, according to investigations, the train leader on train 165, a Mr Günther Sternberg, made fraudulent use of UNRRA identification. Furthermore, the train was to be met by a member of the Jewish committee in Hannover, who advised the British that he had an agreement with the Americans for the travellers to go to the Obcrammergau camp and thence to Palestine, the United States, and various other places.[52]

The British investigation into these two trains reached the highest levels within the Control Commission. Complaints were filed with the Polish military mission in Berlin, and the Americans and the Foreign Office were advised. The intensity of

[48] NA, FO 688/34: note, 18 Sept. 1946, from British Embassy, Warsaw, to the Foreign Office, London.

[49] Bauer, *Flight and Rescue*, 234–6.   [50] Ibid. 223.

[51] According to Bauer, people did not have to pay for their passage with Berihah: ibid. 122.

[52] Later in 1946, the Americans expressed concern about Jewish emigration from Poland to the American zone of occupation in Germany. At a press conference on 8 October 1946, General Joseph T. McNarney, Theatre Commander, reported on conditions in the American zone: 'I believe that the Jews coming into the zone from the East have been misinformed as to our condition here. Whether this information comes from Jewish agencies in Poland or other sources, I cannot say. However, I have taken steps to inform all agencies in connection with the Jewish population in Poland of the real situation in our zone . . . The situation in the U.S. zone grows more critical as winter approaches.' This speech was forwarded to Władysław Wolski, Under-Secretary of State responsible for repatriation affairs, on 8 November: AAN, 522/II-459/34.

the British response can be explained by their keenness to maintain control over the Swallow operation—though the porosity of the liaison teams based in Poland was not adequately problematized by British officials at this stage. (The fact of this porosity became a national scandal in December 1946 when unfit expellees were given permission to continue to travel to Germany but died owing to freezing temperatures.) Furthermore, the British remained sensitive about Jewish emigration to Palestine, and the movement of Jews from Poland was understood as complicating that situation.

However, while the British could not prove that the travellers on the second Swallow train were not German, their response to the arrival of several hundred Jews in the British zone is revealing. After all, the British–Polish agreement specified the expulsion of Germans but did not mention religion. The position of German Jews therefore remained problematic, whereas the flight of Polish Jews was clearly outside the parameters of Swallow.

While, at least officially, the Swallow train incidents did not cause a change in overall British policy regarding the expulsion of Germans from Poland, or in British perspectives on Polish Jews, it did augur renewed concerns about procedures and personnel. On 8 October 1946, in what may be a completely unconnected series of correspondence, Christopher 'Kit' Steel of the political department of the CCG (BE) wrote to Pat Dean of the German department at the Foreign Office regarding the Control Commission's 'Jewish adviser'. In the letter, Steel declared that 'Almost any honest Jew will admit that no Jew can be really objective about Jewish affairs; and anyone who is not objective cannot be expected to advise HMG [His Majesty's Government] reliably.' Subsequent comments on the letter expressed concern that 'we risk having our general directives, designed to prevent the exodus of Jews from E. Europe and illegal migration to Palestine, misapplied or ignored' and also noted the delicate nature of the issue, arguing that the 'matter should be broached orally'.[53] Thus, the conduct of a British Jew was brought into question on the grounds of his Jewishness. The British objective of trying to inhibit migration out of eastern Europe could not be easily reconciled with the Polish government's sympathy for Jewish national aspirations in Palestine. British officialdom's suspicions about the loyalty of a section of their staff can therefore be understood as a response to the difficulty of dealing with Jewish voluntary migration, but the correspondence between the Foreign Office and the CCG (BE) in October 1946 suggests that suspicion of the constructed Other was structural rather than contingent. Indeed, this incident indicates that even though assimilation was encouraged, those who assimilated were tarnished by their other identities, and could be accused of simulating Britishness rather than being truly British. In other words, the equality posited by the liberal assimilatory model was, in part, illusory.

---

[53] NA, FO 371/52654.

CONCLUSION

In this chapter I have traced three episodes between 1944 and 1946 that highlight British imaginings of Polish Jews. These typecasts illustrate the prevalence of 'liberal' antisemitism and, perhaps more surprisingly, the similarity between liberal policies of exclusion and those practised by the emerging communist regime in Poland. In Britain, as Tony Kushner has made clear, liberal ideologies 'were welded to exclusionary national frameworks . . . based on notions of Englishness'. In this framework, 'Foreign Jews, especially those from Eastern Europe, were seen as particularly troublesome and it was believed they would bring antisemitism with them.'[54] The perceived inherently troublesome nature of the Jews was argued by Home Secretary Herbert Morrison in May 1945 to be reason enough for Jewish refugees in Britain to be removed at the end of the war. Indeed, he asserted that 'if the Jews were allowed to remain here they might be an explosive element in the country, especially if the economic situation deteriorated'. He was 'seriously alarmed regarding the possibility of antisemitism in this country'.[55] While acknowledging that the situations of Jewish refugees in Britain and Polish Jews in Poland after the war were not readily comparable, the response of some Polish and British politicians to the Jewish issue was remarkably similar.[56] Just as the report allegedly submitted by Berezowski and written by Knoll wished to see a homeland for Jews outside Poland, so also Morrison declared that 'if arising out of the war . . . territory other than Palestine became available for colonization by refugees, the best solution would be to send the Jews there'.[57] Like Knoll, Morrison envisaged a place somewhere for the Jews, but not there. Unlike Knoll, Morrison was speaking in 1945, when the contours of the post-war settlement were more clearly visible. It behoves us to ask what exactly Morrison was thinking.

The limits of British liberalism so apparent in Robin Hankey's evocation of a 'plague of Jews', Fred Savery's condemnation of Jews' lack of civic pride, and Mr Walker's assumption of Jewish proclivity for the Soviet Union, were not, as the above comments of Herbert Morrison make clear, restricted to the Foreign Office. Indeed, the British position regarding Jews is not so different from that advocated by the Provisional Government for National Unity. Both governments officially protested 'racial' or religious discrimination and made efforts to foster integration to the majoritarian culture and society. In Poland, this took place through the work of the Office of the Government Commissar Relating to the Productivization of the

---

[54] Kushner, *The Holocaust and the Liberal Imagination*, 273.

[55] NA, CAB 95/15: 16 May 1945, Meeting of War Cabinet Committee on the reception and accommodation of refugees.

[56] For an overview of policy towards Jewish refugees during this period, see A. J. Kochavi, *Post-Holocaust Politics: Britain, the United States and Jewish Refugees, 1945–1948* (Chapel Hill, NC, 2001).

[57] NA, CAB 95/15: 16 May 1945, Meeting of War Cabinet Committee on the reception and accommodation of refugees.

Jewish Populace. Both saw assimilation as the only way to assure social harmony. But this is where the comparison with the policy of the Provisional Government of National Unity breaks down. For it is with Knoll's view regarding 'foreign' Jews that British political sentiment has the most resonance. Knoll argued that the return of Jews who had been deported to the Soviet Union in 1940 would not be welcomed as, in part, they would be seen as 'foreign'. Knoll and Morrison for different reasons sought a homeland for Jews, preferably not in Palestine. Both envisioned a future for their countries without a sizeable population of Jews, and both rationalized this view by the evocation that a visible Jewish presence would lead to antisemitism.

It is therefore slightly surprising that while the nationalist sentiment of elements of the Polish government-in-exile has been strongly and rightly criticized for its ethnocentrism, many British officials and politicians have escaped such criticism despite the convergence of views.[58]

The concerns of the Polish political class regarding Jews were not so dissimilar from the positions articulated by British officialdom and politicians in the immediate aftermath of the war. Polish nationalist sentiment, which for sociopolitical reasons sympathized with the Zionist project but was qualified by an awareness of the potential difficulties of Palestine, found a direct echo at the highest level in the British government. The views of the communist-dominated Warsaw government, with emphasis on integration and assimilation, reflected the mainstream 'liberal' position adopted both in the Foreign Office and in relation to British immigration policy more generally. Unity rather than plurality dominated both in Warsaw and in London, though the trajectories to such an end point were markedly different. The Polish government's sympathy for a Jewish homeland in Palestine was the main area in which the Poles and the British diverged.

In demonstrating the similarity of views between the British and various sections of the Polish political class, I have also sought to sketch a geography of engagement. The case studies have emphasized how British liberalism, fostered through socialization, merged with institutional practices and culture to inhibit full comprehension of, and empathy with, alternative world views. The nodes of this landscape included the British embassy in Poland, the Foreign Office, and the Control Commission headquarters, which may be understood as ideological filtering stations where information was processed to affirm 'knowledge' already known. This is not to say that the analysis and commentary of officials such as Hankey and Savery is without merit, but rather that their work is marked by the ideological context in which it was produced—a context defined by British 'liberal' antisemitism and institutional instrumentality.

---

[58] This is not to suggest that ethnocentrism defined all members of the Polish government-in-exile, but merely to recognize that ethnocentrism was fairly common, and—as Libionka has argued in connection with Polish–Jewish relations—reflected a sentiment widespread in Poland itself.

'The Hanging of Judas'; or, Contemporary Jewish Topics

JOANNA TOKARSKA-BAKIR

Who is a liar but he that denieth that Jesus is the Christ?
He is antichrist, that denieth the Father and the Son.

I JOHN 2: 22

THE PEACEFUL AND MERRY COUNTRYSIDE

ALEKSANDER HERTZ, the Polish sociologist, observed that by 1914 the 'peaceful and merry countryside' had practically disappeared, and, in a parallel situation, by 1939 the jungle had relinquished its similarly tranquil qualities.[1] The implication of this statement is that Bronisław Malinowski had described the Trobriand Islands at the very last moment. In roughly the same era, Polish ethnographers achieved their greatest accomplishments: Oskar Kolberg had completed his monumental opus,[2] a number of issues of *Zbiór Wiadomości do Antropologii Krajowej* had

Interviews stored in the archive of the Katedra Etnologii i Antropologii Kulturowej, University of Warsaw, are referred to in abbreviated form. The following key lists the interviewer and the date and place of each interview:

Ch	Krystyna Gieryszewska, 6 Nov. 1989, Chłopice
Cie 1	Krystyna Gieryszewska, May 1990, Cieszacin Wielki
Cie 2	Krystyna Gieryszewska, 7 Nov. 1989, Cieszacin Wielki
Cie 3	Krystyna Gieryszewska, 8 Nov. 1989, Cieszacin Wielki
Cie 4	Krystyna Gieryszewska, May 1990, Cieszacin Wielki
P 1	Krystyna Gieryszewska, 4 Nov. 1989, Pruchnik
P 2	Krystyna Gieryszewska, 5 Nov. 1989, Pruchnik
P 3	Agata Wieczorek, 4 Nov. 1989, Pruchnik
P 4	Agata Wieczorek, 4 Nov. 1989, Pruchnik
P 5	Agata Wieczorek, 5 Nov. 1989, Pruchnik
Pa	Krystyna Gieryszewska and Agata Wieczorek, 1 Apr. 1990, Pajówka
S 1	Krystyna Gieryszewska, May 1990, Siennów
S 2	Krystyna Gieryszewska, May 1990, Siennów
U	Krystyna Gieryszewska, May 1990, Urzejowice

[1] A. Hertz, *Wyznania starego człowieka* (Warsaw, 1991), 56.

[2] O. Kolberg, *Lud: Jego zwyczaje, sposób życia, mowa, podania, przysłowia, obrzędy, gusła, zabawy, pieśni, muzyka i tańce*, 34 vols. (Warsaw, 1857–90); reissued as O. Kolberg, *Dzieła wszystkie*, ed. J. Krzyżanowski et al. (Wrocław etc., 1961–).

appeared, and the first volumes of the important monthlies *Wisła* and *Lud* had been published.

If not after the First World War, then certainly after the Second, the Polish countryside unquestionably lost its idyllic nature. The disappearance of the manor and of the country's Jews, features that had been recognized by some researchers (among them Agnes Heller)[3] as the two essential elements of central European identity, had far-reaching ethical implications.

'Disappearance' is a euphemism describing the brutal force of the totalitarian ideologies that completely transformed the post-war Polish countryside. The genocidal nature of these disappearances became apparent only at the demise of the ideologies. Along with the deaths of the manors and the Jews died the language of propaganda that had served to rationalize rule over the country. Today, unlike fifty—or even twenty—years ago, no sane person would refer to the Galician massacre of 1846 as 'a taking over of the manors', or try to prove the 'historical necessity' of 'a struggle against reactionary forces' to 'strengthen the people's power'. Even colloquial speech has thrown into doubt the communist gauge of 'progressive versus reactionary'. Words such as 'patrician', 'gentry', 'landlord', or 'steward of an estate' have lost their stigma.

Before examining similar changes in relation to 'Jewish topics', let us note that the post-communist purge of the language has been generally accepted by Polish society. No one protests or questions the new linguistic order as officially imposed 'political correctness'.

INTELLECTUALS, COMMON FOLK, AND 'JEWISH TOPICS'

Has a similar change been noticed in relation to 'Jewish topics'? One would think that after the Holocaust no antisemitic or anti-Jewish act could be considered innocent. However, the debate aroused by Jan T. Gross's book *Neighbors*[4] exposed an extraordinarily polarized *sensus communis*, or rather a multi-voiced chorus of 'common senses' that erupts in response to 'Jewish topics' and is conditioned by conflicting political opinions and the social position of the speakers. Competition between diverse visions of Polish and Jewish martyrologies has produced different versions of history, additionally complicated by so-called façade behaviour (displayed as a veiled dislike of Jews). According to some researchers, however, manifestations of this kind of behaviour are somewhat weaker in Poland than, for example, in Germany, Austria, or France.[5]

Research points to an obvious disparity between Polish and German views of

[3] A. Heller, 'Europa Środkowowschodnia', *Gazeta Wyborcza*, 28 Sept. 2000.

[4] J. T. Gross, *Sąsiedzi: Historia zagłady żydowskiego miasteczka* (Sejny, 2000), Eng. trans. *Neighbors: The Destruction of the Jewish Community of Jedwabne* (Princeton, 2001).

[5] See I. Krzemiński (ed.), *Czy Polacy są antysemitami? Wyniki badania sondażowego* (Warsaw, 1996), 150.

antisemitism, both in their respective understanding of this phenomenon per se, as well as in their recognition of its place in history and in relation to national and personal identities.[6] Surveys by Ireneusz Krzemiński's team from the University of Warsaw in the 1990s reveal that among Poles, antisemitism is most widely perceived as 'aversion, dislike, prejudice' (38 per cent), or as 'hatred' or 'intolerance' of Jews (21 per cent). The definition of antisemitism as 'active anti-Jewish behaviour, if only for the sake of propaganda', takes a surprisingly high third place (16 per cent), with the focus not on attitudes and emotions, but on action. According to Krzemiński, 'the process of research revealed that the majority of those polled (who were not members of the intelligentsia) tended to use the word "antisemitism" only when referring to hostile acts'.[7]

'THERE WERE NO CONFLICTS'

What does this third category—of 'active antisemitism' as a definition popular especially among the uneducated—signify when translated into ethnographic reality? It means that those who are asked about their personal or their group's antisemitism can deny it in good faith if they cannot recall examples of those 'hostile acts' by which, in their view, antisemitism is defined.

The more thorough ethnographic research recorded by Alina Cała in *Wizerunek Żyda w polskiej kulturze ludowej*[8] confirms the sociological findings cited above. She observes a frequent phenomenon, familiar from other works on the subject: 'The question whether conflicts ever occurred between the two groups is usually vehemently denied' (*WŻ* 15).

Some statements that she quotes may be examined more closely: 'People intermingled and lived in peace, as good neighbours. They didn't bother anyone, but among Poles "beat the Jew" was a popular catchword—it was the Poles who attacked them. But there were no open demonstrations' (*WŻ* 44). What does this speaker mean by 'open demonstrations'? If the attacks against Jews that he himself mentions were not open demonstrations, does this imply that an 'attack' is considered to be an 'open demonstration' only when committed by a Jew? Krzemiński's focus group of common people defines antisemitism as 'hostile behaviour' against Jews, yet does not view 'attacking Jews' as an 'open demonstration', so it is doubtful that the same kind of logic would recognize 'attacking Jews' as 'hostile behaviour'. Thus, establishing the reality of antisemitism is delayed *usque ad mortem*.

Similar contradictions appear in the following statements cited by Cała:

[6] Krzemiński (ed.), *Czy Polacy są antysemitami?*; W. Benz (ed.), *Rechtsextremismus in der Bundesrepublik: Voraussetzungen, Zusammenhänge, Wirkungen* (Frankfurt am Main, 1991); H.-U. Wehler, *Entsorgung der deutschen Vergangenheit? Ein polemischer Essay zum 'Historikerstreit'* (Munich, 1988).   [7] Krzemiński (ed.), *Czy Polacy są antysemitami?*, 153.

[8] A. Cała, *Wizerunek Żyda w polskiej kulturze ludowej* (Warsaw, 1987). Subsequent references to this work in the main text will be indicated by the abbreviation *WŻ* followed by page number(s).

There were no conflicts. Just minor irritations, not as rude and ugly as nowadays. Like, when Jews wanted to cover their heads in class, local Catholics protested, threatening to keep their children from school. So Jewish pupils had to sit in school without skullcaps. (*WŻ* 40)

[Polish] boys would tug at their sidecurls, and sometimes cut them off. They would throw stones into the sukkahs [tents raised by Jews during the Feast of Tabernacles], yelling and frightening [them]. Sometimes they would trap a crow or a jackdaw, and let it loose into the sukkah, or even the synagogue. They would extinguish the candles. The Jews believed it was a ghost and interrupted [their prayers]. (*WŻ* 40)

and in a statement quoted by other researchers: 'Jews had their sukkahs. During their holiday, they were supposed to drink dew. So the boys would make [fun?] of Jews, pee in the sukkah, and the Jews thought it was dew.'[9]

Besides urination in the sukkahs, other 'jokes' are mentioned, such as tossing frogs, dead animals, and pork into the sukkah, rubbing door handles with pork fat and snot, or disturbing Jewish funerals (*WŻ* 42, 47).

A further statement highlights the contradictions. If the sentences are labelled sequentially, they can be seen to present a parody of logic: $a = {\sim}a, b = {\sim}b, c = {\sim}c, d = {\sim}d$:[10]

No, there were no fights [*a*]. Only sometimes youngsters threw stones into those sukkahs . . . or tossed a brick [${\sim}a$]. Why would a Pole quarrel with them? he borrowed, got into debt, so they grabbed his pig or horse [*b*] . . . Jarosław Jews used to chant: 'The streets may be yours, yet the buildings are ours.' But they didn't hurt anyone, didn't interfere with the Catholics [${\sim}b$]. They know how to win over a customer [*c*], while Poles in shops these days are sometimes plain rude. I can't complain [*c*]. Other folk also got along with the Jews . . . Jews are swindlers [${\sim}c$] . . . At school Poles would shove lard up a Jewish kid's nose [*d*] . . . As a general rule, they got along fine [${\sim}d$] . . . The well-behaved boys didn't harass them— but there were hooligans. Two or three in a class would give Jews a hard time. Parents came to school to pick up their kids. They were let out earlier, us later [${\sim}d$]. (*WŻ* 41)

A similar pattern characterizes the views of a retired town councillor from Przeworsk:

Later they stopped bringing [the baked goods Jews used to offer neighbours on the sabbath] since a new culture was introduced—the antisemitic campaign throughout Poland. Jewish businesses were boycotted, and Polish shops opened . . . It wasn't done brutally or violently, no. Earlier, during the bishop's visits . . . Jews went out with their Torah to greet him. They showed respect. About 1930 they stopped going out [because] Christian youths were harassing the Jews, jeering at them—but there was no fighting. Jews didn't attend town dances. They kept our holy days . . . that's why Poles didn't treat Jews badly. On Corpus

[9] Interview by Krystyna Gieryszewska and Agata Wieczorek, Mar. 1990, in Katedra Etnologii i Antropologii Kulturowej. It is not known where the interview was conducted, as the first page of the transcript is missing.

[10] The logical symbol ${\sim}$ denotes negation of the following element. For example, '$a = {\sim}a$' may be read as 'a equals not-a'.

Christi they hung out rugs on balconies—but no icons or decorations. They avoided leaving their homes, or standing out on their balconies. There were no conflicts then, or fisticuffs. Polish youths and children went to the synagogue to poke fun . . . Jews avoided meeting 'Herods', for they got beaten. (*WŻ* 44)

One could reconstruct the presumed logic of this text in the following way: to prevent conflicts, to show respect to their hosts, Jews too should observe Christian holidays, but discreetly. On no account should they leave home or go out on their balconies (though the precaution was needless, because after all 'There were no conflicts then, or fisticuffs'). Despite the jeering, mentioned twice (while welcoming the bishop and in the synagogue), and beating, mentioned once, the statement about 'lack of violence' is stubbornly repeated. There is a certain logic in this thinking: just as in the denial that 'harassment' of Jews by Poles constitutes an 'open demonstration', so too is a one-sided attack not considered 'fighting', 'conflict', or 'fisticuffs'.

Antisemitic logic requires radical solutions: '[The presence of] the Other is a scandal' not to be tolerated in the long term by the populace of a village or small town. Therefore, in its own best interest, the Other should as soon as possible stop being different, and—in line with the suggestion of 'discreetly observing Christian holidays'—should convert to Catholicism.

ANTISEMITIC REASONING

It is a commonplace that the logic of exclusion judges the members of one's own group and aliens by a double standard. Some of the examples collected by Cała refresh that cliché, revealing its unintended absurdity. As an example of typical Jewish chutzpah ('Before the war they [the Jews] ruled the roost'), the following criminal case is cited: 'When a Polish policeman killed a 2-year-old Jewish child, what hell did they raise! Dragging him through the courts, until he was sentenced to a long period of imprisonment' (*WŻ* 46).

Two other statements represent complaints about Jewish injustice: 'They never helped Poles, though they helped their own—the Jewish council [of elders] distributed money' (*WŻ* 21); and Poles are owed help 'by right': there is no question of reciprocity. Similar logic applies to a complaint about attempts by Jews to retrieve furniture after Poles had taken over formerly Jewish property: 'Once they [Jews] came to me too, for I still live in a formerly Jewish house. They didn't check who it used to belong to. As long as it was Jewish, it was theirs' (*WŻ* 173–4), complains the speaker.

With iron consistency, the logic of exclusion interprets lack of proof as proof. 'They believed in a calf and also in God . . . How [they felt] about Catholics—we don't know; [they were] quiet, didn't scoff, but when they gathered together—it's hard to tell' (*WŻ* 35). The so-called 'Jewish telephone' (*eruv*), the wire connecting the roofs of adjacent Jewish houses to form a symbolic courtyard that would allow the sabbath to be observed, was viewed as a trick: 'Jewish houses were connected by wire crossing the street, forcing the icons in a [church] procession to bow. Poles often cut those wires' (*WŻ* 56). Even ignorance of the Jews' language becomes a proof against them: 'Eighty per cent of their prayers were curses against the worshippers of another religion' (*WŻ* 85), declared someone who certainly had never learned either Hebrew or Yiddish, or indeed any foreign language at all.

PENAL MYTHOLOGY

Despite the numbers of complaints made against Jews, the Polish village was aware of their social deprivation, a consequence of the Diaspora. This assertion can also be reversed: awareness of that deprivation created the need to rationalize it through images of Jewish duplicity. Studies in social psychology and victimology point to the frequent justification of crimes by blaming the victim (e.g. 'She provoked it herself', said of a victim of rape). At stake is the principle of divine justice, embodied in the statement that 'God punishes evil, and rewards good'. In high culture this principle inspired theodicies, but in popular culture and everyday thinking it was penal mythology that resulted.

The most popular explanation of the Jewish Diaspora is found in the myth of the wandering Jew, which, according to Joshua Trachtenberg, appeared for the first time in Europe in the thirteenth century in the figure of Joseph Cartaphilus, allegedly well known in the East as a languishing witness of Christ's agony.[11] The apologetic force of his testimony was from the beginning used against Jews and heretics. In eastern Poland, the concept still remains strong:

When the Lord Jesus was carrying the cross, he wanted to rest in front of a Jewish house. That Jew chased him away and the Lord Jesus cursed him to become an eternal wanderer. And when that Jew walks, his footprints appear as crosses. Ahasuerus was that Jew's name, and wherever he shows up, a plague breaks out. He changes shape every century, gets rejuvenated, and continues wandering. (P 5)

The story of Ahasuerus overlaps with the myth of 'the tribe of Judas' and the punishment it suffers for one of its sons' deeds. In the eyes of their Polish neighbours, the story serves as a basic explanation for the fate of the Jews. Cała writes: 'The majority of those surveyed believe that Jews were accomplices in the death of the Son of God. The punishment for the crucifixion was the dispersion and universal hatred of Jews' (*WŻ* 90).[12] A similar belief is so widespread in Polish folk Christianity that it can be considered as part of the blueprint of that culture. Here are two examples: 'The Lord Jesus put a curse on them and since then they have

[11] J. Trachtenberg, *Diabeł i Żydzi: Średniowieczna koncepcja Żyda a współczesny antysemityzm*, trans. R. Stiller (Gdynia, 1997), 24–6.

[12] See also H. Datner-Śpiewak, 'Struktura i wyznaczniki postaw antysemickich', in Krzemiński (ed.), *Czy Polacy są antysemitami?*, 33 ff.; A. Cała, *Asymilacja Żydów w Królestwie Polskim (1864–1897): Postawy, konflikty, stereotypy* (Warsaw, 1989), esp. the chapters 'Antysemityzm a asymilacja' and 'Dygresje i refleksje'.

been roaming homeless about the world'; 'The Lord sent such a one as Hitler to destroy them. War is never from people, only from God. It's the Lord God who wages war' (Huta Brzuska, 1985; *WŻ* 91).

Folk Christianity reinforces the stereotypical image of Jews: as a rule, justice trumps mercy, and 'an eye for an eye, a tooth for a tooth' remains the principle by which scores are settled. Let us compare two statements. The first is from the Belarusian village of Lebeda:

[Why did the Germans treat the Jews in that way?] . . . They made God suffer. Jews killed the Lord Jesus. So . . . a punishment was inflicted upon them, that's all.
[And is that punishment just?] Of course it's just, if the Lord God demands it! I've been beaten, so I'll beat back, I'll punish the people.[13]

The second statement, from Polish Siennów, is a commentary on the Good Friday ritual of beating and hanging a figure representing Judas, the topic that will be the theme of the second part of this chapter: 'After they'd taken down the Judas, they shouted: "Treachery! Now it's your turn to get a thrashing!"' (S 2). Where Christ himself is viewed as a God of revenge, the 'imitation' of him must assume the form of 'the hanging of Judas'.

'THE RIGHTEOUS SHALL REJOICE WHEN HE SEETH THE VENGEANCE' (Ps. 58: 10)

A striking aspect of penal mythology was the alleged anticipation of the Holocaust by the Jews as just punishment for their sins, especially for that of deicide. These predictions were the specialty of *tsadikim* (*WŻ* 113–15), the only Jews who were universally respected and who ('even though they were Jews') were not subjected to provocation by children or youths. This aspect of the Jewish prophetic myth is characterized by an unusually large number of naïve Christian conjectures. Trachtenberg writes that, even in the Middle Ages, Christianity 'was so deeply convinced of the unquestionable validity of its tradition and teachings, that it was simply unable to accept the existence of an alternative truth. It may seem strange, but there exist compelling testimonies that the Catholic world believed that Jews themselves accepted the legitimacy of Christian doctrine.'[14] The Jews' refusal to acknowledge the coming of Christ caused Poles widespread astonishment, and was explained by Poles as part of a natural Jewish proclivity to deceive. After all, Jews are great experts on the Scriptures, which, in Christian opinion, indisputably foretold Christ's coming.

A typical illustration is provided by Jan Ursyn Niemcewicz in his memoirs:

My father used to argue with Jews, trying by all means to convert them. Once he embarked upon a discussion with an innkeeper, quoting the prophets to attest the coming of Christ.

[13] Interview by Jacek Ciechocki, Nov. 1993, Lebeda (Belarus): Anna Engelking's Belarusian records, unpublished.   [14] Trachtenberg, *Diabeł i Żydzi*, 24.

The debate became heated; in the end the Jew dared to say that Catholics had falsified the Hebrew text, upon which my father, enraged by such audacity, tried to reach for a stronger argument—the Jew's sidecurls—whereupon a servant entered with a pot of chicken soup and interrupted the outburst of temper. My good, devoted father maintained his passion for converting Jews until his late old age . . . not discouraged that in his many years of lively debates not a single Jew was converted.[15]

The analysis of the language used in the Catholic periodicals *Rycerz Niepokalanej* and *Mały Dziennik*, carried out by Ute Caumanns and Mathias Niendorf, presents evidence of the unusual longevity of such antisemitic clichés, which survived unchanged into the 1930s.[16]

The stubborn refusal of Jews to convert despite 'sure-fire proofs' infuriated pious Christians. A church leader came up with an explanation: 'I truly doubt whether a Jew can be a human being, since he doesn't submit to human reasoning, refusing to accept conclusive explanations, divine as well as Jewish', stated Peter the Venerable, the abbot of Cluny.[17] As I have already explored the notion of Jewish inhumanity in my article 'Żydzi u Kolberga',[18] I shall limit myself here to just one typical adage recorded by Kolberg: 'There's no difference between a wolf and a Jew, for neither has a soul.'[19]

Jews were believed to have the power to infect the simple Polish folk with a tendency to deceive[20] as well as with their 'soullessness'. This was apparently the view of Sofroniusz Witwicki, who declared in his book *O Huculach* (1860) that, though the people of the Hutsul region of Transcarpathia were by nature 'lecherous', their intimate association with Jews and underground writers had completely corrupted them, 'making them capable of false statements'.[21] Cardinal Hlond's declaration in his 1936 pastoral letter following a pogrom in Przytyk is testimony to the force of such beliefs. Hlond describes the 'corrupting influence' of Jews on Poles, and recommends their social and moral isolation.[22]

Returning to the ethnographic material, we may cite further examples of the outlook underpinning penal mythology:

[15] Quoted in J. S. Bystroń, *Dzieje obyczajów w dawnej Polsce: Wiek XVI–XVIII*, 2 vols. (Warsaw, 1976), i. 339.

[16] U. Caumanns and M. Niendorf, 'Kolbe a Kielce: Święty, jego prasa i problem pewnego pogromu', in E. and R. Traba (eds.),*Tematy żydowskie: Historia, literatura, edukacja* (Olsztyn, 1999), 100–27.   [17] Trachtenberg, *Diabeł i Żydzi*, 27 n. 16.

[18] J. Tokarska-Bakir, 'Żydzi u Kolberga', in ead., *Rzeczy mgliste: Eseje i studia* (Sejny, 2004), esp. 65.   [19] Kolberg, *Dzieła wszystkie*, lx: *Przysłowia* (Wrocław and Poznań, 1967), 533.

[20] This tendency is presented farcically in a Nativity play, when a Jew, asked about God's birthplace, responds that 'the beech tree [play of words on *buk*, 'beech tree', and *Bóg*, 'God'] is born in a forest near Tomaszów, where it is used by carpenters and coopers to make stools and butter dishes, and I have sticks from it' (Cie 4).

[21] Quoted in Kolberg, *Dzieła wszystkie*, lv: *Ruś Karpacka*, pt. 2 (Wrocław and Poznań, 1971), 449.

[22] See A. Cała, H. Węgrzynek, and G. Zalewska, *Historia i kultura Żydów polskich: Słownik* (Warsaw, 2000), s.v. 'Kościół a Żydzi', 168. See also A. Grupińska, *Ciągle po kole: Rozmowy z żołnierzami Getta Warszawskiego* (Warsaw, 2000), 324–5.

Secretly [Jews] believed in the Mother of God, because when the Germans were shooting, they cried 'Holy Mother, save us!' (*WŻ* 35)

[Jewish] dress was black, mournful . . . They wore mourning clothes for him [Christ], but would not believe in him. Did they understand that they had done evil? (*WŻ* 90)

When during the war Father went to see Mendel in the ghetto, he heard him say: 'And so that blood was on our heads.' (*WŻ* 152)

Jews used to say· 'What was the point of Jews crucifying Christ, when now we have to suffer?' (*WŻ* 152)

The belief in Jewish guilt resonates even in the words of a woman who, at the risk of her own and her four children's lives, took in a Jewish orphan for the duration of the war: 'Wintluk himself often repeated: "Our Jews killed the Lord Jesus and that's why we we are made to suffer so"' (*WŻ* 169).[23]

A similar mechanism functions in alleged Jewish prophesies about the Holocaust:

They had their holy books in which it said that when partridges die out, the end will come for Jews too. The 1942 winter was so bad that all the partridges died and Jews themselves told me that it was the end for them too. (Sichlawa; *WŻ* 92)

The Jews had a prophecy in the Talmud about their extinction: when partridges die, it will be a sign of the impending end of the Jews, but if hares start dying, it will mean the end of the Poles. (Uhrusk; *WŻ* 92)

At the beginning of the war Jews were forced to work. They were employed here on an estate taken over by a certain German. Once a young man was returning from work in the evening past the cemetery, when suddenly he saw a lady with a golden crown, all clothed in gold, and with a golden crescent on her chest. Was it the Virgin Mary, or who? He was terribly scared, and fled, and barely alive reached the shack where the Jews were housed. He couldn't get a grip on himself for a long while, then finally told the others about it. Everyone wondered what it could mean, until one very wise old Jew told them: 'It foretells our death!' Because Jews had their holy books and it said there that when the Good Lady appeared to them, it would mean their death. (Uhrusk; *WŻ* 92)

THE HANGING OF JUDAS

'A SORT OF MAN'

In certain regions of southern Poland, a custom known as 'the hanging of Judas' has survived into the present, and was recalled during the debates about Jedwabne.[24] Let us review its ethnographic morphology:

---

[23] The problem of internalization of these accusations by Jews themselves deserves further study. See Daniel Maria (Oswald Rufeisen), *Połknąłem haczyk Królowej Karmelu: Autobiografia* (Kraków, 2001).

[24] See J. Tokarska-Bakir, 'Obsesja niewinności', *Gazeta Wyborcza*, 12–13 Jan. 2001; R. Pawłowski, 'Jude 2001', *Gazeta Wyborcza*, 21–22 Apr. 2001.

There are no Jews here now, but they were here before the war, and wherever they lived, Judas was hanged on their account. On Holy Thursday young people—it was usually the young ones—prepared an effigy, *a sort of man*, they took trousers and a jacket, stuffed them with hay, and sometimes, if they wanted it to be special, they added two sticks for the legs as handles, to hold it up. Everyone helped. It was fun, first of all fun [to do it], and second because Jews wanted to buy themselves out [of the situation], to have it taken down, so you always got a few zlotys, and before the war every zloty counted. (S 2; emphasis mine)

This tradition is still practised in Pruchnik, for example. There the Judas is sewn together at the co-operative workshop (P 3). Further:

There was a long-standing tradition of commemorating Judas's betrayal of the Lord Jesus. There were experts who would stuff that Judas with straw somewhere in a barn. They used to sew it with a head and legs, stuffed with straw. On Good Friday it would hang from a tree by the church. Now it hangs in the market square. Before three o'clock young boys, 12 or 13 years old, would gather. There was one who judged him, and the Judas was dragged onto the church steps before the three o'clock service. The one who judged him would say: 'Judas, you traitor, you sold the Lord Jesus for thirty pieces of silver. You'll get thirty strokes.' And one of them would hit him thirty times with a stick. The boys stood there with sticks to beat him. Before hanging Judas, they tied a bag with coins onto him to show that he had sold [Jesus] for thirty pieces of silver. They pulled and beat him, and finally dragged him through all the streets. In the end they pulled him to the pond and drowned him. And the people yelled. While they were dragging him, they didn't beat him, but just shouted 'hurrah'. (P 2)

That effigy hangs there from Holy Thursday. On Good Friday at three o'clock sharp, so as to be before vespers, young folks are already waiting, armed with clubs and sticks. Judas is judged and taken to the church steps. There was one youngster, a bit simple, who used to judge him; I don't know who judges him now. It happens each year. He says: 'For selling the Lord Jesus for thirty pieces of silver, you'll get thirty blows.' First *he* hits him thirty times. Then the other children also start beating him, pulling him by a rope along the streets, then to where the ponds are, a kind of bog near the river; there they pretend to drown him or even burn him. They even cut his head off before drowning him on top of that. I didn't especially keep up with it . . . More recently they've burned him, maybe there was nothing to drown him in. (P 1)

On Holy Thursday Poles used to make Judas in effigy, dress him in things stolen from Jews, and hang him on a post in the middle of the marketplace. (Kańczuga; *WŻ* 130)

He had a beard like a Jew, made from a handful of hemp, a hat like a scarecrow, with a money-bag in his hand. (S 1)

The traditional 'jokes' played on Jews were organized by groups of young lads.[25] In Pruchnik, however, that group is already slightly more 'mature': 'There are a few of them there, not so young any more. They carve out the head, with its [characteristic] nose [hawk-like? Jewish?]. [Afterwards] they toss off the head and

---

[25] Cała comments: 'Their behaviour was not approved of, but it was tolerated, according to the principle that "boys will be boys"': *Wizerunek Żyda*, 42. The speaker quoted ibid., n. 4, says succinctly: 'There was no fighting with Jews, for there were no young lads here.'

take it away; they don't make a new one every year, it's not worth the bother. They keep it till the next year; when it wears out a bit, they make another' (P 1). A record from the village of Pajówka confirms that the authors of the ritual are no longer just youngsters: 'At night on Holy Thursday [it was hanged], and hung till morning. It was adults that were involved' (Pa).

WHERE THE HANGING TOOK PLACE

The hanging was done where Jews lived. It used to put the Jews on edge. It was hung high. These days, if someone is mad about something, he may still hang a Judas. Earlier, it was usually done to Jews. Now, if some young lady rejects a man, the fiancé may hang it because she refused to marry him. It has happened that a hanging was done because a girl didn't surrender [to marriage]. (Pa)

Longer ago, before 1935, they used to do the beating outside every Jewish house. There was even one Jew living here who put shutters up, for they would have broken his windows; those shutters are still there. They would beat Judas outside every Jewish home. (P 2)

Before the war they used to beat Judas in front of Jewish houses. There were loads of Jews here. Every Jew had shutters, so he wouldn't be robbed, or have his window panes broken. (P 4)

You would go to a stable and find straw, an old shirt, and trousers. A figure was made out of straw and straw-rope, with a hat, and a flask at its side. From Holy Thursday to the Friday, the Jews kept watch so that it wouldn't be hanged. They used to beat the Jews so that they wouldn't take it down. It hung through Friday and Saturday, and it was only on Sunday that the Jews paid to have it taken down . . . They were as pleased as could be, while the Jews closed their doors and windows . . . A Jew would hire someone and that person would take it behind the barn to burn it. Up until then Jews were well liked, but on that day they went and did the hanging. (S 1)

Once, when we were going to Jarosław for the adoration of the Lord's Sepulchre, we looked, and saw someone hanging in a tree by the church, in tatters, grimy. Well now, how old was I? Perhaps two or three years old. He was so battered, torn . . . Young lads used to get together and make that Judas and drag him and beat him in front of the whole village, and when they'd beaten him up they would bring him to the Jewish house where a tall poplar tree stood. They would hang the Judas high, putting a small pan in his hands filled with soot; when the Jew tried to touch the Judas, soot would spill on him. They always hung it by that Jew's house, they wouldn't hang it anywhere else. (Cie 4)

The Jews didn't like it at all; they had to give someone money to take it down, for it hung very high. It often hung in the priest's garden, opposite where the old inn is now; sometimes it would hang for two weeks. Afterwards there was no beating, it was quiet, but whoever took it down would burn and destroy it. (U)

At night, so that the Jews didn't know about it, they would hang it up and wait to see what would happen, how the Jew would react whose house they'd hanged it at. As soon as the Jew saw it, he wanted to get rid of it, and called one or two [boys?] and offered them 5 zlotys or 2 zlotys, because the Jew couldn't take it down, as it was very high, only someone could do it who knew how to. When they'd made a bargain, the Jew would offer his five [zlotys], but would haggle a little: 'Take it down [the Jew would say].' 'I won't [the Pole would answer], it's risky, I might fall.' The tree was the tallest and hardest to reach, so that the Jew couldn't pull down [the Judas]. I remember, with one family they hung it high in a split poplar tree. It hung there for a long time, because they wouldn't pay, they were poor, so it hung until Sunday. After they'd taken down the Judas, they shouted: 'Treachery! Now it's your turn to get a thrashing!' It wasn't about religion, that hanging, it was just for money. (S 2)

A CAT, NO; A JEW, YES

How old was the ritual?

That Judas has always been, but earlier it was only boys who used to run along with sticks; now girls do it too. For a while it wasn't done; it was banned,[26] but then it was resumed, I don't know exactly when. It was an ancient custom, from generation to generation. I don't know how it started. But, because Judas betrayed the Lord Jesus, that's why it's celebrated. I've seen a picture from 1930, it was the same. A head and body sewn from a sack, and stuffed with straw. I also have a picture taken in 1985, with a note on it: 'Judas the traitor 1985'. (P 1)

The cliché 'Judas the traitor', uttered in the accusatory speech on the church steps, recurs in each account as a mnemonic formula that I shall explore further below. It is summoned by any association with evil, such as a mention of Cain.[27] People are familiar with Judas the traitor from Nativity plays: 'When I watched a Nativity play in Przemyśl, performed by priests long ago, he was terrifying, with massive, dishevelled hair, he gave me such a shock' (Ch). When asked about folk legends of Judas, a woman from Urzejowice stresses the correctness of her beliefs: 'No, there were no [legends], only what we heard from the Church' (U).

In the debate over Roman Pawłowski's article,[28] an outraged Archbishop Józef Życiński rejected Cała's hypothesis that priests incited 'openly antisemitic behaviour', and demanded proof of their participation in the rite.[29] Ethnographic material provides such proofs: 'On Good Friday after Mass, Catholics went to the market square along with the priest, the pharmacist, and the doctor, to cut Judas down, drag him along with a rope, and then throw him into the water' (Kańczuga, 1984; *WŻ* 130). Although this testimony probably relates to the pre-war period,

---

[26] Cf. below on the banning of the custom in Pruchnik.

[27] See J. Tokarska-Bakir, *Obraz osobliwy: Hermeneutyczna lektura źródeł etnograficznych* (Kraków, 2000).   [28] Pawłowski, 'Jude 2001'.

[29] 'Personally, in my whole life I haven't yet met a priest who would spend his time drowning Marzanna or attacking an effigy of Judas. The author gives no arguments to substantiate her strong accusations. She declares nonchalantly: "I think that . . ."': Archbishop Józef Życiński's letter to the editors of *Gazeta Wyborcza*, 23 Apr. 2001. Drowning or burning Marzanna (Morena) is a folk custom still popular in Poland, Slovakia, and the Czech Republic. Its symbolic purpose is to welcome the incoming spring and bury the outgoing winter on the day of the vernal equinox. The rite typically involves setting fire to a female straw effigy of Marzanna, sometimes life-size, or drowning it in a river, or both.

another such instance, from 1989, is couched in the present tense: 'The priest sometimes comes along to it, but not to join in; he only says not to take too long, not to delay vespers' (P 1).

In Pruchnik during the war, the ritual of hanging was discontinued, though it is not known who took the initiative to effect this change: 'Under the Germans we weren't allowed to beat Judas. After the liberation, the Party was against it too. [When was the custom resumed?] Two or three years [ago] they started it again' (P 4). An inhabitant of Cieszacin Wielki presents the history of the rite in her village differently: 'During the occupation, when I was little, it was still going on, but not after the war' (Cie 1). The villager from Urzejowice repeats this opinion, with a peculiar explanation: 'After the war they stopped the hanging, as there were no longer any Jews; two families survived, but they soon moved to America. The hanging had been done to annoy Jews' (U).

Regrettably, those interviewed say nothing about the ways in which Jews reacted to the hanging of Judas during the war, nor do the interviews reveal much about the reactions inspired by the fate of the Jews among their neighbours.[30] Wartime events as introduced into Nativity plays, which were performed without a break despite the occupation, are not a clear source of information on this point either. Strangely, both of the updated versions of the traditional text speak about 'Jewish lice':

During the war and the occupation, at the beginning of that [section of the play, Herod] would say [to the Jew, whom he had asked about the birthplace of Jesus Christ]: 'All you can talk about is beans, wood, and a beech tree, and you stand there like a pig's slipper, with lice going for a walk all over your collar.' Sora [the Jew's wife] runs in and counts: 'One, two, three, in every pile a hundred and thirty-three; they can be sent to Germany by train as a contingent.' (Cie 2)

[Stage directions:] The Marshal keeps hitting the Jew, saying: 'Jew, tell me where God, Jesus Christ, is born.' Moshko [the Jew]: 'Ichtychbuch, ichtychbuch, when you made the hump swell up on my back, couldn't you open your gob all the way? You looked like a herd of swine', while lice are crawling all over him . . . One, two, three, in every pile a hundred and thirty-three; and behind your back they're sent by rail to Germany. [The Louse?:] 'Do you think I'm not a military man? When I jump, I'll jump right over you!' The Jew struggles and kicks. The text about lice was performed during the war. (Cie 3)

A number of testimonies recall a custom similar to the 'hanging of Judas', namely the killing or chasing of a cat:

On Holy Wednesday cats were beaten and put into clay pots, the pots were then tied up and thrown down from a small opening on top of the church. A triangular candelabrum was put up with thirteen candles for the twelve apostles and the Lord Jesus. In remembrance, after

---

[30] This question was raised by Alina Cała (e.g. at *Wizerunek Żyda*, 47), at that time one of Ireneusz Krzemiński's team of sociologists that was just beginning its research on Polish attitudes towards Jews. Now, after more than ten years of study, we have much more information on the subject: see e.g. J. Tokarska-Bakir, *Legendy o krwi: Antropologia przesądu* (Warsaw, 2008), 510–644.

the service, matins on Wednesday, that's when they used to beat those cats. The cats would run away, and they would throw stones after them. (P 4)

But that ritual in Pruchnik came to be banned by the local priest: 'On Good Friday they also used to throw a cat down from the church steeple in a clay pot, but that was brutal; once a cat jumped out and got killed. So the priest forbade it' (P 1). Because the priest defended only the cat, 'Judas' had to count on the mercy of another protector. It turned out to be Stalin, whose name we can assume stands for 'the power of the people': 'Stalin forbade [the hanging of Judas] but people kept on doing it' (S 1).

RISUS PASCHALIS?

Alina Cała introduces her depiction of the hanging of Judas with an extensive preface describing the ritualistic context in which Jews appear in Polish folk culture. She mentions a haymakers' initiation (known as a 'Jewish baptism'), 'Herod' costumes, the custom by which brides borrow something from a Jewish woman before their weddings, and the fertility symbolism of Jewish participation in a wedding and at Easter (*WŻ* 129–30). Cała concludes that symbols of otherness played an important role 'in maintaining continuation of the reproductive cycle'. However, in her description of the hanging of Judas, she distinguishes it from that background, and writes:

The descriptions cited resemble the custom of drowning Marzanna. Folk tradition used to mark thus the coming of spring, and the final victory over the dark forces of winter. It appears that the figure representing Judas was a secondary, superficially Christianized form of that ritual. Therefore it should be explained in a similar way: as getting rid of something that one had been trying to tame during a period of transition. The forces that were to initiate life had become superfluous. They could only do harm and so should be excluded. It was sought to achieve this by means of symbolic aggression against those whose mediation had previously been enlisted. (*WŻ* 131)

This position, representing the 'symbolic paradigm' popular since the late 1970s in modern Polish ethnography, covers only some aspects of the complicated phenomenon of the hanging of Judas. Cała herself must also have recognized this explanation as insufficient, because when discussing ritual in *Gazeta Wyborcza* fourteen years after the first publication of her book, she never mentions 'ritualistic time'. She says, instead,

Dragging and beating a figure representing a human being cannot be viewed as innocent fun. Such entertainment is without a doubt an expression of anti-Judaism. Before the war Judas was hanged in the doorways of Jewish houses and Jews had to buy their way out of it. If they didn't do that, they risked getting a beating. An everyday little pogrom.[31]

This statement must grate for ethnographers fond of the symbolic paradigm. This is obvious from the reactions of an ethnographer from Rzeszów and of some

---

[31] Quoted in Pawłowski, 'Jude 2001'.

Warsaw students of ethnography whose opinions were cited in the article. One confessed, 'I never associated the beating of Judas with a pogrom. Beating itself used to be a ritualistic activity: beating with palm branches at Easter is supposed to bring health. I consider that nowadays that custom has nothing to do with antisemitism.' 'To the present-day inhabitants of Pruchnik, Jews seem so distant that this ritual cannot have anything to do with them', declares a Warsaw student emphatically, evidently never having heard about 'antisemitism without Jews'. 'Where then does the word "Yid" come from in their vocabulary?' asks the reporter. 'They might have heard it on TV, or read it in a newspaper. It's called secondary acquisition of meaning', a college girl replies.[32]

Is the Easter-time laughter at Judas being hung in Pruchnik really nothing but Bakhtin's good old *risus paschalis*, an innocent ritualistic laughter? Is nothing really heard in it besides a 'secondary acquisition of meaning'?

SYMBOLIC LOGIC VERSUS THE LOGIC OF EXCLUSION

Ethnographers who do not sense any vestige of antisemitism in that laughter either define antisemitism in a very peculiar way[33] or are trapped in a shallow, purely symbolic reading of the category of 'otherness'. Today this reading, once a revelation after years of materialistic-dialectical aridity, is clearly insufficient if one is to understand the phenomenon in question. It does not take into account the philosophical ferment of recent decades, expressed in works such as Michael Theunissen's *Der Andere*, Emmanuel Levinas's *Le Temps et l'Autre*, and those of Jacques Derrida and Tzvetan Todorov.

Ethnographers who interpreted otherness only as a symbol (in Poland Zbigniew Benedyktowicz, Ludwik Stomma, J. S. Wasilewski, and others) made a contribution by originally developing W. Robertson Smith's intuition about the ambivalence of the *sacrum*[34] and applying it to the phenomenological understanding of the category of otherness. Benedyktowicz believed that 'in spite of and alongside . . . the unambiguously pejorative connotations, and even in the framework of the same image, in at least as many testimonies we encounter a simultaneous admiration of the other'.[35] Among his examples are a Kashube, a Jew, a Gypsy, a woman, an infant, a German,[36]

---

[32] Ibid.

[33] The ways of defining antisemitism that forever postpone its acknowledgement have been discussed above; see also Krzemiński (ed.), *Czy Polacy są antysemitami?* The argument that beating a figure marked 'Yid 2001' shows no signs of antisemitism reminds me somewhat of the opinion that the term 'Jew' cannot be considered an insult because it is a neutral depiction of ethnicity.

[34] See E. Durkheim, *Elementarne formy życia religijnego: System totemiczny*, trans. A. Zadrożyńska (Warsaw, 1990), 391.

[35] Z. Benedyktowicz, *Portrety obcego: Od stereotypu do symbolu* (Kraków, 2000), 185–8.

[36] The word used here for 'woman' is not the stylistically neutral *kobieta* but *niewiasta*, which in origin meant '(she) who does not know'. The words for 'infant' and 'German'—*niemowlę* and *Niemiec*—both allude in their etymology to the inability to speak.

a pregnant woman, a priest, and God. This broad collection, though permissible and desirable from the point of view of symbolic logic, harbours the risk of accepting similarities without qualifications and of neglecting differences that are laid bare by the logic of exclusion.

Today, now that we know what connects the above-mentioned examples, we should make equally clear what separates them. Why might a Kashube, a woman, an infant, a German, a pregnant woman, a priest, or even God (according to Rudolf Otto, the archetypal *ganz Andere*) be accorded the symbolic status of otherness, whereas only two among the listed—a Gypsy and a Jew—are by way of exception marked with the stamp of *differentness*? To grasp this aspect of the phenomenon, *symbolic logic* must recognize the *logic of exclusion*, and the category of *otherness* has to open up to the category of *differentness*.

Everyday language cannot easily distinguish 'otherness' and 'differentness'. I have no intention of forcing this distinction on ethnography; I merely wish to warn that lack of linguistic precision can make us accept the logic of exclusion as purely symbolic logic. What we can overlook is violence, which is not at all symbolic.

Let us return to the ethnographic material. Beating, pulling by the hair, the ears, or the sidelocks, stone-throwing, and other forms of persecution were so much a part of the pre-war Polish Jewish everyday reality that a reader with today's moral awareness is embarrassed to encounter these testimonies. The accounts quoted in Cała's book repeatedly describe these events as 'jokes', 'tricks', or 'inoffensive pranks', and euphemisms such as 'annoyance', 'provocation', or 'mimicry' are also common. 'Folks laughed at [Jews] going to the synagogue in Rymanów. They wore shaggy hats, and on their foreheads and arms, small boxes carved out of wood. So we stood by the road and laughed—"here come the Jews!"' 'It was kids who aped them the most', says one speaker, who even to this day probably sees nothing wrong in this kind of behaviour. 'At night they had to lock their homes, for youngsters would break their windows, or throw stones onto the roof.'[37] 'Students played tricks on Jews: smeared doorknobs with snot, tossed frogs into the sukkahs through the roof' (*WŻ* 47), and so on. 'When our Christian neighbours were celebrating Christmas, none of us came near the church, for it was dangerous', recalls Chaim Beller in Marian Marzyński's documentary *Sztetl*.[38] 'Many considered it a point of honour to break a Jewish window.'

The passivity of the persecuted is the hardest testimony to read: 'A Jew would never approach a Pole first. A Pole would break a Jew's window, and not only when drunk' (*WŻ* 42); 'Jews were quiet, inoffensive . . . No one was afraid of a Jew. A Jew never murdered anyone . . . Some were sometimes cowardly when Poles annoyed

---

[37] M. Nowik, 'Miejsce komunizmu w życiu społeczności wiejskiej na przykładzie wsi Trześniów, woj. krośnieńskiego', master's thesis (Katedra Etnologii i Antropologii Kulturowej, University of Warsaw, 1977), 85, cited in Cała, *Wizerunek Żyda*, 41.

[38] Broadcast on the Polish television channel TVP2, 28 May 2001, along with Fr. Józef Tischner's commentary of 1997.

them' (*WŻ* 20, 21). That may be the reason why practically any discussion of the Holocaust, including the recent one on Jedwabne,[39] carries a note of reproof for the passivity of the victims.

ACQUIESCENCE

The increasing aggression towards Jews in pre-war Polish society, especially in the 1930s, worried even Polish government ministers. In February 1936, one of them said in the Sejm: 'The number of disturbances of public order by members of the National Party [Stronnictwo Narodowe] rises daily, with more and more frequent casualties; this party quite consciously introduces anarchy into our life, inciting the Polish population against the Jewish minority, and causing many fatalities.'[40] In the period from June 1935 to 1937, this unrestrained behaviour escalated into a wave of pogroms.

Aggression against Jews met with the acquiescence of the Church. Although the Catholic Church publicly declared its anti-racist stance, it nonetheless published *Mały Dziennik* and *Rycerz Niepokalanej*[41] and promoted social and moral segregation,[42] not to mention its tolerance of such priests as Father Stanisław Trzeciak, one of the most radical ethno-nationalists and a virulent antisemite.[43] The Catholic Press Agency disseminated antisemitic leaflets, calling for an economic boycott and the removal of Jewish teachers and students from public schools. A large part of the episcopate considered Jews to be 'propagators of communism', and demanded that they be deprived of citizens' rights.[44] Marek Edelman writes:

Before the war the Church in Poland resembled the infamous Black Hundreds. All the major anti-Jewish and anti-Ukrainian goings-on always started from churches. Father Trzeciak had his church on the Plac Teatralny in Warsaw and all the pogroms started from there. 'Don't buy from a Jew', 'beat the Jew', and so on. On Nowy Świat Street, when I was sitting my school leaving exams I think it was, they beat me up. You couldn't go that way, because the ONR-Falanga congregated there.[45]

And this is how Maria Czapska described the tone of church propaganda at that time:

The Catholic clergy and its press . . . did not oppose antisemitism as required by the principle of loving one's neighbour; on the contrary, it pointed to the threat from 'Judaeo-

---

[39] Cf. Tomasz Szarota in conversation with J. Żakowski: 'Anyway, it is hard to understand—and Gross too makes no attempt to explain it in his book—why 1,500 healthy and strong people being led to death by fewer than a hundred thugs armed with sticks didn't try to defend themselves, or at least to flee': *Gazeta Wyborcza*, 18–19 Nov. 2000. The same motifs often recur in conversations with the soldiers of the Warsaw ghetto; see Grupińska, *Ciągle po kole*. An interesting commentary on this phenomenon is provided by S. Vincenz, *Outopos: Zapiski z lat 1938–1944* (Wrocław, 1993), 105.

[40] Quoted in Grupińska, *Ciągle po kole*, 324.   [41] Caumanns and Niendorf, 'Kolbe a Kielce'.

[42] See n. 22 above.   [43] See Grupińska, *Ciągle po kole*, 325 n. 9.

[44] According to Grupińska, in a memo deposited in the Vatican a Polish diplomat wrote in 1938 about the 'zoological antisemitism of the Polish clergy': ibid. 324.   [45] Quoted ibid. 20–1.

communism' and 'Jewish masonry', warning of the dual ethics of the Talmud and stirring up Polish hostility and suspicion of all Israel . . . Anti-Jewish violence under the leadership of fanatical clergymen has its roots in the distant past of the Catholic Church. Every year during Holy Week, masses of Polish believers heard and still hear in churches descriptions of Christ's agony and the death inflicted on him by Jews. Important Christian holidays were often days of mortal fear for the Jews. Only once a year does the Catholic liturgy publicly pray for Jews. On Good Friday, the singing of the St John Passion is followed immediately by solemn prayers for the Church, the pope, bishops, heads of state, believers of all social classes, prisoners, the sick, travellers, heretics and schismatics, and eventually for Jews, followed only by pagans. The prayer goes: 'Oremus et pro perfidis Judaeis, ut Deus et Dominus noster auferat velamen de cordibus eorum, ut et ipsi agnoscant Jesum Christum Dominum Nostrum' ['Let us also pray for the perfidious Jews, that our God and Lord may remove the veil from their hearts, so that they too may acknowledge Christ our Lord'].[46]

Every year on Good Friday, in the atmosphere of Polish piety that preceded the Second Vatican Council, the 'perfidious Jew' met with 'Judas the traitor'. By the time the above prayer was being read in churches, many effigies of Judas were already hanging over Jewish homes.

ETHNOGRAPHIC AND OTHER QUESTIONS

Let us compare the two sets of quotations presented in the accompanying table (opposite). They all relate to beating, but a comparison shows that not all beating is the same. The left-hand column brings together examples in which beating, as part of a ritual, appears as 'theatrical' behaviour performed by a hired actor, often dressed in disguise. The right-hand column contains examples in which violence does not take on a symbolic character. The last three examples, as ambivalent, have been placed across both columns.

Readers are requested to evaluate the accuracy of the classification for themselves, viewing it from both the Polish and the Jewish perspectives.

*

To conclude, instead of a commentary, I shall quote Sławomir Mrożek:

In 1942, we went on holiday to Żmigród. We—that is, my mother, my sister, and I. In Żmigród my mother's brother, married with one child, had got a job as a dairy manager and rented two rooms with a kitchen on the main square. So we had a place to stay.

The holiday was very successful. First we went by train from Kraków to Jasło, then by a hired cart to Żmigród. The river Wisłoka was good for walks and swimming. In the town square markets were held, so there was something to see. At the manor house were the dairy and the station of the gendarmerie, but Germans hardly ever showed up. I saw them only once, from a distance. They were standing on the bridge and threw a hand grenade into the

---

[46] Quoted in K. Jeleński, 'Problem antysemityzmu', *Kultura*, 1957, nos. 1–2, repr. in *Wizja Polski na łamach 'Kultury', 1947–1976*, ed. G. Pomian, 2 vols. (Lublin, 1999), ii. 123. If I understand correctly, this prayer has not been read since the Vatican's Second Ecumenical Council.

Ritualistic

At that time Jews paid a Christian to be **whipped** and spat on. They called him Haman. (*WŻ* 62)

On Haman's day [Jews] hired a man, drove him out of town, and **threw** stones at him. (*WŻ* 85)

[During Jewish carnival, Jews] paid a farmhand, then **poked** him and **beat** him with reeds. (*WŻ* 89)

[Stage directions for a Nativity play:] The Jew is a hunchback, wears a mask with whiskers and a skullcap. He bows to the front, then to the back. The minister **hits** him on his hump with a bat. (Cie 2)

[Herod in a Nativity play:] Hey you, Field Marshal, hit the Jew with your sword, where God, Jesus Christ, is born. (The Marshal **strikes** the Jew on his hump.) (Cie 2)

[Shepherd in a Nativity play:] If I **kick** you on the backside, you'll fall down at once; I'll **kill** you, I'll **club** you to death, I'll **hang** you on a bush; and if anyone walks or rides past, I'll tell him it's a Jew that's hanging. (Cie 3)

Non-ritualistic

They didn't bother anyone, but among Poles '**beat** the Jew' was a popular catchword—it was the Poles who **attacked** them. But there were no open demonstrations. (*WŻ* 44)

Students often cried '**beat** the Jew!' and would set about **beating** them, play various tricks on them, **tear** their clothes—they had whips with hooks at the end, so when they **hit** a Jew, they destroyed his clothes. (*WŻ* 44)

When Jews come to pray [at the tomb of the *tsadik* Elimelekh of Leżajsk], crowds gather, and kids **throw** stones. (Leżajsk, 1980s; *WŻ* 51)

They used to **beat** the Jews so that they wouldn't take [the hanged Judas] down. (S 1)

The Jews didn't like it at all; they had to give someone money to take it down, for it hung very high . . . Afterwards there was **no beating**, it was quiet, but whoever took it down would burn and destroy it. (U)

Poles didn't care for Jews. On Palm Sunday they **beat** them with palm branches, for Jews feared holy water. (*WŻ* 42)

Jews avoided meeting 'Herods', for they got **beaten**. (*WŻ* 44)

After they'd taken down the Judas, they shouted: 'Treachery! Now it's your turn to get a **thrashing**!' (S 2)

Wisłoka, probably to kill fish. At sunset they barricaded themselves in the manor and didn't go out till dawn.

The summer was sultry, majestic. I designed and built a scale model of a Roman catapult from a picture in an old encyclopedia. I made friends with the neighbours' son, a bit older than me. 'Let's go to Mrs Piwinko's', he suggested. I didn't know who Mrs Piwinko was, but an unerring though vague instinct told me why it was precisely her that we had to go and see. 'Don't be afraid; if anything happens, we'll jump out the window and be off', he tempted me. But I was scared. I was as young as, or perhaps rather as old as, 12.

Once we went to a Lemkian village to buy honey. It was a half-day's trip, and the day was, like all the others, sky-blue and golden. On the rear seat of a hired four-wheeler sat my mother and her brother's wife; I had a seat up front next to the coachman. He was a handsome young man with a happy disposition, or perhaps it was just the presence of two pretty young women that animated him so. We were driving along a rising road with a ridge of wooded hills on the left. From there, at regular intervals, something like clapping or popping could be heard.

Pop . . . and again nothing but the trill of invisible larks in the sky. Pop . . . and the lark again. Pop . . . and so on, time about.

'What is it?', I asked the coachman.

'They're shooting Yids', he answered merrily.[47]

Translated from the Polish by Wiktoria Dorosz

[47] S. Mrożek, 'Wakacje', from the cycle 'Uwagi osobiste', *Gazeta Wyborcza*, 21–22 Apr. 2001.

1968; or, America! America!

REGINA GROL

I WAS CAUGHT UP in the 1968 wave of Jewish emigration from Poland. To rely on a well-worn metaphor, that is when my 'exodus from Egypt' occurred. The four decades that followed were my years of 'wandering in the desert' (in more respects than one) and my search—still continuing—for the 'promised land'.

In one of the ironies of fate, unlike most Polish Jewish refugees of the infamous year 1968, I—with literally about $10 to my name—travelled to the United States in style.[1] Having embarked on a luxury ship, the SS *Rotterdam*, at Rouen in France, I spent five days being wined and dined on that vessel, and berthed at pier 51 in New York City on 8 September 1968. Of the 600 passengers on board, only four, including myself, were in their twenties. The remaining ones, mostly American retirees, were ladies and gentlemen of leisure, proudly displaying their diamonds and mink stoles. The voyage, which entailed lavish meals at the captain's table, struck me as rather surreal.

*

The circumstances surrounding my departure from Poland were a mix of curses and blessings. On the one hand, I left Poland as a persecuted Jew, deprived of Polish citizenship; on the other, I was going to America on a full graduate scholarship, a rare privilege for any Polish citizen in those days.

Having graduated with an MA in English from Warsaw University in 1967, I began teaching at the Warsaw College for Foreign Languages (Studium Języków Obcych), as well as part-time at the Warsaw Polytechnic Institute (Politechnika Warszawska), in the autumn of that year. I hardly ever visited Warsaw University after my graduation. Yet, I did venture there on 8 March 1968, International Women's Day. That holiday is festively observed throughout Poland to this day, with women receiving flowers not only from their boyfriends and husbands, but also their bosses, supervisors, and co-workers. Feeling a debt of gratitude to the

---

[1] In 1968, the limit on foreign currency one could officially purchase at the National Bank of Poland and take out of the country was a mere $5. I managed to buy a few extra dollars from friends whose American relatives had a habit of inserting one-dollar bills into their letters. As mail from the West was routinely inspected, not all the money reached the addressees. Fortunately, some did.

librarians of the English Department collection, who had valiantly assisted me in locating materials for my master's thesis, I saw 8 March as an appropriate occasion to express once again my appreciation. I went to the Warsaw University campus that morning and delivered bouquets of flowers to them.

My mission accomplished, I was briskly approaching the university's main gate, when I found myself confronting a line of auxiliary policemen (members of the ORMO).[2] Their arms locked and their batons prominently displayed, the men advanced steadily, hurling insults at the students. A large number of buses could be seen behind them, with more and more police descending, all in a clearly belli- cose mood. The tension was palpable and the danger of being assaulted imminent. Well familiar with the campus, I quickly ran to a side gate and managed to escape unharmed. A lot of students and other visitors were not so lucky. They were beaten, arrested, and thrown in jail.

I came home shaken up. This was my first direct encounter with organized brute force. My sense of shock continued for weeks as the unfolding nightmare hit closer and closer home. The next day, names of Jewish students, particularly those which did not sound typically Polish, were published in the newspapers to create the impression that Jews were stirring up trouble and creating unrest. I was acquainted with some of the students and knew they were totally innocent.

In the months to come, hundreds of students were expelled from universities, and some were arrested. Purges of Jews from various positions were occurring with increasing frequency. My father, who taught modern history at Warsaw's Teachers' College (Studium Nauczycielskie) on Stawki Street, was fired from his job. His transgression, as he was told explicitly, was teaching his students about the Warsaw ghetto uprising and taking them to the monument to the heroes of that event located just around the corner from the college. He was asked to apologize for his 'offence' (in the spirit of self-criticism (*samokrytyka*) practised quite often in the Soviet Union and its satellites), but he refused. That period was harrowing for my father, whose leftist leanings surfaced even before the Second World War and who believed in the promises of communism, particularly those of ethnic and religious tolerance. He was confronting ideological bankruptcy.

My mother, who until March 1968 had been awarded various prizes as an exem- plary educator, resigned her job as a high-school teacher of Russian when her stu- dents welcomed her one morning by pounding on their desks and chanting 'We will not study the Jewish language!' ('My się żydowskiego uczyć nie będziemy!').

While I retained my jobs, I too experienced a number of very unsettling moments. I recall in particular walking with my mother on Marszałkowska Street, one of Warsaw's major thoroughfares, and noticing the dirty looks directed at her. As we left a shop that sold Chinese arts and crafts, I also heard a derogatory com- ment. Olive-skinned and dark-haired, Mother was the classical Semitic type and the stares and words of the passers-by were unmistakably hateful. Instantly, I drew

[2] Ochotnicza Rezerwa Milicji Obywatelskiej (Voluntary Reserve of the Civil Militia).

closer to my mother and took her by the arm. It was an instinctive reaction to protect her. Given her Holocaust experiences, I felt that she certainly did not deserve to be subjected to such expressions of antisemitism.

Another moment I recall with profound sadness was a scene I witnessed right in my neighbourhood on my way home from work. Two boys, no more than 7 or 8 years old, were fighting. I recognized one of them as my former pupil, whom I had taught English in an extracurricular afternoon class at the neighbourhood school. What I found so disturbing was the nature of the abuse I overheard the boys hurling at each other. The words lodged in my memory to this day were 'You Jew!' ('Ty żydzie!'). I realized then that those children, who could hardly have known who or what a Jew was, were already growing up with the horrible prejudice and were using the term 'Jew' as an insult. I was so upset then that I could not even bring myself to intervene and stop the fighting, which I certainly would have done under normal circumstances.

The direct impact of the 'March events' on me and my family was emotionally devastating. Indeed, I must confess that I left Poland with a profound sense of insult and humiliation. Abuse directed towards Jews was rampant in the months prior to my departure. The state-controlled Polish media were totally unrestrained. All of Poland's economic woes were blamed on individuals with Jewish-sounding names. It was also very painful to read in *Trybuna Ludu*, the Communist Party newspaper, various 'expert opinions' cruelly demeaning to the Jews. One writer, for instance, alleged that Jews stemmed from a colony of lepers in Egypt. Statements echoing *The Protocols of the Elders of Zion* abounded. On the state-sponsored TV news one could see crowds of factory workers yelling insults and carrying banners with antisemitic inscriptions like 'Kikes go to Israel!' ('Mośki do Izraela!'), or more indirect ones, like 'Down with Zionism!' ('Precz z syjonizmem!'). Some, like 'Zionists to Siam!' ('Syjoniści do Syjamu!'), bordered on inanity. The terms 'Zionist' and 'cosmopolitan' were routinely used as synonyms for 'Jew', and carried the most derogatory connotations.

The Communist Party Secretary, Władysław Gomułka, not only condoned the abuse, but had no qualms about making insulting comments of his own, for example by referring to Jews as sympathizers of Israel and denouncing them as the 'fifth column'. Not surprisingly, many Jews who had been most loyal Polish citizens decided to leave the country. Gomułka came to be the Polish version of Rameses.

*

The opportunity to study in the United States was a most unexpected development in my life. Warsaw University had an established tradition of inviting Fulbright Scholars to teach in its English Department. In the academic year 1966/7, Professor Sy Kahn from the University of the Pacific in Stockton, California, was the Fulbright Scholar in residence. I signed up for his American literature classes and he also became my thesis adviser. Shortly after I submitted my master's thesis on 'The Concept of a Hero in Bernard Malamud's Writings', he invited me to his office. I assumed he had suggestions for revisions. Instead, he praised my thesis and, looking me straight in the eye, asked: 'How would you like to continue your studies in the United States?' His university did not have a graduate programme, he promptly clarified, but he knew of several excellent ones. The school he recommended in particular was the State University of New York at Binghamton, which offered graduate scholarships to foreign students. It was too late to apply for the academic year 1967/8, Professor Kahn told me, but he encouraged me to do so for the following year and promised his strong support. I remember that May day distinctly. I rushed home to share the good news with my family and literally jumped for joy.

I followed Professor Kahn's advice and applied to the English Department at SUNY-Binghamton. In early 1968, I received notification of my admission to the graduate programme. My challenge then became to obtain a passport. To get one, I first had to secure a leave of absence from the College for Foreign Languages, my primary employer. Repeatedly, I spent hours waiting in the offices of the Kuratorium (the Education Department) without ever being allowed to see any of the officials. My prior written applications had also been ignored. Without a formal statement certifying that I was granted leave, the passport office refused to issue me a passport and I could not leave the country. While I may have been confronting the standard bureaucratic treatment, I perceived the lack of response and the constant evasions of the various officials as forms of chicanery, the more so because there was other blatant evidence that the antisemitic campaign was in full swing all over Poland. I reached the conclusion that the only way for me not to forgo the incredibly rare opportunity of continuing my studies in the United States was to renounce my Polish citizenship and leave Poland as a Jewish refugee, pretending to head for Israel.

In June 1967, following the Six Day War, the Polish government had cut off all diplomatic relations with Israel. The Dutch embassy in Warsaw handled applications for Israeli visas, which then became the basis for obtaining the infamous 'Travel Document' (*dokument podróży*) one could use as an exit passport. The Document was a one-way permit which stated explicitly that the bearer was not a Polish citizen. To obtain this document one also had to present a paid-for ticket to Israel. Since my destination was Binghamton, New York, and not Israel, I resorted to a subterfuge. I appealed to my relatives in France to send me train tickets from Warsaw to Paris and from Paris to Marseille, as well as a ticket for a passage by sea from Marseille to Haifa. Thankfully, they obliged me, and these were the tickets I presented.

My itinerary was rather unusual, as most other Polish Jews opted for a more direct route to Israel, mostly travelling by train to one of the Italian ports and then by ship to Haifa. Thus, I was treated with much suspicion. After weeks of explanations and much pleading, however, I was allowed to use my French tickets and was issued the Travel Document. By the time I finally held it in my hands, I was a nervous wreck.

To add insult to injury, I was also made to repay a huge sum of money for the allegedly 'free' education offered by the socialist state: 30,000 zlotys, a horrendously high amount, given that 2,000 zlotys was the average monthly salary, was the fee imposed by the Polish authorities on emigrating university graduates in the humanities. The fee was even higher for holders of degrees in the natural sciences. After pleas and negotiations, the sum I was ultimately made to pay was reduced to 20,000 zlotys as I had already taught for a year. Needless to say, I had no funds to meet even this lowered demand. I owe my parents an eternal debt of gratitude for the incredible sacrifice they made by offering me all their savings to pay up that extortion.

These were but some of my pre-departure vicissitudes. Another one concerned obtaining a US visa. When I first went to the US embassy in Warsaw to seek clarification regarding visa application procedures (and I may note that I was very much aware that plain-clothes policemen were watching me as I entered the building), the US consul received me warmly. He seemed most sympathetic. Appalled by Poland's deployment of the same criteria as those behind the Nuremberg Laws in Nazi Germany, as he told me, he was resolved to grant me a 'green card', that is, a permanent residence visa. America, he claimed, needed people like me, young and educated. Yet, when a few weeks later I showed up in his office with the Travel Document in hand, he apologetically admitted his reluctance to instigate an 'international diplomatic incident', given the deteriorating political situation in Poland, and declared he could not give me an immigrant visa after all. Instead, he gave me a tourist visa. Rather than stamping it into the Travel Document, however, he issued it on a small piece of paper (3 by 5 inches) and instructed me to hide it well, assuring me that I could obtain permanent residence once I landed in the United States. Thus, I was leaving Poland as a stateless person, not knowing a soul in all of America, and with merely the hope, but no certainty, of becoming a US citizen.

My family, of course, and a number of my friends came to see me off at the Gdańsk railway station in Warsaw. While engaged in tearful personal farewells, I couldn't help noticing the several trains which zoomed by. They were carrying Polish soldiers to Prague. The 'fraternal army' of the People's Republic of Poland was assisting the Soviet Union in quelling the Czech rebellion. That shameful collusion also contributed to my leaving for America with a heavy heart.

Before I reached my destination, however, I first went to France, where I was entertained for a few days by my father's cousins, whose father had emigrated to France in the 1930s. They promptly returned my Paris–Marseille and Marseille–Haifa tickets to the travel agency, replacing them with a ticket for the SS *Rotterdam*, which turned out to be cheaper than the air fare to New York. My elaborate scheme to get to the United States had worked!

Although the *Rotterdam* was a luxury liner, my trip to New York was not entirely a 'love boat' adventure. I was travelling with a heavy heart, fearful that I might not see my parents, my sister, and my fiancé for years, if ever again. I was also experiencing a state of anxiety about the unknown. Shortly after departure from Rouen, moreover, I found out that one of my two suitcases had been lost. It contained, among other items, my Olivetti typewriter, a priceless possession for me in those days. There was yet another source of additional stress. On the second day of the trip, one of the stewards started making very unwelcome advances towards me. I found him opening my cabin with a master key. While I threatened him I would notify the captain about his outrageous conduct, I had no way of knowing if he would heed my threats. (Mercifully, he did!)

My only contact in New York was Anna Tenzer, the sister of a Warsaw acquaintance of mine, Szmul Tenenblat, the editor of the Yiddish newspaper *Folks-Sztyme*. I did not dare write to Anna from Poland, afraid to give away my 'conspiratorial' plan of not going to Israel but to the United States instead. It was only after obtaining my ticket for the *Rotterdam* that I sent her a postcard from Paris. I had never met Anna, as she had emigrated to the United States some ten years earlier, but Szmul assured me his sister was magnanimous and would welcome me in New York. There was no way of knowing, of course, if she would, nor was I even certain that my postcard, which contained the information about the place and time of my arrival, would reach her in time.

When the *Rotterdam* berthed in New York City harbour, I looked around, scanning the crowd on the ground for anyone who could possibly be Anna Tenzer. I had no idea what she looked like . . . Luckily for me, the postcard I had mailed from Paris just a week earlier had reached Anna. She showed up with her husband, Moniek Tenzer, and let me know she was there with a piercing scream 'Are you from Poland?' Never before was such a dissonant sound so pleasing to my ears. I waved at her and established eye contact. My sense of relief was enormous—there was someone on this foreign shore who could assist me and advise me.

Little did I know that I would subject the kind couple to a very long wait. Of the 600 passengers on board, I was the last one to disembark. The immigration officers in New York had never seen a Travel Document before. They were equally surprised at a visa on such a small piece of paper. I could not blame them for eyeing me with great suspicion. After questioning me and making phone calls to their supervisors and to SUNY-Binghamton, they ultimately allowed me to leave the ship.

Anna and Moniek Tenzer assisted me in more ways than one. They drove me to their house in Brooklyn, fed me, hosted me for two days, and lent me money for the bus fare to Binghamton. (The fare was $13 in those days and my entire dollar budget of $10 had been diminished by $5 on the train from Warsaw, when at the East German border I was forced to pay a $5 fee for a transit visa, or else be threatened with removal from the train. This was a totally unexpected expense and an insult added to injury, since Polish citizens could cross the border without any visas.) As I learned later, Moniek, whose father had died a few days before my

arrival in New York, decided to forgo his filial obligation to go to the synagogue
and say prayers and waited patiently for me to get off the ship. I am most grateful
for the Tenzers' generosity and kindness to this day. I must admit, however, that
when on my second day in America they tried to 'fix me up' with Itzik (Icio),
Moniek's younger brother, who had a drinking problem, I suspected them of an
ulterior motive. This *shidukh* (matchmaking) was not the only surprise that
awaited me.

If truth be told, my exposure to Brooklyn was a real culture shock. I found
myself surrounded by people speaking broken English, with working-class man-
nerisms I was not used to and, most surprising of all, they did not look at all like the
gorgeous actors I had seen in Hollywood movies . . . their appearance was a far cry
from that. 'Where are all the handsome and tall Americans?', I wondered. The
same question crossed my mind at Binghamton, where the vast majority of students were rather short New York City Jews. I soon realized that, although I had
read a great deal of American literature and thought I knew something about
American culture, I had come to a totally foreign land.

Among my other shocking discoveries were the unlimited amounts of food students were allowed to load onto their trays in the cafeterias and the incredible
waste of food I was witnessing all around me. It bothered me to see students engage
in mock fights, tossing rolls at each other, or students throwing mountains of
uneaten food into the garbage. I also had to adjust my monetary scale. Given the
exchange rate back in 1968, the average monthly salary in Poland was $20. Thus,
spending a quarter on a can of Coke or a bag of pretzels dispensed in the vending
machines in my dormitory struck me as most extravagant.

The dress code on campus was yet another culture shock. Both students and
faculty dressed casually, in stark contrast to the fashion requirements in Warsaw,
particularly on my daily route of Nowy Świat Street, where one walked to see and
be seen. In Binghamton, however, even when I thought I had dressed down, I was
repeatedly asked by fellow students, 'What did you dress up for?'

Although fashion etiquette definitely was not the primary reason, I must confess
that after the initial few days of discovery, when the novelty of Binghamton wore
off and my enchantment with the colours of the autumn foliage diminished, I
missed Warsaw terribly. I felt trapped on that campus and in that provincial town.
I missed the big-city atmosphere. Sights of Warsaw, particularly of Nowy Świat,
repeatedly appeared in my dreams for several years to come.

As soon as I settled in my dormitory at Binghamton and enrolled in my courses,
I focused on getting my family out of Poland. My mission was twofold: to persuade
my parents and sister to leave Poland, and to find ways to bring them to the States.
I plunged myself into a letter-writing campaign to HIAS (the Hebrew Immigrant
Aid Society) and other agencies. I wrote to congressmen and senators. (I still have
senator Jacob Javits's letter of reply.) My five-hour bus trips to New York City to
intercede directly were quite frequent. It wasn't until a year later that I bought a

car from a departing French student for a sum total of $50. This bargain, a beaten-up Corvette, almost cost me my life and could have burned down an entire building. I had parked in front of my dormitory, and, as I was pulling out one day, I noticed flames leaping high from the engine at the back of my car. Fortunately, Petr Bjaček, a Czech graduate student, saved the day. He had the presence of mind to yell 'Get out!' and located a fire extinguisher, which saved my life and perhaps the lives of others.

My parents did not know any English. Still, I was hoping to find jobs for them. I also searched for study opportunities for my sister, who had completed three semesters of veterinary medicine in Warsaw. Alas, I soon found out that easing my parents' entry into the United States was a bit of a pipe dream. There was little I could do for them. Likewise, I could be of little help to my sister. Practically no funding was available for foreign undergraduates at that time and there were totally different requirements for veterinary medicine majors. To begin with, in Poland veterinary medicine was a course of study one began as a freshman; in the United States it was a graduate programme. Also, a lot more general education at the undergraduate level was required in the United States as compared to both the Polish and the Italian universities' programmes of study.

Luckily, after leaving Poland in 1969 and following the standard route of Polish Jewish refugees—that is, processing in Vienna and then several months' wait in Rome—my parents managed to settle in Paris and in due course obtained French citizenship. My sister stayed in Italy, enrolling at the University of Perugia, from which she later graduated with a degree in veterinary medicine; it was there that she met her husband. She, in turn, became an Italian citizen. During her initial period in Italy, I helped her to the best of my ability by sending her small sums out of my assistantship, which amounted to $2,500 in 1968 and increased to $2,750 in the following years. I had better luck bringing my fiancé to the United States. He obtained a graduate fellowship in the Philosophy Department at SUNY-Binghamton and joined me fifteen months later. We got married just a few weeks after his arrival.

All along, while trying to help my family and my future husband, I had to do well in my courses. At least a B-grade average was required to have the teaching assistantship renewed for the following year. Not only was I competing with American graduate students, thus being at an obvious linguistic disadvantage, but, as a TA (teaching assistant) in a literature and composition class, I, the foreigner, had to teach American undergraduate students how to write in their native language. At first, that made me feel very awkward and tense. When I got the first batch of my students' papers, however, I relaxed considerably. I recognized there was a lot I could teach them even though English was not my native tongue. Still, my *English Pronouncing Dictionary* was in constant use. I was meticulously checking the pronunciation of unfamiliar words and I spent hours preparing for my classes.

As the first student from behind the 'Iron Curtain' at SUNY-Binghamton, I was viewed as an 'exotic animal' of sorts, that is, with curiosity and caution. While curiosity got me invited to some professors' homes, the university decided to play it safe, and my MA from Warsaw University was not recognized. I had to embark on a second MA programme before I could proceed towards my Ph.D. To capitalize on my knowledge of foreign languages and literatures, I decided to get my second master's in comparative literature. By 1973 I managed to get my Ph.D. and, to my surprise, was offered a teaching position in the Comparative Literature Department at my alma mater for the next academic year.

What I remember most distinctly from my first year at SUNY-Binghamton is that my agenda was drastically different from that of other students. It was certainly distinct from my room-mate's. In the autumn of 1968 there were protests against the Vietnam War on campus. The SDS (Students for Democratic Society) was quite active and vocal, advocating civil rights and other noble causes, and especially 'making love, not war'. After President Nixon's election the mood on campus was sombre. Many students, as well as professors, were visibly upset, if not heartbroken, about the outcome of the election, and many intensified their political activities. Yet, their concerns, I must confess, were on the margins of my interest. I had other issues on my mind. I was trying hard to strike roots in America and help my parents, sister, and fiancé to start a new life as well. These basic existential issues preoccupied me to such a degree that I had no psychic energy left for anything else.

My preoccupations were also in sharp contrast with my room-mate's. She was a very attractive Austrian girl from Graz, who came to the United States for a year of fun. Funded by her well-to-do father, who, as she had told me, called her his 'piggy bank', she viewed her classes as secondary to parties and good times. Indeed, young men were routinely invited to our room. After a few weeks, one of them emerged as the leader of the pack. I would often come back from the library to find my room bolted from within . . . The next year, I arranged to be an RA (resident assistant), which meant additional responsibilities, but ensured a room of my own.

By then I had also obtained immigrant status. A few weeks after my arrival at Binghamton, William Derbyshire, a professor of Russian who took me under his wing, accompanied me to the American Civic Association in downtown Binghamton to file my visa application. The clerk informed us about the immigration law at the time, to wit, that having no relatives in the United States, nor being married to a US citizen, my only option was to apply under the 'Fifth Preference' category, that is, as one having a rare competence few or no Americans could boast. While I instantly thought my chances of obtaining an immigrant visa were nil, Professor Derbyshire, demonstrating typical American positive thinking, was undeterred. In our casual chit-chat on the way downtown I had regaled him with my experiences teaching ancient Greek drama in the literature and composition class. To my total surprise he used that information and, without batting an eye, presented me to the American Civic Association clerk as a great expert in ancient Greek drama. I remained speechless . . . Miraculously, his argument worked. Shortly thereafter, I became a permanent resident, which allowed me to travel to France and see my parents.

Only now, as a parent of grown children, do I fully understand how torturous my decision to go to the United States must have been for my parents, who had lost their entire families during the Second World War. There was no way of knowing if they would ever see me again. It did not help that in August 1968, when I was leaving, the assassinations of John F. Kennedy and Martin Luther King were fresh in their memories and made them see the United States as a wild and danger-ous country. My mother, as both she and my sister told me much later, cried non-stop for two weeks after my departure . . . Fortunately, we were able to reunite, albeit for a short time, after only a two-year hiatus. For a family as close as we were that was a long time. Likewise, the geographical diffusion that followed our depar-tures from Poland required a painful emotional adjustment for all of us.

A lingering sense of injustice regarding the 1968 events in Poland stayed with me for quite some time after my arrival in the United States. Yet I must confess that I felt generally misunderstood in America as well, even by American Jews. I recall distinctly a conversation with another graduate student at a wine and cheese party at Binghamton. Asked why I had left Poland, I poured my heart out, telling her about the antisemitic campaign and the various humiliations experienced by Polish Jews. Having listened intently (or pretending to do so) for quite some time, she asked me, 'All right, but other than for financial gains, why did you come to the US?' I was dumbfounded by that question and realized it was pointless to share my thoughts with Americans. Our frames of reference were so drastically different . . . Financial gain was the last thing on my mind when I struggled to get out of Poland. That sense of not being understood has stayed with me to this day, and my closest friends, not surprisingly, are people who share my background.

Among them are Ala and Włodek Konar, who came to the United States in 1969 and in that summer generously let me stay with them in their apartment in Brooklyn. My graduate scholarship payments ended in May 1969. While my assistantship had been renewed (for five years, as it turned out), to survive until the beginning of the next academic year in September 1969, I desperately needed a job. None were available at Binghamton. After all, thousands of students competed for the few local opportunities. My solution was to go to New York City, where I succeeded in finding a 'brain-dead' office job on Broadway Avenue near 34th Street. My one-and-a-half-hour commute from Brooklyn by subway was a new and not a very pleasant experience, but walks around Manhattan on my lunch breaks were fun. So were my good times with the Konars. It is in their company that in the summer of 1969 I saw man's historic first walk on the moon.

*

Today, four decades after my departure from Poland, I also recognize the many positive outcomes of what back in 1968 I had perceived as my misfortune. I am aware of the cognitive privileges of exile; I am appreciative of the many opportunities America has given me and my children; I realize that the world has opened up to me in ways it definitely would not have, had I remained in Poland. Above all, I know that my years in America have cured me of the inferiority complex I felt in Poland as a Jew. I've learned not to apologize for who I am.

To return to the biblical metaphor, my 'exodus from Egypt' was a blessing in disguise. Although, figuratively speaking, what America offered me, the 'manna from heaven', was unfamiliar nourishment, at least at first, often accepted reluctantly and with a longing for the familiar foods of yore, in retrospect I recognize and appreciate the value of that 'manna'. My forty years 'in the desert' (emotionally and spiritually) were a period of major transitions and self-discovery. Gradually, my regrets and nostalgia for the past have vanished. I have learned to forgive and forget. Eventually, I even had no qualms about becoming a cultural ambassador, promoting Polish literature in the United States as a translator, scholar, and teacher. I also ventured back to Poland for several academic conferences and visits. If truth be told, I considered my stint as a Fulbright Research Scholar in Kraków and Warsaw in the academic year 2001/2 as the triumphant return of an abused citizen.

There are days when I think I may well have reached 'the promised land'. On other days it seems to be a mirage, a Fata Morgana.

'Campo di Fiori' Fifty Years Later: The People Who Remain

A Discussion that Took Place on the Fiftieth Anniversary of the Warsaw Ghetto Uprising

JAN BŁOŃSKI, MAREK EDELMAN, CZESŁAW MIŁOSZ, and JERZY TUROWICZ

THE DISCUSSION printed below was most likely taped in 1993 in the library of Znak Publishers. It was intended to be part of a documentary prepared by Katowice Television on Czesław Miłosz's return to Kraków. However, the talk was not included in the film because of technical difficulties, and the tape then 'disappeared' in the in-house archives. I discovered it by accident in 2003, while Czesław Miłosz was still alive. I transcribed it and gave it to him for approval. We also talked about the different versions of his poem 'Campo di Fiori'. The subject of that poem moved him as much as it had ten years earlier during the discussion.

At the beginning of this discussion, Czesław Miłosz, Jan Błoński, and Jerzy Turowicz converse about the different versions of 'Campo di Fiori'. Its author is inclined to accept the idea that the most powerful rendition for the reader is the first one, which came out through the underground press in 1944 in a small volume titled *Z otchłani: Poezje* ('From the Abyss: Poems')[1] and was circulated in a number of versions, some of which distorted the meaning of the poem. In the volume *Ocalenie* ('Survival')[2] the poet included a 'modified' version of the text, which—in spite of the opinions voiced in this discussion—he accepted as the authoritative, ultimate version and included in the first volume of *Wiersze*, the critical edition published by Znak Publishers.[3] As the editor's note to that text states, the character (*brzmienie*) of the

This discussion, with Joanna Gromek-Illg's introduction, was originally published as 'Ludzkość, która zostaje', *Tygodnik Powszechny*, 1 May 2005. The translation of 'Campo di Fiori' printed as an appendix is from A. Gillon, *Selected Poems and Translations* (New York, 1962), 49–51, modified by Antony Polonsky.

[1] *Z otchłani: Poezje*, ed. J. Wajdelota [T. Sarnecki] (Warsaw, 1944).
[2] C. Miłosz, *Ocalenie* (Warsaw, 1945).   [3] C. Miłosz, *Wiersze*, 5 vols. (Kraków, 2001–9).

poem was discussed in detail with the author. To the uninitiated reader, the differences between the versions are not striking; I think it was not for stylistic or artistic reasons that the author placed so much weight on the changes. The subject of the ghetto uprising was particularly important and painful for him his entire life.

JOANNA GROMEK-ILLG

JAN BŁOŃSKI   Among Czesław Miłosz's poems there is one that occupies a special place in his work, namely 'Campo di Fiori'. It is so special because it was the first reaction in Polish literature to the Holocaust, to the uprising in the Warsaw ghetto. The uprising made it clear to people that the goal of the Germans was the complete, total eradication of the Jews. The poem is also special because it is one of only a few reactions in Polish literature to that horrible event. It was formulated on the basis of the contrast between a merry-go-round where people enjoyed themselves by the ghetto wall, and the siege of the ghetto, the battle being fought on the other side. Built on this contrast the poem speaks also of the loneliness of the dying, referring to Giordano Bruno being burnt at the stake. Could you tell us what particular incident inspired you to write this poem?

CZESŁAW MIŁOSZ   This poem, like some others that were born of moral outrage and anger, was wrenched out of me through a coincidence. I was on my way to see Jerzy Andrzejewski, who lived in Bielany. The tramline went right past where the merry-go-round stood and where you could hear the shots of the insurgents defending themselves. There was a jam on the line and for a long time I looked at what was going on there. I wrote the poem soon afterwards, affected by that experience. Andrzejewski wrote *Wielki Tydzień* ['Holy Week']. People of Jewish origin stayed at his place, traumatized by the events going on because they weren't in the ghetto. Andrzejewski depicted those circumstances in his book. My poem was published in a small anthology called *Z otchłani*, which came out the year after the ghetto uprising, in April 1944, shortly after which it was reprinted in New York.

   The poem has a great many different versions because I lost track of the various copies that were in circulation. There is a book by Natan Gross, *Poeci i Szoa*,[4] in which the chapter entitled 'The Life of a Certain Poem' shows how the different versions circulated. I corresponded with the author, trying to defend the other versions a little. But when Gross was in Kraków last summer, after talking to him I finally conceded that the first version was the most correct one, and that my later amendments were unnecessary. I acknowledged that.

   Which was the first version? The one published in the *Z otchłani* collection during the war. The next one appeared in the anthology *Pieśń ujdzie cało*, published just after the war by Michał Borwicz.[5] After my discussion with

---

[4] N. Gross, *Poeci i Szoa: Obraz zagłady Żydów w poezji polskiej* (Sosnowiec, 1993).

[5] *Pieśń ujdzie cało... Antologia wierszy o Żydach pod okupacją niemiecką*, ed. M. M. Borwicz (Warsaw, 1947).

Natan Gross I reverted to the original version for later editions. What does the difference consist in? Setting aside some small, immaterial points, there is quite a significant change relating to the lines about Giordano Bruno:

> Yet I thought then
> about the loneliness of the dying,
> about how, when Giordano
> stepped onto the scaffold,
> there was not a single word
> in all of human language
> that he could say to the
> people that remain.

> [Ja jednak wtedy myślałem
> o samotności ginących,
> o tym, że kiedy Giordano
> wstępował na rusztowanie
> nie było w ludzkim języku
> ani jednego wyrazu,
> żeby coś zdołał powiedzieć
> ludzkości, która zostaje.]

That's the first version. In the *Ocalenie* volume it was:

> he couldn't find in any language
> a single word
> with which to bid farewell to the people,
> the people who remain.

> [nie znalazł w żadnym języku
> ani jednego wyrazu,
> żeby nim ludzkość pożegnać,
> tę ludzkość, która zostaje.]

The first version is more powerful, isn't it?

JAN BŁOŃSKI Much more powerful, of course.

CZESŁAW MIŁOSZ And that's the version I reverted to. Apart from that, at the very end Gross questioned the version:

> And those, dying, lonely,
> already forgotten by the world.
> Our language became foreign to them,
> like the language of some ancient planet.

> [I ci, ginący, samotni,
> już zapomniani od świata.
> Język nasz stał się im obcy
> jak język dawnej planety.]

In some versions it's 'Their language became foreign to us' ['Język ich stał się nam obcy'].

> Until everything becomes a legend,
> and then after many years,
> on the new Campo di Fiori
> a poet's word will incite revolt.

> [Aż wszystko będzie legendą
> i wtedy po wielu latach,
> na nowym Campo di Fiori
> bunt wznieci słowo poety.]

He pointed out that in the original the last two lines read:

> on the great Campo di Fiori
> a poet's word will incite revolt.

> [na wielkim Campo di Fiori
> bunt wznieci słowo poety.]

It's better, isn't it?

JERZY TUROWICZ Of course.

JAN BŁOŃSKI That means that the whole world is the Campo di Fiori; the poet will incite a revolt against the world. The meaning of the poem has nevertheless been questioned; for example, some people claim that there was no merry-go-round. But even though I was a little boy, I saw that roundabout when I was walking from Stare Miasto to Żoliborz. I remember very well the roundabout standing by the ghetto wall; next to it a barrel organ was playing, and on the other side you could hear gunfire.

CZESŁAW MIŁOSZ It's a very strange feeling for a poet who has written a poem like that, which was as if torn out of him, as if in defiance of his life's work hitherto. I don't want to moralize, to set myself up as a person who judges others. Of course, I acknowledge that I wrote this poem. But it was plucked out of my fate, wasn't it?

JAN BŁOŃSKI You spoke of the loneliness of the dying in that poem. That immediately poses a problem: is this poem in some way directed against Polish society, pointing out its indifference? Here the Jews are abandoned, lonely. I am interested to know how you, Czesław, see this, but also how you [Edelman] would see it.

CZESŁAW MIŁOSZ For me loneliness was the most important element here. The loneliness of the dying. After all, that's the source of the image of Giordano Bruno. I don't know where that image came from, because it wasn't philosophical, it wasn't that Giordano Bruno was for me a hero of the fight for free thought. I remembered the Campo di Fiori, that place where Giordano Bruno was burnt, and the ceaseless bustle of people at the market, enjoying themselves, all around.

JAN BŁOŃSKI I'm interested to know if and when the poem also reached the Jews.

MAREK EDELMAN That's not so simple. It didn't get to us straight away. But let's return to the merry-go-round—this is a matter that is enormously significant. Because it was like this: you have to understand that, for example, the underground Polish powers in London and even the communists didn't want the uprising in the ghetto. They were scared that the uprising would light a flame all over Warsaw. And without hesitation General Grot said: 'Gentlemen, this uprising will not happen because we shall not help you. We're afraid. It's too early.' We never had direct contact with him. There were two intermediaries: the head of the Jewish division, Henryk Woliński, and Aleksander Kamiński, the author of *Kamienie na szaniec*; they were our appointed representatives. In the tragic discussion that took place between the Jewish Fighting Organization and the leadership of the Home Army, we were told: 'You can't do it.' And secondly, 'We don't trust you; we don't have a lot of weapons and we shan't give them to you.' That was one kind of loneliness. I won't talk about ancient history, when different groupings, the Polish Socialist Party and others, wanted to create an uprising, but everyone was subsumed under the London philosophy: don't do it too soon. I can't say all those horrible things, that the only revolver in the ghetto before the uprising came from the communists. That disgusting communist Witold Jóźwiak brought his revolver into the ghetto. And the first shot came from that revolver. We bought weapons ourselves from the Germans on Kercelak Square and in Praga for huge sums of money. That too was loneliness—no one helped us.

The loneliness began much earlier. On 18 January the first shots were fired in the ghetto and two or three Germans died—that was the driving force for the operation at the Arsenal. If it wasn't for the fact that the first German had fallen in open combat, the operation would never have taken place. Everybody—Kamiński, Orsza—says that the mystique of the German helmet had been destroyed. During the uprising itself the Home Army did help, it gave us weapons and so on. But, you have to understand, the Home Army mobilized three platoons opposite the ghetto and for three weeks no one told us about it. They never wanted to have contact with us. On the first day of the uprising in the ghetto that merry-go-round was there, but not turning. It was only on the second day that it started spinning, and that was something really terrible. You could see it spinning from the window, the barrel organ playing, girls' skirts, red and blue with white dots, swirling in the wind. We saw that from the windows and that was our curse. This side was on fire, people were being killed, and there—everyone laughing and having fun.

JAN BŁOŃSKI That's a shocking image. The problem of loneliness arises here, the problem of some kind of historical distance, historical misunderstanding, the divergence of Polish and Jewish society.

MAREK EDELMAN It's not a question of divergence. It ought to be viewed in a completely different way. During the occupation people who were shut away in the ghetto were people of a second class. Not only for the Germans, but for everyone. If 400,000 people can be shut away and eaten by fleas, can die of hunger and not do a thing, they are subhuman. After all, Roosevelt expressly said to the delegation that came to him: yes, it's true that they are being murdered, but don't write that 100,000 have been murdered, because that is a figure that will move no one. Write that little Masza with long curly plaits and big wide eyes was killed by two Germans. That will speak to people. But when thousands die, thousands every day, in full view of people, it becomes trivialized.

CZESŁAW MIŁOSZ It was the aim of the Germans to dehumanize their victims. I remember when the ghetto was being closed off in Warsaw, there were signs on the walls: 'Jews, fleas, typhus', so that those words would become linked.

JAN BŁOŃSKI The poem 'Campo di Fiori' was not only a tribute or a show of horror, it also posed the question of relations between Polish society and Jewish society.

MAREK EDELMAN That poem was a rallying call in the way that Słonimski's 'Alarm' had been in 1939. I got Miłosz's poem by chance through Mitzner, who dealt with the business of reprints. Despite great difficulties we sent a copy of the poem to the forest. And it was those boys—who were dying at the hands of those . . . others, we won't talk about it in detail—who said, 'At last someone has noticed us.' That was the most important thing. Gajcy wouldn't have written that poem, you understand. He was a good poet, but he would never have written a poem like that, because he felt contempt for those people. You understand my point? We looked for people who didn't pour scorn on us. We were dirty, lousy, yet we all spoke and thought like people.

CZESŁAW MIŁOSZ I said that the poem was torn out of me, but of course my pre-war political stance did greatly influence what I wrote during the occupation. When pre-war Poland is idealized, one forgets, for example, about the activity of the gutter press, about the antisemitic movements, about *Prosto z mostu* . . .

MAREK EDELMAN About great poets . . .

JAN BŁOŃSKI Everyone knows that. But overall it must be said that if all Poles had been disposed towards Jews like the poets were, it wouldn't have been quite so bad. In that field there were relatively few antisemites.

MAREK EDELMAN I wouldn't have wanted to be a soldier under Gajcy . . .

JAN BŁOŃSKI Well yes, Gajcy was involved with the ONR-Falanga.

CZESŁAW MIŁOSZ Obviously I knew those young people; I knew Gajcy and I thought that their ideas were completely insane. But still, they were very young, and you can bet that if they had survived, they would have changed their views.

JERZY TUROWICZ I think that, independent of its artistic value, this poem by Czesław Miłosz was hugely important, as the first to touch at the heart of the matter of the attitudes of Polish society towards the genocide of the Jews.

MAREK EDELMAN And not at the heart of issues relating to life?

JERZY TUROWICZ That also. But I mean about the issue which is pertinent in discussions and debates up to the present. We know that even today Poles, Polish society, are accused of being co-responsible for the genocide of the Jews. It is said that extermination camps were set up in Poland because Poles are antisemitic. We know that they are unfairly accused. Extermination camps were located in Poland, and also in Russia, because that's where the greatest concentration of Jews in Europe was; therefore, transporting them elsewhere was pointless since they were to be killed. Moreover, the Germans still wanted, within the limits of possibility, to keep it a secret from the Western world, and, well, Poland was separated from the West by the Third Reich.

However, if we wanted to assert that Poles were not co-responsible, the situation is obviously not that simple. The powerful article by Jan Błoński, 'The Poor Poles Look at the Ghetto', published in *Tygodnik Powszechny*,[6] which also refers to Miłosz's poems, points to the guilt of a large portion of Polish society, a guilt based on indifference. We know that sensitive people, who tried to do something, to save Jews, were only a minority. However, a large part of society behaved indifferently, justifying themselves either with 'It has nothing to do with us', or with 'The Germans are murdering the Jews, but they're also murdering us.' Yet they were making a comparison between situations that were completely incomparable, despite all the losses that the Polish nation suffered. Or they would also say, 'Now they're murdering the Jews, but afterwards they'll murder us.' There is no evidence for the truth of such a statement. The merry-go-round by the wall of the ghetto was a very meaningful image of that

---

[6] J. Błoński, 'Biedni Polacy patrzą na getto', *Tygodnik Powszechny*, 11 Jan. 1987; Eng. trans. 'The Poor Poles Look at the Ghetto', in A. Polonsky (ed.), *'My Brother's Keeper'? Recent Polish Debates on the Holocaust* (London, 1990), 34–52.

indifference. That is not at all to say that, without it, many more Jews could have been saved. Probably more, but not many. Because what chance was there of saving anyone, say, in western Poland, in a little *shtetl* that was 80 per cent Jewish, hasidic, often not Polish-speaking? There the chances of saving someone were next to nothing. The great majority of society really were powerless and helpless. But the indifference—not to mention those extreme cases (fortunately, I believe, few in number) of people who were pleased that the Jewish question in Poland was being solved by Hitler's hand—the indifference is a kind of guilt. And I think that the poem 'Campo di Fiori' showed what kind of challenge to the conscience was posed by the genocide of the Jews, to the Christian conscience and the conscience of humanity as a whole.

JAN BŁOŃSKI I think that you can see this even more strongly in another poem by Czesław Miłosz from this period, also dedicated to the Jews, the poem 'The Poor Christian Looks at the Ghetto' ['Biedny chrześcijanin patrzy na getto']. The poem is very mysterious at first, because it presents an image of rubble, among which lie dead people, among the ruins, among the remains of their homes. In that strange underground, in that Hades, appears a guardian mole, with a little torch on his forehead. The poet compares the mole to a patriarch, as if he is someone from another world, a prophet perhaps, a Jewish prophet. And now he is counting, counting, looking, he knows everything and looks to see if everyone is circumcised or whether there are also uncircumcised among them. And the uncircumcised are the Germans. The one who speaks, the poem's central character, is very afraid that he might also be lying there, and then the patriarch would also count him as a German, as an executioner, a murderer . . .

CZESŁAW MIŁOSZ A division into Christians and Jews . . .

JAN BŁOŃSKI He fears that as a Christian he could be counted as one of death's helpers.

CZESŁAW MIŁOSZ Very much so.

JAN BŁOŃSKI For me it was a poem perhaps even more disturbing than 'Campo di Fiori'. 'Campo di Fiori' is so polished, it is an 'Italian' poem, whereas this one is very moving.

CZESŁAW MIŁOSZ I must say that I have certain difficulties of a moral nature. I look at the problem from a different perspective, because I don't live in Poland all the time, but in America. At any rate that's how it was until recently. I don't read these poems at readings in America because of the generally held opinion that Poles are antisemites. Reading these poems is in a certain sense preaching to the converted. You could see my views on this as my having misgivings of a moral or aesthetic nature. So I, from an American perspective, try to understand what people in Poland think about that time. I don't understand the phenomenon of antisemitism without Jews, I don't understand that about Poland.

MAREK EDELMAN   I read that poem twenty years ago and understood it in a completely different way than today. At that time it was for me a poem directly relating to the period of the war—Hitlerism, the ghetto, and so on. When I read it yesterday—because of course I did not remember it, poetry is a difficult thing, it flits out of your head—I read it not as a poem about the ghetto. It isn't a poem about what happened in Warsaw. It's a poem about humanity, it's a poem about what happens to people generally. After fifty years we have had more Holocausts—I don't want to name them here—a lot more. And you have to understand that that is human life. That is man. That poem isn't about four million Jews who were murdered. It's about man, about life as a whole, it's nature as it is.

Ocalenie was an important book for me, which came out just after the war, the first volume of poetry. I'm not a big expert, because you read poetry and it flies out of your head—but something of it has stayed with me. Back then I thought that it related only to me. But yesterday I saw that it relates to everyone, relates to whether man is good, or bad. I don't know too well what Jansenism is, but I know more or less what it is about. The nature of humanity is contemplated in all these poems and I think that is the most significant thing.

JAN BŁOŃSKI   You can understand the poem in that broad way, but for me it focuses on the hidden pangs of conscience, on that which appears in the subconscious, that which is deep inside man.

CZESŁAW MIŁOSZ   From a certain angle, obliquely, the poem touches on one other issue: the constant reproach directed by Jews at Christians, a charge against the simple folk's understanding of Christianity according to which 'the Jews killed Jesus'. That kind of thinking was in large part the reason for antisemitism.

MAREK EDELMAN   It's not an incidental poem. There is in it a picture of today's world. After fifty years it is even more relevant than it was then.

Translated from the Polish by Anna Solarska

APPENDIX
Campo di Fiori

In Rome, on the Campo di Fiori,
baskets with olives and lemons,
the pavement spattered with wine
and broken fragments of flowers.
The hawkers pour on the counters
the pink fruits of the sea,
and heavy armfuls of grapes
fall on the down of peaches.

Here, on this very square
Giordano Bruno was burned;
the hangman kindled the flame
of the pyre in the ring of the gaping crowd,
and hardly the flame extinguished,
the taverns were full again
and hawkers carried on heads
baskets with olives and lemons.

I recalled Campo di Fiori
in Warsaw, on a merry-go-round,
on a fair night in the spring
by the sound of vivacious music.
The salvoes behind the ghetto walls
were drowned in lively tunes,
and steamy breaths curled high
into the tranquil sky.

Sometimes the wind from burning houses
would bring the kites along,
and people on the merry-go-round
caught the flying charred bits.
This wind from the burning houses
blew open the girls' skirts,
and the happy throngs
laughed on a beautiful Warsaw Sunday.

Perhaps one will guess the moral,
that the people of Warsaw and Rome
trade and play and love
passing by the martyr's pyre.

Another, perhaps, will read
of the passing of human things,
of the oblivion growing
before the flame expired.

But I that day reflected
on the loneliness of dying men,
on the fate of lone Giordano;
that when he climbed the scaffold
he found no word in human tongue
with which to bid farewell
to those of mankind who remain.

Already they were on the run,
to peddle starfish, gulp their wine;
they carried olives and lemons
in the gay hum of the city
And he was already remote
As though ages have passed,
and they waited a while
for his flight in the fire.

And those dying alone,
forgotten by the world,
their tongue grew strange to us,
like the tongue of an ancient planet.
And all will become a legend—
and then after many years
the poet's word shall stir revolt
on the great Campo di Fiori.

                              Warsaw, 1943

Obituaries

Chimen Abramsky
12 September 1916–14 March 2010

CHIMEN ABRAMSKY—a Jewish intellectual, historian of European Jewry, book collector, and bibliographer of world renown—passed away in London at the age of 93. He published relatively little, but his academic legacy was huge: at St Antony's College, Oxford, and University College London (UCL) he trained a whole generation of scholars at a time when Jewish studies was emerging as an academic subject in its own right, establishing itself not only in Israel but in a growing number of universities in the West.

Abramsky embodied a significant chapter of the history he studied and taught. He was born during the First World War in Minsk, then in Russia (now in Belarus), within the region that Jewish culture had traditionally termed 'Litvak'. His father, Yehezkel Abramsky, while still a young man, acquired an international reputation as a highly distinguished rabbinical scholar. In 1929 he was arrested in Moscow, accused of treason, and sent to Siberia for his involvement in Orthodox Jewish religious activities. Thanks to lobbying by Jewish groups in the West and interventions by the Weimar government, he was eventually released and allowed to leave the Soviet Union. The family arrived in London as exiles in early 1932, and two years later, at the instigation of the then Chief Rabbi of England, Joseph Herman Hertz, Yehezkel Abramsky was appointed head of the London Rabbinical Court—a powerful position he invested with fresh rigour and held until his retirement and emigration to Israel in 1951.

Chimen Abramsky never attended school. As a child he was taught at home by private tutors in Yiddish, Hebrew, and Russian, secretly cultivating what was to become a lifelong interest in Karl Marx. On arrival in London as a teenager, he enrolled in an English-language course at Pitman College. He soon mastered English (although he never lost his Litvak Yiddish accent) and was avidly reading, in all the languages at his disposal, on history, politics, and Marxist economics, while at the same time being drawn to a circle of émigré Jewish intellectuals— Yiddish authors, literary critics, and artists—whom he encountered in London's East End. In 1936, with his parents' reluctant blessing, he travelled to Palestine to enrol in the Hebrew University of Jerusalem.

He studied history, Jewish history, and philosophy with Fritz Isaac Baer, Ben-Zion Dinur, and other leading lights of the Hebrew University, while forging lifelong friendships with a number of fellow students, all of whom eventually became prominent Israeli academics, most notably the late Shmuel Ettinger— future head, for many years, of the Hebrew University's Jewish History Department, with whom Abramsky shared at the time a passionate involvement in left-wing campus politics. On one occasion, as he later recalled with relish, he was beaten up by future Israeli prime minister Yitzhak Shamir, then a leading figure in the right-wing underground military organization known as the Irgun.

In the summer vacation of 1939, he returned to London to visit his parents. Trapped there by the outbreak of war, unable to return to Jerusalem to complete his studies, he found employment in Shapiro Valentine, the oldest Jewish book-shop in the East End of London, where he met, and a year later married, the pro-prietor's daughter, Miriam Nirenstein, who had been a member of the Communist Party since 1937. He soon joined the Party himself, despite his family's bitter expe-rience of persecution by Stalin. 'If you were against fascism at the time', he would later say, 'this was the place to go.' Within a short time he became one of the Party's prominent Jewish activists: secretary of the Jewish Committee, editor of its organ, *The Jewish Clarion*, member of the International Secretariat, and chairman of the Middle-East Sub-Committee. He also founded, from his Highgate home, a small publishing company, which published, among other things, the first English edition of George Lukács's *Studies in European Realism*. In 1956, in the wake of the Soviet invasion of Hungary, Miriam Abramsky, alongside thousands of others, left the Communist Party, but Chimen remained steadfast for another eighteen months, which he deeply regretted in subsequent years, resigning only in 1958, after ongoing disagreements with the Party line.

His academic break came in the 1960s. While still a bookseller, and with a grow-ing reputation for his exceptional expertise in this field, he was hired by Sotheby's as a consultant on Hebrew and Judaica books and manuscripts, a position he was to retain for over three decades. During the same period he came in contact with a number of eminent British academics, including E. H. Carr, James Joll, and above all Isaiah Berlin, who discovered in him an intellectual curiosity and erudition matched only by his own, becoming Abramsky's champion and loyal personal friend. When Abramsky's *Karl Marx and the British Labour Movement*, which he co-authored with Henry Collins, was published in 1965, Berlin encouraged him to enter the academic world. On Berlin's recommendation, and without any formal qualifications, Abramsky was elected in the same year senior fellow of St Antony's College, Oxford, and in 1966 was invited to take up a newly created lectureship in modern Jewish history at UCL. To facilitate this, he had briefly to appear before an examining board at the Hebrew University, which awarded him retroactively a *cum laude* MA. Eight years later he was made head of UCL's Department of Hebrew and Jewish Studies, a position he retained until his retirement in 1984.

The Abramsky home was for many years a magnet for socialist and Jewish intel-lectuals—a latter-day 'salon' full of warmth and a genuine sense of camaraderie.

Distinguished professors would mingle with students, all freely engaging in heated discussions until the small hours of the night, while being sustained by a constant flow of food and drink from Miriam's legendary kitchen. Several generations of Marxist scholars and Jewish historians from all over the world were initiated to this circle, drawn to Abramsky, who never failed to astonish them with his command of their own fields of research, and to his remarkable collection of rare books, which he would readily display, often inviting his visitors to reach for them when—at little over five feet—he could not reach them himself. Although he led a secular life, he was deeply attached to the Jewish tradition, and came to feel a strong attachment to the state of Israel.

Following prolonged physical decline, he died peacefully at his home, clutching a small leather-bound Hebrew Bible, which he always kept within easy reach in the last few years of his life.

He is survived by his son, Dr Jack Abramsky, and his daughter, Dame Jenny Abramsky, DBE.

יהי זכרו ברוך

ADA RAPOPORT-ALBERT

Marek Edelman
1919–2 October 2009

IN THE AUTUMN OF 1945 Marek and his wife Alina (Ala) Margolis entered the School of Medicine of the newly founded Łódź University, as did I, but we did not meet at that time. We attended very few lectures, and our shifts at the chemistry lab did not overlap. Moreover, Marek was busy elsewhere, working as a proof-reader for the socialist newspaper *Robotnik*, and writing and publishing his pamphlet *Getto walczy*. I met Ala and Marek in the spring of 1946, when we were assigned to the same shift in the dissecting room. Marek looked rather funny with his small black moustache but turned out to be quite handsome when he shaved it off. I certainly was impressed by Marek, five years my senior, and in the recent past a guerrilla fighter. Having served through the war years with the regular army, I realized how much stronger commitment, initiative, and force of character it took to be a member, and even more so a leader, of a fighting partisan group. And there was about Marek an air of steadiness, of resilience, which, as I realized much later, resulted from the fact that he was a man of almost no illusions.

A quickly grasping mind was another of his traits. Most of us crammed from 8 a.m. to 8 p.m. seven days a week, trying to learn anatomy by heart, and then patho-logical anatomy, reciting the 105 branches of the trigeminus nerve, and the list of conditions in which vitreous degeneration of muscle cells occurred in the uterus. Not so Marek; he grasped everything 'just like that' (a particular movement of the fingers is needed to illustrate this speed of grasping things); to be sure, this way of learning inevitably leaves some gaps. Years later Ala, impressed by Marek's capabilities, said to me: 'Marek is so talented, so talented! If he were such a hard-working person as you are, he would be a genius!'

After our graduation, Ala specialized in paediatrics, her mother's field; Marek and I went to work at the department of internal diseases headed by Professor Jakubowski. We stayed at that department for thirteen years. Marek's professional style differed from mine, but I fully appreciated his qualities: he had a keen eye for the natural phenomena occurring in human disease, an instant grasp of a patient's needs, desires, and psychological problems, and a great ability to lead the patient in a salutary direction.

Marek's Ph.D. thesis was a good example of his abilities: he noticed that patients with valvular heart disease who (for whatever reason) were treated with large doses of prednisone developed an incompetence of the tricuspid valve. He guessed that this was due to the prednisone-induced increase in serum albumins and the resulting expansion of the circulating blood volume; and he proved this was indeed so on a large group of patients.

Both of us left the university department when our master Jerzy Jakubowski retired, but we stayed in touch. Marek was a consultant on internal diseases working with the military hospital's cardio-surgical unit, and from my department at a city hospital I referred to him all patients in need of heart surgery. We also used to see a good deal of each other outside of work, and over the years we had many occasions to talk.

The Edelman family moved from Homel to Warsaw in the great wave of repatriation of 1922. Marek's father, a member of the General Jewish Workers' Alliance—the Bund—died young; his mother, continuing the family's traditions, became the leader of the women's Bund movement. Marek was active in the Bund youth organization.

At a Warsaw gymnasium Marek had to beat off verbal and bodily assaults orchestrated by his classmate Mosdorf, the brother of the leader of the National Radical Camp, a fascist group. Watching Marek much later, I was amazed to see how peculiarly insensitive he was to manifestations of antisemitism. They used to shock and surprise me, but not him. He simply did not expect the world to be better than it really was.

Marek's role in founding the Jewish Fighting Organization in the Warsaw ghetto, commanding the Bund fighting group during the uprising, and leading their escape through the sewers has been reported in a number of books and interviews, and I shall not dwell on this part of Marek's biography. Rather, I would like to mention some earlier episodes.

The printing plant used by the Central Committee of the Bund to communicate with the population of the Warsaw ghetto and warn them of danger was betrayed to the Gestapo, but hours before the Gestapo raid, Marek, aided by Velvel Rosowski and several others, rescued the plant and the precious stock of paper, moving it to another hiding place.[1] In 1940–2 Marek often served as an armed escort to Bund leader Bernard Goldstein on the latter's various missions in the ghetto. This involved frequent brushes with the SS and Gestapo; Marek was 'utterly without fear', wrote Goldstein in his memoirs.[2]

For half a century, on every anniversary of the ghetto uprising on 19 April, Marek travelled to Warsaw to stand before the monument to the Heroes of the Ghetto, and every time found there a gorgeous bouquet of yellow flowers designated for him and placed there by an anonymous hand. Everybody was sad when in the mid-1990s the flowers ceased to appear. It seemed some well-wishing and grateful person had died.

---

[1] B. Goldstein, *The Stars Bear Witness*, trans. and ed. L. Shatzkin (New York, 1949), 88.
[2] Ibid. 160–1.

Marek's ideas, attitudes, and reactions were shaped by the ethos of the Bund: workers' solidarity, the belief in social democracy and humanistic values, internationalism, the distrust of Zionism, the rejection of communism, the conviction that the goal, however great, did not sanctify the means.

Marek's feeling that he shared the responsibility for the Bund's policies was at the root of his refusal ever to leave Poland. 'We dissuaded people from emigrating', he told me; 'nobody in sound mind could imagine a genocide in the heart of Europe—but it happened. I have to stay where they perished.'

I knew that from the very beginning Marek opposed the Soviet domination of Poland. This immediate opposition quite surprised me, and I asked him once: 'Why? As early as 1945, when the Soviets had just liberated you from the Nazi nightmare?' 'I knew', he answered, 'that killings would soon begin.' He was aware of his family's past experiences, the Red Terror of 1918, the executions of 'socialist-revolutionaries' after Dora Kaplan's attempt to assassinate Lenin. It was only later that he learned about the execution of Bund leaders Henryk Ehrlich and Wiktor Alter.

Marek repeatedly told me that he never hated the Germans, and I believed him. He had the sad conviction that under certain circumstances members of any nation could be incited to commit mass murder. However, he reacted with anger and indignation when in the twenty-first century some Germans began their attempt to convince the world that they were the real victims of the Second World War.

Marek was never enthusiastic about Israel but he was saddened and repulsed by the terrorist tactics of Israel's enemies. He wrote an open letter to Palestinian fighters who had been his patients when they were studying in Łódź. He addressed them not as terrorists but as fellow guerrilla fighters, and appealed to them to reject dishonourable tactics. 'We, the ghetto fighters', he wrote, 'never sent our people to a certain death in suicide attacks; and we never attacked civilians.'

One morning in 1968, during the 'anti-Zionist' campaign, Marek was barred from entering the military hospital; that is how he learned that he had been fired from his post. He took this event with enviable calm. I invited him then to come and work at the Madurowicz Hospital, where our common friend Stanisław Gadzicki was the director. I ceded to Marek twenty-two beds in my department.

Our views on medical ethics were identical. I am grateful to Marek for his insightful and enlightening contribution to the euthanasia debate. It has long been known that the Nazi euthanasia programme prepared the methods, the cadres, and the psychological readiness for the Holocaust.[3] It was Marek who pointed to the reverse connection: at a meeting with the philosophers of the French 'New Left', he stated that the Holocaust opened the way to the present proliferation of pro-euthanasia movements. In his words, 'When six million were murdered and Heaven did not fall down on the earth, it became difficult to maintain belief in the sanctity of human life.'

[3] H. Friedlander, *The Origins of Nazi Genocide: From Euthanasia to the Final Solution* (Chapel Hill, NC, and London, 1995).

Marek's courageous joining of the Solidarity movement gained him immense popularity, led later to numerous well-deserved honours, and opened to him international opportunities to raise his voice in defence of human rights, against ethnic hatred and oppression. I was no longer in the country, and we communicated only on the telephone or during his visits to France and Holland and mine to Poland.

He was ailing and in September 2008 I came to see him. He had moved to Warsaw and was staying at the home of close friends, Mr and Mrs Sawicki, who were enormously helpful, offering him all the care he needed, understanding, appreciation, and a warm family atmosphere.

Soon after that visit we had a telephone conversation which deserves to be mentioned here: it was when Barack Obama was elected president of the United States. Marek was ecstatic. I objected that—considering the new president's team—it would not be a great change but more of the same. 'Never mind the politics', said Marek, 'America has elected a black president! We live in a different world than before!' I can recall only one occasion when Marek was similarly elated: it was in 1959, when a Soviet unmanned probe orbited the Moon and we saw the photographs of the Moon's other side, never before seen by human beings. That too was an event that changed the image of the world.

RICHARD FENIGSEN

Glossary

ban (Hebrew: *ḥerem*) The various degrees of religious and social ostracism imposed by rabbinical courts. It was frequently used as a deterrent; transgressors would be threatened with the ban when an edict was promulgated.

Bund General Jewish Workers' Alliance (Bund). A Jewish socialist party, founded in 1897. It joined the Russian Social Democratic Labour Party, but seceded from it when its programme of national autonomy was not accepted. In independent Poland, it adopted a leftist anti-communist posture and from the 1930s co-operated increasingly closely with the Polish Socialist Party (PPS).

commonwealth (Polish: *rzeczpospolita*) The term *rzeczpospolita* is derived from Latin *res publica*. It is sometimes translated as 'commonwealth' and sometimes as 'republic', often in the form 'Noblemen's Republic' (Rzeczpospolita szlachecka). After the union of Lublin in 1569 it was used officially in the form Rzeczpospolita Obojga Narodów (Commonwealth of Two Nations) to designate the new form of state that had arisen. In historical literature this term is often rendered as the Polish–Lithuanian Commonwealth. Also used for the independent state established after 1918.

Congress Kingdom (otherwise Kingdom of Poland or Congress Poland) A constitutional kingdom created at the Congress of Vienna (1814–15), with the Tsar of Russia as hereditary monarch. After 1831 it declined to an administrative unit of the Russian empire in all but name. After 1864 it lost the remaining vestiges of the autonomy it had been granted at Vienna and was now officially referred to as 'Privislansky krai' (Vistula Territory).

Council of Four Lands The principal body through which the Jews governed themselves autonomously in the Polish–Lithuanian Commonwealth (see **commonwealth**). The Four Lands, which changed in the course of the life of this body, which lasted from the late sixteenth century to 1764, referred to the areas which were represented in it. Made up of lay and rabbinical delegates from an increasing number of communities and regions, the Council generally met once a year and was responsible for negotiating with the monarchy the level of Jewish taxation and for apportioning the tax burden among the regions and communities. In addition, it passed laws and statutes on internal educational and economic matters and other general concerns of Jewish life. A separate but similar body existed in the Grand Duchy of Lithuania.

Endecja Popular name for the Polish National Democratic Party, a right-wing party which had its origins in the 1890s. Its principal ideologue was Roman Dmowski, who advocated a Polish version of the integral nationalism which became popular in Europe at the turn of the nineteenth century. The Endecja advanced the slogan 'Poland for the Poles' and called for the exclusion of the Jews from Polish political and economic life.

Endek A supporter of the Endecja (q.v.).

gmina (pl. *gminy*) (see *kehilah*) After the partitions of Poland, the reorganized communal body, which no longer had the power to punish religious heterodoxy, but administered synagogues, schools, cemeteries, and *mikvaot*, was often called the *gmina* (commune).

Such bodies were established in the Kingdom of Poland, the Republic of Kraków, and Galicia. In inter-war Poland, the legal status of the *kehilot* was regulated by statute in October 1927 and March 1930.

halakhah (Hebrew; lit. 'the way') A word used to describe the entire prescriptive part of Jewish tradition and the Jewish law. It defines the norms of behaviour and religious observance.

hasid (pl. hasidim) (Hebrew; lit. 'a righteous man') An adherent of the hasidic movement (see **hasidism**).

hasidism A mystically inclined movement of religious revival consisting of distinct groups with charismatic leadership which arose in the borderlands of the Polish–Lithuanian Commonwealth in the second half of the eighteenth century. The hasidim emphasized joy in the service of God, whose presence they sought everywhere. Originally opposed in a series of bans (q.v.) by the bulk of the Orthodox establishment in Poland, who described themselves as mitnagedim (lit. 'opposers', i.e. of hasidism), the movement soon spread rapidly and became particularly strong in Ukraine, southern Poland (Małopolska or Galicia), and central Poland (the Kingdom of Poland).

Haskalah (Hebrew; lit. 'wisdom' or 'understanding', but used in the sense of 'Enlightenment') A rationalistic movement which emerged in the Jewish world under the impact of the European Enlightenment in the second half of the eighteenth century and continued to the second half of the nineteenth century. It first became important in Germany under the influence of Moses Mendelssohn and soon spread to the rest of European Jewry, first in the west and then, more slowly, in the east. The maskilim (followers of the Haskalah), while retaining the Jewish religion, sought to reduce Jewish separateness from the nations among whom they lived and to increase their knowledge of the secular world. The movement also fostered the study of biblical rather than talmudic Hebrew and emphasized the poetic, critical, and scientific elements in Hebrew literature, aiming to substitute the study of modern subjects for traditional ones. In eastern Europe, it opposed hasidism and what it regarded as the relics of Jewish fanaticism and superstition. It stressed a revived version of Hebrew and was strongly opposed to Yiddish, which it saw as a debased jargon. It also sought Jewish emancipation and the adoption by Jews of agriculture and handicrafts.

ḥeder (Hebrew; lit. 'room'; pl. *ḥadarim*) Colloquial name for a traditional Jewish elementary school in which teaching is conducted by a melamed.

ḥerem. See **ban**.

kahalnik A person who sat on a Jewish communal body (*kahal* or *kehilah*).

kehilah (pl. *kehilot*), *kahal* (pl. *kehalim*) (Yiddish: *kehile*) Although both terms mean 'community', *kehilah* denotes the community of Jews who live in the town, while *kahal* is used to denote the institution of Jewish autonomy in a particular locality. The *kahal* was the lowest level of the Jewish autonomous institutions in the Polish–Lithuanian Commonwealth. Above the local *kehilot* were regional bodies, and above these a central body, the Council of Four Lands (q.v.) for the Kingdom of Poland and a corresponding body for the Grand Duchy of Lithuania. The Council of Four Lands was abolished by the Polish authorities in 1764, but autonomous institutions continued to operate legally until 1844 and in practice for many years after this date in those parts of the Polish–Lithuanian Commonwealth directly annexed by the tsarist empire and until the emergence of the Polish state in the Kingdom of Poland and Galicia. Here the reorganized communal body, which no longer had the power to punish religious heterodoxy, but administered synagogues, schools, cemeteries, and *mikvaot*, was often called the *gmina* (commune). In inter-war Poland, the legal status of the *kehilot* was regulated by statute in October 1927 and March 1930. The legislation gave them control over many aspects of Jewish communal life with both religious and social functions. All adherents of the 'Mosaic faith' were required to belong to a *kehilah*, and one could not withdraw except through baptism or by declaring oneself an atheist.

maskil. See **Haskalah**.

minyan (pl. *minyanim*) The quorum of ten male adults, aged 13 years or over, necessary for public synagogue service and certain other religious ceremonies.

numerus clausus (Latin; closed number) The restriction on the number of Jewish students in high school and university, a feature of educational policy in the tsarist empire and independent Poland, particularly after 1935.

peyes (Yiddish; Hebrew: *pe'ot*) Literally 'corners', but referring to the uncut sidecurls worn by ultra-Orthodox Jewish men.

Po'alei Tsiyon A socialist Zionist Party based on the ideology of Ber Borochov. It split after the Bolshevik revolution into right- and left-wing groupings, the left adopting a pro-communist position.

Sejm The central parliamentary institution of the Polish–Lithuanian Commonwealth, composed of a Senate and a Chamber of Deputies; after 1501 both of these had a voice in the introduction of new legislation. It met regularly for six weeks every two years, but could be called for sessions of two weeks in an emergency. When it was not in session, an appointed commission of sixteen senators, in rotation four at a time, resided with the king both to advise and to keep watch over his activities. Until the middle of the seventeenth century, the Sejm functioned reasonably well; after that, the use of the *liberum veto* began to paralyse its effectiveness. Also used for the local parliament in Galicia (Sejm Galicyjski), which functioned from 1861, when Galicia was granted autonomy, and operated with a severely limited franchise which favoured the Polish nobility as against the peasantry and the Ukrainians in the eastern part of the province.

shehitah Kosher slaughter.

shtadlan (pl. *shtadlanim*) (from Aramaic *shadal*, 'to intercede on behalf of') A representative of the Jewish community with access to high dignitaries and legislative bodies.

shtadlanut The activity of intercession carried out by a *shtadlan*.

shtetl (pl. *shtetlekh*) (Yiddish; small town) The characteristic small town of central and eastern Poland, Ukraine, Belarus, and Lithuania, with a substantial Jewish population which sometimes amounted to a majority. These were originally 'private' towns under the control of the *szlachta*.

szlachta The Polish nobility, a very broad social stratum making up nearly 8 per cent of the population in the eighteenth century. Its members ranged from the great magnates, like the Czartoryskis, Potockis, and Radziwiłłs, who dominated political and social life in the last century of the Polish–Lithuanian Commonwealth, to small landowners (the *szlachta zagrodowa*) and even to landless retainers of the great houses. What distinguished members of this group from the remainder of the population was their noble status and their right to participate in political life in the dietines, the Sejm (q.v.), and the election of the king.

tsadik (Hebrew; lit. 'the just one' or 'a pious man'; pl. *tsadikim*) The leader of a hasidic sect (or community). Hasidim often credited their *tsadikim* or *rebbes* with miraculous powers, seeing them as mediators between God and man.

voivode (Polish: *wojewoda*, 'palatine') Governor of a province, holding a seat in the Senate by virtue of his office. Initially this official acted in place of the ruler, especially in judicial and militiary matters. From the thirteenth century the office gradually evolved into a provincial dignity; between the sixteenth and eighteenth centuries, the voivode conducted the local dietine, led the *pospolite ruszenie* (the *levée en masse* of the *szlachta* in times of danger to the Commonwealth), and occasionally governed cities and collected certain dues. The assistant sub-voivode (*podwojewoda*) often acted as Judge of the Jews.

voivodeship (Polish: *województwo*) A province governed by a voivode (q.v.).

wojewoda. See **voivode**.

yeshiva A rabbinical college, the highest institution in the traditional Jewish system of education. Initially the hasidic movement had been opposed to yeshivas, but in the course of the nineteenth century began to establish such institutions, of which a number were found in Galicia.

Notes on the Contributors

KAREN AUERBACH is a postdoctoral fellow in the Frankel Institute for Advanced Judaic Studies at the University of Michigan. She received her Ph.D. from Brandeis University in 2009 on the basis of a dissertation entitled 'A Window on Postwar Warsaw: The Jewish Families of 16 Ujazdowskie Avenue'.

ISRAEL BARTAL studied at the Hebrew University of Jerusalem and at Harvard University and received his Ph.D. from the Hebrew University. He has been a visiting professor at Harvard, McGill, the University of Pennsylvania, Rutgers, and Moscow State University. He served as the Dean of the Faculty of Humanities at the Hebrew University between 2006 and 2010 and is the chair of the Historical Society of Israel. Among his publications are (with Magdalena Opalski) *Poles and Jews: A Failed Brotherhood* (Hanover, NH, 1992); *Polin*, 12 (1999) (co-edited with Antony Polonsky), which focuses on the Jews in Galicia, 1772–1918; and *The Jews of Eastern Europe, 1772–1881* (Philadelphia, 2005), which has also appeared in Hebrew, Russian, and German.

ELA BAUER is the chair of the Department of Communication and Film at the Seminar Ha-Kibbutzim College in Tel Aviv. In addition, she teaches in the Jewish History Department at Haifa University. Her academic interests include the history and culture of Polish Jewry and the history of the Jewish press. Her recent articles deal with the triangular discourse on the role of Yiddish that played out in the pages of *Hatsefirah*, *Hamelits*, and *Hamagid* in the last decade of the nineteenth century, the Jewish Polish intelligentsia in Warsaw, Jan Gottlieb Bloch and Hayim Zelig Slonimski, and Alexander von Humboldt.

MICHAEL FLEMING is a professor at the Academy of Humanities and Economics in Łódź, Poland, and an associate professor at the Polish University Abroad, London. He has taught human geography at Jesus College and at Pembroke College, Oxford, and has been a visiting researcher at the Pułtusk School of Humanities and at the Institute of History, Polish Academy of Sciences, in Warsaw. His books include *Communism, Nationalism and Ethnicity in Poland, 1944–1950* (London, 2010) and *National Minorities in Post-Communist Poland* (London, 2003).

DOROTA GLOWACKA teaches critical theory and Holocaust studies at the University of King's College in Halifax, Canada. She is the author of *Disappearing Traces: Holocaust Testimonials between Ethics and Aesthetics* (forthcoming from the University of Washington Press), and a co-editor of *Between Ethics and Aesthetics: Crossing the Boundaries* (Albany, NY, 2002) and *Imaginary Neighbors: Mediating Polish–Jewish Relations after the Holocaust* (Lincoln, Nebr., 2007).

REGINA GROL has taught Polish Studies at the University of North Carolina at Chapel Hill (2007–10) and is currently a fellow at the Center for Slavic, Eurasian and East European Studies at the same university. Previously she was a professor of comparative literature at Empire State College, State University of New York, and a visiting professor at Rutgers University as well as at Hunter College, City University of New York. A literary critic and translator of Polish literature, Dr Grol spent the academic year 2001/2 in Poland as a Fulbright Research Scholar.

FRANÇOIS GUESNET is Sidney and Elizabeth Corob Lecturer in Modern Jewish History in the Department of Hebrew and Jewish Studies at University College London. He specializes in the early modern and nineteenth-century history of Polish Jews. His publications include *Polnische Juden im 19. Jahrhundert: Lebensbedingungen, Rechtsnormen und Organisation im Wandel* (Cologne, 1998) and numerous contributions and articles. Most recently, he has edited an anthology of non-fictional Polish writings about the Jews of Poland, *Der Fremde als Nachbar: Polnische Positionen zur jüdischen Präsenz. Texte seit 1800* (Frankfurt am Main, 2009), and a collection of German-language texts by a nineteenth-century Jewish merchant from Włocławek, *Louis Meyer: Hinterlassene deutsche Schriften eines polnischen Juden* (Hildesheim, 2010).

BRIAN HOROWITZ holds the Sizeler Family Chair Professorship at Tulane University in New Orleans. He is the author of many studies of Russian and east European Jewry, including *Jewish Philanthropy and Enlightenment in Late-Tsarist Russia* (Seattle, 2009) and *Empire Jews: Jewish Nationalism and Acculturation in Nineteenth- and Early Twentieth-Century Russia* (Bloomington, Ind., 2009).

AGNIESZKA JAGODZIŃSKA received her doctorate from the University of Wrocław, where she is Assistant Professor in the Department of Jewish Studies. Her main academic interest is the history of Jewish religious and cultural life in the nineteenth century. She is the author of the prize-winning monograph *Pomiędzy: Akulturacja Żydów Warszawy w drugiej połowie XIX wieku* (Wrocław, 2008) and of several articles on Jewish cultural studies.

JEFFREY S. KOPSTEIN is Professor of Political Science and Director of the Centre for European, Russian, and Eurasian Studies at the University of Toronto. He is the author of *The Politics of Economic Decline in East Germany, 1945–1989* (Chapel Hill, NC, 1997). Currently he is completing a book, *Intimate Violence: Anti-Jewish Pogroms in the Shadow of the Holocaust*.

SERGEY R. KRAVTSOV is a research fellow at the Center for Jewish Art at the Hebrew University of Jerusalem. Born in Lviv, Ukraine, he was trained as an architect at the Lviv Polytechnic University. He received his doctoral degree in architectural history from the Institute for the Theory and History of Architecture in Moscow in 1993, and moved to Israel in 1994. He has published essays in the

Journal of the Society of Architectural Historians (2005), *Architecture* (2005), *Jewish Cultural Studies* (2008), *Ars Judaica* (2008, 2010), and *Synagogues of Lithuania* (2010).

RACHEL MANEKIN is an assistant professor of Jewish history at the University of Maryland, and specializes in the social, political, and cultural history of Galician Jewry. She has published articles on Galician Haskalah, Orthodoxy, hasidism, the development of Jewish politics, and the construction of Jewish identity in Galicia.

KARIN NEUBURGER is a lecturer at the Institute for Central and Eastern European Studies at the Hebrew University of Jerusalem. In her research, she deals with modern German, Hebrew, and Yiddish literature and the interrelations between them. Among her publications are articles on Yadé Kara, Yoel Hoffmann, Uri Zvi Greenberg, and Micha Yosef Berdyczewski, and a book comprising an introduction to an annotated translation into German of Greenberg's *Mephisto* (Munich 2007).

ANTONY POLONSKY is Albert Abramson Professor of Holocaust Studies at Brandeis University and the United States Holocaust Memorial Museum. Until 1991, he was Professor of International History at the London School of Economics and Political Science. He is chair of the editorial board of *Polin: Studies in Polish Jewry*; author of *Politics in Independent Poland, 1921–1939* (Oxford, 1972), *The Little Dictators* (London, 1975), *The Great Powers and the Polish Question, 1941–45* (London, 1976); co-author of *The History of Poland since 1863* (Cambridge, 1980) and *The Beginnings of Communist Rule in Poland* (London, 1981); and co-editor of *Contemporary Jewish Writing in Poland: An Anthology* (Lincoln, Nebr., 2001) and *The Neighbors Respond: The Controversy over the Jedwabne Massacre in Poland* (Princeton, 2004). His most recent work is *The Jews in Poland and Russia*, i: *1350–1881* (Oxford, 2009); ii: *1881–1914* (Oxford, 2010).

PRZEMYSŁAW RÓŻAŃSKI obtained his doctorate from the University of Bydgoszcz with a thesis on Polish–American diplomatic relations in the context of the 'Jewish question' in Poland during the First World War and its immediate aftermath. At present he is a lecturer in the Institute of History of the University of Gdańsk, specializing in modern history, particularly in Polish–American–Jewish relations during the inter-war period. He is the author of a monograph, *Stany Zjednoczone wobec kwestii żydowskiej w Polsce, 1918–1921* (Gdańsk, 2007), and of numerous articles. Currently he is working on a new monograph on the influnce of Jewish issues in Poland on Polish–American diplomatic relations between 1922 and 1939.

KAI STRUVE is a research fellow at the Institute of History of Martin Luther University in Halle, Germany. He has published *Bauern und Nation in Galizien: Über Zugehörigkeit und soziale Emanzipation im 19. Jahrhundert* (Göttingen, 2005), and he co-edited, with Elazar Barkan and Elizabeth A. Cole, *Shared History—*

Divided Memory: Jews and Others in Soviet-Occupied Poland, 1939–1941 (Leipzig, 2007). At present he is working on a larger study on violence against Jews in western Ukraine during the summer of 1941.

JOANNA TOKARSKA-BAKIR is a cultural anthropologist and professor at the Institute of Applied Social Sciences, University of Warsaw, and in the Polish Academy of Sciences. She was awarded the Jan Karski and Pola Nireńska Prize by YIVO (2008) and the Father Stanisław Musiał Award (Jagiellonian University, 2010). She is the author of *Rzeczy mgliste: Eseje i studia* (Sejny, 2004) and *Legendy o krwi: Antropologia przesądu* (Warsaw, 2008), amongst other works.

SCOTT URY is senior lecturer in Tel Aviv University's Department of Jewish History, where he is also head of the Stephen Roth Center for the Study of Contemporary Antisemitism and Racism. His work has appeared in *Jewish Social Studies*, *Polin*, the *YIVO Encyclopedia of Jews in Eastern Europe*, and other academic forums, in English, French, German, Hebrew, and Polish. In addition to the present volume, he has also co-edited a special edition of the *European Review of History* on *Cosmopolitanism, Nationalism and the Jews of East Central Europe*. His monograph on the Jews of Warsaw and the revolution of 1905 is forthcoming from Stanford University Press.

KALMAN WEISER is the Silber Family Professor of Modern Jewish Studies at York University in Toronto, Canada. He is the co-editor, together with Joshua Fogel, of *Czernowitz at 100: The First Yiddish Language Conference in Historical Perspective* (Lanham, Md., 2010) and the author of *Jewish People, Yiddish Nation: Noah Prylucki and the Folkists in Poland* (Toronto, 2010).

JASON WITTENBERG is Assistant Professor of Political Science at the University of California, Berkeley. A former Academy Scholar, he is the author of *Crucibles of Political Loyalty: Church Institutions and Electoral Continuity in Hungary* (Cambridge, 2006). His current research focuses on ethnic violence.

MARCIN WODZIŃSKI is Professor of Jewish History and Literature at the University of Wrocław and director of the Department of Jewish Studies at that university. His special fields of interest are the social history of the Jews in nineteenth-century Poland, the regional history of the Jews in Silesia, and Jewish sepulchral art. He is the author of several books, including *Hebrajskie inskrypcje na Śląsku XIII–XVIII wieku* (Wrocław, 1996), *Bibliography on the History of Silesian Jewry*, ii (Munich, 2004), *Haskalah and Hasidism in the Kingdom of Poland: A History of Conflict* (Oxford, 2005), and *Hasidism and Politics* (forthcoming in 2011).

PIOTR WRÓBEL holds the Konstanty Reynert Chair of Polish Studies at the University of Toronto. He received his MA and Ph.D. from the University of Warsaw in 1977 and 1984, respectively. He specializes in the history of Poland and ethnic minorities in east-central Europe.

Index